MAGILL'S CINEMA ANNUAL

MAGILL'S CINEMA ANNUAL 1988

A Survey of the Films of 1987

Edited by

FRANK N. MAGILL

SALEM PRESS

Pasadena, California   Englewood Cliffs, New Jersey

Library of Congress Catalog Card No. 83-644357
ISBN 0-89356-407-9
ISSN 0739-2141

First Printing

PRINTED IN THE UNITED STATES OF AMERICA

PUBLISHER'S NOTE

Magill's Cinema Annual, 1988, is the seventh annual volume in a series that developed from the twenty-one-volume core set, *Magill's Survey of Cinema*. Each annual covers the preceding year and follows a similar format in reviewing the films of the year. This format consists of five general sections: essays of general interest, the films of 1987, retrospective films, lists of obituaries and awards, and the indexes.

In the first section, the first article reviews the career and accomplishments of the recipient of the Life Achievement Award, which is presented by the American Film Institute. In 1987, this award was given to the distinguished actress Barbara Stanwyck. Following this initial essay, the reader will find an interview with writer-director Tim Hunter. The next essay lists selected film books published in 1987. Briefly annotated, the list provides a valuable guide to the current literature about the film industry and its leaders.

The largest section of the annual, "Selected Films of 1987," is devoted to essay-reviews of eighty-five significant films released in the United States in 1987. The reviews are arranged alphabetically by the title under which the film was released in the United States. Original and alternate titles are cross-referenced to the American-release title in the Title Index.

Each article begins with selected credits for the film. Credit categories include: Production, Direction, Screenplay, Cinematography, Editing, Art direction, and Music. Also included are the MPAA rating, the running time, and a list of the principal characters with the corresponding actors. This introductory information on a film not released originally in the United States also includes the country of origin and the year the film was released there. If the information for any of the standard categories was unavailable, the heading is followed by the phrase "no listing." Additional headings such as Special effects, Costume design, and Song have been included in an article's introductory top matter when appropriate. Also, the symbol (AA) in the top matter identifies those artists who have received an Academy Award for their contribution to a film from the Academy of Motion Picture Arts and Sciences.

The section of the annual labeled "More Films of 1987" supplies the reader with an alphabetical listing of an additional 326 feature films released in the United States during the year. Included are brief credits and short descriptions of the films. These films can be located, along with any cross-references, in the indexes.

Following "More Films of 1987" are essays on five retrospective films. These essay-reviews follow exactly the same format as the articles in the

"Selected Films of 1987" section, and in each instance, the original release date is also provided. Because the Motion Picture Association of America (MPAA) was established in 1956, any film released prior to that year will not have an MPAA rating.

Two further lists conclude the text of the volume. The first of these is the Obituaries, which provides useful information about the careers of motion-picture professionals who died in 1987. The second list is of the awards presented by ten different international associations, from the Academy of Motion Picture Arts and Sciences to the Cannes International Film Festival and the British Academy Awards.

The final section of this volume includes nine indexes that cover the films reviewed in *Magill's Cinema Annual*, 1988. Arranged in the order established in the introductory matter of the essay-reviews, the indexes are as follows: Title Index, Director Index, Screenwriter Index, Cinematographer Index, Editor Index, Art Director Index, Music Index, and Performer Index. A Subject Index is also provided. To assist the reader further, pseudonyms, foreign titles, and alternate titles are all cross-referenced. Titles of foreign films and retrospective films are followed by the year, in brackets, of their original release.

The Title Index includes all the titles of films covered in individual articles, in "More Films of 1987," and also those discussed at some length in the general essays and interviews. The next seven indexes are arranged according to artists, each of whose names is followed by a list of the films on which they worked and the titles of the essays (such as "Interview with Tim Hunter, An") in which they are mentioned at length. The final listing is the Subject Index, in which any one film can be categorized under several headings. Thus, a reader can effectively use all these indexes to approach a film from any one of several directions, including not only its credits but also its subject matter.

CONTRIBUTING REVIEWERS

Michael Adams
Freelance Reviewer

Rebecca Bell-Metereau
Southwest Texas State University

Mira Reym Binford
Quinnipiac College

Beverley Bare Buehrer
Freelance Reviewer

Raymond Carney
University of Texas at Dallas

Nika Cavat
Freelance Reviewer

Greg Changnon
Northwestern University

R C Dale
University of Washington

David Desser
*University of Illinois at Urbana-
  Champaign*

Susan Doll
Freelance Reviewer

Nataša Ďurovičová
*John Jay College of Criminal Justice
City University of New York*

Thomas L. Erskine
Salisbury State University

Joan Esposito
Nassau Community College

Jeffrey Fenner
Freelance Reviewer

Gabrielle Forman
Stanford University

Dan Georgakas
*State University of New York
  Empire State College*

Scott Giantvalley
*California State University,
  Dominguez Hills*

Richard Glatzer
Freelance Reviewer

Sidney Gottlieb
Sacred Heart University

Kevin Jack Hagopian
State University of New York at Albany

John Hartzog
California State University, Northridge

David J. Hogan
Freelance Reviewer

Andrew Jefchak
Aquinas College

William Johnson
Freelance Reviewer

John Robert Kelly
Boston University

Ira Konigsberg
University of Michigan, Ann Arbor

Patricia Kowal
*Pennsylvania State University—
  University Park*

Jim Kozak
Freelance Reviewer

Leon Lewis
Appalachian State University

Janet E. Lorenz
Freelance Reviewer

Blake Lucas
Freelance Reviewer

Mary Lou McNichol
Freelance Reviewer

Marc Mancini
Loyola Marymount University

Roger Manvell
Boston University

Cono Robert Marcazzo
Upsala College

Harriet Margolis
Florida Atlantic University

Joss Marsh
*University of California,
  Santa Barbara*

John W. Martin
Freelance Reviewer

John J. Michalczyk
Boston College

Robert Mitchell
University of Arizona

Darrin Navarro
Freelance Reviewer

Terry Nixon
Freelance Reviewer

Chon Noriega
Stanford University

John R. Orlandello
Western Illinois University

Carl Rollyson
*Bernard M. Baruch College
City University of New York*

Paul W. Salmon
University of Western Ontario

David Schwartz
American Museum of the Moving Image

Neil Sinyard
Freelance Reviewer

George Slade
Freelance Reviewer

Ellen Snyder
Freelance Reviewer

Michael Sprinker
*State University of New York
at Stony Brook*

Robert Strauss
Freelance Reviewer

Richard Strelitz
Duke University

Gaylyn Studlar
Emory University

Peter Tasker
British Film Institute

Fiona Valentine
Northwestern University

Gordon Walters
DePauw University

James M. Welsh
Salisbury State University

Joanne L. Yeck
Art Center College of Design

CONTENTS

CONTENTS

MAGILL'S
CINEMA
ANNUAL

Life Achievement Award
BARBARA STANWYCK

Hollywood loves grandes dames. From the early years of the film industry, when local boarding houses would put up notices that read "No Actors," Hollywood has craved and obsessively sought respectability. By luring "great ladies" from the stage or grooming unknowns to be home-grown great ladies, the film industry worked to define the grande dame as a mature luminary of the silver screen, a star to be sure, but one regally polished by time and oozing artistic integrity from every thespian pore. In spite of Hollywood's efforts, perhaps grandes dames really emerge only in retrospect, as their titles are bestowed on them by an adoring, nostalgic public that chooses to forget when these legends have been box-office poison or summer-stock understudies. Longevity, therefore, emerges as a key ingredient to the making of a grande dame of the silver screen.

Barbara Stanwyck is not a grande dame and will probably never be one, although her credentials, including her longevity, would appear to be enough to elevate her automatically to the ranks of actresses such as Katharine Hepburn, Bette Davis, and Lillian Gish. With the American Film Institute's Life Achievement Award, a special Academy Award, and three Emmys, among numerous other accolades, Stanwyck's lack of grande dame status would seem to be either a scandal or her willfully perverse denial of success. Clinging to Barbara Stanwyck, however, is the aura of a dame, not a grande dame. With her flattened, Brooklynesque "a's," her enthusiastic roughriding in Westerns, and her no-nonsense attitude, she seems to lack both the patrician pedigree and the assumed air of grandeur necessary to the image of grande dame as cultural icon. Stanwyck has never quite kicked off the traces of her working-class origins. Instead, beloved by grips and gaffers, scriptgirls and stuntmen, she is a good sport, a trooper, who believes that she is a professional in a business of professionals.

Stanwyck's businesslike attitude toward acting can be traced to her childhood in Brooklyn, New York. Born Ruby Stevens in 1907, to a poor family with too many children (five) and not enough of anything else, Stanwyck literally grew up on the wrong side of the tracks. She was two years old when her mother was killed in a streetcar accident. Her father abandoned the family. She and her brother Malcolm were farmed out to various foster families. Occasionally, Ruby's older sister Millie would take her on the vaudeville circuit with her during the summers. Ruby loved it, but she had to return to school in the autumn. After finishing grammar school, she took a job as a package wrapper for a department store before trying her hand at other unskilled jobs and secretarial school.

Her career in show business began as a mistake when she arrived at the Remick Music Company for an interview for a switchboard operator's position. Instead, a dance audition was being held. She stayed. Soon Ruby was dancing in the back of the chorus at the Strand Roof nightclub for forty dollars a week. Nightclub stints and revue shows followed in the 1923 and 1924 seasons until she joined the Ziegfeld Follies touring company. In 1926, Ruby Stevens was hired by Willard Mack to play the character of a chorus girl in his play, *The Noose*. After considerable rewriting, her role included the enviable climactic speech of the last act. Mack thought her name sounded like that of a "burlesque queen": Ruby Stevens became Barbara Stanwyck. When *The Noose* opened on Broadway in October, Barbara Stanwyck and the play received glowing notices.

After Stanwyck won a role in First National's silent film *Broadway Nights* (1927), producer Arthur Hopkins brought her back to Broadway. Her "rough poignancy" was needed for the female lead in George Manker Watters and Hopkins' *Burlesque* (1927), the story of a troubled vaudeville couple. The play broke box-office records; Stanwyck was a star. An offer came from Hollywood for her to replay her role in *The Noose*, now being remade as a talking picture. Unfortunately, her commitment to *Burlesque* precluded her participation in the film.

Now her career was complicated by another commitment. In 1928, she hastily married "Broadway's Favorite Son," vaudevillean Frank Fay. Twice divorced and hard-drinking, Fay would later become a professional liability to Stanwyck, but in these halcyon days of their marriage, he played a crucial part in establishing her Hollywood career. In 1929, Stanwyck and Fay set out for Hollywood with picture contracts in hand. Stanwyck's first two talking films were *The Locked Door* (1929), a stilted melodrama produced by Joseph P. Kennedy, and *Mexicali Rose* (1929), which was, in the words of Columbia Pictures' publicity department, "the story of a heartless coquette who knew no law but her own turbulent passions." While Fay was achieving great success at Warner Bros., Stanwyck's Broadway-star value in Hollywood was rapidly diminishing. Numerous screen tests led nowhere; unemployment increased her self-doubt. Finally, she was asked to make a test at Warner's, but she knew that it was nothing more than a concession to her husband's star status at the studio.

Whether he remembered her from his own studio's film, *Mexicali Rose*, or saw the Warner's screen test is unclear, but Harry Cohn, head of Columbia, brought Stanwyck to the attention of a young producer-director, Frank Capra. Capra was casting *Ladies of Leisure* (1930). He interviewed Stanwyck but thought her rude and defensive. She had refused to make a test for him and walked out of the interview. Calling Capra to berate him for mistreating his wife, Fay offered to show him her test for Warner's. He saw it and immediately hired her for the first of their five film collaborations.

Capra employed a unique method of shooting to capture Stanwyck's intense projection of emotion. Because of her stage background and limited training, Stanwyck was unable to sustain the emotional peak of her first take in subsequent takes of the same scene. Capra was determined not to lose the quality for which he had hired her: her ability, as he has said, to "grab your heart and tear it to pieces." He would rehearse the other actors without her. He then would shoot the take with multiple cameras set up to capture Stanwyck from every angle. "One-take Barbara" would later overcome the limitation of technique that precipitated this elaborate directorial maneuver, but she would awe directors with her ability to do a scene in one take when demanded.

In *Ladies of Leisure*, Stanwyck plays a young woman of lower-class origins whose gold digging ways are reformed by a socialite artist who uses her as a model and then falls in love with her. Stanwyck and the film were extremely well received. The subsequent films for Capra and Stanwyck, *The Miracle Woman* (1931), *Forbidden* (1932), *The Bitter Tea of General Yen* (1933), and *Meet John Doe* (1941) all would, in varying degree, address potentially controversial subjects: adultery, evangelism, miscegenation, and homegrown American fascism. *Forbidden*, the least successful of their collaborations, is a sentimental film in which Stanwyck plays a librarian who has an affair with a devoted but predictably married man, played by Adolphe Menjou. *The Miracle Woman*, banned in Great Britain for "irreverency," was a rather watered-down indictment of Aimee Semple McPherson-style evangelism. *The Bitter Tea of General Yen* features Stanwyck as a New England missionary who loses her heart to a Chinese warlord. This film was also banned in Great Britain because of its depiction of interracial love. Stanwyck's sensitive portrayal of the heroine was finely shaded, but the film was not a popular success.

Shuttling between Columbia and Warner's in nonexclusive contracts with both studios, Stanwyck acted in 1930's films such as the high-spirited *Night Nurse* (1931), with one of her favorite directors, William Wellman, *Illicit* (1931), a melodrama on the tribulations of free love, *Ten Cents a Dance* (1931), in which she portrays a dance-hall hostess, and *Ladies They Talk About* (1933), in which she plays a gangster's moll. During this period, a pattern was set which would be continued in Stanwyck's later career. Even when her films failed at the box office, as did *Forbidden*, or received poor reviews, as was the case with *The Purchase Price* (1932), she rarely failed to garner critical acclaim. One critic, reviewing *The Purchase Price*, noted that Stanwyck exercised an "uncanny ability to make the most phoney heroines seem like human beings." In these days, when she seemed to be portraying barmaids, waitresses, molls, gold diggers, and gamblers in every other picture, her qualities of sincerity, forthrightness, and naturalness were taxed to the breaking point in making her characters "seem like human beings." By the mid-1930's, her career had stalled and so had her marriage. Fay's drinking had increased as his pictures began to fail and his battles with the studio intensified. Stanwyck was chafing under the studio system's insistence that she accept bad scripts. Increasingly, she faced suspension for refusing films. In 1935, Warner's dropped her. Later that year, Stanwyck dropped Fay. She filed for divorce.

It is fortunate that the Stanwyck of 1935 was a different creature from the wary, intimidated Hollywood newcomer of 1929. She now knew her worth. Free-lancing did not seem a frightening prospect. She went without a job for some six months until producer Edward Small offered her *Red Salute* (1935), a forgettable anti-Communist campus comedy. The film she needed to turn her career in the right direction was George Stevens' *Annie Oakley* (1935). Stanwyck threw herself with relish into the role of Annie, the "World's Greatest Woman Rifle Shot." Although she had been loving, suffering, and emoting in most of her roles, what she really wanted was a film with action. As a child, she had adored Pearl White, the daredevil heroine of action-packed serials. She also loved Westerns. As a result, Annie Oakley is a vibrantly convincing characterization. Under Stevens' guidance, Stanwyck's country sharpshooter emerges as a woman of warmth and simplicity.

Stanwyck's well-received performance in *Annie Oakley* was followed by contracts with Twentieth Century-Fox and RKO Studios. She worked with good directors during this period, including John Ford for *The Plough and the Stars* (1937) and John Cromwell for *Banjo on My Knee* (1936), but, in spite of the big names and big talents involved, these films were not as good as they should have been. In 1937, Stanwyck finally found a role worthy of her talents. Olive Higgins Prouty's novel *Stella Dallas* (1937), which had been filmed as a silent, was to be redone by Samuel Goldwyn. Most of Hollywood's leading actresses coveted the title role, which Stanwyck won.

The story of mother love growing into a transfiguring self-sacrifice, *Stella Dallas* was acknowledged as powerfully emotional material, but by 1937, many regarded it as anachronistic, outdated in its melodramatic excess. Yet, in much the same way that D. W. Griffith transformed the outdated Victorian stage melodrama *Way Down East* (1920) into a cinematic classic, Stanwyck, director King Vidor, and the film's other collaborators, kept *Stella Dallas* from becoming sentimental. For as Stanwyck herself has said, there is a significant difference between sentimentality and honest sentiment.

Stella Dallas centers on Stella Martin, the daughter of a working-class family in a Massachusetts mill town of 1919. Normally loud, exuberantly belligerent, and overdressed, Stella modulates her voice and appearance so that Stephen Dallas, a high-society executive at the plant where her brother works, sees her as a soft-spoken, winsome young woman who wishes to better herself. On the way home from a date, Stella talks of emulating the figures she has seen at the picture show, but Stephen admonishes her to be herself. They kiss. The next morning, she returns to her family as a married woman. Soon, she and Stephen have a daughter, Laurel, but by this time, Stella's lower-class ways are setting her husband's teeth on edge. Stella's desire to change was either a passing fancy or a sexual ploy. She is openly defiant: She knows she has "stacks of style" and does not want to change. She accuses Stephen of never giving in, of always thinking that he is right. Stella willingly lets Stephen move back to New York. Alone, she rears Laurel, who grows up to be a kind and refined child of whom Stella and the occasionally visiting Stephen are both proud. As Laurel reaches adolescence, Stella's inappropriate dress and coarse behavior become hindrances to Laurel's social life. Realizing that she is a liability to her daughter's future happiness in the upper-class setting in which she belongs, Stella tricks Laurel into believing that she no longer wants her. Stella's final triumph is her daughter's wedding, an event to which she has not been invited. With the crowd of common folk standing outside the mansion, Stella watches through the window as Laurel marries her Prince Charming.

Nominated for an Academy Award, Stanwyck's portrayal of Stella forces the film's spectator to walk the tightrope between pity and anger, embarrassment and fascination. Initially, Stella seems fully capable of assuming the more refined manners and dress of her "betters," yet her clothes become more outrageous, her behavior cruder. Her excessive style can be read as a self-willed liability, not the inability to adapt that many critics have cited as the source of her troubles. If Stella's failure to change is interpreted as a defiant slap in the face at Stephen's class expectations—his snobbish, "undertaker" attitude toward life as well as his hypocritical premarital injunction for her to stay as she is—then our pity for Stella must be mediated by other, more complicated feelings. Stanwyck's interpretation of Stella precludes the easy sentimentality which once led male critics to dismiss "the woman's film." Stella's vitality and her independence force the audience to admire and even to question the social goals which Stephen and the audience would normally assume to be best for her.

Stanwyck purposely followed *Stella Dallas* with lighter fare, and her continuing radio work with the Lux Radio Theater eased her suspension in 1937 by both RKO and Twentieth Century-Fox. Like Bette Davis, Stanwyck was often suspended for rejecting scripts, but many of her directors have remarked that after she accepted a role, any role, she always reconciled herself to the limitations of that film project and approached her part with unflagging enthusiasm. Her professionalism extended beyond knowing her lines and being on time. William Holden, who costarred with her on his first film, *Golden Boy* (1939), recounted how her professionalism was linked to her concern for others and to her integrity. Recruited from a college theater, Holden was floundering in *Golden Boy* until Stanwyck began working with him on his lines between takes. *Golden Boy* was a success for both of them and marked the start of an enormously satisfying period of work for

Stanwyck. She followed with Mitchell Leisen's charming comedy, *Remember the Night* (1940). The screenwriter for that film was Preston Sturges, who casually remarked to Stanwyck that she was funny and that he would write a film for her. His offhand remark led to *The Lady Eve* (1941), the vehicle for one of Stanwyck's most accomplished performances.

In her films of the 1930's, Stanwyck had been known to give snappy lines a snappy reading, but she was not associated with comedy. When she attempted a screwball comedy, *The Mad Miss Manton*, in 1938, she had seemed, as one reviewer noted, rather too earthbound and stoic to be playing a dizzy debutante. In *The Lady Eve*, she plays a card sharp who pretends to be an English aristocrat in order to capture the heart of ale heir Hopsy Pike (Henry Fonda). Her pairing with Fonda is inspired. Her savvy con artist calmly watches Hopsy fall all over himself in repressed sexual bliss as he discovers that there is something more to life than studying snakes in the Amazon. Following *The Lady Eve* with Capra's lackluster and heavy-handed *Meet John Doe*, Stanwyck did not strike gold again until Howard Hawks's *Ball of Fire* (1942). In it, she portrays Sugar Puss O'Shea, a gum-smacking stripper who charms a houseful of absentminded professors, including Gary Cooper as a shy linguist. For her portrayal, Stanwyck received her second Academy Award nomination. Wellman's epic Western, *The Great Man's Lady*, followed in 1942, and in 1943, Stanwyck played yet another burlesque queen in Wellman's film version of Gypsy Rose Lee's murder mystery, *The G-String Murders* (1941).

In 1944, like so many times in the early 1930's, Stanwyck took a role that no one else wanted, that of Phyllis Dietrichson in *Double Indemnity*. Stanwyck became the ultimate femme fatale in a film that set the tone for an entire era's vision of the American dream gone wrong. Stanwyck has called Phyllis "the most hard-boiled dame I ever played," but hard-boiled is an understatement. Phyllis plots to kill her husband and enlists the help of cynical insurance agent Walter Neff (Fred MacMurray). After they succeed in their scheme, Phyllis goes after her stepdaughter and then after Neff. Slickly, stupidly self-confident, Neff realizes too late that Phyllis has more brains, more nerve, and less heart than he ever imagined.

Stanwyck's Phyllis is nothing like James Cain's original character in the novel *Double Indemnity* (1943). While Cain's Phyllis is a lithe, freckle-faced young matron whose psychopathia is masked by her deceptively innocent appearance, Stanwyck's Phyllis is a sleek, pageboy blonde who is outrageously bad from the moment she appears, clad only in a bath towel. In Cain's novel, Phyllis loves death and wants to make it her "bridegroom." In the end, she *is* death. Stanwyck's Phyllis is cold-blooded and calculating, but always human. Shockingly, only when she shoots Walter does she discover that she loves him.

In 1946, Stanwyck essayed another sexy, dangerous femme fatale in Lewis

Milestone's *The Strange Love of Martha Ivers*. Her affinity for playing noir females continued to be manifested in her roles in *The File on Thelma Jordan* (1950) and Anatole Litvak's *Sorry, Wrong Number* (1948), for which she earned another Academy Award nomination for her portrayal of a hypochondriac invalid. Stanwyck continued to work actively into the 1950's. She made several Westerns, including Anthony Mann's *The Furies* (1950) and *The Violent Men* (1955), as well as melodramas such as Douglas Sirk's *All I Desire* (1953; reviewed in this volume) and a Sirkian masterpiece on middle-class malaise, *There's Always Tomorrow* (1956), which again teamed her with Fred MacMurray.

After Samuel Fuller's *Forty Guns* (1957), there was a five-year hiatus in her film career. Although she still had a youthful figure and often did her own stunt work, Stanwyck was the victim of age discrimination. Walter Huston had once told her that age was only a number, but she discovered that that number was very important in Hollywood. She remarked that "they don't normally write parts for women my age because America is now a country of youth." Television began to look better and better to her. What she wanted, however, was to star in a Western series with a female protagonist. Encountering opposition, even from her own agent, she settled into guest appearances in dramatic anthology series such as the "Alcoa-Goodyear Playhouse" and episodes of the Western anthology "Zane Grey Theatre" during the 1958 and 1959 seasons. Then NBC offered her her own anthology series, "The Barbara Stanwyck Show," which was modeled on the format of "The Loretta Young Show." Although she received an Emmy for her work in the series, the show was canceled.

Fortunately, Stanwyck did not stay idle for long. She was offered a part in *Walk on the Wild Side* (1962), a film in which she played a Depression-era New Orleans madam with a passion for one of her prostitutes. She received excellent reviews for her startlingly unsympathetic portrayal, but found herself wasted in her next film role as a carnival operator in the Elvis Presley vehicle *Roustabout* (1964). Her last theatrical film, *The Night Walker* (1965), was a William Castle suspense thriller that is notable only for reuniting her with Robert Taylor, to whom she was married from 1939 to 1951.

Stanwyck returned to television with guest appearances until she got what she wanted in 1965, when she became Victoria Barkley in the popular ABC Western series "The Big Valley." The series lasted four seasons, earned for Stanwyck another Emmy, and has become an extremely successful syndicated series. Stanwyck appeared in several made-for-television films in the 1970's; in 1983, she appeared in the much-anticipated television miniseries based on Colleen McCullough's romance novel *The Thorn Birds* (1977). Playing yet another strong-willed matriarch, Stanwyck earned another Emmy at the age of seventy-seven.

In her long career on the stage, in film, and in television, Barbara Stanwyck's sensitive portrayals of everything from taxi dancers to heiresses, mothers to molls, have demonstrated the triumph of a naturalistic acting style combined with a highly professional attitude. It seems as if she has never made an enemy, judging from the high praise that she has received from her peers of every era and medium in which she has worked. It is quite a compliment to be the favorite actress of some of Hollywood's most famous directors, including Billy Wilder, Frank Capra, and Cecil B. De Mille; yet one of the most charming photographs of Stanwyck is from 1941, as she is captured lovingly embracing a small statue, the token of affection from the production crew of *The Great Man's Lady*. As Capra has said, "In a Hollywood popularity contest, she would win first prize hands down."

Stanwyck has always been valued for her egalitarian naturalness off the screen as well as on. She is very much like the best of the characters she has played. In *Annie Oakley*, Annie unknowingly breaks the rules of etiquette by shaking the hand of the czar of Russia. She realizes her mistake and sputters, "Gosh, I suppose that was terrible." The reply to Annie is equally applicable to Stanwyck: "No, you were just yourself. That is why we all love you."

Gaylyn Studlar

An Interview with
TIM HUNTER

One of the most startling and impressive films of 1987 was *River's Edge* (reviewed in this volume), a depiction of the skewed reactions of a group of teenagers to the murder of one of their friends. Based on an actual killing in Milpitas, California, the film was as audacious in its blackly comic tone as in its choice of subject. *River's Edge* is only the third film Tim Hunter has directed, yet already he has managed to put together a distinctive body of work, a group of films dealing with troubled teenagers which far outshine most Hollywood teen fare by virtue of Hunter's honesty, daring, and acute intelligence.

An interest in film came early to Tim Hunter, for his father, Ian McLellan Hunter, was an Oscar-winning screenwriter (*Roman Holiday*, 1953). Yet Hunter did not grow up in the easy Southern California climate. When his father, along with Waldo Salt, Ring Lardner, Jr., and Dalton Trumbo, was blacklisted during the McCarthy witchhunts, the family fled to Mexico City in the hope that Ian Hunter might ghostwrite scripts within reasonable reach of Los Angeles.

After a frustrating year, the Hunters left Mexico to drive cross-country to New York, where they resided for most of Tim's childhood and where Ian Hunter wrote for British television shows such as "Sir Lancelot," "The Buccaneers," and "The Adventures of Robin Hood."

"The kids of other blacklisted writers who were my friends and I had lots of shared secrets," Hunter observes. " 'Robin Hood' was one of *the* big TV shows of that time and we couldn't tell anybody that our parents were writing it. But we had a very strong sense of loyalty to one another and loyalty to principle. What had happened to our families happened because they stood up for what they believed in and didn't name names and didn't capitulate to HUAC [House Committee on Un-American Activities]. That made us all very proud. So I have some good memories of the blacklist because of the sense of community I experienced."

"About age ten," Hunter decided that he wanted to be a film director. Later, he attended the public High School of Music and Art in New York City. He wrote several screenplays while in high school and at college made numerous student films. Having been graduated from Harvard University in the class of 1968, Hunter remained in Boston long enough to make a film for WGBH, the Boston public television station. The film, *Prophetic Pictures*, had two parts, based on a pair of short stories: the title story, by Nathaniel Hawthorne, and Edgar Allan Poe's "Eleonora." Hunter's verdict on the project is nothing if not honest: "It's the worst thing I've ever done."

Nevertheless, Hunter was recruited to be in the first class of the American Film Institute (AFI). Flying to Los Angeles, Hunter was given ten thousand dollars to make *Devil's Bargain*, a 16-mm film based on Raymond Chandler's short story "Goldfish." The film took second prize at the Atlanta Film Festival and was also shown at Edinburgh. Though Hunter likes the film, he calls it, with characteristic irony, "a little short of professional... not the kind of film to make [Steven] Spielberg take notice and assign me to an 'Amazing Stories.'" He left AFI feeling disappointed. Though he acknowledges that others have benefited from AFI, for him the organization was "more like a political lobby than an outfit dedicated to helping kids with postgraduate work."

After his experience with the institute, Hunter accepted a part-time teaching position at the University of California at Santa Cruz, where for four years he organized courses around various film series he booked— series structured around themes, such as love stories or *films noir*, or around the careers of directors such as Alfred Hitchcock. "I'm a voracious film buff and inveterate auteurist," Hunter explains. "I never wanted to teach filmmaking as such but I always thought it was very exciting to turn people on to filmmaking through film and through a sense of the continuity of style and subject that filmmakers can achieve." Some of Hunter's favorite auteurs in the classroom were Frank Borzage, Douglas Sirk, John M. Stahl, and Nicholas Ray. Ray's *Rebel Without a Cause* (1956) in particular seems to have informed Hunter's career thus far, yet while Hunter admits, "I love *Rebel Without a Cause*," he claims that he "never really thought about it in terms of my pictures. Getting into pictures about teenagers just happened, as one project led into another. I never expected to be making pictures about teens."

It was at Santa Cruz that Hunter began collaborating with Charlie Haas, one of his students. Together, the two wrote *The Soul Hit* (1977), a mystery novel that was published by Harper & Row. While still in Santa Cruz, Haas read an article in the *San Francisco Examiner* about young teenagers on a crime spree in a planned community—"Mouse Packs," the paper called the gang. Traveling to Foster City, California, and researching the story, Hunter and Haas began work on *Over the Edge*, a screenplay that "took two, two and a half years to get right. It was tough to get a hook on it. We had a lot of isolated scenes and material. But we didn't quite have the thread to pull it together." Moving to Los Angeles, the two writers worked with Tina Nides at Warner Bros. on structuring the script, sold it to producer George Litto, and financed it through the newly formed Orion Pictures.

Director Jonathan Kaplan (*White Line Fever*, 1975; *Heart Like a Wheel*, 1983) was the son of a blacklisted composer and a childhood friend of Hunter whom Hunter wanted to direct the film. At first, no one would hire Kaplan, because his latest film, *Mr. Billion* (1977), had bombed at the box office. Then, through a pretty twist of fate, *White Line Fever's* television premiere was scheduled directly after the World Series and earned enormous ratings. Kaplan "became bankable that week," and Orion hired him to direct the film.

Hunter remained involved in the project through casting, location scouting, and shooting. It was important to him that the planned community in which the film was set be absolutely authentic. "I like to ground my films in that kind of physical reality," Hunter says. "There's so much that comes out of the environment. The situation in *Over the Edge* was . . . a direct response to the shortcomings of the environment. Developers had planned this whole upper-class bedroom community and nobody had taken into account that one-quarter of the population would be fifteen or younger. There was nothing for them to do."

A similar emphasis was put on finding actors the right age and type to portray the Mouse Pack. "We cast the real kids and I think that is one of the shocking things about the film. . . . The kids who had been involved in the trouble in Foster City were fifteen or younger. We cast it accurately."

The resulting 1979 film was a remarkable work for many reasons. It was perhaps the most anarchic, incendiary work about teenagers since François Truffaut's *Les Quatre Cents Coups* (1959; *The 400 Blows*); it introduced actor Matt Dillon to films; it caused considerable controversy wherever it was released. Yet the film was practically buried by the distributors, primarily because of the violence surrounding Walter Hill's gang picture, *The Warriors* (1979). "I was pleased with the film," Hunter says. "If you can get them made, you're well ahead of the game. I never lose too much sleep over bad distribution. Unless you have a really commercial picture or a sleeper or something, you can nearly anticipate bad distribution. It was a hit on cable and it's been played a lot. So by now a lot of people have seen it. It certainly has its fans."

After *Over the Edge*, Hunter and Haas worked on a computer thriller called "Trap Door," which came close to getting a studio go-ahead but was never actually filmed. Meanwhile, Hunter was pursuing another project, based on S. E. Hinton's novel *Tex* (1979). Back in Foster City researching *Over the Edge*, Hunter had realized that "if these kids read at all, they only read S. E. Hinton." So he looked into the author's published works, rejecting *The Outsiders* (1967) and *Rumble Fish* (1975)—the novels Francis Coppola later filmed—as well as *That Was Then, This Is Now* (1971). Finally, Hunter optioned *Tex* when the book first appeared in galleys. Knowing that Dillon was also a Hinton fan, Hunter sent the book to the actor, who promptly agreed to play the title role in the film. Hunter then spent a lot of time trying to interest producers in the package, but none of them at this time had heard of Hinton. "I brought the package to Disney and Disney had a new president, a guy named Tom Wilhite with a mandate to bring Disney into the modern age a bit. So to them *Tex* represented a property that could be pitched at their traditional audience and yet was more modern, more realistic, and would be taken seriously."

With a budget of five million dollars, Disney Studios agreed to take a chance on *Tex*—and on a first-time director, Tim Hunter. Hunter found the task of translating Hinton's novel to the screen rewarding. "I like melodrama," Hunter explains, "but melodrama is so often reduced to a simple hook that hooks you into a premise. Nine out of ten times you can anticipate the inevitable resolution of the premise. But in Susie Hinton's stuff, she strings together isolated melodramatic episodes that start and finish in their own time and then fold into a larger story, which in turn incorporates a larger view of the world."

The only significant change that Hunter and cowriter Haas made to Hinton's story was to add "something tangible in the last act to make it clear that Tex had learned from his experiences and wasn't going to stand in his brother's way." So Hunter and Haas created the "clunky but serviceable" device of Tex's spiteful theft of his brother's college application, only to fill it out and submit it at the picture's close.

With the part of Tex already cast, Hunter set about finding his two other leads: Tex's brother Mason and sometime girlfriend Jamie. Both parts proved difficult to cast. Hunter finally chose Jim Metzler as Mason. "He was far and away the best of the people we read for the part. We felt he was a little old for it but he had so much soul compared to anybody else." Finding someone with the combination of spunk and sensitivity to play Jamie was equally difficult. "Meg Tilly had been a dancer in the ensemble of *Fame* (1980) and had wound up mostly on the cutting-room floor. She'd done no real acting and nobody knew about her. We were right down to the wire— we'd interviewed a couple of hundred actors and nobody was right [for Jamie]. And we were really grabbing at straws. So my wife Cindy and I made a last-ditch foray into the Academy Players Guide just looking at photographs and Cindy spotted hers. And Meg came in and read for us, and five minutes later she had the part."

How was it working for Disney? "Great," according to Hunter. "They sent our first draft into production and sent my first cut into the theaters." The shooting went smoothly, and *Tex* (1982) did well with both the critics and the public, marking the entry of Disney Studios into mainstream film production. "Overall, *Tex* had a certain calmness to it, a reflective quality about people and how they change"—something Hunter and many filmgoers still value in the picture today.

"I think for the most part movies are thin these days. I really like a story with different values represented and a fair amount of complexity if I can justify it," Hunter says. Perhaps it was his demand for a denser picture than Hollywood ordinarily encourages that explains his next three years of inactivity. Hunter will not elaborate on the various projects that he, as both a writer and a director, turned down after *Tex*. Several of them, he acknowledges, eventually became major commercial successes, yet he does not regret his decisions, because it "doesn't make sense to make a film if you don't have a feel for it."

By 1985, Hunter had become desperate to make another picture. He jumped at the invitation to direct *Sylvester*, the tale of an orphaned girl's bid to become a high-toned jockey—a story, not coincidentally, with many similarities to *Tex*. Hunter enjoyed the opportunity to do "Western-type stuff: the runaway horse scene and the jumping and eventing scenes. People don't get too many chances to shoot that kind of stuff anymore. And in fact even fewer people have had a chance since *Sylvester*."

A weak, derivative film, *Sylvester* had problems beginning with the thin script by Carol Sobieski, which Hunter was encouraged to follow word for word. Hunter was also encouraged to shoot "every conceivable piece of traditional coverage" for his film. He came back with more than half a million feet of film, and "that affects the way a thing looks. It makes the style a little more impersonal, a little more homogenous."

After *Sylvester* (1985), Hunter "expected that I'd have to endure two to three years of inactivity. It was a miracle that *River's Edge* was submitted to me." Yet at first the script did not sound particularly promising. For one thing, its subject was a teen murder, and Hunter had sworn that he would have nothing further to do with teen films. Furthermore, it was a first-time screenwriter's script that had been knocking around Hollywood for two and a half years. Yet when Hunter read Neal Jimenez's script, he was "knocked out . . . floored. I couldn't believe it hadn't been made."

Even though the budget was only $1.7 million, he readily accepted the offer that Hemdale Film Corporation extended. "I was happy to get back to a . . . piece of material with a lot of shock value. I hadn't had a chance to direct a picture myself that had that kind of toughness to it." Hunter saw the characters' callousness as "a reflection of the Reagan years, as an outgrowth of a selfishness in society and of seriously misplaced priorities in society. . . . All of this leads to a dangerous apathy." He welcomed the chance to make such a political comment.

With cinematographer Frederick Elmes, Hunter evolved an expressionist visual style to match certain aspects of Jimenez's script. Because of budgetary concerns, they were encouraged to "figure out in advance what the smallest number of set-ups would be and, more to the point, [how to get] what we really wanted. . . . So *River's Edge* is more of a direct reflection of how I saw the thing than it would have been if I'd had three cameras and another four weeks on the shooting schedule."

Once again, casting proved to be a fascinating part of Hunter's work. The part of Layne, the speed-freak leader of the teenagers, was perhaps the pivotal role in the script. Crispin Glover was one of the first actors to read for Layne, and, though he called to say how much he loved the script, he postponed reading until he could prepare the part thoroughly. Two weeks later, "he came in in character and we all did a triple take. I thought he was very funny, very original. . . . His wackiness lent a lot of credence to his charismatic position within that group of kids. . . . I tend to think that if you've got the energy and charisma to lead a group, you'll find a group to lead. Most people don't have the energy to do anything but follow."

Hunter also liked the idea that Layne would be more unsettling on screen than Dennis Hopper's character, Feck, who "on paper was so much the strangest character." With Glover as Layne, Feck "would become by default the custodian of what little sense of conventional morality there is expressed in the picture. . . . It would make the picture that much more unsettling."

Casting young Joshua Miller as Tim, the perverse, angry witness to the murder, added another aspect to the film. When Hunter first saw the rushes, he realized that one could not tell if Tim were "a boy or a girl in that opening shot. I was really pleased to see it. And Crispin deliberately brought a feminine component to Layne that he was very conscious of. . . . I liked all that androgyny because it . . . revealed the worst aspect of machismo, the utter inability of the male characters to deal with women. They really hated those girls. It just comes out over and over again."

River's Edge, after all, deals with a teenager who hates women so much that he kills one. Hunter wanted the corpse of the murdered girl to be as realistic as possible.

"In the script, Jamie's body was [described] romantically. It was all very Ophelia-like. I did want to convey that dark romanticism, but I wanted a clinical aspect to it also. I didn't want the audience to slough it off as a movie death. . . . So we consulted forensic textbooks and I looked at some morgue photographs. . . . All that stuff was very accurate, right down to the lividity of the blood settling in the bottom of the body over a period of time."

In many ways, *River's Edge* bears a surprising resemblance to Hunter's first script, *Over the Edge*. Here, as a director, Hunter took the same great care that he had taken as a writer in creating a vivid milieu. Yet, whereas the previous film had an instantly recognizable setting—a planned suburban community—*River's Edge* takes place in a lonely, pastoral landscape broken only by convenience stores, schools, and cheaply built, decrepit houses.

"It isn't a city, it isn't a suburb, and it isn't the country. That's why I wanted to shoot it in Tujunga [California]. Because Tujunga really is the land that time forgot, up there in the foothills. It's full of old river-rock houses from a bygone era. And it's full of ex-hippies and ex-bikers. I just felt it would give it a timeless *Our Town* sort of quality. The purpose in this was just the opposite of the one in *Over the Edge*, because in this particular case this problem did not grow out of the specific environment like it did in Foster City. It's a problem of society, and we wanted to universalize that as much as possible. We also wanted not to point the finger in any way at Milpitas, where the real murder took place. It was just a twist of fate that that crime took place in Milpitas. It had nothing to do with Milpitas being a blot on the landscape of America."

"Dangerous," "unsettling"—these are the adjectives Tim Hunter uses to describe *River's Edge*. His goal is to depict teen malaise while at the same time depriving the viewer of a safe perspective from which to watch, and the film succeeds brilliantly. At first, studio heads at Hemdale considered *River's Edge* so subversive that they were reluctant to release it. After several positive film-festival screenings, however, they distributed the film through Island Pictures and found themselves with a cult success on their hands. Many critics found *River's Edge* the most original, disturbing film of the year.

Now writer/director Tim Hunter is anticipating branching out into new territory. He and mystery writer James Crumley have collaborated on a screen version of Crumley's mystery classic *Dancing Bear* (1983) and have since written a script based on the comic strip "Judge Dredd" for producer Edward R. Pressman. In the wake of the enormous success of *La Bamba* (1987; reviewed in this volume), Hunter has also obtained approval from United Artists to go ahead with a longtime dream: a film about the wonders of salsa music. Collaborating with playwright Reinaldo Povod, the author of *Cuba and His Teddy Bear* (1986), Hunter is penning the story of a Puerto Rican *salsero*—"a story with great music, some grit, and a lot of heart."

Asked whether this self-styled "inveterate auteurist" is worried about thematic consistency in his work, Hunter merely shrugs. "You have to go where the good material is," he explains. One thing is certain: Whatever he does in the future, Hunter thus far has displayed a level of intelligence, commitment, and daring that marks him as one of the brightest lights of the contemporary cinema.

Richard Glatzer

SELECTED FILM BOOKS OF 1987

Altman, Rick. *The American Film Musical*. Bloomington: Indiana University Press, 1987. Altman's excellent scholarly analysis provides a history of the Hollywood musical, arranged by thematic type.

Archer, Robyn and Diana Simmonds. *A Star Is Torn*. New York: E. P. Dutton, 1987. Aimed at the mass audience, this book examines the rise and fall of Marilyn Monroe, Judy Garland, and eleven other actresses and female singers who died young.

Arnold, Eve. *Marilyn Monroe: An Appreciation*. New York: Alfred A. Knopf, 1987. Photographer Arnold covered Monroe during her rise to superstardom in the 1950's, and this volume chronicles that period with behind-the-scenes photographs.

Aumont, Jacques. *Montage Eisenstein*. London: BFI Books, 1987. This biographical and critical analysis of Eisenstein focuses on the link between the Russian director's writing and his films.

Bates, Brian. *The Way of the Actor: A Path to Knowledge and Power*. Boston: Shambhala Press, 1987. Bates finds lessons in Eastern mysticism in the careers of thirty actors, including Marlon Brando, Charlton Heston, and Meryl Streep.

Boller, Paul F., Jr., and Ronald L. Davis. *Hollywood Anecdotes*. New York: William Morrow and Co., 1987. This highly readable collection of anecdotes has thirty-one chapters on diverse subjects such as studios and child stars. Each chapter is preceded by a brief essay establishing a context for the anecdotes which follow.

Bonanno, Margaret Wilder. *Angela Lansbury: A Biography*. New York: St. Martin's Press, 1987. Bonanno offers a well-written biography of the popular film and television star.

Brown, Peter H., and Jim Pinkston. *Oscar Dearest*. New York: Harper and Row, Publishers, 1987. Although much of this volume consists of a repackaging of Brown's *The Real Oscar* (1981), it is a compilation of six decades' worth of gossip and scandal that adds up to a diverting, if unorthodox, examination of the Academy Awards.

Brunette, Peter. *Roberto Rossellini*. New York: Oxford University Press, 1987. Arguing that Rossellini is "perhaps the greatest unknown director who ever lived," Brunette offers a detailed and scholarly analysis of the Italian filmmaker's career.

Christensen, Terry. *Reel Politics: American Political Movies from* Birth of a Nation *to* Platoon. New York: Basil Blackwell, 1987. Christensen argues that Hollywood films, even those which appear to be progressive, have always reinforced traditional American values.

Clark, Virginia M. *Aldous Huxley and Film*. Metuchen, New Jersey: Scarecrow Press, 1987. Huxley lived in Los Angeles for twenty-five years, writing screenplays as well as novels. Clark examines the four major screenplays and two film-related novels that Huxley produced during this time.

Cotten, Joseph. *Joseph Cotten, an Autobiography: Vanity Will Get You Somewhere.* London: Colombus, 1987. This is a frank and often-funny account of the actor's life and times.

Cowie, Peter, ed. *International Film Guide 1987.* London: The Tantivy Press, 1987. This annual publication reports on filmmaking activity in fifty-nine countries throughout the world.

Cumbow, Robert C. *Once Upon a Time: The Films of Sergio Leone.* Metuchen, New Jersey: Scarecrow Press, 1987. Cumbow provides a sympathetic analysis of the career of the Italian director whose spaghetti Westerns revolutionized the Western genre.

Davis, Bette, with Michael Herskowitz. *This 'n' That.* New York: G. P. Putnam's Sons, 1987. In Davis' third volume of memoirs, the mood is one of relative serenity, as the actress muses on her past in the aftermath of her recovery from a serious stroke.

De Carlo, Yvonne, with Doug Warren. *Yvonne: An Autobiography.* New York: St. Martin's Press, 1987. The star of innumerable B-films offers a kiss-and-tell autobiography.

Devillers, Marceau. *James Dean.* London: Sidgwick and Jackson, 1987. Production stills and candid location photographs from Dean's films highlight this survey of the actor's brief but brilliant career.

Doane, Mary Ann. *The Desire to Desire: The Woman's Film of the 1940's.* Bloomington: Indiana University Press, 1987. Doane analyzes the Hollywood films of the World War II era which were aimed explicitly at a female audience.

Donahue, Suzanne Mary. *American Film Distribution: The Changing Marketplace.* Ann Arbor, Michigan: UMI Research Press, 1987. In her scholarly study of the changing distribution patterns in the American film industry, Donahue provides an important analysis of an often-overlooked subject.

Duke, Patty, and Kenneth Turan. *Call Me Anna: The Autobiography of Patty Duke.* New York: Bantam Books, 1987. Actress and former child star Duke writes with feeling about her lost childhood and her bouts with manic-depressive psychosis.

Ebert, Roger. *Two Weeks in the Midday Sun: A Cannes Notebook.* Kansas City, Missouri: Andrews and McMeel, 1987. The popular and influential film critic offers this collection of journal entries and drawings produced during the 1987 Cannes Film Festival.

Edwards, Anne. *Early Reagan.* New York: William Morrow and Co., 1987. Focusing on Ronald Reagan's childhood and on his acting career, Edwards' biography is anecdotal rather than analytical.

Gabbard, Krin, and Glen O. Gabbard. *Psychiatry and the Cinema*. Chicago: University of Chicago Press, 1987. The first half of this scholarly volume focuses on images of psychiatry in film. The second half is a critical analysis of specific films from the point of view of a psychiatrist.

Gagne, Paul R. *The Zombies That Ate Pittsburgh: The Films of George A. Romero*. New York: Dodd, Mead and Co., 1987. Gagne's is the first in-depth study of the director of *The Night of the Living Dead* (1968) and other horror classics.

Gale, Steven H. *S. J. Perelman: A Critical Study*. Westport, Connecticut: Greenwood Press, 1987. Gale's work includes an extended discussion of Perelman's screenplays, which have frequently been neglected in previous studies of the humorist's career.

Garland, Brock. *War Movies: The Complete Viewer's Guide*. New York: Facts on File, 1987. Garland provides information on nearly five hundred films about war; entries list cast and credits and offer plot summaries and brief analyses.

Gates, Phyllis, and Bob Thomas. *My Husband, Rock Hudson*. Garden City, New York: Doubleday and Co., 1987. Gates's brief marriage to Hudson was forgotten until the revelation of his homosexuality after his death from AIDS. Here she offers an account of their relationship.

Geduld, Harry M. *Chapliniana, A Commentary on Charlie Chaplin's 81 Movies, Volume 1: The Keystone Films*. Bloomington: Indiana University Press, 1987. In the first of three projected volumes, Geduld provides detailed plot summaries, but no critical analysis, of thirty-five Chaplin films.

Gehring, Wes D. *The Marx Brothers: A Bio-Bibliography*. Westport, Connecticut: Greenwood Press, 1987. Gehring offers a study of the Marx Brothers—including Zeppo and Gummo—and their place in popular culture. The bibliographical essay is a useful review of literature that deals with the comic group.

Gifford, Denis. *British Animated Films, 1895-1985*. Jefferson, North Carolina: McFarland and Co., 1987. Arranged chronologically, this filmography provides information on production credits and plot synopses for nearly thirteen hundred cartoons produced in Great Britain since the turn of the century.

Goldstein, Toby. *William Hurt: The Actor and His Work*. New York: St. Martin's Press, 1987. Goldstein's book is a brief and undistinguished survey of the work of one of the best American actors of the 1980's.

Hamilton, John R. *Thunder in the Dust: Classic Images of Western Movies*. New York: Stewart, Tabori and Chang, 1987. The text by John Calvin Batchelor explicates Hamilton's color photographs from the sets of classic Western films of the 1960's through the 1980's in this handsome coffee-table book.

Harding, James. *Ivor Novello.* London: W. H. Allen, 1987. Novello, who died in 1951, was a major British film star in the 1930's. Harding's biography traces the career of this actor-turned-playwright.

Harris, Thomas J. *Courtroom's Finest Hour in American Cinema.* Metuchen, New Jersey: Scarecrow Press, 1987. Harris analyzes eight examples of courtroom dramas, most of which were released between 1957 and 1961.

Harris, Warren G. *Cary Grant: A Touch of Elegance.* New York: Doubleday Publishing Co., 1987. This biography, the first since Grant's death in 1986, is aimed at the mass audience.

Harvey, James. *Romantic Comedy in Hollywood from Lubitsch to Sturges.* New York: Alfred A. Knopf, 1987. Harvey's work is a detailed and cogent analysis of the screwball comedy genre in its heyday from 1929 to 1948.

Hay, James. *Popular Film Culture in Fascist Italy: The Passing of the Rex.* Bloomington: Indiana University Press, 1987. Using the luxury liner *Rex* from Federico Fellini's *Amarcord* (1974) as a metaphor, Hay offers a scholarly examination of the underlying themes of Italian cinema during the 1930's. He suggests that the search for a new social order was a common motif in the films of the Fascist era.

Helt, Richard C., and Marie E. Helt. *West German Cinema Since 1945: A Reference Handbook.* Metuchen, New Jersey: Scarecrow Press, 1987. In this alphabetical listing of feature-length films produced by West German filmmakers since the end of World War II, each entry contains information on cast and credits, as well as a one-sentence plot summary.

Hepburn, Katharine. *The Making of the African Queen, Or How I Went to Africa With Bogart, Bacall, and Huston and Almost Lost My Mind.* New York: Alfred A. Knopf, 1987. A delightful account of the making of a classic film, Hepburn's memoir became a best-seller.

Higham, Charles. *Brando: The Unauthorized Biography.* New York: New American Library, 1987. This book is a standard unauthorized biography from a veteran of the genre on a subject who is doubtless accustomed to this sort of treatment.

Hutchison, David. *Film Magic: The Art and Science of Special Effects.* Englewood Cliffs, New Jersey: Prentice-Hall, 1987. Aimed at the lay audience, this useful volume devotes a chapter each to such special effects techniques as miniatures and traveling mattes. It also contains an annotated filmography of films that feature noteworthy special effects.

Johnson, Randal. *The Film Industry in Brazil.* Pittsburgh, Pennsylvania: University of Pittsburgh Press, 1987. The complex relationship between art and the state forms the context of this history of Brazilian cinema from the late nineteenth century through the mid-1980's.

Katz, Robert. *Love Is Colder Than Death: The Life and Times of Rainer*

Werner Fassbinder. New York: Random House, 1987. This account of the life of the late German filmmaker stresses biographical details rather than film criticism.

Kidd, Charles. *Debrett Goes to Hollywood*. New York: St. Martin's Press, 1987. Kidd, a veteran researcher into the family trees of British royalty, turns his talents on American celebrities, with surprisingly interesting results.

Knight, Vivienne. *Trevor Howard: A Gentleman and a Player*. New York: Beaufort Books, 1987. This rather pedestrian authorized biography was written prior to the death of the distinguished British actor.

Koppes, Clayton R., and Gregory D. Black. *Hollywood Goes to War*. New York: Macmillan, 1987. The authors examine the relationship between the United States Office of War Information and the American film studios, concluding that the government exerted great influence in Hollywood during World War II.

Kotsilibas-Davis, James, and Myrna Loy. *Myrna Loy: Being and Becoming*. New York: Alfred A. Knopf, 1987. This memoir intersperses the actress' recollections with those of her associates and stresses her political activism as much as her acting career.

Kuenzli, Rudolf E., ed. *Dada and Surrealist Film*. New York: Willis Locker and Owens, 1987. A collection of fourteen essays on the cinema of Luis Buñuel, Man Ray, and other surrealists. The book's final chapter is an extensive biography on Dada/surrealist film in general, as well as on all the important filmmakers of the genre in particular.

Lardner, James. *Fast Forward: Hollywood, the Japanese, and the Onslaught of the VCR*. New York: W. W. Norton and Co., 1987. Lardner tells the story behind the Hollywood studios' unsuccessful attempts to convince the Supreme Court to prohibit private-use home taping in the United States.

Lee, Spike. *Spike Lee's She's Gotta Have It: Inside Guerrilla Filmmaking*. New York: Simon and Schuster, 1987. Lee's film was a surprise hit, and this volume, which includes the screenplay, Lee's journals and production notes, and a lengthy interview, offers useful insights on the black filmmaker's approach to his craft.

Leff, Leonard J. *Hitchcock and Selznick*. New York: Weidenfeld and Nicolson, 1987. Director Alfred Hitchcock and producer David O. Selznick made four films together between 1939 and 1947, quarreling all the while over who was in control of each project. Leff's book is a well-written account of this relationship.

Levy, Emanuel. *And the Winner Is . . . : The History and Politics of the Oscar Award*. New York: Frederick Ungar Publishing Co., 1987. Levy applies techniques of statistical analysis to the Academy Awards in this economic and sociological study of a Hollywood institution.

Luhr, William, ed. *World Cinema Since 1945*. New York: Frederick Ungar

Publishing Co., 1987. Luhr presents a useful collection of essays on the development of cinema since World War II in more than thirty foreign countries.

MacCann, Richard Dyer. *The First Tycoons*. Metuchen, New Jersey: Scarecrow Press, 1987. Here is a scholarly examination of the lives and interactions of the founders of the major American film studios—William Fox, Samuel Goldwyn, Adolph Zukor, and more.

McCarty, John. *The Films of John Huston*. Secaucus, New Jersey: Citadel Press, 1987. This volume, completed prior to Huston's death, covers the actor/screenwriter/director's career through *Prizzi's Honor* (1985). Like similar volumes from Citadel, this book contains a plot summary for each film, along with a summary of contemporary reviews and information on cast and credits.

McDonald, Archie P. *Shooting Stars: Heroes and Heroines of Western Film*. Bloomington: Indiana University Press, 1987. This book provides critical essays on the careers of ten actors known for their Western films, plus a chapter each on women in Westerns and Westerns on television.

McDonough, Tom. *Light Years: Confession of a Cinematographer*. New York: Grove Press, 1987. This memoir includes biographical information on McDonough and his colleagues as well as insights into the art of cinematography.

McFarlane, Brian. *Australian Cinema, 1970-1985*. London: Secker and Warburg, 1987. Although other authors have published books on the earlier days of Australian cinema, McFarlane's work is the first extensive critical survey of the decade in which these films attained international popularity.

MacLaine, Shirley. *It's All in the Playing*. New York: Bantam Books, 1987. This book is the fifth of MacLaine's best-selling accounts of her spiritual odysseys in this world and others.

McMurtry, Larry. *Film Flam: Essays on Hollywood*. New York: Simon and Schuster, 1987. This volume collects twenty-one essays, written in the 1970's, on various aspects of filmmaking. All but four were originally published in *American Film*. At his best, McMurtry offers beautifully astringent commentary on the craft of screenwriting.

Maeder, Edward, ed. *Hollywood and History: Costume Design in Film*. New York: Thames and Hudson, 1987. The archives of the Los Angeles County Museum of Art provided the raw material for this impressive collection of essays on costume design in American cinema.

Marx, Samuel. *A Gaudy Spree*. New York: Franklin Watts, 1987. Marx was a Hollywood screenwriter in the 1930's; this book chronicles the literary life of that era "when the west was fun."

Mast, Gerald. *Can't Help Singin': The American Musical on Stage and Screen*. Woodstock, New York: Overlook Press, 1987. Through chapters on individual songwriters, playwrights, and studios of the 1930's, 1940's, and 1950's, Mast traces the evolution of the American musical, identifying it as the middle ground between opera and burlesque.

Mathews, Jack. *The Battle of Brazil*. New York: Crown Publishers, 1987. Mathews analyzes the prerelease controversy generated by Terry Gilliam's acclaimed black comedy.

Moseley, Roy. *Rex Harrison: The First Biography*. New York: St. Martin's Press, 1987. Written with the cooperation of several Harrison intimates, but not that of Harrison himself, this volume supplants the actor's own *Rex* (1975) as the most authoritative account of the life of the British leading man.

Oumano, Ellen. *Movies for a Desert Isle*. New York: St. Martin's Press, 1987. Forty-two actors, directors, and other celebrities talk about themselves and their favorite films in this entertaining volume.

Palmer, William J. *The Films of the Seventies: A Social History*. Metuchen, New Jersey: Scarecrow Press, 1987. Focusing on eleven films released between 1966 and 1981, Palmer identifies four major themes in the cinema of the 1970's: corporate conspiracy, the futility of war, the inability to control and understand reality, and the failure of postwar existentialism.

Parish, James Robert, and Michael R. Pitts. *The Great Gangster Pictures II*. Metuchen, New Jersey: Scarecrow Press, 1987. Volume 1 was published in 1976; this book provides detailed information on four hundred gangster films released in the following decade.

Pogel, Nancy. *Woody Allen*. Boston: Twayne Publishers, 1987. Pogel's scholarly study of Allen's film career through *The Purple Rose of Cairo* (1985), places Allen in the Chaplinesque tradition of the "little man."

Powell, Michael. *A Life in Movies: An Autobiography*. New York: Alfred A. Knopf, 1987. An important British filmmaker, best known for *The Red Shoes* (1948), covers the first half of his life in this well-written autobiography.

Rainey, Buck. *Heroes of the Range: Yesterday's Matinee Movie Cowboys*. Metuchen, New Jersey: Scarecrow Press, 1987. A good survey of the careers of fifteen film cowboys, including some less well-known actors, Rainey's book also features complete filmographies for each of its subjects.

Riese, Randall, and Neal Hitchens. *The Unabridged Marilyn: Her Life from A to Z*. New York: Congdon and Weed, 1987. This encyclopedia is devoted to the life and career of Marilyn Monroe. Its quirky arrangement makes it a better trivia book than a reference work.

Robbins, Jhan. *Yul Brynner: The Inscrutable King*. New York: Dodd, Mead and Co., 1987. Robbins' biography of the late actor is aimed at the popular audience.

Rockett, Kevin, Luke Gibbons, and John Hill. *Cinema and Ireland*. London: Croom Helm, 1987. This volume represents the most comprehensive survey available of films shot in and about Ireland.

Rogin, Michael Paul. *Ronald Reagan, the Movie, and Other Episodes in Political Demonology*. Berkeley: University of California Press, 1987. American Marxist Rogin traces Reagan's politics to the roles he played as an actor in this collection of essays on politics and film.

Ross, Harris. *Film as Literature, Literature as Film*. New York: Greenwood Press, 1987. Ross provides a fifty-page analysis of the relationship between literature and cinema to accompany a twenty-five-hundred-item bibliography on the subject.

Ryan, Michael, and Douglas Kellner. *Camera Politica: The Politics and Ideology of Contemporary Hollywood Film*. Bloomington: Indiana University Press, 1987. The authors advance the rather unremarkable theory that the liberal attitudes evidenced in Hollywood films in the late 1960's have been supplanted by a more conservative ideology.

Sandahl, Linda J. *Rock Films*. New York: Facts on File, 1987. This reference book provides information on feature films and documentaries about rock and roll. The work covers films released between 1955 and 1986.

Sayles, John. *Thinking in Pictures: The Making of the Movie* Matewan. Houghton Mifflin Co., 1987. Sayles, one of the most creative directors in American cinema, describes in detail the choices a filmmaker faces during the course of a film's creation.

Scott, Jay. *Midnight Matinees: Movies and Their Makers, 1975-1985*. New York: Frederick Ungar Publishing Co., 1987. An irreverent Canadian film critic offers a compilation of articles and shorter reviews of a decade's worth of films.

Server, Lee. *Screenwriter: Words Become Pictures*. Pittstown, New Jersey: Main Street Press, 1987. Server interviews twelve screenwriters; the resulting volume is longer on gossip than it is on useful information about screenwriting.

Skretvedt, Randy. *Laurel and Hardy: The Magic Behind the Movies*. Beverly Hills, California: Moonstone Press, 1987. Focusing on the comic duo's least successful films, Skretvedt argues that Laurel and Hardy's demise was caused by the death of films of two reels, the length best suited to their talents.

Slater, Thomas J. *Miloš Forman: A Bio-Bibliography*. New York: Greenwood Press, 1987. The first book-length study of this important director includes an extensive filmography as well as an annotated bibliography.

Spada, James. *Grace: The Secret Lives of a Princess*. Garden City, New York: Doubleday Publishing Co., 1987. Spada presents a detailed "warts-and-all" account of the life of Grace Kelly.

Steene, Brigitta. *Ingmar Bergman: A Guide to References and Resources*. Boston: G. K. Hall and Co., 1987. This book is a biographical and bibliographical study of the career of the great Swedish filmmaker through *Fanny and Alexander* (1983).

Sterling, Anna Kate, ed. *Celebrity Articles from* The Screen Guild Magazine. Metuchen, New Jersey: Scarecrow Press, 1987. This book collects articles written by prominent actors, directors, and screenwriters between 1934 and 1938 for *The Screen Guild Magazine*.

_____, ed. *Cinematographers on the Art and Craft of Cinematography*. Metuchen, New Jersey: Scarecrow Press, 1987. This valuable compilation of articles published in *The International Photographer* between 1929 and 1937 provides a unique look at cinematography in film's early days.

Stock, Dennis. *James Dean Revisited*. San Francisco: Chronicle Books, 1987. Dean was a strikingly photogenic individual, and these photographs of the actor as he went about his daily life provide more grist for his fans.

Strasberg, Lee. *A Dream of Passion: The Development of the Method*. Boston: Little, Brown and Co., 1987. Strasberg's theories on acting are among the most influential of the twentieth century, and this volume represents his version of the development of the famous Method school of acting.

Swann, Paul. *The Hollywood Feature Film in Postwar Britain*. London: Croom Helm, 1987. Swann analyzes the success of American cinema in England after World War II and explores the medium's role in extending American cultural hegemony in Europe.

Tambling, Jeremy. *Opera, Ideology, and Film*. Manchester, England: Manchester University Press, 1987. A scholarly examination of the treatment of opera in cinema and the effect of one medium on the other.

Tarkovsky, Andrey. *Sculpting in Time: Reflections on the Cinema*. New York: Alfred A. Knopf, 1987. Tarkovsky, who died in 1986, was an avant-garde Russian director. This volume offers his ideas on various aspects of filmmaking.

Taub, Eric. *Gaffers, Grips, and Best Boys*. New York: St. Martin's Press, 1987. This handbook, aimed at a lay audience, is a useful guide to the behind-the-scenes tasks that go into the making of a motion picture.

Taves, Brian. *Robert Florey, the French Expressionist*. Metuchen, New Jersey: Scarecrow Press, 1987. Florey wrote and directed films as diverse as *Frankenstein* (1931) and the Marx Brothers' *The Cocoanuts* (1929). This volume analyzes his lengthy career.

Taylor, John. *Storming the Magic Kingdom: Wall Street, the Raiders, and the Battle for Disney*. New York: Alfred A. Knopf, 1987. Taylor offers a fascinating account of the financial intrigue in and around the Disney empire in the mid-1980's.

Thomson, David. *Warren Beatty and Desert Eyes*. Garden City, New York: Doubleday and Co., 1987. Thomson combines fiction with film criticism and biography in this impressionistic survey of the life and times of Warren Beatty.

Van Doren, Mamie, and Art Aveilhe. *Playing the Field: My Story*. New York: G. P. Putnam's Sons, 1987. One of Hollywood's best-known sex symbols of the 1950's describes her numerous affairs in this "tell-all" autobiography.

Wagenknecht, Edward. *Stars of the Silents*. Metuchen, New Jersey: Scarecrow Press, 1987. A noted authority on silent films offers illuminating biographical essays on eight stars of that era.

Walker, Alexander. *Vivien: The Life of Vivien Leigh*. New York: Weidenfeld and Nicolson, 1987. This well-written biography of the talented actress focuses on her relationship with Laurence Olivier and her battles with mental illness.

Wayne, Jane Ellen. *Gable's Women*. Englewood Cliffs, New Jersey: Prentice-Hall, 1987. Blow-by-blow accounts of Clark Gable's love affairs form the basis of this rather skewed biography.

Wayne, Pilar, with Alex Thorleifson. *John Wayne: My Life with the Duke*. New York: McGraw-Hill Book Co., 1987. John Wayne's third wife provides a better-than-average account of the career of her late husband, both before and after their marriage.

Weiss, Marion. *Martin Scorsese: A Guide to References and Resources*. Boston: G. K. Hall and Co., 1987. This book is a biographical and bibliographical study of Scorsese's career through *After Hours* (1985).

Whiting, Charles. *Hero: The Life and Death of Audie Murphy*. New York: Stein and Day, 1987. Murphy, who was the most decorated soldier of World War II, parlayed his fame into a long, if undistinguished, film career. Whiting argues that Murphy's problems were caused by what has come to be known as posttraumatic stress disorder.

Wild, David. *The Movies of Woody Allen*. New York: Perigee Books, 1987. This is a book of trivia questions for Allen buffs only.

Wolfe, Charles. *Frank Capra: A Guide to References and Resources*. Boston: G. K. Hall and Co., 1987. Wolfe has assembled a biographical and bibliographical study of the career of the great American director.

Woll, Allen L., and Randall M. Miller. *Ethnic and Racial Images in American Film and Television: Historical Essays and Bibliography*. New York: Garland, 1987. This survey of the screen images of twelve racial/ethnic groups is especially useful in regard to groups (such as Arabs and Eastern Europeans) about whom relatively little has been published.

Zucker, Harvey Marc, and Lawrence J. Babich. *Sports Films: A Complete Reference*. Jefferson, North Carolina: McFarland and Co., 1987. Arranged first by sport and then alphabetically by title, this reference volume offers a plot summary plus cast and credit information for more than two thousand films from the silent era through 1984.

SELECTED
FILMS
OF
1987

ANGEL HEART

Production: Alan Marshall and Elliot Kastner; released by Tri-Star Pictures
Direction: Alan Parker
Screenplay: Alan Parker; based on the novel *Falling Angel* by William
   Hjortsberg
Cinematography: Michael Seresin
Editing: Gerry Hambling
Production design: Brian Morris
Art direction: Kristi Zea and Armin Ganz; set decoration, Robert J. Franco
   and Leslie Pope
Special effects: J. C. Brotherhood
Makeup: Carla White
Costume design: Aude Bronson-Howard
Choreography: Louis Faler
Sound: Danny Michael
Music: Trevor Jones
MPAA rating: R
Running time: 113 minutes

Principal characters:
Harry Angel	Mickey Rourke
Louis Cyphre	Robert De Niro
Epiphany Proudfoot	Lisa Bonet
Margaret Krusemark	Charlotte Rampling
Ethan Krusemark	Socker Fontelieu
Toots Sweet	Brownie McGhee
Dr. Fowler	Michael Higgins
Connie	Elizabeth Whitcraft
Sterne	Eliot Keener
Spider Simpson	Charles Gordone
Winesap	Dann Florek

Alan Parker's *Angel Heart* opens late at night in New York City with a
solitary figure, his back to the camera, shuffling down a deserted street. A
cat meows, trapped on the landing of a fire escape. A dog trots down the
street, becoming briefly interested in the cat before moving on. As the camera tracks the dog's progress, it suddenly sweeps across a bloody corpse, lying faceup on the sidewalk, the throat slashed.

This atmospheric beginning, never clearly connected to the plot, not only
sets the tone for the film but also serves as a microcosm for the subsequent
narrative. The steely, blue-gray, glistening darkness of the street, the steam
rising from a manhole (indicative of Michael Seresin's carefully composed

cinematography), and Courtney Pine's moody jazz saxophone playing in the background serve to ground the film squarely within the *film noir* tradition. While the corpse is only one of many such unfortunates to be discovered later, the animals, in particular the cat with its traditional association with witchcraft and the devil, hint at another important strain in the film—the horror picture. In fact, the work represents an attempt, which remains at best uneasy, to achieve a merging of these two distinct genres.

The action takes place in the 1950's. Harry Angel (Mickey Rourke), a shabby private eye, is hired by a mysterious gentleman named Louis Cyphre (Robert De Niro) to find a missing celebrity, a crooner named Johnny Favorite, who disappeared during World War II without paying a debt to Cyphre.

Harry's search takes him first to Poughkeepsie, New York, where he encounters a drug-addicted doctor who once treated Favorite, and then to New Orleans in search of Favorite's mistresses, Margaret Krusemark (Charlotte Rampling), a clairvoyant, and Evangeline Proudfoot, a black herbalist.

Along the way, he meets and makes love to Evangeline's daughter Epiphany (Lisa Bonet), but his investigative efforts are impeded when each of the people he tracks down and questions dies grotesquely. Not until the end of the film is Harry forced to confront the truth that he is, in fact, Johnny Favorite. He suffers from amnesia and has been killing those who knew him in a desperate attempt to avoid having to recognize his true identity and pay his debt to Louis Cyphre, who is actually Lucifer.

Angel Heart is one of a series of recent films set mainly in New Orleans, which has suddenly become a very popular location, evidenced by *Down by Law* (1986), *No Mercy* (1986), and *The Big Easy* (1987; reviewed in this volume). In *Angel Heart*, the city has a distinctly different look from New York. The colors of the decaying New Orleans buildings are much more faded, as if washed out by the torrential downpour during which the narrative terminates. With its African subculture voodoo cults (Dr. John's "Zu Zu Mamou" is on the sound track), the city is a colorful backdrop for a modern retelling of the Faust legend.

Bonet, who plays a daughter in the all-American black family of television's "The Cosby Show," gives an unexpectedly fine performance as a sultry mambo priestess. Her casting in this role, which includes a rather torrid but nevertheless routine lovemaking scene with Rourke, nearly resulted in the film's receiving an X rating. Since the distributor, Tri-Star Pictures, threatened to withdraw its services if this initial rating stood, Parker was obliged to snip ten noncontinuous, offending seconds from the print, after which the Classification and Rating Administration vouchsafed it an R rating. Since those who have seen the unexpurgated version are at a loss to explain what difference those particular ten seconds could possibly make, it seems safe to conclude that the board members were uncomfortable seeing Bonet, whose television image is so wholesome, abandon herself to pleasure in the arms of a man who later proves to be her father. The ratings tiff gave the film a considerable amount of free publicity, making it something of a *succès de scandale* even before its release.

Rourke seems deliberately to choose to star in quirky films such as *Rumble Fish* (1983) and *Nine and a Half Weeks* (1986) that take him away from mainstream cinema. In *Angel Heart* and, more recently, in *Barfly* (1987; reviewed in this volume), he appears to be drawn to extremely sleazy fringe characters. Harry Angel is by no means the standard Hollywood private eye. He is as likely to run from a battle as he is to stay and fight it. He is a man without beliefs who merely wants to survive by doing the mundane divorce and insurance-related cases. Yet, he is capable of showing flashes of the traditional hard-boiled, wise guy private eye in the style of Humphrey Bogart in *The Maltese Falcon* (1941), such as when he questions the drug-addicted doctor, and later when he lights a cigarette by striking a match on the sole of the dead physician's shoe. More often, however, he is clearly in over his head, as when he is seated in the parlor of Pastor John's church, where he first met Cyphre. He looks completely lost, as if he has no idea how to proceed with the investigation; in fact, there seems to be no reason why he would have returned to the church at all. Harry Angel does not have much going for him and it is a credit to Rourke's skill as an actor that he manages to make such a sordid character sympathetic and even compelling.

Angel Heart is far less convincing in its horror-film aspects, despite De Niro's effective portrayal of a refined, almost operatic Prince of Darkness. His total on-screen time is brief. He has one memorable scene, however, in which he takes an excruciatingly long time to peel and then devour, in close-up, a hard-boiled egg, having explained to Harry that the egg is the symbol of the soul. Even his characterization of a punctilious, at times prissy archfiend unravels near the end, when he appears with those all-too-familiar pale yellowish, glistening eyes. When Epiphany's young son, supposedly the offspring of the mambo priestess and the devil, reveals the same satanic eyes, the similarity to *Rosemary's Baby* (1968) becomes uncomfortably pronounced, the visual cliché underscoring a certain tired, unimaginative quality in the denouement.

This is unfortunate because, up to the end, the film poses a number of provocative and unanswered questions. During the opening scene of the street at night, a mysterious voice-over whispers "Johnny! Johnny!" What is to be made of this linking of Johnny and Harry to an otherwise routine urban crime? Is he a killer or a serial murderer? Harry supposedly suffers from amnesia, the result of a brief but traumatic service in World War II, which left his earlier life a blank. As the list of corpses grows, how does he manage to suppress completely any remembrance of these recent killings? When blood rains down on the lovemaking of Harry and Epiphany (no doubt adding to the discomfort of the rating-board members), the viewer wonders exactly whose hallucination it is.

Film critic Molly Haskell argues that the film makes emotional rather than literal sense and there is much truth in this assertion. The narration is infused with repeated images, often in flashback, of fans, shrouded figures, basins of liquid (water or blood), an Art Nouveau staircase, mirrors, and old-fashioned elevators with collapsible iron-grill doors. The fans are particularly disquieting; they are seldom turned on but move gratingly in the breeze, clockwise and counterclockwise. Often, they are window fans and one has to wonder why they remain in place in winter, with snow on the ground and everybody wearing overcoats. Johnny Favorite's New York hotel room on New Year's Eve seems to be the only one on the building's ample façade so peculiarly equipped.

Parker, who also wrote the screenplay, has a number of impressive films to his credit, including *Midnight Express* (1978), and *Fame* (1980), *Pink Floyd the Wall* (1982), and *Shoot the Moon* (1982). Taken together, what is unusual about these works is that they are all quite different in subject matter and tone. Parker is apparently a director who is inspired by diversity. *Angel Heart* represents yet another new tack in this varied and productive career.

John W. Martin

Reviews
Films in Review. XXXVIII, August, 1987, p. 424.
Jet. LXXI, March 2, 1987, p. 16.
Los Angeles Times. March 6, 1987, VI, p. 1.
Macleans. C, March 16, 1987, p. 58.
National Review. XXXIX, April 10, 1987, p. 52.
The New York Times. March 6, 1987, p. C5.
The New Yorker. LXIII, April 6, 1987, p. 85.
Newsweek. CIX, March 16, 1987, p. 72.
Time. CXXIX, March 9, 1987, p. 86.
Variety. CCCXXVI, March 4, 1987, p. 18.

ANNA

Production: Zanne Devine and Yurek Bogayevicz; released by Vestron
  Pictures
Direction: Yurek Bogayevicz
Screenplay: Agnieszka Holland
Cinematography: Bobby Bukowski
Editing: Julie Sloane
Production design: Lester Cohen
Art direction: Daniel Talpers; set decoration, John Tatlock
Music: Greg Hawkes
MPAA rating: PG-13
Running time: 100 minutes

> *Principal characters:*
> Anna.............................Sally Kirkland
> Daniel ....Robert Fields
> Krystyna.......................Paulina Porizkova
> Professor ....Stefan Schnabel
> Baskin ....Larry Pines
> Agent............................Charles Randall
> Tonda............................Steven Gilborn

Not until Sally Kirkland received several major awards, including a
nomination for Best Actress by the Academy of Motion Picture Arts and
Sciences, for her performance in *Anna* did the film shake the persistent
critical reprimands of banality—not altogether surprising, given how thickly
allusions to other films and other genres are layered in the narrative.

From the first shot of the Manhattan skyline, a ringing phone draws the
viewer into a modest apartment. It is answered by a disheveled middle-aged
blonde with a heavy Czech accent: The Off-Off Broadway actress Anna
Radkova (Kirkland) is reminded by her furious agent that one of her rare
auditions is about to begin in fifteen minutes. Arriving in a chic black outfit
highlighting her spectacular legs, the energetic and only slightly ravaged
Anna looks an unlikely candidate for the role of an older woman in what
seems to be the work of a lesser Polish absurdist. The lunatic audition over,
she is accosted by a bundled-up figure, introducing herself in fluent Czech
as a fervent admirer from their former homeland, just arrived in New York
and ready to wash dishes simply to be near her idol. When the young
woman, Krystyna (Paulina Porizkova), faints from hunger on her suitcase
full of old clippings documenting the actress' brilliant career, Anna takes her
home; when her agent lets her know that she has been chosen for the play,
she announces to Daniel (Robert Fields), her "lover, a little," that she is
keeping Krystyna for luck.

With her looks and English groomed by Anna and Daniel, respectively, Krystyna flourishes: A photomontage of the two women bridged by a voice-over letter to Krystyna's younger sister overseas details the enthusiastic embrace of America. While the depressed Anna continues to watch from the wings the repetition of the mad play in which her role turns out to be the understudy for a cast of seven women, Krystyna soon lands a major role in a film by world-famous director Baskin (Larry Pines).

In a part-motherly, part-sisterly mood, Anna confides details from her complicated past to her protégée, telling her that she can "make what she wants of it": from stardom at the crest of the Czech New Wave tech under the tutelage of its best young director, subsequently her husband Tonda (Steven Gilborn), through post-1968 invasion persecution, prison, death of a child, and expulsion from her homeland, to a rejection in New York by the now fully Americanized Tonda. Krystyna seems deeply moved; yet on her first television show, answering a question about her life, she uses the same story, carefully rehearsed, to provide herself with a dramatic past proper for an Iron Curtain star. In a precipitous series of events, the distraught Anna throws out Krystyna from her apartment, finding that in the process she is also losing Daniel, who wants to move to Los Angeles as Krystyna's manager; subsequently she watches an old film of hers burn up as it becomes caught in a jammed projector in a mostly deserted theater. Drunk during her one evening on the stage, Anna curses her audience. Finally, she is seen on a beach where she climbs over a dune, pulls out a gun and, aiming badly, shoots. Emerging in a white dress from the sea in front of a battery of film cameras and a large crew, Krystyna is wounded but runs to embrace the older woman. The two weep in each other's arms while Krystyna's unflappable voice-over letter to her sister describes Anna's behavior as a minor breakdown, her own health problem as insignificant, and tells of their future plans, which involve Los Angeles, film work, and a face-lift for Anna.

Most critics saw the archetypal plot of the young actress stealing the existence of the aging star as a less-than-original compound of themes from *All About Eve* (1950), *A Star Is Born* (1954), *Sunset Boulevard* (1950), and almost every backstage musical ever made. Granting, however, a near-generic status to this premise, it is possible to appreciate instead how these familiar conventions are inflected. From this perspective, Kirkland's portrayal of Anna, the fading star, belongs properly in the same category with Bette Davis' portrayal of Margo Channing, James Mason's portrayal of Norman Maine, and Gloria Swanson's portrayal of Norma Desmond. In the three latter cases, however, the requisite charisma for those roles as fading stars was accrued by Davis, Mason, and Swanson after years of top billing. In her first major film role, Kirkland's task was first to build up the resonance of stardom, cover it with twenty years of failure, and then somehow sum up the contradiction.

It is thus apparent why Polish screenwriter Agnieszka Holland (herself a filmmaker whose best-known work is *Provincial Actors*, 1979) and director Yurek Bogayevicz (whose career began in the Polish experimentalist theater of Jerzy Grotowski) would have chosen to work with a Strasberg-trained actress. In best Method style, Kirkland plays each scene by drawing on two fundamentally disjunct emotions, carefully managing body against objects. During a particularly low point of her existence as understudy, verging on tears, she lies on the floor and gives a maternal pep talk to a cockroach. A new production assistant drops in to tell her how much she admired her performance in an early Czech film; smiling radiantly Anna accepts the compliment, then returns politely to the cockroach. Far from the madness or the wrenching melodrama usually associated with the figure of a fallen star, Anna's failure emerges simply as a function of differences between cultures: Her foreignness is allowed to stand without turning pathetic, deliberate, or comical.

It is proper that characterization would be structured so complexly, given that the key turn of the plot is Krystyna's theft of Anna's "depth," that accumulation of experiences and memories that define an individual's *persona*. This dimension Krystyna lacks completely; indeed, the two photomontage and voice-over sequences, normally devices that allow a heightened intimacy with a character, serve here mainly to document the young woman's absolute banality. Neither vicious nor ambitious, Krystyna is a blank surface that needs depth to be transformed from merely another pretty face (supplied, appropriately, by the world-famous model Porizkova) into a dramatic actress with a complete emotional ensemble.

The dichotomy of depth and surface does not serve only to differentiate the mediums of theater and film in terms of their capacity to represent psychological space. The flattening of Anna's life story by Krystyna is also a process of fitting it into the cliché-laden slots of the American mass media at large. "All East Europeans have bad teeth," opines one character; "I hate Czech films," says another. "Here you'll need a life story," Anna instructs Krystyna, and she advises that it include mention of cruel Communists, bloody uprisings, heroic democrats, and evil Russian ambassadors. While explicitly mocking these generic requirements, the film also makes occasional ironic use of them (ambiguously enough for some reviewers to take the jokes seriously and reproach the two Polish filmmakers for spreading stereotypes about East European culture). Krystyna thus arrives in New York directly from a costume drama about turn-of-the-century immigrants: baggy stockings, braided buns under a babushka, and a disarming but far from perfect smile. Pensively she reveals to Anna that her youth in Czechoslovakia was boring, nothing more than "playing piano [and] milking cows."

What makes *Anna* at once troublesome and fascinating is that the film, like so many European art films in the 1960's, circulates with an additional layer of information that belongs both outside and inside the text itself, ostensibly apparent only to those in the know, but in fact also carefully distributed through select press channels. According to the film's credits, the story of Anna is a thinly veiled biography of Elzbieta Czyzewska, a brilliant Warsaw stage actress whose complicated involvement with the Polish authorities as well as with the Polish film establishment in the late 1960's led her to settle in New York, where she made several unsuccessful attempts to regain a theatrical career. Legendary among emigrés as well as theater cognoscenti (Meryl Streep has acknowledged her debt publicly), Czyzewska was apparently instrumental in arranging the debut of Joanna Pakula in *Gorky Park* (1983). Conversely, Porizkova's own biography, even modified for the film's press packet, is no less melodramatic than the one Krystyna is castigated for "stealing" from her mentor. Left in Czechoslovakia as a young child by her parents, who failed in all of their efforts to get her released through legal channels, she was to be kidnapped by her mother and two Swedish journalists in a rented plane. The action was interrupted by the police, however, and the mother was jailed for several years before the authorities yielded to massive international media pressure and let the family return to Sweden along with a second child born in prison.

Drawing on generic forms acceptable to the American audiences, Bogayevicz and Holland bracketed the problem of cultural authenticity (America's view of non-America as shown in an American-made film) within a more readily accepted plot of struggle for formal authenticity (as a problem of authentic versus artificial depth in performance). Using extra-filmic levers (an already famous model's face, the frisson of a plot *à clef*), Bogayevicz and especially Holland thus redesigned their past experience, making it possible to be rediscovered by America so as to break into world cinema a second time.

Nataša Ďurovičová

Reviews
Films in Review. XXXIX, January, 1988, p. 45.
Life. X, October, 1987, p. 8.
Los Angeles Times. November 13, 1987, VI, p. 1.
New York. XX, November 9, 1987, p. 116.
The New York Times. October 2, 1987, p. C11.
Variety. CCCXXVI, April 8, 1987, p. 16.
Vogue. CLXXVII, October, 1987, p. 82.

AU REVOIR LES ENFANTS
(GOODBYE, CHILDREN)

Origin: France
Production: Louis Malle for Nouvelles Éditions de Films, M.K.2. Productions, Stella Film, and N.E.F.; released by Orion Classics
Direction: Louis Malle
Screenplay: Louis Malle
Cinematography: Renato Berta
Editing: Émmanuelle Castro
Narration: Louis Malle
Art direction: Willy Holt
Makeup: Susan Robertson
Costume design: Corinne Jorry
Sound: Jean-Claude Laureux
Music: Franz Schubert, Moment Musical no. 2, and Camille Saint-Saëns, Rondo Capricioso
MPAA rating: PG
Running time: 103 minutes

> *Principal characters:*
> Julien Quentin.................Gaspard Manesse
> Jean Bonnet......................Raphaël Fejtö
> Mme Quentin...................Francine Racette
> François Quentin........Stanislas Carré de Malberg
> Father Jean ....Philippe Morier-Genoud
> Father Michel.................François Berléand
> Joseph ....François Négret
> Muller...............................Peter Fitz
> Negus.........................Arnaud Henriet
> Mme Perrin ....Jacqueline Paris

It has taken director Louis Malle more than forty years to film the tragic events of a day in 1944 which would become the most important experience of his childhood. *Au Revoir les Enfants* is Malle's poignant, highly autobiographical account of his experiences as a schoolboy in occupied France and his friendship with a young Jewish boy hidden from the Germans by the priests at Malle's exclusive Catholic boarding school. His friend's eventual discovery and arrest—and subsequent death at Auschwitz—left Malle with memories that have haunted him throughout his long and successful career.

Malle has stated in interviews that he believes that he has only recently acquired the skill and experience he needed as a filmmaker to be able to do justice to the story, and his film captures both the everyday antics of adolescent schoolboys and the devastating loss of innocence that accompanies a child's first encounter with the full-scale cruelty and hatred of the adult world. Malle wrote, produced, and directed *Au Revoir les Enfants*, casting unknown and inexperienced young actors in the two central roles and re-creating for the film the world of his childhood under the Nazi occupation.

Malle begins his story with the simple events that constitute life at a boarding school and gradually interweaves the elements that will draw the film toward its shattering conclusion. Julien Quentin (Gaspard Manesse) is the pampered younger son of a wealthy Parisian family, an excellent student, admired by his friends but longing to remain in Paris with his adoring mother (Francine Racette). The students' return to school after the Christmas holidays is marked by the arrival of three new boys, one of whom, Jean Bonnet (Raphaël Fejtö), is assigned the bed next to Julien's. Jean is bright and a loner, and he is teased and harassed by the other boys as he tries to adjust to the school and its routines.

Julien is both resentful of the new boy and fascinated by his intelligent, serious manner, and his own sharp-eyed observations soon lead him to suspect the truth—that Jean is Jewish and is being hidden at the school by the priests. The two form a tentative friendship which is cemented when they become lost together in the woods during an outing and are returned to the school by a group of German soldiers. The school and the surrounding village are filled with constant reminders of the Nazi occupation—such as the black marketeering of Joseph (François Négret), the school's clubfooted kitchen assistant, and an attempt by French collaborators to throw an elderly Jewish man out of a restricted restaurant—and Jean lives in constant fear for his own life and the fate of his family. His fears are realized one morning when Joseph, who has been fired for his black-market dealings, turns informer and the Germans arrive to close down the school and arrest Jean and the two other Jewish students. As Julien and his classmates watch from the courtyard, the three boys and Father Jean (Philippe Morier-Genoud), the school's director and a Resistance sympathizer, are led away. In response to the students' shouts of "Goodbye, Father," the priest replies "Goodbye, children. See you soon,"—as Malle himself informs the audience in voice-over that Father Jean and all three boys died in the concentration camps.

Au Revoir les Enfants is a film about childhood and the loss of innocence (Malle dedicated it to his own three children), yet the picture it paints of children themselves is far from simplistic. The film views the world through Julien's eyes, and his own experience, like Malle's, has been that of the privileged son of wealthy parents. It is his meeting with Jean that helps Julien to see beyond his own small concerns and realize that there are other children in the world whose lives have been shattered and placed in peril in ways he can only imagine. Jean's hardships have left him with an air of dignity and maturity that both puzzles and awes Julien, and the new boy's intelligence and talent mark him as a potential rival. As the two share their passion for literature and the myriad experiences that form the life of a twelve-year-old, however, the friendship between them gives Julien his first taste of a relationship with a schoolmate who is his intellectual equal.

Jean's arrival at the school makes him the target of teasing and ridicule from the other boys—including Julien—who respond to the stranger in their midst with a show of unthinking, boisterous cruelty that has its roots in man's age-old tendency to react to outsiders with fear and hostility. The boys at the school also torment Joseph, with a show of arrogance that implies a very real awareness of the class distinction between them and a young man who occupies the position of a servant. At the heart of this behavior lie the seeds of the ability to think of the world in terms of "them" and "us"—a crucial element in the philosophy of the Nazis—and, indeed, it is Joseph's resentment of his treatment at the school which leads to his eventual collaboration with the Germans. Through his friendship with Jean, however, Julien comes to understand the tragedy of such distinctions when the person who has been designated as "them" is a valued friend.

The film's depiction of the occupying German forces is surprisingly subtle and restrained. Malle realizes that the true horror of the Nazis is best conveyed not through sneering caricatures but through the seeming ordinariness of the men carrying out the anti-Semitic Nazi policies. The soldiers are arrogant—they are conquerors in a defeated country—but it is the twisted, unruffled assurance with which they carry out their aims that strikes a chill as a German officer calmly tells the boys that their fellow students are not French, they are Jewish. For Julien, the humiliation and mistreatment of the Jews is brought home in a moment during the Nazis' search for one of the Jewish students who has escaped. When the soldiers find Julien in the infirmary, they order him to lower his pants while they check to see if he is circumcised, and for a moment, the wealthy young Catholic boy is subjected to the absolute suspension of basic rights which is the Nazis' customary treatment of the Jews. In the Nazis, Julien has before him an example of the very worst traits of which men are capable, and his knowledge of man's capacity for evil will remain with him forever.

If the Nazis are the worst that humanity has to offer, Julien also has before him an example of the best: Father Jean and his fellow priests, who have risked their lives to hide the three Jewish boys. The priests' willingness to sacrifice their own safety to help the boys and Father Jean's immense dignity and courage as he is led away by the Germans provide a moving contrast not only to the Nazis but also to those Frenchmen who are collaborating with the Germans and betraying their own countrymen. For Julien, and indeed for all the students, Father Jean's actions illuminate the dark days of the war with a moral conviction that cannot fail to leave the students unchanged.

Although Louis Malle waited forty years to bring *Au Revoir les Enfants* to the screen, aspects of the experience and of Malle's childhood have found their way into his earlier films. There are unmistakable similarities between Julien Quentin and the young, mother-fixated hero of the director's popular 1971 feature, *Le Souffle au cœur* (*Murmur of the Heart*), although the setting and period are different and the focus of the earlier film is on the relationship between mother and son. *Au Revoir les Enfants'* closest ties, however, are to Malle's Oscar-nominated *Lacombe, Lucien* (1974), the story of a brutish French peasant boy who collaborates with the Germans when he is turned down by the Resistance. The character of Lucien was based on Joseph, the kitchen-boy-turned-collaborator, and the film explores the mentality and motivations of those who chose to side with the Nazis against their own countrymen, a choice which precipitates the tragic climax of *Au Revoir les Enfants*.

In *Lacombe, Lucien*, Malle examines one facet of the childhood memory that would become *Au Revoir les Enfants*, making that film in many ways a preparation for the latter work. Now, however, he has at last taken on the full emotional force of the day in 1944 that so profoundly affected his life, and the resulting film is a devastating and heartfelt portrait of friendship and lost innocence.

Janet E. Lorenz

Reviews
American Film. XIII, January, 1988, p. 7.
California. XIII, February, 1988, p. 35.
The New Republic. CXCVIII, February 22, 1988, p. 24.
The New York Times. February 12, 1988, p. C15.
The New Yorker. LXIV, February 22, 1988, p. 85.
Newsweek. CXI, February 15, 1988, p. 70.
Time. CXXXI, February 22, 1988, p. 94.
Variety. CCCXXVIII, September 2, 1987, p. 18.
The Wall Street Journal. February 11, 1988, p. 28.

BABY BOOM

Production: Nancy Meyers; released by Metro-Goldwyn-Mayer/United Artists
Direction: Charles Shyer
Screenplay: Nancy Meyers and Charles Shyer
Cinematography: William A. Fraker
Editing: Lynzee Klingman
Art direction: Jeffrey Howard
Music: Bill Conti
Costume design: Susan Becker
MPAA rating: PG
Running time: 103 minutes

Principal characters:
J. C. Wiatt	Diane Keaton
Dr. Jeff Cooper	Sam Shepard
Steven Buchner	Harold Ramis
Fritz Curtis	Sam Wanamaker
Ken Arrenberg	James Spader
Elizabeth Wiatt	Kristina Kennedy and Michelle Kennedy

J. C. Wiatt is a Harvard Business School graduate. Known as "the tiger lady" because she is an aggressive career woman angling for a partnership in a Manhattan management-consultant firm, she is also a bundle of anxieties who barely copes with the pressure by sheer force of will. Diane Keaton delivers one of her best comic performances in years in her rendering of J. C. on the verge of hysteria. At a business meeting, her nerves almost get the better of her as she surreptitiously struggles to keep her knee from hitting the corporate table. She looks cool even as her emotional engine is running hot. She is an overachiever, willing to work long hours and to sacrifice nearly all of her personal life for corporate success.

Such is the life that J. C. has chosen. When Fritz Curtis (Sam Wanamaker), one of the senior partners of the firm, questions her closely about whether she is able to give up everything of a personal nature for a partnership, she vehemently insists that she is ready for even more work. If Curtis is doubtful, the reason is that he knows that a man—at least a man of his generation—can have it all: a full life both in business and at home. He has a wife who looks after all family and domestic matters for him. Why, he is not even sure that he knows the names of all of his grandchildren. Can an unmarried woman without this support system really function as effectively as a married, well-cared-for male? Curtis has to know whether J. C. has any desire to have children or to minister to her own man in the way that she now serves her company. J. C. is convinced that her loyalty is to the corporation, but to persuade Curtis, she must act out her aggressiveness. She has to prove herself.

In this context, the film sets J. C. up for failure. She cannot actually work much harder; she has already sacrificed nearly all of her personal life. She and her male live-in partner (Harold Ramis) have minimized sexual intercourse, for example, to a four-minute intermission in their preparations for the next corporate day. It is only by accident—a plot twist—that J. C. comes to realize what is lacking in her life. By a quirk of fate, she is the last living relative of a cousin who bequeaths to her a baby, Elizabeth (played by twins, Kristina and Michelle Kennedy).

Several reviewers have been quick to point out the improbability of a baby arriving from England, accompanied by a government servant who firmly places the child in J. C.'s hands. The film suffers from other lapses in credibility, but they hardly seem to matter, since the focus of the film is J. C., a woman who is particularly susceptible to what happens to her because she has never taken the time to determine what she really wants out of life.

Keaton delivers a masterfully comic performance in the scenes showing J. C.'s initial awkwardness with the adorable baby. She does not know how to talk to or feed the child, and the food ends up on the kitchen wall. J. C. does not even know how to hold a baby: There is a hilarious yet frightening shot of her approaching a revolving door with Elizabeth sort of sloppily hanging from her hip. With the child in tow, J. C. bungles one business deal. She begins to relinquish Elizabeth to an adoption agency, but snatches her back when she realizes that the prospective parents are a fundamentalist couple who are sure to give the child the narrowest of upbringings. Suddenly, J. C. has become as ambitious for her child as she has been for herself. The result is that she loses Steven, the boyfriend who had not bargained on parenthood.

Because J. C. cannot trust Elizabeth to the inept babysitters and housekeepers whom it is her misfortune to hire, she tries bringing her baby to work. In no time at all, she finds herself outmaneuvered by the low-key but wily Ken Arrenberg (James Spader), her young assistant who takes advantage of her absences and lateness. Failing to gain a partnership, J. C. decides to buy the country house of her dreams and to embark on a healthy life of solitude. As in that hilarious Cary Grant film, *Mr. Blandings Builds His Dream House* (1948), the rural retreat turns out to be a disaster, with the roof leaking, the well running dry, and the plumbing breaking down.

J. C. spends nearly the whole film denying most of her profoundest feelings: her love for baby Elizabeth, her hapless sexual attraction to Jeff Cooper (Sam Shepard), a country veterinarian, and her inclination to go it alone rather than in partnership with the older men who have always been her role models. In short, what J. C. tries to suppress is the fact that she cannot control her feelings. When Cooper kisses her rather violently and walks away, she has no response. Although he is usually mild-mannered, he is capable of expressing deep emotion openly and unaffectedly. J. C., on the other hand, has had only her affectations to live with.

As several reviewers point out, *Baby Boom* has many well-executed scenes: J. C. trying to keep a diaper together with electrical tape, J. C. at a business lunch checking her baby as she would check her coat in a cloakroom, J. C. regaining consciousness in a doctor's consulting room and beginning to confide in the white-jacketed male, only to realize, upon seeing a cow on another table, that he is a veterinarian. Stanley Kauffmann, reviewer for *The New Republic*, notes perceptively that Shepard is such a "cinema natural" that he does not have to be much more than a calm presence to set off Keaton's manic gestures and hesitations. In Kauffmann's words, she has the full physical complement of movements needed for this agitated character—"the quick starts, the self-interruptions, the bursts of amusement and perception as if her speech and features were trying to keep up with her racing mind."

If there is a serious fault in the film, it is the facile ending. Having discovered a way of preparing and marketing applesauce for babies in her country abode, J. C. returns to her Manhattan firm and triumphantly turns down its handsome offer to buy out her business. This kind of ending works against the logic of the film, which has concentrated not on the theme of success but on J. C.'s understanding of her true identity. In everything she has done, she has been an ambitious woman; at the very last, she has even become ambitious about knowing herself. The face-off with her former corporate associates seems gratuitous.

The best scenes in the film have to do with the handling of human emotions. This is why baby Elizabeth has such a powerful part to play in the film. More than simply a cute baby, she speaks to the need to acknowledge deep feeling. Toward the end of the film, J. C. enters her house and is greeted by her baby's soft cry of "Mama!" It is a powerful moment, communicating that the naming of J. C. as a mama is in itself enough to justify her decision to leave corporate life. It is not a sentimental scene, in spite of the strong sentiment it evokes. Rather, it epitomizes the values of individuals who do want to rear their own children and to know the names of their grandchildren.

Carl Rollyson

Reviews
Glamour. LXXXV, November, 1987, p. 256.
Macleans. C, October 26, 1987, p. 63.
The New Republic. CXCVII, November 9, 1987, p. 24.
New York. XX, October 12, 1987, p. 91.
The New York Times. October 7, 1987, p. C24.
Newsweek. CX, October 13, 1987, p. 84.
Time. CXXX, October 12, 1987, p. 85.

LA BAMBA

Production: Taylor Hackford and Bill Borden; released by Columbia
   Pictures
Direction: Luis Valdez
Screenplay: Luis Valdez
Cinematography: Adam Greenberg
Editing: Sheldon Kahn and Don Brochu
Art direction: Vince Cresciman
Music: Carlos Santana and Miles Goodman
Song: Los Lobos, "La Bamba"
MPAA rating: PG-13
Running time: 106 minutes

Principal characters:

Ritchie Valens	Lou Diamond Phillips
Bob Morales	Esai Morales
Connie Valenzuela	Rosana De Soto
Rosie Morales	Elizabeth Peña
Donna Ludwig	Danielle von Zerneck
Bob Keene	Joe Pantoliano
Ted Quillin	Rick Dees
Buddy Holly	Marshall Crenshaw
Jackie Wilson	Howard Huntsberry
Eddie Cochran	Brian Setzer

   La Bamba is a tribute to the brief but brilliant career of rock singer and
songwriter Ritchie Valens. Valens died in a plane crash in 1959 after an
eight-month rise to fame. Three of his songs were national hits. One of
them, "La Bamba," has becomes his signature song, for it embodies better
than anything else the energy and the freshness of his art. A traditional
Mexican folk song sung to the bride at weddings, the song's lyrics suggest
pure joy and are expressive of male confidence and charm:

> Para bailar la bamba . . .
> Se necesita una poca de gracia . . .
> Para mi y para ti
> Y arriba y arriba. . . .
> ¡Por ti seré!

> To dance the bamba . . .
> A little grace is needed . . .
> For you and for me
> And up and up. . . .
> For you, I'll be!

Valens, a Hispanic (born Richard Valenzuela), adapted the lyrics and the rhythms of the original song and made it into a rock number that communicates the singer's charisma. In Valens' version, the song becomes his pledge to his fans to move them beyond themselves. In the film, when Valens (Lou Diamond Phillips) sings "La Bamba" at an important rock-and-roll show, the audience rises to its feet, clapping and dancing. *La Bamba* portrays the power of an artist to awaken people, to excite in them a feeling of transcendence. As Luis Valdez, the writer and director of the film, suggested to Elvis Mitchell in an interview published in *The Detroit Free Press*, "the song is about ascending, moving higher and forward."

Part of *La Bamba*'s power derives from the deeply personal commitment of the writer/director and the associate producer, his brother Daniel, who first conceived of a film of Valens' life in 1972. Valens' recordings were technically inferior to what was needed for a motion picture, so the Latino group Los Lobos rerecorded Valens' songs, which Phillips mimed after learning the guitar fingering. The songs are so authentically rendered and the passion of Phillips' acting is so perfect that the mood and temper of the 1950's is expertly conveyed as an organic part of the film.

The best part of *La Bamba* is the story of how Valens became a star. Even as his family works in a migrant laborer camp, his raw talent is apparent. He lives and dreams rock and roll. His enthusiasm wins over his family—especially his mother who becomes his first agent, so to speak, by organizing his first dance concert. Ritchie infuses her with a sense of destiny, with a notion that his life has a purpose that will elevate the family far beyond their menial occupations and concerns. Yet perhaps because of his sense of destiny, Ritchie also foresees that his life will end in a plane crash. His dreams of sudden death periodically wake him out of dreams of success. *La Bamba* was made with the full cooperation of Valens' family, and it is from Valens' half-brother, Bob, that the makers of the film learned that Valens did indeed have such nightmares.

In the film, Valens seems almost too good to be true. He is never rude, never short-tempered, and never bitter about the discrimination he suffers as a Hispanic. In part, this goodness becomes believable because music means everything to him; it makes him good; it makes even his decisions to compromise on certain principles understandable. For example, when he is first discovered by a recording company representative, he refuses to record a song without his group. The agent explains, however, that it is only Ritchie in whom he is interested and that Ritchie must decide—once and for all— whether it is his music that will come first. Later, this commitment to music means overcoming his fear of flying in order to do cross-country concert tours. It also means that Ritchie will have to accept an easier and less Hispanic-sounding surname. Yet the drive of his musical sensibility is so overwhelming that he finally convinces the agent to let him record "La

Bamba," even though the song is "ethnic" and a reminder of the culture from which Ritchie comes.

There are many powerful scenes that show Valens' singing style and his impact on his audiences. There is also an extraordinary scene in a recording studio where Ritchie learns that his raw talent is not enough. He must adapt to the medium of the studio recording; he must sing the same phrases over and over again until they are perfect little pieces in themselves that can be used for editing purposes. Ritchie is clearly frustrated and almost ready to give up, but his agent reminds him of the consequences of his decision to be a professional and to have his songs distributed nationally.

There is a second story in *La Bamba* that is not as well developed: the story of Ritchie's family and of his Hispanic roots. The film begins with the re- union of Ritchie's brother Bob with his family. He is the black sheep, a party- loving, hard-drinking, irresponsible opposite to Ritchie's clean-cut dedica- tion to career and family. Bob looks Hispanic; Ritchie does not. In rather heavy-handed fashion, Bob is presented as the dark twin—almost a stereotypical figure. Yet there is genuine warmth and good feeling between the brothers, which is undoubtedly a reflection of the fact that Bob Morales worked closely with the filmmakers and was willing to have the unflattering aspects of his character revealed. In this case, the director was not con- cerned with improving upon reality and took intact the real, if hackneyed, story of sibling rivalry.

Even in this weaker side of the film, however, there are many excellent scenes. Bob's feelings of love and hate for his brother are convincingly played by Esai Morales. Bob is, in many ways, a very generous brother who is more in tune with his Hispanic origins than is Ritchie, who always puts his music first. The filmmakers are wise to let this theme of ethnic origins play itself out through family relationships rather than making it an overt problem. Ritchie does not even speak Spanish, and a brief trip with Bob to Mexico is a revelation to him. It is where he is stimulated to adapt and per- form "La Bamba."

In the same way, Ritchie's falling in love with a "gringa," Donna, the sub- ject of one of his hit songs, is treated rather lightly in the film. Donna (Danielle von Zerneck) strikes just the right chords as the pretty teenage girl attracted to Ritchie's ingenuous courting of her and deeply hurt by her father's racist dismissal of Ritchie from her life. Von Zerneck is only one of several cast members whose acting is superior to the script. Good acting somehow overrides the clichéd language and makes vivid the 1950's psychol- ogy of the characters.

La Bamba is not a particularly inventive film in cinematic terms, but sophisticated and innovative photography would not be to the point. The story concerns Valens—the force of his personality and his art. Moreover, although *La Bamba* is a period piece, it is also a lament for a gifted human being who transcended his times. Carlos Santana, who wrote some of the original music for the film, was quoted in *The Detroit Free Press* as observing: "The way he played raunchy, man, he was *the* first heavy metal. He was such an innovator for seventeen, who knows where he would've gone if he would've lived?" Santana is right. There is a sense of loss in *La Bamba* that justifies the words of many reviewers who have called Valens' story tragic.

Carl Rollyson

Reviews
American Film. XII, July, 1987, p. 15.
The Detroit Free Press. July 24, 1987, p. 1C.
Films in Review. XXXVIII, October, 1987.
Los Angeles Times. July 24, 1987, VI, p. 1.
Macleans. C, July 27, 1987, p. 47.
The New York Times. July 24, 1987, p. C4.
The New Yorker. LXIII, August 10, 1987, p. 71.
Newsweek. CX, August 17, 1987, p. 66.
Time. CXXX, August 17, 1987, p. 62.
Variety. CCCXXVII, May 20, 1987, p. 16.
The Wall Street Journal. July 23, 1987, p. 28.

BARFLY

Production: Barbet Schroeder, Fred Roos, and Tom Luddy; released by
   Cannon Films
Direction: Barbet Schroeder
Screenplay: Charles Bukowski
Cinematography: Robby Muller
Editing: Eva Gardos
Art direction: Bob Ziembicki; set decoration, Lisa Dean
Makeup: Ken Diaz
Costume design: Milena Canonero
Sound: Petur Hliddal
Music: Paula Erickson
MPAA rating: R
Running time: 99 minutes

> *Principal characters:*
> Henry Chinaski....................Mickey Rourke
> Wanda Wilcox ....Faye Dunaway
> Tully................................Alice Krige
> Detective...........................Jack Nance
> Jim.................................J. C. Quinn
> Eddie ....Frank Stallone
> Janice............................Sandy Martin
> Lilly............................Roberta Bassin
> Grandma Moses ....Gloria Leroy

Films tend either to pity or to burlesque drunks. *Barfly* does neither in
any conventional sense, yet manages to portray the condition as both waste-
ful and hilarious. Based on a semiautobiographical screenplay by the poet
laureate of Los Angeles degeneracy, Charles Bukowski, Barbet Schroeder's
film treats alcoholism with a celebratory humanism—this is perhaps the first
film to respect drunks as people, not problems—yet never glamorizes it.
Bukowski stand-in Henry Chinaski (Mickey Rourke) leads a singularly un-
appetizing life, defined by grime, pointless violence, and daily pirouettes
with dementia. Yet he is comfortable, indeed happy, with and creatively
inspired by his debased existence. Among the film's many wonders, the
greatest is that it leaves the viewer with the opinion that Henry should stay
just the way he is.

This superb, nonjudgmental balancing act between Henry's antisocial
pride and his awful way of life is reflected in every other aspect of the film.
Robby Muller's camera, as it often has for Wim Wenders, captures the
alienating cityscape and gritty drabness of Henry's milieu. Yet at night,

Muller gives a giddy neon sheen to the dirty skid row taverns which Henry, by that hour quite drunk, sees as a Disneyesque playland. Bukowski, as might be expected, provides his spokesman with the most amusing lines and most penetrating insights, but he also exaggerates the inherent stupidity in Henry's behavior: The drunk may win one of numerous, pointless fistfights with a surly bartender, but he usually loses, and his victory is bought with much of his own blood. Rourke's performance is stylized both physically (a constant stoop, face marred with stubble, bruises, and caked blood, hair a stringy, oily mess) and orally (he speaks in a breathy growl). Even encased in such severe mannerism, however, Rourke's portrayal never fails to convince. His Henry is a bizarre character, to be sure, but by his own strange definition of the term, he acts completely naturally.

The story's refusal to acknowledge objective standards of what constitutes good and bad, right and wrong, enjoyment and pain, is evident in the film's opening sequence. Night exteriors of the low-life bars along Western Avenue lead to the neon sign indicating The Golden Horn, with its motto, A Friendly Place, in smaller lights. Inside, the bar is empty except for a bored assistant bartender. In the alley out back, however, can be heard a raucous crowd.

Eddie (Frank Stallone), the macho night bartender, is beating up Henry, with most of The Golden Horn's aged, drink-ravaged regulars cheering him on. Henry refuses to ask for mercy, and Eddie leaves him half dead on the pavement while everyone else goes back inside for a drink. It is suggested that Henry should not be left lying there, but noted that he also hates any kind of help.

The next morning, Henry is back at the Horn, bringing sandwiches for visiting businessmen in return for drinks. Jim (J. C. Quinn), the amiable day bartender, tells Henry that he should stop fighting without a reason. Henry replies that he needs no reasons to win fights, only fuel. With that, Henry shoves half of one of the businessmen's sandwiches into his own mouth. Jim defends Henry's behavior as being as right as anybody's.

Henry returns to his flophouse room, writes some poetry, then passes out. Rising later, he goes down the hall to the bathroom. A detective (Jack Nance) sneaks into Henry's room and photographs the poet's writings. At the Horn that night, Henry antagonizes Eddie into another fight, which Henry wins despite most patrons' wagers to the contrary. Heading down the street in black-and-blue triumph, Henry is stopped by Jim, the only person who bet on him. Jim insists that Henry take some of the money.

In another bar, Henry spends the cash on drinks for a beautiful, lone woman, Wanda Wilcox (Faye Dunaway). She tells him that she hates people, and he replies that he feels better when they are not around. She says she drinks. He lets her know that he is broke, has no rent and no job. They go to Wanda's apartment, where she warns him that she does not want to go through falling in love again. Henry reassures her that no one has loved him yet.

The next day, Henry introduces Wanda to his friends at the Horn. He leaves Wanda there with his income tax refund while he goes to a job interview. It is disastrous, but Henry does not care. He returns to the Horn at the end of the day to learn that Wanda left with Eddie, who offered her whiskey. Henry goes back to her apartment and waits for her until she comes home almost twenty-four hours later. She apologizes for her night with Eddie, blaming it on bad judgment caused by drink. An argument ensues, culminating with Wanda beating Henry bloody with her purse, then storming out.

Later that day, the detective comes to Wanda's apartment, waking the wounded drunk. Henry throws him out, then throws all Wanda's clothes out the window. Wanda calls later to see if he is all right. He runs outside and retrieves her clothes, putting them back in the wrong drawers before she arrives. They make up, despite her perplexity over her disarranged wardrobe. That night, Wanda awakens from an alcoholic sleep, terrified that she has seen the Angel of Death. The next morning, she goes out looking for a job, accompanied by Henry to the bus stop, convinced that her dream was a warning to get straight.

Returning to Wanda's apartment, Henry finds the chic, attractive Tully (Alice Krige) waiting in the hallway. Publisher of *The Contemporary Review of Art and Literature*, which has printed one of his stories, she hired the detective to find Henry. She has a check for Henry, but he has no way to cash it. They drive in her convertible to her bank, then up to her posh home in the Hollywood Hills, where they proceed to drink and make love. The next morning, Tully implores Henry to live and write with her, to which he responds that he belongs on the streets and then leaves.

Henry returns to an angry Wanda, who smells on him Tully's perfume. She is mollified when Henry showers her with the cash from his story, however, and they go to the Horn to celebrate.

In the bar, Henry buys round after round for the house, shocking and insulting Eddie with his ability to pay for it all. In the midst of the party, a tipsy Tully enters. Wanda recognizes her perfume and attacks her. They roll on the floor, slugging and scratching, before being separated. Tully concedes that she knows Henry needs this atmosphere, wishes him luck, and departs. Henry drinks a toast to the gathered, cackling throng—to all of his friends—then everybody heads out the back door to witness another alley fight between Henry and Eddie.

Director Schroeder spent seven years trying to mount *Barfly*, and his affection for the material is evident in every frame. Always enamored of marginal characters—his films *Maîtresse* (1976) and *Les Tricheurs* (1983) brought matter-of-fact understanding to the demimondes of sadomasochistic sex and compulsive gambling, respectively—Schroeder has a particular affinity for Bukowski. From 1980 to 1984, Schroeder conducted fifty video-tape interviews with the author, which have been released commercially.

It is no small wonder, then, that *Barfly* does a better job of capturing the poetry of Bukowski's world than did Marco Ferreri's similar *Tales of Ordinary Madness* (1983). Schroeder aims less for overt shock (nothing in *Barfly* compares with Ornella Muti's self-mutilation and suicide in the earlier film), nor does he take Bukowski's self-destructive rebel stance as seriously as the Italian does.

Complementing Rourke's whacky performance is the finest work from Dunaway that filmgoers are ever likely to see. She takes a totally different, naturalistic approach to Wanda, presenting a woman who seems to have embraced her own alcoholism as fully as Henry has, while doing much less to prove it. The couple's relationship, as turbulent and hazy as it often is, is nevertheless one of the most joyous matings in contemporary cinema. While fooling around together in her dingy apartment, Wanda and Henry can insult, assault, reconcile, and joke with one another more confidently and affectionately than most sober couples; they bring out whatever is left of the best in each other. His carefree nihilism calms her darker fears; she inspires in him generosity and even a vague glimmer of responsibility (he tries to get a steady job so that he can maintain their liquor supply).

The supporting cast, almost exclusively composed of grotesque characters, buttresses the film's basic theory that even the most undignified characters have as much claim to the human label as anybody else does. Of the film's rich lode of amusing, pithy, and memorable Bukowskisms, Jim the bartender's observation that Henry is as right as anybody encapsulates its fundamental argument that life, no matter how misspent, is worth drinking to.

Robert Strauss

Reviews
Daily Variety. May 13, 1987, p. 8.
The Hollywood Reporter. September 22, 1987, p. 3.
Los Angeles Times. November 5, 1987, VI, p. 1.
New York. October 26, 1987, p. 114.
The New York Times. September 20, 1987, C, p. 18.
Newsweek. October 26, 1987, p. 86.

THE BEDROOM WINDOW

Production: Martha Schumacher; released by DeLaurentiis Entertainment
  Group
Direction: Curtis Hanson
Screenplay: Curtis Hanson; based on the novel *The Witnesses* by Anne
  Holden
Cinematography: Gil Taylor
Editing: Scott Conrad
Art direction: Rafael Caro; set decoration, Hilton Rosemarin
Makeup: Stefano Fava
Costume design: Clifford Capone
Sound: Bill Daly
Music: Michael Shrieve and Patrick Gleeson
MPAA rating: R
Running time: 113 minutes

Principal characters:
Terry Lambert	Steve Guttenberg
Denise	Elizabeth McGovern
Sylvia	Isabelle Huppert
Colin	Paul Shenar
Henderson	Brad Greenquist
Quirke	Carl Lumbly
Jessup	Frederick Coffin
Henderson's attorney	Wallace Shawn
State Attorney Peters	Robert Schenkkan
Pool player	Maurey Chaykin
Dancing girl	Sara Carlson
Man in phone booth	Mark Margolis
Judge	Penelope Allen

Alfred Hitchcock frequently insisted on the distinction between the mystery thriller and the suspense thriller. In the former, the criminal is not revealed until the film's end, and audience involvement hinges on an anticipation of this disclosure; in the latter, the audience shares in the knowledge of the true criminal throughout but is held in suspense through the machinations of the narrative and close identification with the hero. *The Bedroom Window*, a stylish and involving thriller written and directed by Curtis Hanson from the novel *The Witnesses* (1971) by Anne Holden, is certainly in the suspense-thriller mode that Hitchcock preferred, and it clearly imitates general patterns and alludes to several of Hitchcock's films. The catalytic situation of the film—accidentally observing a murder through a window—

echoes the central premise of Hitchcock's *Rear Window* (1954). The involvement of an innocent man in a complex web of deception and murders parallels the situations of Hitchcock heroes in many films, including *The Man Who Knew Too Much* (1934), *The Thirty-nine Steps* (1935), *Strangers on a Train* (1951), and *Frenzy* (1972). There is also a variant on the familiar Hitchcockian device of the double chase, in which the hero is pursued by both the real murderer and the authorities who suspect him of the crime; he must, consequently, prove his own innocence to disbelieving representatives of justice, while doing their job in capturing the criminal. In addition, the psychosexual pathology of the murderer in Hanson's film shares definite similarities with two of Hitchcock's most fascinating villains, the mother-dominated and sexually deviant killers of *Strangers on a Train* and *Psycho* (1960).

The Bedroom Window opens with a tilt-down shot on a huge statue of George Washington (echoing Hitchcock's frequent and ironic use of national monuments) to Baltimore's East Mount Vernon Street where Terry Lambert (Steve Guttenberg) pulls up in a flashy vintage car. As Terry enters his apartment, the camera slowly tracks up toward and through the bedroom window. He quickly straightens up the apartment in preparation for the arrival of Sylvia (Isabelle Huppert). Sylvia, his boss's wife, arrives and seems ill at ease, fearing for her reputation and the stability of her marriage to Colin (Paul Shenar), a successful architect. Nevertheless, Sylvia and Terry make love. Later, while he is in the shower, Sylvia hears the cries of a woman outside the bedroom window and sees a young woman being assaulted. She opens the window just as the red-haired and unusually pale-skinned attacker looks up, sees her, and then rushes off. Terry has hurried out of the shower but arrives too late to see the attacker. They decide not to contact the police since this would seriously compromise Sylvia, but Terry notices a newspaper headline the next day about a young woman who was murdered a few blocks from his apartment and suspects that the incident is related to the attack outside his window. Meeting again with Sylvia, he tells her that they must report the assault she witnessed, and since she cannot testify to being in his room, he will tell the police that he witnessed the assault. Terry belatedly calls the police to make a report, and this first seemingly harmless lie sets off a chain of lies which will increasingly implicate Terry in the attack and a series of murders to follow. He will be forced to play dual roles in the film, both of which will damage his credibility and connect him to the crimes: First, as a bogus key witness he will have to lie repeatedly to the police and later perjure himself in court, and, second, as amateur detective he will unwittingly place himself at the scenes of the crimes.

Terry's role as witness begins with an interview by police officers Jessup (Frederick Coffin) and Quirke (Carl Lumbly), to whom he falsely gives

Sylvia's eyewitness account as his own. Soon after, Terry assumes his role as amateur detective, bringing Sylvia to the scene of the first murder. Terry reconstructs the circumstances of the murder in a visually effective sequence which is shot entirely in subjective camera from the point of view of the killer. The point of view is also that of Terry as narrator, and the sequence links him with the killer. Called again as a witness, Terry views suspects in a police lineup, and it is here that he first meets Denise (Elizabeth McGovern), the victim of the assault and a character who will figure importantly in the third part of the film. Neither he nor Denise can positively identify any of the suspects, and they leave separately. Outside in the parking lot, resuming his role of detective, Terry sees and decides to follow the red-haired man from the lineup. Terry trails him to a sleazy waterfront house and watches him go inside. Here occurs another of the film's direct allusions to Hitchcock's *Psycho*; sitting by the window of the house is a mysteriously menacing woman, seen in profile. As the viewer will later learn, this is the home of Chris Henderson (Brad Greenquist), the mother-dominated, sexually deviant psychopath who is responsible for the first assault and murder as well as those to come later.

The characterization of Chris, with its psychological shadings, is the clearest indication of the Hitchcockian thrust of Hanson's screenplay. In the novel *The Witnesses*, the character of the murderer is only sketchily presented, and little is known about him personally or about the circumstances of the murders. Hanson's screenplay presents him as a psychopath compelled to murder women who both arouse and disgust him by overtly sexual displays in public.

Only because Terry assumes the role of detective stalking the suspect does the audience become aware of the motivation for the crimes. This narrative strategy is not central to the film's source novel, and it is clear that Hanson's script is following other cinematic models. In *The Bedroom Window*, Terry, ironically, becomes more clearly a witness than in Holden's novel. In his voyeuristic observance of Chris's behavior he is able to piece together not only motives but also the patterns and methods of the crimes.

Terry's first telling observation of Chris is at The Fells Point Bar, where he watches Chris stare angrily at a young woman with clustered bracelets on her arm who is dancing lasciviously among her friends. When Terry is distracted by a waitress who spills a tray of drinks on him, Chris disappears. Shortly after and nearby, Terry sees police officers wheeling a corpse on a stretcher; as one arm falls loose from the sheet covering it, he sees what looks to be the same cluster of gold bracelets he had earlier seen on the dancing woman at the bar. This second link between Chris and a killing causes Terry to go again to the police and tell them of the bizarre coincidence he has discovered. Again he is caught up in lies because he cannot tell the whole truth. The police decide to attempt to prosecute Chris on the assault of Denise which Terry witnessed. During the dramatically charged courtroom scene that follows, a number of key revelations are made, and the lives of the key players in the film intersect: Chris's clever defense attorney (played menacingly by Wallace Shawn) establishes that Terry is nearsighted and could not have identified Chris since he admitted to not wearing his contact lenses on the night of the assault; Sylvia attempts to prompt Terry's answers to the attorney's test of Terry's vision; and both Chris and Denise observe Sylvia's prompting of Terry and realize that she was, indeed, the witness. His testimony is muddled and inexplicable; he has not only perjured himself but revealed himself to Chris and marked Sylvia as a potential victim of the psychopathic murderer.

Suspicion builds around Terry who, from this point on, will be the prime suspect in the murders. Only Sylvia's coming forth as the real witness could save him. In one of the film's most striking scenes, Terry and Sylvia meet at the city's aquarium, where he implores her to tell the truth. They are photographed against huge tanks of fish and sea turtles as Sylvia coldly refuses to help him any further. The striking framing of the actors against the aquatic imagery seems to be a clever allusion to a similar scene in Orson Welles's *The Lady from Shanghai* (1948) and functions in much the same way. In Hanson's film, the framing of the characters by the huge tanks also suggests entrapment, a world closing in. Sylvia's betrayal is imaged by the giant sea turtles in the background—she, like the turtles, may opt to pull in her head to avoid danger, seeking protection in the hard shell of her marriage and respectability. Her desire for disinvolvement at this point is futile, however, since her role as the true witness was discovered by the murderer in the earlier trial scene. Chris eventually follows Sylvia to a ballet and murders her in the theater, again implicating Terry in the killing since he has also followed Sylvia there to repeat his plea for help. Terry will be left holding Sylvia's bloody corpse; the one person who might have proven his innocence is now dead, and he appears to be her killer.

The elaborate climactic section of the film centers on a plot devised by Denise in which she disguises herself, follows the killer to a dingy bar, and then behaves salaciously in hopes of luring him to follow her home and attempt another murder in the presence of the police, whom Terry will have informed. Her physical transformation echoes that of Kim Novak's in *Vertigo* (1958) and her heroics those of Grace Kelly in *Rear Window*. McGovern's portrayal of Denise is richly detailed in its combination of strength and vulnerability, and she brings a salutary warmth to the film. Her surety and rightmindedness, in fact, make clearer the naïvely inept actions of Terry earlier in the film. During the climactic chase sequence following Denise's encounter with Chris in a cheap waterfront bar, nearly everything goes wrong: Terry's view of the bar is obscured by a truck; he is unable to telephone the police because of a surly patron who will not relinquish the phone booth; he gets into a fight with the man in the phone booth as Denise leaves for home where she, unprotected, will be met by the killer; and, when a policeman arrives to break up the fight and arrest both men, Terry brazenly steals the police car in order to follow Denise. Sound is used effectively in the crosscutting which follows—the eerie silence as Denise is being stalked by Chris in a deserted parking structure is intercut with the howling siren of the stolen police car and the noise of the radio which Terry uses to summon help. In typical chase-sequence form, Terry arrives just as Chris is attempting to strangle Denise. A fight ensues between the two men until Chris manages to escape and get to his truck. The scene ends as Chris crashes into the side of the arriving police car. In a typical Hitchcockian joke, the police are unable to capture the real villain until he literally runs into them.

The Bedroom Window is engaging and satisfying as a thriller for numerous reasons, but it also provides more than mere thrills in its darkly comic yet nightmarish view of a world of illicit love, shunned responsibility, betrayal, deceit, and murder. Hanson's screenplay has clearly added pointed ironies, not present in the source material, which add to the richness of the film. Its quality is enhanced also by the principal players: Guttenberg is charming, sincere, and comically gullible as Terry; Huppert, with her coldly exotic beauty, is effective as Sylvia; and McGovern is convincingly brass yet frightened as Denise. Much of the film's success must also be credited to its rich visual style captured by cinematographer Gil Taylor. Taylor has worked with such celebrated directors as Stanley Kubrick, Roman Polanski, and George Lucas, and his credits include: *Dr. Strangelove* (1964), *Repulsion* (1965), *Cul-De-Sac* (1966), and *Star Wars* (1977). Most important, perhaps, to his collaboration with Hanson on the very Hitchcockian film *The Bedroom Window* is the fact that Taylor was also the cinematographer for Hitchcock's penultimate film, *Frenzy*.

John R. Orlandello

Reviews
Films in Review. XXXVIII, May 1987, p. 297.
Los Angeles Times. January 16, 1987, VI, p. 17.
Macleans. C, January 19, 1987, p. 56.
New York. XX, February 2, 1987, p. 57.
The New York Times. January 16, 1987, p. C6.
The New Yorker. LXII, February 9, 1987, p. 94.
People Weekly. XXVII, January 26, 1987, p. 14.
Time. CXIX, February 16, 1987, p. 76.
Variety. CCCXXV, January 7, 1987, p. 21.
The Wall Street Journal. January 22, 1987, p. 28.

BEST SELLER

Production: Carter De Haven; released by Orion Pictures
Direction: John Flynn
Screenplay: Larry Cohen
Cinematography: Fred Murphy
Editing: David Rosenbloom
Production design: Gene Rudolf
Art direction: Robert Howland; set decoration, Chris Butler
Special effects: Ken Speed and Robert Olmstead
Makeup: Deborah Figuly
Sound: Lee Alexander
Music direction: Budd Carr
Music: Jay Ferguson
Song: Lamont Dozier, "Perfect Ending"
MPAA rating: R
Running time: 107 minutes

Principal characters:
Cleve	James Woods
Dennis Meechum	Brian Dennehy
Roberta Gillian	Victoria Tennant
Holly Meechum	Allison Balson
David Madlock	Paul Shenar
Graham	George Coe
Mrs. Foster	Anne Pitoniak
Cleve's Mother	Mary Carver
Monks	Sully Boyar
Annie	Kathleen Lloyd
Cleve's Father	Harold Tyner
Taxi driver	E. Brian Dean
Pearlman	Jeffrey Josephson
Thorn	Edward Blackoff
Woman in laundry	Jenny Gago

Best Seller is an ambitious *film noir* exercise marked by an outstanding acting duet from James Woods and Brian Dennehy but marred by inconsistent storytelling and injudicious editing. Unlike most thrillers, in which plot considerations overwhelm character development, *Best Seller* seems almost entirely bent on achieving increased psychological depth while its story elements are allowed to unravel out of control. Director John Flynn, ultimately, accomplishes quite a feat: He creates an indelible, pathological male-bonding relationship—perhaps the most outré seen in American crime films since Alfred Hitchcock's *Strangers on a Train* (1951)—in the midst of narrative chaos.

The film opens in Los Angeles in 1972. Three armed men wearing Richard Nixon masks invade the Police Evidence Depository Building, killing three guards and shooting a fourth, Dennis Meechum (Dennehy), who manages to stab one of the assailants before they all escape with a large amount of cash. Meechum survives, writes a best-selling book about the unsolved crime, and is eventually promoted to detective. By 1987, he has written several other popular crime stories, although he currently suffers from a writer's block that started when his wife died of cancer.

While chasing some drug smugglers through the San Pedro piers one day, Meechum finds himself shadowed by a mysterious man wearing sunglasses and a dark suit. The man kills one of the smugglers who is about to ambush Meechum, then disappears. Later, Meechum finds a note attached to his car, instructing him to say thank you.

The following morning, Meechum's teenage daughter, Holly (Allison Balson), tells her father how an old friend of his, who knew everything about their private lives, gave her a ride. She describes the mystery man in the dark suit. Later, at a business luncheon, several publishing types— including Roberta Gillian (Victoria Tennant), an editor—berate Meechum for missing deadlines. Legal action is hinted at strongly.

Following another cryptic note, Meechum meets the mystery man that night on an old tugboat. Cleve (Woods) offers his life story to the burned-out writer, leaving him with a scrapbook filled with clippings about an assortment of seemingly mundane deaths. Several other meetings ensue, in which Meechum almost arrests Cleve for his earlier killing of the dope dealer in San Pedro. Cleve, however, stays Meechum's hand with an outrageous story about how, for years, he was a corporate hit man for one David Madlock (Paul Shenar), owner of a huge conglomerate named Capa International. Cleve claims to have killed everyone in the scrapbook on Madlock's orders and boasts that he was so good at his job that he made all the murders look like natural or accidental deaths. Recently squeezed out of the company—when he thinks that he should have been promoted for doing his job as well as any equivalent vice president of marketing or acquisitions— Cleve wants revenge on Madlock, who is too powerful simply to accuse. If Meechum writes a substantiated book about Cleve's work, Madlock cannot successfully deny his complicity.

Meechum is skeptical of Cleve's story until Cleve reveals that he took part in the 1972 depository heist (but only as a driver, he claims). The take from the robbery, according to Cleve, was the seed money that started Capa International. With Meechum's interest piqued by the idea of revenge against the man responsible for his colleagues' deaths, Cleve observes that the writer is in debt from his wife's cancer treatments and desperately needs a good story. When Cleve tries to make the point that they have a bond—both are killers—Meechum protests that he does not have anything in common with the proudly professional murderer.

During the next several weeks, Cleve takes Meechum on a series of excursions to prove the veracity of his story. They meet Madlock, visit the sites of several of Cleve's crimes in New York and are almost killed when a taxicab they hire blows up. Along the way, Cleve displays his insidious imagination, his gleeful joy in his work, his eerily effective charm, and a mad conviction that he is a prime example of the American success story. A visit to Cleve's parents in Oregon, followed by a heartfelt if somewhat pitiful attempt to buy Meechum's friendship with an engraved watch, reveals a sentimental streak in the callous killer. A visit from two of Madlock's operatives to Meechum's precinct, in which they alternately threaten and attempt to bribe the author-cop, finally convinces Meechum that Cleve's story is true. He starts to write, with the full intention of arresting Cleve when he has finished. Editor Gillian reads the early chapters and loves them; Cleve later terrorizes her in an attempt to learn how Meechum is presenting him.

For no apparent reasons other than the mechanical ones of varying the Los Angeles location and injecting some action into the story, Meechum and Cleve fly to El Paso, Texas, to get some corroborating evidence from a Hispanic laundress (Jenny Gago). The woman is killed, however, along with a number of Madlock's thugs who attack the laundry plant. Cleve returns to Los Angeles first, just in time to save Holly from another Madlock operative, Thorn (Edward Blackoff), who has broken into the Meechum home in search of the manuscript. Although Cleve takes Holly to Gillian's home for safekeeping, Madlock kidnaps the girl anyway.

Upon his return to Los Angeles, Meechum is invited to a charity children's party at Madlock's beach house. Cleve works his way into the lush estate, effortlessly killing numerous guards that he sneers at as being amateurs. As Madlock threatens both Meechums' futures unless Dennis agrees to turn over his manuscript and come to work for Capa International, Cleve frees Holly, then closes in to kill Madlock—the perfect ending for Meechum's book. Panicking, Madlock shoots Meechum in the arm. Holly runs crying to her wounded father but is caught by Madlock, who puts his gun to her head. Cleve drops his gun and is shot by Madlock, who then gives his gun to Meechum, surrendering without resistance.

With his dying breath, Cleve tells Meechum that he should have killed Madlock; it would have made a better ending for the book. Finally feeling a twinge of affection for the man he has so despised, Meechum thanks Cleve for saving Holly. Cleve tells him not to mention it, except in the book, and then dies. The book, *Retribution*, becomes a best-seller.

At one point in the film's editing process, the decision was made to focus exclusively on the relationship between Cleve and Meechum. Although never as teasingly hinted at as in the Robert Walker-Farley Granger relationship from *Strangers on a Train*, Cleve's touching, outlandish, and coolly desperate attempts to win Meechum's affection bear their share of homosexual implications, as do his angry reactions to Meechum's disdain. The latter is spectacularly expressed in one of the film's best-staged set pieces: At Cleve's parents' middle-American farmhouse, Meechum expresses wonder that such nice country people could produce such an aberration of nature. That night, Cleve, the consummate sneak thief, slips into Meechum's room and holds a gun to the sleeping man's temple. He demands respect, but rather than being met with fear, Cleve finds himself looking into the barrel of a raised .45 as well. The sexuality inherent in their supine posture and pointed guns is, as throughout the film, repressed as quickly as it is suggested; they agree to call it a draw, with the threat that the next time a gun is pulled like that, it had better be used.

Cleve, as an aberration of American virtue, provides the film with a running strain of astringent humor. Cleve's insane conviction that he is merely another Yankee businessman, even a hero, is tempered by at least an inkling of life's absurdity. When, after deceiving someone with an elaborate falsehood, he pontificates about how faith in human nature made the United States great, or how someone's comparatively minor attitude problem is part of what is destroying civilization, he must be aware of the satire inherent in his statements.

Woods is certainly aware of it. Cleve is perhaps his most complexly nuanced performance to date. This man is much crazier than Richard Boyle in *Salvador* (1986), yet he is infinitely subtler and smarter. Woods is a time bomb throughout the film, not only because his character is an unrepentant killer but also because he can become violent or oddly tender with the same unpredictable, thoroughly convincing swiftness. It is a monument to the actor's ability that one finds, along with Meechum, the misdirected and unforgivable final sacrifice to Cleve a moving, even noble, gesture.

Dennehy, in an admirably low-key manner, keeps up with Woods's flashier performance every step of the way. Though the more rational of the two men, Meechum's inner conflicts are, arguably, the more severe. His storyteller's instinct, coupled with the need to address his shaky financial status, goes to war with his lawman's ethics and, later, a strong desire for revenge almost every time Cleve opens his mouth. Add to that his continuing sorrow over the loss of his wife, and it is a wonder that Meechum does not explode. That Dennehy manages to keep the character percolating at a well-modulated midpoint between rage and professional restraint—in the face of Woods's incorrigible ability to steal every scene—is quite a wondrous achievement in itself.

Robert Strauss

Reviews

Films in Review. XXXVIII, December, 1987, p. 610.
Los Angeles. XXXII, October, 1987, p. 242.
Los Angeles Times. September 25, 1987, VI, p. 16.
Macleans. C, October 5, 1987, p. 58.
New York. XX, October 12, 1987, p. 93.
The New York Times. September 25, 1987, p. C24.
Newsweek. CX, October 5, 1987, p. 84.
Time. CXXX, October 12, 1987, p. 85.
Variety. CCCXXVIII, September 23, 1987, p. 12.
The Wall Street Journal. September 24, 1987, p. 24.

BEVERLY HILLS COP II

Production: Don Simpson and Jerry Bruckheimer, in association with Eddie
   Murphy Productions; released by Paramount Pictures
Direction: Tony Scott
Screenplay: Larry Ferguson and Warren Skaaren; based on a story by Eddie
   Murphy and Robert D. Wachs
Cinematography: Jeffrey L. Kimball
Editing: Billy Weber, Chris Lebenzon, and Michael Tronick
Art direction: Ken Davis
Music: Harold Faltermeyer
MPAA rating: R
Running time: 102 minutes

> *Principal characters:*
> Axel Foley........................Eddie Murphy
> Billy Rosewood...................Judge Reinhold
> Maxwell Dent...................Jürgen Prochnow
> Captain Andrew Bogomil ....Ronny Cox
> Sergeant John Taggart ....John Ashton
> Karla Fry.......................Brigitte Nielsen
> Harold Lutz.......................Allen Garfield
> Chip Cain........................Dean Stockwell
> Jeffrey Friedman ....Paul Reiser
> Mayor Egan......................Robert Ridgley
> Inspector Todd ....Gil Hill
> Sidney Bernstein ....Gilbert Gottfried

It is noteworthy that Eddie Murphy Productions is a member of the aggregate of the film's producers and that the story was written by Murphy (along with his manager, Robert D. Wachs). The film appears to be little more than the marketing of Murphy, and one suspects that he has his eye on promoting thousands of Mumford High School T-shirts and Detroit Lions jackets (which the Murphy character wears in the California sunshine). Since the film delivers much childish foolishness, *Beverly Hills Cop II* appeals primarily to the young viewer.

It is becoming more and more apparent that Murphy's formerly successful career in film derived in large part from the responsible professionals who directed him: Walter Hill (*48 HRS.*, 1982) and John Landis (*Trading Places*, 1983), in particular. After *Beverly Hills Cop* (1984), the quality of Murphy's work seemed to deteriorate. Michael Ritchie, who has directed some good comedies (*The Survivors*, 1983, and *Fletch*, 1985), also directed *The Golden Child* (1986), which slipped quickly into oblivion, but the film's failure was more more attributable to Dennis Feldman's poor script than to the direction. Tony Scott, who had directed the financially successful *Top Gun* (1986), hired on to direct Murphy in *Beverly Hills Cop II*, but his work is even less competent than that of writers Larry Ferguson and Warren Skaaren.

The viewer who has seen *Beverly Hills Cop* has essentially seen its sequel. Many of the characters from the original film appear again: Sergeant John Taggart (John Ashton), Billy Rosewood (Judge Reinhold), Captain Andrew Bogomil (Ronny Cox), and Inspector Todd (Gil Hill). *Beverly Hills Cop II* begins with a series of parallel cuts from Beverly Hills to Detroit and back again. After the film's opening shot of the red glow of the California sun, the viewer witnesses the first of what will be a series of carefully planned Beverly Hills robberies, which the police and newspapers will call the "Alphabet" robberies.

A tall blonde woman, dressed in white except for her sunglasses, leads a commando raid on an exclusive jewelry store. In less than two minutes, the gang of thieves has seized what it wants; the blonde woman, Karla Fry (Brigitte Nielsen), leaves behind a rose and an envelope which bears the letter A and then shoots down the store's elaborate chandelier. The scene shifts to Detroit, where Axel Foley (Eddie Murphy) is getting dressed for another day of undercover detective work. The viewer follows him as he speeds through the city in a red Ferrari in order to set up a purchase of counterfeit credit cards. Meanwhile, back in Beverly Hills, while Captain Andrew Bogomil is jogging one morning near an oil field, he suddenly discovers something of significance; in his preoccupation, he telephones his old friend Axel and cancels their annual fishing trip. Bogomil has been assigned to the Alphabet case, along with Rosewood and Taggart, but the three detectives are finding life most difficult under a new Chief of Police, Harold Lutz (Allen Garfield). After Lutz suspends him in a fit of rage, Bogomil starts for home, only to run into trouble. Unsuspectingly, he stops to help a motorist in trouble, but the motorist is Karla, who shoots him and leaves him for dead.

It does not take long for Foley to hear about Bogomil; after conning Inspector Todd into increasing his expense money, Foley hops a plane for California. From this point onward *Beverly Hills Cop II* focuses on numerous typical Eddie Murphy bits. First, Axel poses as a Beverly Hills building inspector in order to use a luxurious mansion for his base of operations. Later, when Chief Lutz confronts him, Axel does a routine as a Jamaican psychic. As the plot thickens, he visits a posh gun club, posing as an explosives delivery man; when the trail of the Alphabet robbers leads him to the Playboy Club, Axel poses as a swimming-pool sanitary engineer. Between Murphy's one-man shows, the film's plot advances. Behind the Alphabet crimes lies the master mind of Maxwell Dent (Jürgen Prochnow), who, with his aides, Chip Cain (Dean Stockwell) and Karla, maintains offices at the Beverly Hills Shooting Club. When Axel shows up at the club, Dent guesses his true identity and orders him to be killed. An attempted assassination outside a nightclub fails, but the scene involves the requisite gunfire and car chases.

Rosewood has become, since Axel's initial visit to Beverly Hills, something of a free spirit, and Axel has no difficulty persuading him to join a nighttime break-in at the Shooting Club; Taggart, who is much more conservative, constantly wrings his hands in fear of losing his job. The break-in nets coded information about the ring's future targets, and as Axel predicts, the gang soon descends upon a federal depository. As Axel, Rosewood, and Taggart arrive at the depository, the robbery is in progress: More gunfire and more vehicular stunts ensue.

The robbers' trail leads to the Playboy Club, where Axel publicly antagonizes Dent, picks his pocket, and thereby discovers the identity of Dent's accountant. Axel applies devious pressure to Sidney Bernstein (Gilbert Gottfried), who unwittingly allows the policemen access to Dent's files, and the truth begins to surface: Dent has been selling weapons to a notorious gunrunner; coming up against a cash shortage, he has initiated the series of spectacular robberies.

The film's showdown develops during Dent's robbery of his own racetrack. In the aftermath, Axel discovers the clue which Bogomil had earlier unearthed: Dent hides his weapons in a large warehouse on an oil field adjacent to the racetrack. At at this warehouse that Axel, Rosewood, and Taggart will confront Dent, Karla, and their gunmen. The first of two climactic shoot-outs produces a considerable amount of fireworks (literally). After the warehouse has been secured, Axel goes alone after Dent and Karla. He disposes of Dent, but it is the previously reticent Taggart who kills Karla, just as she is about to dispatch Axel.

The denouement of *Beverly Hills Cop II* is rather unsurprising. The mayor of Beverly Hills, Ted Egan (Robert Ridgley), fires Lutz, Captain Bogomil recovers and becomes Chief of Police, and the mayor calls Todd and praises Foley's work. Rosewood and Taggart bid a fond adieu to Axel as he returns to Detroit.

Although the film was among the biggest box-office successes of 1987, its success relies primarily upon the huge popular appeal of its star and the success of *Beverly Hills Cop*. Director Scott, director of photography Jeffrey L. Kimball, and art director Ken Davis tried to make the film visually interesting—Kimball shoots several scenes, for example, through filters in order to suggest the half-lit underworld that lurks behind and beneath the bright glamor of Beverly Hills. In the final analysis, however, Scott and writers Ferguson and Skaaren rely on tried-and-true formulas for the substance of the film.

The essence of the film, as one would expect, is action—shoot-outs, physical violence, and vehicle chases—and what passes for wit in the minds of the film's writers. Much of the film's humor is of the playground or locker-room variety. Nonstop obscenities and gratuitous sexual wordplay make the film often both offensive and predictable. To Axel, women are nothing more than sexual playthings (there is at least some justice in the fact that Karla gets the advantage of Axel near the end of the film), and it is woefully evident that the only reason that a scene is staged at the Playboy Club is to titillate the viewer with shots of females at play. In the final analysis, *Beverly Hills Cop II* is another example of a sequel's success based on the merits of its predecessor and not on its own strengths.

Gordon Walters

Reviews
Cosmopolitan. CIII, August, 1987, p. 32.
Films in Review. XXXVIII, August, 1987, p. 422.
Jet. LXXII, June 15, 1987, p. 56.
Los Angeles Times. May 20, 1987, VI, p. 1.
Macleans. C, June 1, 1987, p. 55.
The New Republic. CXCVI, June 29, 1987, p. 25.
The New York Times. May 20, 1987, p. C28.
Newsweek. CIX, June 1, 1987, p. 69.
Time. CXXIX, June 1, 1987, p. 73.
Variety. CCCXXVII, May 20, 1987, p. 16.

BEYOND THERAPY

Production: Steven M. Haft for Sandcastle 5; released by New World
 Pictures
Direction: Robert Altman
Screenplay: Christopher Durang and Robert Altman; based on the play of
 the same name by Christopher Durang
Cinematography: Pierre Mignot
Editing: Steve Dunn and Jennifer Auge
Production design: Stephen Altman
Art direction: Annie Senechal
Music: Gabriel Yared
Song: George Gershwin and Ira Gershwin, "Someone to Watch over Me";
 performed by Yves Montand
MPAA rating: R
Running time: 93 minutes

> *Principal characters:*
> Prudence .... Julie Hagerty
> Bruce .... Jeff Goldblum
> Charlotte .... Glenda Jackson
> Stuart .... Tom Conti
> Bob .... Christopher Guest
> Zizi .... Geneviève Page
> Andrew .... Cris Campion

Robert Altman's prolific career as a film director is the chronicle of a creative survivor. In little more than a decade, originating with the release of
M*A*S*H* in 1970 and culminating with his last big-budget feature *Popeye*
in 1980, Altman directed an astonishing total of fifteen feature films. This
rigorous schedule, coupled with Altman's uncompromising artistic tempera-
ment, led to the demise of his independent production company, Lion's
Gate Studios, following the generally negative critical reception and subsequent commercial debacle of *A Wedding* (1978), *A Perfect Couple* (1979),
and *Popeye.* Though shunned by the Hollywood establishment, Altman revived his floundering film career with a fusion of theatrical material, cable
television funding, and a return to the lower budget format of 16-mm production. His first "theatrical" motion picture, *Come Back to the 5 & Dime,
Jimmy Dean, Jimmy Dean* (1982), was a filmed reconstruction of his own
off-Broadway production commissioned by Viacom for its Showtime channel, and it has been followed by successful films of plays by Frank South,
David Rabe, and Sam Shepard. Altman's most recent release, *Beyond Therapy*, continues the director's exploration of this rich vein of theatrical mate-

rial, although this time the weary conventions of the source, a two-act farce by Christopher Durang that debuted on Broadway in 1982, often undermine the admirable efforts of Altman and his cast.

Beyond Therapy follows the escapades of bisexual Bruce (Jeff Goldblum), who contrives to consummate a heterosexual relationship through the personal advertisement section of *New York* magazine. His intended conquest, Prudence (Julie Hagerty), agrees to meet Bruce at a French restaurant, Les Bouchons; she responds to his romantic overtures, until she learns of his sexual predilections. Prudence is disgusted by Bruce's casual admission, and her homophobia actively surfaces with the suggestion that she might be but a brief recreational respite from the monotony of Bruce's primary relationship with his live-in lover, Bob (Christopher Guest). Meanwhile, from her perch on the second-floor balcony of Les Bouchons, Bob's mother Zizi (Geneviève Page) witnesses the meeting and mistakenly assumes that the couple's animated assignation denotes concupiscence. These disclosures precipitate a flurry of activity as each of the principals exit the restaurant seeking solace for bruised psyches. Prudence and Bruce rapidly repair to the counsel and comfort of their psychotherapists while Zizi offers maternal consolation to the deceived Bob, who in turn pursues advice from members of his aerobics encounter group.

This unsubtle opening reveals the flaws of Durang's original play, including the overtly stereotypical characters and the now-commonplace swipes at the trite trendiness of New York culture. The anarchy of the farce is undercut by the author's earnest plea for the acceptance and understanding of the humanity of his characters. Altman manages to breathe life into the story, however, by undermining the play's transparent desire to be inoffensively likable and charming. Altman restores a necessary edge to the characters by imbuing them with a desperate kinetic energy; Goldblum's self-involved Bruce is a catalog of annoying tics and mannerisms, while the wraithlike Hagerty transforms the neurasthenic Prudence into a vertiginous windmill of torso and limbs. Les Bouchons, where the opening scenes unfold, resembles an aviary and the customers exotic species of birds, though none so visually vibrant as Zizi, a colorfully plumed harridan who fearfully flutters and shrieks like a protective brood hen over her solitary offspring. The camera movement creates a sensation of claustrophobia in the restaurant, where the staff as well as customers, as befits a French farce, are vigorously engaged in romantic trysts. The familiar sweeping arcs, overlapping dialogue, and composition-in-depth of the Altman style capture the giddy and inchoate sexual energy of the characters.

Prudence's analyst Stuart (Tom Conti), thinly cloaks his passion for her in the guise of libido liberation and an affected Italian accent, though Prudence will have none of him—her earlier ardor cooled when she discovered at first hand his problem: *ejaculatio praecox*. Charlotte (Glenda Jackson),

Bruce's therapist, offers an equally unsettling view of the unethical behavior and personality disorders of the mental health professional. She is a rigidly insular and infantile regressive who turns a deaf ear to her patients' needs and believes only in anonymously consummated heterosexuality—a credo she has the opportunity to practice daily, although briefly, because of the proximity of Stuart in the adjacent office. Not surprisingly, these therapists offer no cogent advice to Prudence and Bruce, who meet again through magazine advertisements and finally overcome their mutual antipathy and casually consummate their relationship. Bruce invites Prudence to dinner at the apartment he still shares with Bob, thereby callously affronting his former lover. Bob's confrontation with his rival precipitates a suicidal anxiety attack; Bruce's remedy is to send Bob to Charlotte. While Charlotte proves of no practical assistance (she does not believe that Bruce is gay), her homophobia provides a catalyst to Bob's flagging self-worth. In defense of his lifestyle, he pulls a pistol on Charlotte and fires at her—a symbolic assassination since the revolver is loaded with blanks. This outburst—malevolent, violent, yet ultimately harmless—suggests a therapeutic modality to Charlotte, who now counsels Bob to exorcise his repressed anger with a figurative destruction of Bruce and accompanies him to witness the deed at the restaurant.

Meanwhile, Stuart has followed Prudence to Les Bouchons, hoping to dissuade her from continuing her relationship with Bruce (Stuart's already fragile self-esteem has been fractured by her graphic description of his bisexual rival's superior prowess in bed). The climax, shot by Altman in an excruciatingly satiric parody of the slow-motion shoot-out, has Bob empty dozens of rounds (without reloading) at Bruce. Altman's artificial expansion of this temporally transitory scene allows a protracted catharsis that engenders a more honest assessment of the romantic opportunities of each character. At the denouement, Prudence accepts Bruce's marriage proposal and Bob finds a new roommate (ironically, the gay son of homophobic Charlotte). Bruce, whose Francophilia suggested the choice of Les Bouchons for their assignation, promises Prudence a honeymoon in Paris. As they exit to the street, Altman's overhead camera pulls back to reveal the skyline, with the Eiffel Tower centered on the horizon.

The release pattern of *Beyond Therapy* follows the increasingly familiar distribution of a film intended less for theatrical consumption than for its subsequent rental at video outlets. The reviews were decidedly mixed, though the positive assessments were often effusive, and after a brief tour of the festival circuit the film was shelved until its rerelease in the videotape format. The critics who expected a verbatim transcription of the play on to the screen were disappointed at Altman's interpretation, though most praised the acting ensemble. The actors are indeed one of the strongest recommendations of the film, especially Conti and Guest, who bring a surprising dignity and compassion to the two most difficult roles in the film. The criticism of Altman's manipulation of the original material seems especially obtuse, since the director ably employs the source text, which is frequently too frothy and facile to offer the satiric bite required of farce, as effective counterpoint to his visual translation of the play. Altman's deconstruction of Durang, most notable in the director's refusal to exploit the effortless charm of the written roles and the screen *personae*, cuts through the conventional pieties to reveal the more painful processes of gender identification, sexual orientation, and urban alienation. Altman's narrative strategy attempts to graft Bertolt Brecht to Neil Simon, and while not wholly successful, Altman's version ultimately is archly sophisticated where Durang's is slight and sophomoric.

John Robert Kelly

Reviews
American Film. XII, January, 1987, p. 72.
Commonweal. CIV, March 27, 1987, p. 183.
Los Angeles Times. February 27, 1987, VI, p. 14.
Macleans. C, March 9, 1987, p. 57.
Monthly Film Bulletin. LIV, October, 1987, p. 301.
The New Republic. CXCVI, March 23, 1987, p. 25.
The New York Times. February 27, 1987, p. C8.
Sight and Sound. LVI, Autumn, 1987, p. 293.
Time. CXXIX, March 2, 1987, p. D4.
Variety. CCCXXVI, January 28, 1987, p. 22.
The Wall Street Journal. February 26, 1987, p. 20.
The Washington Post. March 2, 1987, p. B12.

THE BIG EASY

Production: Stephen Friedman; released by Columbia Pictures
Direction: Jim McBride
Screenplay: Daniel Petrie, Jr., and Jack Baran
Cinematography: Affonso Beato
Editing: Mia Goldman
Art direction: Jeannine Claudia Oppewall; set decoration, Lisa Fischer
Makeup: Julie Purcell
Costume design: Tracey Tynan
Sound: Mark Ulano
Music: Brad Fiedel
MPAA rating: R
Running time: 101 minutes

Principal characters:
Remy McSwain	Dennis Quaid
Anne Osborne	Ellen Barkin
Jack Kellom	Ned Beatty
Detective Ed Dodge	Ebbe Roe Smith
Detective Andre De Soto	John Goodman
Detective McCabe	Lisa Jane Persky
Lamar Parmental	Charles Ludlam
Bobby McSwain	Tim O'Brien
Judge James Garrison	Judge Jim Garrison
Vinnie "Cannon" Di Moti	Marc Lawrence
Mama	Grace Zabriskie

The "big easy" is a local nickname for the city of New Orleans and also accurately describes the life-style of local detective Remy McSwain (Dennis Quaid), whose family connections with the local police department give him free rein. There are hints of corruption attached to his relationships with the traders, bar owners, and possibly the organized criminals of the area. It seems, however, that Remy has more than one kind of family connection, one that is brought into focus when a local Mafia drug runner is found dead in the harbor. That same day a special inspector arrives at the precinct to investigate allegations of corruption. Remy is dubious about the investigation, but once he meets Special Prosecutor Anne Osborne (Ellen Barkin), he shows an interest in cooperation which seems to have more to do with her physical appearance than with his sense of civic pride and justice. Anne accompanies Remy and Detective McCabe (Lisa Jane Persky) to the scene of the death, which could possibly be a murder, and is later shown some of the town by Remy. Anne is confused by his apparent indifference to the crime that he is investigating and takes a professional interest in the number of favors granted the detective during the night, her first in the city.

They soon develop a passionate sexual attraction despite much initial hostility and some verbal sparring. After a local triple murder which Remy links, by tenuous logic, to the initial killing, and which witnesses say was carried out by three men in an unmarked police car, Anne's position as the investigator of corruption begins to become more compromised. After Remy is tricked by his superior, Jack Kellom (Ned Beatty), into making payoffs to a local bar owner, Anne is forced to prosecute Remy. Her anger at his involvement in police corruption increases when he uses his family connections to destroy the videotape on which she was to rely for evidence in court. The case against Remy has to be dismissed, but a series of threats directed at Anne and him, coupled with the shooting of his brother in an obvious case of mistaken identity, prompt Remy to go against family loyalty and form a partnership with Anne to investigate what is happening. An explosion at a Mardi Gras warehouse helps to convince Remy of widespread police involvement in a drug-dealing racket, especially when he sees an unmarked police car leaving the scene.

Despite spoiling tactics by Kellom, who is soon to marry Remy's mother (Grace Zabriskie), Remy and Anne stumble across a huge drug shipment concealed in a police dockyard. While Kellom tries to destroy the evidence, he becomes involved in a gun battle with detectives Ed Dodge (Ebbe Roe Smith) and Andre De Soto (John Goodman), which results in the deaths of all three.

Director Jim McBride's previous feature film, *Breathless* (1983), demonstrated a particular interest in the character and atmosphere of unusual locations. Observantly detailed on-the-road scenery and the unique texture of life in Venice Beach, California, were used to great effect to add texture to the film. Although it must have been a great temptation to costar New Orleans with the leading characters in *The Big Easy*, such a tactic was resisted. In fact, the audience sees very little of the city streets but does see many smoky, music-filled interiors, as well as some meticulously photographed scenes shot in a Mardi Gras warehouse and at the riverfront, which add to the film's memorable atmosphere. This close atmosphere adds emphasis to Remy's dilemma when his loyalties are so dramatically split; he is so much a part of the city that he feels himself to be the betrayed and the betrayer.

This evocation of atmosphere and Remy's wooing of Anne are greatly enhanced by the sound track of the film, composed of Cajun and Louisiana tunes, as well as songs from the New Orleans mainstream. McBride thought that the sound track was inaccessible, but it has been very successful in record sales and has no doubt enhanced the performance of the film at the box office, which has totaled $20 million, thus more than recouping the estimated budget of $6.5 million.

It is ironic that a film which uses its location to such effect was originally set in a different city. Writer Daniel Petrie, Jr., marketed his screenplay, set in Chicago, as *Windy City*. McBride suggested a rewrite to place the action in the more ambiguous atmosphere of New Orleans. Problems were encountered trying to convince producers to make the film without recognized actors in the lead roles to guarantee box-office interest. After extensive rewrites, the film was finally cast with Quaid and Barkin, both of whom have appeared in cult successes such as *The Right Stuff* (1983) and *Desert Bloom* (1985). McBride comments in *The Hollywood Reporter* magazine that the pace and energy of the performances in *The Big Easy* were encouraged by a screening of Howard Hawks's comedy *His Girl Friday* (1940) for the cast. Not only is the Barkin-Quaid chemistry in the lead partnership effective, it was also fostered in an atmosphere where all the actors were trying to deliver their dialogue as quickly as possible. This sense of fun and the breathless pace generated in the film are a tribute to the skills of the actors and the control of the director. In fact, the whole ensemble of players produces highly personable performances, notably Persky (as McCabe, a role originally written for a man), who is, regrettably, missing from most of the action involving the police corruption investigation. In effect, this isolates Anne as the only fully realized female character in the film, allowing some casual and regrettable sexism to creep into the dialogue from time to time.

It is the relentless pace and verve of the film which helps carry it through some flaws of logic in the plot, such as occasional conclusions rendered ludicrous by lack of facts. Such faults in logic could seriously undermine an ordinary thriller, but here the audience can enjoy a romantic romp and happily suspend disbelief.

The Big Easy has many of the qualities of some of the most popular film classics. With its otherworldly and romantic setting, the relationship of Barkin and Quaid recalls the deep-seated empathy and electric dialogue of the great screwball comedy partnerships. The plot and story line, although not always readily coherent, are reminiscent of the spirit of adventure of the screen's great thrillers.

The success of the film, despite the indifference of some distributors in the United States, has proved that there is still an audience for atmospheric and finely paced films. *The Big Easy* survived the producers' attempts at tampering with its ending, and the director's preferred version was finally released with a fittingly romantic and throwaway finale in the spirit of Remy and Anne's romance and the atmosphere of New Orleans.

Peter Tasker

Reviews

Films in Review. XXXVIII, November, 1987, p. 548.
The Hollywood Reporter. CCC, October 30, 1987, p. 42.
Los Angeles Times. August 21, 1987, VI, p. 1.
Macleans. C, August 24, 1987, p. 49.
The New Republic. CXCVII, September 28, 1987, p. 27.
The New York Times. August 21, 1987, p. C4.
The New Yorker. LXIII, September 7, 1987, p. 100.
Newsweek. CX, August 24, 1987, p. 60.
People Weekly. XXVIII, August 31, 1987, p. 8.
Time. CXXX, August 24, 1987, p. 65.
Variety. CCCXXV, December 3, 1986, p. 23.

BLACK WIDOW

Production: Harold Schneider for Americent Films and American Entertainment Partners; released by Twentieth Century-Fox
Direction: Bob Rafelson
Screenplay: Ronald Bass
Cinematography: Conrad L. Hall
Editing: John Bloom
Art direction: Gene Callahan; set decoration, Jim Duffy, Buck Henshaw, and Rick Simpson
Special effects: Allen Hall and Jerry Williams
Costume design: Patricia Norris
Sound: David MacMillan
Music: Michael Small
Songs: Peter Rafelson, "Magic Island" and "Night Hearts"
MPAA rating: R
Running time: 103 minutes

> *Principal characters:*
> Alexandra Barnes.................Debra Winger
> Catharine......................Theresa Russell
> Paul ....Sami Frey
> Ben ....Dennis Hopper
> William ....Nicol Williamson
> Bruce..........................Terry O'Quinn
> Shin ....James Hong
> Etta...............................Diane Ladd
> Herb.............................David Mamet
> Michael.........................D. W. Moffett
> Sara...............................Lois Smith
> Ricci...............................Leo Rossi

If not eagerly anticipated, the release of *Black Widow* at least aroused more than usual interest among film fans, chiefly because it was the first motion picture from director Bob Rafelson since 1981, and only the second since 1976. Further, *Black Widow* marked the return to the big screen of gifted cinematographer Conrad Hall, who had not lensed a theatrical feature since 1976. Added to these attractions was a splendid cast led by Debra Winger, perhaps the most popular actress in contemporary American cinema, and Theresa Russell, a provocative, chameleonic actress who had impressed cineasts in a variety of challenging roles for a decade. Given these ingredients, one might have reasonably expected something more than the well-mounted piece of pulp entertainment that was delivered. *Black Widow* is effective entertainment, but it becomes tangled in its own pretensions and improbabilities.

Black Widow is a chronicle of the beginnings and the endings of relationships. It opens as the strikingly beautiful Catharine (Theresa Russell) mourns the death of her husband, a prominent New York publisher old enough to have been her father. Catharine alters her *persona* and moves to Dallas, where she marries a successful toy manufacturer (Dennis Hopper). After poisoning her husband's brandy, Catharine is once again a wealthy widow. From Dallas she moves to Seattle, where she goes to considerable trouble to ingratiate herself with and finally marry William (Nicol Williamson), a wealthy scholar.

In Washington, D.C., independent research of restless, deskbound Justice Department investigator Alexandra ("Alex") Barnes (Debra Winger) leads her to suspect a connection between the seemingly unrelated deaths. Alex finally concludes that she is tracing the movements of only one woman. She follows Catharine to Seattle but is too late to prevent William's murder. The chase continues to Hawaii, where Alex takes an assumed name, contrives to meet Catharine, and eventually strikes up a friendship with her. Catharine's suspicions have been aroused, however, by the snooping of Shin (James Hong), a third-rate private detective hired by Alex.

Catharine murders Shin and proceeds to manipulate her latest romantic conquest, Paul (Sami Frey), an attractive developer of luxury hotels. Because Catharine realizes that Alex is a threat, she plays a heartless game of seduction, encouraging Alex's simultaneous attraction to her and to Paul. Alex, who feels womanly for the first time in her life, loses her objectivity.

In a calculated turnabout, Catharine suddenly marries Paul, provoking a jealous outburst (and the gift of a brooch in the form of a black widow spider) from Alex at the wedding. Catharine proceeds to do away with her husband and expertly frames Alex for the crime. When Catharine visits the prison to gloat, however, Alex produces Paul, who is very much alive. Realizing that she has been caught in a very clever trap, Catharine blurts out a confession.

Director Rafelson made his name in the 1970's with emotionally charged films that celebrate unorthodoxy and the rebel spirit. Such films as *Five Easy Pieces* (1970) and *The King of Marvin Gardens* (1972) established Rafelson's interest in ferociously nonconformist characters and his ability to harness effectively the energies of such talented actors as Jack Nicholson and Bruce Dern. Yet Rafelson's remake of *The Postman Always Rings Twice* (1981) is a murky, obscurely motivated film that disappointed his followers. It was hoped in some quarters that *Black Widow* would provide Rafelson with a vehicle with which to reestablish himself as one of Hollywood's more thoughtful and challenging directors, but this was not to be: *Black Widow* is an impersonal, commercial film that could have been directed by any number of competent craftsmen. Well written on a superficial level, the film does have tense, often-clever dialogue and even some wit. Undeniable tension is built between the two women. The engine that propels the story forward, however, is fueled by illogic and improbability; Rafelson had little hope of connecting with the script on a meaningful level.

Structurally, *Black Widow* is a chase film with a chase that has little grounding in reality. So concerned was screenwriter Ronald Bass with character development and interplay that he contrived to have Alex pursue Catharine across the United States on the slimmest of leads. The audience is given no clue as to how Alex becomes convinced that Catharine has moved from Dallas to Seattle, nor how Alex is immediately able to locate Catharine in that city. Following the murder of William, an airline ticket clerk's vague recollection of Catharine is sufficient to prompt Alex to leave her job, sell everything she owns, and travel to Hawaii. Once there, Alex is soon sharing a scuba-diving class with Catharine. One might suppose that this is partly a result of the efforts of the clearly inept detective, Shin, a surmise that prompts more questions: If Shin is inept and disreputable, why does Alex go to him? How does he manage to locate as elusive a felon as Catharine?

For all the script's contrivance and gaps in logic, the relationship between the women is interesting and sometimes provocative. Alex, with her careless manner and androgynous name, is the converse of Catharine, who is seductive and desirable no matter which guise she takes. The sexuality that Alex has denied herself comes easily to Catharine, so Alex's forging of a symbiotic relationship seems inevitable. Alex does more than simply wear Catharine's clothes and borrow her Hawaiian hairdresser: She struggles to assume Catharine's identity and to experience the intense pleasures that Catharine callously discards.

The deterioration of Alex's professional objectivity is well explicated. When Alex feels the growth of her womanly confidence in Hawaii, as Paul responds to her, she does not stop to think why Catharine encourages her to pursue Paul. The possibility that Catharine may be preparing a subtle trap does not occur to her. Alex's bitter confrontation with Catharine later at the wedding is an expression of her dismay at being the sexual loser when, for the first time, she had sensed the possibility of being a winner. The jeweled black widow that she gives to Catharine is not merely a comment on Catharine's murderousness, but a reflection of Alex's female rage. Similarly, the final trap sprung by Alex is more than the scheme of a clever investigator—it is the revenge of a wounded woman.

Winger may be the most natural and accessible of all American leading women; her performance as Alex is thoroughly believable. As Catharine, Theresa Russell has the role that will probably propel her into the cinematic mainstream. Russell, who is married to director Nicolas Roeg, established her reputation with fine work in his *Bad Timing: A Sensual Obsession* (1980) and *Insignificance* (1985). She has specialized in sharply etched, often-troubled characters—beautiful women with fatal flaws. To watch Russell as Catharine is fascinating: The character's dark emotions subtly shift and roil beneath her delicate, provocative features, and the audience is ensnared just as surely as Catharine's victims.

Technical credits, particularly the moodily pastel cinematography of Conrad Hall, are first-rate—incongruously so: The film is simply overproduced and does not warrant the skill and care that was lavished upon it. If it had been made by a first-time director or by a filmmaker known previously for exploitation films, it would have elicited considerable excitement. As it stands, *Black Widow* is little more than agreeable entertainment, the work of talented artists laboring beneath their capabilities.

David J. Hogan

Reviews
American Film. January, 1987, p. 72.
Film Quarterly. XLI, Fall, 1987, p. 54.
Films in Review. XXXVIII, April, 1987, p. 227.
Los Angeles Times. February 6, 1987, VI, p. 1.
The New Republic. CXCVI, March 2, 1987, p. 24.
The New York Times. February 6, 1987, p. C3.
The New Yorker. LXIII, February 23, 1987, p. 111.
Newsweek. CIX, February 16, 1987, p. 72.
Time. CXXIX, February 16, 1987, p. 76.
Variety. CCCXXVI, February 4, 1987, p. 23.

BLIND DATE

Production: Tony Adams; released by Tri-Star Pictures
Direction: Blake Edwards
Screenplay: Dale Launer
Cinematography: Harry Stradling
Editing: Robert Pergament
Production design: Rodger Maus
Art direction: Peter Lansdown Smith; set decoration, Carl Biddiscombe
Special effects: Roy Downey
Makeup: Rick Sharp and Norman T. Leavitt
Costume design: Tracy Tynan
Sound: William M. Randall
Music direction: Al Bunetta and Tom Bocci
Music: Henry Mancini
MPAA rating: PG-13
Running time: 93 minutes

Principal characters:
Nadia Gates .... Kim Basinger
Walter Davis .... Bruce Willis
David Bedford .... John Larroquette
Judge Harold Bedford .... William Daniels
Ted Davis .... Phil Hartman
Stanley Jordan .... Himself

Blind Date is director Blake Edwards' flat-footed attempt to make a screwball comedy for yuppies. The film provides a pallid imitation of the high-pitched, bizarre, and disturbingly violent action of its precursors, Martin Scorsese's *After Hours* (1985) and Jonathan Demme's *Something Wild* (1986). *Blind Date* relies almost entirely on predictable slapstick, never making credible the screwball-comedy formula, wherein madcap female liberates workaday male. The light social satire that one expects from Edwards remains embryonic at best, as though such things were better left for his comedies of midlife crises, notably *10* (1979) and *Micki and Maude* (1984).

Blind Date begins with a shot of an electric guitar and pans right, past an empty bed, to Walter Davis (Bruce Willis) asleep at the kitchen table, which is covered with spreadsheets. The symbolism is clear: Davis, a financial analyst, has given up an uncertain but happy career in jazz for a steady job, a nice car, and a condo. The consequence, however, is an empty bed, since Davis' work denies him both sleep and a sex life. Davis claims, "I'm getting something out of this," but he cannot articulate what that something might be.

That night Davis must help wine and dine an important client, a Japanese industrialist with Old World views on women. The single Davis must find a submissive woman to accompany him to the dinner. Unable to find someone, he reluctantly turns to his brother Ted (Phil Hartman), a slick car salesman, who sets him up with Nadia Gates (Kim Basinger). Davis is warned not to let Gates drink because she becomes "real wild."

Predictably, Davis treats Gates to champagne before dinner. A drunken Gates then proceeds to humiliate Davis' lecherous associate, shower his boss with champagne, and convince the industrialist's wife to divorce her husband for openly keeping concubines and forcing her to dress like a geisha. The alcoholic Gates is supposed to be the wise fool, exposing the double standard and misogyny as she wreaks havoc. The alcoholic, however, lacks the wise fool's transcendent gift of divination, suffering instead from a disease hardly suitable to feminist or other social satire. Edwards, who directed the powerful and poignant *Days of Wine and Roses* (1962), should know this better than anyone else. Further undermining the scene is a racist and sexist portrayal of the Japanese couple. The industrialist is not an efficient capitalist but the monstrous caricature painted by American media, industrialists, and politicians in the wake of a trade surplus. The wife "no speaka Engurish," until she learns from Gates that California divorce laws entitle her to 50 percent of her husband's wealth. The infamous California divorce acts as an instant Berlitz lesson in English for avaricious women the world over.

The remainder of the film involves Gates and the now-fired Davis fleeing from her psychotic former boyfriend David Bedford (John Larroquette). Bedford, a lawyer, is obsessed with the idea that Davis might "drill" Gates, a telling metaphor for sex that is repeated more for laughs than insight into Bedford's psychosis. There follows an endless series of pratfalls, car chases, and hallway high jinks, with Bedford driving through no fewer than three storefronts. Davis is arrested for shooting a gun at Bedford, and the evening ends.

Gates secretly bails out Davis and agrees to marry Bedford if he will defend Davis. In court, the judge proves to be Bedford's unloving father (William Daniels). Bedford privately agrees to leave town if his father drops the charges and holds the impending wedding at his mansion. When Davis learns of Gates's sacrifice, he plans to liberate her with a box of rum-filled chocolates, which she proceeds to devour before heading to the makeshift altar in front of the outdoor pool.

At the altar, Gates giggles and staggers. Now uninhibited, she no longer abides by the sense of honor and sacrifice that guided her while sober. She turns to the seated guests and asks them whether she should be forced to marry someone she does not love. They shout, "No." Not to be outdone, Bedford poses a counter-question, while his father insists on a vote. Before the guests have time to decide Gates's fate, however, Davis calls out from the other end of the pool. In slow motion, Gates turns and both dive into the water as the guests applaud. The two meet underwater and kiss. The scene dissolves to a shot of a beach; the camera pans to the left to reveal Davis playing guitar for Gates, then tilts down to a bottle of cola in a champagne cooler.

The film has come full circle for Davis: from a pan to the right, away from freedom (the guitar) and sex (the bed) to a pan to the left, toward freedom (the guitar) and sex (a kiss). For Gates, however, the ending is problematic. The cola bottle signifies sobriety, but since the film links her alcoholic behavior with feminist insight and activism, the cola bottle also suggests a loss of freedom or autonomy in her relationship with Davis.

At times *Blind Date* appears to be on the verge of a social satire of yuppie values and male chauvinism. The film, however, fails to develop these themes, providing instead a perfunctory run-through of slapstick conventions. The slight narrative causes the film not only to fail in its intentions but to become outright sexist and racist as well.

It is ironic that the actors fail to salvage *Blind Date* as a screwball comedy, given that most of them are major stars on popular television series: Willis in "Moonlighting," a show that best embodies the screwball comedy style of the 1930's; Larroquette in "Night Court," a situation comedy in which he has won two Emmy Awards for his role as, oddly enough, a crazed lawyer; and Daniels in "St. Elsewhere," among others.

The high point of the film has nothing to do with the stars, the dialogue, or the slapstick, all of which are at best adequate. It is the music. Early into the blind date, Davis takes Gates to a recording studio to see his friend, jazz guitarist Stanley Jordan (as himself). The few shots of Jordan's unusual technique, in which he frets and picks simultaneously with both hands, provide a visual and aural pleasure lacking from the rest of the film.

Screwball comedy represents a balance between two excesses—rapid-fire dialogue and slapstick action—often engaging in social and sexual commentary. Ironically, it is the music, usually composed by Henry Mancini, that one remembers most about Edwards' comedies. Furthermore, the members of the Academy of Motion Picture Arts and Sciences have recognized Mancini with twelve Academy Award nominations and four Oscars for scoring Edwards' films, but have not acknowledged the writer-director-producer Edwards.

Chon Noriega

Reviews
Chicago Tribune. April 3, 1987, VII, p. 42.
The Hollywood Reporter. March 27, 1987, p. 3.

Los Angeles Times. March 27, 1987, VI, p. 1.
Macleans. C, April 6, 1987, p. 54.
The New Leader. LXX, April 6, 1987, p. 23.
The New Republic. CXCVI, April 27, 1987, p. 27.
The New York Times. March 27, 1987, p. CII.
Newsweek. CIX, April 13, 1987, p. 77.
People Weekly. XXVII, April 13, 1987, p. 12.
San Francisco Chronicle. March 27, 1987, p. 72.
Time. CXXIX, April 20, 1987, p. 76.
Variety. CCCXXVI, April 1, 1987, p. 14.
The Wall Street Journal. April 2, 1987, p. 26.
The Washington Post. April 3, 1987, p. 23.

BROADCAST NEWS

Production: James L. Brooks; released by Twentieth Century-Fox
Direction: James L. Brooks
Screenplay: James L. Brooks
Cinematography: Michael Ballhaus
Editing: Richard Marks
Art direction: Charles Rosen; set decoration, Jane Bogart
Makeup: Carl Fullerton
Costume design: Molly Maginnis
Music: Bill Conti
MPAA rating: R
Running time: 131 minutes

Principal characters:
Tom Grunick......................William Hurt
Aaron Altman ....Albert Brooks
Jane Craig........................Holly Hunter
Ernie Merriman ....Robert Prosky
Jennifer Mack........................Lois Chiles
Blair Litton........................Joan Cusack
Paul Moore ....Peter Hackes
Bobby ....Christian Clemenson

As the creative force behind such television projects as "Room 222," "Mary Tyler Moore" (and its spin-off "Lou Grant"), and "Taxi," James L. Brooks both emulated and heightened everyday life. These series were popular because viewers found it easy to empathize with characters whose lives, at home and at work, were as unpredictable as their own. Brooks endowed his dramas with endearing humor and palpable moral and emotional virtue; his characters are memorable because of the care invested in making their lives both flawed and eloquent.

Such qualities were amply evident in *Terms of Endearment* (1983), which marked Brooks's debut as a feature-film director and garnered five Oscars (including Best Picture and Best Director). In *Broadcast News* (also nominated by the Academy for Best Picture), Brooks goes back to the office. After getting to know several network journalists at the 1984 Democratic Convention, revisiting the territory he experienced in the early 1960's as a newswriter, Brooks realized that changes in the profession had created a fertile environment for his brand of storytelling. In *Broadcast News,* Brooks parlays elements from *Terms of Endearment* and his television projects into a parable of work and love for the urban-professional 1980's.

Broadcast News bills itself as biographical and begins with sketches of the three protagonists as precocious children and later as high school students. Little Jane Craig (Gennie James), future network-news producer, is shown typing late-night letters to the last three pen pals on her list; her father (Leo Burmester) startles her mid-thought and warns her not to get obsessive in her writing. Aaron Altman (Dwayne Markee), future network correspondent, is introduced as a not-quite fifteen-year-old high school valedictorian who defends himself against bullies with his sharp wit. Tom Grunick (Kimber Shoop) studies hard but is slow to learn. His good looks and pleasant personality will more than compensate for his average intelligence.

With the salient personality traits and employment aptitudes of its three principals summarized, the film shows them next as grown-ups; each is a professional in the world of television journalism. Jane (Holly Hunter, nominated for Best Actress) and Aaron (Albert Brooks, nominated for Best Supporting Actor) are working on a story about a mercenary returning from action in Angola. Jane is also preparing a speech that she is to deliver at a network conference. The film then cuts to her presentation, in which she decries the current state of network journalism. A conscientious and committed professional, Jane calls her audience of network newspeople to task for the decline of issue-based news in favor of entertaining filler stories and higher ratings. Her audience, bored and distracted, suddenly regains interest when she plays a tape of a recently aired "story" that is spectacular in effect but a bit of fluff as far as newsworthiness is concerned. The audience's rapt involvement only proves Jane's point: Thoroughly frustrated, she retreats from the dais as the hall empties of her colleagues. An attractive man stays behind, however, approaching her and introducing himself as Tom Grunick (William Hurt, nominated for Best Actor), a local television anchor who claims to have been impressed by her speech. Flattered and reassured by his attention, Jane asks the stranger to dinner.

The two end the evening in Jane's hotel room, continuing their discussion on journalistic ethics. Jane is attracted to Tom, but their conversation reveals that his career exemplifies the trend toward slickness and superficiality that she deplores. Tom recognizes his weakness, claiming that the profession is rewarding him for something of which he considers himself incapable, to which Jane inquires about his proficiency at backrubs. This vital conflict between professional concerns and personal desires is underlined by Michael Ballhaus' fluid camera work, which pans and circles around Tom and Jane, constantly melding, separating, and repositioning them in the frame; the lack of visual resolve parallels the emotional confusion of the characters.

The scene concludes with Jane, alone in her room after Tom's departure, sitting in bed and talking to Aaron on the phone. Aaron, brilliant but average looking, is both colleague and confidant; he hears out the evening's postmortems and Jane's concerns that she has lost her capacity for seduction. Jane and Aaron share the same high ethics and intellectual acuity and are both driven by the pursuit of truth in broadcasting. Their relationship, however, remains platonic, though comfortable, until Tom, who has been hired by their network as a news anchor, arrives in Washington to complicate the issue.

The office greets Tom with a frenetic welcome while Jane races a deadline to finish a story. Tom can only stand back and marvel at her command of the situation as she pushes her assistants to the limits of their skills and perseverance. In contrast, Aaron calmly writes and tapes the copy for the piece, stopwatch in hand for thirty seconds of quality voice-over. They finish with barely enough time to rush the tape to the control room and put it on the air. Adding to the scene's intensity is a brilliant cameo performance by Jack Nicholson as the network's star anchor from New York.

The frantic aspect of this scene informs the remainder of the film, though it does not graphically re-emerge. Broadcast news is portrayed as a highly demanding profession with no room for inefficiency or indecision. Jane and Aaron are well versed in its necessities, and Tom is quick to realize that he must strive hard to keep pace. His initiation into the big leagues arises when he is assigned to anchor a special report on a sudden crisis in the Middle East.

While Jane coordinates the report and conspires to make everything as simple as possible for Tom, he retires into his office to make his own preparations—calmly unwrapping and donning a fresh shirt and combing his hair. Aaron, whose substantive experience reporting from the region is bypassed for Tom's stylish presence, sits peevishly at home. In a brilliantly comic and poignant scene, he cannot avoid watching the report and getting involved. He telephones Jane at the studio and gives her information, which she synthesizes and conveys as prompts to Tom through his discreetly placed earphone. The electronic link between Tom and Jane as she feeds information to him becomes a sensuous metaphor: Her voice is insinuating, seductive, and redolent of discretionary power. Her finger is seen caressing the button which connects her microphone with his ear, which in turn is intercut with tight close-ups of her mouth. Adding Aaron to the picture as he talks to Jane from his living room, Brooks molds these three distinct personalities into one high-performance broadcast machine. Seconds after Aaron has conveyed his ideas to Jane, they resurface from Tom's mouth, on the air, in one of the film's best evocations of the schizophrenic split between idea and image, conception and delivery, that is the unsavory reality of television news.

As Tom discovered during the report, and Aaron already knew, high-intensity work can provoke high-intensity attraction. This romantic triangle, with its attendant dialectic of career and personal aspirations, is nevertheless destined to remain unresolved; there are no clear winners or losers here. With the emotional matrix loaded to its breaking point, the network intervenes to resolve the dilemma. A massive layoff entirely disrupts the Washington bureau; a large segment of the office is fired, Tom is transferred to London (actually a promotion), Aaron resigns on principle, and Jane is elevated to the position of bureau chief.

Tom suggests to Jane that before he relocates they should go away together on vacation to discover their compatibility outside the work environment. She accepts his offer and is eager to go until Aaron suggests that she review a story Tom produced earlier. The piece was an emotional portrayal of a woman who had been raped, and it contained a shot of Tom responding with tears in his eyes to the woman's painful confession. Jane's investigation of the unedited footage reveals that Tom filmed this emotional response after the interview, then inserted it to give the impression of an immediate and sincere reaction. Jane is aghast at this breach of journalistic ethics and is completely disappointed by Tom. Her romantic interest in him and the vacation flags. She abandons him at the airport and rides away, small and despondent in the backseat of a cab with a ticket to the Tropics in her hand, frustrated again.

In the film's conclusion, the three reunite seven years later. With the tensions of professional ambitions diminished (all three are successful in their careers) and the possibility of a relationship between Jane and Tom or Aaron evaporated (they have found other partners), the viewer is forced to temper away any previous biases about their personalities (especially Tom's) as the three themselves have done. *Terms of Endearment* ended on a tearful note; *Broadcast News* offers little in the way of catharsis, leaving viewers bemused and quizzical instead. Given the professional milieu of the film, however, it is not surprising that viewers' emotions should be kept at bay. By basing the relationships in *Broadcast News* on the image-conscious ethics and morals of television journalism, rather than on the vicissitudes of middle-American daily life, Brooks created a film which posits success and professional integrity as higher virtues, if it does not actually condone them.

George Slade

Reviews

America. CLVIII, February 6, 1988, p. 122.
Commonweal. CXV, January 29, 1988, p. 48.
Los Angeles Times. December 16, 1987, VI, p. 1.
The Nation. CCXLVI, January 23, 1988, p. 94.
The New Republic. CXCVIII, February 1, 1988, p. 26.
The New York Times. December 16, 1987, p. C21.
The New Yorker. LXIII, January 11, 1988, p. 76.
Time. CXXX, December 14, 1987, p. 82.
The Wall Street Journal. December 15, 1987, p. 30.

CRY FREEDOM

Origin: Great Britain
Production: Richard Attenborough for Marble Arch Productions; released
   by Universal
Direction: Richard Attenborough
Screenplay: John Briley; based on the memoirs *Biko* and *Asking for Trouble*
   by Donald Woods
Cinematography: Ronnie Taylor
Editing: Lesley Walker
Production design: Stuart Craig
Art direction: Norman Dorme, George Richardson, and John King; set
   decoration, Michael Seirton
Costume design: John Mollo
Music: George Fenton and Jonas Gwangwa
MPAA rating: PG
Running time: 158 minutes

Principal characters:
Donald Woods......................Kevin Kline
Wendy Woods...................Penelope Wilton
Steve Biko....................Denzel Washington
Bruce........................John Hargreaves
Acting High Commissioner..........Alec McCowen
Ken ....Kevin McNally
Father Kani.........................Zakes Moke
State prosecutor ....Ian Richardson
Dr. Ramphele ....Josette Simon
Kruger..............................John Thaw
Captain de Wet ....Timothy West
Don Card.........................Julian Glover
Jane Woods........................Kate Hardie

   Richard Attenborough is a feeler, not a thinker, and the persuasiveness of
his films lies not in the polemic but in the pathos. *Cry Freedom* is less a
political analysis than a humanitarian tract. Yet, although it makes certain
compromises with commercialism, its central message is clear: It delivers an
unequivocal condemnation of apartheid.
   Based on truth, the film tells the story of an unlikely friendship that
blossomed in the mid-1970's between a South African newspaper editor,
Donald Woods (Kevin Kline), and a black political activist, Steve Biko
(Denzel Washington). They meet after Woods has attacked Biko's politics in
an editorial and been invited by Biko to see for himself how black people in

South Africa are required to live. When Biko is arrested for violating his detention order and later dies in police custody, Woods insists on visiting the morgue with Biko's wife. He takes pictures of the body as evidence that the death was not the result of a hunger strike, as the authorities have claimed, but of murder. His photographs are seized, however, and Woods himself is put under house arrest. When T-shirts soaked in acid are sent to his children through the post, Woods resolves to leave the country with his wife and family and complete a book about Biko that will expose the horrors of the South African political system. With the help of friends, he plots a daring escape.

In choosing this particular story to dramatize his abhorrence of apartheid, Attenborough was inevitably courting controversy. In his book *Filming with Attenborough* (1987), Woods describes how the South African authorities tried to discredit the film before its release by leaking preposterous rumors, for example, that Biko was to be played by Paul Newman with a blackened face. More significantly, the black South African community was disturbed by the fact that the message of their suffering was to be carried by a white liberal. Attenborough's argument was that the film required a white hero if it was to command an international audience. There is no doubt that the film's dual focus on Woods and Biko does create problems, and it is arguable that, in attempting to widen the film's appeal, Attenborough might have diminished its political impact. Nevertheless, one can see his point.

In a sense, Woods is not so much the film's hero as the film's eye—its perspective on events. Unfortunately, the character slips into one of the clichés of current cinema—that of the journalist-hero who, like similar heroes in *Under Fire* (1983), *The Killing Fields* (1984), and *Salvador* (1986), through bitter experience gains a perspective on events in a foreign country which he proceeds to communicate to Western readers.

In fact, Woods's experience is presented almost in the mode of a horror film. The normality of his life is gradually threatened by the intrusion of a monster—the monster of apartheid, certainly, but also the monster of his own conscience that Biko has awakened. Biko's growing influence is suggested by Woods's hiring of black journalists. The gathering threat is then indicated by nocturnal police harassment. By the second half of the film, Woods has almost become Biko—submitting to raids on his home and to house arrest and finally on the run because of his opposition to state policies.

If Woods is the film's conscience, Biko is its charisma, and Washington's performance appropriately upstages Kline's. Attenborough had been impressed by Washington's performance in *A Soldier's Story* (1984), and although Attenborough was criticized for casting an American rather than an African actor in the role, such criticism has mostly been silenced by the excellence of the performance. Washington's Biko has charm as well as steel. This is fortunate because there are some awkward structural obstacles to overcome. Because Biko's ideas often must be presented in the form of a courtroom address or a speech at a political rally, sometimes the film is experienced more as a lecture than as a narrative. Also, because he dies halfway through the film, which then focuses on Woods's escape, Biko is thereafter seen only in some rather clumsily integrated flashbacks. Yet the performance is sensitive and compelling enough to defuse these weaknesses.

Attenborough's direction has all the characteristics one has come to recognize. He is indulgent with actors and, if *Cry Freedom* seems more convincing histrionically than earlier works such as *Oh! What a Lovely War* (1969) and *A Bridge Too Far* (1977), the reason might be that the drama is not deflected in order to accommodate cameos from his acting chums. Tearful farewell scenes slow down the second part of the film, but there are some neat touches that add to the film's texture. For example, when Woods returns home after visiting Biko for the first time, one notices not only the visual contrast between black township and white suburb, but also the unthinking way in which Woods takes his drink from his "coloured" maid without even looking at her. The gradual transition from that careless gesture to the later scene when he rushes to her defense against the police encapsulates the character's movement from objective aloofness to personal concern.

Cry Freedom is structured around three major set pieces. The first is the police raid on the Crossroads settlement in 1975, which Attenborough sets over typed-out credits which seem designed to assert the film's journalistic veracity. The second is Biko's funeral in 1977, a spectacle of grief that serves as the emotional heart of the film. The last, and most controversial, is the re-creation of the massacre of the children at Soweto in 1976, which brings the film to a close and considerably modifies the viewer's response to Woods's successful escape. The film's chronology might be confusing, but the decision to end with this scene was a good one. *Cry Freedom* does not leave its audience with the triumph of one man who escapes: It closes on the tragedy of those for whom escape is not possible. The film's coda is a chilling catalog of the people who died in police custody in South Africa during the preceding decade. Such a melancholy ending cannot have improved its box-office prospects, but it would have been irresponsible not to draw attention to the fact of South Africa's continuing tragedy.

Perhaps because of its structure, the film cannot avoid an overall sense of creeping hopelessness, of isolated acts of individual heroism in the face of persistent brutality, a process that can only end in bloodshed. Moreover, the film could be more hard-hitting than it is. What actually happened to Biko in his cell and the obscenity of the inquest into his death are dealt with rather cursorily. When Sergei M. Eisenstein made a film about political injustice, such as *Potemkin* (1925), he wanted it to feel like a punch on the nose. Attenborough's films feel more like a sorrowful kiss on the cheek.

Yet it would be wrong to end on a negative note. Although *Cry Freedom* does not surmount all the problems in reconciling politics with entertainment, it does convey a worthwhile statement with intelligence and style. The Victorian novelist George Eliot said that the moral function of art was the enlargement of man's sympathies. By that criterion, *Cry Freedom* succeeds. Politically it might not be enough, but cinematically this effort is an honorable achievement.

Neil Sinyard

Reviews

America. CLVII, December 19, 1987, p. 482.
American Film. XIII, January, 1988, p. 62.
Ebony. XLIII, December, 1987, p. 60.
Films in Review. XXXIX, February, 1988, p. 98.
Los Angeles Times. November 6, 1987, VI, p. 1.
The Nation. CCXLVI, January 9, 1988, p. 30.
The New York Times. November 6, 1987, p. C14.
The New Yorker. LXIII, November 30, 1987, p. 101.
Time. CXXX, November 9, 1987, p. 91.
Variety. CCCXXIX, November 4, 1987, p. 10.

DARK EYES
(OCI CIORNIE)

Origin: Italy
Released in U.S.: 1987
Production: Silvia D'Amico Bendico and Carlo Cucchi; released by Island
  Pictures
Direction: Nikita Mikhalkov
Screenplay: Nikita Mikhalkov and Alexander Adabachian, with Suso Cecchi
  D'Amico; based on the short stories "The Lady with the Little Dog,"
  "The Name-Day Party," "My Wife," and "Anna Around the Neck," by
  Anton Chekhov
Cinematography: Franco di Giacomo
Editing: Enzo Meniconi
Art direction: Mario Garbuglia; set decoration, Carlo Gervasi
Costume design: Carlo Diappi
Music direction: Christian Gaubert
Music: Francis Lai
MPAA rating: no listing
Running time: 118 minutes

> *Principal characters:*
> Romano.....................Marcello Mastroianni
> Elisa..........................Silvana Mangano
> Tina..............................Marthe Keller
> Anna............................Elena Sofonova
> Elisa's mother ....Pina Cei
> Pavel ....Vsevolod Larionov
> The Governor ....Innokenti Smoktunovski
> The lawyer ....Roberto Herlitzka
> Kostantin....................Dimitri Zolothukin

Soviet director Nikita Mikhalkov, whose earlier works include *Raba lyubvi* (1976; *A Slave of Love*) and *Neskolo dnei iz zhizn I. I. Oblomova* (1980; *Oblomov*), revealed in a recent interview that before beginning work on a new production, he always takes time to view his favorite film, Federico Fellini's *Otto e mezzo* (1963; *8½*) as inspiration. When the star of *8½*, Italian actor Marcello Mastroianni, sought out Mikhalkov to collaborate on a project, Mikhalkov says he jumped at the opportunity. That the director spoke no Italian and the actor spoke no Russian was, according to Mikhalkov, no problem. They communicated, he said, with their eyes.

Dark Eyes begins in the dining room of an Italian cruise ship, where a disheveled Romano (Marcello Mastroianni), wearing a rumpled suit, sits alone drinking, lost in memories sparked by an old photograph. Romano is stirred from his reveries by the Russian accent of one of the passengers, Pavel (Vsevolod Larionov), who wanders in looking for a drink. Romano excitedly jumps up from his chair, shouting "Sabatchka!" (little dog), the one Russian word he remembers, and invites Pavel to join him.

Romano begins to talk, confiding in this stranger. He tells of having once been a penniless but promising architecture student who married the only daughter of a wealthy banker, Elisa (Silvana Mangano). Once married, he lost all ambition, preferring to live a life of luxury made possible by Elisa's family money. The film then flashes back to the family estate outside Rome eight years earlier.

The audience sees Romano, younger, meticulously groomed and dressed, clowning in the midst of a gathering of family and friends. Tables are piled high with sumptuous displays of food; servants arrange huge vases of flowers; children fly bright, long-tailed kites above perfectly manicured lawns. Throughout the celebration, Elisa is preoccupied by the unsettling news of the impending collapse of the family business. With her anxiety mounting, she searches for Romano, and when she finds him napping, she explodes in anger. Romano, berated for his laziness, has nothing to say for himself, and so responds by leaving to "take the cure" at his favorite spa.

Not surprisingly, the opening scenes at the spa are stylized in a manner strongly reminiscent of Fellini's *8½*. Unfortunately, Mikhalkov lacks Fellini's finely tuned eye for the comically surreal and thus these scenes function merely as an affectionate homage, without offering either the resonance or the metaphorical meaning that pervade Fellini's work.

At the spa, free from the restraints of home and marriage, Romano "cures" himself through a series of nocturnal carousings, until one morning, a quiet, young Russian woman, who is always in the company of her small dog, Sabatchka, catches his eye when the sunlight reflected off a jeweled pin in her upswept hair, momentarily blinds him. Their courtship begins when Romano, feigning trouble with his legs as a joke, finds that the young woman, Anna (Elena Sofonova), has taken his joke seriously. It is this quality in her that attracts him: her ability to believe in everything.

Mikhalkov's rare talent of being able to convey feelings nonverbally, purely through actions and gestures, is most evident when a sudden gust of wind lifts Anna's hat off her head and lands it on the surface of the spa's mud bath. Romano, dressed in his white suit, trudges through waist-high mud, retrieves the hat, and then wades out even farther to pluck a yellow flower floating on the surface.

Anna and Romano's bliss is cut short when she abruptly returns home to Sisoiev, leaving behind only a letter—in Russian, which Romano cannot read. He seeks outs a translator and learns of Anna's loveless marriage to a wealthy man whose money supports her impoverished family. In returning home she has given up the love she has longed for all of her life. Anna, Romano realizes, believes in everything, it would seem, except the possibility of her own happiness. He sets out at once to find her.

Under the guise of establishing a factory to manufacture unbreakable glass, Romano arrives in Sisoiev, stepping off the train in the middle of nowhere, the only signs of life being an old peasant woman, a goat, and a cow. Then, as he turns to the opposite side of the tracks, a brass band begins to play; the entire town has turned out to greet him, bringing him flowers and wreaths, vodka and caviar. The next morning, badly hung-over, he is whisked off to see the Governor (Innokenti Smoktunovski), a pompous egotist whose palatial home is filled with likenesses of its owner, and who, it suddenly becomes clear (when the little dog Sabatchka almost mystically appears at Romano's feet), is his beloved Anna's husband.

At a party that the Governor throws to celebrate Romano's arrival, Anna, torn between passion and duty, sneaks out to hide from Romano. Romano, in turn, sneaks out to find Anna. When he finally catches up to her, the audience hears only one sound: the rattling of empty wine glasses on a silver tray Romano holds. Nervous and excited, he cannot control his trembling hands. Reunited at last, the two vow never again to live apart.

Romano returns home to settle his affairs and finds the family business has gone bankrupt; Elisa is showing the house to prospective buyers. When they are left alone, Elisa confronts Romano with Anna's perfumed letter, asking if there is another woman. Face-to-face with Elisa, Romano begins to nod, but at the last moment he pauses and then whispers, "No." Elisa tears up the letter. Romano stands alone, his back to the camera; his slumped shoulders and bowed head express the collapse of his dreams. Softly, almost imperceptibly, music begins to play; Elisa has put on a record he brought from his trip: the Gypsy songs from Sisoiev. In a bittersweet moment, Romano responds, slowly beginning to spin across the floor, remembering happier times.

On the cruise ship, Romano concludes his story: He never saw Anna again and has since separated from Elisa. Pavel asks him why he will not return to Anna now. "It's the twentieth century," Romano responds; nobody waits for anyone anymore. Pavel disagrees; he is on his honeymoon with a woman he has loved since childhood, who rejected him eight times before finally agreeing to become his wife.

Their conversation ends when a shout warns Romano that only a few minutes remain to set up for lunch. In a heartbreaking moment, both Pavel and the audience realize that circumstances have reduced Romano to the role of a scurrying waiter, who jumps to his feet out of fear of losing his job. Pavel offers his help, but Romano sends him away, urging him to return with his bride so that Romano might have the honor of serving them a special lunch. Topside, Pavel kisses his wife's hand as she sits up in her deck chair. The jeweled ornaments that hold her hair in place gleam brightly in the sunlight. In slow motion, she turns to face the camera; it is Anna.

There is nothing dark about *Dark Eyes*. Mikhalkov fills the screen with images of laughter, play, and passion. He presents a world essentially without villains or treachery, without an underside: The family's opulent estate hides not a trace of decadence; Elisa, far from being a shrew, is a woman of great beauty, warmth, and intelligence; Romano's philandering is less lecherous than childlike and playful.

Mikhalkov balances the narrative's broader comic touches with brief, lyrical images, quiet moments that resonate with an air of solitude, of haunting introspection: An abandoned wheelchair spins slowly in the gray rain; a young girl in St. Petersburg loses her hat to the wind, and for a moment it takes flight, the only semblance of life in the empty square; alone on a balcony, a young musical prodigy leans over the railing to conduct an imaginary orchestra below; Anna, weeping and singing softly to herself, uses her tears to draw faint figures on the wall by her bed. Such images, combined with cinematographer Franco di Giacomo's views of the pastoral Russian plains, heavy with early morning mist, and the stunning surfaces of Romano and Elisa's turn-of-the-century villa, help to convey the film's palpable sense of loss.

Mastroianni, who won the Best Actor Award at Cannes and an Academy Award nomination for his performance, makes an appealingly impish Romano, one who is far more at home with the boisterous carousing at the Sisoiev train station (indeed, the Gypsies seem to be his kindred spirits) than in the tasteful celebration at the family estate, with its white-gloved servants and piano recitals. Mastroianni masterfully conveys Romano's delight in the richness and possibilities of life, juxtaposing it to the world-weariness and ennui that are the baggage of Romano's squandered life and talent.

Mikhalkov and Mastroianni have combined their considerable talents brilliantly to portray a man who has had "everything and nothing," and in so doing they have created a moving and passionate love story, tinged with loss as well as hope, weakness as well as strength, regret as well as joy.

Mary Lou McNichol

Reviews
National Review. XXXIX, November 6, 1987, p. 56.
The New Republic. CXCVII, October 12, 1987, p. 32.
New York. October 5, 1987, p. 116.
The New York Times. September 25, 1987, p. C26.
The New Yorker. LXIII, October 5, 1987, p. 93.
Newsweek. CX, October 5, 1987, p. 84.

THE DEAD

Production: Wieland Schulz-Keil and Chris Sievernich for Liffey Films; released by Vestron Pictures
Direction: John Huston
Screenplay: Tony Huston; based on the short story "The Dead," by James Joyce
Cinematography: Fred Murphy
Editing: Roberto Silvi
Art direction: Stephen Grimes with Dennis Washington; set decoration, Josie MacAvin
Costume design: Dorothy Jeakins
Music: Alex North
MPAA rating: PG
Running time: 83 minutes

Principal characters:
Gabriel Conroy . . . . Donal McCann
Gretta Conroy . . . . Anjelica Huston
Aunt Kate . . . . Helena Carroll
Aunt Julia . . . . Cathleen Delany
Bartell D'Arcy . . . . Frank Patterson
Lily . . . . Rachael Dowling
Miss Furlong . . . . Katherine O'Toole
Miss Higgins . . . . Bairbre Dowling
Miss O Callaghan . . . . Maria Hayden
Mr. Kerrigan . . . . Cormac O'Herlihy
Mr. Bergin . . . . Colm Meaney
Mary Jane . . . . Ingrid Craigie
Mr. Brown . . . . Dan O'Herlihy
Mrs. Malins . . . . Marie Kean
Freddy Malins . . . . Donal Donnelly
Mr. Grace . . . . Sean McClory
Molly Ivors . . . . Maria McDermottroe
Miss Daly . . . . Lyda Anderson

As a young man, John Huston was one of the first Americans to read James Joyce's banned *Ulysses* (1922), in a copy his mother smuggled back from France for him. In later years, Huston often said that this reading influenced him profoundly throughout his creative life. Among all Joyce's work, only "The Dead," the final story in his first published collection of stories, *Dubliners* (1914), attracted Huston as a possible adaptation. He had been thinking about filming it for some thirty years, but he had always found the project too intimidating because of Joyce's narrative unorthodoxies. When Huston finally agreed to undertake the project in 1986, he decided to walk the same narrative tightrope Joyce had used more than seventy years earlier, and he instructed his son, Tony Huston, to follow the original as closely as possible in the scenario that he would construct.

The narrative begins on a snowy night outside a Dublin house in 1904. Various guests are entering the house to attend an annual family-and-friends dinner-dance given by a trio of musical spinsters. The film's focal character, Gabriel Conroy (Donal McCann) and his wife, Gretta (Anjelica Huston), are among them, and as they remove their wraps, Gretta teases Gabriel about his insistence that they both wear galoshes, an innovation recently imported from the Continent. Despite its homeliness, this seemingly trivial footwear forms one of the film's central images, a sort of objective correlative of Gabriel's unconscious desire to insulate and protect himself, not only from the snow, but from the Irish earth itself, and everything it means. The evening will lead to a number of discoveries on Gabriel's part, in effect stripping him of his emotional galoshes and laying him open to a final emotional moment of profound self-revelation.

Joyce called these informing events epiphanies, and he structured his stories in *Dubliners* around them. In "The Dead" he created a work that had virtually no plot and then told that story without recourse to narrative commentary. Without the skeleton provided by plot or the skin furnished by narrative glossing, the story was stripped of its traditional internal and external support systems. Lacking these time-honored shapers, "The Dead" had to rely almost exclusively on themes, images, and characters to lead to Gabriel's epiphany.

The two Hustons honor Joyce's narrative procedure completely in their translation of the story, although they depart from its specific handling of events on a number of occasions. Perhaps to make up for their deviations, they insert two lines into the dialogue to pay homage to their mentor. Although Joyce's narrator never reveals what day the party is taking place, the Hustons specify it in two ways. First, they let the audience hear that one of the guests has been "on the wagon" since the beginning of the year, and that six days have elapsed since he began his regime. Second, a guest tells one of the hostesses to "sit down and proclaim yourself queen" of her own party. The first bit of apparently throwaway dialogue situates the evening on January 6, the date of the feast of the Epiphany, and the second suggests that Aunt Kate (Helena Carroll) act as queen of the celebration, traditional in European secular celebrations of the Epiphany.

The evening's program consists of talking, dancing, and dining, along with various entertainments provided by the hostesses and their guests. During one of the evening's dances, Gabriel is taken to task by a fellow guest, Molly Ivors (Maria McDermottroe), for wanting to spend his summer bicycling on the Continent with friends. Rather than running away from home, she says, he should go to the Arran Islands for the summer and get back in touch with the real Ireland. By linking Ivors' observations to the image of the galoshes—pointedly a Continental innovation—Joyce/Huston suggest that Gabriel figuratively and literally has been fleeing his native soil, using Continental rubber to keep his feet clean. Keeping his feet clean, however, has meant cutting himself off from his native roots in a number of ways.

One of these ways relates to Irish politics, referred to obliquely through several mentions of "committee meetings." These are Hustonian interpolations, not present in the original, and they lend Gabriel's desire to escape to the Continent a certain political fecklessness that adds depth to his character. The novella was written and published well before the revolution, so these interpolations corroborate Joyce's characterization in a way that he might not have anticipated.

By looking to the Continent, Gabriel has also neglected native art, a central theme in the novella. All three of the hostesses, the Misses Morkan—the elderly aunts Julia (Cathleen Delany) and Kate, as well as their younger niece, Mary Jane (Ingrid Craigie)—are or were active as amateur musicians, and much of the conversation at dinner turns on the subject of music, particularly beautiful voices from the past: the voices of the dead that continue to enchant and enrapture their respective listeners many decades after their physical owners have passed away.

Elaborating this Joycean theme of voices from beyond the grave, Tony Huston adds several important variations to what he retained from the original. Among the most striking is the introduction of a new character not present in Joyce's story, Mr. Grace (Sean McClory), whose *raison d'être* in the film is to read a beautiful poem on the subject of broken vows. The poem, full of exquisite oxymoronic images, contrasts lost glorious potentials with present crippled realities, and Gabriel's uneasy glance at Gretta during its recitation suggests that he has at least an inkling of how it encapsulates what he will eventually see as her feelings toward him. As a translation from the Irish of a fourteenth century lament, the poem brilliantly crystallizes the artistic and emotional Irish roots Gabriel has unconsciously severed.

A second and very moving variation also occurs during the entertainments. In Joyce's story, Aunt Julia sings a song to her guests in a clear, strong voice, executing the music's contours and details expertly. In the film, however, the aged Aunt Julia's singing voice has lost all of its sweetness and vibrancy; instead of gliding, it quavers and trembles; instead of warbling, it croaks. As the wrinkled and worn, sweet old lady bravely makes her way through this sensual chanson about a beautiful young bride on her wedding day, the camera turns toward memorabilia scattered around the room, and the viewer, in his mind's eye, almost certainly adds some private images to Huston's ineffable tour of aging and beauty, memory and loss, togetherness and the ultimate separation that time works on both body and soul.

A third important variation occurs at the end of the party. In the original, Joyce gave only a muffled, offstage account of the story's final song, sung under protest by a tenor suffering from a hoarse throat. In the film, Bartell D'Arcy (Frank Patterson) willingly delivers a full-throated and quite beautiful rendition of the traditional dirge "The Lass of Aughrim," in the classic style of the Irish tenor, to oblige (and probably to impress) Gretta. As Gabriel pulls on his galoshes in the hall below, Gretta slowly descends the stairs, listening in rapture to the song. She pauses at a landing, and Gabriel watches her listen, her eyes closed, moving her head ever so slightly in time to the music, finally giving way to tears. When the song ends, she remains under its spell for a moment, then glances down to see her husband watching her from the bottom of the stairs. Almost imperceptibly, she snaps out of her reverie and descends the stairs to join him. Anjelica Huston's performance here is one of utmost subtlety and respect for her character's interior feelings. Like the narrative crafted throughout by her father and her brother, it can sustain multiple readings yet remain impervious to interpretation.

Gabriel, for one, is not sure how to interpret his wife's manner. As they return to their hotel through the snow-filled streets, he worries about Gretta's state of distraction. In the story, Gabriel falls into a virtual rage of possessiveness. Translating Gabriel's rage to the screen would have required one of two approaches, neither of them viable. To have Gabriel act out his possessive excitement would have meant destroying the interiority of the experience as well as its expression, whereas a literal transcription of the original narrative as voice-over would have verged on the ludicrous. Instead, in the Hustons' version, only Gabriel's dejection at his wife's preoccupied withdrawal is evident as they ride through the snowy streets to their hotel. He probably attributes her introspective state to an interest in D'Arcy and his beautiful voice, but the audience cannot be sure. As they do throughout the film, the Hustons observe a remarkable narrative discretion in handling this scene. Here their discretion lends Gabriel's inner thoughts and feelings a moving sense of defeated dignity and make of him a considerably less abject and autobiographically parochial character than Joyce's original.

Once they reach their hotel room, Gabriel presses Gretta to confess the reason for her distraction, and she reluctantly tells him that the song D'Arcy sang at the party has revived her memory of a boy she knew long before she met Gabriel. Amazed at this revelation, he continues to question her about the boy and learns that he died of exposure when he left his sickbed one night to come visit her. Gabriel associates him with the land, with the Irish spirit, and with a devotion and passion completely foreign to himself. Crushed by the fact that Gretta has kept this memory from him for so many years, and by the suspicion that she reciprocated the boy's love, Gabriel gazes out the window at the snow settling over all Ireland.

The narrative concludes with the cinematic equivalent of an indirect free discourse passage by showing what Gabriel is (probably) thinking. A shot of him gazing sadly out the hotel window is interrupted first by a glimpse of Aunt Julia lying dead upon her bed and then by a series of haunting funerary images set in the Irish countryside—Celtic crosses, ruined towers, dead trees, graveyards—all seen in dark silhouette, with the unifying blanket of snow quietly tucking them into their eternal beds, and the final passages of the story are read in voice-over, ending with Joyce's final sentence: "His soul swooned slowly as he heard the snow falling faintly through the universe and faintly falling, like the descent of their last end, upon all the living and the dead."

In repaying his creative debt to Joyce, John Huston left one final gift in this deeply moving film: the opportunity both to grieve for his loss and to celebrate the transcendence of his spirit through his art.

R C Dale

Reviews

Commonweal. CXIV, December 18, 1987, p. 748.
The New Republic. CXCVII, December 21, 1987, p. 26.
The New York Times. December 17, 1987, p. 24.
The New Yorker. LXIII, December 14, 1987, p. 144.
Newsweek. CX, December 21, 1987, p. 68.
Time. CXXXI, January 4, 1988, p. 64.
The Wall Street Journal. December 17, 1987, p. 26.

DIRTY DANCING

Production: Linda Gottlieb; released by Vestron Pictures
Direction: Emile Ardolino
Screenplay: Eleanor Bergstein
Cinematography: Jeff Jur
Editing: Peter C. Frank
Production design: David Chapman
Art direction: Mark Haack and Stephen Lineweaver; set decoration, Clay Griffith
Makeup: Gilbert LaChapelle and David Forrest
Costume design: Hilary Rosenfeld
Choreography: Kenny Ortega
Sound: John Pritchett
Music direction: Danny Goldberg and Michael Lloyd
Music: John Morris
Song: Frank Previte, Donald Markovitz, and John D'Andrea, "(I've Had) The Time of My Life"
MPAA rating: PG-13
Running time: 100 minutes

Principal characters:

Frances "Baby" Houseman	Jennifer Grey
Johnny Castle	Patrick Swayze
Jake Houseman	Jerry Orbach
Penny Johnson	Cynthia Rhodes
Max Kellerman	Jack Weston
Lisa Houseman	Jane Brucker
Marjorie Houseman	Kelly Bishop
Neil Kellerman	Lonny Price
Robbie Gould	Max Cantor
Mrs. Schumacher	Paula Trueman
Mr. Schumacher	Alvin Myerovich
Billy Kostecki	Neal Jones
Vivian Pressman	Miranda Garrison
Moe Pressman	Garry Goodrow

"Tough dancing"—overtly sexual moves that bring the bedroom to the ballroom—was born and reached its peak in the period from 1880 to 1920, in the nexus of a young, urban working class and the new accessibility of sound recordings. That writer Eleanor Bergstein chooses to make such dancing the pivotal symbol upon which *Dirty Dancing* turns is indicative of some of the problems with this slight but critically and publicly well-received film.

It is the summer of 1963—following the Cuban Missile Crisis and before the assassinations of John F. Kennedy and Martin Luther King, Jr. Baby Houseman (Jennifer Grey), a seventeen-year-old liberal idealist who plans on enlisting in the Peace Corps after college, travels with her family—liberal physician father (Jerry Orbach), vague housewife mother (Kelly Bishop), and spoiled sister Lisa (Jane Brucker)—to Kellerman's Borscht Belt resort in the Catskill Mountains.

At the main lodge, Baby happens to see Max Kellerman (Jack Weston) prepping his college-age waiters on their social duties to the daughters of the guests. When dance instructor Johnny Castle (Patrick Swayze) saunters in, Kellerman reminds him that he is to keep his hands to himself. Baby is instantly smitten.

After an evening dance, sickened by the stuffy social atmosphere, Baby leaves the lodge and runs into Billy Kostecki (Neal Jones), a staff member she met earlier. Reluctantly, he lets her follow him into the staff quarters, where the workers are holding a dance of their own. Couples gyrate slowly together and writhe up and down each other's bodies. Baby is shocked and excited. Johnny and his dance partner Penny Johnson (Cynthia Rhodes) arrive. Johnny, rather meanly, asks Baby to dance. On the dance floor, however, he begins to teach her some of the "dirty dance" moves.

The next evening, Kellerman's grandson Neil (Lonny Price) escorts Baby around the resort; his boastfulness, coupled with a glimpse of Lisa's rude treatment at the hands of waiter Robbie Gould (Max Cantor), furthers Baby's alienation from the middle-class surroundings. When Neil takes her to the kitchen for a snack, she spies a sobbing Penny under a table and hurries away with Neil under pretext, only to return for Penny with Johnny and Billy. Learning that Penny is pregnant and Robbie is responsible, Baby is sure that there is a solution. Yet the others mock her naïve optimism; she leaves, humiliated but determined to help.

Baby confronts Robbie, who refuses to help. Baby then goes to her father, whose own altruism is her moral model. Although she will not tell him why she needs $250, Dr. Houseman entrusts his daughter with the money. That night, Baby gives Penny the money. Johnny is cynical about the gesture, saying, "It takes a real saint to ask Daddy." Billy mentions that he can schedule an abortion appointment only for the night that Johnny and Penny are set to dance at the Sheldrake, an important engagement for their careers, and that there is no one available to replace Penny. As a nasty joke, Johnny suggests that Baby substitute for Penny, but Billy and Penny take him seriously, pointing out that there is no other solution and that Baby does have natural agility.

In a long sequence with minimal dialogue, the viewer follows the development of Baby-as-dancer through a series of lessons with Johnny. Finally, it is the night of the Sheldrake performance. Although Baby is stiff at first, forgets a few steps, and is too frightened to perform the lift, Johnny and Baby are a success.

When they return to Kellerman's, they find Penny gravely ill from her back-alley abortion. Baby runs and wakes her father, who saves Penny but mistakenly assumes that Johnny was the father and is now preying on innocent Baby. As Dr. Houseman leaves, he tells Baby that he has lost faith in her and forbids her to associate with the staff. Baby nevertheless returns to Johnny's room and apologizes for her father. He expresses his admiration for her courage and conviction, and she expresses her desire for him. They dance, then make love.

A wealthy guest, Vivian Pressman (Miranda Garrison), who has been amusing herself with Johnny, tells him that she has arranged for one last fling together. Johnny refuses the generous payment that the indifferent or unwitting Moe Pressman (Garry Goodrow) offers him to give his wife one more round of "dance lessons." As a rebounding Mrs. Pressman leaves Robbie's cabin at dawn, she sees Baby leaving Johnny's cabin and realizes why he was no longer available to her.

When Mr. Pressman's wallet is missing that morning, Mrs. Pressman vindictively accuses Johnny. Kellerman tells this story to the Housemans, adding that Johnny has said, as an alibi, that he was alone reading all night. When Kellerman and Neil are about to leave and fire Johnny, Baby confesses that she is his witness, having spent the whole night with him in his room.

Johnny finds Baby later and tells her the news that Mr. and Mrs. Schumacher (Alvin Myerovich and Paula Trueman), an odd, older couple, had in fact stolen Mr. Pressman's wallet but that he is to be fired anyway, for sleeping with Baby. Johnny and Baby say good-bye, both refusing to regret their experience. Johnny drives off.

At the main house, Dr. Houseman stops Robbie to give him his summer bonus. Robbie thanks him for discreetly handling his "little mistake," Penny. Outraged, Dr. Houseman snatches back the money. As Baby sits in a corner with her parents, watching the conclusion of Kellerman's last show of the season, Johnny returns. He grabs Baby, and they mount the stage, halting the show. Johnny announces that he will be performing a dance with "somebody who's taught me about the kind of person I want to be." Baby and Johnny then perform their Sheldrake mambo, with a touch of dirty dancing, to the growing approval of the crowd. As the staff mingles among the guests, the whole floor dissolves into dance. Dr. Houseman apologizes to Johnny and praises Baby. As the film closes, Johnny and Baby are in each other's arms, laughing, and he sings, along with the music, about owing her "the time of his life."

This last detail, a theme repeated many times in the film, is one of the more disturbing aspects of a script which purports, through its sympathetic protagonist, to critique the status quo. While the bourgeois middle class, as seen through Baby's eyes, appears to be not only hypocritical but also oppressive, it is still the farseeing middle class that will work to improve the lives of the working class. At the same time, the reverse stereotype is evident: The sensuality of the working class has a liberating effect on the upper-middle class.

Writer Bergstein chose to set the film in the summer of 1963, a time that witnessed the last remnant of liberalism, before radicalism took hold. Max Kellerman, watching the last show of the summer season, says, "It all seems to be ending." This nostalgic statement seems to offset what could be a positive image, the film's final mingling of rich guests and poor hotel staff. What might be seen as the potential breakdown of class and racial barriers, is instead mourned as an ending of stability.

The film is not without pleasure—mostly from the dance sequences, the talented Swayze, the radiant Grey, and the comical Jane Brucker—but there is not much flair otherwise. Aside from its clichés and excessive ending, *Dirty Dancing* bears only minor resemblance to the period it attempts to portray. Perhaps that resulted because those involved in its production had such ambivalence about that period, as the film's contradictory politics suggest.

Gabrielle Forman

Reviews
Films in Review. XXXVIII, December, 1987, p. 612.
Los Angeles Times. August 21, 1987, VI, p. 1.
Macleans. C, August 24, 1987, p. 50.
The New York Times. August 21, 1987, p. C3.
The New Yorker. LXIII, August 24, 1987, p. 79.
Newsweek. CX, August 24, 1987, p. 60.
Time. CXXX, September 14, 1987, p. 77.
Variety. CCCXXVII, May 20, 1987, p. 104.
Vogue. CLXXVII, August, 1987, p. 64.
The Wall Street Journal. September 3, 1987, p. 17.

DRAGNET

Production: David Permut and Robert K. Weiss; released by Universal
  Pictures
Direction: Tom Mankiewicz
Screenplay: Dan Aykroyd, Alan Zweibel, and Tom Mankiewicz
Cinematography: Matthew F. Leonetti
Editing: Richard Halsey and William D. Gordean
Art direction: Robert F. Boyle
Music: Ira Newborn
MPAA rating: PG-13
Running time: 106 minutes

> *Principal characters:*
> Sergeant Joe Friday .... Dan Aykroyd
> Pep Streebeck .... Tom Hanks
> The Reverend Whirley .... Christopher Plummer
> Captain Bill Gannon .... Harry Morgan
> Connie Swail .... Alexandra Paul
> Jane Kirkpatrick .... Elizabeth Ashley
> Jerry Caesar..................... Dabney Coleman
> Enid Borden .... Kathleen Freeman
> Mayor Parvin........................ Bruce Gray
> Granny Mundy................... Lenka Peterson

Like any highly stylized form of entertainment, the original "Dragnet"
was a target for parody almost as soon as it became a television hit in the
1950's. Its distinctive music, staccato narrative, and intense but flat characters were so recognizable that Stan Freberg, a radio comedian, had to do
little more than produce a standard script for the show with everything just
slightly off to achieve an immediate comic effect. By the time Jack Webb's
signature salutation, "Just the facts, ma'am," had become a national catch-
phrase, the show was beginning to parody its own highly distinctive' features, and while the show is no longer in syndication, it is still familiar
enough to make it useful for commercials requiring almost instant recognition of a familiar form.

The idea of taking Sergeant Joe Friday, the quintessence of 1950's values
and attitudes, out of his decade and into the crazed California landscape of
the late 1980's is the premise behind the production of the film. The obvious
contrasts between the cultural assumptions of the two eras, plus the possibilities for parody of a character who represented an extreme version of
the law-and-order fetish of Dwight D. Eisenhower's America, combined
with the talents for mimicry which Dan Aykroyd perfected while working

on "Saturday Night Live" have resulted in a film that has some wonderfully comical moments. Yet without a story that engages the attention of the audience (such as Michael J. Fox's struggle for survival in *Back to the Future*, 1985), the film drifts away from some striking opening sequences toward a tired and predictable series of chaotic car chases and confrontations between adversaries of little consequence. The only item of interest in the last third of the film is a continuing anticipation of what Aykroyd as Friday might say or do—a confirmation of the success of his depiction of Joe Friday's nephew, the comic center of the entire enterprise.

The conception with which Aykroyd begins is based on the potential for astonishment inherent in the clash between social behavior in the 1980's and the values and principles that Friday lives by—a series of assumptions about life that verged on the unreal even in Webb's heyday. The extraordinary, self-satisfied squareness, the law-and-order rigidity carried to nearly robotic dementia, the complete absence of reflection and the remarkably laconic delivery are exaggerations of generally accepted modes of behavior in the quiet, conformist 1950's. Webb created Joe Friday as a part of an established authority structure, and while his methods have been carried to a brutal excess by others, Friday himself was basically decent, completely free from corruption, oblivious to temptation, and dedicated to the preservation of the standards of a placid, middle-class existence where home and the family are sacred. Aykroyd's almost uncanny reincarnation of this stance, as Friday's nephew returning to work for the Los Angeles Police Department (LAPD), evokes a feeling of nostalgia for an apparently simpler, more innocent time and creates the potential for vast comic confusion as Friday's single-mindedness of purpose proves totally inappropriate for dealing with the wildness of Los Angeles. This aspect of Aykroyd's character works as a kind of comic homage to Webb's almost manic devotion to duty, while, at the same time, it becomes steadily more hilarious as Friday's outmoded approach to police work fails at one situation after another with no effect at all on Friday's immense confidence in himself.

The character remains compelling even after all the potential for parody in Friday's outlook has been exhausted and the absurdity latent in his misconception of his place in the LAPD has been fully exploited. The mark of real genius in Aykroyd's portrayal of Friday is the sustained wit of his narration of the film's meandering story. Friday's reactions to a world he can never quite understand have been written with such invention and verbal dexterity that although he remains convincingly within Friday's psychological frame, Aykroyd is able to comment incisively on life in the United States of the late 1980's. The tone of misguided certainty that invigorates Friday's account is presented with a kind of lunatic logic. Aykroyd knows that comic madness can enable one to see things from an angle unsuspected by most conventional observers. In addition, the maintenance of a deadpan demeanor amid scenes of increasing chaos is a method for crafting comic ambience directly in the tradition of Buster Keaton.

Unfortunately, even Aykroyd is unable to sustain Friday's narrative throughout a two-and-a-half hour film, and the rest of *Dragnet* has nothing to equal it. The triple credit for the screenplay suggests that Aykroyd concentrated on his character while Tom Mankiewicz, the director, and Alan Zweibel handled the rest of the production. The idea of pairing Friday with a street-hip, ultramodern, clearly ethnic partner, Pep Streebeck (Tom Hanks), is a sound application of the "unlikely friendship" technique, but Hanks's relaxed, affable performance does not have the support of a script that develops his character. Streebeck's reactions to Friday's antics are supposed to parallel those of the presumed audience for the film, but Streebeck himself never becomes the counterforce required to propel the film when Friday is at rest. Friday's encounter with and growing attraction to a girl held captive by a cult of biker/devil worshippers, who intend her as a virgin sacrifice, is promising as a humanizing influence, but the developing relationship with Connie Swail (Alexandra Paul) never moves much beyond the initial glow of two shy people sort of falling in love. These relationships are potentially interesting and are organized around Friday's character. The plot of the film, on the other hand, is neither very interesting nor organized around anything at all.

Although a basic premise of the film is that the original Joe Friday's vaunted powers of methodical investigation are ineffectual in dealing with criminals in the 1980's, Aykroyd's bumbling doggedness might have been employed to comic effect if he were actually involved in plausible police work. Instead, in an elaborately contrived scheme that mixes the demonology of *Ghostbusters* (1984) and the high-level corruption of *Into the Night* (1985), Friday and Streebeck stumble through an incoherent story about a smarmy television evangelist, the Reverend Whirley (played with a touch of sinister charm by Christopher Plummer) who is in alliance with a Hugh Hefner clone, the smut peddler Jerry Caesar (played with silk-gowned, lisping pomposity by Dabney Coleman) in an attempt to control the city government and increase their empires. The narrative action through which Connie Swail is rescued, Whirley exposed and defrocked, Caesar unmansioned and jailed, and Friday and Streebeck returned to their station as officers is presented with loud noise, hurtling objects, flashing lights, and little sense. Amid the confusion and clutter of car chases and other elements of the generic action film of the 1980's, a droll caricature of a power-hungry professional woman, suggestively named Jane Kirkpatrick (Elizabeth Ashley) is thrown away. Harry Morgan, the fine actor who played Friday's partner in the original series, is promoted here to captain and given the opportunity to roll his eyes whenever Aykroyd's misguided methodology messes up some serious police work. Morgan's solidity and reasonableness are the closest thing to a standard of adult behavior that exists in the film and provide a calm foundation, at times, to launch the film's flights of satiric fancy.

While most of the details of the instantly forgettable plot blur into oblivion, Aykroyd's marvelous monologues linger. More than simple parody, they have a singular style of their own: distinctively witty, surprisingly literate, dryly comic in their juxtaposition of items from different domains ("How could Jerry Caesar build a modern Gomorrah smack in the city where they recorded 'We Are the World'?"). Morally indignant, curiously naïve, compulsively eager, these routines make a bizarre man almost lovable. Aykroyd's wit is not enough to sustain a feature film, but he does offer the revelation that one of the seemingly most serious characters in American popular culture is actually a closet comedian.

Leon Lewis

Reviews

Films in Review. XXXVIII, October, 1987, p. 490.
Life. X, April, 1987, p. 26.
Los Angeles Times. June 26, 1987, VI, p. 1.
Macleans. C, July 13, 1987, p. 46.
The New York Times. June 26, 1987, p. C3.
Newsweek. CX, July 13, 1987, p. 60.
People Weekly. XXVIII, July 20, 1987, p. 10.
Time. CXXX, July 13, 1987, p. 68.
Variety. CCCXXVII, July 1, 1987, p. 10.
The Wall Street Journal. June 30, 1987, p. 28.

EIGHTY-FOUR CHARING CROSS ROAD

Production: Geoffrey Helman for Brooksfilm; released by Columbia
  Pictures
Direction: David Jones
Screenplay: Hugh Whitemore; based on the book of the same name by He-
  lene Hanff, originally adapted for the stage by James Roose-Evans
Cinematography: Brian West
Editing: Chris Wimble
Art direction: Eileen Diss and Edward Pisoni
Costume design: Jane Greenwood and Lindy Hemming
Music: George Fenton
MPAA rating: PG
Running time: 97 minutes

> *Principal characters:*
> Helene Hanff .... Anne Bancroft
> Frank Doel .... Anthony Hopkins
> Nora Doel .... Judi Dench
> Maxine Bellamy.................... Jean De Baer
> George Martin.................. Maurice Denham
> Cecily Farr....................... Eleanor David
> Bill Humphries .... Ian McNeice
> Megan Wells .... Wendy Morgan
> Brian .... Daniel Gerroll
> Kay .... Mercedes Ruehl
> American customer................. Connie Booth

The twenty-year friendship of a New York writer and a London book
dealer who never meet seems an unlikely subject for an American-financed
film in the 1980's, but that is exactly what *Eighty-four Charing Cross Road*
is. Based on Helene Hanff's 1970 collection of the correspondence between
her and Frank Doel and on the 1982 stage adaptation by James Roose-
Evans, the film celebrates friendship, the love of literature, and Anglo-
philia.

In 1949, while working as a reader of film scripts in Manhattan, Helene
Hanff (Anne Bancroft) wants to buy inexpensive editions of her favorite
works of English literature but cannot find them in New York bookstores.
She needs her own copies so that she will not be tempted to write marginal
notes in books borrowed from libraries. Responding to an advertisement in
the *Saturday Review of Literature* magazine, Hanff sends a list of desired
titles to Marks and Company, an antiquarian bookshop in London, specify-
ing that she will pay no more than five dollars for each. She is shocked

when she promptly receives most of the books, some covered in vellum, at surprisingly low prices. She considers the well-bound volumes almost too elegant for her spartan apartment.

Hanff begins writing letters to the staff of Marks and Company with her orders, and *Eighty-four Charing Cross Road* cuts between scenes from her life and ones showing the daily activities of Frank Doel (Anthony Hopkins) and his coworkers. Hanff ingratiates herself with the booksellers when she learns from Brian (Daniel Gerroll), an English friend, of the severe food rationing in postwar England and has food packages mailed to them from Denmark. The tinned meat, powdered eggs, and fruit they receive are unexpected luxuries.

Cecily Farr (Eleanor David), one of the Marks and Company staff, writes to Hanff secretly, saying that Doel is too reserved to respond to her notes even though he clearly enjoys her very opinionated views of literature and of all things British. Doel is charmed by the outspoken New Yorker even when she expresses frustration that the books he has sent are not the ones she requested. When Hanff asks him to write about London, Doel's side of the correspondence is underway. He shares her joy when she begins to make more money by writing for such television programs as *Ellery Queen* in the 1950's.

The letters become more personal after Doel's wife, Nora (Judi Dench), writes to Hanff to thank her for the frequent food shipments and includes photographs of the couple and their two daughters. The Marks and Company staff members are mystified when nylons suddenly appear in Doel's office—secretly delivered by Hanff's actress friend Maxine Bellamy (Jean De Baer). They are disappointed when Hanff must postpone her long-awaited first trip to England because of an enormous dental bill. Doel dies in 1969, and *Eighty-four Charing Cross Road* ends with Hanff finally going to London and visiting the vacant building where Marks and Company once was, the business having closed shortly after Doel's death.

Eighty-four Charing Cross Road is such an unexpected big-screen venture because it presents rather ordinary people who lead mostly uneventful lives: They read good literature and write letters to one another. Though the film may be directed at that small audience which likes to congratulate itself for being civilized in a decadent age, it is nevertheless entertaining and is made surprisingly cinematic by director David Jones and screenwriter Hugh Whitemore.

Making a film based on letters and a play presents some problems, not all of which can be solved easily. Although *Eighty-four Charing Cross Road* cannot avoid the voiceover readings of the correspondence or the shots of characters writing and reading letters, Jones and Whitemore make it work visually by breaking the film into a series of brief scenes, usually one to three minutes long. (Jones showed his masterful ability to open up a play in his first film, the 1983 adaptation of Harold Pinter's *Betrayal*.) The claustrophobic effects of cutting back and forth between apartment and bookstore are avoided by constantly varying the setting: television studio, Central Park, Columbia University, the coast of England, the Thames Embankment, trains. The filmmakers acknowledge the difficulty and artificiality of their task by having Hanff occasionally talk directly to the camera and by making two letters between Hanff and Doel into a short transatlantic conversation.

Art directors Eileen Diss and Edward Pisoni and costume designers Jane Greenwood and Lindy Hemming pay close attention to period details, creating smooth transitions from decade to decade. George Fenton's music helps set the time and place effectively, except once when he employs a clichéd piece meant to suggest the noise and bustle of New York City. Cinematographer Brian West bathes the film in browns, yellows, and oranges to suggest a perpetual autumn, a period of comparatively cultivated behavior impossible to restore.

Eighty-four Charing Cross Road is both a mood piece and a character study, the story of two opposites strangely attracted to each other. As such, and as one of the few successful cinematic portraits of male-female friendship, it resembles Robert Benton's *The Late Show* (1977) and *Places in the Heart* (1984).

Hanff is a chain-smoking, self-educated, combative New York Jewish intellectual. A woman of contradictions, she never reads fiction, although she writes television scripts. She takes literature seriously, becoming outraged at the Church of England version of a Latin Bible which Doel sends her. She takes herself less seriously. After she stumbles into a political demonstration and is arrested, she arrives at home disheveled and switches on television news to see herself being shoved into a paddy wagon, but laughs at how ridiculous it all is. Unmarried, she has friends for whom she babysits and walks dogs, and a penchant for alcohol. Her writing and her books are her life.

During his forty years at Marks and Company, Frank Doel lives for his work. Though he takes his wife dancing, he lives a mostly sedate, solitary existence. "Very tasty" is all he says to Nora during meals. The reticent Doel is taken out of himself by the verve of Hanff's personality. Since he is almost, through her, leading a fantasy life separate from reality, it is fitting that they never meet.

On one level, the Hanff-Doel friendship consists of her telling him to root for the Brooklyn Dodgers and his asking her to support Tottenham Hotspur, his favorite team. On another, Doel risks upsetting Hanff by sending her a book she has not ordered. She is angry until she reads in it a John Donne sermon which expresses her view of the world. Hanff realizes then that Doel is "the only man alive" who understands her. That *Eighty-four*

Charing Cross Road is a love story becomes clear when Hanff sees *Brief Encounter* (1945), the classic tale of lovers separated forever. Equally important is the love each feels for the culture of the other. Already infatuated with the idea of England, Hanff becomes even more passionate because of Doel's letters, and he is compelled by the force of her American energy.

Bancroft can be a mannered actress, but here she shows remarkable restraint. Although her character is similar to the pushy activist she plays in *Garbo Talks* (1984), Bancroft resists the sentimental manipulations of that film. Instead of forcing the audience to like the character, she allows Helene Hanff to evolve into a fully realized person. This performance is Bancroft's most subtle and the character her most complex since Mrs. Robinson in *The Graduate* (1967).

Anthony Hopkins can also overact, is given to the twitches and stammers of an American Method actor. As Frank Doel, however, he gives his least busy screen performance. Hopkins conveys the calm colorlessness Doel's co-workers see, but he also shows the complexity beneath the bookseller's bland surface. In perhaps the best scene in *Eighty-four Charing Cross Road*, Doel overhears an American customer (Connie Booth), thinks that she might be Hanff, hopes fervently that she is, and is crestfallen when he realizes that she is not. The range of emotions Hopkins reveals in one minute involves more acting skill than many performers are called upon to display in an entire film.

Eighty-four Charing Cross Road might be faulted for not telling enough about Hanff and Doel, but Whitemore, who wrote *Stevie* (1978), another examination of a seemingly uneventful life, and Jones are careful to keep the friendship of the protagonists as the center of attention. That they can tell this story without sentimentality or condescension to either characters or audience is an achievement. The final shot of Hanff's glorious smile once she has finally arrived in England and at Charing Cross Road illustrates the filmmakers' sensitive approach. That Doel is dead and the store empty do not diminish her joy.

Michael Adams

Reviews
Christianity Today. XXXI, July 10, 1987, p. 61.
Films in Review. XXXVIII, April, 1987, p. 230.
Glamour. LXXXV, April, 1987, p. 244.
Los Angeles Times. March 26, 1987, VI, p. 1.
Ms. XV, April, 1987, p. 35.
The New Republic. CXCVI, February 23, 1987, p. 24.
New York. XX, March 2, 1987, p. 100.

The New York Times. February 13, 1987, p. C10.
Newsweek. CIX, February 16, 1987, p. 72.
People Weekly. XXVII, March 30, 1987, p. 12.
Time. CXXIX, March 2, 1987, p. 74.
Variety. CCCXXVI, January 28, 1987, p. 20.
Video. XI, December, 1987, p. 90.
The Wall Street Journal. February 12, 1987, p. 22.

EMPIRE OF THE SUN

Production: Steven Spielberg, Kathleen Kennedy, and Frank Marshall for
  Amblin Entertainment; released by Warner Bros.
Direction: Steven Spielberg
Screenplay: Tom Stoppard; based on the novel of the same name by J. G.
  Ballard
Cinematography: Allen Daviau
Editing: Michael Kahn
Production design: Norman Reynolds
Art direction: Frederick Hole; set decoration, Harry Cordwell and
  Michael D. Ford
Costume design: Bob Ringwood
Sound: Robert Knudson, Don Digirolamo, John Boyd, and Tony Dawe
Music: John Williams
MPAA rating: PG
Running time: 152 minutes

Principal characters:
Jamie (Jim)	Christian Bale
Basie	John Malkovich
Mrs. Victor	Miranda Richardson
Dr. Rawlins	Nigel Havers
Frank	Joe Pantoliano
Jim's father	Rupert Frazer
Jim's mother	Emily Richard
Mr. Maxton	Leslie Phillips
Mr. Lockwood	Robert Stephens
Mr. Victor	Peter Gale
Mr. Chen	Burt Kwouk
Dainty	Ben Stiller
Tiptree	David Neidorf
Cohen	Ralph Seymour
Sergeant Nagata	Masato Ibu

In a television documentary on the making of this first major Hollywood studio production shot in the People's Republic of China, Steven Spielberg describes the 1984 book by J. G. Ballard on which the film is based as a remolding of the author's experience of imprisonment "as if it had been more of an adventure." More applicable to the film than to the book, Spielberg's perception is a key to both the success and the failure of *Empire of the Sun.*

Tom Stoppard's screenplay provides the raw material for yet another

Spielberg film in which a child is both a focus for the action and a lens through which others are seen. Unlike the band of children in *E. T.: The Extra-Terrestrial* (1982) or the boy in *Close Encounters of the Third Kind* (1977) who are privileged beyond most adults in their insight into reality, however, the young protagonist of *Empire of the Sun* moves from innocence to awareness under the fierce conditions of loss of parents and harsh imprisonment in time of war.

Titles set the scene: Shanghai, at the beginning of December, 1941, with the Japanese army dug in around the International Settlement and awaiting the signal of Pearl Harbor while wealthy Europeans continue to live their luxurious lives. The screen then fills with rippling water. Flower petals drift by, and then, from the right, small coffins—clearly children's—bob into view. The film will end, after the war, with a similar image: the screen filled with calmly rippling water and a wooden box drifting in from the right. This box, however, is a suitcase which Jamie Graham (Christian Bale), the main character, has recently thrown into the ocean in the course of a long trek away from his internment camp after the Japanese collapse. It contains magazine clippings and trinkets which had helped him maintain his sense of identity during three and a half years of imprisonment, and by giving it up he has symbolically marked the death of his childhood. Framed between these two images of actual and symbolic death is the working out of Jamie Graham's will to life, the story of a survivor.

Eleven-year-old Jamie is first shown singing in a boys' choir rehearsal in a cathedral. He wears the blazer and cap of an upper-class British school. His singing voice, its volume enhanced on the sound track, has a clear, crystalline beauty. This scene identifies Jamie as a member of the privileged international community, but the quality of his singing voice suggests something special and precious.

The film then sketches in Jamie's luxurious (and loving) home life, the atmosphere of the International Settlement under threat, and his enthusiastic interest in aerial warfare. An effective stylistic device is the photographing of the streets of Shanghai through the closed windows of the family's chauffeured car, during three rides outside the international enclave.

The first is Jamie's return from choir practice as he watches the teeming humanity of Shanghai: street merchants and performers, bar girls and foreign sailors, and the beggars, especially an old man outside his family's residence, banging his metal bowl on the sidewalk. The second ride shows Jamie and his parents in elaborate costumes on their way to a British party, and here the camera moves outside the car and outside other British cars as well, counterpointing the costumed and worried English with the turmoil and misery of the Chinese refugees who have poured into Shanghai. Among them is a street boy, older and bigger than Jamie, with whom Jamie exchanges a long glance, preceded by a sudden smear of blood on the window accidentally slapped there by a man carrying a slaughtered chicken.

The third ride takes place after the Japanese attack. Hands hammer on the windows, while the Japanese march and drive through the terrified crowd. In danger of being crushed by a tank, the family rushes from the car. A comparison with the novel here may help to illuminate Spielberg's project, which is one of simplification to suit the conventions of the Hollywood commercial film, creating an easily grasped thematic movement and, insofar as possible, the concentration of ideas and historical events into a series of personal confrontations.

In the book, Jamie's father (Rupert Frazer) runs down to help wounded English sailors who are trying to swim ashore. Jamie hurries after him, while his mother (Emily Richard) is pushed into a crowd and driven away by Japanese soldiers. Spielberg's conception of Jamie, in contrast, keeps him an innocent, rather unbelievable child in a situation of clear danger. The three leave the car hand in hand, and Jamie's father is torn away by the crowd. Though passionately admonished not to let go of his mother's hand, Jamie does so in order to retrieve a tiny toy airplane that he has dropped. His mother is swept away, and the Jamie of the film will not know till the very end whether his parents have survived. (The imprisoned Jamie of the novel knows that his parents are alive.)

The scene with the toy plane (a Japanese fighter), underscores, at the cost of psychological probability, the boy's fascination with the Japanese air force, a theme present in the novel but stressed much more heavily in the film. By making Jamie behave so childishly, Spielberg tilts the scales for a more dramatic transition to the capable survivor he will become in the detention camp. The sense of process present in the novel, however, is lost. As cinema, the scene is impressively handled—Jamie and his mother being carried away from each other in an uncontrollable crowd recalls the parting of the lovers at the end of Marcel Carné's *Les Enfants du Paradis* (1945), one of several references to classic films. (Among the more powerful is the most direct, when Jamie, alone and searching for food, passes an enormous billboard advertising *Gone with the Wind*, 1939, which, according to the novel, was actually showing in Shanghai at the time.)

A series of thematic reversals follows. Jamie's Chinese amah slaps him in the face when he tells her not to steal a piece of furniture. The street boy reappears, chases him, and steals his shoes. (In the much harsher novel, the equivalent character tries to cut off Jamie's hand to obtain his watch.) Later, at his first detention site, the British prisoners bang their bowls on the ground like the old beggar.

During his internment, Jamie (with virtually no character development) seems the most competently heroic individual in the camp. The camera runs along with him through a sequence where he is shown "organizing" (to use the slang of the German concentration camps), wheeling and dealing one object for another in his drive to survive. Despite his independence, he has two surrogate fathers, who vie for his soul. Basie (John Malkovich), an American merchant seaman whom he has encountered earlier and who rechristened him Jim ("a new name for a new life"), is the ruthless and selfish expert at survival. Dr. Rawlins (Nigel Havers), who tends the sick under impossible conditions, represents the values of British civilization: Jim studies Latin verbs with him. More competent as a prisoner than his tutor, Jim saves Dr. Rawlins' life, through cleverness and cunning submission, when the doctor attempts to stop the camp sergeant from breaking the windows of the hospital.

The treatment of the Japanese provides some of the most moving as well as one of the clumsiest episodes in the film. The various Japanese of the novel are boiled down to a few clear-cut characters, in the camp and in the Japanese airfield adjoining it. When Jim first arrives at the campsite, he is drawn to touch a Japanese fighter plane, in response to which Sergeant Nagata (Masato Ibu), the embodiment of brutal militarism, cocks his rifle. He does not shoot, however, because in a hail of sparks from a welder's torch and with otherwordly music playing in the skies, three Japanese pilots approach through a mist of smoke and return Jim's immediate salute. With the substitution of antennae for flyer's caps, the highly effective scene could easily have come from *Close Encounters of the Third Kind*. Otherworldly in a vein of Christian (or Buddhist) resignation is the episode in which Jim, through the wire, sees three kamikaze ceremonially preparing for takeoff and, in a film whose musical background is sometimes banally conceived, sings for them beautifully in his angelic voice. (This scene, like the preceding and the one next discussed, does not appear in the novel.) The gentleness and vulnerability, as opposed to the grandeur and brutality, of the Japanese is represented by the rather unlikely, film-created character of a young Japanese on the airfield who at one point saves Jim's life. This young man is shot, after the Japanese collapse, by Basie's small band of land pirates as he stands over Jim—in a ridiculously conceived pose—with a drawn sword raised to cut a mango, which he means to share with his English friend.

Despite the bravura successes of the film, its simplifications may at times seem off-putting. Still, when Jim, in a scene not found in the novel (and one that is marvelously acted by the brilliant thirteen-year-old Bale), painfully recognizes and is recognized by the parents he has not seen for three and a half years, it would be difficult to avoid being moved. Spielberg's handling of this scene, making full use of Bale's skill, elevates the film above the typical Hollywood adventure, evoking the pain and the wonder of Jim's grueling coming of age.

Mira Reym Binford

Reviews

Commonweal. CXV, January 15, 1988, p. 20.
Los Angeles Times. December 9, 1987, VI, p. 1.
National Review. XL, February 5, 1988, p. 59.
The New York Times. December 9, 1987, p. C25.
The New Yorker. LXIII, December 28, 1987, p. 93.
Newsweek. CX, December 14, 1987, p. 82.
People Weekly. XXIX, January 11, 1988, p. 10.
Time. CXXX, December 7, 1987, p. 79.
Variety. CCCXXIX, December 2, 1987, p. 10.
The Wall Street Journal. December 9, 1987, p. 36.

FATAL ATTRACTION

Production: Stanley R. Jaffe and Sherry Lansing; released by Paramount
   Pictures
Direction: Adrian Lyne
Screenplay: James Dearden; based on his short film of the same name
Cinematography: Howard Atherton
Editing: Michael Kahn and Peter E. Berger
Production design: Mel Bourne
Art direction: Jack Blackman; set decoration, George DeTitta
Costume design: Ellen Mirojnick
Sound: Les Lazarowitz
Music: Maurice Jarre
MPAA rating: R
Running time: 119 minutes

> *Principal characters:*
> Dan Gallagher .... Michael Douglas
> Alex Forrest .... Glenn Close
> Beth Gallagher .... Anne Archer
> Ellen Gallagher .... Ellen Hamilton Latzen
> Jimmy .... Stuart Pankin
> Hildy .... Ellen Foley
> Arthur .... Fred Gwynne
> Joan Rogerson .... Meg Mundy
> Howard Rogerson .... Tom Brennan
> Martha .... Lois Smith

Fatal Attraction begins with the camera panning the skyline of New York
City and gradually approaching a window in a large building. After the
shade is drawn, the scene switches to the inside of an apartment. This opening shot will remind some viewers of the beginning of Alfred Hitchcock's
Psycho (1960)—indeed, the city of Phoenix, the location of the opening
shots of *Psycho*, is even mentioned by *Fatal Attraction*'s villain, Alex Forrest
(Glenn Close), later in the film as the place where her father presently re-
sides. There are numerous allusions to horror films throughout *Fatal Attraction*, subtly embedded in the work's texture. During the film, as Alex
charges at the hero, Dan Gallagher (Michael Douglas), wildly brandishing a
large kitchen knife above her head and emitting a high-pitched scream, the
viewer is reminded of Norman Bates's supposed mother rushing at poor
Arbogast, with the scream recalling the piercing score in *Psycho*. The ending of the film is a neatly contrived concoction that pulls together visual images from numerous classic horror films. The horrific violence all takes

place in the bathroom, recalling not only the shower sequence in *Psycho*, but also the opening and closing bathroom sequences in Brian De Palma's *Dressed to Kill* (1980); the rising up of Alex's apparently drowned body in the bathtub is a direct allusion to a similar moment in Henri-Georges Clouzot's French horror classic, *Les Diaboliques* (1955) and is reminiscent also of the several resurrections of the human monster at the end of John Carpenter's *Halloween* (1978). *Fatal Attraction* calls to mind Clint Eastwood's *Play Misty for Me* (1971), which has a strikingly similar plot (although more romantic) about a man besieged by a former lover, who also becomes homicidal and must be brutally dispatched. *Fatal Attraction* has more in common with the horror film; yet the film has had a much wider appeal than most horror films (it earned more than $100 million during the first six months of release) undoubtedly as a result of its more realistic characters and setting as well as the social resonance of the film's sexual theme. The film utilizes the perennial plot of good people being attacked by some destructive monster; in this case, however, the monster is a woman scorned. The story is told with the basic filmic techniques used by the best makers of horror films to put their audiences in a state of anticipation and frenzy.

The mobile camera of *Fatal Attraction* seems to search out characters and discover them, then move in on them and trap them within the interior spaces of the initial image. The viewer feels vulnerable and helpless while associating with the characters and constantly suspects that something dreadful is about to happen to them. Dan is sought out by the camera and discovered taking a shower after he has spent the night with Alex, the first indication that he is no longer free and no longer alone. The camera is frequently sneaking up on Dan and his family, often when they are together in a single room, and frequently when he is alone, answering the phone. The viewer's involvement with Dan and sense of being trapped with him is at key moments in the film intensified by subjective techniques. At one point in the film, Alex leaves her apartment building from a point-of-view shot that represents Dan's perspective, then the camera pans to the left, allowing the viewer to see him enter her building. Once he is inside her apartment, his movements are followed with the jolting bounce of the hand-held camera, creating the effect that the viewer too has intruded with Dan into the mad woman's personal space. The film is edited at times with a skillful interaction of images to bring the audience to a dreaded traumatic moment. The climax of the film renders a state of extreme tension by crosscutting between the two women in the bathroom and Dan, who is downstairs. The crosscutting is orchestrated with the upstairs shots—the bath, the faucet, the fogged mirror, the women struggling, Alex's knife slashing her own thigh—playing off the downstairs shots of Dan—the teapot, the water leaking through the ceiling, and the dog. Director Adrian Lyne and his director of photography, Howard Atherton, have achieved a finely wrought, self-consciously exploitative film that manipulates the audience with great cunning and technique.

The technical achievements of *Fatal Attraction* have made James Dearden's screenplay, which by itself might seem thin and melodramatic, into a modern parable that has shocked audiences and provoked debate. Much of the action transpires in New York City, a place of noise, crowds, business, and money, from which Dan and his family later flee for the decent life of the countryside. Dan has a beautiful wife, Beth (Anne Archer), and a charming little girl, Ellen (Ellen Hamilton Latzen), but he lives in a world of promiscuity and adultery. He is advising the publishing firm where Alex is an editor about the legal rights for publishing a book that discusses, by implication, the adultery of a United States congressman. With her blonde Medusa hairdo, rampant sexuality, and unquenchable need, Alex seems to be a contemporary symbol of the misplaced female in the male business world.

Dan and Alex begin their relationship with wild and frenzied lovemaking that moves from her kitchen to the bedroom and finally to the elevator. The next day, when the two are running in the park, Dan suddenly collapses and pretends to be dead, paralyzing Alex with fright. She explains that her father died from a heart attack right in front of her when she was seven but then claims that she too is pretending since her father is still alive. Alex prevents Dan from leaving that night by cutting her wrists. He bandages her wounds and stays with her, departing the next morning after she promises that she will be all right. Alex's pursuit of Dan during the coming weeks culminates with her announcement to him that she is pregnant and has no intention of aborting their child; she is thirty-six, and this is her last chance to be a mother. When Dan later sneaks into Alex's apartment to find out more about her, he discovers a newspaper article concerning her father's death at the age of forty-two in 1959. After Dan has moved with his family to the country, Alex tracks him down and brutally kills his child's pet rabbit, forcing Dan to confess the situation to his wife. Posing as a family friend, Alex whisks Ellen off from school one day and takes her to an amusement park. While the two ride on a roller coaster, Beth drives around town in a state of near-hysteria looking for her daughter and crashes into another car. Upon learning of the accident, Dan rushes to the hospital, where he is reconciled with his wife. He then goes to Alex's apartment in a rage and nearly strangles her. In the final sequence of the film, while Beth is preparing a bath and Dan is downstairs making her a cup of tea, Beth discovers Alex in the bathroom clutching a knife. When Dan notices the bath water leaking through the ceiling, he rushes to his wife's rescue, and after a struggle, he apparently drowns Alex in the bathtub. Alex suddenly rises from the bath water, however, knife in hand, finally to be shot dead by Beth.

Much has been written by critics concerning the social themes that have made the film such a success. The most popular interpretation is that the film embodies a cultural reaction against the sexual liberation of the years prior to the spread of acquired immune deficiency syndrome (AIDS) by presenting the prolonged punishment of Dan, the unfaithful husband and the final destruction of Alex, the licentious female. Such a reading is supported by the emphasis the film places on Dan's perfect family and the animalism of his early relationship with Alex. Their lovemaking in the kitchen is a wonderfully sardonic desecration of the center of family life.

Dan is passive for much of the film, telling Alex right at the start that she must decide whether the two of them will have an affair; and it is his wife, Beth, who must finally terminate Alex and the threat to the family by appropriating the traditional American symbol of masculinity—the gun. Beth is a remarkably attractive woman; in one scene Dan seems to worship her body as she sits scantily attired at her dressing table, the camera finding its way to the lower portion of her torso. Though at no point during the film does Dan actually make love to his wife. He is emasculated not only by Alex's power over him ("So you're frightened of me," her voice laughs at him), but also by his wife finally having to assume the traditionally male role of guardian of the family.

Alex lost her father when she was seven and has never recovered from that abandonment; she now wishes to replace her father with Dan. He is incapable of playing the role of her father, however; in his own life he has lacked such a model, he tells Alex, relating that his father's only moment of closeness to him occurred during a performance of *Madam Butterfly*. On every level of the film, patriarchy is defeated, and at the conclusion, matriarchy is triumphant when the virtuous mother shoots dead the pregnant intruder from the urban world of promiscuity and sin. The film has been seen as an attack on feminism, but it is certainly an encomium to the indomitable female spirit. The empowered woman has now put the family in order by destroying her sex's immoral and promiscuous image, an image, ironically, celebrated by the Hollywood film industry in recent years.

Ira Konigsberg

Reviews

Commonweal. CXIV, October 9, 1987, p. 565.
Films in Review. XXXVIII, December, 1987, p. 609.
Ms. XLI, December, 1987, p. 78.
The New Republic. CXCIV, October 19, 1987, p. 27.
The New York Times. September 18, 1987, p. C10.
The New Yorker. LXIII, October 19, 1987, p. 106.
Newsweek. CX, September 28, 1987, p. 76.
Time. CXXX, September 28, 1987, p. 69.
Time. CXXX, November 16, 1987, p. 72.

THE FOURTH PROTOCOL

Origin: Great Britain
Production: Timothy Burrill; released by Lorimar
Direction: John Mackenzie
Screenplay: Frederick Forsyth, with additional material by Richard Burridge; based on the novel of the same name by Forsyth
Cinematography: Phil Meheux
Editing: Graham Walker
Production design: Allan Cameron
Art direction: Tim Hutchinson; set decoration, Peter Howitt
Special effects: Peter Hutchinson
Makeup: Lois Burwell
Costume design: Tiny Nicholls
Sound: Chris Monro
Music: Lalo Schifrin
MPAA rating: R
Running time: 119 minutes

> *Principal characters:*
> John Preston . . . . Michael Caine
> Major Petrofsky . . . . Pierce Brosnan
> Irina Vassilieva. . . . . Joanna Cassidy
> Borisov . . . . Ned Beatty
> General Karpov . . . . Ray McAnally
> Brian Harcourt-Smith . . . . Julian Glover
> Sir Nigel Irvine . . . . Ian Richardson
> Sir Bernard Hemmings . . . . Michael Gough
> George Berenson . . . . Anton Rodgers
> Eileen MacWhirter . . . . Betsy Brantley
> Tom MacWhirter . . . . Matt Frewer
> General Govorshin . . . . Alan North
> Kim Philby . . . . Michael Bilton

The Fourth Protocol is a Cold War suspense thriller with an intricate, if not always lucid, plot. Its international cast, which includes the ubiquitous Michael Caine, portrays acts of sex, violence, and espionage in ways calculated to entertain a mass audience. Based on a 1984 best-selling novel by Frederick Forsyth, who wrote the film's screenplay and also served as coexecutive producer, The Fourth Protocol is a hybrid of several other British spy films. With its glamorous agents, race-against-time chase scenes, and a plot involving a threat to the world power balance, the film captures some of the flavor of an early James Bond adventure. On the other hand, its depiction of British intelligence as a world of disenchantment, red tape, and petty rivalries achieves some of the verisimilitude found in Sidney Lumet's *The Deadly Affair* (1967) and Martin Ritt's *The Spy Who Came In from the Cold* (1965).

The film begins with a mysterious death. Kim Philby (Michael Bilton), the notorious British spy-turned-traitor, arrives for a meeting with General Govorshin (Alan North), chairman of the Soviet State Security Committee (KGB), and is executed instead. Elsewhere in the Soviet Union, Major Petrofsky (Pierce Brosnan), a rising star in the KGB, is summoned to meet Govorshin and learns that he has been selected for a secret mission which will earn for him undreamed honors.

In London, British agent John Preston (Caine) uncovers a Soviet plot to obtain secret documents of the North Atlantic Treaty Organization (NATO). Preston's methods, however, anger his boss, Brian Harcourt-Smith (Julian Glover), deputy head of British counterintelligence, because they betray a lack of respect for authority and threaten Harcourt-Smith's promotion prospects. Harcourt-Smith disposes of Preston by reassigning him.

General Karpov (Ray McAnally), deputy head of the KGB, is disturbed to learn that Govorshin has mounted an operation in Great Britain without his knowledge. Borisov (Ned Beatty), Karpov's friend and colleague, reports that he has been stripped of his resources, including his best agent, Petrofsky. Borisov speculates that Govorshin may be trying to embarrass or remove Karpov.

Petrofsky, masquerading as an Englishman, arrives in Great Britain, rents a house next to an American air base, and takes delivery of assorted packages from a series of couriers. One of the couriers is accidentally killed, and his death comes to Preston's attention. Among the courier's effects is a disk of polonium, a metal used to detonate atom bombs. Preston's activities again displease Harcourt-Smith and he is suspended. Convinced he has uncovered a Soviet plot to assemble and explode an atom bomb within Great Britain, Preston meets secretly with Sir Nigel Irvine (Ian Richardson), head of British foreign intelligence and *bête noire* of Harcourt-Smith, and secures permission to continue his investigations clandestinely.

Karpov, having discovered the involvement of Philby and a Soviet scientist in Govorshin's operation, reviews his findings with Borisov. If Govorshin's plan to explode an atom bomb near an American air base succeeds, the United States will be blamed for a nuclear accident and NATO will collapse. If Petrofsky is caught, the Soviet Union will be accused of breaking the secret Fourth Protocol (whose terms are not explained in the film) to the 1968 Nuclear Nonproliferation Treaty signed by the United States, Great Britain, and the Soviet Union, and the Cold War will intensify. Either outcome would result in a shift in the world power balance likely to justify Govorshin's hard-line policies and thus to secure the KGB chief's position.

Karpov, mindful that he must proceed carefully if he is not to endanger his own position, resolves to bide his time.

Soviet scientist Irina Vassilieva (Joanna Cassidy) joins Petrofsky in England, bringing with her a replacement polonium disk. At the agent's house, they assemble the bomb, then mechanically make love. Immediately afterward, Petrofsky carries out his orders to kill Vassilieva. Meanwhile, Preston learns that a KGB communications specialist has entered Great Britain on a forged passport and tracks him to the site of a secret Soviet transmitter. Petrofsky visits this location, then returns to his house, unaware that Preston is following him. Petrofsky receives the signal to activate the bomb but pauses on discovering that his own death forms part of Govorshin's plan. Preston, accompanied by a special task force, bursts into the house. Petrofsky is hastily killed by one of Preston's assistants, who explains to the outraged Preston that he was acting under orders.

Later, Irvine holds a furtive meeting with Karpov. Preston arrives and accuses them of having made a deal to ensure the failure of the operation. He further claims that their actions were governed solely by career interests. Disgusted, Preston walks away from these unlikely allies to concentrate on what matters to him most—his son.

It is not always fair to judge a film in terms of fidelity to the novel from which it is derived. It is nevertheless instructive to compare the film and book of *The Fourth Protocol* because of what is learned about the kinds of compromises made in the interests of box-office success. For example, the film depicts sexual encounters which are absent from the book. The novel's Russian bomb expert is a male who shares only a few terse exchanges with Petrofsky. In the film, he has metamorphosed into a beautiful female willing to indulge the agent's otherwise unsatisfied sexual urges. In another episode, with no narrative significance, Petrofsky socializes with an American couple and is tormented by desire for the wife. Both sequences seem designed to exploit the proven sex appeal of Brosnan, who formerly starred in the television series "Remington Steele" and narrowly missed becoming Roger Moore's successor as 007 in the James Bond films. The film also contains several violent deaths, including Philby's, which do not appear in the book. Forsyth's original is not without its brutal slayings, but violence has a much more pervasive presence in the screen version. The film necessarily simplifies the novel's plot, but the choices made occur at the expense of clarity. For example, the book's painstaking account of the plan's political underpinnings is eliminated, with the result that the audience is left in the dark as to the precise nature of the Fourth Protocol.

Characterization often suffers in films designed to keep a mass audience attentive, and *The Fourth Protocol* is no exception. The script squanders the talent of outstanding character actors such as McAnally and Beatty in roles which are little more than hooks on which to hang the action. Caine, who is no stranger to the spy genre, having appeared in the Len Deighton trilogy *The Ipcress File* (1965), *Funeral in Berlin* (1966), and *Billion Dollar Brain* (1967) as well as the more recent *The Whistle Blower* (1987), offers a believable portrayal and provides the film with its few flashes of humor. At no point, however, does the script permit him to display the kind of virtuosity he demonstrated in *Sleuth* (1972), *California Suite* (1978), *Educating Rita* (1983), and *Hannah and Her Sisters* (1986). The female characters are uniformly one-dimensional.

John Mackenzie, who earlier directed the energetic British gangster film, *The Long Good Friday* (1980), is less adventurous on this occasion and allows the action to lose momentum. The climactic scene, in which nuclear disaster is narrowly averted, is a wasted opportunity to build tension and excitement. Lalo Schifrin's score is lackluster and mainly serves to signal changes of pace or to add atmosphere to the appearance of sinister Russians against frosty landscapes. The dominant impression created by the film is that of routineness, which is surprising given Forsyth's direct involvement in the production.

The Fourth Protocol may not contain many major surprises, but the subtextual note of similarity between those whom the cinema has traditionally presented as opposites makes the film of more than passing interest. Intelligence chiefs, no matter what their political coloration, are depicted as being motivated more by careerism than by ideology. Their underlings have in common a function as pawns in the power games played by their superiors. Obedience to authority may be the guiding principle of the KGB, but then the rule-bound environment of the British intelligence system has little room for independent-mindedness. Reinforcing this theme of similarity between opposites is the absence of an effort to denote the characters' nationalities through language. The American and Irish actors who portray Russians speak in their natural accents and are not required to deliver their lines in broken English. This willingness to eschew some of the more entrenched clichés of the Cold War thriller makes *The Fourth Protocol* seem, at times, almost boldly innovative.

> *Fiona Valentine*
> *Greg Changnon*

Reviews

Cosmopolitan. CCIII, September, 1987, p. 52.
Films and Filming. CCCXCI, April, 1987, p. 36.
Films in Review. XXXVIII, November, 1987, p. 546.
Los Angeles. XXXII, September, 1987, p. 204.
Los Angeles Times. August 28, 1987, VI, p. 1.

Macleans. C, September 14, 1987, p. 54.
The New Republic. CXCVII, September 28, 1987, p. 26.
The New York Times. August 28, 1987, p. C19.
Newsweek. CX, September 14, 1987, p. 82.
People Weekly. XXVIII, September 7, 1987, p. 14.
Variety. CCCXXVI, March 18, 1987, p. 18.

THE FRINGE DWELLERS

Origin: Australia
Released: 1986
Released in U.S.: 1987
Production: Sue Milliken; released by Atlantic Releasing Corporation
Direction: Bruce Beresford
Screenplay: Bruce Beresford and Rhoisin Beresford; based on the novel of the same name by Nene Gare
Cinematography: Don McAlpine
Editing: Tim Wellburn
Production design: Herbert Pinter
Art direction: Stewart Way
Costume design: Kerri Barnett
Sound: Max Bowring
Music: George Dreyfus
MPAA rating: PG
Running time: 98 minutes

Principal characters:

Trilby	Kristina Nehm
Mollie	Justine Saunders
Joe	Bob Maza
Noonah	Kylie Belling
Bartie	Denis Walker
Phil	Ernie Dingo
Charlie	Malcolm Silva
Hannah	Marlene Bell
Audrena	Michelle Torres
Blanchie	Michele Miles
Eva	Kath Walker
Skippy	Bill Sandy

Bruce Beresford, along with Peter Weir, has emerged as one of the world-class filmmakers of the contemporary Australian cinema, a leading light of the so-called Australian "New Wave." Such a categorization is actually a misnomer: The filmmakers who brought Australian cinema to world attention in the mid-1970's cannot be said to represent a "new wave" of filmmaking, for they were preceded by no "old wave," no genuine, significant Australian cinematic tradition. The typical historical pattern in world cinema has been for leading directors of emerging national cinemas to be lured away from their native lands to Hollywood, and such has been the case with Weir and Beresford. Beresford's Hollywood career has been notable—*Tender Mercies*

(1983) and *Crimes of the Heart* (1986) are major films by any standards, and *King David* (1985), although something of a disaster at the time, will perhaps prove more interesting to viewers in years to come. Still, *The Fringe Dwellers* is evidence that Beresford has by no means abandoned his native land. *Tender Mercies* aside, *The Fringe Dwellers* is Beresford's best film since *Breaker Morant* (1980).

The term "fringe dwellers" refers to the aborigines who live in shanty towns on the outskirts of prosperous cities. Many aborigines, who make up approximately one percent of Australia's population, actually live in cities, typically in substandard housing; about 15 percent of aborigines live in fringe camps, which may be seen as contemporary attempts to preserve some aspects of their earlier tribal life-style. Some very small percentage of aborigines, mostly full-blooded members of the remnants of the ancient tribes, live on reserves. (About two-thirds of those considered aborigine are of mixed descent.) In Beresford's film, the fringe camp is on the edge of the town of Murgon, in rugged Queensland.

The film is highly episodic in structure, building up its details and characterizations slowly, in cumulative fashion. The film is reminiscent of *Tender Mercies* in that it is structured around everyday activities. Although *The Fringe Dwellers* is more dramatic and far less austere than *Tender Mercies*— it does have moments of action and some violence—it relies on the rhythms of real life to make its points. Some of the accents are a bit difficult, and slang expressions take some getting used to—the speech of the character Skippy (Bill Sandy), who maintains close ties to the tribal past, is often impenetrable—but they add another layer to the film, providing not only authenticity, but also a privileged glimpse into lives that would otherwise be utterly foreign and unfamiliar to most twentieth century American viewers. The film's message is thus less a plea for racial harmony and tolerance than a revelation of how aboriginal life is led, how it feels from the inside.

The main character is Trilby Comeaway (Kristina Nehm), a very handsome, strong-willed teenage girl who wants to live like an ordinary, middle-class Australian. Trilby, like many a rebellious, intelligent teenager, is determined to make something of herself. The obstacles that she faces are formidable—the prejudice of some whites and the cycle of poverty and ignorance in which many contemporary aborigines are trapped. She has ambivalent feelings about being black, a mix of self-hatred and resentment against whites. Early in the story, she expresses annoyance toward a group of aborigine boys who come to talk to her and her cousins, Audrena (Michelle Torres) and Blanchie (Michele Miles). Her cousins reproach her: "Don't know what you expect—Mel Gibson, Bryan Brown?" They then go into a predominantly white ice-cream shop, where Trilby and her cousins overhear white girls complaining about them. When a middle-aged white man castigates the white girls for their attitude, Trilby lashes out at him, saying, "I don't want people defending me." This attitude manifests itself later after she slaps a schoolmate who makes disparaging remarks about aborigines. She is angry that she is not punished by the school authorities for her violence. If she were white, she claims, she would have been punished.

Trilby's goals, on one level, are quite modest. She envisions herself as an office worker living in the city after she attains her school certificate—no small accomplishment for an aborigine, as viewers learn. In the meantime, she convinces her sympathetic yet wary mother, Mollie (Justine Saunders), and her likable, decent, too easygoing father, Joe (Bob Maza), to apply for a house in a white middle-class neighborhood in town. They move into a suburban cottage, but their unease is apparent. A white neighbor invites Mollie to tea, but Trilby is mortified when her mother describes her visit. Enraged to learn that the white neighbor has given the family some old clothes, Trilby ostentatiously sets fire to them in plain sight of the neighbor. Mollie soon begins to feel lonely. In a memorable juxtaposition of shots, a vignette of Mollie's friends playing cards back at the fringe camp cuts to Mollie alone in her house, vacantly flipping through a magazine.

Their experiment in middle-class living soon turns disastrous. First, much to Trilby's resentment, Joe's brother, Charlie (Malcolm Silva), and his family move in. None of them has any understanding of paying rent and bills. Trilby's dissatisfaction turns to outright hostility when she becomes pregnant by Phil (Ernie Dingo), a handsome stockman who wants to marry her. Events turn dark when Joe, on his way to pay the long-overdue rent, loses the money in a card game and leaves home; the family moves back to the fringe camp. Trilby's newborn daughter dies. Although the death is officially declared an accident, the combination of expressionistic lighting, jump-cuts, and a low-angle dolly-in to Trilby holding her baby, with flashcuts from earlier scenes, suggests a deliberateness on her part. The scene is certainly ambiguous, and the viewer perhaps wants to attribute Trilby's actions to accident or to severe stress. This response is a tribute to the film's ability to make the viewer care for Trilby, to see things from her point of view. When, at the end, she leaves on a bus for the city, one is still shaken by her actions but hopeful for her future.

Similarly, the feelings and actions of other characters become understandable as the film progresses. One can identify with Joe as he is subjected to peer pressure. Jeering at him for succumbing to the wishes of women, other men continually entice him into drinking beer with them or playing cards. Skippy wonders why Joe wants to live in the white suburb. "What do you want to be," he asks, "a flaming white man, mowing the lawn, washing the car?" Although the film could be accused of stereotyping Joe as a lazy black man, it shows that at work he is assigned the worst jobs. Though he was a successful boxer when he was younger, back-breaking day labor is now the best he can manage. Trilby's older sister, Noonah (Kylie Belling), works as a nurse-in-training. Although popular with the patients and sympathetic to their needs, she is having trouble with the written exam, especially the mathematics components. In this case, the kindness of a doctor and of the head nurse enables Noonah to keep her job as they provide tutoring for her. Bartie (Denis Walker), Trilby's little brother, has enormous artistic talent. A sympathetic schoolteacher provides him with a sketch pad and tells him there is no reason in the world that he cannot later attend art school. It becomes clear, however, that there *is* a reason why he may not attend school, why Noonah almost had to leave nursing, why Trilby came close to marrying Phil when she was pregnant. To Trilby's declaration that she does not want to end up as so many other aborigines have, Phil responds that she is different. Trilby wonders, "Yeah, well, maybe they were all different once." The cycle is hard to break.

While the dignity, kindness, and love of the aborigines and the often shortsighted, condescending, outright racist attitudes of many whites are vividly depicted in *The Fringe Dwellers*, the film's ultimate implication is that middle-class life is highly desirable. The only alternative is seen in the character of Skippy, who by film's end has returned to his ancestral homeland in the rugged outback, where, in full tribal paint, he waits to die. There is also the character of Eva (Kath Walker), an aged woman who also has much of the tribal essence about her. She lives, seemingly contentedly, in the fringe camp. Are Skippy and Eva, however, to be taken as genuine alternatives to white Australian middle-class life? Nene Gare, the aborigine author of the novel *The Fringe Dwellers* (1961), clearly recognizes, as does Beresford, that life in the fringe camps is a marginal existence. The film takes no stand on reserve life, but instead calls for the integration of aborigines into middle-class life, should they desire it. In fact, it may be taken as a sign of the film's integrity that the viewer is led to question Trilby's motives and recognize her self-hatred. The film's focus on the aborigine experience may leave its viewers equipped to deal with issues and problems of white-black relations in Australia without romanticization and oversimplification.

David Desser

Reviews
Los Angeles Times. January 24, 1987, VI, p. 12.
Ms. XV, March, 1987, p. 20.
The New York Times. January 23, 1987, p. C13.
Seventeen. XLVI, April, 1987, p. 87.
The Wall Street Journal. January 22, 1987, p. 28.

FULL METAL JACKET

Production: Stanley Kubrick; released by Warner Bros.
Direction: Stanley Kubrick
Screenplay: Stanley Kubrick, Michael Herr, and Gustav Hasford; based on
 Hasford's book *The Short-Timers*
Cinematography: Douglas Milsome
Editing: Martin Hunter
Production design: Anton Furst
Art direction: Rod Stratfold; set decoration, Stephen Simmonds
Special effects: John Evans
Makeup: Jennifer Boost and Christine Allsopp
Costume design: Keith Denny
Sound: Edward Tise
Music: Abigail Mead
MPAA rating: R
Running time: 118 minutes

> *Principal characters:*
> Private Joker .... Matthew Modine
> Animal Mother .... Adam Baldwin
> Private Pyle .... Vincent D'Onofrio
> Gunnery Sergeant Hartman .... Lee Ermey
> Eightball .... Dorian Harewood
> Cowboy .... Arliss Howard
> Rafterman .... Kevyn Major Howard
> Lieutenant Touchdown .... Ed O'Ross
> Prostitute .... Papillon Soo Soo

It has been more than a decade since the end of the Vietnam War, and, as
the years begin to provide chronological and emotional distance from the
troubling events of that era, filmmakers are gradually weighing in with cinematic portraits of the conflict that cost countless lives and threw America
into a period of political turmoil. The Best Picture Oscar awarded to *Platoon* (1986) and the appearance on prime-time television of *Tour of Duty*,
the medium's first Vietnam series, both signify the degree to which audiences in the 1980's are prepared to accept the war as a subject for dramatization.

Stanley Kubrick's films have operated consistently outside the mainstream
of popular filmmaking, and the application of his brilliant cinematic style to
any subject has long been a source of fascination to his admirers. From his
blackly satiric look at the world on the brink of nuclear war in *Dr. Strangelove* (1964) to his chilling screen version of Anthony Burgess' *A Clockwork*

Orange (1971), Kubrick has challenged his audiences with startlingly original visions of difficult subjects. The announcement of a Kubrick Vietnam film, then, gave rise to much speculation and anticipation from those who were eager to see how the great director would approach this most sensitive and haunting of topics.

The answer is a full-on frontal assault, a film so powerful that it transcends the trappings of its actual setting and becomes a film about all wars and the terrible blow they deal to the human spirit of those who fight them. Based on Vietnam War veteran Gustav Hasford's book *The Short-Timers* (1979) and adapted for the screen by Kubrick, Hasford, and Michael Herr, the author of the book *Dispatches* (1977), *Full Metal Jacket* forces the viewer relentlessly through the experiences of a group of marines, beginning with basic training and continuing through the horrors of the war. The film opens with a shot of young marine recruits seated in barber's chairs having their heads shaved upon their arrival at Parris Island. Stripped of their hair and clothing—and hence their civilian identities—the recruits are plunged into a rigorous, often-humiliating period of basic training at the hands of a ferocious, inventively foul-mouthed drill sergeant named Hartman (Lee Ermey, a real-life drill sergeant originally hired as a technical adviser on the film). It is a process that will harden them for battle, turning them—as the sergeant says with pride—into killers.

The basic training segment comprises the film's first forty-five minutes and centers primarily on two recruits, the intelligent, wisecracking Private Joker (Matthew Modine) and Private Pyle (Vincent D'Onofrio), an overweight, slow-witted young man whom Sergeant Hartman singles out for his most abusive harassment. Pyle improves slowly under Joker's patient supervision until hc is caught with a forbidden jelly doughnut by Hartman, who decides to punish the entire barracks for Pyle's mistakes. The plan culminates in Pyle's savage, nighttime beating by his fellow recruits and his subsequent slide into a dangerous mental collapse. On the recruits' final night in the barracks, Joker finds Pyle in the latrine with his rifle, now clearly well over the edge into madness. When Sergeant Hartman arrives, Pyle shoots him, spares Joker, and, in one of the film's most horrifying and graphic scenes, turns the rifle on himself.

The scene shifts abruptly to Vietnam, where Joker and his friend, Rafterman (Kevyn Major Howard), are reporters for *Stars and Stripes*. The time is the eve of the Tet offensive, which erupts around the pair's hitherto secure camp, and the two are sent to cover troop action near Hue. There they meet Cowboy (Arliss Howard), Joker's friend from boot camp, and the members of his unit, including a black soldier nicknamed Eightball (Dorian Harewood) and the viciously aggressive Animal Mother (Adam Baldwin). After the group is interviewed by a documentary news crew (asked for his comments on the war, Joker deadpans, "I wanted to meet interesting, stimulating people from an ancient land . . . and kill them."), Joker and Rafterman accompany Cowboy's unit on its sweep through Hue, which has been reduced to smoking ruins by the fighting. When the men are pinned by sniper fire and Eightball and another man are hit, the others watch helplessly as the sniper fires repeatedly into the bodies of their wounded comrades, until Animal Mother defies his orders and goes in after them. The others follow and Cowboy is shot, dying in Joker's arms.

The men split up to search for the sniper, and Joker locates the source of the attack—a young Viet Cong girl who has been shot by Animal Mother. As the girl lies on the ground, gravely wounded and begging to be killed, the men decide to leave her. Joker, however, balks at the suggestion and is taunted by the others to "waste her," which he does. It is an act of both compassion and revenge, and it catapults the young soldier irrevocably into that deadened emotional state necessary for survival in circumstances of such brutality. His metamorphosis now complete, Joker has become the hardened survivor that was the final goal of his basic training.

The key to the film's central theme is provided by its title. A "full metal jacket" is a special type of shell casing formulated to keep bullets intact as they enter the body. In the context of the film, that is precisely what the rigors of basic training are intended to provide for the marine recruits—an outer casing so hardened that it will survive the horrors to which the men will inevitably be subjected. The first step in the process is Parris Island, where they are stripped of their identities, broken down through humiliation and fatigue, and built back up into marines—"born again hard," as Sergeant Hartman terms it. The war completes the process, effectively numbing the soldiers' emotions to the point where they are able to withstand the loss of comrades, for whom there is no time to grieve, as well as sights which would leave civilians in a state of sickened shock. It is a condition which is indispensable for a state of war but devastatingly destructive to the basic tenets of humanity.

The complexity of this deadly process and the terrible paradoxes it involves are referred to obliquely throughout the film. When Joker is asked by a superior officer to explain the meaning of the peace symbol and the "born to kill" lettering on his helmet, he replies, "I think I was trying to say something about the duality of man." This duality is at the heart of Private Pyle's slide into insanity even as he becomes a good marine, and in the irony of the discovery that the sniper is a woman, when earlier references to women in the film are purely sexual in nature. The duality is also present in Joker's shooting of the sniper, an act that encompasses such a broad range of emotions that it shuts down his ability to feel anything beyond joy at still finding himself alive.

Kubrick's method of conveying this message is to take the audience through the men's experiences. As the marines are brutalized by what they see, so, in effect, is the audience brutalized. His camera spares the viewer nothing, holding unblinkingly on scenes of such horror that the visual impact is nearly overwhelming. Yet the film never falls back on the emotional conventions of most war pictures. Nothing is learned about any of the men's lives outside the military; there are no voice-over letters home, no foxhole reminiscences about parents or sweethearts left behind, and no clichéd tugs at the heartstrings. Although *Full Metal Jacket* is less stylized than most of the director's films, there are moments of ironic detachment, many of them musical (such as the shots of medical helicopters picking up wounded soldiers to the tune of the nonsensical "Surfin' Bird" or of the soldiers singing the *Mickey Mouse Club* song in the film's final scene, that find a black, chilling humor in the images of death and destruction.

What sets *Full Metal Jacket* apart from most Vietnam films is that it is both antiwar and apolitical. Politics has no place in the fabric of the film— its concerns run much deeper. For Joker and his friends, the final outcome of the war will not be measured in terms of ground won or lost or allies secured or vanquished. In Kubrick's vision, it is their humanity that is at stake, and the cost to their souls will be immeasurable.

Janet E. Lorenz

Reviews
Films in Review. XXXVIII, December, 1987, p. 611.
The Hollywood Reporter. CCC, June 22, 1987, p. 3.
Los Angeles Times. June 26, 1987, VI, p. 1.
Los Angeles Times Magazine. June 28, 1987, p. 18.
The Nation. CCXLV, August 1, 1987, p. 98.
The New Republic. CXCVII, July 27, 1987, p. 28.
New York. July 13, 1987, p. 54.
The New York Times. June 21, 1987, II, p. 1.
The New York Times. June 26, 1987, p. C3.
The New Yorker. LXIII, July 13, 1987, p. 75.
Newsweek. CIX, June 29, 1987, p. 64.
Time. June 29, 1987, p. 66.
Variety. CCCXXVII, June 24, 1987, p. 12.

THE FUNERAL
(OSŌSHIKI)

Origin: Japan
Released: 1984
Released in U.S.: 1987
Production: Yasushi Takaoki and Yutaka Okada for Itami-N.C.P.; released
　by New Yorker Films
Direction: Juzo Itami
Screenplay: Juzo Itami
Cinematography: Yoneza Maeda (color) and Shinpei Asai (black and white)
Editing: Akira Suzuki
Art direction: Hiroshi Tokuda
Sound: Minoru Nobuoka
Music: Joji Yuasa
MPAA rating: no listing
Running time: 124 minutes

> *Principal characters:*
> Wabisuke Inoue . . . . Tsutomu Yamazaki
> Chizuko Amamiya . . . . Nobuko Miyamoto
> Kikue Amamiya . . . . Kin Sugai
> Shinkichi Amamiya . . . . Koen Okumura
> Shokichi Amamiya . . . . Shuji Otaki
> Satomi. . . . . Ichiro Zaitsu
> Ebihara. . . . . Nekohachi Edoya
> Aoki. . . . . Takashi Tsumura
> Yoshiko Saito. Haruna Takase
> The priest. . . . . Chishu Ryu
> Inose . . . . Kaoru Kobayashi

　　Although *The Funeral* was shown at several North American film festivals
in 1985 and 1986, it was not until 1987 that Juzo Itami made an impression
on United States audiences. That year *The Funeral*, his first film, and
Tampopo (1986; reviewed in this volume), his second film, opened in the
United States in reverse order, while his third, *Marusa no Onna* (1987; *A
Taxing Woman*), was shown at the New York Film Festival and scheduled
for release early in 1988. Some similarities between the three films—their
energy, their often cockeyed humor, and the presence of both Nobuko
Miyamoto (Itami's wife) and Tsutomu Yamazaki (who somewhat resembles
Gregory Peck) in the leading roles—helped to reinforce the impression of a
consistent new talent.

　　In fact, Itami is new only to the director's chair. Now in his fifties, he began acting in films in 1960 and was seen on American screens in the subdued role of the banker Tatsuo in Kon Ichikawa's *Sasame Yuki* (1983; *The Makioka Sisters*) and more prominently as the father in Yoshimitsu Morita's *Kazoku Geemu* (1983; *The Family Game*). Itami has also hosted a television talk show and published several books of essays. His father, Mansaku Itami, had been a director of period films in the 1930's. The topic that Juzo Itami chose for his directorial debut arose from his own experience of arranging the funeral of Miyamoto's father.

In *The Funeral*, Wabisuke (Yamazaki) runs a company that makes television commercials, in which he and his wife Chizuko (Miyamoto) also act. They lead a prosperous, Westernized suburban life. Chizuko's father, Shinkichi (Koen Okumura), dies of a heart attack, and her mother, Kikue (Kin Sugai), wants a traditional funeral ceremony to be held at Wabisuke and Chizuko's home. Since Wabisuke and Chizuko are unprepared for death in general and a traditional funeral in particular, the rest of the film consists of a series of misadventures as they try to cope with each item on the mortuary's agenda. They must collect Shinkichi's body from the hospital (deciding whether it should be placed in the coffin before or after transportation), bring in a Buddhist priest (Chishu Ryu) to chant prayers, hold a wake for relatives and friends, receive ceremonial donations of money, close the coffin with everyone ritualistically tapping a nail, escort the coffin to the crematorium, and finally give speeches to honor the deceased.

In these activities, Wabisuke and Chizuko are helped—and often confused—by a variety of characters, including Wabisuke's office manager Satomi (Ichiro Zaitsu), the ubiquitous and soft-spoken funeral director Ebihara (Nekohachi Edoya), Wabisuke's employee Aoki (Takashi Tsumura), who films the proceedings in black and white, and Shinkichi's incipiently senile brother Shokichi (Shuji Otaki). They even seek help from a videotape on how to conduct a funeral ceremony. Meanwhile, there are other characters who disrupt the proceedings to a greater or lesser extent; the lesser of these include rambunctious children and a woman acquaintance of Shinkichi who makes a longer and louder display of grief than anyone else; the greatest disruption comes from Wabisuke's mistress, Yoshiko (Haruna Takase), who threatens to create a scene until he has sex with her in the bushes. The film ends when Wabisuke, who has been dreading his responsibility of making a speech at the closing ceremony, is asked by Kikue to let her speak instead; humor then subsides into gentle acceptance of death.

There are several weaknesses in the structure of *The Funeral* that Itami avoided in his subsequent films. The series of almost self-contained episodes becomes repetitive, so that the action flags about two-thirds of the way through. When the guests at the wake overstay their welcome, the film begins to overstay its welcome, too. It does brighten up again, but Wabisuke's dread of giving a speech (implausible in a professional actor) is too flimsy an element of suspense for its resolution to provide a satisfying ending. Although *A Taxing Woman* is linear and includes many brief episodes, it also has a suspenseful plot line that extends from start to finish. *Tampopo* continually digresses from its main plot line, but into such wild comedy that it has the fascination of a firecracker. In *The Funeral*, the digression involving Yoshiko is out of key with the rest of the film, yet not far enough out to fascinate.

On the other hand, *The Funeral* offers inventive and genuinely comic scenes throughout. It opens with amusing ambiguity: Is Shinkichi an acerbic curmudgeon whom Kikue tolerates, or is he playing a role that Kikue enjoys? In the crematorium scene just before the end, family members join Inose (Kaoru Kobayashi), the cremator, who discourses on such trade secrets as the need for a higher temperature with diseased bodies than with healthy ones. Much of the humor in between emerges from deft details such as Satomi's laughter when he goes to pay the hospital bill for Wabisuke and finds that it is much less than they expected, and the funeral director's continual manipulation of his eyeglasses, which have flip-up sunshades and slip-in reading lenses. On balance, *The Funeral* is both enjoyable and remarkably assured for a first film. It is certainly far more successful than another recent film by a first-time Japanese director on a related topic—Yoshishige Yoshida's *Promesse* (*A Promise*, 1985), which takes a serious and eventually turgid approach to an old man's mercy killing of his sick wife.

Not that Itami's comic handling of a serious topic is new or unusual in Japanese filmmaking. The presence in *The Funeral* of Ryu, a favorite actor of director Yasujiro Ozu, is a reminder that Ozu not only started by making farces but also invariably included comic or even farcical scenes in his serious films, from the opening of *Tokyo no Gassho* (1931; *Tokyo Chorus*) to the brief hoax in his last film, *Samma no Aji* (1962; *An Autumn Afternoon*), wherein a man, newly married to a younger wife, dies of a heart attack. Other leading directors have gone further. Keisuke Kinoshita not only mixed politics, poverty, unwed motherhood, and modern art into his comic satire *Karumen Junjosu* (1952; *Carmen's Pure Love*), but also inserted comedy into his downbeat *Nihon no Higeki* (1953; *A Japanese Tragedy*). Ichikawa, though best known in the United States for such thoroughly serious films as *Biruma no Tategoto* (1956; *The Burmese Harp*) and *Nobi* (1959; *Fires on the Plain*), is also a master at teaming farce with tragedy: The supercharged hilarity of his *Manin Densha* (1957; *The Crowded Train*), about competitiveness in overcrowded Japan, powers a satire more grim and abrasive than anything Itami has yet attempted.

The conflict between traditional and Western ways is also a recurrent theme in Japanese films, and here Itami proves both novel and effective. In the beginning of the film, he neatly sandwiches the two cultures by introducing Wabisuke and Chizuko in traditional costume as they perform in a commercial that is accompanied by rock music; as an added untraditional touch, the commercial involves an optical illusion that makes Chizuko appear twice her husband's size. Having learned of Shinkichi's death, they hurriedly change into their usual Western clothes (and sizes). Thereafter the Western viewer finds it easy to follow the various funerary ceremonies because they first have to be explained to Wabisuke and Chizuko.

The acting is generally so smooth that it is easily taken for granted. Miyamoto's role is more subdued than in *Tampopo* or, particularly, *A Taxing Woman*, since Chizuko takes the misadventures more calmly than Wabisuke. Yamazaki, who plays two different kinds of tough guys in those films, here gives a convincing portrayal of insecurity behind a worldly façade. Zaitsu, Edoya, and Ryu all skillfully demonstrate the effectiveness of restraint. In fact, none of the performers displays any awareness that he or she is meant to be comic, and that is one reason that much of *The Funeral* is very comic indeed.

William Johnson

Reviews
Los Angeles Times. November 20, 1987, VI, p. 18.
The New York Times. October 23, 1987, III, p. 14.
San Francisco Examiner. November 18, 1987, V, p. 1.
Variety. May 15, 1985, p. 22.
The Village Voice. November 3, 1987, p. 76.

GABY—A TRUE STORY

Production: Pinchas Perry; released by Tri-Star Pictures
Direction: Luis Mandoki
Screenplay: Martin Salinas and Michael James Love; developed by Luis Mandoki as told to him by Gabriela Brimmer
Cinematography: Lajos Koltai
Editing: Garth Craven
Art direction: Alejandro Luna; set decoration, Olivia Bond
Sound: Robert Grieve
Music: Maurice Jarre
MPAA rating: R
Running time: 114 minutes

Principal characters:
Gaby	Rachel Levin
Florencia	Norma Aleandro
Sari	Liv Ullmann
Michel	Robert Loggia
Fernando	Lawrence Monoson
Luis	Robert Beltran
Fernando's mother	Beatriz Sheridan
David	Tony Goldwyn
Gaby (three years old)	Paulina Gomez

In telling the story of poet Gabriela Brimmer, a woman who exercises a fierce will in carving out her place in life despite the severe disability of an extreme case of cerebral palsy, director Luis Mandoki reveals a sensibility that is capable of both tough-mindedness and considerable delicacy of feeling. The tough-mindedness is evident when considering how physical affliction is usually regarded when it becomes a cinematic subject. Commonly, such stories—which are often, like this one, based on someone's actual experience—take the subtly patronizing perspective that the protagonist exists sentimentally to uplift the audience through his or her struggle. The recounted experience then becomes an example of the human spirit triumphing over adversity, with any gains magnified and glorified and any defeats trivialized into tear-jerking superficiality, with no attention to any deeper implications. Mandoki's perspective is quite different. He admires his heroine without sentimentalizing her—more properly, he perceives her situation, even at its saddest, as not uniquely tragic in the scheme of things and not so much inspiring as illuminating. It is this illumination that reflects his delicacy of feeling, for to Mandoki the character's individual passage and her relationships evoke much about varying attitudes toward living. His perceptions embrace but transcend conventional ideas about physical sickness, affliction, and abnormality. One of the thrusts of the narrative is to show that the heroine is, in a vital sense, the least "crippled" of the characters.

Mandoki's lucidity is not notably in evidence in the first part of the film, which centers on three-year-old Gaby (Paulina Gomez) and her parents, Michel (Robert Loggia) and Sari (Liv Ullmann). Apart from the fact that they are Austrian Jews who have relocated to Mexico City to escape the Holocaust, the viewer learns little about the parents at this point, and Mandoki does nothing more than obliquely sketch in the motif of a culture clash between them and their Mexican neighbors, who are narrowly Catholic in a way that forces the refugees into an apparent emotional isolation, although this cultural gap later becomes a major force in the primary action. Sari briefly serves as narrator, although most of the film will not be from her point of view. Still and mysterious, Gaby's place in the action is undefined.

Mandoki's apparently unfocused and fragmentary treatment, however, does not long obscure the fact that he has a clear idea about what he perceives to be the center of the story. This center emerges when the character of Florencia (Norma Aleandro), a simple, Mexican maid, is introduced. Soon, Florencia becomes the narrator of the film, and, with Gaby, a co-protagonist. Though an outsider to the family's culture, Florencia is the one who takes care of and nurtures Gaby, draws out the alive mind within the almost totally paralyzed body (Gaby cannot speak and can only slightly move one leg) and, as the years pass, comes to define her own existence by her devotion to Gaby. Much of the film's interest derives from the absorbing treatment of this character, played with impressive subtlety and restraint by Argentine actress Norma Aleandro (by contrast with her intense emoting in *The Official Story*, 1985, which made her international reputation). As the film proceeds, Florencia builds what can only be described as a symbiotic relationship with Gaby, uncomfortable for both of them at times, but never broken. This simple woman is her charge's opposite. She defines herself by being emotionally muted and personally repressed to the point of wanting to repress passion in others. Yet in this limited figure, there is a magnificent capacity for unconditional love, so in experiencing the narrative, it would be unwise to look altogether negatively on the cultural and religious values that have forged her.

By contrast, the adult Gaby (Rachel Levin) is restless, always in the process of forming and then redefining her identity. Sometimes bitter about life, she transforms the bitterness through her creativity, writing compelling and sensitive poetry. She rebels against staying in a school for the disabled and becomes a successful student at the university. She is in touch with all of her needs and actively seeks to satisfy them, which becomes especially compelling when she initiates intimate relationships with men. Gaby has one brief affair with another disabled student, Fernando (Lawrence Monoson), which is aborted by his over-protective, dominating mother (Beatriz Sheridan), and later, at the university, strikes up a warm friendship with a physically sound man, Luis (Robert Beltran), who rejects her when she offers herself sexually. By choice, Gaby finally withdraws to a quiet existence with Florencia at the family home, yet even in this melancholy conclusion, the strongest impression one has of her is of an aliveness on every level—mental, physical, and spiritual—that any of her fellow humans would envy.

In the greater part of the film, which begins when Gaby is introduced as a young woman (the intervening years are elided), Mandoki's initially oblique rendering of the narrative gives way to a somewhat more direct approach, and it becomes possible to perceive a pleasing stylistic purposefulness in his even tone, a reticence to emphasize dramatic highs and lows, and an apparent disinterest in building the material so that there is a sense of climactic release and finality. His revelations are discreet and dispersed almost casually in the flow of the film, but they are compelling. In addition to his insights into Gaby and Florencia, Mandoki penetrates other characters, sometimes at points when they have come to seem peripheral in relation to the main story. Very skillfully, he allows Sari to emerge as a quietly frightened and disappointed woman who retreats into introversion and solitary exile after the death of her husband and soon dies herself; he shows Michel giving strength and a clear-eyed appreciation of reality to Gaby while failing adequately to sustain himself with these same qualities; he touches on the uneasy aloofness of Gaby's brother, David (Tony Goldwyn); and he arouses compassion for the well-meaning but finally weak Fernando without making the character pitiable and without turning the character's mother into a one-dimensional caricature. Intriguingly, it is the other women, apart from Gaby, who lead the saddest, most constricted lives in the film, but the ambiguity of Florencia's self-effacement—however neurotic her motivation, she does support another's quest for self-expression—intimates that in Mandoki's vision, inequalities in self-realization are, while not ideal, profoundly a part of the fabric of life.

Gaby—A True Story may impose itself on the viewer as an episodic narrative, and its compositions and editing might seem to lack any special grace. Yet, the barely perceptible rhythm and distinctive mood Mandoki's directorial personality encourages do evoke all that he wants to express, which is considerably more than can be found in a conventional film. Not only does he appreciate subtleties of character, subtleties which he illuminates in order to redefine the audience's sense of what is and is not human limitation, but also he is very observant of cultural reality and the extent to which it is imposed, the extent to which it is unconsciously integrated within personality, and the extent to which it may be transcended. One such moment of transcendence, especially compelling in its execution, exemplifies the film's power of resonance. It is the startling, briefly glimpsed moment of lovemaking between Gaby and Fernando (in which she must wrench herself out of her chair and throw herself onto a hard floor). Almost every reviewer made glowing allusion to this scene, perhaps less because it is surprising than because it is so much more erotic and evocative of sexual passion than most conventional love scenes. Mandoki also displays a good sense of its reverberations on the whole, for the viewer's enhanced appreciation of Gaby forces a greater distance from the established point of view of the puritanical Florencia, who inevitably reacts to the affair with distaste.

Mandoki made the film in his native Mexico with a largely Mexican crew, but in English, and with backing from a company in the United States (Tri-Star) and the collaboration on both sides of the camera of an international group of artists. Among those participating, an especially inspired choice was Levin, who plays Gaby. Levin's professional career had been halted a decade earlier when she herself became afflicted with a neuromuscular disorder, Guillain-Barre syndrome, which caused near-total paralysis, but from which she ultimately recovered almost completely. It may be, as some observers have suggested, that the parallel between the experience of the actress and that of the character helped facilitate an especially convincing identification with deepened the reality of the interpretation. More important, though, in harmony with his broader ideas about the subject, Mandoki surely chose Levin because of her beauty, vibrancy and sensuality—all of which may have gained in intensity because of this opportunity for renewed expression of her art. The empathy that the actress solicits for her character derives from the viewer's active attraction to her unquenchable vitality, assertive creative spirit, and direct physical appeal. Indeed, the film's most indelibly seductive images are those of a barefoot Gaby typing with her toes.

Blake Lucas

Reviews
Films in Review. XXXIX, January, 1988, p. 41.
Los Angeles. XXXII, December, 1987, p. 295.
Los Angeles Times. November 13, 1987, VI, p. 10.
Macleans. C, November 30, 1987, p. 67.
The New York Times. October 30, 1987, p. C8.
Variety. CCCXXVIII, September 23, 1987, p. 26.
The Wall Street Journal. October 29, 1987, p. 30.

GARDENS OF STONE

Production: Michael I. Levy and Francis Coppola for Tri-Star Pictures; released by Tri-Star Pictures
Direction: Francis Coppola
Screenplay: Ronald Bass; based on the novel of the same name by Nicholas Proffitt
Cinematography: Jordan Cronenweth
Editing: Barry Malkin
Production design: Dean Tavoularis
Art direction: Alex Tavoularis; set decoration, Gary Fettis
Special effects: Robin Hauser
Makeup: Monty Westmore, Bernadette Mazur, and Brad Wilder
Costume design: Willa Kim and Judianna Makovsky
Sound: Richard Beggs
Music: Carmine Coppola
MPAA rating: R
Running time: 112 minutes

> *Principal characters:*
> Sergeant Clell Hazard ....James Caan
> Samantha Davis..................Anjelica Huston
> Sergeant Major Goody Nelson.....James Earl Jones
> Jackie Willow ....D. B. Sweeney
> Captain Homer Thomas ....Dean Stockwell
> Rachel Feld ....Mary Stuart Masterson
> Betty Rae ....Lonette McKee
> Sergeant Slasher Williams ...Dick Anthony Williams
> Lieutenant Webber ....Sam Bottoms
> Colonel Feld ....Peter Masterson
> Mrs. Feld ....Carlin Glynn

Although death and destruction seem to underscore virtually every scene in it, *Gardens of Stone* is a war film without combat. Unfolding primarily in and around the National Cemetery in Arlington, Virginia, director Francis Coppola's drama examines the Vietnam experience from the perspective of the Old Guard, a precision burial team that carries out ceremonial rituals on behalf of the young corpses that arrive daily from Southeast Asia.

The film bears little resemblance in style, tone, or scope to Coppola's other treatment of the Vietnam War, the spectacularly violent *Apocalypse Now* (1979). The earlier picture, patterned after Joseph Conrad's brooding, symbolic novella *Heart of Darkness* (1902), vividly showed the devastation of deep jungle warfare. *Gardens of Stone*, based on Nicholas Proffitt's generally realistic novel of the same name, demonstrates not the horrors of battle but the anxiety, frustration, and grief of career soldiers who wait for new assignments but get only new bodies to bury.

Through screenwriter Ronald Bass's treatment of the Proffitt story, Coppola structures his film around the burial of Jackie Willow (D. B. Sweeney), a former enlisted man who gets an officer's commission and eventually the Vietnam assignment for which he had hoped. Aside from brief glimpses of his funeral scene, Coppola tells the story in chronological flashback.

Private First Class Willow receives typically harsh treatment from the veterans at Fort Myer, Virginia, adjacent to Arlington, but even the most crass and critical among them can see that the young man is a cut above the other young soldiers newly assigned to the base. He is further set apart from the latter in that he wants nothing more than to go to Vietnam. He believes that one man in the right place can make a difference. His militant idealism catches the notice of Sergeant Clell Hazard (James Caan), a mild-mannered but tough combat veteran who once had been a close army buddy to Willow's father. Clell still loves the army but nevertheless voices some disillusionment with the way the brass has allowed a senseless war to continue without showing much eagerness to win it or give it sensible direction. He tries to tone down the youngster's urgency about personally contributing in Southeast Asia.

Having once been an army brat himself, novelist Proffitt has a keen ear and careful memory for the language of hard-drinking, aging non-coms. Bass's script retains much of the raucous, profane character of their speech. They are warriors who, when not fighting, play at being warriors, or simply play. Clell's chief partner in leisure is another old friend, the huge, black Sergeant Major Goody Nelson (James Earl Jones), a colossus of good nature with cavernous vocal tones that resonate through the barracks as he conducts inspection, effectively terrorizing most of the young troops he oversees.

Clell meets Samantha Davis (Anjelica Huston), an attractive reporter for *The Washington Post*, and for their first date they enjoy a homemade meal. They are joined that evening by Goody and his attractive friend, Betty Rae (Lonette McKee), an administrative assistant to Senator Sam Ervin. The ambiguities of political attitude expressed by the men take the liberal Samantha by surprise. The servicemen seem regretful that their kind is needed in the modern world, even though they readily admit their own dedication. Betty Rae, on the other hand, seems fairly conservative, even as she flashes her sultry smile.

The reporter, though distrustful and even intolerant of servicemen, begins to mellow, because she is physically attracted to Clell. The sergeant is clearly lonely (his wife left him long ago, taking their child) and relatively gentle. Their affair falters, however, when Clell accompanies Samantha on a news assignment and is reproached by an antiwar activist named Brubaker. Clell tries to calm the man but is virtually goaded into physically attacking him. The sergeant's extraordinary hand-to-hand combat skills quickly send Brubaker to the hospital. Samantha is shocked and disgusted, but eventually she and Clell reconcile.

When Jackie's father dies, Clell shares his grief and becomes, in a sense, his surrogate father. The veteran tries to dislodge from the youngster's mind the dream of performing significantly in combat, but Jackie's purpose grows stronger. While off duty, Jackie rekindles a relationship with Rachel Feld (Mary Stuart Masterson), the high school sweetheart who had broken up with him in the recent past. The tensions apparent at their reunion are explained when the young soldier picks her up for a dinner date. Her father is a former general who once had guaranteed Jackie an appointment to the United States Military Academy at West Point if he promised not to marry Rachel for four years. Rachel, knowing her father's reprehensibly aristocratic streak, had tried to convince Jackie that the bargain was false. She ultimately had forced him to make a choice between marrying her then and there or, effectively, marrying the army.

Jackie had not really understood then, but now he does. Before long they marry, despite Rachel's objections to his military commitment. Jackie goes to officer candidate school, receives his commission, and eventually gets shipped to Vietnam, which he describes in letters to her and to Clell. At the end of the flashback, the news arrives that he has been killed in action, and Clell condemns himself for not being able to exert more control on the youngster's preparedness. The funeral that started the film is then completed, and Lieutenant Jackie Willow's tombstone becomes the newest sprout in the Arlington "stone gardens."

At its best, *Gardens of Stone* presents an impressive pageantry of grief and lamentation which indirectly reflects the terrible waste of vigorous, youthful life. The scenes at Arlington, featuring the precision movements of the honor guard, the horse without rider, the flag-covered coffin are shot smoothly by cinematographer Jordan Cronenweth so that the overall effect of each is lasting. In the Arlington scenes, the film seems to commemorate centuries of bravery and honor, extending emotional respect for those present but remembering others like them.

At its worst, the film lags as a result of shoddy construction. Like Proffitt's original, Coppola's depiction of intensity in human relationships never gets beyond basic stages, because none of the relationships—aside from that between Clell and Goody—is ever effectively sustained. Neither Clell's romance with Samantha nor Jackie's with Rachel generates evidence of the power of friendship, let alone the fire of passion. It is the kind of multileveled story which requires the tightest economy of dialogue and a correct ordering of episodes—the way scriptwriter Daniel Taradash reworked the unwieldly James Jones novel *From Here to Eternity* (1951) in 1953.

Performance levels vary. As Jackie, D. B. Sweeney is pop-eyed and stiff when he should be, but also when he should not. Mary Stuart Masterson's Rachel, on the other hand, at times spells out the fierce love she carries, almost against her will, behind a façade of principled resistance. As the Behemoth of different wars, Jones plays Goody Nelson with rumbling delight and understanding, but he is clearly most comfortable when spewing barracks vulgarity or raising his big face to the ceiling in unbridled laughter. Caan's return to the screen after a five-year absence is for the most part a cautious, sensitive new beginning in the key role of Clell Hazard. Despite its errant script, Coppola's *Gardens of Stone* is in the main a disquieting study of the agonies of war, as seen from the last station of that agony.

Andrew Jefchak

Reviews
America. CLVI, June 20, 1987, p. 506.
American Film. XII, January, 1987, p. 72.
Commonweal. CXIV, May 22, 1987, p. 320.
Films in Review. XXXVIII, August, 1987, p. 423.
Los Angeles Times. May 8, 1987, VI, p. 1.
The New Republic. CXCVI, May 25, 1987, p. 24.
The New York Times. May 8, 1987, III, p. 32.
The New Yorker. LXIII, May 18, 1987, p. 84.
Newsweek. CIX, May 11, 1987, p. 79.
Time. CXXIX, June 15, 1987, p. 74.
Variety. CCCXXVII, May 6, 1987, p. 12.

THE GATE

Production: John Kemeny; released by New Century/Vista Film Company
Direction: Tibor Takacs
Screenplay: Michael Nankin
Cinematography: Thomas Vamos
Editing: Rit Wallis
Art direction: William Beeton; set decoration, Jeff Cutler and Marlene
    Graham
Special effects: Randall William Cook
Makeup: Craig Reardon
Music: Michael Hoenig and J. Peter Robinson
Song: Vincent Carlucci, "Love Will Find a Way"
MPAA rating: PG-13
Running time: 91 minutes

> *Principal characters:*
> Glen .... Stephen Dorff
> Al .... Christa Denton
> Terry .... Louis Tripp
> Mom .... Deborah Grover
> Dad .... Scot Denton

One should be grateful for good things where one finds them. Behind the rather routine horror-film scaffolding of *The Gate* lies a charming fantasy-fable about love. Amid the sex, violence, drugs, and rock and roll of nearly all the films which Hollywood aims at the "youth market" (a demeaning term which suggests images of children hung up like slabs of beef), one is occasionally fortunate to come across the work of filmmakers who are interested in something other than pandering. In *The Gate*, writer Michael Nankin and director Tibor Takacs have made a sincere attempt to say something shamelessly positive to and about young people and their relationships with one another and with their parents.

The film's protagonist, Glen (Stephen Dorff), lives in a comfortable suburban home with his mother (Deborah Grover), father (Scot Denton), and sixteen-year-old sister, Alexandra (Christa Denton), better known to all as "Al." Glen's family life is stable and what most viewers would consider normal: Dad works, Mom maintains the home, Glen goes to school and squabbles with Al. The boy is typical of young teenagers in another sense as well, insofar as he possesses an active imagination which focuses primarily on his hobby of launching toy rocket ships.

Sometimes Glen's fantasy causes problems for him and his family. His rocketry is often a nuisance, and his sleep is interrupted by nightmares. The first sequence of the film is in fact Glen's vision, which the viewer shares, of a grotesque tree that dwarfs his home. Glen awakens to find himself in familiar surroundings, but his dream proves to be prophetic. There is indeed a huge dead tree in the yard behind the family home. A crew of workmen uproot the tree, leaving in its place an impressively deep pit. The workmen fill the hole with soil, and it seems that their job is finished.

Glen's parents decide to take a vacation trip, leaving Al in charge of things at home. Glen has a skirmish of sorts with some of Al's friends, who want to take advantage of the parents' absence in order to throw a party. Al, however, recognizes the impropriety of her friends' attitudes and sides with her brother when two of her chums make fun of him.

So Glen and Al are alone in their house when the trouble begins. They discover that the hole left in their backyard when the tree was removed has reappeared; moreover, the seemingly bottomless pit gives off an eerie light, and later, swarms of ugly moths ascend from the depths of the chasm.

Glen seeks the expert advice and support of his bosom pal, Terry (Louis Tripp). Terry is innocently attracted to heavy-metal music and demonology. He wears a cut-off denim jacket emblazoned with the logo of a rock group called "The Killer Dwarfs"—a name whose irony will go unnoticed by the boys. Terry is fascinated by the pit in Glen's backyard, and its mysteries permit him to display his expertise. Terry recognizes that this hole in the ground is no ordinary hole: It is "the gate," a passageway from Hell to the surface of the Earth. Glen's friend makes this discovery by careful analysis of a song on a recording which he owns, an album released by a satanic band called Sacrifyx. Eventually, Terry comes to examine the pit and casually observes that Glen, Al, and he are dealing with demons.

As any viewer will guess, evil forces threaten the youngsters, gradually manifesting themselves in various forms. The kids attempt to take refuge in the house, but the walls of the home offer no resistance to the nastiness which has been freed from the bowels of the Earth. Ugly creatures beat at the windows at first, then appear beneath Glen's bed. These frightening manifestations, however, are only the beginning of the assault. It culminates with the invasion of the Demon Lord himself, a six-armed, four-eyed behemoth, accompanied by his minions, vicious little beasts with sharp teeth.

The final twenty minutes of *The Gate*, a pyrotechnical display of cinematic special effects (orchestrated by Randall William Cook and Craig Reardon), focus on young Glen's heroism. The Demon Lord not only makes a shambles of Glen and Al's home, but the evil being also threatens to make off with Terry and Al—until Glen comes to the rescue. Terry and Al are saved by Glen's willingness to lay down his life for his sister. "Love Will Find A Way," as one of the film's background songs explains.

Certainly the work of the young principal players of *The Gate* has much to do with the film's success. Dorff, Denton, and Tripp unaffectedly portray average kids, occasionally given to mischief but, by and large, kind, thoughtful, and responsible. One has the sense that director Takacs, a Canadian for whom *The Gate* represents his initial major American release, had the insight to stand back and allow these talented youngsters to do their jobs.

Nankin's script and the film's special effects exploit the blurred distinction between nightmare and reality, especially from the perspective of a small child—although adult viewers are easily drawn into the narrative and visual traps as well, primarily through cinematographer Thomas Vamos' liberal use of point-of-view shots. Given the traditions of the genre within which Nankin is working and the surreal atmosphere that the film establishes, it is pointless to quibble about the credibility of the plot or to poke fun at the special effects, which are, in fact, quite nicely done.

The Gate features some familiar horror-film set-ups. The opening sequence recalls the settings of such films as *Halloween* (1978) and *The Exorcist* (1973) insofar as one is placed in middle-class suburbia and in a milieu of secure-family life into which the menace of evil will intrude. In addition, *The Gate*'s first sequence manipulates the viewer in a fashion which is almost ritualistic to horror-film aficionados. One is quickly introduced to the dream motif of the film, and, at the same time, one becomes aware of the fears of the film's protagonist.

What sets *The Gate* apart from run-of-the-mill teen horror films is that Glen and his sister, despite the usual sibling horseplay, truly care for each other. How many adolescent girls go shopping and return, as Al does, with a surprise gift for little brother? Even more unusual—in contrast to the classic teen film in which mean, negligent adults victimize young people—is the fact that the parents of Glen and Al expect responsible behavior from their children and are not afraid to exert authority—which the children welcome. The walls of their home are covered with portraits of smiling faces. Even Terry, whose parents seem to play little role in his life (the viewer never sees Terry's father), is a dependable boy and a loyal friend, given only to rather quirky preoccupations.

The Gate is accurately rated PG-13: Some of the film's dream sequences and especially the film's final twenty minutes are probably too unsettling for small children. Older youngsters, however, will profit from the film's lessons, and *The Gate* will have surprising appeal for everyone except those who thirst for another slasher film.

Gordon Walters

Reviews
Chicago Tribune. May 18, 1987, V, p. 3.
Cinema Canada. July, 1987, p. 25.
Los Angeles Times. May 19, 1987, VI, p. 3.
People Weekly. XXVII, June 8, 1987, p. 10.

THE GLASS MENAGERIE

Production: Burtt Harris; released by Cineplex Odeon Films
Direction: Paul Newman
Screenplay: Tennessee Williams
Cinematography: Michael Ballhaus
Editing: David Ray
Production design: Tony Walton
Art direction: John Kasarda; set decoration, Susan Bode
Music: Henry Mancini
MPAA rating: PG
Running time: 134 minutes

> *Principal characters:*
> Amanda Wingfield ....Joanne Woodward
> Tom Wingfield ....John Malkovich
> Laura Wingfield....................Karen Allen
> Jim O'Connor...................James Naughton

Tennessee Williams' *The Glass Menagerie* (1944) is one of those American stage classics, like Eugene O'Neill's *Long Day's Journey into Night* (1956) and Arthur Miller's *Death of a Salesman* (1949), that is a temptation to actors and directors. The rich material encourages exploration and lures formidable artists into attempting definitive interpretations, or at least very worthwhile ones. These plays are given far more than what would be a normal number of productions—even for American classics—and not only on stage but also on screen.

The original New York production of the play in 1945 is part of Broadway's legend because of the comeback performance of Laurette Taylor in the role of a meddling mother whose son works in a warehouse but writes poetry in a cabinet of the men's room during his breaks, and whose shy daughter limps and spends much of her time alone with her collection of glass animals. This odd family had been abandoned by its husband-father almost sixteen years before. A considerable amount of the mother's energy is spent worrying about her daughter's future; at one point she importunes her son to bring home for his sister a gentleman caller, who proves to be the fourth and final character in this small-cast play. These characters, according to many commentators, have great vitality because this is Williams' most autobiographical and, hence, most deeply felt play.

The work continues to stand up under the frequent explorations and renditions of major interpreters. Among them have been Gertrude Lawrence and Jane Wyman (who played the mother and daughter in the 1950 film), Shirley Booth, Helen Hayes, Katharine Hepburn, Eddie Dowling,

Kirk Douglas, Hal Holbrook, Michael Moriarty, and Sam Waterston. As a Mozart piano concerto is inexhaustible and reveals different rewarding facets depending on whether it is played by Murray Perahia or Vladimir Ashkenazy, or any of a host of other pianists, so *The Glass Menagerie* shines in different ways depending on who is in its cast and who is its director. Although the great Geraldine Page turned down opportunities to play the principal role in this particular film adaptation, saying that she had seen Laurette do it and had nothing to add, it is right that such a gem be displayed again and again in various revealing settings. Paul Newman's film production is a worthwhile addition to past interpretations of the work, and like most of them it has its particular strengths and weaknesses.

The success of any version depends to a great extent on the performance of the actress playing the mother, Amanda Wingfield (Joanne Woodward). A great role, like a great concerto, has its delicate and its boisterous passages; the character of Amanda ranges from moments of tender concern to moments of frustrated rage. Woodward is deeply moving when Amanda is most vulnerable; one wishes she were tougher when Amanda is fighting to have her way.

When her son Tom (John Malkovich) is driven by her incessant nagging to a vituperative outburst which culminates in his calling her "an ugly babbling old witch," Amanda's hurt is palpable. Although it is easy to understand the frustration and sense of claustrophobic hopelessness that has caused Tom, finally, to erupt, one's sympathy by the end of that segment is also strongly with Amanda. One cares about both characters because they care about each other, even while they fight. There is no joy taken when one succeeds in wounding the other.

Woodward has other poignantly realized moments such as when Amanda admits to Tom that she loved his father, and on the night before the gentleman caller's visit when she has her daughter (Karen Allen) wish on the moon for happiness and good fortune. At such times the intensity of her caring is most apparent.

In another segment, Amanda comes home and finds Laura pretending to practice her typing after just learning that Laura has not attended typing classes for six weeks. The expression on Woodward's face promises a storm, but the storm never comes, at least, not with the fullness of her gentler moments. Hepburn's raspy voice and feistiness, in a film of the play made for television in 1973, made her bouts of will with her children more effective moments of dramatic conflict. Hepburn, too, can be eminently vulnerable, and that combination proved highly satisfactory in this role. She is perhaps the best of the screen's Amandas.

Woodward, despite her excellent work, does not make the role of Amanda her personal property. Another member of this fine cast, however, Malkovich, has remarkably taken possession of not one but two classic roles in the American dramatic repertoire: Biff in *Death of a Salesman*, which he did on Broadway and television with Dustin Hoffman, and now Tom in *The Glass Menagerie*.

Malkovich's own interesting idiosyncrasies serve well the character of Tom, who is an eccentric malcontent wanting to free himself from mundane necessities so that he can create literature. Nonconformist and artist that he is, Malkovich was able to find strong emotional connections between himself and that part of Tom. The several monologues that Tom delivers, however, pose a problem: All of them are potentially awkward for the medium of film, and some of the phrases they contain sound literary or theatrical to the 1988 ear, rather than conversational. Tom is a poet, however, and Malkovich reads these phrases as if he were composing, trying out words to describe what he sees and thinks. This approach keeps intact the seamless reality of an outstanding performance.

Allen as Laura looks right for the role and is consistently credible. The gentleman caller, Jim O'Connor (James Naughton), effectively goes through a transition from condescension and superficial politeness to a higher plane of truthfulness and concern for Laura's needs.

These four actors achieved their results under the nurturing guidance of Newman, who has developed considerably as a director since his bland television film *The Shadow Box* (1980), a production that somehow managed virtually to obliterate many of the searing dramatic clashes that made the stage production of the Michael Cristofer play so satisfying. Newman now seems to be going through the process of building his cinematic vocabulary. Sometimes he chooses devices that are too artful or too literal for his purpose, as when he unnecessarily bottom lights Tom's face during parts of the tirade in which he describes himself as an underworld character who goes to opium dens. At other times, though, he finds exactly the right device to say something about a character or a moment, as when he alternates circular tracking shots—first one way and then the other—around Laura to suggest the inner turbulence she feels because she realizes that her soon-to-be gentleman caller might be the same Jim O'Connor she had a crush on in high school.

Problems of adaptation are inevitably discussed whenever a film is made from a play. When the actor playing Tom in a stage production of *The Glass Menagerie* says that the play is not realistic (as he does in his opening monologue), he is preparing the audience to accept the essential truth of characters, situations, and settings even though stage presentation is necessarily artificial. Film is a realistic medium, however. The audience expects to see not an actual two-dimensional painting of a housefront, but rather a moving picture of an actual three-dimensional building. The first frames of this film, in fact, show the front of an old decaying and vacant city tenement with its shabby stoop and the rubbish-littered pavement along its side. It has never been represented this way on stage, and probably could not be, because the action in a flash must shift back to the time in which the building was lived in by the Wingfield family. Why, then, keep the lines that say the play is not realistic when it is necessarily being presented realistically? Newman and Tony Walton, who was responsible for the production design and costumes, have taken pains to achieve a wonderful evocation of period; it was appropriate that they did so. Desire to be faithful to the text should not have prohibited the excision of lines that are inappropriate for the medium being used.

Whatever quibbles one might have with aspects of interpretation, the film's strengths and its fidelity to its source would make it an excellent intro- duction for students unfamiliar with the play. More than that, the always credible, sometimes powerful, sometimes touching performances of the four players make this film worth repeated viewings by avid filmgoers and by admirers and students of the drama of Tennessee Williams.

Cono Robert Marcazzo

Reviews
Films in Review. XXXIX, January, 1988, p. 44.
Glamour. LXXXV, December, 1987, p. 159.
Los Angeles Times. November 4, 1987, VI, p. 1.
Macleans. C, September 28, 1987, p. 42.
The New Republic. CXCVII, November 23, 1987, p. 25.
The New York Times. October 23, 1987, p. C14.
People Weekly. XXVIII, November 23, 1987, p. 14.
The Times Literary Supplement. January 22, 1988, p. 86.
Variety. CCCXXVII, May 13, 1987, p. 139.
The Wall Street Journal. October 21, 1987, p. 34.

GOOD MORNING, VIETNAM

Production: Mark Johnson and Larry Brezner; released by Touchstone Pictures
Direction: Barry Levinson
Screenplay: Mitch Markowitz
Cinematography: Peter Sova
Editing: Stu Linder
Production design: Roy Walker
Art direction: Steve Spence; set decoration, Tessa Davies
Music: Alex North
MPAA rating: R
Running time: 120 minutes

Principal characters:

Adrian Cronauer	Robin Williams
Edward Garlick	Forest Whitaker
Tuan	Tung Thanh Tran
Trinh	Chintara Sukapatana
Lieutenant Steve Hauk	Bruno Kirby
Sergeant Major Dickerson	J. T. Walsh
General Taylor	Noble Willingham

Good Morning, Vietnam seems to be the title of two films; one stars Robin Williams (he received an Oscar nomination for Best Actor), and the other is a treatment of the "Vietnam Experience." That the two projects are in fact the same film is an idea that does not seem to be palatable to many pundits and critics. Perhaps a full frontal assault on the sensibilities of the audience and a manifest disregard for chronology and rules are the best way to illuminate those tumultuous times. Like most films that appear to span genres, *Good Morning, Vietnam* is vulnerable to the scorekeepers but endearing to filmgoers.

The film's roots are, on the one hand, the iconoclastic military comedy as exemplified by television's *M*A*S*H** and *The Phil Silvers Show*, and on the other, the period pieces of director Barry Levinson (*Diner*, 1982; *The Natural*, 1984; and *Tin Men*, 1987, reviewed in this volume). In those earlier films, however, there was an understanding of choices that people have to make, even if they are not heroic. In *Good Morning, Vietnam*, such sympathy is lacking, and it follows more faithfully the cynicism of its military predecessors.

Good Morning, Vietnam is filled with disrespect, if not contempt, for officers, but not for all of them, just 98 percent. In general, it is a contempt for regulations, that brass-plated code of rules, and for those to whom the regulations become the commandments. The heroes are those who can subvert, or at least circumvent, the principles and reveal the foolishness of those who would promulgate the absurdity. Indeed, the film seems to veer off course to take a gratuitous poke at Richard Nixon, not the President or the Vice President, or even the candidate, but at the projection of his image onto the collective conscious of the Vietnam generation. When the film becomes a standard army comedy, it is buoyed up by the exuberance of Williams' comedy, not by any intrinsic humor (which is not in itself a flaw). A film which seeks to evoke need not be original; on the contrary, it should be true to its roots, only exaggeratedly.

As an army comedy, *Good Morning, Vietnam* is a classic confrontation of the good-hearted individual against a system, at once absurd and pernicious but, unlike *Tin Men*, there is little sympathy for the system and especially not for the bosses or enforcers, personified here by Sergeant Major Dickerson (J. T. Walsh) and Lieutenant Hauk (Bruno Kirby), both of whom are veterans of Levinson's productions. They are the stereotypical, humorless bureaucratic drudges, venal and self-serving, dedicated to enforcing senseless rules merely to maintain a perverse order. They are held in check (and in contempt) by their superior, the avuncular General Taylor (Noble Willingham). There is humor inherent in the confrontation between man and bureaucratic juggernaut; what distinguishes the humor here from the run-of-the-mill variety is the intensity of Williams' responses and the overreaching venality, including sending Adrian Cronauer (Williams) into an ambush and certain death. It does not seem fair that Cronauer will have to pay with his life for his irreverence, even if he has been attacking the lifestyle chosen by Hauk and Dickerson. It is indicative of the film that it restricts its magnanimity to the Vietnamese and the grunts in the rice paddies. It is an indication of the film, not an indictment, as there is no requirement that a film, like life, must be fair.

The most compelling aspect of the film is its ability to portray the day-to-day life of the soldiers, who, although scared and lonely, continue soldiering. The men were not constantly at war, but they were away from home, and they needed reminders of both. In the street scenes and with rock and roll, Levinson depicts a sense of the awesome and terrifying adventure of being on the edge of death. These pastiches are reminiscent of both "Music Television" (MTV) and the solid recreations of times past that Levinson so successfully achieved in *The Natural*, *Young Sherlock Holmes* (1985), *Tin Men*, and *Diner*. It is a success because it allows even the nonveteran to sense the alienation of the GI and the Vietnamese from what their situations had become.

If there is an underlying theme to this film, it is the need not only to make sense of an absurd situation but also to establish a comfortable milieu. Levinson paints and orchestrates this environment, but he stops short of scripting it, whether by design or by omission, one cannot say. Nevertheless, it is a powerful concept, one made more graphic by his depiction of the Vietnamese and their cities and towns (the scenery is more than occasionally breathtaking), as well as the evident self-alienation of Cronauer. He is a man possessed on the air; he is disaffected as a soldier and as an American, yet he tries to enlist his classful of Vietnamese in such quintessential Americana as invective, scatological abuse, and baseball. There is no point in trying to analyze the motivations of Cronauer, as it is difficult to distinguish Williams from Cronauer. That there is or was a real Cronauer is a red herring; the character works because the viewer knows Williams to be wild. In the film, he does not play against type, a form used all too often to create characterizations by contrast. He plays true to form, and thus confuses those who have difficulty distinguishing between characters and actors, who are themselves recognizable characters. Williams may be a wild man, a maniac, but he is under control, and so is Cronauer. Part of the tension of the film emanates from the mixing of the Cronauer side of the character with the Williams side; more accurately, it is the tension in both the Williams actor and the Cronauer character between the rational and the hysteric parts. It should be argued that if either of them were out of control, then neither would have achieved what they have—a measure of respect from their peers and an acknowledgement of their ability and reliability from their backers and higher ups.

The Cronauer-Williams identity crisis is an offscreen affair; it has echoes on the screen, however, in the character of Tuan (Tung Thanh Tran), who is both a friend to Cronauer and a Viet Cong operative. The relationship between Cronauer and Tuan is central to the plot because it defines Cronauer's position in relation to the Vietnamese. Tuan is the man who introduces Cronauer to native food, allows him to meet his sister Trinh (Chintara Sukapatana), and eventually is the reason that Cronauer has to leave Vietnam. He makes it possible for Cronauer to see and experience the real Vietnam as well as the untouched one, but like the American soldiers who will not tolerate Tuan's presence in their bar, Cronauer is consistently being reminded that he too is out of place and unwanted.

To a lesser extent, Trinh is also troubled by her places in both the old country and the new. She professes to admire the old ways and traditions, yet she is learning English, the language of a culture whose presence in her country will be brief, though troubling. The viewer does not learn more about her other than that she is a devoted daughter and family member. Her role in the film is more substantial because of her powerful yet understated performance.

One of the bravura performances of the film is that of Forest Whitaker, who portrays Cronauer's orderly, Edward Garlick. The role is that of the young innocent who is not destined to be part of the establishment, but not ready to rebel. His style and his oversize shape perfectly fit into the part of the foil or straight man.

It is not the romantic entanglement that is the heart of the film; rather, it is the more traditional romantic relationship between the individual and the self and the individual and the nation. The Romantic Age was a time of nationalism, and a time of the hero, of individualism and of individual nations. The idea of war and the portrayal of war was essentially a Romantic one; the major characters in the film are propelled into their destinies by nonrational drives. Cronauer is not acting rationally when he upsets his superiors and is far more off-the-wall with them than he is in private. It is his personal revolt against a system; his own search for heroism. His persecutors in Armed Forces Radio, Hauk and Dickerson, are more the kind of people who would continue fighting the Civil War than the sort who would write the Declaration of Independence—they hold very romantic ideals about how life works, not rational ones. That the viewer does not see any internal conflict in them is unfair, but it is going to be a long time before a bureaucrat is portrayed kindly, especially since functionaries do not tend to write, produce, direct or in any way serve in a creative capacity.

It is also a romantic notion to think rhapsodically about one's homeland and customs. The themes of nationalism and nostalgia for a passing culture are explored through the characters of Tuan and Trinh. More pointedly, however, it was also Cronauer who wanted to believe in a country and be part of some mythologically good place, but could not fit in. Both Cronauer and Williams realize that it is impossible to idealize a country that seems to consist of productive efficiency and ruthless consumerism. There are no possibilities for Wagnerian myths from that material, and hence no fodder for dreams and visions.

Director Levinson has a feel for the gulf between what one wants to believe and how one is forced to live. The 1960's was a time of coming to grips with the concept of ideals. How could the United States be a land of the free when American soldiers were dying so that some other Americans might be almost free; how could it be a land of opportunity when there was official poverty? In *Tin Men* and *Diner*, Levinson tackled the knotty question of how one lives a life of shortened horizons. If one's job is to sell shoddy aluminum siding, realizing that it is more than a job but a calling, how does one make peace with the soul? Levinson's antidote suggests that one act a little crazy, both to relieve the tension and to show the disparity between how one lives life and what options there are in life. Levinson is superb at casting people whose inner workings and public *personas* are consonant with that issue; certainly Williams is one who needs craziness to cope, and there is little question that Richard Dreyfuss and Danny De Vito are of the same cloth.

In the end, the film seems less directed than produced, but that should not be taken as a criticism of Levinson. It is perhaps too much to ask of anyone but a specialist to be able to analyze with dispassionate passion the maelstrom that was Vietnam. Levinson's ambiguity and confusion are appropriate to the situation; a more unified image would be too personal to view. The film makes its box office as an army comedy; it makes its mark by its tone and the style of its players.

Richard Strelitz

Reviews

Commonweal. CXV, January 29, 1988, p. 49.
Glamour. LXXXVI, March, 1988, p. 253.
Los Angeles Times. December 25, 1987, VI, p. 1.
The New Republic. CXCVIII, February 8, 1988, p. 26.
The New York Times. December 23, 1987, p. C11.
The New Yorker. LXIII, January 11, 1988, p. 78.
People Weekly. XXIX, January 18, 1988, p. 8.
Time. CXXX, December 28, 1987, p. 74.
Variety. CCCXXIX, December 23, 1987, p. 15.
The Wall Street Journal. December 24, 1987, p. 5.

GOTHIC

Origin: Great Britain
Production: Penny Corke for Virgin Vision; released by Vestron Pictures
Direction: Ken Russell
Screenplay: Stephen Volk
Cinematography: Mike Southon
Editing: Michael Bradsell
Production design: Christopher Hobbs
Art direction: Michael Buchanan
Makeup: Pat Hay
Costume design: Victoria Russell
Music: Thomas Dolby
MPAA rating: R
Running time: 90 minutes

> *Principal characters:*
> Mary Godwin .... Natasha Richardson
> Percy Bysshe Shelley .... Julian Sands
> Lord Byron .... Gabriel Byrne
> Claire Clairmont .... Myriam Cyr
> Dr. Polidori .... Timothy Spall

Ken Russell began his directorial career in the early 1960's with a series of biographical films for British television, examining the lives of Sir Edward Elgar, Frederick Delius, and Isadora Duncan, among others. On the big screen, he has offered highly stylized impressions of Pyotr Tchaikovsky, in *The Music Lovers* (1971); sculptor Henri Gaudier and writer Sophie Brzeska, in *Savage Messiah* (1972); Gustav Mahler, in *Mahler* (1974); Franz Liszt, in *Lisztomania* (1975); and Rudolph Valentino, in *Valentino* (1977). The controversial filmmaker returns to real lives in *Gothic*, and although he has called this depiction of Romantic writers a horror film rather than a biography, it continues his obsession with the neuroses of artists as it purports to explain how young Mary Wollstonecraft Godwin Shelley came to write *Frankenstein* (1818).

The setting is the Villa Diodati in Switzerland, in 1816, and *Gothic* opens with tourists looking through telescopes at the summer home of the notorious Lord Byron (Gabriel Byrne), described by one as "mad, bad, and dangerous to know." The tourists hope to catch a glimpse of the adultery and incest they know to be occurring in the poet's villa; the irony is that even more unconventional behavior is about to take place.

Byron is soon joined by his friend Percy Bysshe Shelley (Julian Sands); Mary Godwin (Natasha Richardson), Shelley's mistress and future wife; and

Claire Clairmont (Myriam Cyr), Mary's stepsister and Byron's pregnant lover. As they arrive, Shelley is pounced upon by young admirers, and throughout the film, he and Byron behave like a pair of spoiled, self-obsessed rock stars. Byron even greets his guests by reciting his poetry. (Russell has covered this territory before, having presented Franz Liszt as a pop idol.)

Gothic is seen from the point of view of Mary Godwin, the most innocent and sane of the protagonists. She is made uneasy by Byron's kissing Shelley on the forehead, by the goat her host keeps indoors, and by Dr. Polidori (Timothy Spall), Byron's homosexual friend who tempts confrontation by calling Shelley "the greatest English poet of his generation." Mary's dilemma is to be both a willing participant—up to a point—in the ensuing decadence and a detached, though not impartial, observer. Russell, never one for subtlety, emphasizes that Mary is out of her element with a shot of fish flapping about in an empty pool.

Byron asks his guests, "Is fear a game?" During the night the characters use ghost stories, sex, and drugs—Shelley is addicted to laudanum—to frighten one another and themselves. Byron is the leader, seemingly trying to discover if he can destroy the others before he annihilates himself. Claire refers to his clubfoot as a cloven hoof, and it is clear that Russell and screenwriter Stephen Volk see him as devilish, though perhaps as less evil than possessed by demons of his own imagining. Byron's influence on the behavior of the others can be seen when Shelley climbs naked onto the roof during a violent thunderstorm.

Byron and Shelley say that they are bored with life, and everyone is obsessed with death in different ways: Polidori with thoughts of suicide; Byron with Augusta, his dead, beloved half sister; Mary with the premature infant fathered by Shelley. After Byron humiliates him, Polidori attempts to kill himself several times. While making love to a maid, Byron has her wear a mask of Augusta. Shelley, more than half in love with easeful death, says that he can smell the grave. Mary has visions of the deaths of the others.

As the night progresses, the fears of the five have been so heightened that none can separate reality from hallucination. Their worse nightmares have seemingly come true, especially for Mary, who sees Henry Fuseli's painting *The Nightmare* (1781), depicting a demon on the chest of a sleeping woman, come alive. (Fuseli was a close friend of her mother, Mary Wollstonecraft.) Mary, Shelley, and Polidori encounter another creature, the embodiment of their fears. More than anything, Mary dreads the future, saying that the creature will see them to their deaths.

Russell is often criticized for being out of control. The chaos in *Gothic*, however, is entirely that of the characters, since the director creates strong images to unify the film's many elements. The persistent rain and lightning, doors that close by themselves, and creatures such as rats, snakes, and leeches appearing in unlikely places are appropriate for setting the mood for a horror film in which anything is likely to happen. Mary's falling in the mud upon her arrival at the villa prefigures her being besmirched by the events of the night. Shelley's bathing his face in a bowl of goldfish foreshadows his death by drowning. A suit of armor with a huge phallus underscores the use of sex as a weapon. A dead fetus emphasizes the obsession with death and the premature demises of Shelley and Byron.

Early in *Gothic*, Claire sings, "I Died for Love." From *Women in Love* (1970) to *Crimes of Passion* (1984), Russell's films deal with the pain and often-fatal effects of love. Claire loves Byron, but he considers her merely a momentary diversion. Polidori also loves the brooding poet but is foolish enough to think that his affection may be returned. Mary loves Shelley but worries that he may care as much for Claire or Byron as for her, realizing that he is too wrapped up in himself to love her deeply. There is no reason to disbelieve Byron when he says that he loves no one; he prefers longing for his lost Augusta.

This close relationship between love and death is perfect for an examination of Russell's favorite subject: the anguish of the artist. He implies that Byron and Shelley live dissolutely not as an escape from the agony of creating poetry but as a means of living life to its limits to have the understanding to create great art. Mary is not performing unintentional research that will lead to *Frankenstein*; she is experiencing, in Russell's view, that pain necessary for the creation of her novel.

"My story is a story of creation," says Mary, and creation is the major subject of *Gothic*. The film constantly makes observations about at least three types of creation: childbirth, art, and God. (Polidori both loves and fears religion.) Creation, as seen by Russell and Volk, is agonizing and mysterious. Mary says that creation, whether of children or art, is a form of punishment. Neither mother nor artist can be certain about what has been created.

Russell and his collaborators are clearly not that interested in historical accuracy. The director twists the truth about his subjects to fit his vision of them. The character with whom he most identifies then is the demon-ridden Byron, who finds no solace in either art or decadence. As an explanation of how *Frankenstein* came to be written, *Gothic* may be even more inaccurate than the account given at the beginning of James Whale's *The Bride of Frankenstein* (1935), but that is of no concern to Russell. He is interpreting lives rather than re-creating them.

Since *Gothic* is concerned as much with mood as with theme, the work of production designer Christopher Hobbes, art director Michael Buchanan, and cinematographer Mike Southon is important for establishing and maintaining the claustrophobic tension engulfing the characters. All do excellent jobs of transforming the country house in Hertfordshire where *Gothic* was filmed into a vision of hell.

Music is also important to this horrific mood, but composer Thomas Dolby offers only what is often a bad electronic imitation of Sergei Prokofiev's score for *Alexander Nevsky* (1939) and at other times a compilation of camp horror effects. The music cannot compare with John Corigliano's similar but effective score for Russell's *Altered States* (1980).

A film such as *Gothic* poses problems for the actors since the temptation to overact is great. Unfortunately, Sands, Spall, and, especially, Cyr give in to temptation. Byrne's Byron has some presence—aided by his usually being positioned in the center of the frame—but not the charisma which might suggest poetic genius.

For *Gothic* to be bearable, Mary must be sympathetic, and Richardson displays a surprising dignity amid the debaucheries without holding herself aloof from the material. Though she lacks the beauty her mother, Vanessa Redgrave, had at her age, Richardson has the same ability to convey intelligence and command attention. She is also refreshingly unselfconscious and unmannered, a major attribute in a Russell film.

Gothic's reviewers have drawn many parallels between it and *The Devils* (1971), Russell's most sex-and-violence-laden film, but the work it most recalls is *Dante's Inferno*, his 1967 television treatment of the Pre-Raphaelites. With his addiction to laudanum and obsession with his dead wife, Dante Gabriel Rossetti resembles both Shelley and Byron. Say what he might about *Gothic* as a horror film, Russell cannot deny that it continues his frequently enthralling concern with the excesses of the artist.

Michael Adams

Reviews
America. CLVI, May 30, 1987, p. 445.
Chicago Tribune. May 22, 1987, VII, p. 39.
Los Angeles Times. April 24, 1987, V, p. 1.
New Statesman. CXIII, February 27, 1987, p. 24.
The New York Times. April 10, 1987, p. C16.
Newsweek. CIX, April 27, 1987, p. 79.
People Weekly. XXVII, April 20, 1987, p. 14.
Time. CXXIX, April 20, 1987, p. 76.
The Wall Street Journal. April 21, 1987, p. 36.
The Washington Post. May 6, 1987, p. B11.

HIGH TIDE

Origin: Australia
Production: Sandra Levy for Hemdale Film Corporation; released by Tri-Star Pictures
Direction: Gillian Armstrong
Screenplay: Laura Jones
Cinematography: Russell Boyd
Editing: Nicholas Beauman
Production design: Sally Campbell
Art direction: Ian Allen
Costume design: Terry Ryan
Sound: Ben Osmo
Music: Mary Moffiatt and Ricky Fataar
MPAA rating: PG-13
Running time: 101 minutes

Principal characters:
Lilli . . . . Judy Davis
Bet . . . . Jan Adele
Ally . . . . Claudia Karvan
Mick . . . . Colin Friels
Col . . . . John Clayton
Tracy . . . . Monica Tropaga
Lester . . . . Frankie J. Holden
Mary . . . . Toni Scanlon
Jason . . . . Marc Gray
Michelle . . . . Emily Stocker
Mechanic . . . . Mark Hembrow

High Tide represents the first teaming of director Gillian Armstrong and actress Judy Davis since the 1980 release of *My Brilliant Career*. In *High Tide*, Davis plays Lilli, a singer who has spent most of her adult life on the road. Fourteen years before the film's action, she had given birth to a daughter, Ally (Claudia Karvan). Overwhelmed by grief after her husband's subsequent death, however, Lilli had relinquished the child to her mother-in-law, Bet (Jan Adele), and thrown herself into the life of a traveling musician.

The film's early scenes crosscut between mother and daughter. It opens in a noisy nightclub where the center of attention is a singularly bad Elvis Presley imitator and his three wigged backup girls. Lilli is one of these. Next, the viewer gets a brief glimpse of Ally, lying in a shallow tidal pool in her wet suit. She is a surfer who loves the ocean with intense passion.

Next, Lilli reappears with her coperformers. Her mischievous razzing of her boss, Lester (Frankie J. Holden), soon costs her her job. Declaring defiantly that she is glad to be "free again," she walks out to find that her car will not start.

Ally lives with Bet, a fish-factory worker, in a trailer park in New South Wales. She is discovering boys, one boy in particular, Jason (Marc Gray), whom she has taken to kissing behind an old bus. She is a lively and charming girl who likes nothing more than to go to the disco with her friends. Bet, however, is a protective guardian and worries about such places. She is more comfortable having Ally follow her and her boyfriend, Col (John Clayton), to the local club, where she sings American songs in talent shows. One of these shows takes place on the same night as the Elvis routine, and Ally sees for the first time the woman who is her mother.

By the next evening, Lilli has been fired and her car has been towed to a local shop; she proceeds to rent a trailer at the park where Ally and Bet live. Ally finds her in the public bathroom under a sink, drunk and singing Bob Dylan's "Dark Eyes." As Ally and Jason help Lilli back to her trailer, Lilli pretends to know how to read palms and offers some free advice to the young lovers. Despite the woman's state, Ally likes her and begins to befriend her.

The next day, as Ally helps Lilli with her laundry, Bet appears and immediately recognizes her daughter-in-law. Bet's immediate reaction is terror: Lilli must have come to take her daughter away. Once Ally is safely out of earshot, Bet angrily confronts Lilli. She does not want the girl to know that Lilli is her mother (Bet had told the child that her parents died together). She even offers to pay Lilli's garage bill to get her on the road immediately.

Lilli, however, has no intention of taking her daughter; she has grown too fond of her freewheeling way of life to take on the responsibilities of motherhood again, and she assures Bet that she will not identify herself to Ally. Still, Lilli is intrigued by the strange twist of fate that has reunited her with her daughter.

When Lilli's car is fixed, the bill is twice what was quoted to her, and she cannot pay it. She reluctantly takes a striptease job at the club for the forthcoming weekend; the pay is enough to get her car back and to see her on the road again. Meanwhile, there is not much for her to do, and she finds herself surreptitiously watching her daughter at every opportunity—peeking through a window, or under a shower door as the girl shaves her legs.

A subplot in the film involves a handsome fisherman, Mick (Colin Friels), who has befriended Lilli. He is the only one in whom Lilli can confide throughout her ordeal, and it may be that his sole function in the film is to give Lilli a way to verbalize her thoughts. It is he who eventually tells Ally who Lilli is, and though the viewer could fault him for breaking Lilli's trust, the primary emotion evoked is relief that someone has finally revealed the truth.

In a memorable beach scene, Ally confronts her mother, who tries unsuccessfully to deny the relationship. Lilli has decided to follow Mick north, where he is planning to start a small business. At the last minute, Lilli invites her daughter to come along. The two are on the road in a matter of minutes. A few miles down the road, however, Ally insists on returning to say her farewells to Bet. The parting proves relatively painless; Bet has been expecting it.

On the road again, Lilli and Ally stop for dinner, and Lilli goes to the rest room as Ally finds a table. While Ally waits, Lilli returns to her car and starts it, ready to barrel on, leaving her daughter behind. She stops herself, though, and returns to Ally, hugging her from behind the chair, clearly happy with her choice.

Davis' role as Lilli is the center of the story. Critics repeatedly praised her strong performance. Had *High Tide* been more widely released in the United States, it is likely that Davis would have been nominated for an Academy Award.

High Tide distinguishes itself from other relationship films in being a very visual work. Much of the shooting was done on cloudy days to make use of the contrast between the lush greens and blues of the seaside and the desolate grays of the sky. More than making the film pretty, however, Armstrong, in conjunction with cinematographer Russell Boyd, utilized the camera poetically. Long, fluid tracking shots reflect Lilli's traveling life. One shot starts as a close-up of Bet watching Lilli and Ally drive away. Bet shrinks into the distance as the car pulls away and the camera turns its attention to the lines on the road, speeding by.

The significance of the title is never made totally clear. An analogy might be drawn between Ally's surfing and the opportunity which presents itself so unexpectedly to her mother. A moment's hesitation can cost the surfer a great wave, and at the trailer park Lilli faces just such a moment. In the end, she finds the courage to ride the wave.

Darrin Navarro

Reviews

Chicago Tribune. November 12, 1987, V, p.8.
The Hollywood Reporter. December 17, 1987, p. 3.
Los Angeles Times. December 18, 1987, VI, p. 29.
The New York Times. February 19, 1988, p. C5.
The New Yorker. LXIV, February 22, 1988, p. 84.
Newsweek. CXI, February 1, 1988, p. 54.
Time. CXXXI, February 1, 1988, p. 71.
Variety. CCCXXVII, May 20, 1987, p. 44.
The Wall Street Journal. March 3, 1988, p. 14.

HOLLYWOOD SHUFFLE

Production: Robert Townsend for Conquering Unicorn; released by Samuel
Goldwyn Company
Direction: Robert Townsend
Screenplay: Robert Townsend and Keenen Ivory Wayans
Cinematography: Peter Deming
Editing: W. O. Garrett
Art direction: Melba Katzman Farquhar
Choreography: Donald Douglass
Sound: William Shaffer
Music: Patrice Rushen and Udi Harpaz
MPAA rating: R
Running time: 82 minutes

    Principal characters:
    Bobby Taylor .... Robert Townsend
    Lydia...................... Anne-Marie Johnson
    Bobby's mother.................. Starletta Dupois
    Bobby's grandmother .... Helen Martin
    Stevie........................ Craigus R. Johnson
    Producer........................... Lisa Mende
    Donald/Jerry Curl .... Keenen Ivory Wayans
    Tiny .... Ludie Washington
    Mr. Jones .... John Witherspoon

Actor Robert Townsend had been working as an extra in New York, but the parts available to him, as a black actor, tended to be pimps, pushers, and street hoods. His frustration led to the inspiration of making a film to expose this situation, while giving himself a meaty and nonstereotypical role. He managed to put together $100,000 (including forty thousand dollars drawn from cash reserves on various credit cards, as he explained in the very amusing trailer) and write and direct a film satirizing this deplorable state of affairs.

With this minuscule budget and a repertory company of black actors, most of whom play multiple roles, Townsend's *Hollywood Shuffle* effectively illustrates the obstacle of stereoptyping facing many black actors. Through some clever writing and numerous witty inspirations, Townsend satirizes Hollywood and its treatment of blacks in film.

The story portrays many of the dreams and difficulties faced by aspiring actors of all races, as well as the struggles confronting many young black people in the 1980's. Bobby Taylor (Robert Townsend) is a young actor who lives at home with a working mother (Starletta Dupois), an outspoken grandmother (Helen Martin), and an adoring elementary-school-age brother (Craigus R. Johnson). He has a minimum-wage job at the Winky Dinky Dog hot dog stand—a job which his frequent auditions are increasingly jeopardizing, while his grandmother keeps telling him that the post office is hiring. He is dedicated, however, to succeeding as an actor, even if that means seeking a role in an exploitative film about a black gang (which seems about fifteen years out of date). This film's comically bizarre dialogue is an outrageous pastiche of black grammar and slang such as could be written only by someone whose knowledge of blacks comes solely from television and film stereotypes (as the screenwriter of the film-within-a-film admits sheepishly at the end).

Hollywood Shuffle traces Bobby's eventually successful quest for a role in this film, including his hilarious struggles with the aforementioned dialogue and his assorted confrontations with others in the entertainment industry. The climax of the plot comes during the shooting of this film-within-a-film, when Bobby, playing the embarrassingly stereotypical lead in front of his disgusted grandmother and aghast brother, realizes that he is selling out and quits the film. His integrity, however, does not destroy his career but simply takes it in another direction for the time being: Apparently following his grandmother's advice, he dons a letter carrier's uniform—but only to star in a Postal Service recruiting commercial. (Rather sloppily, this commercial and the film's acknowledgments refer to the United States Postal Service as the United States Post Office, a term superseded at the beginning of the 1970's, while Bobby's lines in this commercial refer to a "mailman" rather than a "letter carrier," the official and nonsexist label since the same decade.)

As with most satire, however, the thrust of the film lies less with the plot than with several witty set pieces that reveal Bobby's daydreams about the various consequences of his career choices and the problems of selling out. He sees himself in a commercial for a black acting school (run by white men), in which aspirants learn stereotypical black dialect as if they were studying the Queen's English at the Royal Academy of Dramatic Arts, and are coached in such standard black roles as slaves, butlers, criminals, and street hoods.

Then Bobby and a friend picture themselves as film critics à la Gene Siskel and Roger Ebert in a parody called "Sneakin' In at the Movies," commenting on takeoffs of Steven Spielberg's Indiana Jones epics (with an amazingly close Harrison Ford clone), Clint Eastwood's Dirty Harry series, *Amadeus* (1984), and finally a horror film called *Revenge of the Street Pimps*, the only one of the four which wins their unqualified acclaim. The humor here comes from seeing the familiar format with the criticism given in street dialect rather than the sophisticated banter of Rex Reed and company.

Bobby also sees himself starring in a black-and-white *film noir* detective picture—not as Sam Spade, for obvious reasons, but as Sam Ace. This sequence seems the least inspired and the most overextended.

A more devastating fantasy sequence stems from Bobby's increasing doubts about what his film role will contribute to the demeaning view of blacks. He imagines the National Association for the Advancement of Colored People (NAACP) heading a protest against him while even his loved ones turn away from him. These images, though humorous in the context of the film, lead him to make a serious statement by withdrawing from the film-within-a-film.

As has been noted by Stanley Kauffmann and others, this film is an indication that blacks have become confident enough about their position in society that they can laugh at it, without feeling constant anger and indignation. This is a trend evidenced by the success of George C. Wolfe's play *The Colored Museum*, a hilarious satire on various aspects of contemporary and past black life, dealing with the serious question of ethnic identity versus assimilation. Another film, *She's Gotta Have It* (1986), also offers a humorous portrayal of contemporary black life-styles, while disproving Robert Townsend's claim that he would probably be the only black male to kiss a woman on-screen in the mid-1980's.

She's Gotta Have It is also remarkable for its depiction of a lesbian character who is neither a laughingstock nor a villain. In contrast, *Hollywood Shuffle*, which seems to be arguing for greater sensitivity to minorities and a rejection of stereotyping, treats homosexuals as comic butts through action, characterization, and dialogue.

In fact, a gay filmmaker has much more cause to criticize Hollywood than a black filmmaker has. Numerous black actors are major stars—and not only Eddie Murphy, who is the film-within-a-film's model of a black man. Moreover, blacks have been appearing for years in roles as doctors, bank officials, courtroom personnel, spaceship crew members, store clerks, military officers, and so on—on television as well as in film. Granted, proportional to their numbers in the population at large, black people (as well as members of other minorities, racial or sexual) appear much less frequently in leading roles than Caucasians. Progress, however, is clearly being made: The most successful American television show of the 1980's, "The Cosby Show," features a middle-class black family headed by a doctor (the father) and a lawyer (the mother), certainly positive images for blacks and nonblacks to appreciate. At the same time, a film such as *The Color Purple* (1985), presenting an entirely black-oriented story, however much it was criticized on various counts, proved highly popular with audiences, while stars such as Whoopi Goldberg, Lou Gossett, Jr., and Gregory Hines headline in hit genre films that have a wide appeal.

Hollywood Shuffle has already helped Townsend's career significantly. His follow-up directing effort, *Raw* (1987), is a film of a live Eddie Murphy performance: a successful production that has further enhanced Townsend's bankability but has disappointed many admirers of *Hollywood Shuffle.*

Scott Giantvalley

Reviews
Ebony. XLII, July, 1987, p. 54.
Essence. XVIII, May, 1987, p. 28.
Film Comment. XXIII, March, 1987, p. 11.
Jet. LXXII, June 1, 1987, p. 58.
Los Angeles Times. April 24, 1987, V, p. 1.
The New Republic. CXCVI, May 4, 1987, p. 26.
The New York Times. March 20, 1987, p. C8.
Newsweek. CIX, April 6, 1987, p. 64.
Time. CXXIX, April 27, 1987, p. 79.
Variety. CCCXXVI, March 18, 1987, p. 16.

HOPE AND GLORY

Origin: Great Britain
Production: John Boorman; released by Columbia Pictures
Direction: John Boorman
Screenplay: John Boorman
Cinematography: Philippe Rousselot
Editing: Ian Crafford
Production design: Anthony Pratt
Art direction: Don Dossett; set decoration, Joan Woollard
Special effects: Phil Stokes
Costume design: Shirley Russell
Sound: Ron Davis
Music: Peter Martin
MPAA rating: PG
Running time: 112 minutes

> *Principal characters:*
> Bill Rohan .... Sebastian Rice-Edwards
> Grace Rohan .... Sarah Miles
> Clive Rohan .... David Hayman
> Dawn Rohan .... Sammi Davis
> Mac .... Derrick O'Connor
> Grandfather .... Ian Bannen

Hope and Glory, which won an Academy Award nomination for Best Picture, is Boorman's most personal film to date. It is entirely and very closely based on his childhood recollections of the London Blitz (war broke out when he was six) and was promoted as such. Faber and Faber's issuing of the script prefaced by Boorman's introduction and frank personal memoir heavily underscored his authorship of the film. Furthermore, the film itself not only advertises its autobiographical genesis but also offers wry glimpses of the filmmaker's mind in the making. Its child's-eye view of the Blitz (so much more subtly and lightly handled than in Steven Spielberg's overblown and costly epic *Empire of the Sun*, 1987; reviewed in this volume) has a specifically visual filmic playfulness. Along with young Bill Rohan (Sebastian Rice-Edwards), the viewer sees the family's suburban front room through the wrong end of Dad's binoculars, enjoys a knee-high voyeuristic perspective on scantily clad women trying on clothes, and experiences his guilty wish-and-fear dreams—of eliminating relatives and failing to show himself a man—rendered in black-and-white. That use of black and white is stylistically linked to episodes surely of the utmost importance to Boorman as auteur. Also in black and white are snippets from the Saturday afternoon matinee show that starts the film, and British romantic film offerings reminiscent of David Lean's *Brief Encounter* (1946). Little Bill Rohan is from the film's opening a child of motion pictures: He is undeterred by his grandfather's dismissal of a film crew they drive past near his riverside cottage in Shepperton (still a center of the British film industry)—"Playing silly buggers with a war on!"—and toward the film's close appropriately takes on the role of family photographer at his sister's wedding.

Hope and Glory opens immediately before the declaration of war: Filmfed Bill has not as yet experienced war's alternative spectacle. On that historic day, September 3, 1939, the family gathers respectfully around the radio. Immediately, as throughout the film, adult seriousness is punctured: Bill's sister Dawn (Sammi Davis) drowns out the broadcast with vociferous demands for her stockings. Perhaps the adults do not take war in quite the spirit the British government intended. For Bill's middle-aged father, Clive (David Hayman), the war offers an opportunity to flee drab suburban clerkdom in quest of a lost self image of manliness; for his mother, it brings relief from the presence of a husband she does not truly love and the rekindling of her romance with his best friend, whom she does love. Neither parent has quite lived up to the ideals of grace and gentility.

His father's registering for the military leaves Bill suspended between three separate worlds. On one side, there is the world of women: preeminently his romantic but Britishly decent mother, whose social standing slipped as a result of her marriage (a fine performance by Sarah Miles, whose casting cleverly plays off her upper-class image), and his hormone-crazed fifteen-year-old sister, whose abandonment to her Canadian soldier-lover on the nearest bombsite he accidentally witnesses. "War has put an end to decent things," the adults half confess, half exult.

The second world is school, that microcosm of British authoritarianism, here marvelously deflated. In one sequence, rebellious Bill receives a lashing on the hands. Intercut with shots of the head master's cane descending are shots of this same petty tyrant gleefully intoning, "Oh God, bring destruction on our enemies." Bill's class teacher seeks to instill belief in the dying Empire. Gesturing toward a map of the world, she barks: "Men are fighting and dying to save all the pink bits for you ungrateful little twerps." Air raids bring anarchic release and anarchic humor. Lessons continue in the shelter; with gas masks on, the multiplication table sounds like a flurry of obscene bodily noises.

The third world is the emotional center of the film: the all-boy world of the bomb sites as adventure playgrounds, rich in pickings of shrapnel, bullets, and lost possessions. Here, Bill experiences a ritual initiation into the gang that rules the ruins, one that is also a comic initiation into manhood and sexuality. "Repeat after me," the head tyke solemnly demands, "bugger off, sod, bloody." The ceremony over, all turn to the serious business of smashing rubble to the swelling strains of big band music.

Bill and the family experience the lurid beauty of the London sky at night, the terrors of the ill-built shelter in the garden, the excitement of the German pilot who alights on the vegetable allotments, the runaway barrage balloon that dances across their rooftops, and the relief of near-misses. Finally, their home too is bombed and burnt out. Abruptly, the old suburban life is over and the family evacuates to the mother's gracious childhood home—grandfather's Thameside cottage—and a pastoral idyll commences. It is the beautiful summertime; school is out. Only a chronic food shortage reminds them the war is merely a few miles away, in London. From the breakfast table, the eccentric grandfather (gloriously overplayed by Ian Bannen) attempts to shoot rodents in the garden. It is left to the magic of war, however, to provide food: A bomb explodes in the river, and Bill fills the family rowboat with fish.

While Bill learns the ways of the river, his teenage sister has learned more of the facts of life. Her lover has been posted, they have quarreled, and now she is pregnant. Nevertheless, a happy ending is in store for both, as her Canadian leaves his post (without permission) to marry her. The whole family gathers by the river, at peace for once, to celebrate. Bill's mother and her three sisters play music that floats across the lawn where the boy joins his grandfather and father (home on leave) for cricket. This ritual, an initiation into manhood and peculiarly British mysteries, ends with a triumph: Bill stumps his father by bowling him a devious "googly." At exactly the same moment, a female ritual is fulfilled when his sister goes into labor.

Then, it seems, the idyll is over. A protesting Bill is driven to school by his grandfather for the new term. Instead, a perfect day is in store: A stray bomb has flattened the school (a tyke streches his arms to the sky in an ecstasy of gratitude: "Thank you, Adolf!"). With a quiet voice-over, above the patriotic strains of "Land of Hope and Glory," the film closes: "My school lay in ruins, and the river beckoned with the promise of stolen days."

Hope and Glory might seem overloose and episodic, but, as even a synopsis reveals, it is actually carefully structured. It rises far above the level of quality television drama or even soap opera to which some imperceptive critics consigned it (overemphasising the fact that it was at one time a television project), though still showing traces of its earliest origins in the bedtime stories Boorman once told his own children. The production has none of the epic sweep of his *Excalibur* (1981), but it is not short on production values—Rosehill Avenue disappears into an infinity of ugly suburban boredom; the solid, million-dollar, 650-foot-long street set was the largest made for a British film since the war. Visually, the film recaptures the colors of wartime: drabness alternates with vivid lipstick and bomb-fire colors. The river scenes sparkle with light, and the grandfather's emerald lawn has upon it the glow of an Edwardian summer. At this point, the film veers dangerously close to whimsy. The visual idyll, however, is tempered by the crackle of dialogue. Throughout, music adds another layer to the comedy: patriotic strains (at the end), big band tunes (in the bomb sites), Richard Wagner's "Siegfried's Rhine Journey" (the German pilot's descent), and "The Dance of the Apprentices" from *Die Meistersinger* (the barrage balloon episode).

Though the film is ostensibly so very British and anti-British, its themes are actually universal. Boorman may have desired to express his affectionate admiration for his mother and her three sisters; what emerges on film is also more simply a male fascination with the mysterious female. The same applies to Bill's relationship with his father. The "googly" is the film's most important recurrent motif of initiation; it even appears in Bill's black-and-white fear dream of failing the test of manhood. The technique of throwing a "googly" was first taught Bill by his father on the day he went to war. Hence his moan, "I taught him how, and now he turns it against me." Grandfather's reply underlines the point: "It's the law of life. Cruel, isn't it?" Although the film's domination by female characters makes it superficially unlike most of Boorman's work, pre-eminently those trials of male endurance *Point Blank* (1967) and *Deliverance* (1972), its essential narrative structure of initiation and displacement of the father strongly recalls *The Emerald Forest* (1985), which (appropriately) starred Boorman's own son, and makes it an integral part of his oeuvre.

Joss Marsh

Reviews
Commonweal. CXIV, December 4, 1987, p. 704.
Films in Review. XXXIX, January, 1988, p. 42.
Los Angeles Times. October 30, 1987, VI, p. 1.
The New Republic. CXCVII, November 2, 1987, p. 28.
The New York Times. October 9, 1987, p. C23.
The New Yorker. LXIII, October 5, 1987, p. 91.
Newsweek. CX, October 19, 1987, p. 84.
Sight and Sound. LVI, Autumn, 1987, p. 291.
Time. CXXX, October 19, 1987, p. 76.
Variety. CCCXXVII, July 15, 1987, p. 14.

HOUSE OF GAMES

Production: Michael Hausman; released by Orion Pictures
Direction: David Mamet
Screenplay: David Mamet; based on an original story by Jonathan Katz and
  Mamet
Cinematography: Juan Ruiz-Anchia
Editing: Trudy Ship
Art direction: Michael Merritt
Makeup: Pamela Westmore
Costume design: Nan Cibula
Sound: Anthony John Ciccolini III
Music: Alaric Jans
MPAA rating: R
Running time: 102 minutes

> *Principal characters:*
> Dr. Margaret Ford . . . . Lindsay Crouse
> Mike . . . . Joe Mantegna
> Joey . . . . Mike Nussbaum
> Dr. Littauer . . . . Lilia Skala
> Businessman . . . . J. T. Walsh
> Young woman with book . . . . Willo Hausman
> Prison-ward patient . . . . Karen Kohlhaas
> Billy Hahn . . . . Steve Goldstein

A chilly mood informs this dark fable about the absence of knowingness within the too-conscious mind. Compelling interested attention throughout, the film-directorial debut of acclaimed playwright and screenwriter David Mamet resists too much penetration, for it is so profoundly pessimistic that its most persuasive resonances are of emptiness, desolation, and a kind of death. One feels immediately the stillness of the air, the abstract and sculptural sense of an ambiguous, posing humanity, and the subterranean viciousness that quietly waits amid the placid surfaces of contemporary reality. In this atmosphere, a psychiatrist and author, Dr. Margaret Ford (Lindsay Crouse), signs a copy of her book, *Driven*—a study of obsessive behavior—for an intense young woman (Willo Hausman) who edgily proclaims how helpful and transformative its contents have been for her. The compositions, sound track, and playing are cool and neutral, but the image already suggests content other than that being projected—it is like an image of a torrent of tears suddenly frozen and placed behind glass.

Soon, an intricate plot will be devised around the character of the psychiatrist, but while it engages through clever twists and turns, its only real interest is in its introduction of a male double for the female protagonist. An attractive, though hard-edged and forbidding, confidence man, Mike (Joe Mantegna) is, as much as Margaret, an astute student of human nature. The great difference between them as the narrative proceeds is that his motives seem more conscious. The way in which Mike is introduced into the film is intriguing; there is no mistaking how contrived Margaret's involvement with him is, even when it has been fully explained later as the first step in an elaborate scheme designed not only to part her from her money but also to devastate her emotionally. Alertness to aspects other than this undisguised contrivance is important because the exposition will then become rewarding and indicate what kind of attention should be given to the principal relationship between Margaret and Mike.

Single-mindedly, Mamet has one concentrated purpose to pursue in the film, and that is for everything to reflect, in some way, the contradictory and tormented inner being of Margaret. Before Mike ever appears, four characters in a row double her in some way. First, there is the intense young woman, who, by the film's end, seems like Margaret's psychological twin, for they are both outwardly poised and self-composed but inwardly out of control. Then there is a prison-ward patient (Karen Kohlhaas), whom Margaret is earnestly trying to heal. The patient's dream is carried, as if it were Margaret's own, to Margaret's friend and mentor, Dr. Littauer (Lilia Skala), who, as a woman, seems like a role model. Her observation of Margaret's inner distress, however, which the other signals through amazing slips of the tongue which seemingly occur each time the two women get together, never transforms into active protectiveness. Though sensitive and sympathetic, Dr. Littauer is impotent to act in her friend's interest; one presumes that she was Margaret's psychiatrist while the younger woman was in training, which means that she has never helped her to do anything other than put on a mask. The fourth double is the reflection of that mask, patient Billy Hahn (Steve Goldstein), who confesses to Margaret in bitter anguish that his compulsive gambling has destroyed him because Mike, the man to whom he owes money, is going to kill him. Billy, it is finally learned, has been acting (he is working with Mike). It is a performance in a different register from the one Margaret projects to the world—the poised psychiatrist who understands obsession—but hers has no more tangible reality in the final analysis. From female reflections, the film has progressed into darker male ones, and Mike, the true double, is the darkest and most male.

By now, Margaret's own masculine qualities—her short haircut, her dress, the hard lines given her face by her makeup—should be comprehensible; without these attributes she would seem ridiculous in the world she enters, which is so coarsely masculine. As it is, her femininity abruptly becomes very pronounced by contrast with the new atmosphere and new characters. Though no empathy has been solicited for her by Mamet, she elicits it anyway because of the unashamed vulnerability with which, in the middle of the narrative, she responds to Mike's assessment of her sexual needs; she directly acknowledges that she wants to be, in effect, enslaved.

Before the sexual interlude there is a tense, rigged card game, which Margaret is intended to expose, and afterward there is a more elaborate con game in which she is set up as an apparent killer and must pay off a "ghost" source. Margaret's mission in entering Mike's world was never really to act for Billy, although that was her conscious intention. It was to be discovered—in the sense of being revealed in her psychological nakedness—by her male double. Perhaps, similarly and even more unconsciously, Mike's true mission was not to execute a classic professional con game and the bagful of money it would bring, but to be discovered by Margaret. If he has, as the viewer learns, studied her from a distance, why has he overlooked her powers of perception, not to mention her obsessive drive to concentrate on *anything* without rest until she understands it? She learns what he has done and murders him, then retreats behind her mask once again, now so impenetrable that (in the last scene) she steals a gold cigarette lighter while having lunch with Dr. Littauer and does not make one of her memorable Freudian slips.

Is the action meant to be as puzzling as the House of Games—literally, a cheap gambling parlor, though, vitally, the place where Margaret first meets Mike and feels the lure of his world—which gives the film its title? The confidence games are initially a puzzle but later seem like cheap, seamy tricks, so unpleasant in detail that even their cleverness does not provoke admiration. The characters' lives, or at least the kind of interaction which here exclusively composes their lives, appear no different. With a small amount of effort, Mamet has articulated his metaphor of human existence as a house of games—not a very utopian thought, to say the least. Is he not, however, also suggesting, more despairingly, that the psyche itself is the home of impenetrable contradiction and emotional fragmentation that no amount of outer poise, psychological insight, and evolved intuition will ever bring to light? In effect, is it not a truly eerie, endlessly unsettling, and cruelly mocking house of games which pervades and undermines all attempts at positive human endeavor? It is the explicit thrust of the film to show that Margaret has such a psyche and that, manipulated by others and beyond her control, it ravages her. Yet, beyond this self-destruction, the viewer might find something appealing in her, a thwarted desire for openness and a poignant need to experience the love which she inadvertently acknowledges that her father denied her. By contrast, there is the negative reflection, Mike, seemingly undefined by emotional needs and using his ruthless perceptions to control events until he is physically destroyed. More subtly but just as provocatively, he, too, is the pitiable prisoner of his unexamined inner self. In a conversation that Margaret overhears and that precipitates the climax, he speaks with deep distaste of the sexual encounter with her which, it appears, was a necessary part of his scheme. At the heart of his seeming impersonality is a pathological misogyny and, by extension, misanthropy, for scorn of woman is a scorn of all that makes man creative and vigorous; his real need is not to exercise his cleverness but simply to hurt. It is a sad spectacle to witness how passive his male partners are in the face of his sneering adolescent demeanor—the older, softer partner Joey (Mike Nussbaum), the phoney businessman (J. T. Walsh), and the callow Hahn. If these men are representative of maleness, then who can blame Margaret for shooting Mike, less because he has conned her than because of his contempt for her as a woman.

House of Games was widely compared to *film noir*, or considered a modern variant, but despite the sense of fatality, doom, and human destructiveness in the *film noir* cycle, there was always, too, some sense of a failed positive alternative, even within a morally lost protagonist (*Night and the City*, 1950; *Kiss Me Deadly*, 1955) or within a male-female relationship in which at least one partner is treacherous (*Double Indemnity*, 1944; *Criss Cross*, 1949). The landscape of Mamet's film is too spiritually arid to suggest such a positive alternative. Dispassionate and reflective, it suggests more readily, and in an impressive way, the modern European cinema (which may partly explain why it met with a mixed critical response and failed to find a wide audience). Nor is Mamet stylistically following *film noir*, with its extreme compositions and intricate black-and-white lighting. Aided by the clear and simple color hues of cinematographer Juan Ruiz-Anchia, Mamet visualizes a world as stable and calm in appearance as his characters are stable and calm in their external demeanor. Everything in his cinematic treatment exists to provide contrast to the disturbing tensions which float beneath the surface, so behavior is opaque and the characters speak in a flat, declamatory manner. It is an imaginative approach, paying off richly in the film's sustained mood and in the offbeat allure of Crouse (Mamet's wife, who has not before been such a provocative cinematic presence), as well as establishing Mamet as a new American director of innate talent and great promise. Given the bracing freshness of this film within the prevailing conformist tendencies of 1980's Hollywood, the highly unsettling nature of Mamet's vision surely warrants some forbearance.

Blake Lucas

Reviews
Commonweal. CXIV, December 4, 1987, p. 703.
Los Angeles Times. October 15, 1987, VI, p. 1.
Macleans. C, October 26, 1987, p. 63.
The New Republic. CXCVII, November 16, 1987, p. 22.

New Statesman. CXIV, November 27, 1987, p. 37.
The New York Times. October 11, 1987, I, p. 94.
Newsweek. CX, October 19, 1987, p. 85.
Time. CXXX, October 19, 1987, p. 76.
Variety. CCCXXVIII, September 9, 1987, p. 14.
The Wall Street Journal. October 15, 1987, p. 30.

HOUSEKEEPING

Production: Robert F. Colesberry; released by Columbia Pictures
Direction: Bill Forsyth
Screenplay: Bill Forsyth; based on the novel of the same name by Marilynne
   Robinson
Cinematography: Michael Coulter
Editing: Michael Ellis
Production design: Adrienne Atkinson
Art direction: John Willett and John Stuart Blackie; set decoration, Jim
   Erickson
Special effects: John Thomas
Makeup: Sandy Cooper and Maurice Parkhurst
Costume design: Mary-Jane Reyner
Sound: Ralph Parker
Music: Michael Gibbs
MPAA rating: PG
Running time: 117 minutes

Principal characters:
Sylvie	Christine Lahti
Ruth	Sara Walker
Lucille	Andrea Burchill
Aunt Lily	Anne Pitoniak
Aunt Nona	Barbara Reese
Helen	Margot Pinvidic
Sheriff	Bill Smillie
Grandmother	Georgie Collins
Young Ruth	Tonya Tanner
Young Lucille	Leah Penny

Housekeeping is a study in normalcy—or rather, what some people believe is normal. It is set in the 1950's in a sleepy, isolated Northwest town
called Fingerbone. Two young sisters, Ruth (Sara Walker), the painfully shy
dreamer who narrates the film, and the younger, more fastidious Lucille
(Andrea Burchill) are about to be orphaned in a scene typical of director
Bill Forsyth's deadpan humor. After dropping her children at their grandmother's, Helen (Margot Pinvidic) drives her car off a cliff into the same
glacial lake that earlier consumed the passengers of the legendary Fingerbone Train Wreck.

   Seven lonely years later, Ruthie and Lucille are abandoned once again,
when Grandmother (Georgie Collins) dies. Aunts Lily (Anne Pitoniak) and
Nona (Barbara Reese), enticed by free room and board, arrive from Spo-

kane, but there is a problem: They hate the isolation and eeriness of Fingerbone. So it is with great anticipation that the girls await the arrival of their mother's sister Sylvie (Christine Lahti), a kind and charmingly distant free spirit. Sylvie is a mysterious woman who seems totally at peace with herself. As the film unfolds, she is faced with the conventionality and harsh scrutiny of the people of Fingerbone.

Convinced that Sylvie holds the key to all unanswered questions, the girls are immediately mesmerized by their newfound guardian. Yet Sylvie is vague and distant. The fact that she never removes her coat immediately makes her suspect in the eyes of Lucille and Ruthie. So, when Sylvie goes out for an early morning walk which takes her back to the train station, the girls follow her. Sylvie reassures them that she was only trying to warm up and that the station was the only place open. The girls escort her back to the house, after making sure that Sylvie is outfitted with new gloves and a scarf to fight off the chill of Fingerbone. Aunts Lily and Nona quickly flee, leaving Sylvie, Ruthie, and Lucille to get acquainted.

Then, as if symbolic of the coming of a new life and the washing away of the old, it begins to rain for four days. While Sylvie merely accepts the flood as part of the natural ebb and tide of life and rejoices, dancing in the water with Ruthie, young Lucille grows increasingly depressed, longing for a more ordinary existence. After she is sent home for cheating on an exam, Lucille cannot face going back to school. The girls spend their days at the lake, hoping that someone will notice that they are missing. Finally one day, they spot Sylvie, and there is a sense of relief, since all the while they were waiting to get caught. Sylvie, however, is not out looking for the girls but stares at the sky as she makes her way up the hill to the railroad bridge. The girls are terrified as they watch Sylvie tiptoe across the bridge, balancing precariously on the edge. They are convinced that Sylvie is planning suicide, exactly as their mother had done years before. Sylvie is surprised that school is out already, but when the girls confess that they have been playing hooky, Sylvie replies, "But I didn't know that."

The girls stop going to school altogether; they hide out in the woods and sing "Oh, My Papa," puffing on imaginary cigarettes. Disappointed by Sylvie's unconventionality, Lucille confronts her as they sit in the dark amid the growing stacks of newspapers and empty tin cans that Sylvie collects. The next morning, the girls find Sylvie sleeping on a park bench in the middle of town.

Lucille, uncomfortable with her aunt's quirky habits, decides to take active steps to get herself back into mainstream life. This decision drives a wedge between the girls. Unable to rescue her sister from Sylvie, Lucille moves out of the house and in with her home economics teacher. Sylvie, who until this point has never tried to interfere in the girls' relationship, takes Ruthie to her special place where Sylvie leaves marshmallows for the wild children who hide in the woods. The two spend the night in a rowboat on the lake, waiting for the night train. Sylvie stands in the boat, feeling the power of the train overhead as she hangs onto the trestle. When morning comes, Sylvie and Ruthie ride the boxcar back to town. A woman on the train remarks to Sylvie, "She's a good girl. Just like you always said."

When Lucille expresses concern for her sister's safety, Ruthie tells her that everything is fine. Soon, visits from both the sheriff (Bill Smillie) and three of the town's busybodies prompt Sylvie to stay up all night cleaning the house. In the morning, Sylvie sends Ruthie to school looking spick-and-span, but Ruthie returns to learn of an upcoming custody hearing. That night, the two frantically burn the collection of newspapers in a bonfire outside, and when Sylvie sends her inside to bed, Ruthie decides to play a game of hide and seek on her aunt. Late at night, the sheriff encounters Ruthie in the orchard, telling him to leave. In the closing scene, Sylvie and Ruthie pack two small suitcases, set fire to the house, and run off across the railroad bridge, disappearing into the night.

Scottish director Forsyth resists sentimentality by avoiding hazy, romantic filters and shooting this piece with gritty realism. He allows his audience to understand equally both sisters and the choices each makes rather than imposing his own preferences. Both Ruthie and Lucille need acceptance. It is simply that one of them cannot find it through conventional society. *Housekeeping* marks Forsyth's first North American effort. His previous work includes *Gregory's Girl* (1981), *Local Hero* (1983), and *Comfort and Joy* (1984), all shot in Scotland. Meticulously filmed, *Housekeeping* is both entertaining and compelling.

While it is difficult to watch Lahti as Sylvie and not think of the more quirky, highly individual Diane Keaton, the actress originally slated for the role (certain lines of dialogue were clearly written with Keaton's delivery in mind), Lahti does an admirable job of walking that fine line between creativity and insanity. The two young Canadian actresses Sara Walker and Andrea Burchill are captivating as the sisters torn between conformity and self-expression.

The reviews of *Housekeeping* were generally positive, although it was interesting to note that the critics disagreed in their perceptions of Sylvie's character. Some believed that she was potentially dangerous and obviously insane. This observation seems more a reflection of the reviewer's character than of the film's. If it is easier to live life following the rules, conforming to societal expectations, then perhaps it is more comforting to regard people like Sylvie, and consequently Ruth, as a threat, lonely lunatics who will never know the responsibilities of a conventional life-style. Yet, for those "misfits" in the viewing audience, *Housekeeping* offers a reaffirmation of their blessed nonconformity.

Patricia Kowal

Reviews
America. CLVIII, February 6, 1988, p. 122.
Films in Review. XXXIX, February, 1988, p. 102.
Macleans. C, December 14, 1987, p. 67.
The Nation. CCXLVI, January 16, 1988, p. 66.
The New Republic. CXCVIII, January 18, 1988, p. 26.
The New York Times. November 25, 1987, p. C11.
The New Yorker. LXIII, December 14, 1987, p. 147.
Newsweek. CX, December 7, 1987, p. 89.
Savvy. VIII, December, 1987, p. 22.
Time. CXXX, November 23, 1987, p. 101.
Variety. CCCXXVIII, October 7, 1987, p. 22.
Vogue. CLXXVII, December, 1987, p. 72.

IN THE MOOD

Production: Gary Adelson and Karen Mack for Kings Road Entertainment; released by Lorimar
Direction: Phil Alden Robinson
Screenplay: Phil Alden Robinson; based on the story by Bob Kosberg, David Simon, and Phil Alden Robinson
Cinematography: John Lindley
Editing: Patrick Kennedy
Production design: Dennis Gassner
Art direction: Dins Danielsen; set decoration, Richard Hoover
Costume design: Linda Bass
Sound: Russell Williams II
Music: Ralph Burns
MPAA rating: PG-13
Running time: 98 minutes

Principal characters:
Ellsworth "Sonny" Wisecarver	Patrick Dempsey
Judy Cusimano	Talia Balsam
Francine Glatt	Beverly D'Angelo
Mr. Wisecarver	Michael Constantine
Mrs. Wisecarver	Betty Jinnette
Mrs. Marver	Kathleen Freeman
The Judge	Peter Hobbs
Carlo	Tony Longo
Uncle Clete	Douglas Rowe
Chief Kelsey	Ernie Brown
Wendy	Kim Myers
George	Brian McNamara
Alberta	Dana Short

In the Mood, originally released under the title *The Woo Woo Kid*, represents the initial directorial effort of screenwriter Phil Alden Robinson, the scenarist of the successful screwball comedy *All of Me* (1984). *In the Mood* chronicles the hapless, true-life escapades of Sonny Wisecarver (Patrick Dempsey), a fifteen-year-old Lothario from Long Beach, California, who captured the fancy of the American public in 1944 through a series of highly publicized adventures with married and significantly older women. While the naïve Sonny is firmly situated as the focus of the narrative, his high jinks are often secondary to the manner in which they are effectively exploited by the media. Robinson's film faithfully incorporates material developed from newspaper accounts, newsreels, and the actual courtroom transcripts of the

events and depicts both the duplicitous journalists and their eagerly credu-
lous readers, weary and dispirited from the lengthy war effort, as cocon-
spirators in the creation of the myth that envelopes and ultimately punishes
the protagonist.

The story opens with a black-and-white newsreel montage of the year,
including shots of soldiers, a newspaper vendor, current headlines of world
figures, battles, a Hollywood murder, and reports of sightings of Japanese
planes off the coast of Seattle—a curious admixture of tragic and hysterical
reportage—while Sonny, the narrator, prepares the audience for his unsolicited entry into this public arena. His mordant observations on his experience, although filtered through the hindsight of four decades, dissipate any
nostalgia for the era. There is a curious temporal dislocation in the frequent
voice-over passages that punctuate the film, since Sonny is clearly an adult
describing a distant past, yet he distinctly utilizes the same voice as the
fifteen-year-old Sonny. This technique effectively undercuts the irony of his
observations, including the memories of his family that open the film as it
segues from black and white into the pastel hues of his residence in Southern California in 1944. Mr. Wisecarver (Michael Constantine), a taciturn
domestic despot, quickly expunges any semblance of frivolity or spontaneity
under his roof; when Sonny is discovered marking his height against a door
frame, the youth is required to erase the evidence with his tongue.

Sonny wisely spends most of his time outside the home. His access to un-
limited supplies of gasoline, a severely rationed commodity, gives him status
among an older, more sophisticated crowd that frequents the home of his
neighbor, Judy (Talia Balsam), for early afternoon dance parties. Sonny, an
incorrigible truant with no particular intellectual aptitude, other than the
creativity applied to induce fevers that exempt him from academic pursuits,
initiates a friendship with Judy, a common-law wife and mother of two. For
Judy, these afternoons in the company of the vital and attractive, if somewhat naïve, Sonny provide her with a desperately needed respite from her
husband, Carlo (Tony Longo), a monosyllabic, uncouth lout. Romantic passion clearly plays a minor role in their relationship; Sonny is depicted as
completely untutored in the strategies of serious courtship while Judy is too
frightened by her husband to initiate anything beyond platonic contact with
the youth.

After Carlo turns violent, Sonny rescues Judy and offers her an escape:
Two of his friends, George (Brian McNamara) and Alberta (Dana Short),
are about to elope to Arizona, and Sonny suggests that the four of them
embark on the adventure. Robinson presents this scene as purely coincidental and improbably chaste; Judy appears tempted only by the solicitous and
courteous manner of Sonny, while he seems incapable of any meaningful reflection on their dilemma. This approach clearly encourages an ironic reading of these characters, yet the scenario seems incapable, as do the actors,

of suggesting anything beyond the simple record of events. This unambiguous strategy is obdurately maintained throughout the film, and any real sexual ignition between the principals is quickly extinguished, thereby eliminating blind passion as a motivation for their impulsive action. While this lack of passion renders the production more palatable to a wide audience, it also dramatically undercuts the essence of the story. Judy is especially shortchanged in this depiction, since she never examines the jeopardy it presents to her family; as they flee to Arizona to marry, the audience has yet to be informed that she has abandoned two young children in the progress. Thus, the more complex implications of their illegal marriage have been effectively reduced to the dimension of a teenage prank (an interpretation encouraged by the apparent proximity in age of actors Balsam and Dempsey).

The nature of the story shifts abruptly during the honeymoon. After apparently a single night of connubial congress, the couple is arrested and returned to California, where she faces charges that could result in lengthy incarceration—Sonny is a minor and Judy already has a common-law husband. Judy, rather improbably, becomes sophisticated at manipulating the media, and the sexual angle, reticently depicted in earlier scenes, now becomes the nexus of the plot as she eagerly regales the reporters with testimony of Sonny's "wooing" techniques. The press exploits his prowess, dubbing him the "Woo Woo Kid," and Sonny finds himself idolized by women and teenagers throughout the country. The film strikes a more consistently light and entertaining mood as it explores the exploitation of the media and the effects of this sudden and unsolicited fame on Sonny. Older women now pursue him as he struggles to maintain his anonymity. During a brief convalescence at a hospital, nurses incessantly minister to the new sexual celebrity; lines form to offer him private sponge baths. During the court hearing, the judge (Peter Hobbs) inadvertently contributes to the growing myth by misreading an innocent remark offered by Mrs. Wisecarver (Betty Jinnette) about Sonny's abnormal "size," sending the courtroom into hysterics as the bailiff is dutifully dispatched with a measuring stick to confirm her report. Although all the charges are eventually dropped, Sonny is adjudged an "oversexed punk" and a threat to public decency and is banished from town for the summer.

While toiling at a fish cannery for the summer, the landlady (Kathleen Freeman) at his rooming house, an apoplectic harridan, places Sonny under constant surveillance. The flirtatious Francine (Beverly D'Angelo), another target of the landlady's moral opprobrium, sympathizes with Sonny's plight and befriends him. Francine too has been misunderstood; she insists that her overtly sensuous public demeanor and dress conflict with her private moral rectitude. In her case, however, the advertising was accurate, as she lures the still-innocent youth into fleeing the confining boarding house for a rendezvous in Paradise, California. After a night of passion in Paradise, the couple awakes to find that they are front-page news in the local newspapers. The gallant Sonny, eager to spare Francine's reputation, offers himself to the constabulary, whereupon he is promptly arrested. Robinson seems to lose control at this point; only the film's inertia drags it lifelessly to its conclusion. The director pointlessly wastes time chronicling the terms of Sonny's imprisonment at the hands of cheerful Police Chief Kelsey (Ernie Brown), an avuncular soul affectionately known as Papa Bear. The return to the original courtroom for the predictable denouement affords no new insight into the character of Sonny, nor does the very brief sequence at a youth camp where he is subsequently detained under court order. Sonny quickly escapes to Nevada, where broke and dejected he seeks shelter for the night, only to be expelled by Wendy, an usherette, to whom, the viewer learns in a voice-over, he will be married after a four-week courtship. The speed with which these final events are narrated never allows the actors to convince the audience that the story has any import, any validity. The film is quite short, well under one hundred minutes, a length that suggests that Lorimar Telepictures tailored the film to suit the commercial exigencies of prime-time network programming.

While *In the Mood* has an undeniable charm, most notably for the evocative production design of Dennis Gassner and the often elegiac cinematography of John Lindley, the overall effort seems to have been miscalculated, as evidenced by the distribution history of the film, first released under the title *The Woo Woo Kid* and subsequently pulled from theatrical distribution. The heart of the story, the character of Sonny Wisecarver, is neither intelligently developed nor cogently motivated, and thus he remains an enigma. One of the major problems is the casting and direction of Dempsey, a modestly talented twenty-year-old actor who cannot begin to suggest the physical or emotional composition of a fifteen-year-old character. Apparently, a compromise was reached—Dempsey, who looks every bit of twenty, would play Sonny as an affable yet unimaginative dolt. It does not work, however, nor does the misconceived notion that a fifteen-year-old would narrate the film from the present, as if recalling a distant memory. By insisting on an essentially naïve quality to Sonny, the director creates an innocent victim, a proposition that cannot work without a wicked sense of irony; the script offers none of that necessary sardonic incongruity. The subject of precocious sexuality, the apparent motivation for the script, is barely more than an unfortunate series of coincidental events immoderately inflated by an exploitative media. Sonny's motivation and psyche remain unexplored territory. Many of the minor roles, however, are perfectly assayed, especially Constantine and Jinnette as Sonny's parents; in their very brief roles these actors supply the kind of off-beat energy and shrewdly understated mania that this film cannot sustain. *In the Mood* becomes too conservative and inoffensive for its subject matter. It ultimately reduces unusual events to manageable proportions and knocks off the rough edges of a unique personality to suit a figure who might fit more comfortably into the small glowing box in every living room of America.

John Robert Kelly

Reviews

Films in Review. XXXVIII, December, 1987, p. 617.
Los Angeles. XXXII, October, 1987, p. 241.
Los Angeles Times. September 18, 1987, VI, p. 12.
The New York Times. September 16, 1987, p. C27.
Newsweek. CX, September 28, 1987, p. 77.
People Weekly. XXVIII, October 12, 1987, p. 12.
Time. CXXX, September 28, 1987, p. 69.
Variety. CCCXXVII, May 20, 1987, p. 107.
The Wall Street Journal. September 17, 1987, p. 32.

INNERSPACE

Production: Michael Finnell for Amblin Entertainment, Steven Spielberg, Peter Guber, and Jon Peters (executive producers); released by Warner Bros.
Direction: Joe Dante
Screenplay: Jeffrey Boam and Chip Proser; based on a story by Chip Proser
Cinematography: Andrew Laszlo
Editing: Kent Beyda
Production design: James H. Spencer
Art direction: William Matthews; set decoration, Richard C. Goddard
Special effects: Michael Wood, Michael Edmonson, James Fredburg, Alfred Broussard, Mike Paris, Joe Sasgen, and David Wood
Special visual effects: Dennis Muren, William George, Harley Jessup, and Kenneth Smith
Makeup: Rob Bottin
Costume design: Rosanna Norton
Music direction: Kenneth Hall
Music: Jerry Goldsmith
MPAA rating: PG
Running time: 118 minutes

Principal characters:
Lieutenant Tuck Pendelton . . . . Dennis Quaid
Jack Putter . . . . Martin Short
Lydia Maxwell . . . . Meg Ryan
Victor Scrimshaw . . . . Kevin McCarthy
Dr. Margaret Canker . . . . Fiona Lewis
Mr. Igoe . . . . Vernon Wells
The cowboy . . . . Robert Picardo
Wendy . . . . Wendy Schaal
Pete Blanchard . . . . Harold Sylvester
Dr. Greenbush . . . . William Schallert
Mr. Wormwood . . . . Henry Gibson
Ozzie Wexler . . . . John Hora
Dr. Niles . . . . Mark L. Taylor
Editor . . . . Orson Bean
Duane . . . . Kevin Hooks
Dream lady . . . . Kathleen Freeman
Messenger . . . . Archie Hahn
Wendell . . . . Shawn Nelson
Rusty . . . . Grainger Hines

Innerspace is a preposterous science-fiction feature that would be an unmitigated disaster were it not for Joe Dante's direction and wonderful performances by Dennis Quaid and Martin Short. Short also appeared in *¡Three Amigos!* (1986), where he held his own against the comic talents of Steve Martin and Chevy Chase, no easy task. *Innerspace* establishes Short as a top-rate comedian. His straight man, Quaid, will be remembered for his work in *The Right Stuff* (1983) and *Enemy Mine* (1985). Director Dante has to his credit the runaway hit *Gremlins* (1984), which grossed more than $200 million.

In *Innerspace*, Quaid plays Lieutenant Tuck Pendelton, a military renegade who drinks too much and does not follow orders. He has agreed to take part in a top-secret miniaturization experiment in which he is to be shrunk to microscopic size, then injected into the body of a rabbit named Bugs. This experience is to be his goofy adventure in "innerspace," but things go wrong—seriously wrong. Screenwriters Jeffrey Boam and Chip Proser are fully in tune with the absurdity of the plot and are able to exploit the silliness of the idea in an amusing and agreeable way.

The project is sabotaged after Pendelton and his command module have been miniaturized and deposited into a hypodermic serum. A hit team of thugs and competing scientists break into the laboratory, intent on technological thievery. The head scientist, Pendelton-laden syringe in the pocket of his lab coat, escapes and is chased by a bionic hit man. In a shopping mall, they collide with timid supermarket clerk Jack Putter (Martin Short), and the scientist, who has been seriously injured by the hit man, jabs the needle into Putter's rump. Thereafter, Pendelton is inside Putter, eventually able to see through Putter's eyes and to communicate through Putter's inner ear. There is no way that the young man can understand what has happened to him, and when he starts to hear Pendelton's voice, the poor man thinks that he is going crazy.

Clearly, the plot is remarkably absurd, but the story is treated as surreal comedy, and the treatment makes it tolerable. Dante is sure of the effect that he wants to create, and he knows how to get laughs. The challenge is to recover a stolen microchip that Pendelton needs in order to escape his dilemma (and his host) and return to normal size. Putter picks up a sidekick when he enlists Pendelton's girlfriend, Lydia Maxwell (Meg Ryan), to help locate the missing chip. Meanwhile, Pendelton's oxygen supply is running low, and his hours are numbered.

The plot goes haywire when the bionic hit man is also miniaturized and injected into Putter. His mission is to kill Pendelton and recover the second chip that Pendelton has with him. How the villain gets miniaturized without the second chip is a mystery that the screenplay does not bother to explain. Pendelton and the villain carry on a running battle in Putter's digestive tract, and the hit man is finally destroyed by Putter's upset stomach.

The corporate villain of the film, Victor Scrimshaw, is played by cult actor Kevin McCarthy, who also played the hero in the original film version of *The Invasion of the Body Snatchers* in 1956. His evil sidekick, Dr. Margaret Canker, is played by the British actress Fiona Lewis.

What is most amusing about *Innerspace* is the way Short's character changes once he has the flamboyant Pendelton under his skin. The film is surely crazy but good-natured and frequently funny. For that reason it was a moderate success in the early summer market of 1987. One reviewer accurately described *Innerspace* as "a *Mad Magazine* version of *Fantastic Voyage*," an earlier exercise in science-fiction miniaturization, made in 1966, but unprotected by a satiric framework. The *Fantastic Voyage* gimmick is wedded to another comic idea, the inner comedy suggested by *All of Me* (1984).

Innerspace was the second summer 1987 release from Steven Spielberg's Amblin Entertainment organization. The first, an insufferably cute Bigfoot comedy called *Harry and the Hendersons*, was only moderately successful. The strongest drawing card for *Innerspace* was the casting, though in this regard the film had little to offer beyond Quaid and Short. The rest of the cast were tied to one-dimensional roles, the best reduced to caricatures— villains and sidekicks alike.

Quaid went on to star with Ellen Barkin in *The Big Easy* (reviewed in this volume), a much more substantial picture that opened in August of 1987, and then next with Cher in *Suspect* (reviewed in this volume), one of the best offerings of a strong fall season. In this context, his performance in *Innerspace* as Tuck Pendelton, the military-macho miniaturized astronaut, pales in significance. Still, the inner-and-outer rapport he establishes with the mild-mannered hypochondriac played by Short in *Innerspace* has just the right satiric edge.

The film belongs mainly to Short, however, who has to suggest a character transformation convincingly after Pendelton has entered his life and invaded his consciousness. Because of Pendelton's arrogance and self-confidence, Putter's timidity vanishes. The transformation is fun to watch. Moreover, when Pendelton first speaks to Putter from the inside, the hysteria that results is hilarious; Putter is convinced that he is possessed. Indeed, Desson Howe, reviewing *Innerspace* for *The Washington Post*, pointed out that, although he is "ostensibly the movie's comic foil, Short becomes the main attraction," and also suggested that if anything was wrong with this film, it is that it was "too short on Short."

Writing for *The New Yorker*, Pauline Kael aptly described *Innerspace* as a "stupid-crazy-funky" comedy. In her view, the film was too "starved for craziness" and held down by a "slow-moving script," but she praised the three leads (including sidekick Ryan) as being "just about everything they should be."

Reviewing the film for *Newsweek*, David Ansen objected to the "cartoonish villains" and the " 'anything goes' school of plotting" but concluded that when it sticks to its premise as a "daffy biological buddy movie," *Innerspace* is "a joy to watch." *Time* critic Richard Corliss was equally enthusiastic and drew a favorable comparison between *Innerspace* and "the hippest Martin-and-Lewis comedy." As summer comedy goes, *Innerspace* was a superior and successful offering.

James M. Welsh

Reviews

Films in Review. XXXVIII, October, 1987, p. 491.
Los Angeles Times. July 1, 1987, VI, p. 1.
Macleans. C, July 13, 1987, p. 46.
The New York Times. July 1, 1987, p. C17.
The New Yorker. LXIII, July 27, 1987, p. 65.
Newsweek. CX, July 13, 1987, p. 60.
Time. CXXX, July 13, 1987, p. 68.
Variety. CCCXXVII, June 24, 1987, p. 13.
The Wall Street Journal. July 2, 1987, p. 16.
The Washington Post. July 1, 1987, p. D1.

IRONWEED

Production: Keith Barish and Marcia Nasatir; released by Tri-Star Pictures
Direction: Hector Babenco
Screenplay: William Kennedy; based on his novel of the same name
Cinematography: Lauro Escorel
Editing: Anne Goursaud
Production design: Jeannine C. Oppewall
Art direction: Robert Guerra; set decoration, Leslie Pope and Elaine
   O'Donnell
Costume design: Joseph G. Aulisi
Music: John Morris
MPAA rating: R
Running time: 145 minutes

> *Principal characters:*
> Francis Phelan . . . . Jack Nicholson
> Helen . . . . Meryl Streep
> Annie Phelan . . . . Carroll Baker
> Rudy . . . . Tom Waits
> Oscar . . . . Fred Gwynne
> Billy Phelan. . . . . Michael O'Keefe
> Peggy Phelan . . . . Diane Venora
> Katrina. . . . . Margaret Whitton
> Reverend Chester . . . . James Gammon
> Junk man . . . . Hy Anzell

Director Hector Babenco's *Ironweed* and William Kennedy's novel *Ironweed* (1983) are two entirely different entities. Although the latter, a Pulitzer Prize-winning novel, is the foundation for the former, *Ironweed* the film is an example of the perplexing intricacies involved in translating literature into film. More than one reviewer, however, noted that Kennedy's direct contribution to the film version increases the irony in its failure to capture the qualities that made the novel such a critical success. These qualities proved difficult to translate to the moving image, since much of the novel's appeal resided in the rich suggestiveness of its language, which described the inner life of its alcoholic protagonist and his subjective encounters with the fantastic, the unknowable, and the unfathomable.

While some critics blamed the fundamental inappropriateness of any attempt to translate Kennedy's novel to the screen, others blamed Babenco, whose earlier critical successes included the modestly budgeted but highly acclaimed foray into politics and fantasy, *Kiss of the Spider Woman* (1985), and *Pixote* (1980), the story of street life among abandoned Brazilian children. Babenco, some critics suggested, possessed a Latin American sensibility that was incompatible with both the Depression-era setting of Kennedy's novel and the author's Irish-Catholic blending of guilt and black humor. Nevertheless, Babenco's demonstrated ability to handle the fantastic in *Kiss of the Spider Woman*, as well as the unflinching realism of *Pixote*, could easily be used as evidence of directorial virtues well suited to guiding a film version of Kennedy's book.

Ironweed showcases the acting of Nicholson as Francis Phelan, former baseball player and family man who, after accidentally killing his infant son, spends the next twenty-two years running from his guilty past. The film opens in the icy blue of predawn, downtown Albany, New York, in October of 1938. Arising from a back alley, Francis awakens, not to greet a new day but to start a new round in his battle for daily survival. The sound of a baby crying is heard, but this phantom noise is merely the first in a series of phantoms which haunt Francis' booze-sodden existence.

Francis joins others gathered outside the local skid-row mission run by Reverend Chester (James Gammon). He meets his friend Rudy (Tom Waits), whose clean suit might, in other circumstances, be a sign that he has met with good luck, but Rudy has been in the hospital. The doctors have given him a new suit and a death sentence: He has cancer and does not have long to live. Francis and Rudy take work shoveling dirt at the cemetery. The few dollars' pay will buy a bottle and a place to sleep. At the cemetery, Francis stops at the grave of his infant son, Gerald. Riding back to town on the trolley, Francis imagines that he is again a youth standing amid the striking trolley-car workers. A chance throw of a rock and Francis killed a scab driver who was doing nothing more than standing at the controls of a car. Francis' thoughts return to the present, but he continues to see the man he killed as a ghost who will later be joined by the ghosts of two boxcar hobos Francis killed in self-defense. These ghostly figures, with their luminous, glowing wounds and pale faces, appear Felliniesque in their white suits and are among the most critically controversial aspects of the film. Several critics thought their presence was distracting and crudely conceived as a vehicle to literalize Francis' guilt.

At the mission, Francis finally locates Helen (Meryl Streep), his companion for the past nine years. With her harsh street talk, paranoia, and strangeness, Helen constantly attempts to recall her earlier life, in which she was, she says, the refined daughter of a well-to-do family. In their search for a place to sleep, Helen, Francis, Rudy, and some of their friends go to a bar where they run into Oscar (Fred Gwynne), an old acquaintance who no longer drinks. Now a singing bartender, he encourages Helen when she talks of her experience as a radio singer. In a moment combining fantasy and reality, Helen takes the stage and belts out a song dedicated to Francis, "He's My Pal." Her talent and training are obvious; she has not been lying about her past. Her fleeting recapturing of former success is a fantasy, however, shared only with the film audience. The viewer sees the actual end of her song, with the bar patrons indifferent to her pathetically used up voice and nervous stage presence.

Still searching for a place to spend the night, Helen and Francis visit a drunkard husband and wife who manage to keep an apartment. The husband is interested in Helen, and the slovenly wife appears to be amenable to bedding down with Francis. Seeing that a bed for the night will involve the exchange of sexual favors, Helen insists that they leave. She and Francis viciously fight on the street. They reconcile, and he finds an abandoned car in which she can sleep, but the dollar he gives to its resident bum will not be enough for his own rent. After Francis leaves, Helen is forced to submit to the sexual advances of the man in order to keep her place in the car. When she leaves in the morning, she goes to confession, then finds some money on the church floor that enables her to redeem her possessions from the pawnshop and rent a clean hotel room.

Francis has obtained a job as the helper to a junk man (Hy Anzell) who loves life. He finds himself in the neighborhood where he was reared and where his wife and two grown children still live. As Helen is cleaning up and preparing for his return, Francis prepares himself to visit his wife, Annie (Carroll Baker). Annie does not recognize him at first, but it becomes clear as they talk that she is willing to take him back into her life. He has a chance for redemption, but Francis no longer seems to want anything, including redemption. When she asks him what he needs, he can only reply: a new shoelace. Nor does acceptance by his sympathetic son, Billy (Michael O'Keefe), and finally by his embittered daughter, Peggy (Diane Venora), provide him with the hope that he needs in order to change. He tells Annie that he knows his staying would not work. He leaves as quietly as he appeared.

Francis finds Rudy sleeping on the street. They pass time at a shanty town. Amazingly, Francis can finally speak of his loss. He tells his drunken, uninterested companions of his accidentally dropping his son and recalls his kindly wife who "never told a soul I did it." The meaning of Francis' story is lost on them, however. Suddenly, vigilantes arrive to torch the shacks and drive the bums out of Albany. Rudy is viciously attacked, but Francis manages to drag him away. By the time they reach a hospital, Rudy is dead. Francis leaves him in order to find solace with a bottle and with Helen, but when he discovers Helen in her rented hotel room, she is dead of alcohol poisoning. In his drunken state, he incoherently promises her that he will get her a tombstone—a promise that, like all the others in Francis' life, will never be kept. *Ironweed* ends with Francis returning to the rails to escape Albany. He throws away his bottle, but Francis' escape from liquor, like his escape from his past, is doubtless a temporary and futile gesture.

Described as "a joyless classic" by Pauline Kael and greeted with reviews that characterized it as serious, somber, and slow, *Ironweed* missed receiving the kind of critical enthusiasm which its investment ($23 million) and its participating talent might have seemed to ensure. In spite of the disappointing critical reception given the film, the acting of Nicholson and Streep was greeted with widespread praise and with nominations by the Academy of Motion Picture Arts and Sciences for Best Actor and Best Actress. Streep, in particular—so often the subject of a rather begrudging admiration for her acting technique coupled with a sense that she does not hold the screen with the authoritative style that signals a truly charismatic Hollywood presence—finally received unreserved praise for both her technique and her charisma. Nicholson also was widely praised, with some critics noting, however, that the role of Francis did not fully exploit what is most captivating about Nicholson: his energy and his humor. Thus, *Ironweed* became marked as that rarest and most financially dangerous of modern Hollywood products—a film that is too serious.

Gaylyn Studlar

Reviews
Los Angeles Times. December 18, 1987, VI, p. 1.
Macleans. CI, February 15, 1988, p. 57.
The New Republic. CXCVIII, January 25, 1988, p. 28.
The New York Times. December 18, 1987, p. C24.
The New Yorker. LXIII, January 11, 1988, p. 78.
Newsweek. CX, December 21, 1987, p. 68.
People Weekly. XXIX, January 11, 1988, p. 12.
Time. CXXX, December 21, 1987, p. 74.
Variety. CCCXXIX, December 16, 1987, p. 10.
The Wall Street Journal. December 17, 1987, p. 28.

ISHTAR

Production: Warren Beatty for Columbia-Delphi V; released by Columbia
   Pictures
Direction: Elaine May
Screenplay: Elaine May
Cinematography: Vittorio Storaro
Editing: Stephen A. Rotter, William Reynolds, and Richard Cirincione
Production design: Paul Sylbert
Art direction: Bill Groom, Vicki Paul, Peter Childs, and Tony Reading; set
   decoration, Steve Jordan and Alan Hicks
Special effects: George Gibbs
Makeup: Bob Jiras and Alan Boyle
Costume design: Anthony Powell
Music: John Strauss
Songs: Paul Williams and Elaine May
MPAA rating: PG-13
Running time: 107 minutes

   Principal characters:
   Lyle Rogers .... Warren Beatty
   Chuck Clarke..................... Dustin Hoffman
   Shirra Assel .... Isabelle Adjani
   Jim Harrison .... Charles Grodin
   Marty Freed .... Jack Weston
   Willa Rogers .... Tess Harper
   Carol .... Carol Kane

   There are certain jazz singers whose distinctive vocal achievement is their
ability to sing just slightly between the notes: ahead of or behind the beat of
a tune. Elaine May's characters might similarly be described as making their
idiosyncratic presence felt by means of their movements against the grain of
the work in which they exist. They live (and sometimes they die) in the
cracks between the regular patterns of actions and events that one finds in
other films. Furthermore, as in a good jazz performance, the expressive ec-
centricity of the performances of May's characters can make something
interesting of even the most unpromising material.
   Such characters, however, present problems for audiences and critics. Just
as the music of Louis Armstrong, Charlie Parker, or Billie Holiday does not
make for easy listening, such a conception of narrative and character does
not make for easy viewing. May's characters will not be reduced to standard
types; they stay elusive and unpredictable. As many of the adverse reviews
of *Ishtar* pointed out, the principal characters are extremely hard to pene-

trate. It is quite difficult to know what makes them tick or exactly why they say and do certain things in the course of the film. May's off-key, off-beat characterizations are representations of identities in flux and confusion. Her characters do not understand themselves well enough even to state their problems. They are too subtly and profoundly confused to know what their confusions are.

Accordingly, a true defense of May's work would not argue that a viewer must merely "allow for" the shagginess of the performances and the sprawl of the scenes. The vagaries of purpose of May's characters and the anecdotal looseness of the development of her scenes are not imperfections that might have been corrected with more directorial care. They are the essence of the interest of work which is an exploration of the destinies of characters who cannot make up their minds about their lives. May's characters have too many mixed feelings and conflicting allegiances to be ground down in the mill of the formulaic plot and the schematic characterizations of most other movies. They are continuously trying out new roles and new identities for themselves and are continuously dissatisfied with their past efforts. They casually, anxiously make themselves up as they go along, changing their minds about themselves and their relationships to others, just as an audience may keep changing its mind about them.

Seen in this light, it is no accident that in *Ishtar* May chooses as her central characters a pair of figures who are professional stage performers engaged in acts of creative improvisation in front of an audience. All the important characters in May's work attempt to improvise their identities as if they were dramatic performers of their own lives. In her earlier work— *Mikey and Nicky* (1976), *The Heartbreak Kid* (1972), and *A New Leaf* (1971)—though her characters were not professional performers, all of her central figures functioned as hustlers, confidence men, scam artists, and storytellers attempting to get their acts together and take them on the road.

The stars of *Ishtar* differ from these earlier performers, then, only in that they make their living by professional, and not amateur, improvisation. Chuck Clarke (Dustin Hoffman) and Lyle Rogers (Warren Beatty) are failed, frustrated songwriter-performers who take their dismal lounge act on the road to Morocco (which May calls Ishtar) out of desperation to get a booking. Just prior to their arrival in Ishtar, an ancient map is discovered at the site of an archaeological dig. It announces the arrival of two divine messengers who, according to the legend, will usher in the millennium. That is the world into which May's two innocents abroad naïvely wander.

It is a classic comic setup, and May milks Chuck and Lyle's nearly terminal case of mistaken identity for every hilarious ramification possible. On the one side, the local terrorist organization seizes on the discovery of the map in an attempt to use the "divine messengers" to incite the people and legitimize an overthrow of the government. On the other, the local despot mobilizes to shore up his corrupt regime and to prevent the impending coup by having the "divine messengers" secretly murdered. Last, but far from least, the local operatives of the Central Intelligence Agency (CIA) and the Soviet State Security Committee (KGB) move in to play both sides against the middle to their own advantage. Each of the rival factions is alternately out to threaten, bribe, or wheedle the undynamic duo into allegiance to their side, or, failing that, to eliminate them.

Much of the film is given over to a series of almost indescribably elaborate double and triple crosses, which apparently left audiences almost as bewildered as May's song and dance men. Lyle and Chuck are caught in the middle of a Byzantine plot (a critical metaphor which May, as it were, literalizes) with international geopolitical ramifications. May then tops all of it by having the pair fall in love with one of the terrorists, Shirra Assel (Isabelle Adjani).

The attempt to reduce *Ishtar* to a plot summary is like using a metronome to follow the syncopations of a good jazz piece. In effect, what May explores is the predicament of two characters trapped in a series of plots—both the plots organized by the CIA, the KGB, and the other groups within the film, and the plot of May's film itself—from which they must attempt to escape. It is as if Indiana Jones (or Harrison Ford) were asked to lever himself out of the silliness of *Raiders of the Lost Ark* (1981), instead of merely surrendering to it.

How does one escape the plot of one's own film? Only with the greatest difficulty, as the reply goes. In May's work, it is those potential imaginative openings, those saving fissures and cracks that matter most: the moments when a figure is not reducible to being a semiotic function of the plot. For May, the redeeming moments are the inadvertent admissions of weakness, vulnerability, and need that occasionally break through the proud exteriors presented to the world. May's greatest achievement in *Ishtar* is her ability to tease out those secret, small vulnerabilities and strengths in her central characters. It is in those fleeting and almost invisible expressions of their true feelings that Lyle and Chuck momentarily liberate themselves from the dumbness of their own film and the stupidity of their situations.

Chuck is a self-declared ladies' man—smooth, polished, glib, confident. Yet it is his moments of breakdown—the fault lines beneath his lady-killer patina—that May is interested in revealing. His attempted suicide scene early in the film tells much more about him than his "How to Pick Up Girls" aplomb in the local singles spot. Lyle is a self-conscious klutz, a nerd, but it is his sincerity, his good-heartedness, his can-do spunkiness underneath all of his nebbishness that emerges in times of crisis.

Ishtar is a critique of American innocence in general and of the emotional immaturity and superficiality of the American male in particular. Lyle and Chuck are American idealists in over their heads with confusing emotional and social realities which they try to wish or dream away. They take their place in the rogues' gallery of American boy-men which May has been delineating throughout her career (never more profoundly than in *Mikey and Nicky*).

Lyle and Chuck inhabit a world that is stranger and crueler and emotionally more complex than they can understand. Some of the most touching (and ludicrous) moments in *Ishtar* are those in which—while terrorists or intelligence agents gather to murder them in the desert—these two American Adams utterly fail to understand anything that is happening around them. In one scene, as if they were not wandering lost in the Sahara but sitting in an air-conditioned singles bar on the Upper West Side, they argue about whose "girl" the terrorist Shirra Assel is, based on who saw her first and to whom she talked the most. In another scene, while high-tech hired killers stalk them in helicopters, they fret about whether the dye in their Arab caftans is carcinogenic. As they crawl along in a sandstorm, literally dying of thirst, they hash out the lyrics to a new song: "My lips are on fire (with my desire)."

Perhaps never has the American entrepreneurial faith in being free to make oneself up as one goes along been more devastatingly and hilariously questioned. May makes a comedy out of what she previously treated tragically in *Mikey and Nicky*. *Ishtar*'s comedy tells the audience how hard it is to dislike such innocence, no matter how wrong it is. Doomed as they are, Lyle and Chuck are almost enviable in their optimism and their boundless faith in themselves. As anchormen smile through national crises of confidence on the evening news, May suggests that perhaps laughter is more appropriate than tears as a response to America. In May's black comedy, the American male innocently laughs his way to apocalypse, trying to make his charm pass for self-knowledge.

Yet *Ishtar* is a far from perfect film. There were rumors, before the film's long-postponed release, of fights between the principals, of radical editorial cuts and revisions, of massive deletions of parts of the original script and of extensive rewritings and reshootings of other parts. It is hard not to feel that some of these problems took their toll on the finished film. There are gaps and confusions in the narrative and strange ellipses within particular scenes. Most important, the presentation of the relationship between Lyle and Chuck is simply too cursory to accomplish all that May obviously intended. Although a few scenes reveal some of the adult emotional confusions under the boyish surfaces of Chuck's and Lyle's lives, truly complex emotional moments are fairly scarce in *Ishtar*. The first twenty-five minutes and about fifteen minutes of the desert-wandering scenes contain virtually everything of interest in the film. One can respect May's intentions, even while believing that the film as it was made never quite lives up to them.

The superficiality in the presentation of the relationship between the principals for most of *Ishtar* is all the more surprising in the light of May's earlier triumph in *Mikey and Nicky*. In that film she daringly lavished what seemed like infinite time and space on the presentation and development of a complex relationship between two characters and explored a subterranean emotional realm in which male rivalry, envy, and jealousy were hopelessly mixed up with love, friendship, and admiration. May moves in to explore the same psychological territory in *Ishtar*, but for some reason she does not go nearly as far as she did in the earlier film in showing the conflicts and contradictions that develop out of the clash of innocence and experience. In comparison with that masterwork, *Ishtar* seems all the thinner.

Perhaps the most damning thing that can be said about the film is that the scenes that audiences and critics apparently remember are the blind-camel slapstick between Charles Grodin and Warren Beatty or the munitions-auction gibberish spouted by Dustin Hoffman—scenes that have almost no emotional resonance. However entertaining the occasional comedy may be, one had expected from the creator of *Mikey and Nicky* much more than Abbott and Costello pratfalls and camel jokes. One had hoped for a darker and far more searching investigation of American manhood, American innocence, and American dreaming from this great artist.

Raymond Carney

Reviews
America. CLVI, June 6, 1987, p. 466.
The Christian Century. CIV, July 1, 1987, p. 598.
Films in Review. XXXVIII, August, 1987, p. 422.
Life. X, May, 1987, p. 62.
Los Angeles Times. May 15, 1987, VI, p. 1.
Macleans. C, May 25, 1987, p. 54.
The National Review. XXXIX, July 3, 1987, p. 52.
The New Republic. CXCVI, June 8, 1987, p. 26.
The New York Times. May 15, 1987, p. C3.
The New York Times. June 7, 1987, p. H24.
The New Yorker. LXIII, June 1, 1987, p. 102.
Newsweek. CIX, May 18, 1987, p. 76.
Time. CXXIX, May 18, 1987, p. 85.
Variety. CCCXXVII, May 13, 1987, p. 19.
The Wall Street Journal. May 14, 1987, p. 26.

JEAN DE FLORETTE

Origin: France
Released: 1986
Released in U.S.: 1987
Production: Pierre Grunstein for Renn Productions/Films A2/RAI 2/DD
  Productions; released by Orion Classics
Direction: Claude Berri
Screenplay: Claude Berri and Gérard Brach; based on the novel *L'Eau des*
  collines, by Marcel Pagnol
Cinematography: Bruno Nuytten
Editing: Arlette Langmann, Hervé de Luze, and Noëlle Boisson
Art direction: Bernard Vezat
Music: Jean-Claude Petit
MPAA rating: PG
Running time: 122 minutes

> *Principal characters:*
> César Soubeyran .... Yves Montand
> Jean de Florette .... Gérard Depardieu
> Ugolin .... Daniel Auteuil
> Aimée .... Élisabeth Depardieu
> Manon..................... Ernestine Mazurowna
> Pique-Bouffigue.................. Marcel Champel
> Philoxène....................... Armand Meffre

French filmmaking has influenced the American market in waves—first in the 1930's with such directors as Jean Renoir and Marcel Carné, and later during the 1960's, with New Wave and avant-garde filmmakers, such as François Truffaut, Jean-Luc Godard, Agnès Varda, Alain Resnais, and Louis Malle. Their work played mainly at art houses and for intellectual audiences; nevertheless, it influenced the style and content of mainstream American filmmaking in the late 1960's and early 1970's. After a steady, gradual decline in the popularity of French films, Claude Berri's screen adaptation of Marcel Pagnol's epic novel *L'Eau des collines* (1962-1963; water of the hills) represents a colossal work. The acclaimed project, filmed simultaneously in two parts, *Jean de Florette* and *Manon of the Spring* (1987; reviewed in this volume), cost $17 million dollars, a price tag that makes it the most expensive French production made before 1988.

Jean de Florette, released three months before its sequel both in France and in the United States, does not pretend to stand alone; its ending leaves audiences begging for more. Claude Berri created one of the most successful foreign films of the 1980's in a work with stunning clarity, style, and purpose. The film's strong points are its brilliant characterization, its clear capturing of the harsh yet beautiful countryside of southern France, and its insistent grappling with fundamental issues of good and evil, trust and betrayal, survival and defeat. While many French films leave American audiences baffled about who the villains and heroes are or what the central conflict is, *Jean de Florette* contains no such ambiguity. The only feature of the film which might disconcert American viewers is the intentionally slow pace; the editors' long takes and cinematographer Bruno Nuytten's long shots of parched hills and fields overwhelm the human figures struggling to live on them.

The book *L'Eau des collines* is in keeping with the Marseilles Trilogy, a film epic that Pagnol wrote and produced: *Marius* (1933), *Fanny* (1948), and *César* (1949). In a real-life battle that parallels the struggles depicted in the film, Pagnol's widow resisted selling the rights to the book to Berri for six years. The notion of making a two-part film with each section being released separately over a three-month period was a daring one. Yet, with the support of Orion Classics, the French Socialist government, assistance for television rights from French television, and money from various production companies, the thirty-six-week filming was funded. Excellent box office returns and rave reviews substantiated Berri's faith in the commercial and artistic merit of the project.

The film opens by introducing Ugolin (Daniel Auteuil), a 1930's farmer who wants to grow carnations on his arid family farm in the south of France. His canny uncle César Soubeyran, played with aplomb by Yves Montand, convinces him that his dreams are too small, that he should restore his farm to the glory that once was in his family, with orchards, vineyards, and flowers covering the barren fields. In order to realize this vision, he needs more water, which could be obtained if the long-standing enemy neighbor would only sell his property (which is lying fallow anyway). The neighbor, who refuses even to consider selling, conveniently dies and wills his property to the naïve, endearing Jean (Gérard Depardieu), who is delighted to leave his clerical job in the city to enjoy the dubious pleasure of farming the Provençal countryside just north of Marseilles.

From the very beginning, it is clear that these are more than simple stereotypes of fools, knaves, and tools. Jean represents many things, including the artist; he is the man who appreciates beauty for its own sake. His sensitive and loving nature shines through in his relationship with his retired opera-singer wife, Aimée, played with sweet candor by Élisabeth Depardieu. His idealism extends to his belief in learning, for he bases his farming practices on the latest books and scientific methods.

Jean also places faith in God, nature, and his fellow human beings, a generosity which proves to be totally unfounded. His neighbors cover with concrete the spring that would save his drought-stricken crops, and townspeople and neighboring farmers stay silent, loyal to their own despicable kind by not revealing their knowledge of this treachery. Meanwhile, Jean, Aimée, and their daughter, Manon (Ernestine Mazurowna), work with indomitable energy, archetypes of hope and heroism. César, Ugolin, and the locals stand in contrast as three types of evil: the coldly calculating manipulator; the simple-minded tool, who has sympathetic impulses but neither the intelligence nor the will to act on them; and finally the complacent crowd, content to watch passively.

Élisabeth Depardieu's presence lends refinement and artistic delicacy to the role of Aimée, a woman in love with a man who well deserves her devotion. Ernestine Mazurowna makes an intense, almost mournful Manon, whose observation of the family and neighbors is as stoic as it is unobtrusive. Both females display a greater savvy and a more natural instinct about people than Jean. Despite Ugolin's apparent friendliness and eagerness to help, Aimée and Manon distrust him and find his very presence repulsive. Having been a victim of superficial judgments himself, Jean advises them not to dislike Ugolin simply because he appears homely and simple. In a touching scene in which Jean tells his lovely daughter of the beauty that may reside within a hideous exterior, the audience is tempted to believe Jean's assessment, even though in this case a distasteful appearance is a fair indicator of the inner self. As the ones who see clearly, who survive disaster and hardship, Aimée and her daughter are identified with the land, which remains both obdurate and vital in spite of the machinations of men.

The actors' finesse in playing both sides of relatively flat characters sustains the momentum of the film. Depardieu's Jean combines a kind of robust lustiness with the characteristics of a martyred victim. His apparent innocence runs counter to his alcoholism and his bitterness as a hunchback, a man cursed by nature and by God. Just when he is at the point of despair, he returns with his boundless love of life and possibilities. Daniel Auteuil's Ugolin is another character who is less simple and selfish than he first appears. With a name redolent of the "pangolin" (anteater), his desires seem almost animal, until he reveals his dream of growing carnations. As he falls under the spell of Jean's good-hearted friendship, he seems on the verge of betraying his uncle and his own selfish interests in favor of decency and human sympathy. With the help of a coolly played César, Ugolin maintains his greed and squelches his more honorable emotions. Montand's César has all the graying good looks and solicitude of a charming favorite uncle, but he appears to be devoid of emotion except for a taste for revenge. In a metaphor for the progress of the peasant, Ugolin turns his back on art, sentiment, justice, and even science, in favor of the basest of motives, pure commercial greed.

The film abounds with suggestive overtones, playing on language, allusion, and sound. When Jean speaks of the "paradise of Zola," the audience is forewarned that this naturalistic piece will end in humiliating defeat for its protagonist. In a richly ironic and humorous scene, Ugolin, truly an "authentic" peasant, confuses Jean's description of "authentic farming" with growing something called "othentics," a plant that Ugolin puzzles over for some time. Ominous storm clouds and thunder building up in real life and racing through fitful dreams make the long-needed rains appear threatening. The musical theme based on Giuseppe Verdi's *La forza del destino* underscores the sense of impending doom, as viewers watch Jean's experiments first prosper and then wither and die.

Just as the audience is unsure whether rains moving in are real or dreamed, it is also fooled by a series of minor reversals. The high-priced rabbit that seems to be a worthless purchase actually does breed handsome offspring, but they die in the drought, with Jean letting the few survivors loose before they perish with the rest. The bookish, scientific farming methods that the Soubeyrans predict will fail actually succeed bountifully at first, only to fall prey to drought later in the season. The seeming wealth and well-being of the family, with their citified clothes and furnishings, disintegrates into abject poverty. The ultimate humiliation comes when Jean asks Aimée for her gold locket to be pawned, whereupon she confesses that she has already sold it and that it was actually only gold-plated.

Berri's film is composed of long shots and longer takes, with characters moving through the frame in the same labored way that they pace up and down the vast, rocky terrain of Provence. Interior shots, taken at medium distance, create a sense of claustrophobia and meager light, in sharp contrast to the washed-out brilliance of sunbaked hillsides. While some may find Berri's filming style too flat or his characters too clearly good or evil, he creates a sense of human beings locked in timeless struggles, moving at the same pace that Sisyphus must have rolled his boulder up the mountainside.

Rebecca Bell-Metereau

Reviews
Commonweal. CXIV, July 17, 1987, p. 420.
Films in Review. XXXIX, February, 1988, p. 101.
Los Angeles Times. July 17, 1987, VI, p. 1.
The New Republic. CXCVII, July 6, 1987, p. 26.
The New York Times. June 21, 1987, p. C3.
The New Yorker. LXIII, July 13, 1987, p. 76.
Newsweek. CX, July 13, 1987, p. 61.
Time. CXXX, July 20, 1987, p. 75.
The Wall Street Journal. July 9, 1987, p. 26.
Washingtonian. XXII, August, 1987, p. 69.

THE LAST EMPEROR

Origin: England/Italy
Production: Jeremy Thomas (AA); released by Columbia Pictures
Direction: Bernardo Bertolucci (AA)
Screenplay: Mark Peploe (AA) with Bernardo Bertolucci (AA)
Cinematography: Vittorio Storaro (AA)
Editing: Gabriella Cristiani (AA)
Production design: Ferdinando Scarfiotti (AA)
Art direction: Gianni Giovagnoni, Gianni Silvestri, and Maria Teresa Barbasso; set decoration, Bruno Cesari (AA) and Oswaldo Desideri (AA)
Special effects: Yang Jingguo, Gino de Rossi, and Fabrizio Martinelli
Makeup: Feng Guixiang and Zhang Wanziang
Costume design: James Acheson (AA)
Sound: Les Wiggins
Music: Ryuichi Sakamoto (AA), David Byrne (AA), and Cong Su (AA)
Songs: Johann Strauss, "Kaiser Walzer"; Hank Drake and Harry Akst, "Am I Blue"
MPAA rating: PG-13
Running time: 162 minutes
Running time in U.S.: 166 minutes

Principal characters:

Pu Yi (adult)	John Lone
Wan Jung	Joan Chen
Reginald Johnston (R. J.)	Peter O'Toole
The governor of the prison	Ying Ruocheng
Amakasu	Ryuichi Sakamoto
Chen Pao Shen	Victor Wong
Big Li	Dennis Dun
Eastern Jewel	Maggie Han
Tzu Hsui	Lisa Lu
Wen Hsiu	Wu Jun
Pu Yi (age 3)	Richard Vuu
Ar Mo (wet nurse)	Jade Go

When Bernardo Bertolucci first approached the Chinese about making a feature film in China, he had two possible projects in mind: an adaptation of André Malraux's *La Condition humaine* (1933; *Man's Fate*, 1934), a book about the dispute between Mao Tse-tung and Chou En-lai, and *The Last Emperor*, a film to be based on Pu Yi's autobiographical *From Emperor to Citizen* (1964), a collaboration between Pu Yi and Communist hacks, one of whom, Li Wenda, was to be named as adviser to the film. Although Chinese officials rejected the Malraux novel because it was too politically sensitive, Bertolucci did receive, probably because of his left-wing politics, government permission and cooperation for the filming of the last emperor's story. According to Bertolucci, the Chinese, who had final approval of the screenplay, made only a few factual changes in his script.

In *The Last Emperor*, Bertolucci presents not only the story of Pu Yi (John Lone), but also the development of twentieth century China, since Pu Yi's life (1905-1967) spanned the period of the Chinese warlords, revolutionary leader Sun Yat-sen, Chiang Kai-shek, and the Communist takeover. Although he does not stress the historical background, since his primary focus is on Pu Yi, Bertolucci shows the audience how historical forces beyond the protagonist's control shaped Pu Yi, who became a puppet for a series of masters but who nevertheless continued his unrealistic quest to regain his lost power. Although Bertolucci has maintained that Pu Yi's story is one of the metamorphosis of a dragon into a butterfly, there is some question about the emperor's transformation.

The Last Emperor begins in 1951 with Pu Yi's return from the Soviet Union, where he had spent five years in prison, to a Chinese Communist camp for political prisoners in need of "re-education." As Pu Yi and his fellow prisoners await processing, he unsuccessfully attempts suicide, an action that triggers a series of flashbacks to the events which preceded his capture in 1946.

The first of the flashbacks (which are intercut with the prison scenes) is to the Forbidden City, where he was enthroned as emperor in 1908. The scenes from early childhood, photographed in rich yellows and reds, contrast vividly with the stark drabness of the prison scenes, although the colors are heightened artificially as the young Pu Yi (Richard Vuu) is emotionally, literally, and cinematically a prisoner as well as an emperor. Pu Yi never controls his destiny and is instead a puppet manipulated by others, first by the Dowager Empress, Tsu Hsui (Lisa Lu), who names him, for her own purposes, to succeed her, then by the eunuchs who both serve and shape him. Because he has been taken from his mother and has only minimal contact with his family, he is a lonely child who is suckled by his wet nurse (Jade Go) until he is eight years old, when she too is taken from him. Before the arrival in 1919 of Reginald Johnston (Peter O'Toole), his Scottish tutor, Pu Yi's environment has established his character in true Freudian fashion.

In the flashbacks, Bertolucci establishes several themes and motifs which help characterize Pu Yi and account for his behavior. At pivotal points in his development—when his wet nurse is taken away, when he attempts to follow his father and younger brother, and when he wants to leave the Forbidden City—he has gates closed before him, shutting him in and making him a prisoner. (When his first wife returns to him in 1946, just prior to his capture, she also closes the door on him, shutting him out of her life.) Adding to the sense of entrapment are the caged pets—the cricket and the mouse—that become images of his own situation. The two motifs are linked dramatically and symbolically when Pu Yi, frustrated at having the gates closed on him again, kills his pet mouse by throwing it against the gate. Even when he is expelled from the Forbidden City in 1924 and the gates do open for him, those literal gates are succeeded by additional metaphorical gates—he does not reach America nor does he escape the Soviets.

Bertolucci also uses screens, sheets, and obstacles to block the audience's view of what happens, thereby suggesting the difficulty of knowing Pu Yi's inner life. In order to reveal the sexual impact the eunuchs have had on Pu Yi, whose homosexuality is only intimated, Bertolucci uses a sheet game in which Pu Yi must guess a eunuch's identity by touching the eunuch, who is covered by a sheet. This game is repeated after Pu Yi's marriage when his wife, Wan Jung (Joan Chen), and consort, Wen Hsiu (Wu Jun) join him under the sheets in his only apparently successful heterosexual love-making—even this game, however, is interrupted by the fire the eunuchs start in the storeroom.

The only positive male influence in the young Pu Yi's life is provided by Reginald Johnston (R. J.), whose tutoring helps his charge to see both literally (he overcomes eunuch objections and receives eyeglasses for Pu Yi) and metaphorically (he exposes Pu Yi to the Western world and helps him look beyond his palace prison). Under R. J.'s tutelage, Pu Yi recognizes the corruption within the Forbidden City and determines to effect reforms by expelling the fifteen hundred eunuchs, appointing new councillors, and reducing his staff; the audience is also aware, however, of how little real power he has because he must rely on armed forces outside the Forbidden City to expel the eunuchs. In effect, Bertolucci constantly reminds the viewer of Pu Yi's dependence on the forces outside the walls.

When he is expelled from the Forbidden City in 1924, Pu Yi merely exchanges one interior set for another and is in fact rarely photographed outside. His new manipulators become the Japanese, who virtually imprison him in Tientsin and plan to use him for their eventual invasion of Manchuria, Pu Yi's homeland.

In 1931, the Japanese install Pu Yi, the Manchu Dragon, as their puppet ruler of Manchuria, or Manchukuo. To stress the emptiness of Pu Yi's rule, Bertolucci films the coronation outdoors in an isolated wasteland in a set that features only a throne. After the ceremony, Bertolucci returns to his claustrophobic indoor sets, replete with darkness and shadows. Once more a ruler, Pu Yi is again a prisoner, for the Japanese expect him to endorse their policies. When he later returns from a visit to Japan, he finds himself virtually stripped of power; his subsequent attempt to inform his staff of his decisions leads to their departure and to his speech to an empty room. Meanwhile, his domestic situation has worsened because Wan Jung, now an opium addict, has become pregnant by his driver, and Pu Yi's attempts to claim paternity are rejected by the Japanese, who later murder the healthy child and send Wan Jung away.

When Manchuria is invaded by Soviet troops, Pu Yi is captured, interned in the Soviet Union, and finally returned to the Chinese Communists. The scenes of Pu Yi's re-education, which have been intercut with the flashbacks, demonstrate how a dragon may indeed be transformed to a butterfly. The governor of the prison (Ying Ruocheng) is intent on making Pu Yi confront his actions, acknowledge his guilt, and become a useful citizen in the New Order. To that end, he removes Pu Yi from his followers and family and forces him to undertake chores incompatible with his station in life. By photographing Pu Yi as he exercises with hundreds of fellow prisoners, Bertolucci depicts him as a cog in a machine, not as a distinctive individual. The outside lighting, which seems to brighten during Pu Yi's re-education, also suggests that the last emperor has seen the light, or the truth. While the cinematography suggests a transformation, the script is more ambiguous; the well-intentioned and humane governor questions the transformation, indicating that Pu Yi has changed superficially only in order to survive. This ambiguity also occurs in two later sequences just before his death in 1967. During the Cultural Revolution he attempts to aid the governor, whom the Red Guards are persecuting, but Pu Yi's demeanor contains enough royal presumption to raise doubts about his being a "butterfly." Similarly, when he visits the Forbidden City and steps surreptitiously over the restraining rope to ascend to the throne, his motives are unclear. Is it curiosity or the unquenchable desire to return to the past and to power?

The Last Emperor, like Bertolucci's earlier successes *Il Conformista* (1970; *The Conformist*) and *Ultimo Tango a Parigi* (1972; *Last Tango in Paris*), concerns a weak man placed in an untenable situation, overwhelmed by forces beyond his control; and, like *Novecento* (1976; *1900*), it spans much of the twentieth century and details middle-class decadence and the rise of the proletariat. Because of its successful blending of biography and national history, its topical relevance, and its cinematography, *The Last Emperor*, which won all nine Academy Awards for which it was nominated— making it one of the most honored films in Oscar history—marks a dramatic return to form by Bertolucci, whose career had been in a decline. Though the political militancy of his earlier films is somewhat muted in *The Last Emperor*, Bertolucci remains an effective spokesman for leftist humanism.

Thomas L. Erskine

Reviews

America. CLVIII, January 9, 1988, p. 17.
Commonweal. CXIV, December 18, 1987, p. 747.
Los Angeles Times. November 20, 1987, VI, p. 1.
The New Republic. CXCVII, December 14, 1987, p. 22.
The New York Times. November 20, 1987, p. C3.
The New Yorker. LXIII, November 30, 1987, p. 98.
Newsweek. CX, November 23, 1987, p. 81.
Sight and Sound. LVI, Winter, 1986/87, p. 38.
Time. CXXX, November 23, 1987, p. 100.
Variety. CCCXXVIII, October 7, 1987, p. 16.
The Wall Street Journal. November 25, 1987, p. 12.

LETHAL WEAPON

Production: Richard Donner and Joel Silver; released by Warner Bros.
Direction: Richard Donner
Screenplay: Shane Black
Cinematography: Stephen Goldblatt
Editing: Stuart Baird
Production design: J. Michael Riva
Art direction: Eva Bohn and Virginia L. Randolph; set decoration, Marvin
  March
Special effects: Chuck Gaspar
Makeup: Scott Eddo
Costume design: Mary Malin
Sound: Bill Nelson
Music direction: Christopher Brooks
Music: Michael Kamen and Eric Clapton
MPAA rating: R
Running time: 110 minutes

> *Principal characters:*
> Martin Riggs .... Mel Gibson
> Roger Murtaugh .... Danny Glover
> Mr. Joshua .... Gary Busey
> The General........................ Mitchell Ryan
> Michael Hunsaker.................... Tom Atkins
> Trish Murtaugh .... Darlene Love
> Rianne Murtaugh .... Traci Wolfe
> Amanda Hunsaker................. Jackie Swanson
> Nick Murtaugh .... Damon Hines
> Carrie Murtaugh .... Ebonie Smith

Lethal Weapon is a police action-adventure film in which two mismatched detectives, one black and one white, become buddies in the face of a common threat: heroin dealers. The plot and premise are simple and have been used to comedic effect in recent films such as *48 HRS* (1982) and *Running Scared* (1986). Like these films, *Lethal Weapon* combines realistic setting, detail, and dialogue with overblown and improbable action scenes. *Lethal Weapon*, however, is not a comedy, the mismatch being psychological rather than situational. The film's sensitivity to character development is more akin to Norman Jewison's *In the Heat of the Night* (1967), the first police film with black and white leads. Here the initial resentment between the detectives is based on a color-blind sense of professionalism, however, making *Le-*

thal Weapon one of the more positive images of blacks and whites working together.

Martin Riggs (Mel Gibson), a narcotics detective who becomes emotionally unstable after his wife is killed in a car accident, is transferred to the homicide division and is assigned a new partner, Roger Murtaugh (Danny Glover). Riggs resents being removed from the action, while Murtaugh resents the threat Riggs poses to his middle-aged complacence. Murtaugh lives in the suburbs with his wife and three children, owns a fishing boat, and has just turned fifty—too old to deal with a partner "on the edge." The younger Riggs lives in a trailer on the beach, drinks beer for breakfast, and wavers between suicide and psychosis. Riggs even keeps a special hollow-point bullet for the purpose of killing himself.

Murtaugh and Riggs investigate the apparent suicide of Amanda Hunsaker (Jackie Swanson), a twenty-two-year-old prostitute who jumped from her apartment window. Even before her jump, however, Amanda proves to have been poisoned while high on cocaine. Her father, Michael Hunsaker (Tom Atkins), demands that Murtaugh find and kill the people responsible for his daughter's death, because he once saved Murtaugh's life in Vietnam. When Riggs kills Amanda's drug dealer in a shoot-out, Murtaugh is satisfied that the case is closed and invites Riggs to his house for dinner.

The dinner scene expands on an experience both men share: Vietnam. Murtaugh has put the war behind him and become an all-American, middle-class family man. The death of Riggs's wife, however, destroyed Riggs's attempt to join mainstream American life. Now, like Sylvester Stallone's Rambo, he is a self-acknowledged killing machine on the fringes of society.

The next morning, Riggs convinces Murtaugh that a prostitute who witnessed Amanda's jump might have delivered the poisoned cocaine to Amanda. As Riggs and Murtaugh approach her house to interrogate her, it explodes. The switch used to trigger the explosives reminds Riggs of the kind the CIA used in Vietnam. Furthermore, a neighborhood youngster saw a meter man at the house with a Special Forces tattoo identical to one on Riggs's arm. Vietnam has come home to Los Angeles.

Murtaugh confronts Hunsaker, who confesses that he uses his bank to front a heroin operation run by the same former CIA agents, soldiers, and mercenaries who secretly ran the Vietnam War from Laos. Amanda was killed to convince Hunsaker not to leave the operation. Hunsaker is about to tell Murtaugh about the shipment due to arrive at the end of the week, when albino strongman Mr. Joshua (Gary Busey) shoots him from a helicopter.

The General (Mitchell Ryan), who heads the heroin operation, and Mr. Joshua kidnap Murtaugh's eldest daughter, Rianne (Traci Wolfe), in order to safeguard the heroin shipment. Murtaugh realizes that his daughter will be killed no matter what he does. In order to save her, he must trust the unpredictable but highly trained Riggs. The two almost succeed in ambushing the captors during a desert rendezvous, but they are captured. Murtaugh is shot in the shoulder.

Murtaugh and Riggs are taken back and interrogated in the nightclub that functions as another front for the heroin operation. The General rubs salt in Murtaugh's wound and threatens to rape his daughter in his presence. Meanwhile, Mr. Joshua and a Vietnamese assistant torture Riggs with electric shocks. When Mr. Joshua leaves, Riggs uses his legs to strangle the assistant. The General is laughing at Murtaugh's threats, telling him that "there are no more heroes in the world," when Riggs enters, throws the dead assistant at two guards, grabs a gun, and frees Murtaugh and his daughter.

The ensuing shoot-out provides catharsis to the torture sequence, validating Riggs's code that there are no rules or laws except survival and vengeance. The General and Mr. Joshua must die. Murtaugh shoots and kills the General as he tries to escape in his car. Riggs and Murtaugh then chase and capture Mr. Joshua at Murtaugh's house before he can harm the family. Riggs will not settle for a simple arrest, however, instead offering Mr. Joshua a "shot at the title." The final fight sequence is supposed to showcase Riggs using three unusual forms of martial arts, but it fails to provide the intended climax. The searchlight from a police helicopter and the mist from a spewing fire hydrant make it almost impossible to see the two fighters, while the editing fragments the fight into a series of fast-moving body parts.

In the end, Riggs lets Mr. Joshua live, but not for long. As Murtaugh embraces the exhausted Riggs, Mr. Joshua wrestles a gun from the officer handcuffing him. Murtaugh and Riggs draw in unison, shooting Mr. Joshua. This scene, shot in slow motion, provides the climax that the fight sequence does not. The slow motion reveals a balletic harmony between Murtaugh and Riggs, each trying to save the other. As the film slowly returns to normal speed, Riggs collapses into Murtaugh's arms.

The film ends on Christmas Day. Riggs visits the grave of his wife, then stops by Murtaugh's house to give him a present: the hollow-point bullet. Riggs tries to leave, but Murtaugh begs him to join the family for Christmas dinner; Riggs accepts the invitation.

Throughout *Lethal Weapon*, people exclaim that there are no more heroes in the 1980's. Men are too sensitive. Riggs, after all, cries for his dead wife and is almost driven to suicide. What eventually galvanizes Murtaugh and Riggs into heroic lethal weapons is a threat to family: the kidnapping of Rianne. Unfortunately, most film reviewers did not believe that use of a black family could justify such violent defense, dismissing the Murtaughs as an attempt to capitalize on the great success of "The Cosby Show." The assumption is that happy and cohesive black families are solely a television reality. There is an added irony in that Roger Murtaugh was originally written as a white character.

A. M. Rosenthal, associate editor of *The New York Times*, wrote an editorial condemning the portrayal of the CIA and Special Forces (formerly called the Green Berets) in *Lethal Weapon*. According to Rosenthal, the Vietnam CIA and Special Forces veterans are the new villains in film, iconographically equivalent to the Nazis. This is an odd assertion at a time when films such as *Platoon* (1986), *Full Metal Jacket* (1987; reviewed in this volume), and *Hanoi Hilton* (1987) redefine the Vietnam War as what one reviewer calls "the touchstone of manhood." *Lethal Weapon* is no exception. All the main characters in the film, good and bad, are Vietnam veterans. While most films take "our boys" back to Vietnam to make men out of them, however, *Lethal Weapon* is content to stay at home and show the "Vietnamization" of American men and society. When Mr. Joshua demonstrates his willpower by holding his hand over a flame, he reminds the viewer more of G. Gordon Liddy than, as Rosenthal insists, a Nazi. In short, he is all-American.

Chon Noriega

Reviews
Chicago Tribune. March 6, 1987, VII, p. 35.
Films in Review. XXXVIII, May, 1987, p. 299.
The Hollywood Reporter. March 2, 1987, p. 3.
Jet. LXXII, April 6, 1987, p. 58.
Los Angeles Times. March 6, 1987, VI, p. 4.
Newsweek. CIX, March 16, 1987, p. 72.
The New Republic. CXCVI, April 13, 1987, p. 24.
The New York Times. March 6, 1987, p. C7.
People Weekly. XXVII, March 23, 1987, p. 8.
Time. CXXIX, March 23, 1987, p. 86.
Variety. March 4, 1987, p. 20.
The Village Voice. March 10, 1987, p. 60.
The Wall Street Journal. March 5, 1987, p. 26.
The Washington Post. March 6, 1987, WE, p. 27.
The Washington Post. March 6, 1987, II, p. 1.

THE LIVING DAYLIGHTS

Origin: Great Britain
Production: Albert R. Broccoli and Michael G. Wilson; released by Metro-Goldwyn-Mayer/United Artists
Direction: John Glen
Screenplay: Richard Maibaum and Michael G. Wilson; based on a short story of the same name by Ian Fleming
Cinematography: Alec Mills
Editing: John Grover and Peter Davies
Production design: Peter Lamont
Art direction: Terry Ackland-Snow; set decoration, Michael Ford
Special effects: John Richardson
Costume design: Emma Porteous
Sound: Colin Miller
Music: John Barry
Song: Pal Waaktaar, "The Living Daylights"
MPAA rating: PG
Running time: 130 minutes

Principal characters:
James Bond	Timothy Dalton
Kara Milovy	Maryam d'Abo
General Georgi Koskov	Jeroen Krabbe
Brad Whitaker	Joe Don Baker
General Leonid Pushkin	John Rhys-Davies
Kamran Shah	Art Malik
Necros	Andreas Wisniewski
Saunders	Thomas Wheatley
Q	Desmond Llewelyn
M	Robert Brown
Moneypenny	Caroline Bliss

Since the appearance of *Dr. No* in 1962, fans of the James Bond films have seen the series, a comic-book fantasy to begin with, become less realistic and more cartoonish. This degeneration has resulted in part from the personality of the star of the seven Bond films since Sean Connery left the series after *Diamonds Are Forever* (1971). While Connery is a rugged, inoffensively masculine performer, Roger Moore has been merely an adequate light comedian, more adept at quips than action, especially as he has aged. Moore's Bond films have been tailored both to his talents and his inadequacies, with inventive stunts and special effects taking an increasingly central role. As the stunts have grown more spectacular—though none has topped the skiing Bond's leap off a mountain at the beginning of *The Spy Who Loved Me* (1977)—the filmmakers believed that they had to top themselves in each new 007 adventure. *The Living Daylights,* while still crammed with exciting action, returns the series to the most realistic level in years with Moore replaced by Timothy Dalton, younger, more athletic, and more serious than his predecessor.

As with all recent Bond films, *The Living Daylights* opens with spectacular action. A team of British commandos is making an assault against a military base on Gibraltar, but one is a double agent who begins killing his apparent comrades. James Bond (Dalton), one of the commandos, struggles with this villain on a Land Rover careening along the narrow roads circumscribing the Rock. The sequence ends with the truck hurtling into the sea and Bond saved by the tiny parachute he has packed—even after it catches fire. He lands on the yacht of a bikini-clad young woman who has been complaining into a telephone that she wants a real man.

Bond appears next at a concert in Bratislava, Czechoslovakia, where he notices Kara Milovy (Maryam d'Abo), a beautiful young cellist. Bond is behind the Iron Curtain to aid in the defection of General Georgi Koskov (Jeroen Krabbe) of the Soviet State Security Committee (KGB). When Bond sees that the escaping Koskov is about to be shot by a sniper, he disobeys orders and only wounds rather than kills the sniper because it is Kara. (This part of the plot is based upon the 1966 Ian Fleming short story which gives the film its title.) In one of the more humorous segments of *The Living Daylights,* Bond and his cohorts smuggle the nervous, doubtful Koskov out of Czechoslovakia by encasing him in a sledlike capsule and propelling it through the Trans-Siberian natural gas pipeline.

Bond contacts Kara and realizes she has been betrayed by her lover Koskov, who intended for the British to kill her while she pretended to pose a threat to him. Bond sets about planning her escape from Czechoslovakia, which ends with their speeding down a snowy mountainside on her cello case while he uses her Stradivarius cello to guide it as they dodge the bullets of their pursuers. One of the pleasures of the Bond films is that the filmmakers know that such a chase cannot end merely with 007 reaching safety. As he, Kara, and the case cross the Austrian border, he tosses the priceless cello over the frontier barrier and catches it on the other side.

What follows is an uncharacteristically tame romantic interlude. When they check into Bond's favorite Vienna hotel, the fictional character most associated with the sexual revolution asks for two bedrooms instead of his usual suite. He and Kara even ride through the city in a horse-drawn carriage like tourists. There was considerable press speculation upon the film's release that this chaste Bond resulted from the realities of the age of acquired immune deficiency syndrome (AIDS), but his creators have denied this motivation. His more traditional courting of Kara is a reflection of the filmmakers' conception of 007 as a more serious man who tries to avoid using people. This new seriousness is also shown by the horror in Bond's face when one of his fellow British agents is sliced in half.

Meanwhile, back in England, Koskov is at the center of another escape, this one engineered by Necros (Andreas Wisniewski), a methodical Aryan assassin. Koskov has never intended to defect to the British but to Brad Whitaker (Joe Don Baker), a ruthless American arms dealer based in Tangier, Morocco. (The commando at the beginning of the film is one of Whitaker's men.) Unlike previous Bond villains, Whitaker and Koskov do not plan to take over the world. They merely want to make a fortune running weapons and opium.

With the help of General Leonid Pushkin (John Rhys-Davies), head of the KGB, Bond and Kara track the villains to Afghanistan where Whitaker's drug smuggling originates. There, the hero and heroine are further assisted by moujahadeen rebels led by Kamran Shah (Art Malik). A too-lengthy battle sequence ends with Kara, who does not know how to fly, piloting a cargo plane while Bond fights with Necros on a large net hanging out the rear of the aircraft. This scene is shot by director John Glen so that the viewers can see that real people are actually dangling outside a real plane hundreds of feet in the air.

Glen, a former editor and second-unit director in charge of his fourth Bond film, handles the action sequences with more skill than previously. Cinematographer Alec Mills, editors John Grover and Peter Davies, and production designer Peter Lamont, also in his fourth Bond effort, assist in making *The Living Daylights* the most technically proficient 007 adventure in some time. The plot and characters created by screenwriters Richard Maibaum, who has written or cowritten twelve Bonds, and Michael G. Wilson are the most interesting and entertaining since *The Spy Who Loved Me*.

The villains of *The Living Daylights* are much more believable than is usual in the Bond series. Koskov is a sybarite with no political beliefs and no morals. He prefers women and wine to danger and hopes to attain his objectives with as little risk as possible. Krabbe, that rare performer who can be dashing and klutzy at the same time, makes Koskov an amusing villain without diminishing him as a threat to Bond. Whitaker is a megalomaniac desperate for power. Obsessed with things military, Whitaker chooses only to play soldier since he is incapable of the discipline associated with such a life. Baker portrays Whitaker as a campier version of his cynical Central Intelligence Agency (CIA) agent in *Edge of Darkness*, the 1985 British miniseries that has revitalized his sagging career.

Serviceable performances are also turned in by Rhys-Davies, one of the most dependable character actors of the 1980's, and the bearded Malik, almost unrecognizable as the actor who plays Hari Kumar in the Public Broadcasting Service (PBS) miniseries *The Jewel in the Crown* (1984).

D'Abo's Kara is the sensitive, naïve kind of woman necessary to bring out Bond's tender side. Compared to Tanya Roberts, Maud Adams, Lois Chiles, and similar performers who have provided Bond's love interest in recent years, d'Abo is a good actress, but she has little screen presence and is instantly forgettable. In her brief appearance as the new Moneypenny, secretary to M, Bond's boss, Caroline Bliss makes more of an impact.

The twenty-fifth anniversary of the start of the Bond film series is an appropriate time to introduce a new actor to portray the invincible hero. No one is likely to play 007 as well as Connery, perhaps the most effective casting ever of a popular fictional character. With only one chance to play Bond, in *On Her Majesty's Secret Service* (1969), George Lazenby had insufficient opportunity to show his capability. A poor choice to begin with, Moore played Bond almost exactly as he did Simon Templar in the 1960's television series "The Saint." Moore's 007 is more dandy than superhero. The first choice as the new Bond, Pierce Brosnan—unavailable to take the role because NBC held him to his commitment to the "Remington Steele" television series—would have been more of the same.

While the massive publicity surrounding the choice of Dalton as the new 007 subtracted three years from his age as given in most reference works, it also presented him as an unknown Shakespearean stage actor, ignoring his supporting roles in such big-budget films as *Lion in Winter* (1968), *Mary, Queen of Scots* (1971), and *Agatha* (1979) and larger parts in American television miniseries such as *Centennial*, *Mistral's Daughter*, and *Sins*. Dalton is a much better actor than Moore but can be rather wooden, a humorless version of Harrison Ford. He works best when stiffness is appropriate to his role, as with his Rochester in a BBC dramatization of *Jane Eyre*.

Given these limitations, Dalton, who had rejected the role three times, is a fairly effective Bond. Albert R. Broccoli, producer of fifteen Bond films, thought that 007 had become too remote from reality, and Dalton prepared for the role by reading all the Fleming novels and finding a very human secret agent. Dalton's interpretation ignores the character's obsession with food, drink, clothes, cars, and sex, choosing to see him as as world-weary idealist, a man of principles trapped in a world without principles. This Bond is more introspective. He refuses to shoot Kara not because she is a beautiful woman but because he has just heard her play the cello with such feeling. The possibility of being fired by M for disobeying orders is almost a relief since he would be rescued from a world where such decisions of life and death must be made.

After one film, Dalton is no threat to Connery's status as the consummate 007. While he is closer than any of his predecessors to Fleming's original conception, he is still not exactly what Bond's creator had in mind. Since Fleming described Bond as a young Hoagy Carmichael, someone along the lines of Ben Cross or Daniel Day-Lewis might have been a better choice. As things stand, however, Dalton is an improvement over Moore, and *The Living Daylights* is the best Bond adventure in years.

Michael Adams

Reviews
Films in Review. XXXVIII, October, 1987, p. 489.
The Humanist. XL, November/December, 1987, p. 43.
Los Angeles Times. July 31, 1987, VI, p. 1.
Macleans. C, August 3, 1987, p. 49.
New York. XX, August 10, 1987, p. 54.
The New York Times. July 31, 1987, p. C3.
Newsweek. CX, July 27, 1987, p. 56.
People Weekly. XXVIII, August 31, 1987, p. 8.
Rolling Stone. July 16, 1987, p. 37.
Time. CXXX, August 10, 1987, p. 55.
Variety. CCCXXVII, July 1, 1987, p. 10.
The Wall Street Journal. July 28, 1987, p. 30.

THE LONELY PASSION OF JUDITH HEARNE

Origin: Great Britain
Production: Peter Nelson and Richard Johnson for HandMade Films; released by Island Pictures
Direction: Jack Clayton
Screenplay: Peter Nelson; based on the novel of the same name by Brian Moore
Cinematography: Peter Hannan
Editing: Terry Rawlings
Production design: Michael Pickwoad
Art direction: Henry Harris; set decoration, Josie MacAvin
Costume design: Elizabeth Waller
Sound: Alistair Crocker
Music: Georges Delerue
MPAA rating: R
Running time: 110 minutes

Principal characters:
Judith Hearne .... Maggie Smith
James Madden...................... Bob Hoskins
Aunt D'Arcy...................... Wendy Hiller
Mrs. Rice .... Marie Kean
Bernard........................... Ian McNeice
Father Quigley .... Alan Devlin
Mary.............................. Rudi Davies
Moira O'Neill..................... Prunella Scales
Edie Marinan .... Aine Ni Mhuiri
Miss Friel .... Sheila Reid

In the three decades since *The Lonely Passion of Judith Hearne* was published in 1955, there have been several attempts made to bring Brian Moore's stark, poignant first novel to the screen. Deborah Kerr, Vanessa Redgrave, Shirley MacLaine, Faye Dunaway, and Joanne Woodward were all considered for the role of the unhappy Irish spinster, while a planned stage adaptation was offered first to Katharine Hepburn and later to Geraldine Page and Shirley Booth. The casting of Maggie Smith in the title role, however, seems a particularly fortuitous meeting of actress and character. Smith received an Oscar in 1969 for her performance in *The Prime of Miss Jean Brodie*, a film about an unmarried woman of a very different sort, and she has a unique talent for portraying women who are fragile, eccentric, and emotionally isolated.

The film also pairs Smith with Bob Hoskins, one of the best British actors to win international recognition in recent years, and in a story that depends very much on the believability of its two central characters, the interplay between Smith and Hoskins is crucial. Set in Ireland, the story itself is small in scale, a quiet drama centering on the final, crushing disappointment in the life of a lonely spinster. Yet inherent in Moore's story is an understanding of the full range of human emotions that can exist in seemingly ordinary lives.

Judith Hearne (Maggie Smith) is a middle-aged piano teacher left alone after years of caring for her stern, demanding Aunt D'Arcy (Wendy Hiller). Arriving at the latest in a long line of Dublin boardinghouses, she meets its owner, Mrs. Rice (Marie Kean), her fat, pampered son, Bernard (Ian McNeice), and Mrs. Rice's brother, James Madden (Bob Hoskins), who has spent the last thirty years in the United States and is full of largely fabricated stories of his successes overseas. Hoping to attract his notice, Judith encourages his boasting and suggests that he accompany her to morning Mass. Although in reality she finds him brash and common, Judith begins to see Madden as her last chance for marriage and an end to her own bleak and unhappy existence.

For his part, Madden is far more interested in the expensive jewelry that his sister's new boarder wears than he is in Judith herself. Madden's taste in women runs more to the boardinghouse maid, Mary (Rudi Davies), whom he punishes after catching her with Bernard. He invites Judith to the pictures, however, and afterward tells her of his plans to open an American-style restaurant, mistaking her enthusiasm for a willingness to invest in the project. The spiteful Mrs. Rice soon disrupts their already confused relationship by informing her brother of Judith's true financial circumstances and accusing Judith of hoping to marry Madden for his own small savings, a turn of events which sends Judith on a drinking binge while Madden forces himself on Mary. The situation worsens, exacerbated by Bernard's cruel treatment of Judith, and she continues drinking heavily, at last humiliating herself in front of Madden and leaving the boardinghouse for a hotel.

Judith visits an alcoholic friend, Edie Marinan (Aine Ni Mhuiri), in a clinic, sneaking her a bottle of whiskey which the two of them share. Suffering a crisis of faith and unable to control her drinking, Judith finds no comfort in a talk with her priest, Father Quigley (Alan Devlin), and finally collapses at the church altar. She is taken to the clinic as a patient, where she is visited by Madden, who still believes that she may have money to invest in his plan. Judith confronts him angrily, but the two part as tentative friends with Madden leaving Judith his new address in town. When Judith leaves the clinic, however, she throws his address out the window of the cab in a gesture that marks the final abandonment of her hopes and illusions.

Judith Hearne is a memorably touching character, an unremarkable woman in straitened circumstances whose plight nevertheless has great emotional impact. The status of single women has undergone a considerable change in the decades since Moore's book was written, yet the film arouses the viewer's sympathies for its lonely, timid protagonist despite the fact that yesterday's "spinsters" have been supplanted by today's "single career women"—quite a different image altogether. For Judith, however, who in failing to find a husband has failed to fulfill the primary goal of her upbringing, life offers little beyond the drab walls of her boardinghouse room. Hers is an existence marked by bullying landladies and condescending employers, a secret weakness for Irish whiskey and Sunday afternoons spent with a school friend whose family ridicules Judith behind her back.

Judith is also devoutly Catholic, and her faith has both sustained her and left her with feelings of guilt and shame over her drinking. Her crisis of faith occurs when she can no longer find solace in prayer and forgiveness in the face of the bleak future ahead of her, and her inability to believe in God leaves her utterly without recourse in the emptiness that surrounds her. Her desperate exchange with Father Quigley, in which the priest indicates that even his own faith is not absolute, precipitates Judith's emotional and physical collapse as she gives voice to the anguish and confusion she feels.

Maggie Smith's performance in the role is subtle and affecting. Her hesitant, nervous manner, her self-denigrating "It's only me" as she enters a room, and her sad, eager flirtation with Madden all convey the essence of a woman frightened by life and desperately searching for a way out of her loneliness. Smith is also superb in the film's more emotional scenes, as Judith fights and loses her battle with the bottle, cries out in despair against God, and berates Madden with an embittered recounting of her life's disappointments. Judith Hearne is a complex character—a woman of intelligence and deep feelings who has repressed her emotions and who can rationalize her way past her religious objections to drinking by promising that she will take "just a little nip"—and Smith invests her with sympathy and understanding.

Bob Hoskins is also excellent as the blunt, ambitious James Madden, a man whose dreams of success in America have ended in failure but who has managed to retain the conviction that his big break needs only a bit of luck—and Judith's financial backing. Madden is never intentionally cruel—he believes that he has made his motivations clear to Judith—but he is utterly lacking in the sensitivity that might have kept a more perceptive man from misreading Judith's hopes or visiting her at the clinic to pitch his plan one final time. He hides his past failures beneath bluster and boasting, mentioning his connections with "the hotel business" when he was in reality a doorman, and brutally forces himself on Mary the maid while convincing himself that she is agreeable to his advances. Madden emerges, in Hoskins' portrayal, as a callous, pugnacious, and self-deluded man who is nevertheless still capable of a gesture of pity toward Judith in the film's closing scenes.

Despite the strong performances of Smith and Hoskins, however, *The Lonely Passion of Judith Hearne* is at times wildly uneven in tone. Although the film's subject matter is complex and engrossing, director Jack Clayton's style is surprisingly heavy-handed. The story's few moments of humor are overplayed and obvious, Judith's drinking binge is clumsily staged, and the character of Bernard is a grotesque parody of a lazy, deceitful "momma's boy"—a characterization which undercuts the power of the scene in which Bernard humiliates a drunken Judith. The film has also been given, unnecessarily, a more upbeat ending than the book, which ended with Judith still a patient in the clinic. Yet the film captures the flavor of Ireland in its shots of pubs and city streets, priests and old women dressed in black, making it an inconsistent combination of absorbing character study, atmospheric settings, and ill-advised stylistic choices.

The Lonely Passion of Judith Hearne is at its best in its depiction of Judith's life and unfulfilled dreams, an accomplishment for which Maggie Smith's performance can claim the lion's share of praise. In spite of its sometimes disappointing lapses in directorial subtlety, the film is sustained by its two fine central portrayals and a story that remains intelligent and moving.

Janet E. Lorenz

Reviews
California. XIII, February, 1988, p. 33.
Cosmopolitan. CCIV, February, 1988, p. 40.
Los Angeles Times. December 23, 1987, VI, p. 1.
The New Republic. CXCVIII, January 25, 1988, p. 29.
The New York Times. December 23, 1987, p. C15.
The New Yorker. LXIII, December 28, 1987, p. 92.
Newsweek. CXI, January 11, 1988, p. 57.
People Weekly. XXIX, February 1, 1988, p. 8.
Time. CXXXI, February 1, 1988, p. 71.
Variety. CCCXXIX, December 16, 1987, p. 11.

MADE IN HEAVEN

Production: Raynold Gideon, Bruce A. Evans, and David Blocker; released by Lorimar
Direction: Alan Rudolph
Screenplay: Bruce A. Evans and Raynold Gideon
Cinematography: Jan Kiesser
Editing: Tom Walls
Production design: Paul Peters
Art direction: Steven Legler; set decoration, Rosemary Brandenburg and Lynn Wolverton
Special effects: Max W. Anderson
Makeup: Edward Ternes
Costume design: April Ferry
Sound: Ron Judkins and Robert Jackson
Music: Mark Isham
Song: Neil Young, "We've Never Danced"
MPAA rating: PG
Running time: 102 minutes

Principal characters:
Mike Shea/Elmo Barnett . . . . Timothy Hutton
Annie Packert/Ally Chandler. . . . . Kelly McGillis
Aunt Lisa. Maureen Stapleton
Annette Shea. . . . . Ann Wedgeworth
Steve Shea. James Gammon
Ben Chandler . . . . Don Murray
Brenda Carlucci . . . . Mare Winningham
Tom Donnelly . . . . Timothy Daly
Wiley Foxx . . . . Amanda Plummer
Donald Sumner . . . . David Rasche
Truck driver . . . . Neil Young
Stanky . . . . Tom Petty
Shark . . . . Ric Ocasek
Mario the Toymaker . . . . Tom Robbins
Emmett Humbird. . . . . Debra Winger
(uncredited)
Lucille . . . . Ellen Barkin
(uncredited)

Maverick filmmaker Alan Rudolph made a name for himself in the 1980's with two eccentric romantic fantasies, which were critically acclaimed for their visual style and nontraditional narratives. Though Rudolph had enjoyed some recognition during the 1970's, these two films, *Choose Me*

(1984) and *Trouble in Mind* (1985), established him as an independent writer and director who could appeal to an art-house crowd. Despite this non-mainstream reputation, Rudolph also directed a few commercial features for major studios, including *Roadie* (1980) and *Songwriter* (1984). *Made in Heaven*, produced under the auspices of Lorimar, seems to lie, although precariously, between Rudolph's independent efforts and his commercial endeavors.

Made in Heaven is yet another romantic fantasy made more fanciful by its use of Heaven as subject matter. The story line, like the plots of *Choose Me* and *Trouble in Mind*, concerns the pursuit of true love in spite of the pain and disillusionment that can often accompany it. The film opens in a small Southern town just after World War II. Mike Shea (Timothy Hutton), his girlfriend Brenda (Mare Winningham), and his parents (James Gammon and Ann Wedgeworth) attend a showing of Alfred Hitchcock's *Notorious* (1946). During the film, Brenda declares that she and Mike lead dull lives in comparison to the characters in Hitchcock's suspense classic. Her sentiments seem to be echoed by the black-and-white cinematography in which the beginning of *Made in Heaven* is shot. As the film unfolds, however, her statement soon proves to be not only ironic but also false.

Misfortune befalls Mike when Brenda leaves him to marry her employer and he is turned down for a job as a teller in a local bank. Mike decides to start a new life in California but gets no farther than one hundred miles from home when he is drowned while rescuing a young mother and her two children. To his shock and disbelief, Mike discovers that he has gone to Heaven. The new life he so desired becomes much more than he bargained for, signified by a switch from black-and-white cinematography to color.

In Heaven, Mike rediscovers those he lost while on Earth, including his Aunt Lisa (Maureen Stapleton), who helps him adjust to his situation. More important, he meets Annie (Kelly McGillis), an unborn soul who has not yet been to Earth. Mike and Annie fall in love, but their upcoming wedding—a marriage literally made in Heaven—is interrupted when Annie learns that it is her time to be born on Earth. Desperate not to lose his one true love, Mike strikes a bargain with Emmett Humbird (Debra Winger), an emissary of God. Mike will be reborn on Earth as a new being who will have no prior knowledge of Heaven or Annie. He will have thirty years to find Annie, though he will not know for whom or what he is searching. If they do find each other, they will know the same happiness they had in Heaven; if they do not, they will be doomed to loneliness and misery.

Annie is born as Ally Chandler, the daughter of a financially successful toy manufacturer, while Mike is reborn as Elmo Barnett, the son of an unwed mother from the wrong side of the tracks. Their positions as opposites on the social ladder only make it that much more difficult to find each other. The middle section of the film intercuts scenes illustrating the differences in their lives as they reach adulthood during the late 1960's. Ally attends college, meets and marries a young filmmaker, and becomes a successful toy designer for her father's company. Elmo leaves home, serves in the army during the Vietnam War, and then drifts across the country without goals or ambition.

Many of the characters and objects that had meaning to Mike and Annie in Heaven resurface on Earth to become part of their lives as Elmo and Ally. For example, Annie's fascination with toys in Heaven foreshadows Ally's career as a toy designer on Earth. While growing up, Ally has an imaginary friend named Mike. As an adult, she writes a novel called *The Care and Feeding of Mike*, a book that Elmo is shown reading while he drifts across the country during the 1970's. In Heaven, Mike finds a shovel, which he uses to help build a dream house (a life) for himself and Annie. He asks Emmett Humbird, God's emissary, if the shovel will have meaning to him when he is reborn on Earth. Emmett replies that it could, but that it might be symbolic of something else he will find on Earth, such as a guitar or trumpet. As Emmett predicted, a trumpet takes the place of the shovel as Elmo builds his life by learning to play the instrument. He records an album, of which the title song is "We've Never Danced," which was the last thing Annie said to Mike in Heaven before she was reborn on Earth as Ally.

Despite their class differences, both Elmo and Ally experience loneliness and despair. Elmo's lack of direction before he discovers the trumpet is symbolized by his aimless wanderings on the road, that frequently used metaphor for life. In Elmo's case, the road spirals downward into a kind of Hell as unsavory characters take advantage of him. He is led out of the depths by a visit from Emmett, who warns him that he is drifting, and by a chance meeting with Mr. and Mrs. Shea, his parents from his former life. The Sheas buy the trumpet for him, which he uses to improve his life. Ally's lowest point occurs when her husband leaves her because he cannot compete with her success and abilities. She finds her niche after her father dies, and she takes over the toy company.

All these events lead to the present, when Elmo, now a successful musician, meets Ally, divorced and humbled by her experiences, on a street in Los Angeles on his thirtieth birthday. Elmo and Ally's road to happiness, filled with obstacles and potholes, is a universal symbol, representing the battles and setbacks everyone faces in trying to build a fulfilling life. As a pre-credit title states, "The story you are about to see could be true. You may even know some of the people."

Throughout *Made in Heaven*, Elmo and Ally are searching for true love, much like Eve and Mickey in *Choose Me* and Hawk and Georgia in *Trouble in Mind*. Though each of the films features lighthearted moments and amusing episodes, the mood of all three films is melancholic. The characters in these films have an unshakable faith in love, but Rudolph puts them through a series of heartbreaking events that would test the faith of any believer, accounting in part for the downbeat mood. While the couples in *Choose Me* and *Trouble in Mind* do not quite find complete happiness, the pairing of Elmo and Ally at the end of *Made in Heaven* provides a traditional happy ending. The boy gets the girl.

Though Rudolph's depiction of Heaven could be termed surreal, the sets of *Made in Heaven*—not surprisingly—are whimsical, dreamlike representations of a paradise. The closest setting stylistically to those in *Choose Me* and *Trouble in Mind* is that of Stanky's bar, a smoky beer joint filled with dangerous characters and loose women. Here Elmo is tempted into committing theft by the seductive Lucille (Ellen Barkin). Stanky's, with its hot, red lighting and smoky atmosphere, clearly represents Hell, with Lucille as the Devil. A song on the sound track during this scene, entitled "Up Jumped the Devil," reinforces this interpretation. The scene is played for comedy, however, not tragedy.

The colorful patrons of Stanky's recall Rudolph's penchant for offbeat casting and his use of eccentric secondary characters to introduce an element of satire or irony. Stanky, the owner of the bar, is played by rock singer Tom Petty, whose harsh features and lanky body physically suggest the cynicism and potential cruelty of the character. Rock musicians Ric Ocasek of the Cars and Neil Young also make brief but significant cameos.

The oddest aspect concerning the cast is the omission of screen credit for Debra Winger's tour-de-force portrayal of Emmett, the very male emissary of God. The credits list Emmett as played by "Himself," which helps maintain the fantasy of the film. Ellen Barkin plays the evil Lucille, again without billing. Interestingly, these uncredited actresses are portraying those characters who embody absolute goodness and pure evil.

The reviews were mixed for *Made in Heaven*. The critics who disliked the film were divided between those who thought the Heaven sequences were too whimsical and those who thought the Earth segments were too dark. Perhaps what they were responding to ultimately were the compromises Rudolph had to make on his personal style to accommodate a mainstream Hollywood production. Still, the film fits comfortably with his other work and reveals some fascinating bits and pieces upon repeated viewings.

Susan Doll

Reviews
Chicago Tribune. November 6, 1987, VII, p. 31.
The New York Times. November 6, 1987, p. C16.
Newsweek. CX, November 16, 1987, p. 108.
People Weekly. XXVIII, November 30, 1987, p. 18.
The Wall Street Journal. November 12, 1987, p. 36.

MAKING MR. RIGHT

Production: Mike Wise and Joel Tuber for Barry and Enright; released by
   Orion Pictures
Direction: Susan Seidelman
Screenplay: Floyd Byars and Laurie Frank
Cinematography: Edward Lachman
Editing: Andrew Mondshein
Production design: Barbara Ling
Art direction: Jack Blackman; set decoration, Scott Jacobson and Jimmy
   Robinson II
Special effects: Bran Ferren
Makeup: Janet Flora
Costume design: Rudy Dillon and Adelle Lutz
Sound: Howard Warren
Music: Chaz Jankel
MPAA rating: PG-13
Running time: 95 minutes

   Principal characters:
   Dr. Jeff Peters/Ulysses . . . . John Malkovich
   Frankie Stone . . . . Ann Magnuson
   Trish . . . . Glenne Headly
   Steve Marcus . . . . Ben Masters
   Sandy . . . . Laurie Metcalf
   Estelle Stone . . . . Polly Bergen
   Dr. Ramdas . . . . Harsh Nayyar
   Don . . . . Hart Bochner
   Ivy Stone . . . . Susan Berman
   Suzy Duncan . . . . Polly Draper
   Tux Salesman . . . . Robert Trebor

   A clever, if not quite comically inspired, hybrid, space-age women's picture cum postfeminist *The Bride of Frankenstein* (1935), *Making Mr. Right*
alternates between strained humor and delightful detail almost from scene
to scene. Both lighthearted and despairingly pessimistic in its view of modern relationships, the film exudes director Susan Seidelman's comparatively
fresh point of view and manages to get away with old complaints about the
battle of the sexes and some hoary locker-room gags purely because of her
feminine perspective. Whenever the motion picture's one-joke premise, that
the only way to find a good man is to build one, starts to flag, the visual wit
of Rudy Dillon and Adelle Lutz's costumes and the carnival-ride surrealism

of the set designs carry the viewer smiling on through.

Performance artist/comedienne Ann Magnuson plays Frankie Stone, a Miami Beach public-relations whiz whose eccentric personal habits (she dresses like a high-tech cigarette girl and shaves her legs while driving her red convertible to work) belie her skill at orchestrating successful media campaigns, primarily for politicians. After breaking up with her lover (and soon-to-be former client), the craven Congressman Steve Marcus (Ben Masters), Stone attends a business meeting with a delegation from the National Aeronautics and Space Administration (NASA) contractor Chemtech, led by Dr. Ramdas (Harsh Nayyar). They want her to design a popularization campaign for Ulysses (John Malkovich), an extraordinarily humanlike android built for multiyear deep-space missions. Ramdas figures that if Ulysses becomes a media darling, his company's government contracts will never be threatened.

Agreeing to take the job, Frankie visits Chemtech's underground research and development facility, where she first encounters the childlike, socially awkward Ulysses. He introduces himself by grabbing her breasts and asking, "What are these?" Instinctively, she shoves him away, causing him to malfunction. Dr. Jeff Peters (also played by Malkovich) storms into the room. In his usual grumpy, misanthropic manner, the genius-inventor—who built Ulysses in his own image—removes the android's head and grumbles about how he knew the very concept of a woman would confuse his creation.

Gradually, Frankie learns more about Ulysses' intellectual development and begins trying to teach him some social graces (something Dr. Peters, who has none, believes is unnecessary). Meanwhile, Frankie's flaky, nymphomaniac friend Trish (Glenne Headly), fleeing her actor husband, Don (Hart Bochner), after he has made tabloid headlines with his extramarital affairs, has installed herself in Frankie's apartment. Trish is not the only one with romantic problems: Marcus, who has taken up both emotionally and professionally with Frankie's former assistant Suzy Duncan (Polly Draper), comes to Chemtech to try to win back his former promoter's heart. Not wanting to appear lonely, Frankie introduces the befuddled Dr. Peters as her new boyfriend.

Devastated by the encounter with Marcus, Frankie later drowns her sorrows with a quart of ice cream and a Diet Coke in an abandoned Chemtech cubicle. Ulysses happens to find her, gives her a relaxing foot massage, and informs her that she is the most attractive (even if she is the only) woman he knows.

The next morning, Peters has his own difficulties with a man-hungry fellow employee, Sandy (Laurie Metcalf). She literally chases the disinterested scientist through parking lots and hallways, until he agrees to see her that evening. Later, while working, Peters is appalled when Ulysses kisses him and expresses his love for him; Frankie is teaching the robot all the emotional ticks that Peters has worked so hard to expunge from his own personality.

That evening, Ulysses escapes from Chemtech and hides in the back seat of Frankie's car. He jumps out in a mall parking lot, and a frantic Frankie pursues him into the shopping area. Alternately corralling and losing her innocent charge, Frankie ultimately returns to Chemtech, hoping that the errant machine will come home on its own. Instead, Ulysses encounters Sandy, who, mistaking him for Peters, decides to begin their date early. Unintentionally, the unsophisticated android humiliates her in a jewelry store and ruins her dress in a restaurant, after which Sandy is more than eager to drop him off at Frankie's house.

Later, Frankie returns home to find a hysterical Trish sobbing and pointing to the kitchen floor, where Ulysses lies, pants down, head turned 180 degrees, and unconscious. Trish explains that they were making love, when suddenly something terrible happened. She is absolutely mortified when Frankie removes Ulysses' head and screws it back on correctly. Driving the revitalized android back to Chemtech, Frankie tells him about how difficult and humiliating the search for love can be. Ulysses replies that it would be simple if he were human: He would love her.

Pressured by her mother (Polly Bergen) to bring a date to the wedding of her younger sister Ivy (Susan Berman) and a Hispanic busboy, Frankie recruits a reluctant Peters to be her and Trish's escort. As the beachside reception congas into the night, Ulysses once again escapes Chemtech and works his way toward the party. Congressman Marcus is among the wedding guests and persists in trying to rekindle sparks with Frankie, while the uncomfortable Dr. Peters finds himself explaining physics to the surprisingly interested Trish. Both Ulysses and Don soon crash the party, seeking their estranged women. Ulysses tells Frankie that he loves her, confirming it with a passionate kiss which is videotaped before a big fight breaks out among the gathered jealous men. In the melee, Ulysses is flung into the pool, where he short-circuits in front of hundreds of witnesses.

The press has a field day with the antics of Ulysses and his human girlfriend. The disgraced Frankie is forced to give up the Chemtech account. Back in the lab, Ulysses moons over Frankie during flight-simulator training. Worried that his invention is now too emotionally distraught to accomplish his mission, Peters tells Ulysses that the woman never loved him. At a press conference on the day before his scheduled blast-off, Ulysses tells the gathered audience—including the unwelcome Frankie—that his human feelings, those minor errors, have been corrected.

The next day, ice cream and Diet Coke in hand, Frankie tearfully watches the rocket lift off on television. Her doorbell rings; it is Peters. Or is it? He kisses Frankie, tells her that he loves her, and collapses. She slaps Ulysses back into shape, and he apologizes for his habit of falling apart at the wrong times.

Crying tears of joy, Frankie echoes the last line of *Some Like It Hot* (1959): "Nobody's perfect." On television, the rocket pilot tells mission control that his seven-year journey truly feels like the most exciting thing in the world, the exact way Peters described it to Ulysses during flight training. Asked if he feels lonely out there, Peters radios back, "No. You see, I'm not very good with people."

Without being schematic about it, Seidelman laces the theme of loneliness throughout *Making Mr. Right*: There is Ulysses' sense of isolation in his sterile Chemtech environment and Dr. Peters' pride in his own dehumanized antiemotionalism, not to mention every other character's desperate search for a fulfilling relationship. It is also an extension as well as something of a satire of the standard Seidelman motif of finding oneself by identifying with a fantasy other, just as the groupie played by Berman tried to do through her *persona* of Wren in *Smithereens* (1982) and suburban housewife played by Rosanna Arquette did by swapping selves with the street-survivor played by Madonna in *Desperately Seeking Susan* (1985).

At the center of *Making Mr. Right*'s galaxy of stereotyped characters (nerdy scientist Peters, lovably naïve Ulysses, dumb blonde Trish, superficial politician Marcus, aggressive and unattractive Sandy) is an unexpectedly complex, low-key performance by expert caricaturist Magnuson. Even when displaying Frankie's eccentric personal quirks, Magnuson never gives the impression of playing either cute or obvious; she is an admirably adult professional with a full range of adult feelings and—out of place in this film— mature self-control. Yet she seems as at home in the film's live-action, cartoon world as any of the more garish characters; a fine testament to Magnuson's range and an outstanding lead-acting debut.

Malkovich also does an impressive job with his less-nuanced but diametrically contradictory dual roles. Indeed, he brings all the shading one can reasonably expect to the unbelievably sweet-natured naïf and the curmudgeonly technocrat. With Peters, Malkovich is able to inject the same kind of intensity that has characterized his more dramatic work without taking away from his, previously untapped, expertise at farce.

As in *Desperately Seeking Susan*, Seidelman has once again put an unusually convincing spin on some rather trite, inherently unbelievable material. Not as successfully as the last time, to be sure, but perhaps more daringly. By marrying a ridiculous premise to unremittingly bleak emotional conclusions and some downright cruel humor, she set herself an uneasy task from the outset. Nevertheless, she manages to maintain a light, often giddy, tone throughout, despite such dangerous material. It is hard to imagine any male director displaying such delicacy and finesse.

Robert Strauss

Reviews

Glamour. LXXXV, June, 1987, p. 154.
The Hollywood Reporter. March 19, 1987, p. 3.
Los Angeles Times. April 10, 1987, VI, p. 1.
Macleans. C, April 13, 1987, p. 49.
Ms. XV, May, 1987, p. 22.
The New Republic. CXCVI, May 4, 1987, p. 26.
The New York Times. April 10, 1987, p. C8.
Newsweek. CIX, April 13, 1987, p. 77.
Time. CXXIX, April 13, 1987, p. 78.
Variety. CCCXXVI, March 25, 1987, p. 18.
The Village Voice. April 21, 1987, p. 52.
The Wall Street Journal. April 9, 1987, p. 30.

MANON OF THE SPRING
(MANON DES SOURCES)

Origin: France
Released: 1986
Released in U.S.: 1987
Production: Pierre Grunstein for Renn Productions/Films A2/RA1 2/DD
  Productions; released by Orion Classics
Direction: Claude Berri
Screenplay: Claude Berri and Gérard Brach; based on the novel *L'Eau des
  Collines*, by Marcel Pagnol
Cinematography: Bruno Nuytten
Editing: Geneviève Louveau and Hervé de Luze
Art direction: Bernard Vezat
Makeup: Michèle Deruelle and Jean-Pierre Eychenne
Costume design: Sylvie Gautrelet
Sound: Pierre Gamet
Music: Jean-Claude Petit
MPAA rating: PG
Running time: 113 minutes

> *Principal characters:*
> César Soubeyran .... Yves Montand
> Ugolin Soubeyran .... Daniel Auteuil
> Manon .... Émmanuelle Béart
> Bernard Olivier .... Hippolyte Girardot
> Aimée de Florette............. Élisabeth Depardieu
> Delphine.......................... Yvonne Gamy
> Baptistine...................... Margarita Lozano
> Pascal .... Pierre Jean Rippert
> Pamphile......................... André Dupon
> Priest........................... Jean Bouchaud

When Marcel Pagnol's *Manon des sources* was released in France in 1952,
the nostalgic four-hour film was considered a Provençal epic. In its shortened, commercial version, however, the film disappointed Pagnol and his
wife, Jacqueline (Bouvier) Pagnol (who played the sensuous Manon), as
well as French audiences. The film, set near the Aubagne and Marseilles so
familiar to the writer, essentially highlighted the human cruelty and revenge,
along with the eternal hope, of provincial villagers of approximately two
decades earlier. This was a time and place now almost completely obliter-
ated, all in the name of progress. Claude Berri's *Manon of the Spring*,
inspired by both Pagnol's original film and his two-volume work *L'Eau des*

collines (1963; *Jean de Florette* and *Manon of the Spring*, 1988), reveals an acutely similar freshness and dynamism. Despite major financing ($17 million), lush color (with Bruno Nuytten as director of photography), and technological advances of special effects (including seasonal changes), the recent adaptation still provides contemporary filmgoers with vicarious experiences of a local tragedy that takes on universal proportions.

Berri, respected in France for his last five Césars (French Oscars) for *Tchao Pantin* in 1983 and in the United States for *The Two of Us* (1967) and *Sex Shop* (1972), had petitioned Jacqueline Pagnol for six years before acquiring the rights to adapt *L'Eau des collines* to the screen. To respect Pagnol's literary tone and format, Berri decided to make a cinematic diptych situated in Southern France, the first film to be entitled *Jean de Florette* and the second, *Manon des Sources*.

In *Jean de Florette* (1987; reviewed in this volume), the patriarchal César (Yves Montand), known as Papet or Grandpa, unhappily finds himself the penultimate member of the Soubeyran family. He serves as self-appointed mentor for his unsophisticated nephew Ugolin (Daniel Auteuil). Together they concoct a cruel plan to obstruct the spring of the industrious and sensitive hunchback, Jean de Florette (Gérard Depardieu), in order to force him to sell his property to Ugolin. A faulty explosive kills Jean while he is digging for water in the drought-stricken South. His young daughter, Manon, (Émmanuelle Béart), is virtually left to fend for herself as Ugolin purchases the deceased's property at an exorbitantly low price for the cultivation of carnations.

Manon of the Spring opens with Ugolin prosperous in his carnation business, for the Soubeyrans unblocked the spring for the much-needed water supply. While César begins to lament that the noble family line ends with them, Ugolin becomes enraptured at the sight of Manon bathing in a lush, pastoral setting. In a quasi-voyeuristic fashion, he continues to spy on her and then tries to woo her with the wise counsel of his uncle. Unfortunately for Ugolin, Manon becomes attracted to the charming young schoolteacher Bernard Olivier (Hippolyte Girardot), who collects minerals in the area where she tends her flock.

Upon discovering the Soubeyran's manipulation and destruction of her father, Manon, in a spirit of revenge, blocks the major water supply for Ugolin's carnations as well as for the village. Filled with feelings of utter remorse and burdened with unrequited love, Ugolin hangs himself.

Manon's mother, Aimée (Élisabeth Depardieu), an opera singer, returns for her daughter's marriage to Bernard. Shortly afterward, through his old blind confidante, Delphine (Yvonne Gamy), César learns that Jean was actually his own son by Florette de Camoins. In repentance for his despicable deed causing the death of Jean, César wills his estate to Manon, his granddaughter. The same night, he peacefully dies in his bed.

Berri's simultaneous production of these two films, which must be considered a unit, is an amazing feat. Very elaborate financing and marketing techniques helped Berri bring the Pagnol work to the screen. The staging of this pastoral drama is unique and closely connected with the financing. Shooting during a period of thirty-six weeks entailed countless risks—poor weather, extended contracts, regional brush fires, and above all, almost inaccessible areas for realistic sets that would correspond to a rural setting of the early 1930's. The results of this painstaking attention to detail and final effect immediately strike the eye. Despite the setting in provincial France of fifty years ago, the narrative evokes a timelessness in the characters, issues, and tone of the film. This is undoubtedly a result of the spirit of Pagnol in the work, the careful synthesizing of the two-volume novel, and the poetic cinematography of Nuytten, who created an enchanting Provence of howling winds, sudden storms, and fierce droughts. The music of Jean-Claude Petit serves as continuity for this epic, alternating between the cautiously subtle and the lavishly heroic. The inclusion of the theme from Giuseppe Verdi's *La forza del destino* provides both a lyrical and ironic motif to both works.

Much of the success of *Jean de Florette*, and especially of *Manon of the Spring*, derives from the acting. Montand as the Machiavellian César is most convincing. A noble strain runs through the Provençal blood of this member of the moribund family. His crafty and destructive plotting, however, ultimately brings about his own total destruction. Although Montand first became known in the United States for his role of the French lover in American films such as *Let's Make Love* (1960) with Marilyn Monroe, and then for his political roles in the thrillers of Constantin Costa-Gavras, such as *Z* (1969), he captures well the regional nuances in the character of the elderly César. Costa-Gavras, who cast Montand as a detective from Marseilles in *The Sleeping Car Murders* (1965), believes that the actor steps back into his own personal past in Southern France of almost fifty years ago in order to relive it as a Soubeyran.

In the role of Ugolin, Auteuil earned a well-deserved César for Best Actor in 1987. Auteuil, a handsome and polished young man, took on the traits of a complex, rustic Ugolin, unknowingly led by his uncle to the brink of despair. Childlike in his pursuit of the hand of Manon, Ugolin is nevertheless crafty and self-serving. His dim-witted appearance and awkward social mannerisms alienate the viewer on one hand but evoke sympathy for him on the other. His earlier, Judas-like behavior in the treatment of Jean, coupled with his failure in love, leads him to his tragic demise by hanging.

Manon, played by Béart, daughter of the French singer Guy Béart, is an enigmatic figure. Although she is a shepherdess, she possesses a rare beauty, as well as profound intellectual skills acquired from her father, Jean. At times, Béart as the *enfant sauvage* appears too physically attractive and mentally distant from the character of a rustic Provençal teenage girl, but perhaps not more so than the original Manon, Jacqueline Pagnol. Often compared to a youthful Brigitte Bardot or Cathérine Deneuve, Béart impressed French audiences and won a César for Best Supporting Actress.

The intrinsic value of *Manon of the Spring* lies in its power to relate to the audience on several levels. In the area of French culture, geography, and history, the film provides vivid insight into the Southern France that was once rural, slow-paced, and timeless. Growing industrialization, the popularity of secondary residences, the mandatory move of the youth to the larger cities in quest of work and education, and the loss of regional customs and languages have all had their impact on this tranquil corner of France. These sociological changes make the experience of viewing *Manon of the Spring* one of nostalgia. The moral dimension of this powerful saga is crucial, for it reveals the silent conspiracy of the villagers who know that the Soubeyrans were responsible for Jean's fate. On another level, Berri's work captures human tragedy in its most ironic form, wherein the victimizer becomes the victim. Finally, the film is a poignant look into the darker side of human nature in terms of manipulation, xenophobia, and revenge. Showing the dramatic conversion of César for religious and psychological reasons underscores the fact that, on occasion, justice and innocence may triumph in the end.

This regional epic emerges at a moment when the public has been exposed to several scintillating films of this genre—Richard Attenborough's *Cry Freedom* (1987; reviewed in this volume), Bernardo Bertolucci's *The Last Emperor* (1987; reviewed in this volume), and Steven Spielberg's *Empire of the Sun* (1987; reviewed in this volume). The simultaneous filming and clever marketing of *Jean de Florette* and *Manon of the Spring* have resulted in a nostalgic, melodramatic, yet penetrating human study of complex relationships that crosses national, temporal, and geographical borders.

John J. Michalczyk

Reviews
Chicago Tribune. December 23, 1987, VIII, p. 23.
The Christian Science Monitor. July 3, 1987, p. 19.
Film Journal. November/December, 1987, p. 48.
Films in Review. XXXIX, February, 1988, p. 101.
National Review. XXXIX, December 18, 1987, p. 54.
The New Republic. CXCVII, November 23, 1987, p. 24.
The New York Times. November 6, 1987, p. C25.
Newsweek. CX, November 9, 1987, p. 77.
The Wall Street Journal. November 12, 1987, p. 36.

MATEWAN

Production: Peggy Rajski and Maggi Renzi; released by Cinecom Pictures and Film Gallery
Direction: John Sayles
Screenplay: John Sayles
Cinematography: Haskell Wexler
Editing: Sonya Polonsky
Production design: Nora Chavooshian
Art direction: Dan Bishop; set decoration, Anamarie Michnevich and Leslie Pope
Costume design: Cynthia Flynt
Music: Mason Daring
MPAA rating: PG-13
Running time: 100 minutes

> *Principal characters:*
> Joe Kenehan .... Chris Cooper
> Few Clothes Johnson .... James Earl Jones
> Elma Radnor .... Mary McDonnell
> Danny Radnor...................... Will Oldham
> Sid Hatfield .... David Strathairn
> Sephus Purcell .... Ken Jenkins
> Bill Hickey.......................... Kevin Tighe
> Tom Griggs .... Gordon Clapp
> Hardshell Preacher .... John Sayles
> C. E. Lively........................ Bob Gunton
> Cabell Testerman .... Josh Mostel
> Bridey Mae Tolliver .... Nancy Mette

Set in the hill country of Matewan, West Virginia, in 1920, *Matewan* chronicles a bloody coal-miners strike against a company opposed to union activity. The miners' inability to gain anything more than momentary success—and even this at great price—reflects John Sayles's realistic assessment of the history of the labor movement as well as a somber assessment of the human condition in general.

The difficult and dangerous life of the mine worker is dramatized by the opening scene in the film, where a gritty, coughing miner labors patiently in an ominously dark, closed-in space to set an explosive charge. Another more far-reaching danger is the real threat, however. The company has again lowered the price it pays for coal and in anticipation of organized resistance has imported black and immigrant Italian workers to keep the mines open.

In spite of all the talk about the union, there is very little unity in town. The Hardshell Baptist preacher, played by Sayles himself in an exaggerated hellfire-and-brimstone manner, inveighs against the union as "the enemy of all that is good and pure." Even within the community of workers there is division and strife: The townspeople conceive of their most immediate enemies as the blacks and the Italians. Danny Radnor (Will Oldham), at almost fourteen years old a dedicated union man and preacher, does his best to set the town in the right direction: In a sermon, he chastizes Christ for not heeding the needs of the workers. A full explanation of what a union should stand for, however, comes from Joe Kenehan (Chris Cooper), a union organizer.

Joe is not allowed into the workers' meeting, however, until he passes a test showing his knowledge of union history; ironically, this is administered by C. E. Lively (Bob Gunton), whose constant antagonism to Joe is explained later when he is revealed to be a provocateur hired by the company. Once inside, Joe advises the workers to organize and build support, which means opening the union to the blacks and Italians. He also warns against violence, knowing that the company would like nothing better than to goad the workers into an armed battle. It is this latter warning that proves most difficult to heed, especially after the arrival of two particularly vicious agents hired by the company: Bill Hickey (Kevin Tighe), a smiling, psychopathic veteran from World War I, and Tom Griggs (Gordon Clapp).

The film is basically structured as a series of crises that are narrowly averted by a variety of means until a final conflict arises that cannot be averted. The first confrontation between the miners and the owners, for example, comes when Hickey and Griggs attempt to evict a family of workers from their company-owned house—an incident that alludes to the climactic scene in *Salt of the Earth* (1954), a classic film about striking miners to which Sayles is clearly indebted. The eviction is stopped by an unlikely ally of the workers, Sid Hatfield (David Straithairn), the local sheriff who is unintimidated by the company strongmen and uninterested in the bribes offered to him. His last name links him to a local family, making his support of the townspeople more plausible, but also tying him to the legendary Hatfield-McCoy feud, which identifies him as a person unable to withstand a pull to deadly violence.

Sayles builds dramatic excitement in the film not only by repeating a pattern of tension and release but also by increasing the seriousness of each crime. Even more threatening than the attempted eviction of the family is the explosive situation that arises when the blacks and Italians march to the mine and face the strikers who are determined to prevent them from working. In one of the emotional climaxes of the film, the blacks and Italians throw down their tools and are welcomed into the union. Earlier in the film, Few Clothes Johnson (James Earl Jones), the leader of the blacks, was angered more by being called a scab than by the foul racial epithets. Racial and ethnic prejudice runs deep, but not so deep that it cannot be overcome by the workers' newly awakened sense that their shared misery at the hands of the company is more important than their different colors or cultures. At this point, Danny voices his optimistic, although premature, conviction that the company will crumble.

The company does not, however, relinquish so easily; they attack the workers' camp at night. During the day, when most of the men are away at a meeting, Hickey and Griggs lead a few deputies in to harass those left behind. The final crisis that the workers are able to avoid revolves around Joe, who is never quite welcomed into the community as a result of his not being a miner and because, as one worker puts it, he expects too much of them. His nonviolence is a strenuous burden, especially in the face of escalating attacks by the company. In addition, he is constantly undermined by the plots of C. E. Lively, who not only speaks out repeatedly for violent confrontation, a message eagerly received by the angry and impatient workers, but also forges a letter to make it seem that Joe is a spy planted by the company. Few Clothes draws the task of killing this apparent traitor in their midst, and in a prolonged, extremely tense scene he talks nervously in the woods with Joe, struggling to build up his determination to shoot him. The truth about Joe will be revealed, but not until the last moment: Sayles crosscuts between this scene and one of Danny preaching an allegorical sermon which conveys to everyone in attendance (except the drunken Hickey and Griggs) that Joe is in fact innocent. The message sent to Few Clothes to stop the execution reaches him just in time, but this is the last occasion when violence is prevented.

In the final section of the film, Sayles lulls the audience into a kind of brief reverie in order to make the final turn to violence particularly shocking. The workers play baseball (an archetypal pastoral sport), and one of the Matewan widows not only gives a rabbit to one of the Italian women but also offers her a useful spice she may not be familiar with—garlic! This lightly comic mood ends abruptly, though, with the murder of young Hillard (Jace Alexander) for stealing a few pieces of coal with Danny. He is brutally tortured and his throat is cut by orders of C. E., who realizes that there is "nothing like a young boy dying to stir things up."

Throughout *Matewan*, Sayles not only plays with the conventions of the traditional Western but also provides an ironic commentary. Nowhere is this more evident than at the end, where the band of hired gunmen marches down the main street of town toward the sheriff, calling to mind familiar scenes from *High Noon* (1952), *Shane* (1953), and *Gunfight at the O.K. Corral* (1957). The battle that follows, though, is not a cleansing ritual or a satisfying victory over evil, but a disturbing, graphically portrayed massacre of good and evil. Sayles fills the scene with emblems of pain and futility, not heroism: Testerman lies writhing in the street with an uncomprehending look on his face and a gunshot wound in his belly; Elma weeps over the body of Joe only moments after she disobeys the pacifism he preached by killing Hickey; and Hillard's mother (Jo Henderson) fires shot after shot into a fallen man, never quite able to avenge the death of her son. Perhaps one soul has been saved in the battle: Danny lowers his rifle and allows a terrified gunslinger to swim to safety across the river. Danny survives mainly to be a witness to the following years of strife and violence. His concluding voice-over narrative tells of the brutal death of Hatfield, ambushed later by C. E. and another party of hired guns, but his most important message is that the legacy of the union is not victory but continuing struggle, a struggle unto death.

Sayles places this struggle in a larger context by ending the film not with Danny's narration but with a gospel song that runs through the closing titles. Much of the power of *Matewan* comes from Sayles's careful handling of music and the subtheme of religion. In the beginning, he characterizes each group of workers by their particular musical instruments—the townspeople have a guitar and a fiddle, the Italians a mandolin, the blacks a harmonica—and the clash of these sounds predictably gives way to harmony as they come together in song. Far more subtle and effective, though, is Sayles's use of spirituals during critical moments. Danny, otherwise a confident speaker and preacher, fumbles for words as he tries to eulogize his dead friend Hillard, but the spiritual that ends the funeral is eloquent and moving. The same can be said about the spiritual that closes the film, contrasting the hills of Mingo County with the hills of Galilee.

Matewan is a somber film from beginning to end, visually as well as thematically. There are few bright colors, and cinematographer Haskell Wexler very effectively sets many of the most dramatic scenes in dim light or near-darkness: One gets the sense that a day of bright sunlight would change the lives of these people, but that day will never come. It is much to Sayles's credit that he resists the temptation of the satisfying, happy ending (a decision he writes about in his book, *Thinking in Pictures: The Making of the Movie "Matewan,"* 1987). As a result, *Matewan* may not be a pleasurable film, but it is profoundly true to life, the fictional counterpart to Barbara Kopple's equally disturbing documentary on the apparently never-ending struggles of mine workers, *Harlan County U.S.A.* (1977), surely a major influence on Sayles.

Sidney Gottlieb

Reviews
Commonweal. CXIV, November 6, 1987, p. 626.

Films in Review. XXXVIII, December, 1987, p. 614.
Horizon. XXX, September, 1987, p. 12.
Los Angeles Times. September 11, 1987, VI, p. 1.
Macleans. C, October 12, 1987, p. 56.
The Nation. CCXLV, October 17, 1987, p. 427.
The New Republic. CXCVII, September 7, 1987, p. 24.
The New York Times. August 28, 1987, p. C3.
Newsweek. CX, September 14, 1987, p. 82.
Rolling Stone. October 8, 1987, p. 27.
Time. CXXX, September 14, 1987, p. 77.
Variety. CCCXXVII, May 20, 1987, p. 18.
The Wall Street Journal. August 27, 1987, p. 20.

MAURICE

Origin: Great Britain
Released in U.S.: 1987
Production: Ismail Merchant; released by Cinecom Pictures
Direction: James Ivory
Screenplay: Kit Hesketh-Harvey and James Ivory; based on the novel of the same name by E. M. Forster
Cinematography: Pierre Lhomme
Editing: Katherine Wenning
Production design: Brian Ackland-Snow
Art direction: Peter James
Makeup: Mary Hillman
Costume design: Jenny Beavan and John Bright
Music: Richard Robbins
MPAA rating: R
Running time: 135 minutes

Principal characters:

Maurice	James Wilby
Clive	Hugh Grant
Alec	Rupert Graves
Dr. Barry	Denholm Elliott
Mr. Ducie	Simon Callow
Mrs. Hall	Billie Whitelaw
Lasker-Jones	Ben Kingsley
Anne Durham	Phoebe Nicholls
Risley	Mark Tandy
Ada Hall	Helena Mitchell
Dean Cornwalis	Barry Foster

James Ivory and Ismail Merchant have built a reputation with *The Bostonians* (1984), *A Passage to India* (1984), and *A Room with a View* (1986) for making films faithful in spirit to the novels on which they are based. They have advanced that reputation with *Maurice*, their third adaptation of novels by E. M. Forster.

Especially striking is their refusal to be disloyal to their source even though the novelist's perspective in *Maurice* is an increasingly unpopular one resulting from the backlash caused by the fear of acquired immune deficiency syndrome (AIDS). Someone must have questioned whether this was the best time to make a film with a homosexual hero, one who courageously rejects society's conventions to embrace the life which is natural to him; such a story is not likely to win the approval of, or to stir in the way intended, the apparently growing segment of society that perceives homosexuality as an aberration punishable by God. Nevertheless, James Ivory and his coscreenwriter, Kit Hesketh-Harvey, do not shrink from their responsibility to Forster's novel.

Another remarkable fact is that the Ivory-Merchant team has several times produced products that are admirably cinematic despite their literary origins and their often-literal rendering of many of the books' particulars. In *Maurice*, except for the overlong pauses after fades, which self-consciously suggest the ends of chapters in a book, the medium is used skillfully but unostentatiously. When Maurice (James Wilby) decides to go to hypnotist Lasker-Jones (Ben Kingsley) for a cure, the low-angle shot of the doctor as he moves his index finger slowly back and forth trying to mesmerize his patient not only presents him from Maurice's point of view but also subtly magnifies and distorts him, suggesting his foolishness and the futility of his procedure. Cuts to the reclining Maurice, who is trying desperately to cooperate in letting himself be hypnotized, emphasize this impression. Other effective filmic devices include a long shot of Maurice standing at a second-story window in a heavy rainstorm and in a moment of abandon putting his head and half his torso out into the drenching downpour, followed by a cut to Alec Scudder (Rupert Graves), the young undergamekeeper who has been standing in the rain secretly observing the gentleman he admires, and whose point of view was being presented in the preceding frames; these and numerous shots throughout the film put the viewer in the right place to understand intimately what the characters are feeling.

The fact that the film's action deals mostly with affluent people gives Ivory, his production designer Brian Ackland-Snow, costume designers Jenny Beavan and John Bright, and art director Peter James plenty of opportunity to create lush images of wealth. Elegant table settings, rich dress both casual and formal, glimmering automobiles, and a magnificent estate (although at one point the roof leaks onto the grand piano) with its impressive grounds: All contribute to the visual feast. The impeccable taste of Ivory and his designers is always in evidence.

Still more important is Ivory's sensitive handling of a difficult story. *Maurice* is concerned with self-discovery and self-definition. The plot follows its protagonist through periods of realization concerning his sexual inclinations, turmoil after he is rejected by the first friend to whom he has declared his "unspeakable" love, doubt resulting in efforts to rid himself of his "sickness," and finally, acceptance of his sexual identity. One senses early in the film that Maurice is fundamentally honest. At the elementary school Maurice attends, the teacher, Mr. Ducie (Simon Callow), deciding to fill in for the boy's absent father, takes him for a walk on the beach and, with careful explanation as to their operation, draws in the sand with a stick the male and female organs of reproduction. The befuddled boy, after following the lesson attentively, declares that he does not think he will ever marry. Some years later at Cambridge University, Dean Cornwalis (Barry Foster) is playing host to several students in his quarters. The camera focuses primarily on Maurice while another student translates a passage in which one man describes his love for a male friend. The reading provokes smirks from all except Maurice, who realizes that the words accurately describe his feelings for his friend Clive (Hugh Grant). An earlier sequence in the dean's quarters shows students engaged in intellectual repartee, with one in particular, Risley (Mark Tandy), holding sway over the others; although his arrogance and aristocratic manner are intimidating, Maurice contradicts him. The cumulative effect of these and other incidents is to establish Maurice as someone who is willing to risk censure in his pursuit of truth.

Once he declares his love for Clive, Maurice is willing to give that love physical expression, but Clive, although the first to make his feelings known, insists on keeping the relationship platonic. Clive eventually succeeds in repressing his homosexual inclinations, marries a proper lady, and works toward a respectable life with a future place in Parliament a possibility. Maurice, shattered by Clive's rejection, determines to cure himself. What follows is an amusing sequence with the family physician, Dr. Barry (Denholm Elliott), who assures Maurice that he is mistaken to think such rot about himself. He refuses even to discuss the matter. Maurice then sees Lasker-Jones, who, although ineffectual, is at least open-minded. During one of their meetings, he makes a statement to the effect that England has always been disinclined to accept human nature.

The severity of British law at that time with regard to sexual deviation is demonstrated in an incident which does not occur in the novel. Risley is entrapped into making advances to a guardsman in an alleyway outside a pub; he is arrested on a morals charge, brought to trial, disgraced, and given the so-called light sentence of six months at hard labor. This addition to Forster's story helps one to understand Clive's fear and reversal to socially acceptable behavior but to respect the courage of Maurice's opposite decision.

Maurice, however, is not presented as a flawless, one-dimensional hero useful in the advocacy of homosexual-related causes. He is capable of spitefulness and self-deception. When he suspects that Clive is attracted to his sister Ada (Helena Mitchell), he becomes jealous and treats her cruelly. When Clive puts an end to the unorthodox side of their relationship, Maurice is not above sniveling and petulance. Later, there is a period in his relationship with Scudder when he fears the possibility of blackmail. The fact is, though, that Scudder initially had no such intention; the idea occurs to him because of Maurice's distrust.

Circumstances in *Maurice* do not seem contrived in order to make some simplistic point. One way to have turned this film into an overly neat and shallow lesson against the injustices of a repressive society would have been to depict Clive's marital relationship as a disaster in contrast to Maurice and Scudder's successful union. While Clive's wife Anne (Phoebe Nicholls) seems silly and sexually unresponsive in her early scenes, she gains some strength as the film progresses, however, and eventually seems capable of true affection and sustained commitment. Clive may not have a life of passionate lovemaking and perfect contentment ahead, but whether he would have chosen differently under a law that permitted homosexuality is problematic. Maurice and Scudder, on the other hand (despite the romantic lighting of their reunion in the boathouse), will have to confront serious problems: the difference in their backgrounds and the inevitable tension that will result because of their relationship's unfortunate illegality.

One senses that Ivory, faithfully mirroring Forster's novel, is trying to see and present these characters and their situations accurately. The director's integrity is complemented by the work of an excellent cast, able to explore and project many nuances of character and the potentially elusive intricacies of relationships.

Cono Robert Marcazzo

Reviews
Films in Review. XXXVIII, December, 1987, p. 615.
Los Angeles Times. October 1, 1987, VI, p. 1.
The Nation. CCXLV, October 31, 1987, p. 498.
National Review. XXXIX, November 6, 1987, p. 59.
The New Republic. CXCVII, October 5, 1987, p. 28.
New York. XX, September 28, 1987, p. 136.
The New York Times. September 18, 1987, p. C18.
The New York Times. October 3, 1987, p. C13.
The New Yorker. LXIII, September 21, 1987, p. 103.
Newsweek. CX, September 21, 1987, p. 76.
Sight and Sound. LVI, Autumn, 1987, p. 290.
Time. CXXX, October 12, 1987, p. H4.
Variety. CCCXXVIII, August 26, 1987, p. 15.

MOONSTRUCK

Production: Patrick Palmer and Norman Jewison; released by Metro-Goldwyn-Mayer
Direction: Norman Jewison
Screenplay: John Patrick Shanley (AA)
Cinematography: David Watkin
Editing: Lou Lombardo
Production design: Philip Rosenberg
Art direction: Barbra Matis and Dan Davis
Costume design: Theoni V. Aldredge
Sound: Dennis L. Maitland
Music: Dick Hyman
MPAA rating: PG
Running time: 102 minutes

Principal characters:
Loretta Castorini	Cher (AA)
Ronny Cammareri	Nicolas Cage
Cosmo Castorini	Vincent Gardenia
Rose Castorini	Olympia Dukakis (AA)
Johnny Cammareri	Danny Aiello
Rita Cappomaggi	Julie Bovasso
Perry	John Mahoney
Raymond Cappomaggi	Louis Guss
Old Man	Feodor Chaliapin
Mona	Anita Gillette
Chrissy	Nada Despotovich
Shy Waiter	Joe Grifasi

Moonstruck is an offbeat, comical, and warmly romantic film that looks at love and family life with a freshness and originality that are rare among current films. Directed by Norman Jewison from a screenplay by playwright John Patrick Shanley, the film, which received three Academy Awards, abounds with memorably well-developed characters and a daringly larger-than-life style that never slips into the realm of caricature. It is a romantic comedy in which the romance profoundly changes its lovers and the comedy grows out of the characters themselves—a happy interweaving of story elements that the film carries off with wit and assurance.

Moonstruck is set in Brooklyn, New York, where Loretta Castorini (Cher) works as a bookkeeper. The Castorinis are a close-knit family— Loretta still lives with her parents, Rose (Olympia Dukakis) and Cosmo (Vincent Gardenia), and the household also includes her grandfather (Feodor Chaliapin) and his five dogs—and many of the film's scenes take place in the Castorini kitchen, the center of the family's life. A widow in her late thirties, Loretta is practical, resigned to her life, and full of sensible advice for the fiancé she likes but does not love, Johnny Cammareri (Danny Aiello). When the middle-aged, weak-willed Johnny leaves for Italy to visit his dying mother, who opposes his marriage, he asks Loretta to invite his estranged younger brother, Ronny (Nicolas Cage), to their wedding, which can only take place after his mother is dead. Ronny, a baker, is passionate, brooding, and deeply embittered by an accident—for which he blames Johnny—which cost him his left hand and, consequently, his girlfriend. Loretta and Ronny are attracted to each other immediately and they make love soon after their first meeting as a brilliant full moon illuminates the night sky. The following morning, however, Loretta's customary levelheadedness reasserts itself and she is stricken with guilt as a result of her actions. She soon discovers that she is not alone in her romantic confusion when her mother confides that she is sure that Cosmo is having an affair.

Loretta has agreed to go with Ronny to the opera—his greatest passion—before the two put their brief affair behind them forever, and she blossoms during her preparations for the evening, buying a new dress and permitting her hairdresser to dye her strands of gray hair. Following a performance of Giacomo Puccini's *La Bohème*, Loretta and Ronny encounter Cosmo and his mistress, Mona (Anita Gillette), in the lobby of the Metropolitan Opera House, where father and daughter react to each other with a combination of anger, bewilderment, and guilt. Rose has spent the evening in a restaurant dining with a college professor named Perry (John Mahoney), a lonely man who has just been unceremoniously dumped by the latest in a long line of young lovers. The two discuss the complexities of relationships between men and women and Perry is drawn to Rose's wisdom and strength of character, but she declines his romantic overtures.

Swept away by the emotions of the evening, Loretta at last acknowledges her feelings and again spends the night with Ronny, returning home the next morning knowing that she must break off her engagement to Johnny, who has returned unexpectedly from Italy. Both brothers arrive at the Castorinis, along with Loretta's Aunt Rita (Julie Bovasso) and Uncle Raymond (Louis Guss), but before Loretta can speak, Johnny announces that his mother has made a miraculous recovery and the wedding must be called off. Ronny proposes to Loretta, who accepts, and Rose confronts Cosmo, obtaining his promise to end his affair. With the family gathered around the kitchen table, Cosmo pours drinks for everyone and offers a toast, "A la famiglia!"—to the family.

That *Moonstruck* is indeed a comedy is perhaps not readily apparent from a description of its plot, and it would no doubt be possible to film a straight drama based on the same general story lines: A woman falls in love with her fiancé's brother, and a wife confronts her adulterous husband. Yet the film turns these themes into a celebration of life's possibilities and a sympathetic portrait of human fallibility. Shanley's script, which received an Academy Award for Best Original Screenplay, is affectionate toward all of its characters; there are no villains in *Moonstruck*, only imperfect men and women who are confused by the emotions they feel.

The characters themselves are the source from which the story and its humor arises, and they are exceptionally well realized both in Shanley's writing and the actors' performances. The film revolves around the two strong women at its center, and Cher and Olympia Dukakis won the year's Oscars for Best Actress and Best Supporting Actress for their fine portrayals of Loretta and her mother, Rose. Both characters are intelligent, outspoken, and self-possessed. Loretta has accepted the misfortune which left her a young widow and has resigned herself to a life without passion or love. Her relationship with Johnny is almost maternal in nature; clearly, she will take his mother's place in his life after their marriage. Her meeting with Ronny, however, awakens in Loretta the emotional needs she has ignored since her husband's death. Ronny's passion and energy give rise to an answering spark in her, creating a conflict for Loretta between the direction she has sensibly chosen for her life—do not marry for love, her mother has warned her, or you will have your heart broken—and the impetuous, overwhelming possibility of a life with Ronny. That it is clear from the start which path she will finally choose does nothing to detract from the film's joyous depiction of her bewildered reawakening to the power of love. Cher brings a sensitivity and an assurance to the role which are disarmingly effective.

Dukakis is also outstanding as her mother. For Rose, life's major decisions lay in the past. Her dilemma now is a philosophical one: Why, she wants to know, do men have affairs? The answer at which she arrives after much reflection is both simple and universal—because they fear death—and she promptly informs Cosmo that no matter what he does he will still die, like everyone else. Rose possesses a wry insight into human nature and a healthy measure of good common sense, and although she is hurt by Cosmo's affair, she is a woman who is not afraid to demand the respect to which she is entitled.

The entire cast works together in fine ensemble form; a fact which adds greatly to the story's already strong emphasis on the complex ties which bind families together. The Castorinis are a colorful, Italian-American family; they are expressive, emotional, and rich in their sense of tradition and generational continuity. Loretta's aunt and uncle are present for any important family occasion, and her immigrant grandfather lives in a state of contained but unremitting warfare with Rose that provides some of the film's most amusing moments. The importance of family, from Loretta's talks with her mother to the bad blood between Johnny and Ronny to Cosmo's eventual recognition that he must end his affair, permeates *Moonstruck* with a warmth that helps define the film's characters and their place in the world.

Moonstruck's heightened style takes its cue from Ronny's passion for opera and the trip to the Met, which forms the centerpiece of his relationship with Loretta. The film itself is operatic in tone—a source of great humor within the story—and the characters often express themselves on a grand emotional scale. Jewison is a director whose dramatic films are often powerful but lacking in subtlety, and *Moonstruck*'s tone of comic overplaying proves to be a change of pace ideally suited to his style; the subtlety here takes the form of character nuance while the story is given freer rein. Loretta's first meeting with Ronny, which begins in the bakery and ends in his bedroom, is filled with wildly passionate declarations on both sides, first of Ronny's anger toward his brother and then of the irresistible attraction the two feel for each other. Their encounter ends the following morning when Ronny announces that he loves Loretta and she slaps him—twice— and yells, "Snap out of it!" The incongruity of ordinary lives depicted on an operatic scale gives the film a wonderfully offbeat quality, an eccentric originality that is also present in the film's sound track, which includes passages from *La Bohème* and Dean Martin singing "That's Amore."

Adding to the film's charm are the references to magic and superstition running throughout. The most potent of these is the extraordinary full moon which appears the night that Loretta and Ronny first make love. Loretta's Uncle Raymond has seen such a moon only once before, when Cosmo was courting Rose, and its beauty arouses passion not only in Ronny and Loretta (and Raymond and Rita), but also in Loretta's grandfather, who takes his five dogs down to the river to teach them to howl at "la bella luna." Loretta is also superstitious by nature, convinced that her first husband's death was the result of bad luck brought on by the fact that they were married without a proper church wedding. The luck Loretta needs, however, is love, and she finds it with Ronny.

Moonstruck is a film which manages to be both unabashedly romantic and deliciously witty in its observations on human nature. The film has a confidence that grows from its thorough knowledge of its characters, who spring to life as fully developed and as engaging as any screen family in recent memory. This is a story about following one's heart and the joy of self-discovery, the give and take of family life, and the profound changes which love can bring, all of which are presented with a warmth and humor that illuminate the film just as the moon illuminates the night sky.

Janet E. Lorenz

Reviews
Films in Review. XXXIX, February, 1988, p. 97.
Macleans. C, December 14, 1987, p. 65.
The New Republic. CXCVIII, February 8, 1988, p. 26.
The New York Times. December 16, 1987, p. C22.
The New Yorker. LXIII, January 25, 1988, p. 99.
Newsweek. CX, December 21, 1987, p. 69.
People Weekly. XXIX, January 18, 1988, p. 8.
Time. CXXXI, January 11, 1988, p. 80.
Variety. CCCXXIX, December 16, 1987, p. 10.
The Wall Street Journal. January 5, 1988, p. 22.

MY LIFE AS A DOG
(MITT LIV SOM HUND)

Origin: Sweden
Released: 1985
Released in U.S.: 1987
Production: Waldemar Bergendahl for Svensk Filmindustri; released by
    Skouras Pictures
Direction: Lasse Hallström
Screenplay: Lasse Hallström, Reidar Jönsson, Brasse Brännstrom and Per
    Berglund; based on the novel of the same name by Reidar Jönsson
Cinematography: Jorgen Persson
Editing: Christer Furubrand and Susanne Linnman
Art direction: Lasse Westfelt
Sound: Eddie Axberg and Goran Carmback
Music: Bjorn Isfalt
MPAA rating: PG-13
Running time: 101 minutes

> *Principal characters:*
> Ingemar .... Anton Glanzelius
> Uncle Gunnar .... Tomas von Brömssen
> Mother .... Anki Liden
> Saga .... Melinda Kinnaman
> Aunt Ulla .... Kicki Rundgren
> Berit .... Ing-mari Carlsson

My Life as a Dog is director Lasse Hallström's fifth of eight films to date.
Reminiscent of other famous childhood films, such as François Truffaut's
The 400 Blows (1959), Federico Fellini's *Amarcord* (1974), and compatriot
Ingmar Bergman's *Fanny and Alexander* (1983), it shares their generally optimistic tone and the view that a child can weather a stormy, painful youth
filled with disappointing adults. Yet this film is different, for its protagonist,
Ingemar (Anton Glanzelius), has taken charge of his own maturing, having
achieved, apparently on his own, a set of specific imaginative techniques for
coping with inner and outer chaos.

The film covers a brief period in the life of twelve-year-old Ingemar, a
nervous child whose mother is dying of tuberculosis and whose father works
loading bananas in South America. The narrative is interrupted throughout
the film by two recurrent scenes: Ingemar and his vibrant mother relaxing
by the side of a lake, with a voice-over of Ingemar remembering the way he
made her laugh and wishing that he had told her everything before she died,
and a shot of a clear, starry sky, with a voice-over of Ingemar comparing his

sorrows to the worse ones he has read about in the newspaper. He remembers, for example, the missionary clubbed to death by Ethiopian natives as she preached; the motorcycle daredevil trying to jump over thirty-one buses, but killed on the thirty-first; the man in Boston who had a kidney transplant, got his name in the papers, but died anyway; and especially Laika, the Russian dog that starved to death in outer space. Deciding that in comparison his situation is not so bad, Ingemar is able to survive.

Typical childhood episodes begin the film. Ingemar's older brother, treating his friends to an impromptu sex education, invites Ingemar to demonstrate conception by sticking his penis into a narrow-necked bottle. Predictably, the bottle becomes stuck; Ingemar is unharmed but humiliated when an adult neighbor comes to his rescue. Later, Ingemar wets the bed when his brother awakens him from sleep with a point-blank toy rifle shot. They hide the wet sheets under the kitchen sink and proceed to make breakfast, but an archetypal maelstrom of parental rage ensues when Mother finds it. She chases them around, swatting, swearing, and yelling so loudly that Ingemar's girlfriend closes the window lest the child-welfare authorities think that they are being abused. Soon after, Ingemar and his brother are packed off to relatives to give their ailing mother a much-needed rest.

Ingemar goes to live with Uncle Gunnar (Tomas von Brömssen) and Aunt Ulla (Kicki Rundgren) in the village of Åforf (where Hallström filmed those sequences, using locals for many of the supporting roles). Leaving behind the two things he loves most—his mother and his dog—Ingemar enters a confusing but remarkable new territory.

On one of Ingemar's first days with his life-loving relations, Ulla sheds a soiled dress on the spot, and Gunnar, amorous and irrepressible, goes down on all fours after her, imitating a dog. Ingemar immediately joins him on the floor, barking. When Gunnar chases Ulla into the bedroom and slams the door, a puzzled Ingemar is left outside. An unflappable elderly woman, Mrs. Arvidsson, sits knitting throughout the spectacle. The ancient Mr. Arvidsson, who is maddened by his neighbor Fransson's incessant roof mending, has Ingemar read aloud to him from a women's lingerie catalog, which he shoves under the mattress whenever his wife comes to the door. Gunnar, a kindly though exasperatingly infantile man, is constructing a "summer home"—a crooked gazebo on his neighbor's property. As he builds, he drives Ulla crazy by playing, over and over, a Swedish recording of "Oh, What a Lovely Bunch of Coconuts."

Gunnar has a crush on Berit (Ing-mari Carlsson), a buxom blonde who works with him in the glass factory. Berit impresses Ingemar into service as a chaperone while she poses nude for a local artist who is sculpting the "Ur-mother." Ingemar is banished to a closet where he can chaperone without seeing her, and, in perhaps the film's most amusing scene, he climbs onto the roof, peers down at her through a skylight, then slips and crashes through it to the floor, as she rolls out of his way just in time to avoid him and the falling glass. Ingemar plays soccer with a local team, and one of his teammates, Saga (Melinda Kinnaman), a girl pretending to be a boy, is in love with him. They box together, Saga usually winning, and he helps her escape detection by taping flat her tiny breasts.

Back home, Ingemar's mother is dying, and he visits her. The shots of him watching at the window as she is taken away in an ambulance and of his face at the door of his house as a neighbor begins to break the news of her death are masterpieces of understatement. He goes back to Gunnar and Ulla, but they, being too crowded with new housemates, send him off to live with Mrs. Arvidsson, whose husband has by now died. In one of the film's most touching sequences, Saga takes Ingemar up to a hayloft and shows him her breasts, then invites him, unsuccessfully, to display himself. Hallström tested two thousand girls for the part, and in Kinnaman he found the perfect sexy tomboy.

For a while Ingemar seems adjusted, but when he discovers that his dog, Sickan, allegedly being boarded in a kennel, has been put to sleep, he undergoes a mild breakdown. When Ingemar suffers from a strange, double-identity confusion, imitates a dog, and speaks of causing "her death," it is not clear whether he means Mother's or Sickan's. Fleeing to the tiny summer home, he locks himself in and comes out only much later after Gunnar breaks in to extract him.

During the film's final shots, against the backdrop of the telecasted Ingemar Johansson-Floyd Patterson championship boxing match, Ingemar seems recovered, his confidence in himself restored when his namesake wins the fight. Soon he is in a homemade space module sliding down a rope with Saga who, resigned to her gender, sports a dress. The contraption swings into a puddle of cow muck, but they survive, and a few scenes later are sleeping peacefully together on a couch as the radio blares out the sounds of the fight.

The film has a deceptively simple veneer: a childish sound track, naïve, conventional camera work, and the look of a country fairy tale filled with lanky, almost unrealistically rustic types, from pug-nosed Ingemar and his buck-toothed aunt to a child with chartreuse hair. At time it seems to strive a bit ineptly for a Fellini-like carnival effect, for example, when one of the factory workers rides a unicycle on a tightrope while balancing an axe on his head, or when the whole town turns out to spy on old Fransson's skinny-dip in the freezing river.

Hallström, however, is genuinely concerned with the longing for psychic as well as physical space and distance from relatives and neighbors who necessarily annoy one another when packed together too closely. He is very good at conveying the subtle emotions of longing through close-ups. This is especially evident in the shots of the fatigued, dying mother, of Saga trying to seduce Ingemar, and of Gunnar hungrily watching Berit in the factory.

My Life as a Dog is a charming, deeply humanistic film. Perhaps its main limitations are its characters' unalloyed kindness and its individualistic perspective. It contains death, pain, and disease, but none of the moral evil, the sheer meanness that deepened the visions of *Fanny and Alexander*, *Amarcord*, or *The 400 Blows*. Furthermore, much of Ingemar's pain stems ultimately from economic conditions: Factory-caused overcrowding propels him out of Gunnar's house and into the late Arvidsson's bed.

Ingemar's trick is to distance himself, both physically and psychically, just enough to remain sane, but not so much as to starve, emotionally or literally. An adult coping this way might be accused of apolitical withdrawal, of tranquillity at any price. For a twelve-year-old, this primitive stoicism is a remarkable step toward real wisdom.

Joan Esposito

Reviews
Commonweal. CXIV, July 17, 1987, p. 420.
Los Angeles. XXXII, May, 1987, p. 250.
Los Angeles Times. May 14, 1987, VI, p. 1.
Macleans. C, June 15, 1987, p. 51.
National Review. XXXIX, June 19, 1987, p. 56.
The New Republic. CXCVI, May 25, 1987, p. 24.
New Statesman. CXIII, April 17, 1987, p. 23.
New York. XX, May 11, 1987, p. 70.
The New York Times. March 24, 1987, p. C14.
Newsweek. CIX, May 25, 1987, p. 72.
Variety. CCCXXIII, June 25, 1987, p. 5.
Vogue. CLXXVII, June, 1987, p. 32.
The Wall Street Journal. April 30, 1987, p. 28.
The Washington Post. May 11, 1987, p. B7.
Whole Earth Review. Summer, 1987, p. 119.

NADINE

Production: Arlene Donovan; released by Tri-Star Pictures
Direction: Robert Benton
Screenplay: Robert Benton
Cinematography: Nestor Almendros
Editing: Sam O'Steen
Production design: Paul Sylbert
Art direction: Peter Lansdown Smith and Cary White; set decoration, Lee Poll
Costume design: Albert Wolsky
Sound: David Ronne
Music: Howard Shore
MPAA rating: PG
Running time: 88 minutes

> *Principal characters:*
> Vernon Hightower .... Jeff Bridges
> Nadine Hightower .... Kim Basinger
> Buford Pope .... Rip Torn
> Vera .... Gwen Verdon
> Renée .... Glenne Headly
> Raymond Escobar.................... Jerry Stiller
> Dwight Estes....................... Jay Patterson
> Floyd .... Mickey Jones

Robert Benton is known for his solid dramas such as *Bonnie and Clyde* (1967), which he wrote with David Newman, *Kramer vs. Kramer* (1979), and *Places in the Heart* (1984), both of which he wrote and directed. The comedy *Nadine* harks back to his 1977 sleeper, *The Late Show*, a clever murder mystery and comedy starring Art Carney and Lily Tomlin. While the script of *Nadine* has some great lines and benefits from the chemistry between Jeff Bridges and Kim Basinger, the result is not as successful as *The Late Show*.

Nadine Hightower (Kim Basinger) is a lovely beautician who once posed for some art studies which she thought were destined for *Playboy* magazine. Now she wants them back but the sleazy photographer, Raymond Escobar (Jerry Stiller), will not cooperate. When Escobar is murdered and Nadine finds a set of photographs in his hands, she runs off with them, only to find that they are confidential state maps of the proposed routes for two new highways.

Anxious to find her photographs, she enlists the aid of her estranged husband, Vernon (Jeff Bridges), a born loser whose misplaced sense of optimism has convinced him that his bar, the Bluebonnet Lounge, will soon be a hot spot. She tricks him into breaking into Escobar's studio even though it has been sealed by the police and is under surveillance. Nadine's search is ended when they are surprised by a policeman. They escape by acting as a team and through Vernon's considerable driving skills.

Arriving safely at Nadine's home, each admires the way the other handled the situation at the studio, and they feel the old attraction again. Determined to seduce Vernon, Nadine changes into a black negligee. While she is changing clothes, Vernon finds the photostats in her purse. He immediately knows what they are and drives off just as Nadine reenters the room. She has little time to feel disappointed, as she is then kidnapped by Floyd (Mickey Jones) and taken to Buford Pope (Rip Torn), local crime kingpin and Escobar's killer. Pope has Nadine's photographs and has figured correctly that she must have the maps. Not finding them with her, Pope sends his goons to find Vernon.

Meanwhile, Vernon has gone to see his third cousin once removed, Dwight Estes (Jay Patterson). Although Dwight is not happy to see him because Vernon owes him $820 plus interest, he quickly realizes the value of the maps. When he tries to include himself in the deal, Vernon tells him that he can have the maps only after he raises fifty thousand dollars from his rich friends.

Once Floyd finds Vernon and delivers him to Pope, neither a beating nor Nadine's pleas nor the threat of rattlesnakes, left by some snake worshipers, can induce him to tell where he has hidden the maps. Vernon takes control, however, when he grabs the box of snakes and threatens to set them loose on the floor unless Floyd surrenders his car keys. He and Nadine escape when he actually does toss the snakes onto the floor.

With Nadine still in her negligee, they go to Vernon's trailer home. Realizing how much he cares for her opinion, Vernon worries that Nadine may think that he is what Pope called him: a two-bit loser. Reassuring him of her confidence, Nadine starts to tell him that she is pregnant with his baby, but she stops when he begins pipe-dreaming about the money the maps will earn for him. Nevertheless, the shared threat of danger makes them feel close, and they make love.

In the morning, trouble comes their way again as Renée (Glenne Headly), Vernon's fiancée, shows up at the trailer. At Vernon's urging, Renée has stolen his mounting, unpaid bill from her boss, the Lone Star beer distributor. As Nadine secretly watches with increasing fury, Renée not only teases Vernon with the bill but also runs off with Nadine's negligee, which she thinks is a gift for her. Vernon tries to mollify Nadine, telling her that he has a plan for getting it back. "Trust me!" he pleads.

Disgusted, Nadine goes to the beauty shop and asks her boss Vera (Gwen Verdon) for an advance so that she can leave Austin. When Vernon appears, Vera reveals that Nadine is pregnant. That gives Vernon and Nadine something to fight about, but the arguing stops when they see Floyd and his buddy coming for them. They elude them by taking refuge in an abandoned mission, and after a series of tense and comic misadventures with a brittle ladder, they escape once more by acting as a team. The tension of the situation makes them confess their love for each other, but once the danger passes they revert to bickering.

Nadine and Vernon go to Dwight's house, where they find that his new partner is Buford Pope. Holding Nadine hostage, Pope sends Vernon and Dwight to the Bluebonnet Lounge for the maps. Vernon's attempts to retrieve the firearms hidden at the bar and turn the tables on Dwight are thwarted when Renée storms in. She is outraged because she has discovered that the negligee is not only the wrong size but also a used garment; therefore, she is breaking off the engagement. Her parting words include telling Dwight about the shotgun Vernon keeps in the cooler. As performed by Glenne Headly, the scene is a comic gem.

Back at the salvage yard, Dwight gives Pope the maps and Vernon's gun. Finally in possession of the maps, Pope doublecrosses Dwight and orders Floyd to shoot him. Dwight resists, and Vernon takes advantage of the scuffle to overcome Floyd. When Pope sees the change in the situation, he shoots Floyd without hesitation. A cat-and-mouse chase through the salvage yard ensues as the Hightowers fight for their lives and the maps. They emerge victorious, causing Pope to moan about a lifetime's work ruined by a pair of nitwits.

In police custody, Nadine and Vernon learn that Buford Pope is being charged with the murders of Escobar and Floyd and that Vernon is suspected of having stolen the maps. Even as he denies having them, a folder is found in his jacket. It contains Nadine's photographs, however, not the maps. As Vernon casts a look of amazement at Nadine, she tells him, "Trust me!"

Having won a New York Film Critics Award for his *Bonnie and Clyde* script, Oscars for both his writing and directing of *Kramer vs. Kramer*, and yet another Oscar for his *Places in the Heart* screenplay, Benton's directorial and writing credentials are first-rate. Perhaps that is why the general reaction of critics to *Nadine* was one of disappointment. Most thought that although the stars, Bridges and Basinger, gave solid, enthusiastic performances, *Nadine* was not the hit that they had anticipated. For Basinger it was another fine performance in a line of mediocre films that included *No Mercy* (1986), *9½ Weeks* (1986), and *Blind Date* (1987; reviewed in this volume). Bridges has faced a similar situation since his Oscar-nominated role in *Starman* (1984) and the highly successful *Jagged Edge* (1985); his performance in *Eight Million Ways to Die* (1986) and *The Morning After* (1987) were not well received by critics. In *Nadine*, it was the supporting actors,

Torn, Stiller, and Headly, who were cited for their comedic contributions. The photography by master cinematographer Nestor Almendros, who had also photographed *Kramer vs. Kramer* and *Places in the Heart*, was considered excellent; the authentic 1950's settings were appreciated, and the original score was deemed appropriate. As comedy goes, *Nadine* is lightweight. While there are some very amusing lines and situations, the story is contrived and predictable.

Ellen Snyder

Reviews

Los Angeles. September, 1987, p. 206.
New York. XX, August 24, 1987, p. 113.
The New York Times. August 7, 1987, p. C8.
The New Yorker. LXIII, August 24, 1987, p. 81.
Newsweek. CX, August 10, 1987, p. 58.
People Weekly. XXVIII, August 10, 1987, p. 8.
Time. CXXX, August 17, 1987, p. 62.
Variety. CCCXXVII, July 15, 1987, p. 14.
Vogue. CLXXVII, September, 1987, p. 132.
The Wall Street Journal. LXVIII, August 6, 1987, p. 22.

NO WAY OUT

Production: Laura Ziskin and Robert Garland; released by Orion Pictures
Direction: Roger Donaldson
Screenplay: Robert Garland; based on the novel *The Big Clock* by Kenneth
  Fearing
Cinematography: John Alcott
Editing: Neil Travis
Production design: Dennis Washington
Art direction: Anthony Brockliss; set decoration, Bruce Gibeson
Special effects: Jack Monroe and Terry Frazee
Makeup: Michael A. Hancock
Music: Maurice Jarre
Song: Paul Anka and Michael McDonald, "No Way Out"
MPAA rating: R
Running time: 114 minutes

> *Principal characters:*
> Tom Farrell .... Kevin Costner
> David Brice .... Gene Hackman
> Susan Atwell .... Sean Young
> Scott Pritchard .... Will Patton
> Senator Duvall .... Howard Duff
> Sam Hesselman .... George Dzundza
> Major Donovan .... Jason Bernard
> Nina Beka .... Iman

There has been a rash of films in the 1980's which deal with corrupt authority—in local government, including its police arm, and all the way up the bureaucratic ladder to high-level offices of the national government. The films include *The Big Easy* (1987; reviewed in this volume), *The Untouchables* (1987; reviewed in this volume), *Marie* (1985), *Witness* (1985), *Missing* (1982), and a host of others. *No Way Out*, loosely based on Kenneth Fearing's novel *The Big Clock* (1946), takes the viewer to a very high place, the office of United States Secretary of Defense David Brice (Gene Hackman), and shows the pervasive corruption that can reside even there.

Are such films a direct legacy of the Reagan years, as *All the President's Men* (1976), *Serpico* (1973), *In the Year of the Pig* (1969), and others are part of the inheritance of the Nixon years? It seems so. Conservative eras—particularly those that are tainted with scandal (Watergate/Iranscam)—spawn works by filmmakers who sometimes seem intent on toppling those institutions they find offensive, or, at least, undressing them and shining a glaring light on their shameful nakedness so that one can rebuke or, perhaps, merely gaze at them. The intentions of those who made *No Way Out* seem to be more the latter: voyeuristic rather than corrective or revolutionary.

Although the film's plot involves cover-up and abuse of power on a national level in an age when the reality of such events is all too apparent, *No Way Out* is not informed with any purpose more serious than to provide good, hair-raising entertainment. The producers, particularly (one must suppose) Robert Garland, who doubles as screenwriter and coproducer, were counting on current events to lend their film extra zest and plausibility, to cause the general public, with some allowance for hyperbole, to share their premise that, even though circumstances may differ, similarly hideous goings-on occur in high places. Nevertheless, in *No Way Out*, there is a notable absence of the moral indignation that infuses director Roger Donaldson's other film about political corruption, *Marie*. Perhaps the difference in approach can be accounted for by the fact that *Marie* is a true story, while *No Way Out* is clearly fiction. In any case, the outpouring of films thematically like *No Way Out* may be a somewhat painless indicator of need for reform outside the realm of fiction, yet only a few films do the job of making genuine protest.

The scandalous incident which serves as the plot's core is the secretary of defense's accidental slaying of his beautiful mistress, Susan Atwell (Sean Young). In a jealous rage he pushes her over a banister; she falls through the glass-top table below and is killed instantly. This event leads to an elaborate cover-up, recommended and put into motion by the secretary's general counsel, Scott Pritchard (Will Patton).

There can be some satisfaction in watching potentially horrifying incidents with the distance that would naturally exist between one's emotions and an animated cartoon with an adventure theme. Indeed, *No Way Out* is a cartoon with real actors instead of drawings. It is one that adds to its cast of good and evil characters two or three characters with some moral complexity, thus arousing more viewer interest than a James Bond film, which seems to display no gray ground between the black and white. Still, one should expect *No Way Out* to be what it primarily is, escapist fare, if the film is to have its rewards.

Among the rewards are skillfully executed chases in which the film's protagonist, Lieutenant Commander Tom Farrell (Kevin Costner), while fleeing the villains, slides on his posterior down the diagonal ledge alongside a crowded escalator, rolls over the hood of a moving automobile, and almost flies Tarzan-like through the branches of a tree. There is also the violent car chase that has become obligatory for films of this genre. One might be reminded of the coyote pursuing Road Runner.

Another reward is the performance of Costner. He looks like the clean-cut boy next door, but one who has grown up, to everyone's surprise, adept at both the sexual and martial arts. Costner's pleasing screen presence serves him well in the role of a naval career officer, extremely able and likable, who is appointed to a high-level job by Secretary of Defense Brice, only to find that he is caught in a seemingly no-win situation, pitted against the depravity of men who have the power to hurt unalterably.

Hackman's performance as the secretary of defense, particularly in the early scenes, provides the basis of credibility for the entire film. He convinces the viewer that this is the way a man of great power who knows how to use it might act. According to how a situation serves his purpose, he can seem genuinely concerned or be rudely abrupt; he uses duplicity to keep a political opponent at bay; and he is skillfully manipulative, getting others to do his bidding even at considerable inconvenience to themselves. It is regrettable that Hackman's performance becomes less interesting in later scenes, after the death of Susan Atwell, when the script permits him to do little more than fear exposure and wallow in self-pity for extended periods of time.

The film's one brilliant performance is that of Patton as Scott Pritchard, a man in the bureaucratic stratosphere. He skillfully manipulates the secretary of defense and, toward the end of the film, warns a fast-learning but still-defiant Tom Farrell that he has no idea what men of power can do. Pritchard has been giving horrific demonstrations of that potential throughout much of the film, and as it builds toward its climax, his obsessive desire to protect his boss from scandal prompts him to use means that are increasingly cruel and arrogant. The performance reaches a level of intensity, extreme in the manner of Jay Robinson's Caligula in *The Robe* (1953). Both are risk-taking performances, which go all the way to the end of the limb and, instead of falling, maintain beautiful balance.

Young as Susan Atwell, the secretary of defense's unfortunate mistress, who complicates her life—while she still has it—by engaging in a simultaneous affair with his young appointee, Tom Farrell, is competent and appealing.

No Way Out is dedicated to the memory of John Alcott, who died in an accident soon after completion of his work as the film's director of photography. He merits a memorial especially on the strength of his past work, such stunningly photographed films as *Barry Lyndon* (1975) and *Greystoke: The Legend of Tarzan, Lord of the Apes* (1984). His shooting of *No Way Out* is never less than capable, and it should be considered a virtue that the cinematography does not call attention to itself, but rather lets the viewer focus on the unfolding plot. The same might be said of Roger Donaldson's unobtrusive direction. He tells the story, which is a complex narrative, efficiently, always sustaining interest and often generating dramatic tension.

The film's surprise ending, which the filmmakers have asked the press not to spoil, seems an afterthought hastily added to give the viewer one final punch before the screen darkens.

Cono Robert Marcazzo

Reviews
Film Comment. XXII, November, 1986, p. 4.
Films in Review. XXXVIII, November, 1987, p. 545.
Los Angeles Times. August 14, 1987, VI, p. 1.
National Review. XXXIX, September 25, 1987, p. 59.
The New York Times. August 14, 1987, p. C3.
The New Yorker. LXIII, September 7, 1987, p. 98.
Newsweek. CX, August 24, 1987, p. 60.
Time. CXXX, August 17, 1987, p. 62.
Variety. CCCXXVIII, August 12, 1987, p. 12.
The Wall Street Journal. August 13, 1987, p. 18.

NUTS

Production: Barbra Streisand; released by Warner Bros.
Direction: Martin Ritt
Screenplay: Tom Topor, Darryl Ponicsan, and Alvin Sargent; based on the
   play of the same name by Tom Topor
Cinematography: Andrzej Bartkowiak
Editing: Sidney Levin
Production design: Joel Schiller
Art direction: Eric Orbom; set decoration, Anne McCulley
Music direction: Jeremy Lubbock
Music: Barbra Streisand
MPAA rating: R
Running time: 116 minutes

> *Principal characters:*
> Claudia Draper................... Barbra Streisand
> Aaron Levinsky.................. Richard Dreyfuss
> Rose Kirk .... Maureen Stapleton
> Arthur Kirk .... Karl Malden
> Dr. Herbert A. Morrison............... Eli Wallach
> Francis MacMillan .... Robert Webber
> Judge Stanley Murdoch............ James Whitmore
> Allen Green....................... Leslie Nielsen
> Clarence Middleton................. William Prince
> First Judge...................... Dakin Matthews

Like many other courtroom dramas, *Nuts* is constructed as a series of tense confrontations and powerful revelations. On whatever level of seriousness, plays and films which address the civilized workings of justice—and Tom Topor's work has now enjoyed incarnations in both mediums, having originated on the stage in 1980—consistently benefit from two pervasive, complementary axioms of their genre. They deal with the pursuit of truth (and so are innately high-minded), and they have evolved out of a tradition in which artistic license allows all manner of theatrics, on the witness stand and off (and so are innately entertaining). In the cinema, for example, *Anatomy of a Murder* (1959) sustains a richly dramatic and highly intricate narrative while subtly asserting as its subject the imprecision of even the most purposeful inquiry into the truth of a given situation. The expectations of high-mindedness and entertainment that the audience brings to the genre both actually become essential elements of the work and help to provoke a sophisticated response. By contrast, *Nuts* projects an aura of high-mindedness so extreme that an attitude of simple self-righteousness seems to lurk beneath the surface of its depiction of flamboyant drama in the courtroom. Though mildly enjoyable, it is finally undermined by a superficiality which not only exposes hollow moralizing but, even more damagingly, results in a lack of credibility.

The film's focus is on Claudia Draper (Barbra Streisand), an uptown, upscale prostitute who has killed a client (Leslie Nielsen). It does not focus on her murder trial (although, unlike the play, it leaves no doubt about her innocence, as flashbacks reveal that the killing was an act of self-defense); rather, the primary event on view is a hearing to determine her mental fitness to stand trial. Her mother, Rose Kirk (Maureen Stapleton), and stepfather, Arthur Kirk (Karl Malden), have employed a high-priced attorney, Clarence Middleton (William Prince), to argue that she is not fit to stand trial and should remain in a mental institution. Claudia, however, has had no voice in this strategy, and, outraged by what she rightfully perceives to be unfair treatment, she physically attacks Middleton in court, prompting him to resign. The judge (Dakin Matthews), as required by law, appoints a public defender, Aaron Levinsky (Richard Dreyfuss), who happens to be present, and Levinsky, though initially disinterested, has enough integrity to approach Claudia with an open mind. Ultimately, he takes her side and, in a subsequent hearing, defends her right to stand trial.

This second hearing, following some investigation of Claudia's life by Levinsky and some interaction between them, makes up the major part of the film, which from this point closely follows the play (in which the entire action was the second hearing, with allusions to the earlier events). The modifications in narrative structure cause the second hearing to play differently in certain respects. Though both play and film show an out-of-control, conceivably unbalanced woman treating almost everyone, including Levinsky, as adversaries, the film has painstakingly shown the provocations for this behavior. Thus, though there is some loss of suspense as the drama unfolds—though certainly no loss of conventional dramatic tension and potent psychological undercurrents—there are also apparent gains. Claudia goes through the second hearing with increased sympathetic identification from the viewer, who understands that her madness is illusory, admires her already evident perceptiveness and intelligence, and knows that she deserves not only to win the hearing but also to be ultimately vindicated of the murder charge. Yet these apparent gains are symptomatic of attitudes that finally disfigure *Nuts* and assure its artistic failure.

On the face of it, the second hearing has all the elements that it needs to be engaging drama. In addition to its two underdogs—vulnerable, abused, but essentially strong Claudia and hardworking, underpaid, and underestimated Levinsky—there are the smug but essentially decent district attorney, Francis MacMillan (Robert Webber), the well-intentioned psychiatrist, Dr. Herbert A. Morrison (Eli Wallach), the sensible and patriarchal Judge

Stanley Murdoch (James Whitmore), the anguished, defeated mother, and the highly respectable stepfather, whose tense concern for Claudia masks difficult emotions and unacknowledged fears. The testimony unfolds, with dramatic results. Demonstrating admirable discernment, Levinsky questions Arthur Kirk—against Claudia's will—and unmasks a long-held secret of his sexual abuse of her as a girl, which he has never consciously admitted even to himself. Eventually, Morrison's testimony is undermined and Claudia is found by Judge Murdoch to be capable of understanding the charges against her and of standing trial. A written postscript indicates that she was successfully defended by Levinsky at her trial.

The sexual abuse element has little to do with the question of Claudia's sanity, although it does have a relationship to her choice of profession and the circumstances which prompted the killing. Nevertheless, it is arguably the emotional center of the film. Observing how it is treated helps afford some insight into the texture of the film. In the play, Arthur Kirk ends his testimony in a state of disbelief, badly shaken but still convinced that he had not overstepped in his conduct with Claudia, and as Claudia is seen (in both play and film) as having allowed the abuse out of her desperate need for love, there are intimations that the unmasked abuse had an element of ambiguity. Yet, although the actor who plays Kirk, Karl Malden, is certainly capable of registering ambiguity, the character's actions are treated in the film as more insidiously conscious in nature. In the film, then, Kirk is left without benefit of a shred of sympathy from the filmmakers, who have shorn him of all human complexity.

If Kirk has become simply a villain, then there must be a hero—or, in this case, heroine. There lies the problem with *Nuts*, a problem which seems more severe the more one scrutinizes the film. As played by Streisand, Claudia is a woman who, however neurotic and abrasive, is waiting throughout the narrative to throw off her victim identity and take her place in the world as a profoundly independent and admirable individual. The result is that the pretext for the drama—the justice system's capacity for error in assuming insanity and therefore depriving a person of important rights— becomes relatively meaningless. The assertion-of-independent-womanhood theme does not fare well either. Streisand is a showy actress—appealingly so in her better vehicles such as *Funny Girl* (1968)—and projects Claudia's hysteria with maximal intensity. As the viewer has already perceived the character as intelligent and self-preserving, such hysteria seems to be against her own interests; it would seem more reasonable, though less dramatic, for her simply to let Levinsky make her case. Claudia's courtroom histrionics were a part of the play, too, and because of the ways in which Streisand's interpretation cause the character to fragment into incoherence, it becomes retrospectively evident that the credibility of Topor's work was always questionable.

Cohesion and complexity are difficult to achieve when a single personality is allowed to dominate a film. Self-defeating excesses of ego are the only explanation for why someone of Streisand's undeniable talent would so undermine a project on every level. As producer, she quarreled with and fired director Mark Rydell, then quarreled with but somehow finished the film with his replacement, Martin Ritt. Of her three jobs on the film, only one, her score, was undertaken with discretion and artfulness.

Apart from Streisand, performances in *Nuts* are convincing, flavorful efforts by a group of thoroughly professional veterans—Webber, Whitmore, Wallach, Dreyfuss, Stapleton, and Malden—even if the characters lack dimension. Though most of these players have had richer opportunities, Dreyfuss actually fills out his role to a degree barely suggested in the screenplay, providing Levinsky with nuances of personality which tantalizingly intimate that the entire project might have been infinitely more interesting with more surehanded guidance and a greater concern for delicacy of artistic texture.

Overall, Ritt was probably a better choice for director than the flashier, more mannered Rydell. A sober personality, Ritt actually fares best with unpretentious material (*The Long, Hot Summer*, 1958; *Casey's Shadow*, 1978), being too simplistic and heavy-handed to do justice to the social statements he often seems interested in making. *Nuts*, however, was doomed to risibility as a social statement because of Streisand's intentions. Ritt does bring some control and craftsmanship to the realization of the action, though he is guilty of some excesses of his own in the overheated flashback of the murder and occasionally in the present-tense action—one wonders why he cuts from a long overhead shot in which the camera slowly moves over everyone involved in the courtroom proceedings to a meaningless close-up of Rose Kirk as she testifies. Overall, Ritt works well with the interpolations by the two screenwriters who extended Topor's text, Darryl Ponicsan and Alvin Sargent, especially in the case of Levinsky's solitary visit to Claudia's apartment, the film's single excellent scene. The evocative decor and ambience of this setting and Levinsky's subtle reactions briefly remind one of the supple and fascinating ways in which the cinema may impart something of the complexity and richness of human experience. Unfortunately, the promise of that early scene is betrayed in the thoughtless simplifications that follow.

Blake Lucas

Reviews
Films in Review. XXXIX, February, 1988, p. 100.
Los Angeles Times. November 20, 1987, VI, p. 1.

Macleans. C, November 30, 1987, p. 66.
The New Republic. CXCVII, December 14, 1987, p. 23.
The New York Times. November 20, 1987, p. C16.
Newsweek. CX, November 23, 1987, p. 83.
People Weekly. XXVIII, November 23, 1987, p. 14.
Time. CXXX, November 30, 1987, p. 104.
Variety. CCCXXIX, November 18, 1987, p. 14.
The Wall Street Journal. December 3, 1987, p. 28.

OUTRAGEOUS FORTUNE

Production: Ted Field and Robert W. Cort for Touchstone Pictures, in association with Silver Screen Partners II; released by Buena Vista
Direction: Arthur Hiller
Screenplay: Leslie Dixon
Cinematography: David M. Walsh
Editing: Tom Rolf
Production design: James D. Vance
Art direction: Sandy Veneziano; set decoration, Rick T. Gentz
Costume design: Gloria Gresham
Music: Alan Silvestri
MPAA rating: R
Running time: 100 minutes

Principal characters:
Lauren . . . . Shelley Long
Sandy. . . . . Bette Midler
Michael. . . . . Peter Coyote
Stanislov Korzenowski . . . . Robert Prosky
Atkins . . . . John Schuck
Frank . . . . George Carlin
Weldon. . . . . Anthony Heald

At the time that *Outrageous Fortune* was released, it achieved the highest opening-weekend grosses in the history of Disney Studios. The company had basically floundered through the 1960's and 1970's after its founder, Walt Disney, died in 1967. While other studios were capturing children's cinema-going dollars with such hits as *Star Wars* (1977) and *E.T.: The Extra-Terrestrial* (1982), Disney seemed incapable of producing new films that would win back this core audience, which had once been almost exclusively theirs.

This continuing bad track record among other factors caused a considerable amount of corporate infighting. Finally, in 1984, a new management team headed by Michael Eisner (formerly of Paramount Pictures) and Frank Wells (formerly of Warner Bros.) took control. By 1986 Disney Studios was again producing films that could capture audiences, but with a difference. Under the banner of their new Touchstone Pictures logo, Disney started to release films aimed at more adult tastes. With *Down and Out in Beverly Hills* (1986), Disney had the first R-rated film in its history and its first successful new film in many years.

Outrageous Fortune is yet another in the growing line of successful films released under the auspices of the revamped Disney studios. Like several of its predecessors, *Outrageous Fortune* is a mainstream comedy which is consistently delightful and more than a bit bawdy. Much of the film's ribald explicitness can be directly attributed to the flamboyant acting style of Bette Midler and some playfully funny dialogue and scenes created by newcomer screenwriter, Leslie Dixon. While the more traditional of the Disney motion-picture fans may have been a bit nervous, Midler and Dixon manage to pull it all off with a curious innocence. *Outrageous Fortune* combines several proven Hollywood film premises. It is an adventure-chase film as well as a buddy film. Unlike traditional Hollywood buddy films, however, this one breaks new ground by having two women as perpetrators of the action, comedy, and bonding.

Lauren (Shelley Long) is a prissy, intellectual, struggling actress who is in debt to her parents for thirty-two thousand dollars for the various lessons in which she has indulged herself in preparation for her chosen career. When she hears that a Stanislavsky-like acting teacher will be offering classes, she once again goes to her parents for funding. To establish the relationship between Lauren and her parents, Dixon never lets the viewer see them. They are understandably reluctant to let their daughter into their apartment, and all negotiating is done through the building's intercom.

Also interested in taking the acting classes of Stanislov Korzenowski (Robert Prosky) is Sandy (Bette Midler), whose acting credits consist of a part in *Ninja Vixens* and a performance for the benefit of a phone-company representative who was supposed to disconnect her phone. The two women are as opposite as can be imagined, from Lauren's refined speech and elegant manner to Sandy's colorful insults and saucy, wiggling walk.

What the women do have in common is that they are both having an affair with the same man, Michael (Peter Coyote). Michael is the perfect lover: He is considerate, attentive, eligible, and, as implied in one broad scene, well endowed physically. When he is killed by a bomb, both distraught women go to the morgue to identify his body. They not only discover that Michael has been seeing both of them, but also, after seeing the remains of the charred corpse, discover that it is obviously not Michael's.

Sandy and Lauren now join forces to track down Michael; they want him to choose between them. (Because Midler and Long have created such believable characters, and because the film's comedy develops out of these characters, the extraordinary twists and turns of the plot are easily made credible.) Eventually the two women learn that Michael is a double agent who was using them to smuggle microdots to his KGB contact, their acting teacher Korzenowski. To add to the confusion of the manhunt, Michael is being pursued not only by Sandy and Lauren but also by the KGB and the Central Intelligence Agency; both agencies are after the airborn defoliant he is holding for ransom.

Coyote is an eminently capable actor who has no problem making the chameleonlike Michael plausible as both the romantic hero and the dastardly double agent. The film, however, is stolen by the pairing of the strutting Midler and the gliding Long. Long's Lauren is, in many ways, merely a more ruffled version of Diane Chambers, the character she played on the successful and well-written television series *Cheers*. She is a comedienne capable of convincingly delivering intellectual humor, deftly carrying off slapstick, and expressing more eloquence with the lift of an eyebrow than many actors do with pages of dialogue.

Similarly, Midler's Sandy is little more than another incarnation of the flouncing, shamelessly risqué, live entertainer who has bowled over audiences for years with her singing act. Although she captured an Academy Award nomination for her first film role, in *The Rose* (1979), Midler's career seemed to stall afterward until it was rejuvenated by Disney Studios. She made both *Down and Out In Beverly Hills* and *Ruthless People* for them in 1986. (The first ranked as number ten among box-office winners of 1986, the second ranked number eight.)

The pairing of these complete opposites, characters who were essentially familiar, may have contributed to the immediate box-office power of *Outrageous Fortune*. Audiences were interested to see how these very antagonistic protagonists would play against each other and how they could ever accomplish anything together.

The dialogue given to Midler and Long seems so in keeping with their characters that it sounds ad-libbed, but according to Dixon, the script she delivered to the studio was shot almost exactly as written. Dixon's witty and often-wicked screenplay is carried off perfectly by Midler and Long; the scenes she creates for them not only provide comedy, action, and a bit of mystery, but also open a rich vein of women's humor—including the continuous cat fighting which runs throughout the film. In midchase, closing in upon Michael, Sandy and Lauren stop to try on clothes at a New Mexican trading post run by Frank (George Carlin), a burned-out refugee from the 1960's. When Sandy and Lauren finally arrive at a climactic scene in which they will confront Michael, both stop to check their makeup.

Another theme running through Dixon's script is the world of acting. (In fact, the film's title comes from Hamlet's "To be or not to be" soliloquy, appropriate since the prince of Denmark is a role Lauren sets as a goal for herself.) Sandy and Lauren use their acting talent to portray "Cagney and Lacey" policewomen when they shake down a drug dealer with a toy gun and walk off with his money. In another scene, they try to elicit information out of an airline employee by using fake accents and acting talents so bad that their supposed dupe gives them their first acting review.

By the end of the film, Sandy and Lauren have found Michael and saved the North American continent from defoliation. They have also admitted to themselves that, although they have little in common, they have been through so much together they have become friends. Action-adventure films with a rich vein of humanist comedy are not unknown to director Arthur Hiller. Just as in *Outrageous Fortune*, the plots of Hiller's *Silver Streak* (1976) and *The In-Laws* (1979) center on a pair of seemingly mismatched people who overcome their differences while pursuing a common goal. He takes the time to establish the personality of the main characters and the antagonism between them. He takes the same care in showing them in the environment to which they are accustomed and with which they know how to cope. He then binds them together and moves them into a totally different environment, one in which the coping becomes much more difficult and amusing. Tracking Michael through the busy streets of New York provides some entertaining scenes, but the humor is much stronger when Sandy and Lauren have to chase him through the vast, alien, and remote mesas of New Mexico.

Hiller keeps *Outrageous Fortune* moving at a fast and funny pace. With combinations such as the superb team acting of Midler and Long and the talented writing of Dixon, it would seem that Disney is cementing its place as a maker of good adult comedies that please both audiences and critics.

Beverley Bare Buehrer

Reviews
The Christian Science Monitor. February 4, 1987, p. 25.
Commonweal. CIV, March 27, 1987, p. 182.
Films in Review. XXXVIII, May, 1987, p. 294.
Los Angeles Times. January 30, 1987, VI, p. 1.
The New Republic. CXCVI, March 2, 1987, p. 24.
New York. February 9, 1987, p. 96.
The New York Times. January 30, 1987, p. C5.
The New Yorker. LXIII, February 23, 1987, p. 112.
Newsweek. CIX, January 26, 1987, p. 76.
Savvy. VIII, March, 1987, p. 74.
Time. CXXIX, February 2, 1987, p. 73.
Variety. CCCXXVI, January 28, 1987, p. 20.

PLANES, TRAINS, AND AUTOMOBILES

Production: John Hughes; released by Paramount Pictures
Direction: John Hughes
Screenplay: John Hughes
Cinematography: Don Peterman
Editing: Paul Hirsch
Production design: John Corso
Art direction: Harold Michelson; set decoration, Jane Bogart and Linda Spheeris
Costume design: April Ferry
Sound: Jim Alexander
Music: Ira Newborn
MPAA rating: R
Running time: 93 minutes

Principal characters:
Neal Page........................... Steve Martin
Del Griffith .... John Candy
Sue Page........................... Laila Robbins
State trooper Sergeant Kudner ..... Michael McKean
Taxi racer .... Kevin Bacon
Chairman....................... William Windom
Car rental clerk.................... Edie McClurg

John Hughes has made a name for himself as one of the most successful and prolific directors of the 1980's. His films are not only popular but also profitable. Part of the reason for Hughes's success is that his films have an uncanny knack of entertaining and appealing to that most coveted of filmgoing groups, teenagers. Previous films directed by Hughes, *Sixteen Candles* (1984), *The Breakfast Club* (1985), *Weird Science* (1985), and *Ferris Bueller's Day Off* (1986), quickly garnered favor among younger filmgoers. They easily identified with Hughes's teenage protagonists and enjoyed the wild screen antics these characters performed.

Hughes's films also appeal to adolescent audiences by making good use of popular music. Many of the films with which he has been involved have led to popular record albums and Top 40 hits. To capitalize on this phenomenon, Hughes created his own music label, Hughes Music, which is distributed by MCA Records. While the upbeat sound track is available for *Planes, Trains, and Automobiles*, it has not generated an identifiable song and does not seem destined to be the lucrative seller his other albums were.

Hughes's film accomplishments have gained for him a deal with Paramount Pictures, which has allowed him to produce films under the Hughes Entertainment banner. It was through this arrangement that he directed

Ferris Bueller's Day Off, produced *Some Kind of Wonderful* (1987; reviewed in this volume), and wrote and produced *Pretty in Pink* (1986).

His fourth film under this contract is *Planes, Trains, and Automobiles*. In this film, Hughes assumes the triple task of writer, director, and producer and marks his first real venture into the realm of films aimed at an adult audience. Hughes's previous films did manage to attract a fair share of older audiences mainly because of their lively, comic, and charming themes. Their subject matter, however, was still primarily the world of teenagers. In *Planes, Trains, and Automobiles*, teenagers are a scarce commodity.

In this film, Hughes has created a gag-filled road film in the tradition of Bob Hope and Bing Crosby. Unlike the Hope and Crosby pictures, however, *Planes, Trains, and Automobiles* has minimal singing, much warmth, and a gentle message. By concentrating on two completely opposite characters traveling in the worst of conditions, the film offers a physical and allegorical journey through adversity to self-discovery.

Neal Page (Steve Martin) is an advertising executive on a business trip in New York City two days before Thanksgiving. He only wants to return home to Chicago, see his daughter in her school play, and enjoy the holidays with his family. (Chicago is a favorite setting for Hughes's films.) Unfortunately, what should have been a brief two-hour plane ride turns into a nightmare odyssey, subject in every way to Murphy's Law: If it can go wrong, it will.

Neal's meeting runs late, he trips over a trunk on the sidewalk, someone steals his cab, and his plane is delayed and then rerouted to Wichita, Kansas, because of a snowstorm. When the flight attendant refuses to honor his first-class ticket, he is seated in coach. It proves to be a hardship made even worse by his seatmate, who is an overweight loudmouth who relaxes by removing his shoes and apparently malodorous socks. Del Griffith (John Candy), a shower-ring salesman, is the complete antithesis of the fastidious and reserved Neal. Binding two dissimilar people together is an established comedic formula, but between Hughes's script and Candy's and Martin's characterizations, the film never seems stale or ordinary.

Hughes has based this improbable journey on two characters who are rendered credible by the expert comic abilities of Martin and Candy. Martin, hot from his critical success as C. D. Bales in *Roxanne* (1987; reviewed in this volume) and as Dr. Orin Scrivello, the sadistic dentist in the remake of *Little Shop of Horrors* (1986), continues his string of entertaining and popular comic characters with his portrayal of Neal Page. He brings to Neal a convincing surface stoicism which disguises his growing, suppressed anger. He invites easy audience identification and provides a sound basis for his character's reactions, no matter how preposterous the situation. These are the kinds of stifled responses perfect for Martin's brand of humor and comic timing.

For Candy, *Planes, Trains, and Automobiles* offers a tricky role which, in the hands of lesser comics, could be very ineffectual. Del is initially introduced as an obnoxious bore, the kind of character audiences love to dislike. It is Candy's task, however, to make Del likable by the end of the film, or it will be totally unbelievable. Candy achieves this in several ways. Although Candy portrays Del as irritatingly gregarious, he also allows the audience to perceive his sincerity and inexhaustible cheerfulness. He may be overly friendly as far as Neal is concerned, but it has given Del, the more adept of the two travelers, friendly acquaintances everywhere he goes.

It is that friendliness which procures for Del a motel room in overbooked Wichita and makes him generously offer to share it with Neal. It is a gesture which provides great comic scenes for the two actors, and it is the audience's first chance to see the compassion behind Del's bluster and the loneliness behind his camaraderie.

In the motel room there is only one bed, which the two are forced to share. While Neal showers, Del leaves beer cans on the vibrating bed. When the cans explode on Neal's side, Del uses all the towels to clean up the mess, leaving a dripping Neal only one washcloth with which to dry himself. Once in bed, Del cracks his knuckles and various other joints and makes disgusting noises clearing his sinuses. Neal is finally pushed to his limits and confronts Del with a volley of stored-up grievances. The hurt in Del's eyes becomes obvious. He has now garnered a degree of sympathy from the audience which will absolve him of his forthcoming transgressions.

Del and Neal have an off-again on-again relationship. Neal tries several times to extricate himself from Del's companionship, but because of convenience or necessity (or guilt on Neal's part) they are fated to travel together. When they discover that they have been robbed of their cash, Del is tied even closer to Neal. Del may have the connections, but Neal is the only one with credit cards to finance their trip to Chicago.

More adversity comes as the two nearly freeze in the back of a pickup truck, board a train destined to break down miles from the highway, and catch a bus where sing-alongs are the entertainment. It is a scene which perfectly depicts the differences in the two men. Neal offers bewildered riders his elitist suggestion that they sing "Three Coins in a Fountain." It is a suggestion which is met with complete silence. The embarrassed Neal is quickly rescued by Del, however, who begins to sing a song they all know, the theme from "The Flintstones."

When Neal and Del accidentally set fire to their rental car and Neal's credit cards, any chance of friendship seems to have gone up in smoke. Neal trades his expensive wristwatch for a motel room and leaves Del to sleep in the burnt shell of their incredibly still-drivable car. Hughes has the audience listen in on Del's shivering conversation with his absent wife, Marie. Here he realizes how he has smothered Neal and consequently lost his friendship.

Neal also gains some insight and finally generates a degree of empathy for Del. In a conciliatory gesture, he invites Del to share his motel room for the night. Through all the adversities and antagonisms, both men have been forced to explore psychological as well as geographical terrains on the road to Chicago. The two dissimilar men have emerged friends.

As a Chicagoan, Hughes often made the trip to New York under the auspices of his jobs as a copywriter and as editor of *The National Lampoon* magazine. Consequently, the nightmarish world of the traveler he creates in *Planes, Trains, and Automobiles* is at once authentic, familiar, and plausibly magnified for maximum humorous effect.

Hughes tells an amusing and fast-paced story in *Planes, Trains, and Automobiles* and has managed to balance laughable, physical sight gags with heartwarming humor. Martin and Candy carry the film the way no two other actors could, and Hughes uses them to full advantage. Hughes's hilarious, if exaggerated, scenes will strike chords of recognition in every filmgoer who has wanted to extract revenge on a rude rental car agent, an airline that loses baggage, or a talkative traveling companion whose tiresome stories have no point.

Beverley Bare Buehrer

Reviews
Chicago Tribune. November 25, 1987, V, p. 6.
The Christian Science Monitor. December 30, 1987, p. 20.
Los Angeles Times. November 25, 1987, VI, p. 1.
Macleans. C, December 14, 1987, p. 67.
The New Republic. CXCVIII, February 8, 1988, p. 26.
New York. XX, December 7, 1987, p. 152.
The New York Times. November 25, 1987, p. C19.
People Weekly. XXVIII, December 14, 1987, p. 14.
Time. CXXX, November 30, 1987, p. 104.
Variety. CCCXXIX, November 25, 1987, p. 14.

PREDATOR

Production: Lawrence Gordon, Joel Silverman, and John Davis for Americent Films and American Entertainment Partners; released by Twentieth Century-Fox
Direction: John McTiernan
Screenplay: Jim Thomas and John Thomas
Cinematography: Donald McAlpine and Leon Sanchez
Editing: John F. Link and Mark Helfrich
Production design: John Vallone
Art direction: Frank Richwood, Jorge Saenz, and John K. Reinhart, Jr.; set decoration, Enrique Estevez
Sound effects: R/Greenberg, supervised by Joel Hynek and Eugen Mamut; thermal vision effects supervised by Stuart Robertson; creature created by Stan Winston
Makeup: Scott Eddo
Costume design: Marilyn Vance-Straker
Sound: Manuel Topete
Music: Alan Silvestri
MPAA rating: R
Running time: 107 minutes

    Principal characters:

Dutch Schaefer	Arnold Schwarzenegger
Dillon	Carl Weathers
Anna	Elpidia Carrillo
Mac	Bill Duke
Blain	Jesse Ventura
Billy	Sonny Landham
Poncho	Richard Chaves
General Philips	R. G. Armstrong
Hawkins	Shane Black
The Predator	Kevin Peter Hall

Arnold Schwarzenegger has established himself as a star of action-packed adventure films which are fast-paced, contain only a touch of humor, and are rife with violence. In such films as *Conan the Barbarian* (1982), its sequel, *Conan the Destroyer* (1984), *Commando* (1985), and *Raw Deal* (1986), Schwarzenegger has fashioned a particular screen *persona*, that of a man of unusual strength and skill who embarks on a mission or quest. These missions most often involve the pursuit of an adversary of equal strength who has somehow threatened or intruded on his existence. Schwarzenegger becomes a hunter, who ruthlessly tracks down and destroys his powerful enemy. Even in *The Terminator* (1984), which features Schwarzenegger in his only role as a villain, he plays a hunter sent from the future to track and destroy a human from the present. Ironically, the two films he made in 1987, *Predator* and *Running Man*, turn the tables on Schwarzenegger and feature him not only as the hunter but also as the hunted.

The theme of the hunter and the hunted echoes throughout the film *Predator*, which was originally titled *Hunter*. Many reviewers assumed that the film's title referred to the space alien who stalks Schwarzenegger and the other characters. In fact, the title describes Schwarzenegger's character and that of the alien as both alternate between being the predator and the prey.

Except for a precredit shot of the alien's space capsule being ejected from the mother ship, the film begins as a typical action-adventure tale. Dutch Schaefer (Schwarzenegger) lands in a Central American country with his special paramilitary rescue team. There he meets with General Philips (R. G. Armstrong) and his old buddy Dillon (Carl Weathers), a former member of his team who now works for the Central Intelligence Agency (CIA). Dutch's new mission is to hunt down and rescue a cabinet minister and his aide who have accidentally crashed across the border into hostile territory and fallen into guerrilla hands.

Against the background music of Little Richard's "Long Tall Sally," the rescue team, along with Dillon, prepares for its mission before the helicopter drops the men across the border in some unnamed, hostile Central American country, loosely masquerading as Nicaragua. The men chew tobacco, tell vulgar jokes, show off their lightning reflexes, and shave their faces without benefit of shaving cream. The scene's purpose is twofold: It serves as a bit of comic relief before the horrors of the rest of the film unfold, and, more important, it depicts the rock-hard toughness of Dutch's team—Mac (Bill Duke), Blain (Jesse Ventura), Billy (Sonny Landham), Poncho (Richard Chaves), and Hawkins (Shane Black). A squad of highly trained weapon-and-survival specialists, Dutch and his team are presented as the ultimate hunters.

After the squad lands and treks into the dense jungle foliage, Billy, an American Indian who serves as the team's scout, discovers the footprints of six Green Berets who seem to be headed for the guerrilla camp. Dutch suspects that Dillon has not been straight with him about the mission, but Dillon claims no knowledge of any Special Forces operation in the area. Soon thereafter, Billy comes across three of the soldiers' bodies, which have been skinned alive and hung from a tree. Dillon immediately blames the rebel forces, but Billy remains unconvinced, noting that the evidence left behind does not support that conclusion. The team brings out their heavy artillery, including large, fully automated weapons and a rotating-barrel machine gun nicknamed "Painless" by the men. Their expertise at assessing the situation and silently traversing the harsh terrain lends credibility to their skills as hunters.

Just as the audience is assured that the team is invincible, however, a few shots of Dutch and his men from a subjective camera angle suggest otherwise. The subjective shots are in thermal vision, specially developed for the film to represent the space alien's vision. The alien's eyesight does not respond to light, as with humans, but instead depends on a heat-sensing device (presumably inside the alien's helmet) that reads the heat patterns of animate objects and reproduces those patterns in color. The shots of Dutch and the team in thermal vision and from a subjective angle suggest that something unfamiliar is stalking them. The hunters are now the hunted.

Dutch's team surrounds the guerrilla camp and attacks just as a pack of animals might charge their prey, a visual metaphor that was surely intentional. The rebels are no match for the highly trained squad and their state-of-the-art military equipment. Unfortunately, the team is too late, for the hostages have already been killed by the guerrillas. After the raid, Dutch discovers that Dillon lied about the true nature of their mission. Instead of a cabinet minister and his aide, the hostages were CIA agents involved with dirty tactics. The exact nature of the CIA's plan is never adequately explained (one of the film's weaknesses), but as one of the characters states, "Something big was going to happen here." The only rebel left alive is a young woman, Anna (Elpidia Carrillo), whom Dillon insists the team take back with them. In expert fashion, Dutch and his paramilitary unit have successfully tracked down the hostages, hunted down the enemy, and captured their prey.

As the team prepares to move out, however, the alien predator (Kevin Peter Hall) silently watches them, studying their moves, weapons, and bits of conversation, just as the rescue team had studied the guerrillas only moments before. Again, the predators become the prey.

The alien pursues them at closer range, silently moving through the trees at high speeds. He moves undetected via a cloaking device that enables him to mimic whatever environment he inhabits, one of the more memorable special effects in the film. When he swings through the trees, a slight rippling effect is created, making him appear a part of the greenery. When he is motionless, he is completely invisible. The alien is presented as a better predator than the humans, because not only does he have powerful weapons but also he uses elements of nature to help him stalk his prey. In comparison, Dutch and his men look out of place as they lug their massive military hardware through the dense jungle.

The alien's first attack occurs when the rebel hostage, Anna, attempts to escape from the team and Hawkins runs after her. Hawkins is shot by the alien's laserlike weapon and then dragged into the jungle. Moments later, Dutch and the men find the woman, unharmed but splattered with Hawkins' blood. All that is left of Hawkins are a few internal organs and his weapons. The rescue team's high-tech weapons are no match for the alien predator, just like the rebels' weapons and tactics were no match for Dutch and his men.

The remaining members of the team surround themselves with a protective circle of flares and explosives until a rescue helicopter can pick them up. By using his cloaking device, the alien is able to penetrate their fortress, in the same way that the rescue team was able to penetrate the rebels' camp. The men are killed and dragged away one by one, with Mac's death being particularly disturbing. As the alien draws near, Mac begins weakly singing "Long Tall Sally," the song the men were listening to when they were preparing for the mission. The song recalls those early scenes of masculine posturing, but Mac's version ironically reminds the viewer that these men are not so tough.

Eventually only Dutch and Anna survive. Dutch realizes that the predator is literally hunting them when he notices that the alien will not attack an unarmed man (or woman), because that would be no sport. Dutch lures the alien away, while Anna escapes unarmed toward the helicopter checkpoint. The predator pursues him into a lake. When Dutch emerges from the other side covered in thick, black mud, he realizes that the alien's heat-seeking device cannot penetrate the mud. The alien moves past him, without detecting his presence.

Dutch, without the benefit of his high-tech, military hardware, prepares to battle the alien predator with weapons made from the jungle environment. While Dutch sets his traps (now the alien is the prey), the audience is given a clue to the alien's motivations. High atop the trees, he is shown ripping the skull out of one of his victims and burning the flesh off of it. He then carefully places the skull next to his other hunting trophies. The scene echoes something Anna told Dutch when she was recalling a similar predator who had attacked her village long ago. The Spanish name for the predator translates as "The Dim One Who Makes Trophies of Man."

The climactic battles between Dutch and the alien shows off both Schwarzenegger's physical presence and Stan Winston's creature design. The alien, without his cloaking device, wears a protective armor, but he discards it to fight one-on-one with Dutch—a more sporting challenge. Dutch defeats the hideously ugly creature by utilizing some of the alien's tactics. Just as the alien had used nature, particularly the dense foliage, for camouflage to stalk his victims better, so Dutch covers himself with mud to hide from the alien. As Dutch is about to strike the final blow, he finds he cannot kill the fatally wounded alien in cold blood. In frustration, he wonders aloud who the alien is. The alien responds with a chilling answer: "I am what you are."

The film concludes when the alien activates a powerful explosive attached to his arm, blowing himself up in the process. Dutch escapes and is rescued by the helicopter, which has also picked up Anna.

Though parallels between predator and Dutch (and by extension his men) have been made throughout the film, even depicting both to be fair fighters, it is the alien's final words that drive home the point. The creature's hideous appearance can be seen as an outward manifestation of his hideous hobby—hunting down human beings as prey and collecting their skulls. When Dutch hears the alien's final words, he realizes that he too is a hunter of men and sees himself in the ugliness of the creature's face. In terms of Schwarzenegger's roles in his previous films, which have usually featured him as a hunter of unusual strength and skill, *Predator* makes for an ironic and pointed commentary on his *persona*.

Susan Doll

Reviews

Chicago Sun-Times. June 12, 1987, Weekend Section, p. 31.
Chicago Tribune. June 12, 1987, VII, p. 45.
Christian Herald. CX, September, 1987, p. 54.
Cinefantastique. December, 1987, p. 36.
Los Angeles Times. June 12, 1987, VI, p. 6.
The New York Times. June 12, 1987, p. C6.
People Weekly. XXIX, June 29, 1987, p. 10.
Variety. CCCXXVII, June 17, 1987, p. 16.
Video. XI, February, 1988, p. 65.
Video Review. VIII, February, 1988, p. 62.

PRICK UP YOUR EARS

Origin: Great Britain
Production: Andrew Brown for Civilhand/Zenith; released by the Samuel Goldwyn Co.
Direction: Stephen Frears
Screenplay: Alan Bennett; based on the book of the same name by John Lahr
Cinematography: Oliver Stapleton
Editing: Mick Audsley
Production design: Hugo Luczyc-Wyhowski
Art direction: Philip Elton; set decoration, John Kirby Spotswood
Special effects: Optical Film Effects
Makeup: Elaine Carew
Costume design: Bob Ringwood
Sound: Tony Jackson
Music direction: John Harle
Music: Stanley Myers
Song: Stanley Myers and Richard Myhill, "Dancing Hearts"
MPAA rating: R
Running time: 110 minutes
Running time in U.S.: 111 minutes

Principal characters:
Joe Orton	Gary Oldman
Kenneth Halliwell	Alfred Molina
Peggy Ramsay	Vanessa Redgrave
John Lahr	Wallace Shawn
Anthea Lahr	Lindsay Duncan
Elsie Orton	Julie Walters
William Orton	James Grant
Leonie Orton	Frances Barber

Prick Up Your Ears is a strange and, in its very particular way, demanding and complex British "bio-pic." Joe Orton's brief career as a maverick, subversive composer of satiric farce, violently cut short by murder at the age of thirty-four, lasted only from 1964, when his radio play, a first venture entitled *The Ruffian on the Stair*, was produced by the British Broadcasting Corporation (BBC), to 1967, when his partner of some sixteen years killed him. By that time, Orton was the acclaimed author of *Entertaining Mr. Sloane* (1964) and *Loot* (1965), surreal comedies of the outlandish and outrageous couched in such carefully styled and satirically mannered, euphemistic dialogue that many have suggested that he was the Oscar Wilde of the twentieth century. All there is in common between Orton and Wilde is the brevity of their period of great success in the London theater, the tragic break in their careers, and their acknowledged homosexuality. Culturally, they were as far apart as the British class system could separate them: Wilde, elitist and delighting in the socialite society he lightly satirized; Orton, culturally deprived ("I'm from the gutter, and don't you ever forget it, because I won't"), loathing bourgeois respectability in all classes, his carefully acquired stylishness the perfume that only served to emphasize the sewer beneath the skin.

Orton (played in the film by Gary Oldman) was born in 1933, the eldest son in a loveless, provincial working-class family in Leicester, England. His birthplace is a prosperous industrial city one hundred miles north of London; it is also a university city with keen support for both professional and amateur theater—culturally conventional, no doubt, but scarcely the absolute cultural desert it has been made out to be as a result of Orton's loathing. Unsuccessful educationally, he left school at sixteen and worked in an office; nevertheless, he developed a passion for amateur acting and for reading. Two years later, in 1951, he managed to get himself accepted by the Royal Academy of Dramatic Art (RADA) in London, although he was to adopt the career of writer and dramatist rather than that of actor. It was at RADA, however, that he met the socially superior, well-educated, middle-class student, Kenneth Halliwell (in the film, Alfred Molina), a man seven years his senior, who became his lover. Halliwell developed Orton's taste in literature, including the work of Ronald Firbank, the mannered and cultish writer, who was to influence Orton's attitude on style. Orton remained a voracious reader, feverishly educating himself during the next ten years and helping Halliwell to write novels that proved unpublishable. They lived on Halliwell's inheritance from his parents and Orton's social security payments and created their own outrageous life-style, which later included obscenely defacing stolen public library books, a petty crime for which they were in 1962 finally imprisoned and, significantly, separated for six months. It was while in prison that Orton, now around the age of thirty, discovered his independence, and began to write in his own style. The initial result was the radio play aired by the BBC, *The Ruffian on the Stair*.

Certainly Orton, Halliwell's changeling, had needed his mentor to guide and educate him, but when his burst of talent began, Halliwell became the equivalent of a neglected wife, the once-valued but now-abandoned teacher and counselor. After 1964, Orton's work became well known, much discussed and denounced, and also courted; he no longer wanted the talentless, monogamous Halliwell, except as housekeeper in their little Islington apartment in North London, where they lived the final eight years of their lives. Orton's new mentor became literary agent Peggy Ramsay (played by Vanessa Redgrave), who understood the true nature of his talent. *Entertain-*

ing Mr. Sloane and *Loot* followed in rapid succession; Orton was even invited to script a film for the Beatles and the humble apartment saw the arrival of a gleaming Rolls Royce and liveried driver to pick him up for script conferences. In his need to shake himself free from the friend and lover he had outgrown, Orton became wildly promiscuous, even haunting certain remote public lavatories earmarked as sites for "brotherhood" saturnalia, at a time when pederasty was still illegal in Great Britain. Halliwell remained for the most part morosely at home, only permitted to share in occasional trips to Tangier, where young and likely lads were to be had by the score for a pittance in the warm and brilliant sunshine.

All this and more lubricious details appear in *Prick Up Your Ears: The Biography of Joe Orton*, sedulously researched since 1970 by American writer John Lahr and his wife and published in 1978, a decade after his subject's violent end. Lahr was in 1987 to edit Orton's late-life diaries, covering the eight months from December, 1966, to August, 1967; the diaries were available to him while he was writing the biography. The entries detailing Orton's infidelities and the record of his growing alienation from Halliwell were left around the cramped apartment for Orton's still infatuated lover to find—a touch of sheer cruelty on Orton's part. Halliwell, after killing Orton, left a brief, sad note before taking his own life with an overdose of Nembutal: "If you read this diary all will be explained. KH. PS. Especially the latter part."

The film itself concentrates on the rise and fall of their relationship. Orton's self-discovery as a writer, his assiduous self-education (initially dependent on Halliwell's tutelage), and the nature of his sudden success, once he had established his style and related it to his philosophy of life ("People are profoundly bad and irresistibly funny"), are all taken for granted as background to the action of the film. Drama is about relationships, and the record of a man establishing within himself his literary persona is not dramatic as such. The film is the result of the creative partnership of an extremely talented team: Lahr, the biographer; Alan Bennett, the screenwriter (a long-established man of the theater and the writer of the successful film *A Private Function*, 1984); Stephen Frears, the director (his best known of many films, *My Beautiful Laundrette*, 1985); and the key players, Oldman (Sid in the film, *Sid and Nancy*, 1986), Molina, and, in the small but influential part of Orton's agent, Redgrave. The suggestive title *Prick Up Your Ears* (the last word is an anagram for "arse") was Orton's intended title for a future farce. (Ironically, it was Halliwell who had originally thought of it, as he had thought of other titles for Orton's work.) Lahr, Bennett, and Frears each inevitably brought a different slant to the collective understanding of Orton and Halliwell's relationship. The weak link in the chain is possibly their unresolved view of Halliwell. In appearance, he somewhat resembled Orton in size and looks, although he was bald. Molina, an admirable actor, is a tall and bulky man, with a moon face, sad eyes, and a high-pitched, volatile voice and manner; inevitably, he interprets Halliwell as a nervous, at times near-comic "stage" homosexual, ridden with anxiety and, later, subject to vituperative expressions of resentment. He never looks, or acts, however, like a person who could have been driven by inner compulsions to batter the head of his lover into pieces.

Another factor that lessens the emotional impact and developmental drive of the film is its constant shift in structure. It moves, with much adroit planning, from one facet of Orton's life with Halliwell to another and even incorporates the period after their deaths, when Lahr, the biographer—a character in the film (played by Wallace Shawn)—discusses the subject with the Orton family in Leicester, while Peggy Ramsay (another character) is interviewed, revealing her memories in flashback, Redgrave's strong personality every so often stealing the film.

Although Bennett's script is a model of orderly continuity for significant scenes that are occasioned by various people's recollections, the film seems in consequence to be impelled forward by a researcher's impulse rather than by the sheer dynamic development in the lovers' relationship, especially when it is threatened by Orton's increasing independence. The screenplay's overall virtue remains that it allows Orton to be himself, without any molding, emasculation, or apologetics for his behavior. The film is therefore frequently shocking, as Orton would have wished it to be, as well as outrageously funny—as in the incident, taken from the later diaries, of Orton stealing his mother's false teeth at her funeral in order to present them to the actor who plays the character in *Loot* who snaps his dead mother's dentures like castanets.

The film is without question an artistic success for Frears, whose first film, *Gumshoe* (1972), an original subject inspiring a fine performance from Albert Finney, was followed by several productions on film for television, with Bennett a frequent collaborator. *My Beautiful Laundrette* was originally made for Great Britain's channel 4 on television, but it enjoyed success in the United States as an art-house film. *Prick Up Your Ears* was made with the modest budget of $3.5 million; it has an outstanding performance by Oldman, who has confessed to an "eerie connection" with Orton, whom he closely resembles. Oldman projects successfully Orton's anarchic, chameleonic charm, but with an expression that, smiles or no smiles, reveals absolute resolution to achieve success on his own terms. Without any sign of compunction, Orton leaves Halliwell to fester in his own, personal failure as a writer and to realize, if he can, that his one success was to have produced Orton. This fact clearly emerges in Oldman's handling of the character with whom he feels so closely identified, coming as he does from a similar background. Oldman was reared in South London, in a home with no books or family visits to the cinema. He says that he was inspired to realize himself through acting after seeing, during his adolescence, Malcolm McDowell's performance in Lindsay Anderson's film *If . . .* (1968). He claims that, when he experienced the initial urge to go to drama school, he had never even seen a play performed.

With its occasional poetic moments—the sun-drenched scenes by the sea in Morocco, the strange Halloween atmosphere during the shadowed saturnalia in the public lavatory—and with its mordant wit, its lines culled by Bennett from the Orton diaries, *Prick Up Your Ears* undoubtedly reveals much of Orton's anarchic personality. Yet the unbearable, jealous pain that drove Halliwell to kill the man he deeply loved in so hideous a manner is not realized in this film, which Bennett has called "a film about marriage," Frears, a "rags-to-riches story," and Lahr, "a murder mystery."

Roger Manvell

Reviews
Films in Review. XXXVIII, August, 1987, p. 426.
Horizon. XXX, April, 1987, p. 61.
Los Angeles Times. May 1, 1987, VI, p. 1.
The Nation. May 9, 1987, p. 618.
The New Republic. CXCVI, April 20, 1987, p. 28.
New Statesman. CXIII, May 22, 1987, p. 23.
The New York Times. April 17, 1987, p. C17.
The New Yorker. LXIII, May 4, 1987, p. 128.
Newsweek. CIX, April 20, 1987, p. 89.
Time. CXXIX, April 20, 1987, p. 76.
The Washington Post. May 16, 1987, p. G8.

THE PRINCESS BRIDE

Production: Andrew Scheinman and Rob Reiner; released by Twentieth Century-Fox
Direction: Rob Reiner
Screenplay: William Goldman; based on his novel of the same name
Cinematography: Adrian Biddle
Editing: Robert Leighton
Production design: Norman Garwood
Art direction: Richard Holland; set decoration, Maggie Gray
Music: Mark Knopfler
MPAA rating: PG
Running time: 100 minutes

Principal characters:

Westley	Cary Elwes
Inigo Montoya	Mandy Patinkin
Prince Humperdinck	Chris Sarandon
Count Rugen	Christopher Guest
Vizzini	Wallace Shawn
Fezzik	Andre the Giant
The Grandson	Fred Savage
The Princess Bride (Buttercup)	Robin Wright
The Grandfather	Peter Falk
Miracle Max	Billy Crystal
Valerie	Carol Kane

Director Rob Reiner's *The Princess Bride* is a fantasy-adventure tale aimed at the PG market. Does that make it like *This Is Spinal Tap* (1984), *The Sure Thing* (1985), or *Stand By Me* (1986)? Is it like *Raiders of the Lost Ark* (1981), *Jewel of the Nile* (1985), or *Labyrinth* (1986)? The answer is a firm yes and no. It does bear a thematic relationship to Reiner's previous films, but the focus has been altered by his choice of collaborators; similarly, the film has its roots in the adventure-film genre but is done from a different perspective from that of the ones noted above.

Like other films aimed at the PG market, *The Princess Bride* offers a strong linear plot that is easy to follow; after all, what can be simpler than a chase, or in this case a pursuit? There are, in fact, several simultaneous pursuits—Westley (Cary Elwes) after Buttercup (Robin Wright), Westley after Vizzini (Wallace Shawn), and Inigo Montoya (Mandy Patinkin) after Count Rugen (Christopher Guest)—which provide the film with a structure, a series of loosely woven threads that are neither too complex nor too intertwined to be followed easily. This structure is quite different from the framing device of the film, that of a story being told to a boy (Fred Savage) on the verge of adolescence by his cynical grandfather (Peter Falk). It is a method not dissimilar from the one used in *This Is Spinal Tap* and one that is well-suited for engaging a broad swath of audiences. The boy provides a running commentary on the film in progress and thus allows Reiner to have both a child's perspective and that of a cynic (the post-*MAD* magazine child). It is a luxury that Spielberg cannot master and that Lucas does not attempt; they provide PG fare that is either too sweet and wholesome or too scary.

If the plot is primary, albeit thin, then the substance of a film should be found in the characters and their development. This is not so, however, in *The Princess Bride*. The viewer does not get to know Westley, the peasant boy who becomes "the pirate dread Roberts," except to see that his boyish earnestness has become a disarming insouciance, just like the devil-may-care heroes of other adventure films. Even more telling, the viewer does not know much or learn more about Buttercup except that she is faithful to the memory of her Westley. There are two characters with a deviousness that portends depth—Vizzini, the would-be mastermind, and the Prince (Chris Sarandon). The latter is evil and cruel without apparent cause, while the former is motivated by a need to show his cleverness, although he is but a pawn in the Prince's game. Since they have to act and cause situations instead of react, their characters are more dimensional, but that is usually the case with literature—the villains are more interesting.

In a sense, the characterizations are similar to those found in other Reiner films that are told primarily from a male's vantage point, sometimes to the point of excluding female characters (as in *Stand By Me* and *This Is Spinal Tap*). Yet another echo from Reiner's previous films is the existence of a mentor, a character who acts as a role model to the hero. Westley owes much to The Pirate Roberts, from his life to his way of life; indeed, without him there would be no Westley character. There is a fascination in Reiner's films with the concept of leaders and roles, and more often than not, the roles discussed are those relating to an external world as opposed to an internalization or identity search.

The Princess Bride is a combination of texture and tone. The substance of the film is the idea of the film itself—that it should be enjoyable by a family yet not devoid of interest. To a certain extent, it achieves this difficult end by using character actors instead of characters, in the fashion that some have come to associate with Shelley Duvall's "Fairy Tale Theater" series (hour-long made-for-television films). Indeed, the strongest characters are those created by the actors with forceful personalities outside *The Princess Bride*, such as Billy Crystal (who plays Miracle Max), Shawn (as Vizzini) and Andre the Giant (who plays Fezzik), which is in marked distinction to the two nominal leads Westley and Buttercup. That there are so many successful portrayals is a tribute to the skill of the director and the casting procedure as well as to the importance of ensemble work over star-vehicle films.

The acclaim if not success of "Fairy Tale Theater" and *The Princess Bride* lies in their tone, not straight yet not mean spirited, a romp with good intentions. The sets are breathtaking, both in the visuals and the way in which it is clear that some of the work is being performed on a sound stage. That combination of outdoors grandeur (filmed in Ireland) and indoor work sets up another frame, making the viewer appreciate even more the value of both types of sets.

If texture is hard to define, it is even more difficult to explain tone. In *The Princess Bride*, the tone seems to be the result of considerable interaction between William Goldman, the novelist (*Soldier in the Rain*, 1960; *Marathon Man*, 1974; *The Color of Light*; and others) and screenwriter (*Harper*, 1966; *Butch Cassidy and the Sundance Kid*, 1969; and *All the President's Men*, 1976) and director Reiner. The book *The Princess Bride* was published in 1973 and differs considerably from the film; given Goldman's reputation, it is implausible that the book was unknown in Hollywood prior to 1987. Although the writing credits are Goldman's alone, it is clear that the tone and content probably developed during discussions between writer and director and gives evidence of the wisdom that attends working in Hollywood for twenty years. In this sense, the tone appears to be unified and filtered jointly through writer and director, showing only flashes of the individuals.

Certainly discussion of tone must include mention of the sound track by Mark Knopfler, which is understated but lush, owing as much to his spare and haunting guitar work as it does to his use of muted string arrangements. Like the best sound tracks, it augments but does not intrude. It does its job, but so effortlessly that its true virtues may escape notice.

The Princess Bride is effective because it is so well anchored in the viewer's projections of what should be happening in a fantasy and so skilled at extrapolating credibly from them. For example, location and set scenes are often juxtaposed and intercut; the location shots set the scene while the work on what is visibly a soundstage makes the fantasy more visceral. It makes sense, and hence is effective to show real cliffs being scaled and then to cut to a manufactured scene for the sword fight atop the cliffs.

Even the exposition of themes is effective; unlike most fantasy films, the format is not that of a quest or of overcoming evil or thwarted love. Rather, it seems to be one that is somewhat constant in Reiner's work, that of respect coupled with self-respect. It can be argued that those were the themes in *This Is Spinal Tap*; it is certainly more transparently so in *Stand By Me* and *The Sure Thing*. It is a theme to which the audience can relate even as it is being amused, as the striving for respect from one's peers while maintaining one's dignity is a constant while growing up. One can see this in the actions of Westley, Inigo Montoya, and also in Vizzini (if not his entourage). One hears it in the exchanges between the boy and his grandfather with their continual sparring for mutual respect, a concept that was not in the book and thus must be attributed to the influence of Reiner.

The film must be deemed successful because it achieves more than it needed to, from a commercial perspective. If the film was made to entertain, it does, bounteously. If it was made to reach a broad audience, it succeeds handsomely; the overall story is fine for the younger ones, although the torture scene is too much for children by leaving nothing to the imagination. Adults can marvel at the performances (not acting, but performances) or at the way the film taps into the collective recollections of how such stories should be. If the film was made to show that adventure need not be a cliffhanging tour-de-force or that fairy tales can be staged without recourse to fantasy or Monty Pythonesque debunking, it is a triumph. The film is a success because it is interesting to watch and interesting to discuss, a feat not very often achieved in the PG market. The film is a success because Reiner is so conversant with the conventions of comedy and film that it is second nature to him. The transference of his intent and ideas to the screen is nearly flawless, allowing the viewer to enjoy the film on a variety of levels. It brings back to the screen a sense of professionalism, which in this case is derived from Reiner's stance as an insider whose film sense comes from personal experience, not dreaming of it in darkened theaters far removed from the business of Hollywood. It is the difference between someone reared on the product of Hollywood and someone reared in Hollywood; between someone trying to re-create the magic of film and someone creating magic in film. Reiner's background allows him to make a film which above all must be entertaining but also must have content, and the audience is thereby rewarded more fully. It is a film made by people with an innate and genuine feel for film as opposed to those trying to look over their shoulders at the past. *The Princess Bride* does not cite past films in the manner of Spielberg; it draws from a more general well—the mind, heart, soul, and concerns of the director and writer. There is much to be said for a system that allows such films to be made.

Richard Strelitz

Reviews

Films in Review. XXXIX, January, 1988, p. 42.
Los Angeles Times. September 25, 1987, VI, p. 1.
Macleans. C, October 5, 1987, p. 58.
The New York Times. September 25, 1987, p. C10.

The New Yorker. LXIII, October 19, 1987, p. 110.
Newsweek. CX, October 5, 1987, p. 85.
People Weekly. XXVIII, September 28, 1987, p. 14.
Time. CXXX, September 21, 1987, p. 74.
Variety. CCCXXVIII, September 16, 1987, p. 12.
The Wall Street Journal. September 24, 1987, p. 24.

RADIO DAYS

Production: Robert Greenhut; released by Orion Pictures
Direction: Woody Allen
Screenplay: Woody Allen
Cinematography: Carlo Di Palma
Editing: Susan E. Morse
Production design: Santo Loquasto
Art direction: Speed Hopkins; set decoration, Carol Joffe and Les Bloom
Costume design: Jeffrey Kurland
Music: Dick Hyman
MPAA rating: PG
Running time: 88 minutes

Principal characters:
Narrator . . . . Woody Allen
Joe . . . . Seth Green
Mother . . . . Julie Kavner
Father . . . . Michael Tucker
Bea . . . . Dianne Wiest
Abe . . . . Josh Mostel
Ceil . . . . Renee Lippin
Sally . . . . Mia Farrow
The Masked Avenger . . . . Wallace Shawn

"The Masked Avenger," "Name That Tune," "The Shadow," Glenn Miller, Carmen Miranda, and Cole Porter were some of the magical voices and sounds that entered the homes and captured the hearts and imaginations of millions of Americans through that miracle of human invention, the radio. During the 1930's, the 1940's, and half of the 1950's, radio shaped the sensibilities of the nation as it delivered its daily dose of romance and reality, entertainment and culture, news and diversion by the magic of invisible electronic sound. In *Radio Days*, a narrator (Woody Allen) explains that the days of radio and the world it created are finished: "Now it's all gone. Except for the memories." Thus Allen announces his task: to evoke for his audience the magic of those vanished radio days through the power of his memories.

The opening sequence of the film is a brilliant piece of filmmaking that uses the full resources of the medium to express the enchantment of radio. The film begins with a blank image. Allen's disembodied voice conjures up a fairy-tale world ("Once upon a time many years ago . . .") as the viewer sees a puzzling image of flashlights in the dark. Unfolding is a scene of burglars robbing his neighbor's house in Rockaway when Allen was a youngster. The phone rings and one of the burglars gropes in the dark to answer it. Using the unique capacity of the film medium instantly to change location, Allen jump cuts to a shot of a radio show, "Guess That Tune," where the announcer is on the phone telling a listener that he has been selected to guess the name of the song currently airing. With another jump cut, Allen's joke is apparent: The burglar is in fact the listener chosen to play the game, and the tune he must guess is appropriately "Dancing in the Dark." Scrambling to turn on the radio, which glows in the dark as it comes alive with sound, the thieves drop their work and become immersed in the show. By crosscutting, Allen shows the interaction between them and the radio show as they succeed in correctly naming all the tunes and winning the grand prizes, which are delivered the next day to the shocked victims of the burglary. Allen's wonderful comic point is that in the days of radio, everyone was captivated by the irresistible magic of radio.

After this masterful opening comic tribute to radio, Allen relates that he will present two kinds of childhood memories associated with radio: personal experiences growing up in a lower-middle-class Jewish family in Rockaway and "inside stories" about radio stars which he has collected throughout the years.

The richest incidents that Allen strings together are those involving his family. One of his most delightful family memories is of his youthful plot to get fifteen cents for the secret-compartment ring offered by his favorite radio crime fighter, the Masked Avenger. Joe (Seth Green), his childhood *persona*, hatches a plot during Hebrew school to steal the donation money meant for the creation of the state of Israel but naturally gets caught. In a zany slapstick scene, he is cuffed around by the outraged rabbi and his father (Michael Tucker) as he learns that his moral decline is the result of the pernicious influence of radio. The rabbi voices the enduring complaint about electronic media: They induce "bad values, false dreams, lazy habits." The young Joe brilliantly disarms the rabbi with an immortal line he learned from one of radio's chief moral heroes, the Lone Ranger: "You speak the truth my faithful Indian companion."

Allen especially treasures the memories of his unmarried Aunt Bea (Dianne Wiest), who constantly dreams of finding the perfect man. In contrast to her sister (who says, "I like to daydream, but I have my two feet planted on my husband"), Bea never allows her dreams to be diminished by reality. She nourishes her fantasy life on the wonderful, romantic music of the 1940's, whose soothing sounds continually transform her Rockaway world. In a series of clever comic reversals, however, Allen shows how the radio which feeds her romantic dreams frequently becomes the means of thwarting them. In the best of such scenes, Bea goes on a date with a new beau who wines and dines her in high style. They end the evening in the archetypal romantic situation: alone in a car out of gas on "lovers' point."

With mood music softly playing on the radio, they begin to make love. Suddenly, a frantic voice interrupts them and declares that Earth has just been invaded by martians. Aunt Bea's hero becomes a coward and rushes off, leaving her to hear the end of Orson Welles's famous radio hoax. Such reversals never defeat Aunt Bea, who continues throughout the film to chase her dreams, dancing to the always up-beat tunes of the 1940's.

Juxtaposed to Allen's family memories are his inside stories about the radio stars, whose glamorous world of upper-Manhattan glitter stands in sharp contrast to Rockaway. He unifies these anecdotes by centering on Sally, the cigarette girl (Mia Farrow), and her comic rise from sexual plaything of Roger (of "Breakfast with Irene and Roger") to radio star Sally White, gossip reporter.

The characters in Allen's two worlds meet only over the airwaves, as any actual contact would shatter the illusions they all need. The film's closing scenes, a series of crosscuts, show both worlds ringing in the new year of 1944. In spite of the limits of their lower-class position, Allen's family is happy scraping by together. Even though Aunt Bea does not have a date, she is not desolate or alone; she is part of a family that, despite the gap between their radio-sustained dreams and reality, still love one another. The family accepts with good humor the mother's observation that the world is divided into "those who drink champagne at night clubs and us who listen to them drink champagne on the radio."

Radio Days ends with a last look at the stars "who drink champagne at the night clubs." The Masked Avenger (Wallace Shawn) and the now-famous Sally White enjoy the glamour of the New Year's Eve party with the other Beautiful People. In the middle of their celebration, Sally leads them on a triumphant return to the rooftop that was the scene of her sexual exploitation as a lowly cigarette girl. On the roof, as the New Year is about to ring in, the Masked Avenger ruefully reflects on the transitoriness of their fame and of all things human: "I wonder if future generations will ever even hear about us. It's not likely. After enough time everything passes."

Radio Days is Allen's nostalgia film, a whimsical celebration of his childhood world where dreams and aspirations were powerfully shaped by golden voices and sounds that are no more. *Radio Days* expresses a longing most people in the 1980's share—a longing for an age of innocence when one could dance to the soothing tunes of Cole Porter and easily separate the good guys from the bad guys, thrilled by the reassuring voice of the Masked Avenger: "Beware evil-doers wherever you are." Such innocent days are gone forever; thanks to *Radio Days*, however, the memories remain.

John Hartzog

Reviews
Commonweal. CXIV, February 27, 1987, p. 111.
Macleans. C, February 9, 1987, p. 47.
Ms. XV, March, 1987, p. 17.
The Nation. CCXLIV, February 21, 1987, p. 229.
National Review. XXXIX, March 27, 1987, p. 67.
The New Leader. LXX, February 9, 1987, p. 19.
The New Republic. CLVI, March 9, 1987, p. 24.
The New Yorker. LXIII, March 9, 1987, p. 96.
Newsweek. CIX, February 2, 1987, p. 7.
Time. CXXIX, February 2, 1987, p. 73.

RAISING ARIZONA

Production: Ethan Coen for Circle Films; released by Twentieth Century-Fox
Direction: Joel Coen
Screenplay: Ethan Coen and Joel Coen
Cinematography: Barry Sonnenfeld
Editing: Michael R. Miller
Production design: Jane Musky
Art direction: Harold Thrasher; set decoration, Robert Kracik
Costume design: Richard Hornung
Sound: Allan Byer
Music: Carter Burwell
MPAA rating: PG-13
Running time: 94 minutes

> *Principal characters:*
> | | |
> |---|---|
> | H. I. McDonnough | Nicolas Cage |
> | Ed | Holly Hunter |
> | Nathan Arizona Sr. | Trey Wilson |
> | Gale | John Goodman |
> | Evelle | William Forsythe |
> | Glen | Sam McMurray |
> | Dot | Frances McDormand |
> | Leonard Smalls | Randall (Tex) Cobb |
> | Nathan Jr. | T. J. Kuhn |
> | Florence Arizona | Lynne Dumin Kitei |

Joel Coen's and Ethan Coen's *Raising Arizona* covers some territory often neglected in American comedy. The first startling feature is the presence of babies, not just one but five of them. A second peculiarity is the film's characters, who are ordinary working and criminal class, not sinister murderers or glamorous drug dealers. These elements might not seem so unusual if they were not brought to life in the kind of clever filmic footwork one usually expects from avant-garde cinema, not from the invisible editing style of most American comedies. *Raising Arizona* straddles these two worlds in a film that pleases mainstream audiences and film-school critics alike. Some viewers praise its fresh, upbeat humor and others admire its offbeat technical finesse, but most reviewers agree that the work firmly establishes the young Coen brothers as a highly influential force on the Hollywood scene.

The background and personal tastes of the Coens would not augur well for their success in the standardized world of American filmmaking. The Coens deliberately target the odd, the wacky effect, in their characters, their plot, and most of all in the look of the filmmaking itself. Enamored of technique and structure, puzzling out the best way to produce the unexpected, the Coens first revealed their innovative genius in *Blood Simple* (1985), a bloody almost-black comedy that won a Grand Jury Prize at the United States Film Festival, one of the most prestigious awards for independent filmmakers. Ethan's Princeton University background in philosophy may not appear in the duo's choice of subject matter, but Joel's film studies at New York University shine through the dazzling camera work and attention to technical detail. Their strong collaboration in directing, screenwriting, and producing makes the designations of director and producer a mere formality. What saves them from the obscurity of avant-garde filmdom is their flexibility and utter indifference to subject matter, viewing the elements that attract audiences—blood, babies, car chases, crimes—as mere fodder for the filmmaking process, their ultimate obsession.

In the eleven minutes before the audience sees the opening title and credits of *Raising Arizona*, the yodeling voice of William Preston Robertson intones the sad tale of H. I. McDonnough, a man doomed by ineptitude and lack of imagination to get caught repeatedly robbing convenience stores. Holly Hunter plays Ed (short for Edwina), a police officer whose voice and heart soften as she takes mug shots of H. I. each time he returns for incarceration. He receives speedy parole each time; he always uses an unloaded gun. After his third release, he marries Ed, and all goes well until the couple learns that Edwina's insides are, in H. I.'s imitation of the doctor's words, a "barren place" where his "seed can gain no purchase." These fancy phrases issuing from the mouths of simple folk contributes ironic humor, but it causes some critics to accuse the filmmakers of condescending to their subject. The characters remain almost subhuman, with their attempts at enjoying all-American homelife an empty imitation of customs and emotions they do not fully understand.

The couple's sense of what kinds of trappings, friends, and behavior are necessary for happiness grows out of the culture itself. The kind of society that spawns convenience stores and Huggies produces caricatures such as H. I. and Ed, who are convinced that they need a baby to be a happily married couple. Unable to adopt because of H. I.'s record, the couple decides to rob the Arizona family of one of their highly publicized quintuplets. Ed justifies the theft by stating that the Arizona family already has more than they can use; H. I. and Ed are simply performing a kind of Robin Hood redistribution of baby wealth.

The film makes other passing jabs at the political and social structure. Early in the film, H. I. explains that he tried to stop robbing convenience stores, but with Ronald Reagan in the White House, it was hard for people like himself to survive. His black roommate in prison recites a litany of the food his family ate to survive, moving down the evolutionary scale from crawdads to sand. Nathan Arizona, Sr., father of the kidnapped quintuplet, typifies the successful entrepreneur, whose commercials for his unpainted furniture store promise the lowest prices available "or his name ain't Nathan Arizona." In fact, his name proves to be Nathan Huffhines, and throughout the ordeal he seems much more concerned with sets—quintuplet sets, kitchen sets, dinette sets—than he is with his child. H. I.'s boss, Glen (Sam McMurray), and his wife, Dot (Frances McDormand), also view children as possessions, in their case to stave off boredom, just as Glen tells H. I. that wife swapping does. As naïve characters, H. I. and Ed truly believe in the American myth of the happy family. Only they and the other criminals, including prison escapees Gale (John Goodman) and Evelle (William Forsythe), seem genuinely enraptured by the sheer wonder of the little creature they have captured. The upright citizens remain untransformed by the baby's beautiful innocence.

Mercenary motives drive the plot, with Gale and Evelle stealing baby Arizona for the reward, followed by the nightmarish appearance on the scene of baby bounty hunter, Leonard Smalls (Randall "Tex" Cobb), a motorcyclist apparently from Hell. He first appears to H. I. in a dream, a brilliant montage of crosscutting between overhead shots of a fitfully sleeping H. I. and blasts of fire as the demoniac Leonard rides onto the scene. Although some critics find his character outlandish, his presence fits thematically as the personification of evil greed, and his role as pursuer creates juicy opportunities for the Coens to play with standard conventions of villainy and chase scenes.

Sound is so crucial to *Raising Arizona* that it almost constitutes a character in itself. From the singsong twang of H. I. and Ed to the recurring screams of Gale and Evelle, each character has a set of aural associations that operate as formulas. The most complex and innovative sound surrounds the evil motorcyclist Leonard, first in the shocking roar of fire in H. I.'s dream, and later in his scene with Nathan Arizona, Sr. A combination of clinking chains and rushing wind crescendos to a startling climax as Leonard moves to capture a fly in midflight, holding in his blackened fingers the fly's body in extreme closeup, inches from Nathan's nose. A similar effect occurs when Leonard realizes that H. I. has pulled the ring on one of his hand grenades. Immediately before the explosion, Leonard emits a rumbling bass growl, which explodes into a deafening long shot of his fiery demise. Leonard's bronzed baby shoes landing on the pavement echo with the faraway sounds of a baby crying, only to dissolve into the frame of the Arizona household window, where H. I. and Ed are returning the stolen baby. The Coens create this kind of haunting synesthesia with the technical ingenuity of soundman Allan Byer and cinematographer Barry Sonnenfeld.

Much of the joy of making and watching *Raising Arizona* derives from the clever devices employed throughout the film. In order to achieve a baby's-eye view, the Coens invented what they call "Shakycam," which mildly jostles the visual image, as opposed to the conventional Steadicam, which smooths the bumps and allows flexible camera motion with no jolts. The film also contains a variety of reverse filming and time-lapse photography segments. A sunset scene is accelerated by shooting one frame every three seconds over the period of a forty-minute sunset. In another dramatic sequence shot in reverse, Gale and Evelle drive to a screeching halt inches from baby Arizona, who sits placidly in his car seat on the yellow median roadline. To achieve this effect during filming, they rocked the car and then backed it up, creating the appearance of an abrupt stop that no stunt driver would dare perform.

The cleverness of the Coens' film is not restricted to the filmmaking process; their script reveals numerous wordplays, allusions, and turns of phrase that bring to mind the old-fashioned accolade of wit. The characters speak in commercials, clichés, and poetry. A merchant describes diapers as "self-contained and fairly explanatory" and Ed calls Leonard a "warthog from hell," a phrase and concept lifted from Flannery O'Connor. The sparkling phrase, "O. K., then," solemnizes H. I.'s three releases from prison and his marriage to Ed.

While all the verbal play and preoccupation with technique could be viewed as devaluing its homely characters, the film's ending suggests more benevolence in the Coens' attitude toward their subject. H. I. and Ed do the right thing by returning the baby, and H. I. dreams of a future in which he has done right by his family, in a place very much like Arizona. Never willing to remain too serious or sentimental, the film ends with H. I.'s addendum, "Maybe it was Utah." The Coen brothers, for all of their fancy filmwork and sophisticated satirizing of American tastes, come from America's heartland and express the wholesome values born of being reared in Minnesota, where belief in the decency of common people survives. Maybe it was Michigan.

Rebecca Bell-Metereau

Reviews
The Christian Century. CIV, July 1, 1987, p. 598.
Commonweal. CXIV, April 24, 1987, p. 242.
Film Comment. XXIII, March, 1987, p. 19.
Los Angeles Times. March 20, 1987, VI, p. 1.
Macleans. C, March 23, 1987, p. 69.
National Review. XXXIX, May 8, 1987, p. 52.
The New Republic. CXCVI, April 13, 1987, p. 24.
The New York Times. March 11, 1987, p. C24.

The New Yorker. LXIII, April 20, 1987, p. 81.
Newsweek. CIX, March 16, 1987, p. 73.
Rolling Stone. May 21, 1987, p. 59.
Time. CXXIX, March 23, 1987, p. 86.
Variety. CCCXXVI, March 4, 1987, p. 18.
The Wall Street Journal. March 26, 1987, p. 34.

RIVER'S EDGE

Production: Sarah Pillsbury and Midge Sanford for Hemdale Film Corporation; released by Island Pictures
Direction: Tim Hunter
Screenplay: Neal Jimenez
Cinematography: Frederick Elmes
Editing: Howard Smith and Sonya Sones
Art direction: John Muto; set decoration, Anne Huntley
Music: Jurgen Knieper
MPAA rating: R
Running time: 99 minutes

> *Principal characters:*
> Layne............................Crispin Glover
> Feck ....Dennis Hopper
> Matt ....Keanu Reeves
> Samson ....Daniel Roebuck
> Clarissa ....Ione Skye Leitch
> Tim..............................Joshua Miller

At a time when even Hollywood seems to be tiring of teen exploitation films, along comes *River's Edge*, a teen drama that manages to be passionately serious while avoiding any trace of complacency. The closest analogues to this film are *Over the Edge*, a 1979 Jonathan Kaplan film which *River's Edge* director Tim Hunter scripted, and Nicholas Ray's classic *Rebel Without a Cause* (1956). Yet *River's Edge* is *Rebel Without a Cause* stripped of any possibility for heroic action. The kids of this film inhabit a muddled world, and in their attempts to give it meaning they shuffle through emotions as if flipping channels on the remote control. That *River's Edge*, a film about a group reaction to a friend's murder, results in a black comedy is a testament not only to director Hunter's daring but also to the relentless logic of his vision.

The film is based on an actual incident that took place in Northern California: A boy strangled his girlfriend and showed the corpse to several of his classmates, none of whom felt compelled to report the event to the police. *River's Edge* begins the moment after the murder has been committed. Samson (Daniel Roebuck), the killer, is not cowed by what he has done; he brings his friends to view the body the way another boy might flaunt his dad's new Porsche. It is only late in the film that the viewer receives any insight into Samson's psychology. Samson killed his girlfriend Jamie because she had insulted his dead mother. He felt triumphantly alive and in control after the murder, but that feeling of control rapidly gives way to one of deadly emptiness. Yet *River's Edge* is not particularly concerned with Samson's pathology. Rather, its subject is the widening significance of Samson's crime, its influence on the more "normal" high-school students whom Samson brings to see the corpse.

Twelve-year-old Tim (Joshua Miller) witnesses the riverside murder from a nearby bridge while "strangling" his baby sister's favorite doll. Seemingly unfazed by the crime, he later uses his knowledge to edge his way into the older boys' world of dope and intrigue. Layne (Crispin Glover), a speed freak, interprets the situation as a test of friendship. Jamie is dead, Layne insists; what matters is that Samson be protected from the police—an ironic priority, since Samson seems simply to be waiting for the police to arrest him. Though Clarissa (Ione Skye Leitch) cannot find it in her heart to cry for her dead friend, she does think that the authorities should be notified. Yet she lacks the courage to telephone them. Only Tim's older brother Matt (Keanu Reeves) is finally moved to telephone the police. His action sparks the hatred of his younger brother, who feels so momentously betrayed that he finds a gun and almost kills Matt.

In addition to the teenagers, Feck (Dennis Hopper), a paranoid, middle-aged dope dealer, becomes embroiled in the murder, thanks to Layne, who brings Samson to Feck's house to hide. A one-legged former biker, Feck claims to have murdered his girlfriend years ago; he insists that the police are still after him. What Feck believes exonerates his behavior is that he, unlike Samson, killed out of love. Annoyed but also touched by Samson's blankness, Feck finally puts the killer out of his misery by shooting him on the banks of the river, exactly where Jamie was strangled.

Imbued as it is with violence and the potential for violence, *River's Edge* is nevertheless much more a study of emotional isolation than it is an action film. As the most active character in the film, Layne would seem to be its protagonist. It is Layne who decides that Samson must hide, and his frenzied attempts to dispose of the body and raise money to get Samson out of town structure much of the film. But Layne's thinking is phenomenally unclear, his devotion to Samson based more on films he has seen than any real bond of friendship. The image of him alone in his decrepit Volkswagen in the middle of the night, making frantic circles in the street, becomes a perfect metaphor for the meaninglessness of his sound and fury.

The film's heart lies with Matt, who suffers, like Layne, from a sense of emotional disorientation but who is too honest to bandage himself with a purely fabricated sense of purpose. Bit by bit, like a child learning to crawl, Matt gropes toward a reckoning with the murder. Helping his baby sister to bury her "murdered" doll, he feels the need of a funeral for Jamie as well and telephones the police. He later tells his schoolmate Clarissa that he only called because he thought everyone else would too. Yet he finds that his action only sets him apart from everyone—from his brother, Layne, his mother, even the police, who initially view him as a suspect. His telephoning the police does not manage to save Samson from death at the hand of Feck. Neither does it serve, in the final scenes, to diminish Matt's anomie. In the moral wasteland of *River's Edge*, a telephone call becomes the closest thing to a heroic action. Yet Tim Hunter and screenwriter Neal Jimenez are careful not to falsify the world they have created by inflating the significance of Matt's action.

Neither have they chosen to reassure the audience by suggesting that the older generation has any answers. The so-called adults in this film are the human wreckage of the love generation: Feck, who dances with an inflatable love doll while reminiscing over his missing leg and his dead girlfriend; Matt and Tim's mother, who pays the bills for her deadbeat boyfriend while accusing her son of stealing from her marijuana stash; and a high-school teacher who shrilly extols his generation's valor in protesting the Vietnam War, then, after hearing of Jamie's death, practically has a nervous breakdown in the classroom, berating his students and himself for their lack of feeling.

The extremes to which Hunter pushes his adult characters adds a disturbingly comic tone to the film. Initially a threatening character, Feck in particular becomes a source of grim comic relief as he describes losing his leg in a motorcycle accident. Hoping that the doctors will come and sew it back on, he watches helplessly as an ambulance drives up and crushes it. Crispin Glover's performance as Layne adds remarkably to the black comedy. Though *River's Edge* was generally lauded critically, Glover was often singled out for giving an inauthentic performance. His long hair flowing out from under a knit cap, his thin hands pantomiming his every speech as if he were speaking to an audience of the deaf, Glover's Layne certainly seems inauthentic. Yet surely that is the point: This boy is inventing emotions, not feeling them. One need only substitute as Layne a more brooding, masculine actor like the Matt Dillon of *Tex* (1982), Hunter's directorial debut, to see how much the edgy, unpredictable tone of *River's Edge* derives from Glover's inventive performance.

Still, Glover's is one in a whole company of fine performances. Joshua Miller is equally astonishing as Tim, perhaps the most angry and jaded twelve-year-old ever seen in a feature film, and Keanu Reeves's Matt manages to project a nascent truthfulness and depth while still seeming wholly at home among these characters. Only the film's female characters seem hastily drawn. While the boys, with the exception of Layne, all have an ordinary, unscrubbed look that perfectly suits the film's setting, the girls are too pretty and their performances are thin. When Clarissa seduces Matt in a park the night that he calls the police, the film for a brief moment starts to look like a teen exploitation comedy. The scene has an important thematic purpose; intercut with a flashback depicting the murder, it shows that Matt, unlike Samson (and, by implication, unlike Layne and Feck), is capable of relinquishing control and loving a woman. Yet Leitch fails to suggest any motivation for Clarissa; her seduction remains in the realm of male fantasy.

The milieu of *River's Edge* is at once oddly generalized and frighteningly particular. The heavy metal music that blares from the radio, the traffic signs that decorate Tim and Matt's room, the decaying ski condominium that is their mother's house, the brooding darkness of the riverside—all remain vividly in the mind after the film ends. Yet at the same time this film could be taking place almost anywhere in the United States. The audience is never certain whether the film is set in a small town, a suburb, or farmland—its convenience stores, schools, and parks are such omnipresent fixtures. Never does the viewer see a Main Street or even a shopping mall—never a crowd of people—and the effect is to create a strange kind of vacuum around these teenagers. Yet their talk is peppered with references to the media, tying them into the fashions of the moment, giving them a whole range of fictions against which to compare their lives. *River's Edge* brilliantly depicts the way that cable television is homogenizing so much of nonurban America, while only increasing the aching sense of isolation.

Tex, Hunter's first film as a director, marked both the beginning of Walt Disney's entry into mainstream Hollywood and the first in a series of films based on S. E. Hinton novels, yet its directorial style was occasionally flat and its script preachy. *Sylvester* (1985), a female version of *Tex*, seemed to indicate that Hunter was bent on directing sentimental coming-of-age films. Who could have predicted that *River's Edge*, Hunter's third teen film, would be the film in which he finds his directorial voice? Its outrageous bleakness reminds one of Flannery O'Connor's short stories; its cinematic austerity echoes Robert Bresson. With this contemplation of the spirit and the flesh, Tim Hunter has set himself apart from the Hollywood of strained Spielbergian fantasy and marked himself as a director of courage and amazing vigor.

Richard Glatzer

Reviews
Film Comment. XXIII, July, 1987, p. 70.
Films in Review. XXXVIII, August, 1987, p. 425.
Los Angeles Times. May 7, 1987, VI, p. 1.
National Review. XXXIX, June 19, 1987, p. 55.
The New Republic. CXCVI, June 8, 1987, p. 26.
The New York Times. May 8, 1987, p. C28.
The New Yorker. LXIII, June 15, 1987, p. 77.
Newsweek. CIX, June 1, 1987, p. 68.
Time. CXXIX, June 1, 1987, p. 73.
Variety. CCCXXIV, September 3, 1987, p. 16.

ROBOCOP

Production: Arne Schmidt and Jon Davison; released by Orion Pictures
Direction: Paul Verhoeven
Screenplay: Edward Neumeier and Michael Miner
Cinematography: Jost Vacano
Editing: Frank J. Urioste
Production design: William Sandell
Art direction: Gayle Simon; set decoration, Robert Gould
Special effects: Dale Martin
Makeup: Carla Palmer
Costume design: Erica Edell Phillips
Sound: Robert Wald
Music direction: Steven Scott Smalley
Music: Basil Poledouris
MPAA rating: R
Running time: 103 minutes

> *Principal characters:*
> Robocop/Murphy .... Peter Weller
> Lewis .... Nancy Allen
> Dick Jones .... Ronny Cox
> Clarence Boddicker .... Kurtwood Smith
> Bob Morton .... Miguel Ferrer
> The Old Man .... Daniel O'Herlihy

In his American debut, Dutch director Paul Verhoeven has made a science-fiction film so excessively violent that it was originally rated X. At first glance, *Robocop* appears to be yet another remake of *The Terminator* (1984), but *Robocop* does more than imitate a successful genre based on violent action and special effects. As with Verhoeven's previous films, which include *Soldiers of Orange* (1979) and *Spetters* (1981), violence becomes a means to an end and not simply an end in itself.

Robocop satirizes media-saturated corporate America. Yet in so doing, *Robocop* criticizes films of its own genre. The relentless action and violence become disconcerting within a satiric context. The violence can never be self-righteous as it is in other Hollywood action-revenge films such as *Rambo* (1985) and *The Terminator*.

For a year prior to filming *Robocop*, Verhoeven lived in Los Angeles, which proved an ideal place to absorb some of the more vulgar aspects of American culture. Perhaps more influential than Los Angeles was the space shuttle *Challenger* explosion of 1986, which Verhoeven saw as "a metaphor for the American situation," briefly revealing the interests and actions of big business and government.

Like most science-fiction films, *Robocop* takes place in the near future in order to comment better on the present. *Robocop* begins with a television news program whose motto is, "You give us three minutes and we'll give you the world." That Leeza Gibbons, real-life reporter for the glib television show "Entertainment Tonight" plays a news anchor further suggests that the news has become mere pabulum. Additional media breaks are inserted throughout the film and use the entire screen in order to give it the appearance of a large television set. In fact, pixels are clearly visible on the screen. In one news break, a "Star Wars" platform misfires, burning down Santa Barbara and killing two former presidents who have retired there. A commercial advertizes NUKEM, a game that pits family members against one another in nuclear brinkmanship.

The media breaks provide a counterpoint to the story in *Robocop*. In effect, television interrupts the film to comment on how popular culture sustains the nuclear arms race. These comments apply also to the film itself, since *Robocop* is about a military contractor expanding its powers beyond the military-industrial complex. The corporation, OCP, also runs the Detroit Police Department and plans to build Delta City, an affluent enclave within Old Detroit. At the OCP boardroom, Dick Jones (Ronny Cox) demonstrates the ED-209 series, a large robot that will make Old Detroit safe while OCP builds Delta City. ED-209 will also become the "hot military product for the next decade," after it has proven itself capable of "urban pacification."

ED-209 malfunctions and shoots the OCP employee chosen to confront it, leaving his bloodied corpse stretched out across the model of Delta City. The top executives, however, are cool amid the confusion: The Old Man (Daniel O'Herlihy) tells Dick that he is very disappointed, while Dick reassures him that "it's just a glitch." The scene provides a perfect visual metaphor for urban renewal in a military-based economy. In order to hedge his bets, the Old Man gives upstart Bob Morton (Miguel Ferrer), who designed an alternative project, permission to use the next police officer killed to create Robocop. Bob does not have to wait long. Lewis (Nancy Allen) and her new partner, Murphy (Peter Weller), chase police-killers Clarence Boddicker (Kurtwood Smith) and his gang to an abandoned steel mill. Lewis and Murphy are captured. As Lewis watches, Clarence slowly tortures Murphy and leaves him for dead.

The scenes during which Murphy is rushed to the hospital and transformed into Robocop are shot from his point of view so that the audience experiences Murphy's dehumanization. The screen goes black, and the audience hears the doctor say that there is no pulse and give the time of death. A second later the screen returns, but as a video or television screen with large pixels. The screen fades and appears to struggle to remain on. The screen continues to go black and return at each step in Murphy's transformation into Robocop, a cyborg with a total body prosthesis and a computer memory. *The Terminator* briefly used subjective camera with a video screen to portray cybernetic vision. *Robocop*, however, makes extensive use of subjective camera, establishing a distinct point of view comparable to the satiric media breaks.

When Robocop is unveiled and allowed to stand and walk, the film continues to use subjective camera so that the only glimpse of Robocop is from a monitor that he passes. At the police station, Robocop is given a systems check of his prime directives, which appear in Robocop's visual system: to serve the public trust, to protect the innocent, and to uphold the law. There is a fourth directive, but it is classified.

Back at OCP headquarters Bob, now a vice president, visits the executive lounge, where he brags and insults Dick, unaware that he is listening from a stall. Dick confronts Bob, giving him a lesson in how the military-industrial complex operates. ED-209 was a better project, he claims, because even if it did not work, OCP could have sold spare parts to the military and made even more money. Later, Dick hires Clarence to torture and kill Bob.

Robocop slowly pieces together his past and identity. He even visits his now-empty house. The scene uses Robocop's point of view, with flashbacks appearing in film rather than in the video that characterizes his vision. The shift from video to film signals the reemergence of human perceptions in Robocop, but since these perceptions are confined to intangible memories, Robocop feels more loss than gain. All that is left is revenge. He leaves the house in search of Clarence.

Robocop catches up to Clarence in a cocaine factory, where he is making a purchase. Robocop is about to kill Clarence when he is stopped by his prime directives and arrests him instead. In the meantime, a terrified Clarence has confessed and implicated Dick Jones in Clarence's operation and Bob's murder. Later at OCP headquarters, Robocop tries to arrest Jones but begins to malfunction. Jones explains that he included a fourth directive in which any attempt to arrest a senior officer of OCP results in shutdown. He admits to having Bob killed but reminds Robocop that he is just a product and can do nothing about it. Jones pushes a button and ED-209 enters and attacks Robocop, injuring him before he can escape. Robocop finds Lewis, who drives him to an empty steel mill so that he can repair himself. When Robocop takes off his helmut, he exposes his face and the computer that has replaced much of his brain. The first shot of Robocop's face is through a dirty, broken mirror that Lewis holds. Once again, the film portrays Robocop's development from his point of view.

Meanwhile, Dick frees Clarence from jail and orders him to kill Robocop, because he recorded their confessions. In order to sweeten the deal, Jones offers Clarence the drugs, gambling, and prostitution concessions for the two million workers that will be living in trailers while they build Delta City. Clarence is armed with military weapons. As Jones states, "We practically are the military."

Clarence and his gang confront Robocop and Lewis at the old steel mill. The otherwise standard shoot-out scene features one unusual death, when one of Clarence's accomplices drives into a vat of toxic waste and emerges grotesquely deformed. In the end, Robocop kills Clarence. Lewis is badly shot, but there is a suggestion that she will be "fixed" into a Robocop, perhaps in the already planned sequel.

Robocop enters the OCP boardroom and informs the Old Man that Dick Jones is wanted for murder and that his program will not allow him to arrest Jones. To corroborate his charges, Robocop plays a recording of Jones's confession on the sixteen-screen console in the boardroom. Jones takes the Old Man hostage. Robocop is unable to shoot Jones until the Old Man cries out, "Dick you're fired," invalidating directive four. When the Old Man compliments Robocop and asks his name, he replies, "Murphy." He has regained his human identity.

The ending, however, leaves several problems unresolved. Since Murphy is still part machine and computer, he is still subject to directive four and therefore cannot act against OCP and its senior officers. The military-industrial complex, which *Robocop* shows to extend its influence into more and more aspects of everyday life, is neither changed nor challenged. Robocop seeks revenge for his own murder and in the process uncovers collusion between the street criminals, big business, and government (notable for its absence). Yet in the end, the Old Man is still in power.

Chon Noriega

Reviews

Cosmopolitan. CCIII, October, 1987, p. 43.
Films in Review. XXXVIII, October, 1987, p. 492.
Los Angeles Times. July 17, 1987, VI, p. 1.
Macleans. C, July 27, 1987, p. 47.
The New York Times. July 17, 1987, p. C10.
The New Yorker. LXIII, August 10, 1987, p. 72.
Newsweek. CX, July 20, 1987, p. 58.
Time. CXXX, July 27, 1987, p. 75.
Variety. CCCXXVII, July 8, 1987, p. 10.
The Wall Street Journal. July 23, 1987, p. 28.

ROSA LUXEMBURG

Origin: West Germany
Released: 1986
Released in U.S.: 1987
Production: Eberhard Junkersdorf; released by New Yorker Films
Direction: Margarethe von Trotta
Screenplay: Margarethe von Trotta
Cinematography: Franz Rath
Editing: Dagmar Hirtz
Production design: Jan Kadlec
Art direction: Bernd Lepel and Karel Vacek
Costume design: Monika Hasse
Sound: Christian Moldt
Music: Nicholas Economou
MPAA rating: no listing
Running time: 122 minutes

> *Principal characters:*
> Rosa Luxemburg .... Barbara Sukowa
> Leo Jogiches .... Daniel Olbrychski
> Karl Liebknecht .... Otto Sander
> Luise Kautsky .... Adelheid Arndt
> Karl Kautsky .... Jurgen Holtz
> Clara Zetkin .... Doris Schade
> Kostia Zetkin .... Hannes Jaenickhe

Rosa Luxemburg takes as its subject the most prominent female Marxist of the twentieth century. The setting is Berlin of the 1910's when the twin specters of revolution and world war hang over the nations of Europe. A major question is whether the mammoth Social Democratic Party of Germany (SPD) will refuse participation in a war effort on ideological grounds or will agree to war on the basis of nationalism. At the center of the dispute is writer and orator Rosa Luxemburg (Barbara Sukowa), an internationalist who stridently opposes wars that pit workers against workers. "Red" Rosa becomes a leading figure in an organizational schism that ultimately leads to the formation of the Communist Party of Germany. Although she argues that a revolutionary bid for power in 1919 is premature, her activism and prominence lead to her execution by the German military.

The tempestuous Luxemburg, a kind of socialist Joan of Arc, has long intrigued German filmmakers. At the time of his death in 1982, Rainer Werner Fassbinder was working with a script about Luxemburg written by Peter Märtescheimer, whose previous credits include Fassbinder's *Die Ehe der Maria Braun* (1978; *The Marriage of Maria Braun*). Fassbinder's producer offered the project to Margarethe von Trotta for completion on the basis of her experience as an actress under Fassbinder's direction, three scripts she had written for her husband, Volker Schlondorff, and her direction of films such as *Strohfeuer* (1972; *A Free Woman*), *Die Bleierne Zeit* (1981; *Marianne and Julianne*), and *Heller Wahn* (1983; *Sheer Madness*). Von Trotta accepted the project but soon discarded the Märtescheimer script for not offering the portrait of Luxemburg she wanted.

Von Trotta proceeded to devote approximately eighteen months to reading Luxemburg's twenty-five hundred personal letters some four or five times each. She was seeking the individual motivation that would humanize a woman who had become a historic icon. As she pursued her reading and conferred with Luxemburg experts, the director became convinced that Luxemburg's private life should eclipse the public events with which she was so clearly associated. After spending another six months writing, von Trotta produced a script that focused on a narrow span of time and kept historical events in the background.

The decision to accent the personal has been the basis of most criticism of the film. For anyone not familiar with German political history, many of the scenes will lose their potential impact or will be perceived on a superficial level. In one ballroom sequence, for example, all the leading figures of the SPD are presented. The dialogue and camera work are very clever, but they will be lost on viewers unfamiliar with the personalities being depicted. This dependency on knowledge not contained within the film is characteristic of the entire script.

The problems generated by this cinematic study become acute when world war actually erupts. There is virtually nothing in the film to delineate the genuine turmoil within party ranks as the SPD opts to vote for war credits, much less the general crisis of the entire European Socialist movement. The subsequent formation of the Third International, the impact of the Russian Revolution, and the theories of Bolshevism are barely alluded to. Even the rebellion that leads to the execution of Luxemburg and Karl Liebknecht (Otto Sander) receives abbreviated screen time.

Further weakening the political dimension of the film is the absence of mass public rallies or scenes to show the popular base of the various factions. The film offers little sense of why the German government would consider Luxemburg dangerous. She appears to operate on a Chautauqua-type speaking circuit rather than threatening the stability of the state. Von Trotta's consistent assumption of detailed knowledge on the part of a popular audience lessens the tragic dimensions of Luxemburg's fate.

The emphasis on the subjective Luxemburg, however, does have its rewards. If the viewer loses something of the fiery revolutionary, he gains a woman with a remarkable sense of ethics, a person who is harder on herself than on others. Luxemburg is utterly fanatical about truthfulness in private relationships. She rejects Leo Jogiches (Daniel Olbrychski), her lover, not because he has had occasion to sleep with other women, but because he has lied to her about his behavior. The Jogiches love affair haunts the film and it is understood that unlike other female revolutionaries such as Emma Goldman, Luxemburg retained a romantic conception of love that was essentially monogamous.

Another side of Luxemburg brought out clearly is her friendships with women. The viewer sees Luxemburg working closely with Clara Zetkin (Doris Schade) in the women's section of the SPD, but unlike Zetkin, Luxemburg refuses to be confined to the role of leader of women only. Zetkin joins Luxemburg, Liebknecht, and Jogiches in creating the Spartacist League, and in 1919 she will write the first work on the martyred leaders. The film treats effectively the comradeship of the two revolutionaries and sensitively explores a brief affair Luxemburg has with Kostia Zetkin (Hannes Jaenickhe), Clara's son.

Some attention is also given to Luise Kautsky (Adelheid Arndt), the wife of one of the SPD's leaders. Even after Luxemburg breaks with Karl Kautsky on political grounds, the women continue to see each other, as their relationship is not mere political courtesy. In 1929, Luise Kautsky would write an appreciative memoir of these years in her *Rosa Luxemburg*.

Considerable screen time takes place in prison or in scenes where Luxemburg is alone. These scenes often explore her genuine love for animals and flowers. Luxemburg's aesthetic sentiments fuse naturally with her political convictions. A woman so enthralled with the world of nature has to be outraged by the exploitation of human beings. The viewer understands that she could never feel the kind of intellectual arrogance common to recent German revolutionaries, nor would she address workers in a condescending tone.

Important as these insights are, essential objective data is blurred. In 1916, Luxemburg returned to Germany from Warsaw, which was then part of the czarist empire. She thought that much could be learned from the experience of Russian revolutionaries. This placed her in the left wing of the SPD. Despite her admiration for Russian revolutionaries, Luxemburg raised objections to some of the views of Vladimir Ilyich Lenin, and her theoretical positions have become touchstones in Marxist debate. None of this is evident in the film, however. Lenin is virtually a nonperson, and Luxemburg the brilliant essayist is discussed but never convincingly revealed. This failure to capture Luxemburg's intellectual stature is a surprising defect in a film so devoted to feminist issues.

Another point that is downplayed is that Luxemburg was a Polish Jew. Given the subsequent rise of Nazism in Germany, one looks for what the situation might have been in the 1910's. The director has stated that ethnic and religious issues were not critical in that period, but the issue demands more attention than is given in the film.

Additional difficulties stem from the nonchronological narration which has intricate backward and forward leaps in time. While not meant to be deconstructive, the film avoids the socialist-thriller style of Constantin Costa-Gavras and the kind of political spectacle Bernardo Bertolucci created in *1900* (1976). The major effort is to locate the human dynamic at the core of revolutionary commitment. In this sense, the film concerns the modern business of showing that the personal is political and the political is personal. While the director intends Luxemburg's life to be a reflection on the problems of contemporary times, she does not want that life to be seen as a rigid catechism of dos and don'ts.

The film's images can be deceptively simple. In the opening shot, Luxemburg, who has a slight limp, is seen walking in a prison yard accompanied by a one-legged black crow. Hanging on her office wall as she edits the newspaper of the ill-fated Sparticist League is Vincent Van Gogh's "Crows over the White Field." Bringing considerable verve to such scenes is Sukowa, who manages a slight Polish accent within otherwise impeccable German, exactly as the historical Luxemburg spoke. Von Trotta fans will note how different the humanist Luxemburg is from the self-vindicating narcissistic Marianne played by Sukowa in *Marianne and Julianne.*

Given its subject matter and cinematic approach, *Rosa Luxemburg* was destined to have mixed reviews. Perhaps because it emphasized antiwar and feminist concerns rather than revolutionary socialism, the film fared decently at the box office. Nevertheless, many critics took the film to task on historical grounds, wanting a textbook biography rather than the interpretive work that von Trotta had created. The director has stated that the film may have been premature for her talents, but that it was politically on time, particularly for German radicals.

Dan Georgakas

Reviews
Cineaste. XV, No. 4, 1987, p. 24.
Films and Filming. Number 383, August, 1986, p. 39.
Films in Review. XXXVIII, November, 1987, p. 549.
Los Angeles Times. June 5, 1987, VI, p. 10.
Ms. XV, May, 1987, p. 22.
The Nation. CCXLIV, April 25, 1987, p. 546.
The New Republic. CXCVI, May 18, 1987, p. 24.
New Statesman. CXII, September 5, 1986, p. 24.
New York. XX, June 1, 1987, p. 96.
The New York Times. May 1, 1987, p. C10.

ROXANNE

Production: Michael Rachmil, Daniel Melnick, and Steve Martin; released
by Columbia Pictures
Direction: Fred Schepisi
Screenplay: Steve Martin; based on the play *Cyrano de Bergerac* by Ed-
mond Rostand
Cinematography: Ian Baker
Editing: John Scott
Production design: Jack DeGovia
Art direction: David Fischer; set decoration, Kimberly Richardson
Makeup: Michael Westmore
Costume design: Richard Bruno and Tish Monaghan
Music: Bruce Smeaton
MPAA rating: PG
Running time: 107 minutes

> *Principal characters:*
> C. D. Bales..........................Steve Martin
> Roxanne..........................Daryl Hannah
> Chris............................Rick Rossovich
> Dixie.............................Shelley Duvall
> Sandy ....Shandra Beri
> Chuck.............................John Kapelos
> Andy ....Michael J. Pollard
> Mayor Deebs ....Fred Willard

Steve Martin brings his own brand of panache to this modern-day rework-
ing of the nineteenth century French play *Cyrano de Bergerac* by Edmond
Rostand. The heroic tale of the swashbuckling captain of the guards, whose
monstrous nose makes hopeless his love for the beautiful Roxanne, is re-
shaped by Martin, as screenwriter, executive producer, and star, into a
gentle romantic comedy with a traditional Hollywood ending. Nevertheless,
Roxanne retains the wit and flavor of the original play, finding equivalents
for nearly all the major characters and situations. In addition, Martin's physical and verbal humor finds full expression in the comic irony of a man
bursting with talent but seen only as a discomforting oddity.

Martin's previous film characterizations have drawn principally on the farcical and bizarre, though some, most notably *The Man with Two Brains*
(1983) and *All of Me* (1984), have a soft, romantic underside. In *Roxanne*,
Martin focuses directly on the realistically drawn romantic relationship.
Running gags and physical and verbal non sequiturs appear, both with Martin and his supporting actors, but they are kept in the background, quietly

expressing a world slightly out of kilter, as on a midsummer's night. The trials of love are drawn from the original play, but the spirit of the film and the end result are Martin's.

Roxanne does not attempt a faithful interpretation of the play, as did the 1950 film *Cyrano de Bergerac*, starring José Ferrer. Instead, *Roxanne* transfers the central theme, that the quality of a man cannot be judged from his external appearance but only from the spirit and virtue in his soul, to totally new surroundings. The setting is Nelson, Washington (filmed on location in British Columbia), a small ski resort town during the summer off-season. Cyrano becomes C. D. Bales (Steve Martin), local fire chief and leader of a Keystone Kops sort of brigade of volunteer firemen. Roxanne (Daryl Hannah) is a summer visitor, an astronomer who has brought her telescope to the clear mountain skies to await a new comet she believes she has discovered. The cosmic imagery of the play is retained in the dialogue and visuals for the film's star-crossed lovers.

The film opens one evening in early summer as C. D., walking down the street and carrying a tennis racket, encounters two loutish ski bums carrying their skis and poles. They take notice of his very large nose, make a point of it, and provoke C. D.'s very short temper on this touchy subject. With a call to arms, C. D. dispatches the louts, racket against ski poles, calling his shots as he does so. Thus, he is introduced as a man who is hypersensitive about his obvious abnormality and capable of handling a situation both physically and verbally.

At the fire station, C. D. rescues his inept volunteers, who have accidentally started a fire, and then responds to a call of distress from a beautiful woman, Roxanne, who has arrived nude at the station, having locked herself out of her house. With the ease of a modern Douglas Fairbanks, C. D. scales the house and vaults into an upper window. Unlocking the door for Roxanne, he calmly stays to get acquainted. C. D.'s love is immediate, but Roxanne, though responding to his wit and intelligence, does not see it.

Instead, Roxanne is physically attracted to Chris (Rick Rossovich), a handsome, professional fire fighter who has recently joined the brigade. Chris avoids meeting Roxanne, and she mistakenly believes him to be a quiet man of hidden depths. Actually, Chris is a simple fellow, so intimidated by Roxanne that the very thought of speaking to her causes him to throw up.

Roxanne confides to C. D. her interest in Chris. Although his illusions are broken, C. D. agrees to help her and suggests to Chris that he write a letter to express what he cannot say. Chris, however, composes so juvenile a note that C. D. feels compelled to write the kind of letter a woman such as Roxanne should receive. Both to his joy and chagrin the letter is a complete success.

C. D. then helps Chris meet Roxanne by wiring him with an earplug connected to a shortwave. This allows C. D. to transmit the appropriate lines to Chris, who is standing outside Roxanne's window, until interference from a local police call severs the connection. Left to his own devices, Chris can think of nothing but platitudes and crude overtures. When Roxanne angrily retreats into her house, C. D. appears to woo her back with his words. Standing in the shadows and pretending to be Chris, he has his victory in completely expressing his love and seeing Roxanne succumb to him. Chris seizes the situation, however, and climbs into Roxanne's willing arms and spends the night with her.

The next day, Chris admits to C. D. that he is not comfortable with Roxanne, since he is not the man she thinks he is. When Roxanne returns to her university for a week to confirm the existence of her comet, C. D. writes her letters every day, which are signed by Chris. Meanwhile, Chris meets Sandy (Shandra Beri), and they discover an immediate rapport based on common interests. When Roxanne returns, C. D. tries to keep up the pretense, but Chris writes his own farewell note and leaves town with Sandy. Dixie (Shelley Duvall), C. D.'s friend and confidante, learns of the letters and reveals the hoax to Roxanne, who explodes with indignation at C. D.'s manipulation of her emotions.

Lost in his despair, C. D. is distracted by the smell of smoke. Leading his men through the streets, he follows his nose to a local barn which is ablaze, with the town mascot trapped inside. For once the volunteers work perfectly together, and the prized cow is saved. Later, as C. D. contemplates the world from atop a roof, Roxanne appears below with her own confession of love. Like the comet predicted far in advance but only just seen, Roxanne finally realizes that more than the words it is their author she loves.

The major deviation of the film from the original play is in the conclusion. Martin has devised a romantic denouement for his C. D. Bales, which the real Cyrano could never have had. Panache is traded for a happy ending, and the hero settles for the simple life. While *Roxanne* never seeks the deeper meanings of the play, where Cyrano fights his ultimate duel with death itself, the film has its own personal side, sincere and consistently developed along the lines of a more accessible romantic love.

Roxanne is beautifully packaged with Ian Baker's wide-screen, panoramic photography and Bruce Smeaton's gentle music. Baker and Smeaton have worked together with Australian director Schepisi on all of his films, including *The Chant of Jimmy Blacksmith* (1978) and *Barbarosa* (1982), two of the most evocative and thematically rich films of recent years. In *Roxanne*, however, much as in Schepisi's previous effort, *Plenty* (1985), the direction is both unimposing and anonymous.

The strengths of the film reside in the comic inventiveness of Martin and the skillful mixture of humor and character detail in the narrative. The viewer sees both the aplomb of C. D., naming the jokes he has collected about his appearance to deflate the expected pain, and the sorrow of C. D., alone with a bird perched comfortably and lovingly on his nose. Hannah's Roxanne is also given an extra dimension, not so much interior but larger than life. As in *Splash* (1984), Hannah has the ability to evoke a woman who is more than human, a rare, precious being. In *Roxanne*, she is a celestial character first seen awash in the moonlight, an image that transfixes both C. D. and the audience.

Terry Nixon

Reviews
Los Angeles Times. June 19, 1987, VI, p. 1.
National Review. XXXIX, July 31, 1987, p. 51.
The New Republic. CXCVI, June 29, 1987, p. 24.
The New York Times. June 19, 1987, p. C3.
The New Yorker. LXIII, June 15, 1987, p. 77.
Newsweek. CIX, June 22, 1987, p. 73.
Time. CXXIX, June 15, 1987, p. 74.
Variety. June 9, 1987, p. 3.

THE SECRET OF MY SUCCESS

Production: Herbert Ross for Rastar; released by Universal Pictures
Direction: Herbert Ross
Screenplay: Jim Cash, Jack Epps, Jr., and A. J. Carothers; story by A. J. Carothers
Cinematography: Carlo Di Palma
Editing: Paul Hirsch
Art direction: Edward Pisoni and Peter Larkin; set decoration, Susan Bode
Costume design: Joseph C. Aulisi
Music: David Foster
MPAA rating: PG-13
Running time: 110 minutes

> *Principal characters:*
> Brantley Foster .... Michael J. Fox
> Christy Wills........................ Helen Slater
> Howard Prescott.................. Richard Jordan
> Vera Prescott .... Margaret Whitton
> Fred Melrose....................... John Pankow
> Barney Rattigan .... Christopher Murney
> Art Thomas...................... Gerry Bamman
> Donald Davenport.................. Fred Gwynne

The title of *The Secret of My Success* suggests Frank Tashlin's satire *Will Success Spoil Rock Hunter?* (1957). In Tashlin's film, Tony Randall played an advertising executive whose sudden rise to prominence is the vehicle for a cutting satire on the American dream. The film's targets include television, materialism, and the fickle nature of celebrity. The word "success" becomes a double-edged sword, viewed with a healthy dose of irony and cynicism.

The Secret of My Success, however, is a satire with little sense of irony. The pronoun of the title refers as much to the film's phenomenally successful star, Michael J. Fox, as it does to the character he plays, Brantley Foster. While the film appears, at first, to be a lampoon of the business world, it is not much more than an attempt to cash in on the enormous real-life success of its star, and it does so by glorifying a character quite similar to that of Fox's "Family Ties" sitcom character, Alex Keaton.

As it details the sudden rise of Brantley Foster, a college graduate from Kansas who becomes the head of a major corporation within two weeks of arriving in New York, *The Secret of My Success* would like to have it both ways. It wants to be seen as a lampoon of the business world, but it glorifies

Foster's gung ho attitude in such a way that the film's view of big business is about as realistic as the portrayal of boxing in *Rocky* (1976).

Brantley Foster is bright, self-confident, and obsessed with money. While he has the makings of a successful businessman, he is also young, sensitive, and innocent. He believes in hard work, but he is also naturally gifted, and things come to him with amazing ease. Brantley arrives in New York to the vibrant beat of the film's rock sound track. Manhattan is viewed as an exciting place, with everything to offer. The opening montage of the city, with sleek skyscrapers and sidewalks filled with beautiful women, has the style of a television commercial. Throughout the film, Carlo Di Palma, who photographed *Hannah and Her Sisters* (1986) for Woody Allen, presents New York in lush, glowing images.

Still, everything is not rosy at first for Brantley, who lives in a cheap, cockroach-infested apartment. The job he was supposed to have upon his arrival no longer exists, and when he makes the rounds to employment agencies, he is criticized for his lack of experience. "I can be older, I can be taller, anything," he tells his interviewers, eager to adapt to the circumstances. The film flashes back to Brantley at home in Kansas, boasting to his parents, "I'm going to come back in my own jet."

Brantley gets a job in the mail room of a multinational conglomerate corporation which is run by Howard Prescott (Richard Jordan), a very distant relative and a ruthless executive. During their brief first meeting, Brantley assures Prescott, "I know I can do anything if I just had a chance."

Immediately after this scene, Brantley sees Christy Wills (Helen Slater), the company's token woman executive, at a water fountain. In a fantasy sequence, he imagines their romantic meeting in an empty hallway. This scene is followed by a romantic, sunset montage of New York; things are beginning to look up for Brantley. Throughout the film, Christy is viewed as little more than an object for Brantley to acquire. She is a fantasy for him, and his pursuit of her is paralleled throughout the film with his pursuit of business success.

The film is essentially a series of conquests for Brantley, who is portrayed as having common sense, drive, and ingenuity that nobody else in the entire company seems to possess. Christy, for example, is shown as being insecure and exhausted with her workload. Also, the audience learns that she has been having an affair with Prescott; the secret, one is led to assume, of *her* success.

Despite his youth and inexperience, Brantley is completely confident with women and able to make them feel secure and loved. While working in the mail room, he is ordered to drive home Vera Prescott (Margaret Whitton), Howard's wife, in the company limousine. In the car, he compliments her looks, and when they arrive at the Prescott estate, she seduces him. Vera is unhappily married and has a poor self-image. Brantley, however, knows exactly what to say to make her feel good. He assures her, "You're beautiful, you're intelligent, you're sensuous."

Meanwhile, back at the office, Brantley plans his rise to the top. He has been taking home company reports and documents and staying up late at night studying them. By scrutinizing interoffice memos during his mail room hours, he has discovered waste and mismanagement in the company's organization. After learning about some executive layoffs, he schemes to move into a vacant office. Soon, he has assumed a second identity, using the name Carlton Whitfield, and he finds a niche in the bureaucracy.

Brantley tries to maintain his mail room position at the same time, and the double identity becomes a source of predictable plot complications, as well as some strained madcap humor. Brantley must change back and forth from his mail room clothes to his executive clothes, and his favorite method of doing so, rather than simply using a bathroom, is to get into an elevator and pull the alarm, forcing the elevator to stop between floors and giving him exactly enough time to change outfits. While the sight of Fox frantically undressing in an elevator may be good for a cheap laugh, the situation is completely pointless.

Brantley adapts quite easily as Carlton Whitfield. He instantly finds a worthy project. The company is the target of a hostile takeover, and Prescott wants to economize by closing the unprofitable Midwestern distribution center. Yet Brantley/Carlton believes that the company should expand in the Midwest and fight the takeover attempt by becoming bigger and stronger. He works late into the night, preparing a report about his expansion plans. He explains to Christy, "Expansion is a positive reaction to the forces of the universe." Soon "expansion" becomes a double entendre for his plans with Christy and the company.

The film has numerous identities of its own. It is a satire, a romance, and a screwball comedy, with a complicated series of love triangles. (Vera is in love with Brantley, who is in love with Christy; Christy is in love with Brantley-as-Whitfield and is trying to end her affair with Prescott.)

The complications come to a head during a weekend party at the Prescott estate. Unaware that Whitfield and Brantley are the same person, Prescott invites Brantley to his home for the weekend, because he knows that Vera is in love with him and he wants Vera distracted so that he can pursue Christy. The result of all of this is a clumsy nighttime bedroom-hopping scene, in which Prescott and Brantley find themselves together in Christy's bed.

Before this, however, Brantley/Carlton has had time to spend much of the weekend talking with important bankers and financiers, winning allies by sharing his brilliant ideas about business. Nowhere in the film is Brantley's business acumen questioned. The characters never doubt that this college graduate from Kansas can become a savvy, innovative executive virtually overnight. Brantley knows it all. He is caring and sensitive with women, and he can turn a corporation around in two weeks.

One could dismiss the film's simplicity by arguing that it is merely a modest comedy set in the business world and is not meant to be taken seriously. Yet even a screwball comedy presents some kind of worldview. Tashlin's film, mentioned above, exhibits a sharp cynicism about the business world. Hal Ashby's *Being There* (1979), another rags-to-riches story, starred Peter Sellers as a complete cipher who grew up watching television and became a success because people interpreted his empty replies and blank gestures as signs of genius. Yet with *Being There* the audience always knew that the Sellers character was less than he appeared.

The problem with *The Secret of My Success* is that it is too much in love with Brantley Foster's vision of success to betray any skepticism. Indeed, no fault is found in any of his actions. He works hard, is resourceful, and favors positive goals, such as expansion and growth. The film ends with Brantley going to the opera in a limousine with Christy; once again, this materialistic splendor is presented with the tone of a television commercial.

Living up to its title, *The Secret of My Success* was one of the most successful films of 1987. It was released in the early part of the year, months before the stock-market crash of October, 1987, sent the Dow-Jones Average plummeting by five hundred points in a single day. If anything, the crash was a case of reality catching up with an overly optimistic and expansive bull market; the business world cannot run on mere optimism and simple solutions. One wonders whether *The Secret of My Success* would have been such a success if it had been released after the crash.

David Schwartz

Reviews
Commonweal. CXIV, May 22, 1987, p. 318.
Films in Review. XXXVIII, June, 1987, p. 362.
Los Angeles Times. April 10, 1987, VI, p. 1.
The New Republic. CXCVI, May 11, 1987, p. 24.
New Statesman. CXIV, July 3, 1987, p. 21.
The New York Times. April 10, 1987, p. C14.
The New Yorker. LXIII, May 4, 1987, p. 130.
Time. CXXIX, May 4, 1987, p. 97.
Variety. CCCXXVI, April 8, 1987, p. 16.
The Wall Street Journal. April 9, 1987, p. 30.

SEPTEMBER

Production: Robert Greenhut and Jack Rollins and Charles H. Joffe (executive producers); released by Orion Pictures
Direction: Woody Allen
Screenplay: Woody Allen
Cinematography: Carlo di Palma
Editing: Susan E. Morse
Production design: Santo Loquasto
Art direction: Speed Hopkins; set decoration, George DeTitta, Jr.
Costume design: Jeffrey Kurland
Sound: James Sabat
Music: Frank Loesser; John Green and Edward Heyman; Sam Coslow and Arthur Johnston; Leo Robin, Richard A. Whiting, and Jewell Chase; Irving Berlin; Jerome Kern, Otto Harbach, and Oscar Hammerstein II; Al J. Neiburg, Doe Daugherty, and Ellis Reynolds; Will Hudson, Eddie De Lange, and Irving Mills; Robert Katscher and B. G. De Silva; and Cole Porter
MPAA rating: PG
Running time: 82 minutes

> *Principal characters:*
> Howard......................... Denholm Elliott
> Stephanie....................... Dianne Wiest
> Lane .... Mia Farrow
> Diane .... Elaine Stritch
> Peter .... Sam Waterston
> Lloyd............................ Jack Warden

Woody Allen's *September*, released at the end of 1987, was a critical and commercial failure, virtually disappearing from theaters after only about one month in limited release. Reviewers and audiences alike have always been capricious in their tastes, and it is usually left to the perspective of time to accord proper understanding to an individual film within the context of a body of work. Even so, the generally derisive tone of print and broadcast media critiques at a time when Allen's prestige was at a peak was startling, if only because the conscientious craftsmanship that has distinguished all Allen's mature work is so tangibly present in *September*. The apathy of fans who are generally eager to see anything he does was also somewhat perplexing, though characterization of the film as unappealingly gloomy partly accounts for it. Perhaps, for the moment, accolades and adulation had been exhausted on Allen's two immediately preceding efforts, *Hannah and Her Sisters* (1986) and, to a lesser extent, *Radio Days* (1987; reviewed in this volume). It is also possible, however, that Allen, though he enjoys an unusual degree of autonomy among commercially viable American filmmakers and is thought of as a major artist by a wide consensus, has not entirely surmounted the preconceptions of others about what kind of films he should and should not make.

September, while expressively moody, is an unpretentious and completely accessible drama. More than other Allen films it is emotionally direct and possessed of an elegant formal simplicity. The characters reveal much pain, but they afford pleasure also. Throughout, one senses an unusually honest projection of an artist's most personal feelings.

Briefly, the action is confined to a Vermont country house where Lane (Mia Farrow) is living following recovery from a nervous breakdown. Her older neighbor, Howard (Denholm Elliott), loves her, openly but without hope, while she loves Peter (Sam Waterston), a would-be novelist staying at her guesthouse. Peter has encouraged her affection but is currently falling in love with her visiting friend, Stephanie (Dianne Wiest), a married woman who nevertheless wants to respond to Peter's advances but hesitates on Lane's account. Lane's mother, Diane (Elaine Stritch), once a film star, comes to visit with her physicist husband, Lloyd (Jack Warden). With all the characters assembled for a languorous evening party, emotions begin to surface. Stephanie finally has an affair with Peter, and Lane, when she finds out about it later, feels betrayed by both of them. At the same time, the perceived truth of a long-ago event—the shooting of one of Diane's earlier husbands by Lane—is revealed to be a lie; Lane, then only a girl, had cooperated in hiding the fact that her mother was the actual killer. Conflicts and confrontations are pursued only tentatively, however, as no character has the will or strength to unsettle the status quo. Lane is in the process of selling the house as September approaches, and after the other characters have departed, Lane and Stephanie wistfully speculate about the future.

The ideas about life, love, sex, death, neurosis, emotional scars, and self-delusion which Allen articulates through these characters are not new in his work. In fact, he built his reputation—even in his silliest and most fanciful early films and in his career as a stand-up comedian—by making jokes about these subjects. To some extent, humor was a way of keeping at bay excessive anxiety and morbidity. The most immediately impressive thing about *September* is the soulful openness with which the characters behave, relate, and express themselves. For example, there is the attraction of Peter and Stephanie, so well observed and well played that it possesses a palpable sexual heat, even though it is described in only a few carefully paced dialogue scenes and a single kiss. Effective, too, is Lloyd's brief, restrained commentary on the malevolence of a senseless universe (an Allen obsession that the filmmaker typically strains to impose); Jack Warden's earthy, natural manner makes the concept, for once, genuinely provocative. Allen shows an appreciation and acceptance of individual personality throughout. Diane may be a selfish and insensitive mother, but her brashness and free spiritedness make it impossible not to like her. Howard, a character who might have been a familiarly pathetic type if handled carelessly, displays a gentle Old World charm and gallantry that are truly touching. Most appealing of all is Farrow's halting and timid yet achingly sincere Lane, so dignified and unafraid in her exposure of vulnerability and fragility.

Through his characters' manner—subtly self-dramatizing but reflective of their deepest, innermost selves—Allen persuasively intimates that the first step toward changing an unhappy human condition is to be truthful about painful emotions. It may be that not much has changed at the end of the film, but in giving voice to their frustrations, angers, and yearnings, these characters are affirming a hopeful, noncynical vision of a world in which they might yet comfortably exist. Such a positive vision may seem ironic in a narrative filled with woe, but it is perceptible enough to suggest that Allen, however humorously affable he may always have been about his darker perceptions, has now matured to a point that his ambivalences need not be resolved in either glib platitudes, which have previously made life-affirming moments in his work superficial, or hollow philosophical notions of man's innate confusion and despair, which he has long found seductive.

Allen's playing of hypochondriac Mickey Sachs in *Hannah and Her Sisters* was perhaps the most amusing manifestation of his on-screen *persona*, but retrospectively it is apparent that Allen can easily represent himself without being physically present within a film. Intriguingly, Cecilia (Farrow) in *The Purple Rose of Cairo* (1985) mingles with a cinematic fantasy world as Allen's own character did in *Play It Again, Sam* (1972; written and starring Allen but directed by Herbert Ross), while both Joey (Mary Beth Hurt) in *Interiors* (1978) and Lane in *September* physically resemble him, although they are women and conceived more seriously. As with Lloyd's articulation of Allen's philosophical speculations, these female characters artistically objectify Allen's sense of himself. Tending increasingly to become a behind-the-scenes presence, Allen is becoming less self-indulgent and increasingly purposeful. His absence in *September* draws attention to the pervading wit and inventiveness of his writing and the beauty of his direction. The cast—including players new to Allen, as well as Farrow and Wiest, whose talents have blossomed under his guidance—is uniformly superb, and the warm visualization of the setting to which the action is confined is steadily absorbing. Allen's magnificently deliberated long takes and fluid camera movements, combined with Carlo di Palma's vibrant lighting, Susan E. Morse's graceful editing, and a wonderful use of source music (on-screen piano playing, as well as records which feature Ben Webster's inimitable romanticism) give the film a singularly entrancing atmosphere. Contrary to some accounts, however, the ambiance and action are not derived from either Anton Chekhov or Ingmar Bergman; these are characters of a specific time and place who are surely as aware as Allen is of emotions evoked by the worlds of those artists.

September was widely compared to *Interiors*, even though it does not repeat the error of the generally laudable earlier drama's insistent solemnity and owes at least as much to the lighter *A Midsummer Night's Sex Comedy* (1982), which was also concerned with romantic yearning and tension among six characters in a country setting. The earlier film was strained and only intermittently charming, so it was certainly reasonable for Allen to take a different, graver approach in *September*. Tellingly, that approach has resulted not only in more richly realized characters and a potent charge of melodrama but also in more wit and humor. Perhaps because of the counterpoint between the characters' melancholy self-dramatizing and the inadvertently amusing things they often say, *September* is frequently hilarious without its genuinely sad situations ever becoming ridiculous. A good example of the film's humor occurs when Diane rambles authoritatively about Lane's last failed romantic relationship with a man she identifies as Jess, and Lane finally breaks in with the punch line: "His name was Jack!"

Bafflingly, this enlivening humor was ignored almost universally, as if Allen had not intended it. Yet Allen was unable to repress his comic side completely even in *Interiors*, while his more ambitious comedies have clearly taught him much about the potential for stimulating interplay between serious material and an innately witty sensibility. Nevertheless, once an artist has established himself, he should be given latitude to evolve in any direction. This is especially true for Allen, who may have ascended too easily to acclaim but seems increasingly worthy of it. Stylistically, *September* is the Allen film which to date most fully reveals a personal, seriocomic voice, one that transcends the influence of Bergman as surely as it transcends the influence of Bob Hope.

Blake Lucas

Reviews
Chicago Tribune. December 18, 1987, VII, p. 17.
Los Angeles Times. December 18, 1987, VI, p. 1.
Macleans. C, December 21, 1987, p. 61.
National Review. XL, March 4, 1988, p. 52.
The New Republic. CXCVIII, February 1, 1988, p. 27.
The New York Times. December 18, 1987, p. C3.
The New Yorker. LXXXI, January 25, 1988, p. 100.
Newsweek. CXI, January 4, 1988, p. 52.
Time. CXXX, December 21, 1987, p. 74.
Variety. CCCXXIX, December 16, 1987, p. 10.
The Wall Street Journal. December 24, 1987, p. 5.

SOME KIND OF WONDERFUL

Production: John Hughes, Michael Chinich, and Ronald Colby for Paramount Pictures; released by Paramount Pictures
Direction: Howard Deutch
Screenplay: John Hughes
Cinematography: Jan Kiesser
Editing: Bud Smith and Scott Smith
Production design: Josan Russo
Art direction: Greg Pickrell; set decoration, Linda Spheeris
Special effects: Louis Cooper
Makeup: Zoltan
Costume design: Marilyn Vance-Straker
Sound: David MacMillan
Music: Stephen Hague and John Musser
Song: Mick Jagger and Keith Richards, "Miss Amanda Jones"
MPAA rating: PG-13
Running time: 93 minutes

Principal characters:
Keith Nelson .... Eric Stoltz
Watts .... Mary Stuart Masterson
Amanda Jones .... Lea Thompson
Hardy Jenns .... Craig Sheffer
Cliff Nelson .... John Ashton
Duncan the Skinhead .... Elias Koteas
Shayne .... Molly Hagan
Laura Nelson .... Maddie Corman
Carol Nelson .... Jane Elliot
Cindy Nelson .... Candace Cameron

The sixth and possibly last of the high school comedies John Hughes has been popularizing since *Sixteen Candles* (1984), *Some Kind of Wonderful* exhibits everything the audience has come to expect from the successful writer/producer's canon: heartache, anger, class struggle, anxiety, and a painful assessment of a world bent on making youth miserable.

Eric Stoltz plays Keith Nelson, a poor but good-hearted high school senior who collides with social adversity at every turn. He is menaced by thuggish schoolmates, harassed by a tomboy sidekick, and hassled by insensitive teachers. Though he has a definite aptitude for art, his father, Cliff Nelson (John Ashton), pushes him toward the more respectable goal of attending business college.

Keith's emotional trials do not really start until he meets the lovely

Amanda Jones (Lea Thompson), a much wealthier classmate. Recovering from a breakup with Hardy Jenns (Craig Sheffer), her philandering boyfriend, Amanda initially embraces Keith's earnest advances. Her upper-middle-class friends are appalled, and she is slowly ostracized from them.

Keith, meanwhile, is feeling pressured by his own friends. His friend Watts (Mary Stuart Masterson), who practices the drums compulsively, warns him that Amanda is from a clique of "users" and that a boy who dates above his class is destined for heartbreak. She also hints that she may be interested in starting a romance with Keith.

All Hughes's films have similar story lines, but the plot of *Some Kind of Wonderful* borrows almost too liberally from *Pretty in Pink* (1986), the previous collaboration between Hughes and director Howard Deutch. Like *Pretty in Pink*, *Some Kind of Wonderful* centers on teenagers from different social classes who fall in love with each other and the efforts of their friends to pull them apart. While *Pretty in Pink*'s protagonist was a poor girl, the protagonist here is male. In fact, the sexes of virtually all the main characters have been reversed. Hughes's trademark nonconformist, played by Anthony Michael Hall in *Sixteen Candles* and John Cryer in *Pretty in Pink*, is now female. James Spader's obnoxious elitist from *Pretty in Pink* has been reincarnated in *Some Kind of Wonderful* as jut-jawed Shayne (Molly Hagan).

These similarities are probably indicative of Hughes's exhaustion with the genre. His three subsequent projects—*She's Having a Baby* (1988), *Planes, Trains and Automobiles* (1987; reviewed in this volume), and *Big Country* (1988)—feature markedly older heroes. *Some Kind of Wonderful* is one of Hughes's weaker screenplays. It functions more as a clearinghouse for themes, ideas, and devices left over from his five previous teen efforts than as an entity unto itself.

Yet the inventive humor in the film tends to eclipse much of the slow-moving plot and muddled motivation. The press material prepared by Paramount Pictures quotes actress Masterson drawing comparisons between Hughes and William Shakespeare. Oddly, the comparisons make sense. Shakespeare, after all, dealt almost exclusively with familiar plots. It was his genius for enhancing the timeworn that inevitably added so much beyond the initial inspiration. So it is with Hughes. The pastiche of well-drawn satellite characters who conflict with Hughes's protagonists, for example, is always extraordinarily amusing.

The brightest spots in the film surely belong to Duncan the Skinhead (Elias Koteas), a likable, lumbering, violently tactless, leather-clad punk anarchist who at first embodies the concept of physical threat, then transmogrifies into Keith's most ardent protector. Duncan stomps through the film like a grinning, psychotic locomotive—but with intrinsic moral fiber. Not to be bothered with the subtleties of class distinction, Duncan appears at strategic points throughout the film to right essential wrongs. As Duncan, Koteas walks the line between lowlife and avenging angel perfectly, alternating effortlessly between the twin roles of bully and clown. The actor, with his dangerous, maniacal charm, suggests a happier Robert De Niro or, with his shaved, angular head, a somewhat goofier Marlon Brando.

Maddie Corman is also effective as Keith's acidic, manipulative, almost Machiavellian little sister. Strongly reminiscent of the sister character played by Jennifer Grey in Hughes's *Ferris Bueller's Day Off* (1986), Laura Nelson takes special competitive pleasure in her brother's failings and proves too adept at making quite a witty irritant of herself. Only when Keith takes his first step up the social ladder does Laura begin to realize the essential worth of a brother whom she refers to as "the human Tater Tot."

Of special note, however, is Masterson's performance as Keith's best friend. The moods of her character, Watts, are rich and varied, and Masterson never makes a false move, more than matching the performances that her predecessors Hall and Cryer brought to similar roles.

Stoltz and Thompson, playing romantic leads opposite each other for the third time—the others being *The Wild Life* (1984) and *Back to the Future* (1985), before Stoltz was replaced in mid-production by Michael J. Fox—offer the film a solid emotional center. Thompson exemplifies every schoolboy's dream with radiance and vulnerability. ("The girl is sex," explains Keith's sister.) Stoltz too turns in a likable performance, but one is constantly struck by the incongruity of this good-looking man as a social misfit. Like Robert Redford, Stoltz simply exudes too much elemental charisma to play an outcast.

Director Deutch, in his second collaboration with Hughes, proves again that he can add strong realistic texture so often absent in Hughes's own directorial efforts. Windows do not shatter when someone screams, as they do in *The Breakfast Club* (1985). Nor are people as easily duped as they are in *Ferris Bueller's Day Off*. The dearth of absurdity is a welcome change in this Hughes film; it is enjoyable to see him elicit laughs solely from character and dialogue.

As with all of his films, this John Hughes production features a rich and integral soundtrack of mostly newer music. Especially well utilized is the wondrous Mick Jagger/Keith Richards song "Miss Amanda Jones," performed by the March Violets as a recurring theme for the song's namesake. One song not on the sound track, interestingly, is the one that inspired the film's title.

Hughes and Deutch clearly have genuine empathy for the troubled youthful characters who populate their films. There is none of the bland, thick-skinned comic indifference so many other filmmakers bring to the same type of film. Hughes, in particular, has been criticized by many for taking so seriously the travails of adolescence, but, in truth, it is precisely that seriousness that drives his work. He seems to remember with unusual clarity the raw, unanesthetized nervousness of young adulthood and what it was like to combat daily life without the hard-won defenses one inevitably acquires to dull the pain of rejection, inadequacy, and abuse.

Jim Kozak

Reviews
Films in Review. XXXVIII, May, 1987, p. 299.
Los Angeles Times. February 27, 1987, VI, p. 1.
The New York Times. February 27, 1987, p. C17.
Newsweek. CIX, March 16, 1987, p. 72.
People Weekly. XXVII, March 9, 1987, p. 12.
Seventeen. XLVI, May, 1987, p. 65.
Time. CXXIX, March 9, 1987, p. 86.
Variety. CCCXXVI, February 25, 1987, p. 277.
The Wall Street Journal. February 26, 1987, p. 20.
The Washington Post. February 28, 1987, p. G1.

STAKEOUT

Production: John Badham; released by Touchstone Pictures
Direction: John Badham
Screenplay: Jim Kouf
Cinematography: John Seale
Editing: Tom Rolf and Michael Ripps
Production design: Philip Harrison
Art direction: Richard Hudolin; set decoration, Rose Marie McSherry
Special effects: John Thomas
Makeup: Sandy Cooper
Costume design: Mary Vogt
Music: Arthur B. Rubinstein
MPAA rating: R
Running time: 105 minutes

> *Principal characters:*
> Chris Lecce .... Richard Dreyfuss
> Bill Reimers .... Emilio Estevez
> Maria McGuire .... Madeleine Stowe
> Richard "Stick" Montgomery.......... Aidan Quinn
> Phil Coldshank....................... Dan Lauria
> Jack Pismo .... Forest Whitaker

Despite its popular and financial success in 1987, *Stakeout* is, at bottom, Hollywood filmmaking at its shabbiest, most exploitative, and most formulaic.

Director John Badham's film tries to be a police-procedural thriller, a buddy film, and a romantic comedy. Unfortunately, Badham and screenwriter Jim Kouf chose to emphasize, according to Hollywood's box-office-oriented values, action instead of character development.

Were it not for the presence of Richard Dreyfuss and Madeleine Stowe, who quite simply carry the film, *Stakeout* would be a completely flippant, pedestrian, cops-chase-the-crazy-crook film.

Chris Lecce (Dreyfuss) and Bill Reimers (Emilio Estevez) are the stereotypical team of experience-hardened, laid-back police detective and his younger, do-it-by-the-book partner. The film's initial sequences preface the appearance of Lecce and Reimers by focusing on the prison break of killer Richard "Stick" Montgomery (Aidan Quinn). Montgomery is abetted in his escape from confinement in Wyoming by a friend who masquerades as a delivery man; the two crooks overpower prison guards, lower themselves down a wall, and make their getaway in a medical supplies truck.

On Stick's prison-cell wall police find a photo of his girlfriend, Maria

McGuire (Stowe); the picture provides lawmen with Montgomery's possible post-escape destination.

The viewer meets Lecce and Reimers as they ply their trade in Seattle. In *Stakeout*'s first action-comedy sequence, Chris and Bill chase a thug through a seafood-processing plant. Chris falls into a pile of fish and is swept into a huge funnel. He exits within a factory complex where an inevitable shoot-out ends with Lecce arresting the criminal.

Upon their return to the precinct headquarters, their superior officer informs Chris and Bill that they are to assist the FBI in the apprehension of Stick Montgomery. Their assignment is to stake out the home of McGuire by establishing surveillance from the house across the street. Lecce and Reimers draw the night shift; two other detectives, Jack (Forest Whitaker) and Phil (Dan Lauria), are their daytime counterparts.

Lecce and Reimers are not looking forward to a week of what they expect to be humdrum observation. Once the two cops see the beautiful Maria enter her home, however, no viewer is surprised that Chris and Bill, who have visual access to almost every room of her house by means of their telescope, become lecherous voyeurs.

Now that Chris lusts after Maria, the film's plot acquires one new dimension: Chris is going to become increasingly involved with his official subject. First of all, he sneaks into her home for a hurried search, then he poses as a telephone repairman in order to wiretap her phones. The next evening, he sees Maria in a neighborhood supermarket, gives her a ride home, and she invites him to dinner. Bill jealously observes his partner's pleasant evening from his post across the street. The friendship of Chris and Maria is cemented when Chris (unknown to Maria) uses his official influence to help rehabilitate her delinquent younger brother.

The film's narrative builds toward the climactic confrontation between Lecce and Reimers and Montgomery by exploiting the gathering momentum of increasingly numerous crosscuts. As Chris falls in love with Maria, Stick makes his way closer and closer to Seattle. The time-honored cinematic tradition of using parallel editing to heighten suspense works reasonably well in *Stakeout* and is a much less obtrusive means of stimulating the viewer than are the dutch angles which photographer John Seale exploits at moments of peak excitement in the narrative.

As Chris grows enamored of Maria, he and Bill both face moral dilemmas. Chris's conscience bothers him because Maria does not know who he really is; Bill is annoyed that Chris has compromised his professional integrity. Chris's dilemma is resolved when a drunken intruder breaks into Maria's house and threatens her. Chris hurries to the rescue and calms the man by employing his crisis-intervention skills. Maria is so impressed with Chris's savoir faire that she seduces him into spending the night with her.

Writer Kouf then sinks to one of his lowest tricks by presenting Chris's nightmare as reality. The viewer is trapped into believing that Montgomery has arrived at Maria's house and finds her and Chris in bed together. As Stick puts a pistol to Maria's head, Chris awakens in a cold sweat. This kind of tawdry manipulation of the viewer does nothing to increase one's respect for the film as a whole, but Kouf is capable of even worse lapses of taste.

After Chris awakens in the bright light of morning and in Maria's arms, he suddenly realizes that he is caught in a major bind: How is he going to leave Maria's house without being identified by Jack and Phil?

Chris has the idea of borrowing a red straw bonnet and a shawl from his lover, and he makes an attempt to escape in disguise. Although Jack and Phil do not recognize Chris, it is not difficult for them to see that a strange man peculiarly dressed in women's clothing is coming out of Maria's front door quite early in the morning. Chris takes off, police cars careen to the scene from several directions, he does battle with a neighbor's dog, and finally takes refuge in a backyard garbage dump, whence he is rescued by Bill.

Meanwhile, Stick has arrived for real in the Seattle area. By now he has been spotted by the police, and Kouf and Badham indulge in several minutes of perfunctory car-chase stunts and gunplay. The climax of this sequence is the flight, shot in slow motion, of Stick's car into a river. The police assume that he has drowned, but the viewer knows better.

Chris has decided to confess to Maria that he is a police officer. Maria feels that she has been made to look foolish, the lovers argue, and Chris leaves Maria's house. When Maria returns to her living room, she is rudely greeted by Stick.

Chris comes back in order to try to patch up things with Maria and abruptly meets his adversary. The detective stalls for time by persuading Montgomery that he too is a former convict. Bill has tried to catch Montgomery unawares, but the killer forces Chris to drive all of them to an oceanside marina where he plans to kill the cops.

Stakeout's showdown materializes in a logging mill where Chris and Stick stalk each other amid menacing buzzsaws and treadmills. The silliness climaxes when, just as Montgomery is positioned to shoot Chris, Maria strikes him with a wooden beam. Chris ends the action by killing Stick.

The last fifteen minutes of *Stakeout* are a worthless recycling of scenes which have been seen countless times in similar films. A fist fight between Chris and Stick on a pilotless boat is an example of utterly perfunctory padding; Kouf, Badham, Dreyfuss, Quinn, and Estevez are literally just going through the motions.

Stakeout is good entertainment only when Dreyfuss, Stowe, and Estevez are allowed to stay in one place and talk to one another. Dreyfuss is comfortably settling into character roles (as he demonstrated in *Tin Men*, 1987; reviewed in this volume), and he is at his best in *Stakeout* as the poor slob whose woman has just left him, taking even the window shades from their apartment. Stowe is talented and pretty, gifted with a gorgeous smile. Estevez adequately serves here as straight man in his odd-couple relationship with Chris.

By retreating into an action-pays-the-rent rut, Kouf gives a lesson in what all too frequently goes wrong with Hollywood films and stifles what would have otherwise stood solidly as an amusing, off-beat romance.

Gordon Walters

Reviews

Films in Review. XXXVIII, November, 1987, p. 543.
Los Angeles Times. August 5, 1987, VI, p. 1.
Macleans. C, August 17, 1987, p. 51.
The New York Times. August 5, 1987, p. C21.
The New Yorker. LXIII, August 24, 1987, p. 80.
Newsweek. CX, August 10, 1987, p. 56.
People Weekly. XXVIII, August 17, 1987, p. 10.
Time. CXXX, August 17, 1987, p. 62.
Variety. CCCXXVIII, August 5, 1987, p. 13.
The Wall Street Journal. August 13, 1987, p. 18.

STREET SMART

Production: Menahem Golan and Yoram Globus; released by Cannon Films
Direction: Jerry Schatzberg
Screenplay: David Freeman
Cinematography: Adam Holender
Editing: Priscilla Nedd
Production design: Dan Leigh
Art direction: Serge Jacques; set direction, Raymond Larose and Katherine Matthewson
Costume design: Jo Ynocenio
Music: Robert Irving III
MPAA rating: R
Running time: 96 minutes

> *Principal characters:*
> Jonathan Fisher................Christopher Reeve
> Fast Black.....................Morgan Freeman
> Punchy............................Kathy Baker
> Alison Parker ....Mimi Rogers
> Ted Avery ....Andre Gregory
> Reggie ....Erik King
> Leonard Pike ....Jay Patterson
> Harriet ....Anna Maria Horsford
> Joel Davis ....Frederick Rolf
> Art Sheffield.................Michael J. Reynolds

In the latter decades of the twentieth century, a variety of factors, including the absence of affordable housing and the deterioration of basic services, have turned the modern American city into an urban wilderness where a permanent underclass coexists uneasily with an anxious and wary group of well-educated professionals. These relatively prosperous people rely on the technological benefits of an advanced industrial society to shield themselves from the realities of survival that must be confronted by a less fortunate but growing minority of citizens. As their comforts and diversions separate them from the people who must scramble and hustle on mean streets, there is, paradoxically, a corresponding increase in their interest in these people. While remaining generally indifferent to the moral implications of this social division, their fascination with what appears to be a rough-hewn energy, dynamic sexuality, and often dazzling style—the fabled power of the primitive—draws them into daring forays into the street realm from which they have generally tried to escape.

Jonathan Fisher (Christopher Reeve), a successful journalist working for a magazine that strongly (and intentionally) resembles *New York* magazine, is a prime example of this phenomenon. As *Street Smart* opens, he is having difficulty finding a project that might interest his editor, Ted Avery (Andre Gregory), but when he proposes a profile of a Times Square pimp, Avery responds with an almost malicious enthusiasm, fully aware that the magazine's subscribers include many upscale readers who are vicariously excited by the wild side of life. Fisher's own inspiration comes from his attraction to the life of the streets, an inclination sparked by a growing malaise that has been developing from the vapid nature of his generally superficial existence. After a few inconclusive visits to sleazy saloons, where he is completely out of his element, a preposterous version of a slumming suburban yuppie, Fisher decides to fabricate a story about an ultra-pimp, Tyrone, an act fully in accordance with his glib cleverness and lack of scruples—traits that probably enabled him to reach his present position. Without concern for or even awareness of journalistic ethics, an attitude representative of a world in which ethical questions have been dismissed as irrelevant and where such evanescent qualities as style and posture seem of paramount importance, Fisher is able to delight Avery and capture the magazine's audience with his creative version of Tyrone's life.

In a parallel but unconnected world, Fast Black (Morgan Freeman), a small-scale pimp, petty gangster, and streetwise hustler, uses a bit too much force to control an obstreperous customer who is bothering one of his whores and accidentally kills the man. As the police develop their case, the magazine article begins to seem to them like a direct connection to the facts behind the man they have charged with the crime. The district attorney then demands to see Fisher's notes. Fisher does not want to admit that he has no corroboration for the story, but he is intrigued by Fast Black, especially since he has become involved with one of Fast Black's girls, a soulful but fiery young woman called Punchy (Kathy Baker). Avery is delighted by the possibility of publicity for the magazine and suggests that Fisher invite Fast Black to a chic soiree. In a situation in which everyone is ready to manipulate everyone else, Fisher finds himself completely unable to control or even influence events when Fast Black, realizing how useful and malleable Fisher is, begins to take advantage of all of his opportunities.

Freeman has been nominated for an Academy Award for Best Supporting Actor, and although Reeve is generally adequate as a weak pretty boy lacking any real self-awareness or depth, both his character and his performance are overwhelmed by Freeman's interpretation of Fast Black. Freeman has the advantage of working with a character who seizes the audience's attention from the first moment he is on the screen, a character whose world of mystery and danger contrasts so heavily with the predictable social milieu of Fisher and his acquaintances. Freeman goes beyond the unpredictability and menace, however, to make Fast Black the only character in the film with a sense of range and dimension. In addition to his aura of lurking violence, he has a kind of daunting charm that he uses like another weapon. Those acquainted with Fast Black—Fisher, Avery, the guests at the dinner party, the women he knows, his henchmen—all appear to be captivated by him and to enjoy the sense of life at a higher intensity. When he shows Fisher his world—the life of the street, the playground, and the hangout— he cannot resist strutting, and his pride in his dingy realm humanizes him, at least until the fundamental viciousness of his nature is fully revealed.

The power projected by Fast Black, instead of launching him as an interesting antagonist for Fisher, tends to dominate the journalist. Fisher's vagueness makes him not only weaker than Fast Black but also less important. When he finally becomes aware of the moral compromises of his life, he does not have the depth to do anything about them. If *Street Smart* were Fast Black's story, this inability to effect change would not matter, but Fisher's adventures form the narrative consciousness that the audience must use as a guide. Fast Black is always seen from the outside, while Fisher's character is sometimes probed for motive and impulse. Fast Black is only on the screen when he is involved in a situation that affects Fisher, while Fisher has a life separate from Fast Black. The camera is positioned to present Fisher's view of the world, and Fast Black is an intruder in his space, entering the frame from odd angles around Fisher, who tends to occupy the center. Reeve effectively indicates stress by compressing this space and by diminishing his stature so that as Fisher he seems smaller than Fast Black (although Freeman is actually smaller in size), but this strategy tends to decrease even further Fisher's ability to resist Fast Black. To balance his physical inferiority, Fisher needs the capacity to learn from experience and must have access to a moral dimension that makes ethical considerations important. Fast Black is consumed by the ethic of the self, while Fisher should be increasingly troubled by the ethical dilemma that he has created for himself. This aspect of Fisher's life never really emerges.

The shallowness of Fisher's character is compounded by the presentation of his world: The bland, plastic decor of his home is an appropriate contrast to the dark, shadowy domain where Fast Black lives, but the pattern of Fisher's life is so vapid that it is hard to establish a sense of gravity or concern for the decisions he makes. He is surrounded by inconsequential people who include Alison Parker (Mimi Rogers), the woman who shares his living space, his coworkers, and casual friends. Fisher's indifference to Parker and his vague disgust for her quivering uncertainty subverts his show of concern for her when Fast Black's henchman, Reggie (Erik King), slashes Parker as a warning. Fisher is also supposed to be genuinely troubled when the district attorney and Avery want to use him for their own purposes, but there is no sense of a man struggling with problems that have only unsatisfactory solutions. The ethical issues involving journalism, opportunism, commitment, and integrity are blurred as the film fails to examine the issues it raises. Instead, it moves toward an abrupt resolution in terms of the violent conflict between Fisher and Fast Black.

The scheme that Fisher devises—a deception that forces Reggie to turn against Fast Black—is unconvincing, and his tactics which should show that he has become street smart, are merely an illustration of his continued awkwardness and ineptitude in the streets. The burst of violence that finishes Fast Black is dramatic but unlikely, and the irony of Fisher's triumph over Fast Black by using one of the pimp's own methods is lost because Fisher is still the same smirking know-it-all that he was at the film's beginning. Jerry Schatzberg's direction displays a good feel for the rhythms of the city, although nothing like the depth of Martin Scorsese's depictions in *Mean Streets* (1973) and *After Hours* (1985). Strong performances from the cast include a breezy and appealing one by Baker as Fisher's real erotic interest and a striking one from Gregory, who is perfectly cast as the suave, polished editor who has an offhand disregard for the consequences of his actions— a fine symbol for the triumph of surface over substance.

The angle of vision is that of an almost indifferent outsider, but lacks the mantle of wisdom which might justify such a position. The result is to make the film nondescript rather than above or beyond it all. The most vital images are of Fast Black, vibrant in his street world. When these are gone, nothing of real interest remains.

Leon Lewis

Reviews
Films in Review. XXXVIII, May, 1987, p. 298.
Glamour. LXXXV, April, 1987, p. 243.
Los Angeles Times. March 20, 1987, VI, p. 19.
Macleans. C, April 20, 1987, p. 54.
The New York Times. March 27, 1987, p. C8.
The New Yorker. LXIII, April 20, 1987, p. 82.
People Weekly. XXVII, March 30, 1987, p. 12.
Texas Monthly. XV, May, 1987, p. 156.
Variety. CCCXXVI, March 4, 1987, p. 18.
The Wall Street Journal. March 26, 1987, p. 34.

SUSPECT

Production: Daniel A. Sherkow; released by Tri-Star Pictures
Direction: Peter Yates
Screenplay: Eric Roth
Cinematography: Billy Williams
Editing: Ray Lovejoy
Production design: Stuart Wurtzel
Art direction: Steve Sardanis; set decoration, Arthur Jeph Parker
Special effects: Joe Ramsey
Makeup: Richard Dean
Costume design: Rita Ryack
Sound: Don Sharpe
Music direction: Eric Tomlinson
Music: Michael Kamen
MPAA rating: R
Running time: 120 minutes

> *Principal characters:*
> Kathleen Riley............................Cher
> Eddie Sanger......................Dennis Quaid
> Carl Wayne Anderson................Liam Neeson
> Judge Matthew Helms ....John Mahoney
> Charlie Stella......................Joe Mantegna
> Paul Gray ....Philip Bosco
> Grace Comisky ....E. Katherine Kerr
> Morty Rosenthal ....Fred Melamed
> Marilyn ....Lisbeth Bartlett

Peter Yates has directed films that rank with the best of the decade. Following his hit *Breaking Away* (1979), he directed the critical successes *The Dresser* (1983) and *Eleni* (1985). Though Yates is British (born in Ewshott, Surrey, a graduate of the Royal Academy of Dramatic Art), *Breaking Away*, set in Bloomington, Indiana, was about as authentic a piece of Americana as has ever been produced on film. *The Dresser*, arguably his masterpiece, was a model adaptation of Ronald Harwood's English play about an actor trying to hold body and soul together for one last performance of William Shakespeare's *King Lear* during World War II, when Great Britain was being bombed by the Germans. *The Dresser* showcased the talents of Albert Finney and Tom Courtenay, both of whom earned Oscar nominations for Best Actor of 1984. In 1987, Yates was not so fortunate with *Suspect*, which might have had an outside chance for an Academy Award nomination if its star, Cher, had not eclipsed her performance with another, later release, *Moonstruck* (1987; reviewed in this volume), directed by Norman Jewison.

Clearly, 1987 was a banner year for Cher. She was much subordinated to her male lead in *The Witches of Eastwick* (1987; reviewed in this volume), which took John Updike's novel and transformed it into a showcase for Jack Nicholson, but that summer release was soon followed by *Suspect* and *Moonstruck* in the fall. While both of these were genre pictures, putting them at a disadvantage in the Academy Award competition, the romantic comedy *Moonstruck* was so strong that it managed to overshadow *Suspect* and earn a nomination for Best Picture.

Suspect, a psychotic thriller, was also overshadowed by the tremendously popular *Fatal Attraction* (1987; reviewed in this volume). *Suspect* is one of several films made during 1987 that focuses on anxiety-ridden career women (though not to the extreme of *Fatal Attraction*), police work, detection, and corruption in the criminal justice system. *The Big Easy* (1987; reviewed in this volume), set in New Orleans, is similar in this regard and also stars Dennis Quaid, who plays Cher's romantic lead in *Suspect*. As one of the year's several thrillers, *Suspect* competed with the stylish *Someone to Watch over Me* (1987) and with the popular *Stakeout* (1987; reviewed in this volume). Like *No Way Out* (1987; reviewed in this volume), *Suspect* contains an unexpected plot reversal.

Yet *Suspect* is, foremost, a courtroom drama—and the best of its kind for the year. It is, moreover, a film that addresses social injustice while telling its tale of romance, murder, and political intrigue. Perhaps the script was too ambitious in what it attempted to cover. Reviewers in New York and Washington were critical of the screenplay. Janet Maslin of *The New York Times*, for example, objected to its "obvious and sloppy plotting."

There was no such accord, however, with regard to Cher's performance. Hal Hinson of *The Washington Post* objected to her "dogged, joyless performance," while Maslin found her "smart, tough, no-nonsense performance" to be "crisply compelling." Writing in *The New Yorker* Pauline Kael objected to "the lamebrained job she does in court," adding "she'd be lost if one of the jurors—a handsome, semi-cynical young lobbyist who knows his way around the bureaucracy—didn't do the detective work that helps her out." She went on to protest the logic of having a woman lawyer at the center of the film who ultimately needs a man to protect her and do her thinking for her. Like *Fatal Attraction*, *Suspect* does not present a very favorable image of female competence in the working world.

As lobbyist Eddie Sanger, Dennis Quaid gives a reasonably convincing portrayal of a cynical Washingtonian. *The Washington Post* revealed that Quaid was coached by Washington lawyer-lobbyist Steven Martindale. ("I taught him how to be superficial," Martindale said.) Quaid also interviewed a former senator, Gaylord Nelson, to learn more about the typical behavior of Washington pundits. Dennis Quaid seems perfectly at ease with his role.

Suspect shows two very different aspects of life in Washington, D.C., the world of the political and the powerful, on the one hand, and the world of the street people, the destitute and the derelict, on the other. The script, by Eric Roth, focuses on a murder trial. A Justice Department secretary who was carrying a considerable sum of money has been found murdered along the banks of the Potomac River. This murder is also linked to the suicide of a Supreme Court justice.

The state's evidence points to a deaf-mute Vietnam veteran (Liam Neeson) whose trauma and misfortune have forced him to lead the life of a derelict and whom the police find huddled under the Whiteburst Freeway with the dead secretary's purse. A parking lot attendant near the Key Bridge remembers finding the derelict in the victim's car the night she died. It looks like an open-and-shut case, complicated by the fact that the defendant is uncooperative, unable to communicate effectively, and possibly crazy.

Cher plays public defender Kathleen Riley. A legal workaholic who has concluded that life may be passing her by, she needs a vacation; she wants a man and eventually a child before it is too late. Frustrated and unfulfilled, she is assigned this apparently unwinnable case. When she realizes that her surly, unmanageable client is a pathetic deaf-mute who claims to be innocent, she gets interested in the case. She has no staff to help her build her case and no supporting evidence. The prosecuting attorney, Charlie Stella (Joe Mantegna), is hostile, and the judge (John Mahoney) wants the case quickly settled and off his docket.

With the help of lobbyist Eddie Sanger, who ends up on the jury, Kathleen begins to discover evidence that may be helpful to her client. The problem is that legal ethics forbid her from meeting with the juror, and the strict judge suspects that something is amiss. When he cannot prove any ethical wrongdoing (though he notices them both at the Library of Congress, suggested by a nicely edited montage), he sequesters the jury. Alert viewers may conclude that the judge may have something more than a purely professional interest in the case. Kathleen, meanwhile, is dangerously close to solving the mystery, and her life is therefore in danger. The murderer has killed twice already and is closely following her progress. Eddie, now her lover, breaks away from his jury duty to assist in a last-minute rescue. The plot line is intentionally misleading and results in a surprising reversal.

Despite some high praise for Cher's work, the lifeless nature of her character in *Suspect* simply could not showcase her talents as well as the thirty-seven-year-old widow she played in *Moonstruck*, whose dry sense of humor was better shaped to the star's natural inclinations. Arguably, Kathleen Riley might have been more of a challenge for Cher to play, but when interviewed by *Film Comment* (February, 1988), she seemed curiously indifferent to her role in *Suspect*.

Still, her 1987 films did much to further Cher's acting career. Besides the major interview just mentioned in *Film Comment* (with Harlan Jacobson), she was profiled by Bruce Weber for *The New York Times Magazine* (October 18, 1987) and by Stephanie Mansfield for *The Washington Post* (October 26, 1987). In mid-December of the previous year, J. Randy Taraborrelli had published his book *Cher: A Biography*, which focused on her earlier life and career, first as Cherilyn Sarkisian of El Centro, California, and then as Sonny Bono's deadpan sidekick, a kind of hippie bimbo who could harmonize. Taraborrelli appropriately covers her early disastrous flirtation with motion pictures under Sonny's tutelage, her career as a Las Vegas superstar, and her serious film acting career through *Mask* (1985). By that time she had already proved herself as an actress by earning an Academy Award nomination as Best Supporting Actress in *Silkwood* (1983), under the direction of Mike Nichols. Thus, her performance in *Suspect* hardly constitutes a career landmark.

Despite the manipulation and flaws of character development, the plot of *Suspect* generally makes sense (although one wonders how an audience of lawyers might react to Kathleen Riley's grandstanding in court) and manages to contrive a tense finale. *Suspect* was certainly one of the year's best thrillers. *Fatal Attraction* was, however, much more successful, both with the audience and with the Academy of Motion Picture Arts and Sciences.

James M. Welsh

Reviews
Films in Review. XXXIX, February, 1988, p. 98.
Los Angeles Times. October 22, 1987, VI, p. 1.
Macleans. C, November 16, 1987, p. 71.
New York. XX, November 2, 1987, p. 94.
The New York Times. October 23, 1987, p. C14.
The New Yorker. LXIII, November 16, 1987, p. 145.
Newsweek. CX, October 26, 1987, p. 86.
People Weekly. XXVIII, November 9, 1987, p. 14.
Variety. CCXXVIII, October 21, 1987, p. 15.
The Wall Street Journal. October 22, 1987, p. 36.
The Washington Post. October 23, p. B1.

SWIMMING TO CAMBODIA

Production: R. A. Shafransky; released by Cinecom
Direction: Jonathan Demme
Screenplay: Spalding Gray
Cinematography: John Bailey
Editing: Carol Littleton
Art direction: Sandy McLeod
Music: Laurie Anderson
MPAA rating: no listing
Running time: 87 minutes

Principal character:
Spalding Gray............................Himself

With *Swimming to Cambodia*, director Jonathan Demme and performer Spalding Gray have accomplished what might have been thought impossible: They have made a thoroughly engaging cinematic event out of one man (Gray) sitting at a desk and talking to the camera. Gray uses his experience of a minor acting role in *The Killing Fields* (1984) as a jumping-off point to explore the political climate that preceded the United States' involvement with the Cambodian conflict, the voluptuousness and threat of Thailand, and the hedonistic pleasures that Westerners find within its borders. He also examines his own ambivalence toward politics, his increasing awareness of how international conflicts affect all the world's inhabitants, the collision of his Waspish Manhattan sensibility with mystical Eastern philosophies, and the ways in which the realities and illusions of filmmaking reflect and distort those of war. Demme's camera never deviates from his subject, but by utilizing subtle lighting, editing, and sound effects, he manages to delve into the haunting, sharply amusing, and altogether mesmerizing properties of Gray's storytelling technique.

Swimming to Cambodia has no direct precedents. One might think of it as a concert film such as *Stop Making Sense* (1984), also directed by Demme and steeped in the Manhattan-based performance-art tradition. *Stop Making Sense*, however, though a state-of-the-art example of its genre and with stimulating rock music as its core, lost most of the Talking Heads' distinctive mixed-media visuals in the confusion of trying to cover so much performing activity. *Richard Pryor Live in Concert* (1979) and *Richard Pryor Live on the Sunset Strip* (1982) were one-man shows like *Swimming to Cambodia*, but they essentially functioned as documentaries of the comic talents of Pryor, who used a complete catalog of full-body gestures in his performing style. *Swimming to Cambodia* takes a conceptual approach to its star's performance, and Gray confines his means of expression to hand gestures, facial expressions, and vocal intonations (he remains seated the entire time). Robert Altman's *Secret Honor* (1985), though a one-man show, was essentially a play, carefully scripted to explore the disintegrating mind of Richard Nixon (played by Philip Baker Hall) as he attempted to justify his Watergate activities hours before resigning as President of the United States. Gray, though retaining the basic structure of his monologue, speaks extemporaneously and allows the viewer to experience events through the ever-changing first-person perspective of Gray himself. Louis Malle's *My Dinner with André* (1981), primarily a discussion of ideas, is perhaps closest in spirit to *Swimming to Cambodia* but is stylistically dry. (One would imagine a conversation between two people to be more potentially cinematic than a monologue.)

Swimming to Cambodia begins simply enough: Spalding Gray walks down the streets of SoHo, arrives at The Performing Garage wearing jeans and a plaid shirt, and takes his seat at a simple wooden desk which contains only a microphone, a tall glass of water from which he occasionally sips, and the Ronald McDonald notebook from which he begins to read. "Saturday, June 18th, 1983. Waheen, Gulf of Siam, Thailand." Gray sets the tone of the piece by telling a rather incidental, descriptive anecdote about a group of the film's crew sitting around the hotel pool on their first day off in a long time, being served Kloster beer by the smiling, scrambling Thai waiters (the Thais described as "the nicest people money can buy"). This introduction allows the audience to become accustomed to the singular and potentially alienating qualities of Gray's monologue format while, at the same time, Gray sets an image of the mostly British film crew as pleasure-seeking colonialists who are enjoying themselves in a barbed wire enclosed hotel that becomes an oasis for hedonists, surrounded by prowling bandits and rabid dogs, and is analogous to a "pleasure prison."

Gray then tells of being invited to a party at the Gulf of Siam by Ivan (Devil in My Ear) Strasberg, the South African head of the second camera unit. Ivan brings a Thai stick, a particularly strong form of marijuana, which brings on vivid hallucinations of anxiety for Gray, made real for the viewer through the magical command of Demme's imaginative technique. The sound track, composed by Laurie Anderson, is filled with the slow hiss of marijuana tokes which degenerate into grating, grinding metallic noises. The lighting flashes slowly, as if a whirring ceiling fan were intermittently blocking out overhead light, while Gray rapidly recedes and then jumps forward in the frame. Renee Shafransky, Gray's girlfriend (and producer of *Swimming to Cambodia*), thinks that he is playfully building sand castles while, in fact, he is experiencing a very bad effect of the drug, the first example of many in which Gray uses the recurring motif of illusion versus reality. That occurs, Gray explains, the night before shooting his big scene in *The Killing Fields*. Gray relates how he came to be cast in *The Killing*

Fields and how director Roland Joffe feverishly described to him the history of Cambodia and the political climate that led to America's involvement in the region. Joffe had described Cambodians as having been such a beautiful, calm people that they "lost touch with evil," thereby making themselves vulnerable to hostile invaders.

Gray describes the convergence of elements that resulted in revolution in Cambodia: the development of the deranged Khmer Rouge forces in the mountains and jungles of Cambodia, trained to fight by the Viet Cong but led by the half-insane Pol Pot, who was determined to destroy the urban city dweller (seen by him as the root of all evil). He recalls that the Kent State tragedy grew out of a demonstration against the specific invasion of Cambodia by United States troops. Gray says:

> So five years of bombing, a diet of bark, bugs, lizards, and leaves up in the Cambodian jungles, an education in the Paris environs in strict Maoist doctrine with a touch of Rousseau, and other things that we will probably never know about in our lifetime including, perhaps, an invisible cloud of evil that circles the Earth and lands at random in places like Iran, Beirut, Germany, Cambodia, [and] America, set the Khmer Rouge up to carry out the worst auto-homeo-genocide in modern history. . . . Whenever I travel, if I can take the time, I travel by train."

Gray tells stories and anecdotes that seem randomly drawn but overlap each other, doubling back on themselves and echoing throughout the film. Explanations of history segue into stories of filming *The Killing Fields*, which become tales of his upbringing (he was reared in upper-middle-class Rhode Island, then moved to Manhattan because he wanted to live on an island off the coast of America, since he found the very idea of America too overwhelming) metamorphosing into arguments with his girlfriend and upstairs New York neighbors. Gray is the most popular high school history teacher, the most neurotic New York artist/intellectual, and one's favorite foulmouthed drinking companion. As his stories collide and converge, his psyche seems to have exploded in much the same fragmented way as the war itself.

Demme, along with cinematographer John Bailey, editor Carol Littleton, and composer Laurie Anderson, creates a style that does much more than preserve Gray's monologue: It enhances and empowers his oratorical skills. In person, Gray can ramble; his words float away, and one's mind begins to wander. On film, the landscape of his face is so interesting and expressive that his words gain intensity. Demme is able to capture the spontaneity of Gray's creativity with the compactness of hindsight. With his technicians, Demme casts shadows and sets moods. For example, Gray tells of an encounter he had with a racist, sexist, anti-Soviet naval officer and sociopath whom he met on a train. The man divulges to Gray that he is stationed in Philadelphia, where he sits chained in a waterproof chamber next to a green button, high on "blue flake cocaine," eagerly waiting to press the button that will launch missiles aimed at the Russians. The sequence is filmed in shot-countershot, with Gray playing the frenzied, sadistic officer as well as his own incredulous self. The result is both amusing and terrifying. Demme's artistry nudges the viewer and enables him to visualize Gray's stories as they are described. *Swimming to Cambodia* is, in every nuance of the word, a sensual experience.

The last portion of the film deals primarily with Gray's experience shooting *The Killing Fields* on location in Bangkok, which is standing in for Phnom Penh. He describes the Bangkok sex shows as carnivals of absurd and outrageous sexual behavior, with women employing everything from Coke bottles to Ping-Pong balls. He also conveys the bitter irony of actors, clinging desperately to their book-learned Method acting techniques, trying to recall emotional memories amid staged scenes of carnage while the reality of human suffering is prevalent everywhere. He stays in Thailand after his scenes are finished shooting because he has not yet experienced a Perfect Moment, which he thinks is necessary when traveling in order to provide a sense of closure, a cue that it is time to move on. For Gray, this moment arrives when he is swimming in the Indian Ocean and becomes caught in a particularly powerful riptide: Closer to death than he may ever have been in his life, he experiences this sense of perfection. Gray, who has likened the experience of trying to comprehend the horrifying recent history of Cambodia to a task equal to swimming to Cambodia, at last finds understanding. His Perfect Moment, which forms a perfect metaphor for the attraction of war to generation after generation, comes in his perception that life is most enhanced when confronted with death. As he observes, however, "Who needs metaphors for hell when this happened here on this earth?"

Jeffrey Fenner

Reviews
Los Angeles Times. April 3, 1987, VI, p. 1.
Macleans. C, April 27, 1987, p. 62.
The Nation. CCXLIV, April 18, 1987, p. 518.
The New Republic. CXCVI, March 23, 1987, p. 24.
New Statesman. CXIV, September 4, 1987, p. 22.
The New York Times. March 22, 1987, II, p. 19.
The New Yorker. LXIII, April 6, 1987, p. 84.
Newsweek. CIX, April 6, 1987, p. 64.
Time. CXXIX, April 27, 1987, p. 79.
Variety. CCCXXVI, March 11, 1987, p. 123.

TAMPOPO

Origin: Japan
Released: 1986
Released in U.S.: 1987
Production: Juzo Itami, Yasushi Tamaoki, and Seigo Hosogoe; released by
  New Yorker Films
Direction: Juzo Itami
Screenplay: Juzo Itami
Cinematography: Masaki Tamura
Editing: Akira Suzuki
Music: Kunihiko Murai
MPAA rating: no listing
Running time: 114 minutes

> *Principal characters:*
> Goro........................Tsutomu Yamazaki
> Tampopo ....Nobuko Miyamoto
> Man in the white suit................Koji Yakusho
> His mistress......................Fukumi Kuroda
> Gun ....Ken Watanabe
> Pisken..........................Rikiya Yasuoka
> Shohei ....Kinzo Sakura
> Tabo ....Mampei Ikeuchi
> Master of ramen-making ....Yoshi Kato
> Rich old man.......................Shuji Otaki

Tampopo is as much a satirical essay as it is a narrative, for interspersed
with episodes of the story proper, and interconnecting with it in odd, offhand and metaphorical ways, are a number of brief self-contained sketches.
Of these, several—one of which opens the film—feature the man in the
white suit (Koji Yakusho) and his moll (Fukumi Kuroda).

The main plot of the film centers on the young widow Tampopo (Nobuko
Miyamoto) and her rise to top noodle-cookdom. One stormy night in
the wastelands of urban Tokyo, a lean, solemn-faced truck driver, Goro
(Tsutomu Yamazaki, who resembles Clint Eastwood in his more taciturn
moments) stops for a rest at Tampopo's noodle shop. The gentle-faced
widow (her name means "dandelion"), her son, and her worthy ambition
to serve the best noodles in Tokyo take his fancy, but the food does not. A
latter-day Shane, Goro undertakes the task of initiating her into the mysteries and ritual of correct ramen making and noodle making. En route, his
affection for her will deepen (he will defeat a local rival, and she, in return,
will proffer clean underwear from her dead husband's belongings), but the

film will not betray the conventions of the Western, and cowboy-hatted Goro (his truck sports horns) will drive off alone onto the freeway.

Many of the film's episodes are excuses for comic and grotesque sketches. Goro and Tampopo seek advice from those highest and lowest on the social ladder—noodles prove great social equalizers. They receive advice from street people, and earn the devoted help of a rich man (Shuji Otaki) and his master cook (Yoshi Kato) after they save the rich man's life by using a vacuum cleaner to empty his stomach after a binge. Essential to Tampopo's progress is the wise old master, the *sensei*, initiate in the noodle mystique, who will teach her the process from the making of the dough to the clarifying of the ramen, and the serving of bowls so artfully arranged that they deserve the comparison to Jackson Pollock paintings made early in the film.

Everything in Japan has its ritual aspect: tea drinking, suicide, flower arranging, and the serious business of eating. The wise old man instructs Goro's sidekick in the requisite manner of approaching a bowl of noodles: regarding the slivers of pork on top "affectionately" while slurping the noodles (noise is obligatory) that have been "activated" by the ramen. The vocabulary applied to noodle making is no less ludicrously high-brow; unlikely characters converse in the terms of gourmet food magazines. Noodles that fall short of supreme excellence are nevertheless "sincere." As Tampopo continues her slow and frustrating struggle upward, she achieves noodles that are at last "beginning to have substance" but that, alas, still "lack depth" (for noodles are "synergetic things"). Yet, despite all obstacles, the dream is finally fulfilled: She becomes not only the best but the fastest and most chic noodle maker in Tokyo. She is queen of a noodle parlor that is distinctly up-market, a middle-class haven created by the unlikeliest fellowship, including the local contractor with whom Goro fought earlier (who has real flair when it comes to ambience).

Casually interwoven in this frothy story are vignettes that deepen the satire on the middle classes, exploring how man's innate obsession with nurture has become crazily distorted. The film is always ready to digress, sometimes needing only the excuse of a young executive hurrying to an appointment. (In this scene, the camera leaves Goro and follows the businessman.) The nervous executive is late for an important lunch. Lateness causes him to be clumsy; he drops things, his ears burn, and his prospects of a good impression dwindle. At the restaurant the menus are distributed, but they are printed entirely in French. (Some stay upside down.) The biggest of the corporate fat cats orders a safe bet: sole, salad, and a Heineken beer. One by one, each bigwig orders the same meager fare. In his element at last, the young man thinks to retrieve his standing and inquires after the chef, orders the house specialities, chooses exactly the right wine, and is complimented by the waiter on his savoir faire. He looks around for approval at five enraged, embarrassed, cartoon-red faces. Meanwhile, elsewhere in the plush hotel restaurant, a group of yuppie wives are attending a class in how to eat Italian spaghetti silently and delicately. The greedy old Adam inside is too much for them, however, and by the meal's end even the instructor is slurping, smacking, gurgling, and holding the bowl to her lips with both hands.

Elsewhere in the hotel, a gangster in a white suit of impeccable cut engages in an amorous repast with his mistress that makes the eating scene in *Tom Jones* (1963) look like a vicarage tea party. He lingers over comestibles cupped in the hollow of her naked belly. They bring themselves to a passionate climax by passing a raw egg yolk from mouth to mouth. This scene is not the film's first sight of this glamorous and greedy couple. The opening shot is of a motion-picture theater seen from the perspective of the screen. The couple arrives, while underlings prepare a table for an exquisite picnic with champagne. They take their seats in the empty front row and then notice "us," the audience. The man in the white suit steps forward: "Oh, so you're watching a movie, too?" he asks. *Tampopo*'s send-up of its filmic origins continues throughout, with the parody Western plot of the main story, overblown playing of romantic scenes, fanciful resorting to transitional tricks such as irising in and out and mockery of the gangster genre in the last scene in which the glamorous couple appear. The man in the white suit is gunned down by rivals near an adventure playground (another whimsically inappropriate suburban setting); bright red blood (tomato sauce?) stains his pristine suit. As he dies, he babbles not of the mob, love, or eternity, but of food—pork stuffed with yams, meticulously prepared. The obsession endures unto death.

Unpretentious, free-form, capricious, burlesque, outrageous, earthy, and unembarrassed, *Tampopo* is played for all it is worth by a competent cast. Most impressive is Itami's wife, Miyamoto, as Tampopo, touching in her quiet, ordinary and solitary womanhood in what is largely a male-dominated fictional (and real) Japanese world. While the film may not be in the same class with Marco Ferreri's classic sex-and-food comedy *La Grande Bouffe* (1972), in which gourmets becomes gourmands and try to eat themselves to death, it shares that film's determination to deflate middle-class pretensions and is quirkily thoughtful to a degree that puts most American comedies to shame. That is a hallmark of Itami's films. His three sharp studies of modern Japanese customs have made him one of that country's most popular directors. Unusual among Japanese producers and directors, Itami has been able to secure independent financing for his films. (*Tampopo* cost a mere $1.6 million.) In his *Oshoshiki* (1984; *The Funeral*, reviewed in this volume), another Japanese sacred cow is comically dissected: Mourners watch videotapes for tips on correct funereal behavior. No less irreverent is *Marusa no Onna* (1987; *A Taxing Woman*), his follow-up to *Tampopo*, a satire on another Japanese passion, tax evasion. The three films are fine examples of a new vein of eccentric humor in Japanese cinema. They explode or exaggerate traditional images of the Japanese as convention-bound workaholics: Itami's Japanese are lustful, obsessive, tax-fiddling epicures.

Itami came late to directing, shooting *Tampopo* in his early fifties. His many other careers have included those of actor, boxer, band organizer, magazine editor, translator (from English), essayist, and talk-show host (one particularly suspects traces of the last two in this free-form film). Another possible influence is his father, a well-known director of samurai films who died when Itami was twelve. As in the Western, in the samurai film a lone-wolf law-bringer must help a beleaguered community survive, much as Goro helps Tampopo and her son before heading for the wide-open space of the freeway again. It therefore seems appropriate that the Western genre provides the framework of *Tampopo*: It both mirrors the concerns and structures of Japan's own samurai genre and is the most American of genres. One of the subtexts of *Tampopo* is the tension in modern-day Japan between what has survived of traditional prewar Japan and the incursions of American influence. This polemic is a subtext Itami knows how to read well, since his own generation lived it.

Joss Marsh

Reviews
Commonweal. CXIV, August 14, 1987, p. 458.
Los Angeles Times. June 24, 1987, VI, p. 1.
Macleans. C, August 31, 1987, p. 46.
The New Republic. CXCVI, June 1, 1987, p. 26.
The New York Times. March 26, 1987, p. C19.
The New York Times. May 22, 1987, III, p. 18.
The New York Times. May 24, 1987, II, p. 1.
The New Yorker. LXIII, June 1, 1986, p. 101.
Newsweek. CIX, June 15, 1987, p. 71.
Time. CXXX, August 3, 1987, p. 65.
Variety. CCCXXIV, September 3, 1986, p. 20.
The Wall Street Journal. May 28, 1987, p. 28.

THREE MEN AND A BABY

Production: Ted Field and Robert W. Cort; released by Touchstone Pictures
Direction: Leonard Nimoy
Screenplay: James Orr and Jim Cruickshank; based on the film *Trois Hommes et un couffin*, by Coline Serreau
Cinematography: Adam Greenberg
Editing: Michael Stevenson
Production design: Peter Larkin
Art direction: Dan Yarhi; set decoration, Hilton Rosemarin
Music: Marvin Hamlisch
MPAA rating: PG
Running time: 101 minutes

> *Principal characters:*
> Peter Mitchell . . . . Tom Selleck
> Michael Kellam . . . . Steve Guttenberg
> Jack Holden. . . . . Ted Danson
> Sylvia. . . . . Nancy Travis
> Rebecca . . . . Margaret Colin
> Mary . . . . Lisa Blair/Michelle Blair
> Detective Melkowitz . . . . Philip Bosco

Three Men and a Baby marks the convergence of two powerful trends in the American cinema of the 1980's. The first of these is the emergence of a subgenre that might be called the "baby film." The "baby film" firmly anchors itself to a conspicuous sociological circumstance: In 1987 an entire generation of baby-boomers finally settled into their own parenting responsibilities. This subgenre of Hollywood films seems especially drawn to examining how child rearing affects the freedom of choice presented by modern life. Not suprisingly, such films as *Raising Arizona, Baby Boom* (both released in 1987 and reviewed in this volume) and *She's Having a Baby* (1988) conclude that "having it all" is no easy matter, that compromises are difficult but essential given the joyous chaos of child rearing. The second trend evident in *Three Men and a Baby* is the recent rash of Hollywood adaptations of French comedy hits for American audiences. Here the progenitor is Coline Serreau's *Trois Hommes et un couffine* (1985), which received a nomination for Best Foreign Film Oscar. In *Three Men and a Baby*, the two trends combine to profitable effect: Within two months after the film was released, it had earned more than $100 million in box-office receipts.

The story turns on the life-style of three roommates: Peter Mitchell (Tom Selleck), an architect; Michael Kellam (Steve Guttenberg), a cartoonist; and Jack Holden (Ted Danson), a globe-trotting actor. It is immediately clear that the three protagonists are hedonistic career bachelors, yet each quickly reveals a distinct personality: Peter, the oldest, is a curmudgeon who treasures his carefully structured sense of order and is strongly proprietary of the trio's apartment, which he designed. Michael is the youngest, a sensitive, childlike fantasist. Jack is confused and insecure. The filmmakers underscore the kinetic, driven nature of the lives of the trio by unnaturally speeding up the opening party scene through camera undercranking. Amid the energetic festivities, a friend of Jack asks him to care for a package that he will have delivered the next day. Distracted, Jack agrees.

The next day, Peter opens the door to find a baby on his doorstep, apparently the "package" that Jack (who has left for Turkey on a shoot) has told him that he can expect to be delivered. The accompanying note to Jack from Sylvia, the mother, who identifies the infant as Mary (played by twins Lisa and Michelle Blair) and the father as Jack.

The film's next twenty minutes are certainly its most compelling and entertaining as Peter and Michael try to placate the crying child. Michael struggles with diapering, Peter wanders through the baby section of the local grocery store, confused, and Mary urinates on the trio's designer couch. What makes this sequence especially effective are the actors' ingenuous reactions to the baby's "performance." Unlike many films that feature infants, this one does not resort to trick editing and looped-in sound to "cheat" the child's performance. As a result, the scenes with Mary have a near-improvisational impact and an honesty rarely seen in films.

Shortly after Mary's appearance, a small package arrives—the real package that Jack promised to look after. Michael and Peter, busy with baby, toss it aside without bothering to ascertain its contents as their normal life gives way to chaos. Neither the landlady nor Peter's girlfriend Rebecca (Margaret Colin) is willing to help: Two women refuse to undertake mothering responsibilities; two men have, in effect, become homemakers.

Help seems to arrive when two strangers arrive at the door for the package. Relieved, Michael and Peter hand over Mary. The strangers, confused, nevertheless accept the child. When, a few moments after they have left, Peter finds the smaller package hidden in the folds of a sofa, he and Michael realize their mistake; tripping on the stairs as he races to retrieve Mary, Michael drops the "real" package, which opens to reveal drugs. The two drug dealers are putting the baby in the trunk of their car when a policeman approaches; the dealers escape, leaving Michael with Mary, drugs, and an inquisitive policeman who is soon joined by Detective Melkowitz (Philip Bosco).

Peter and Michael manage to extricate themselves from the situation, but not for long. While they are with the police, the dealers return, ransack the apartment, and leave a note threatening to harm the child if the drugs are not handed over. Jack finally returns from Turkey; he explains that he had no idea what was in the package he agreed to accept. The three men then concoct and execute an implausible plan: They meet the drug dealers at a construction site, maroon them in an elevator, and stage their arrest.

Writers James Orr and Jim Cruickshank have engineered a three-act structure for *Three Men and a Baby*, each with a different tone: the first and most effective establishes the fish-out-of-water premise; the second is a chase; the third and resolving act begins with Jack's attempt to 'be a responsible parent: "I'm an actor," he says, "I can do a father." Yet he cannot do the parenting alone. The full (though unorthodox) family is needed to care for the child. In the process, each character grows: Peter becomes possessive and protective of Mary; Jack ceases to be the philandering, absent father; Michael rechannels his childishness into responsible caring. A thoroughly charming montage sequence conveys this newfound sensitivity, as does Peter's interaction with a professional nanny whom he judges insensitive to Mary's needs.

The bachelor family tableau is shattered with the return of Sylvia (Nancy Travis), Mary's mother, who has decided to take the child with her to England. Another montage conveys the sadness into which Mary's absence has plunged Jack, Peter, and Michael. They chase Sylvia and Mary to the airport, but it is apparently too late. A few hours later, however, Sylvia returns to the bachelors' apartment. "I have to work," she explains,"but I know that I can't do that alone *and* look after Mary." The three offer to make a home for Sylvia and Mary in their apartment.

This resolution resembles a sitcom, unlike Serreau's original film, which shows Sylvia asleep in the bachelor apartment, sucking her thumb, as Mary toddles in. The American reinterpretation of this ambiguous and thought-provoking ending is clearly geared to the box office. Unfortunately, in diluting the more controversial approach of the French original (in characterization, approach to the drug subplot, and cinematography as well as resolution), the remake loses a theme which made the original both poignant and provocative: Today's society is unprepared to address the needs of its young.

Adam Greenberg's cinematography is correct though uninventive; Marvin Hamlisch's music buttresses the film in a workmanlike manner (the French version is virtually devoid of music); Michael Stevenson's editing is nimble yet unobtrusive. Under Nimoy's direction, however, the trio of Selleck, Guttenberg, and Danson meshes surprisingly well. For Selleck, especially, *Three Men and a Baby* is the breakthrough film that proves his ability to move beyond his well-known "Magnum, P.I." television *persona*.

Marc Mancini

Reviews
Chicago Tribune. November 25, 1987, V, p. 4.
Good Housekeeping. CCV, November, 1987, p. 106.
Los Angeles Times. November 25, 1987, VI, p. 1.
New York. XX, December 7, 1987, p. 152.
The New York Times. November 25, 1987, p. C24.
Newsweek. CX, November 30, 1987, p. 73.
People Weekly. XXVIII, December 14, 1987, p. 14.
Redbook. CLXX, November, 1987, p. 44.
Variety. CCCXXIX, November 25, 1987, p. 14.

THROW MOMMA FROM THE TRAIN

Production: Larry Brezner; released by Orion Pictures
Direction: Danny DeVito
Screenplay: Stu Silver
Cinematography: Barry Sonnenfeld
Editing: Michael Jablow
Production design: Ida Random
Art direction: William Elliott; set decoration, Anne McCulley
Costume design: Marilyn Vance-Straker
Music: David Newman
MPAA rating: PG-13
Running time: 88 minutes

> *Principal characters:*
> Owen .... Danny DeVito
> Larry .... Billy Crystal
> Momma .... Anne Ramsey
> Margaret......................... Kate Mulgrew
> Beth .... Kim Greist
> Lester........................ Branford Marsalis
> Joel .... Rob Reiner

In Alfred Hitchcock's suspense thriller *Strangers on a Train* (1951), Bruno Anthony (Robert Walker) is an amiable psychopath in elegant pinstripes. Purely by chance, he meets a young tennis star, Guy Haines (Farley Granger), on a train. "Criss cross, criss cross," he liltingly intones as he inches nearer to Guy to invade his personal space, the first step to invading his life with a plan that Guy casually dismisses as raving. Without Guy's knowledge, Bruno proceeds to swap murders with him, his father's killing in exchange for that of Guy's shrewish wife.

In *Throw Momma from the Train*, the spirit of Bruno is reborn in the decidedly unelegant presence of Danny DeVito, better known to audiences as the venomous half-pint cabbie boss in television's "Taxi." DeVito plays Owen, a childish little man who plays with miniature trains and quietly formulates his plans for murdering his abusive mother (Anne Ramsey), a bulbous-faced tyrant in a faded chenille houserobe. As well as starring in *Throw Momma from the Train*, DeVito directs this surprisingly clever black comedy that readily acknowledges its debt to Hitchcock.

Unlike *Strangers on a Train*, the film does not open at a train station but in the cramped apartment of a frustrated college writing teacher, Larry (Billy Crystal), who will play Guy Haines to Owen's Bruno. For months he has been trying to complete a novel but cannot get past the first line: "The night was. . . ." He turns on the television and sees his former wife, Margaret (Kate Mulgrew), on a talk show. She has stolen his last four years of work to publish it as her own novel, *Hot Fire*. Not only does she reap a multimillion-dollar book bonanza, but she also boldly vilifies Larry and their "prisonlike marriage" on national television.

Larry is devastated. His community college teaching job provides little inspiration, and he humiliates himself in front of his adult students when he screams that he wants to kill his former wife. His writing class includes Owen, whose interest centers on the murder mystery. Larry avoids reading Owen's acutely inept stories to the class, so Owen follows Larry—first to the Laundromat, then to his home, and even to his romantic rendezvous with an anthropology teacher, Beth (Kim Greist)—seeking advice on his writing. Larry finally tells Owen that his writing problem hinges on the issue of motivation and that to understand the relationship between alibi and motivation in murder he should see Hitchcock's *Strangers on a Train*. Owen does and immediately calls Larry to tell him that he understands the message: "Criss cross, criss cross."

Larry does not grasp that Owen, like Bruno, is readying himself to swap murders. Larry's problems are compounded when his agent, Joel (Rob Reiner), summarily drops him. Then he receives a call from Owen, who is in Hawaii stalking Larry's former wife. On an excursion boat, Owen finds her alone, but before he has a chance to strangle her, she conveniently falls overboard. Owen gives Larry the good news of the "murder" over the phone. At first, Larry is disbelieving, but when he hears a radio bulletin that Margaret is missing, he is hysterical: He is all motive and no alibi. While Larry avoids the police, they begin to question his friends and students, who tell what they know: Larry hated his former wife and swore to kill her. Larry's only dubious defense comes from his neighbor, Lester (Branford Marsalis), who says that he knows Larry did not do it for the simple reason that Larry never does anything.

Until Margaret's murder, the film's tone is surprisingly dark. It is dominated by Larry's frustration with his own failure and with Margaret's successful betrayal of him. Her wealth and celebrity status are contrasted with Larry's life of utter banality: his trip to the Laundromat, his ennui in the face of talentless students, his cramped one-room efficiency apartment. Larry's frustration is increased by his ambivalence. It is clear that his feelings for Margaret are very confused. As more than one character in the film remarks, Larry envies her, hates her, and probably still also loves her.

In contrast to Larry, Owen begins the film as a fascinating psychopath who, like Hitchcock's Bruno Anthony, seems truly unhinged: He is ready to kill Momma, Larry's wife, and even Larry, after the latter has snubbed him in class. Living with Momma in an old Victorian house on a hill above downtown Los Angeles, Owen is childlike but sinister, and the reasons for his dementia are clear. Momma is demanding, repressive, paranoid, and unhinged herself. She is also curiously astute. When Larry tells her that he is Owen's friend, she replies, "Owen doesn't have a friend," evidence of both her cruelty and her knowingness. As a consequence, Owen's malice toward his mother becomes the most normal thing about him. She is a monster, and he is a trapped, abused child, half-grown, literally and figuratively. Because Owen's hatred for her is given ample justification, many of the most amusing episodes in the film are those in which he either halfheartedly attempts to, or fantasizes about, murdering her. Imitating Claude Rains's actions in *Notorious* (1946), Owen prepares her a teacupful of Pepsi-Cola laced with lye, but he reconsiders and bats it from her lips at the last possible moment. Then, in a variation on Hitchcock's *Dial M for Murder* (1954), he fantasizes stabbing her straight through the head with a pair of scissors.

Larry agrees to meet with Owen when he finds the police at his apartment. After a wild car chase, they arrive at Owen's house, where Owen unsuccessfully tries to pass off Larry as cousin Paddy. Momma sees through this ploy but begrudgingly accepts Larry's presence. His sympathy for Owen aroused by the latter's pathetically lonely recollections of his kindly father, Larry agrees to murder Momma. Owen goes bowling and leaves Larry to kill Momma. Once again, he wavers.

Returning from the bowling alley, Owen meets the police at the front door. When he realizes that Momma is still alive, Owen directs them to the pantry where Larry is hiding. His discovery is diverted by Momma's rantings that she knows they have come to take her away. The police leave. Larry then falls down a flight of stairs (like Detective Arbogast in *Psycho*) into a cellar trap meant for Momma. Eschewing either sentimentality or fear, Momma barks at Owen to bury the body before its odor pervades the house, but Larry is revived in time to see Momma phoning the police. She has glimpsed his picture on the television news.

The next scene finds Momma, Owen, and Larry sitting on a train bound for Mexico. He and Owen engage in some good-natured banter about the opening line of Larry's novel. Momma offers a better version. Larry goes berserk and he chases her over the train, until both Owen and Larry have a change of heart. They save her from being swept off the train, but in the final irony, Momma kicks Larry off onto the rails.

Recovering in a hospital, Larry hears the news that Margaret is alive and well after being rescued by a fishing boat. She has sold the motion-picture rights to her ordeal for $1.5 million. Larry decides to write the story of his encounter with Owen. A year later, he is finishing his novel when Owen appears. Momma is dead of natural causes, and Owen has completed his own book about their adventure together. Larry begins to strangle him until he discovers that the book is a children's pop-up picture storybook. In the film's last scene, with Owen and Beth at his side, Larry lives out the pop-up book's last page. Vacationing at the beach, Larry basks in the glow of the tropical sun and his best-selling novel, *Throw Momma from the Train*.

Received with mixed reviews but impressive box-office returns, including a $7.3-million draw in its initial week of release, *Throw Momma from the Train* relies on engaging performances from DeVito and Crystal, with the latter's finely shaded portrayal of Larry in the film's early scenes suggesting the kind of bitterness and emotional ambivalence that makes Hitchcock's innocent characters seem guilty even when they are not. His performance promises a complexity that the film never quite delivers. Most of the acting praise, including a nomination for Best Supporting Actress, went to Ramsey for her amazing performance as Momma, an archetypal bad-mother figure every bit as frighteningly perverse as Mrs. Bates in *Psycho*.

In spite of its dark beginning and its homage to the art of murder, *Throw Momma from the Train* too quickly turns from black comedy to whitewashed sentimentality, and as one critic quipped, its "fangs turn out to be made of rubber." The film refuses to allow any of its characters to be guilty of anything, unlike *Strangers on a Train*, in which Bruno efficiently murders Guy's wife and then merrily goes about trying to frame Guy. Owen turns from an unpredictable lunatic into a lovable lump who actually says that he misses his dead Momma. Here, the film undermines its own narrative logic as well as its hope of sustaining the deliciously forbidden fruit of a truly black comedy that offers its audience the nasty pleasure of playing out murderous impulses which most human beings are too guilt-ridden or repressed to admit, much less act upon. It is in this respect that *Throw Momma from the Train* deviates most from its tribute to Hitchcock and robs the viewer of those darker pleasures which the master of suspense knew how to deliver so disturbingly well.

Gaylyn Studlar

Reviews
Chicago Tribune. December 11, 1987, VII, p. 58.
Los Angeles Times. December 11, 1987, VI, p. 1.
Macleans. C, December 21, 1987, p. 61.
The New Republic.CXCVIII, February 8, 1988, p. 26.
The New York Times. December 11, 1987, p. C15.
Newsweek. CX, December 21, 1987, p. 69.
People Weekly. XXIX, January 11, 1988, p. 13.
Time. CXXXI, January 11, 1988, p. 80.
Variety. CCCXXIX, December 16, 1987, p. 11.
The Wall Street Journal. January 5, 1988, p. 22.

TIN MEN

Production: Mark Johnson for Touchstone Pictures; released by Buena Vista
Direction: Barry Levinson
Screenplay: Barry Levinson
Cinematography: Peter Sova
Editing: Stu Linder
Art direction: Peter Jamison; set decoration, Philip Abramson
Makeup: Irving Buchman
Costume design: Gloria Gresham
Sound: Bill Phillips
Music direction: James Foanberg
Music: David Steele, Andy Cox, and Fine Young Cannibals
MPAA rating: R
Running time: 112 minutes

Principal characters:
BB	Richard Dreyfuss
Tilley	Danny DeVito
Nora	Barbara Hershey
Sam	Jackie Gayle
Cheese	Seymour Cassel
Wing	J. T. Walsh
Stanley	Alan Blumenfeld
Bagel	Michael Tucker
Moe	John Mahoney
Mouse	Bruno Kirby
Gil	Stanley Brock

Barry Levinson's previous film, *Diner* (1982), told the story of a group of young adults from Baltimore's laboring classes whose preferred late-night meeting place was a diner on the harbor. The film's pronounced nostalgia for an era prior to the social upheavals and urban violence that shattered America's postwar calm (one of the opening subtitles pointedly dates the action: Christmas, 1959) and the gentrification that transformed the face of the inner cities from the 1970's onward, was tinged with a gentle malaise. The overriding message of *Diner* was that this world was slipping into the past.

By comparison, *Tin Men* seems strangely future-oriented—describing a time that is now past but which, for the characters in the film, remains to be lived. The period and place are roughly the same—Baltimore in 1963—but the characters are older, the generation that came of age not in the early 1960's but during and after World War II, when the American economy was entering the most spectacular growth phase in its history. For the people of this generation, the steadily rising tide of expectations and material success seemed to have no end in sight. John Kennedy was still president, big Detroit-built cars were the norm, and money flowed freely. When Tilley (Danny DeVito) and BB (Richard Dreyfuss) drive off together in the film's closing sequence, an enormous arch looms up in the background and is frozen in the final shot. A symbolic rainbow? Tilley and BB's plans to start over in a new business, possibly a car dealership selling the then-novel Volkswagen "Bug," indicates just that, as if the social and economic disasters that were to shock the American middle classes during the next twenty years were nowhere on the horizon. What is one to make of this patent misperception that effectively banishes from consciousness all the historical lessons gained since the 1960's?

The key to both films lies in their resolute masculinity, yet *Tin Men* abandons the critical distance that *Diner* established in relation to its subjects. Levinson stopped short of harshly criticizing the illusions of middle age. Still, the film is not devoid of ironic jabs at the foibles of the "tin men" (local argot for the hucksters who convince ordinary people that their houses will be improved by covering the original brick with aluminum siding). From the opening sequence when BB asks the Cadillac salesman why cars are always called "she," through the posturing threats and verbal abuse, to the false climax when Tilley challenges BB to a game of eight ball to decide the fate of his wife, Nora (Barbara Hershey), *Tin Men* pokes fun at the self-delusions of a culture cemented by male bonding, where the principal sign of fellowship is the corrosive, lacerating humor one enjoys at the expense of one's mates.

An important line in the film is Nora's riposte to Tilley when he remarks on the oddity of her showing up at the diner, hitherto an exclusively male preserve. Tilley observes that only six months ago no women would have been seen there. Nora replies: "Don't I know it." Women in the film are consigned to marginal roles, both economically and emotionally. Even Nora's one self-assertive moment, her repudiation of BB for his cruel trick of seducing her only to get revenge on Tilley, is finally nullified by their reconciliation. When BB loses the pool game and confesses to Nora, her rage is quickly dissipated when he informs her that he has no intention of keeping the bargain requiring him to give her up. Love conquers all, as Nora decides that standing by her man ranks higher than righteous indignation at his callous disregard for her feelings, or even her dignity.

In the end, Levinson is kind to his protagonists. Both Tilley, the loser and archetypal "little man," and BB, the consummate huckster whose salesmanship extends to the schmoozing he musters to hook Nora into committing adultery, are punished for their sins, but neither is ultimately wrecked. As they exclaim simultaneously in the car trailing into the future: "I've got an idea." Their newly forged friendship, the deeper identification of one man with another that overcomes their previous rivalry and animosity, projects hope rather than nostalgia, optimism rather than loss. One imagines a sequel set circa 1980, with the two reminiscing in the same diner, not rich but not pathetically poor either, comfortable in a middling sort of way, perhaps slightly regretful about missed opportunities but ultimately content and unthreatened either economically or psychologically.

All this is not to diminish Levinson's considerable stylistic achievements. As in *Diner*, the screenplay is witty, well-timed, and entirely coherent. The periodization is again skillfully realized, primarily through costumes and automobiles, although reproducing the feel of the late 1950's is made easier by the fact that many sections of Baltimore have not altered appreciably in more than a quarter century (many of the row houses and down-at-heel bars and cafés are still there). Music, which played such a prominent narrative role in *Diner*, is here another piece of historical authenticity, a sign that Levinson knows this world intimately. He is clearly a talented, scrupulous filmmaker, adept at establishing character and setting while holding on to what is fast becoming an archaic skill: telling a story. His films recall the romantic comedies of the 1930's and 1940's, the line of sophisticated sexual rivalry that has effectively vanished in the wake of the newer screwball genre dominated by the misadventures of horny, silly teenagers.

Given the obvious superiority of Levinson's films to the bulk of Hollywood's current pulp productions, one feels almost churlish in criticizing *Tin Men*. Yet it is precisely Levinson's intelligence which disappoints. It is not that happy endings are verboten in the 1980's. *Desperately Seeking Susan* (1985), *Something Wild* (1986), and *Blue Velvet* (1986) all end more or less happily for the principals, yet none of the objections posed here would apply so directly to them. What distinguishes these more lucid comedies from Levinson's comparatively innocent productions is their steadfast refusal of any claims to historical or ideological realism. *Tin Men* stridently (and *Diner* more mutedly) proclaims itself a mirror of the period and the people it depicts. While it judges them, it refrains from denouncing the world they have built and the values they embrace. Indicative of Levinson's failure of nerve is the treatment of BB, who is given his moment of heroic resignation twice: once in confessing to Nora that he has treated her shabbily and again in taking the fall for all the other tin men by giving Stanley (Alan Blumenfeld), an inept gumshoe for the Home Improvement Commission, all the evidence he requires to convict BB of improper selling practices. Sexist, huckster, and braggart, BB nevertheless emerges a hero of sorts. The projection of his moderately bright future as a car salesman—however ironic when set against the opening scene—is entirely consonant with the film's loving presentation of ordinary guys simply trying to make a buck.

Romance thrives on stark oppositions between good and evil, and *Tin*

Men has its villains: Wing (J. T. Walsh), the sleazy, smooth-talking boss who sells out Tilley to save his own skin, soothing his conscience by giving Tilley a rather limp golden handshake; Stanley, the hapless snitch; and the members of the Home Improvement Commission, who sit perched at a table in front of the witnesses under investigation, physically disagreeable, not very bright, certainly no better, the film seems to say, than those they are indicting. Most heinous of all, however, is the federal government, represented by two anonymous, impersonal agencies: the Social Security Administration, for whom Nora toils in a vast hall of numberless identical desks, making next to nothing (or so Tilley claims), and the Internal Revenue Service, the grasping, pitiless nemesis that deprives Tilley of his home when he fails to pay his taxes promptly and even impounds his Cadillac when he is having his business license revoked.

This is a film about working and living in the modern state, where one must always be looking over one's shoulder to be certain that those with initiative, imagination, and heart never get too far ahead of the game. Never mind that tin men victimize their customers or that these men never stoop to notice the army of women laboring for inferior wages all around them (save to ogle or proposition them). The real bad guys are the bureaucrats, the laws and regulations, ultimately the state itself, which controls and inhibits the operation of free enterprise—although never enough to prevent a good hustler like BB from moving across the street to ply a different trade with the same skills.

Perhaps *Tin Men* is really a 1980's film after all, for its strongest message is the same one that brought a B-film actor to the highest office in the land: What the country needs most is to get government off the people's back. Only one question remains: Who will most have benefited from this so-called populism? Just who are "the people"?

Michael Sprinker

Reviews
Commonweal. CXIV, April 10, 1987, p. 215.
Films in Review. XXXVIII, May, 1987, p. 300.
Los Angeles Times. March 6, 1987, VI, p. 1.
The Nation. CCXLIV, April 4, 1987, p. 445.
The New Republic. CXCVI, March 30, 1987, p. 24.
The New York Times. March 6, 1987, p. C3.
The New Yorker. LXIII, April 6, 1987, p. 82.
Newsweek. CIX, March 2, 1987, p. 78.
Time. CXXIX, April 6, 1987, p. 80.
Variety. CCCXXVI, March 11, 1987, p. 23.
Video. XI, December, 1987, p. 87.

THE UNTOUCHABLES

Production: Art Linson; released by Paramount Pictures
Direction: Brian De Palma
Screenplay: David Mamet; inspired by the television series of the same name
Cinematography: Stephen H. Burum
Editing: Jerry Greenberg and Bill Pankow
Art direction: William A. Elliott; set decoration, Hal Gausman
Visual Consultant: Patrizia Von Brandenstein
Costume design: Marilyn Vance-Straker
Music: Ennio Morricone
MPAA rating: R
Running time: 119 minutes

> *Principal characters:*
> Eliot Ness........................Kevin Costner
> Jimmy Malone.....................Sean Connery (AA)
> Al Capone ....Robert De Niro
> Oscar Wallace ....Charles Martin Smith
> George Stone.......................Andy Garcia
> Frank Nitti ....Billy Drago
> Mike ....Richard Bradford
> Payne...............................Jack Kehoe
> George...........................Brad Sullivan
> Ness's wife ....Patricia Clarkson

This film brought together two formidable talents: David Mamet, winner of many major awards for playwriting, and Brian De Palma, arguably the most talented of the boomer generation of "film brat" directors. This collaboration of great talents promised a great film, rich in the lean, true-to-the-ear dialogue on which Mamet has built his career, and equally rich in the dense visual textures audiences have come to expect of De Palma. Indeed, the film begins with a striking scene that seems to confirm that promise. De Palma frames Al Capone (Robert De Niro) and his entourage from directly overhead as Capone holds court like Louis XIV at his levee. Spread out as his barber shaves him, only the horizontal Capone has any corporal substance in the scene. The others—his mobsters and the press—are all compressed by the overhead camera angle into anonymous, characterless spots as Capone spouts boastful half-truths to the admiring press. When the barber accidentally nicks Capone, drawing a drop of blood, the scene is set for that first speck of red to spread until eventually the screen is awash in blood.

In the next sequence, a young working-class girl takes a bucket into a neighborhood saloon to fetch her father's beer. Capone's men enter and threaten the owner, who refuses to capitulate to their demands. The scene, while competently dialogued and directed, lacks the conceptual integrity of the first sequence, replacing its inventive qualities with their very opposite: predictability. The moment the viewer sees the girl approaching the saloon, he knows that she will not leave the place alive. The film lapses from invention into cliché in the blinking of an eye, and the dialogue is barely heard as the viewer reluctantly waits to see how the girl will meet her violent end.

Unfortunately, from this point onward, the film tends to follow the low road of the second scene rather than the high one promised by the first. Mamet butts together strings of underdeveloped, elliptical scenes mostly based on plots derived from Westerns, while De Palma does his best to invigorate them visually. For the most part, Mamet's failure to flesh out and interconnect these shopworn scenes means that De Palma has to work with material so truncated that he cannot lend it much visual texture or development. Instead of the rich tapestrics of visual density typical of his best work, he seems reduced to working only a few visual motifs—mostly in costume colors—along with his familiar red.

Mamet's chief source of inspiration for his character configuration, closely tied to the plot, seems to come from the Hawksian formation-of-a-group Western. In the Howard Hawks films, a small group of unlikely paladins would gather and then ride forth into the corrupted land to do battle with the dragon. The genre promises and should deliver an elaboration of the group ethos and its dynamics. Although this picture goes through the motions and spends much time detailing the formation of the group, two of its four members never receive adequate treatment. The two underdeveloped Untouchables are a federal tax accountant, Oscar Wallace (Charles Martin Smith), and a young Chicago cop fresh out of the police academy, George Stone (Andy Garcia). Poor Stone gets probably fewer than a dozen lines in the whole film, half of them dedicated to making him a south-side Italian and the other half denying him the chance to articulate his dedication to the cause. Smith fares somewhat better with his role of a bookish accountant suddenly learning to like all this male violence. Although the role as written lacks depth and skirts caricature, Smith gives his character a certain idiosyncratic enthusiasm that brings him nicely to life.

Although the film's title and much of its structural reasoning is based on the group, it nevertheless fails to develop the problem either in ethical or interpersonal terms. Instead, the film's central ethical problem of corruption is invested almost entirely in the character of Eliot Ness (Kevin Costner), who must undergo his initiation into adult life in Prohibition Chicago. Will this idealistic, untested young man be able to stand straight and true in the face of the dragon, or will he be withered by its fetid breath, which has fouled and corrupted all of Prohibition Chicago?

Although Mamet's script works hard to put Ness through a series of tests, Costner plays his character without noticeable variation, without any visible internalization or expression of what is happening to him. It is a one-note performance, played without understanding or development. Costner never gives the slightest hint of any moral conflict, of even thinking flickeringly for a moment of capitulating to bribery, intimidation, or any of the other suasions brought to bear upon him during the course of the film. Although this central character occasionally declares that things are bad out there, he behaves as if he is out for a Sunday stroll in the park instead of descending into Hades on a heroic journey.

Costner's weakness at portraying his character is made all the more glaring by Sean Connery's full understanding of Jimmy Malone, the nearly burned-out beat cop who will show Ness the ropes, or rather the clue through this corrupt labyrinth. Malone has resisted corruption all of his life, and now he is nearing retirement with a beat cop's pension as his reward. Malone moves from wariness to reluctance to commitment, knowing full well that choosing Treasury work may well mean a terrible death rather than a quiet retirement. Connery, who won an Academy Award for Best Supporting Actor, lends his character both dignity and quiet relish, a thankfulness that at last he can do something that a cop should be doing.

If Malone represents the quiet anonymity of honesty and decency, he forms the perfect obverse of Capone. From the film's striking first shot on, Capone swaggers and grandstands for the press, who seem to dote on his every word. The script insistently parallels Capone's handy manipulation of the press with Ness's initially faltering, eventually successful use of the media to chronicle his own career. Thus, attraction for the media, along with the violence he generates, forms Capone's side of Ness's mimetic triangle. The character configuration, then, provides Ness with two older men as exemplars and lets him choose the good one, while behaving in certain respects more and more like the bad one.

At the same time, the script very insistently contrasts Ness's family with Capone and his various entourages, always directly cutting from or to a scene with one to a scene with the other, presumably to contrast the homely love, tenderness, and goodness of the first to the flashy, venal, violent evil of the second. These severely underdeveloped scenes, like so many other ingredients of the script, fail to find any but the most mechanical of anchors in the film's central character. Given Ness's apparent untouchability, the family provides an area of vulnerability through which Capone can try to wreak his revenge on Ness. Once this potential becomes real, however, Mamet simply has the family moved away into hiding, where they remain out of sight—and pretty much out of mind—for the duration of the picture. Therefore, despite the inclusion of the family in the film, it never really becomes much more than an abstract idea. The truth is, although De Palma and Mamet both pay lip service to the family, this is strictly a film about men.

This becomes amusingly apparent when suddenly the viewer finds himself out West, watching the Untouchables joining forces with a troupe of Royal Canadian Mounted Police to play cowboys and robbers with a team of Capone's rumrunners who are about to smuggle a truckload of booze across the border. This extended sequence betrays the generic origins of the screenplay in the Hollywood Western as clearly as if it were branded W in its every frame, and although the sequence is one of the few in the film that receives adequate protracted treatment, it stands out like a cowboy at a Mafia convention. The film's urbanity, so intensively elaborated up to this point, comes to a crashing halt with its first Fordlike shot of Mounties spread across a western ridge. Even if it does show the filmmakers longingly peeking through the narrative's cracks at the film's real heart, the sequence totally betrays the notion of genre purity and points up a regrettable amount of self-indulgence on both their parts.

The Untouchables is so intensely a film about men that it almost methodically excludes women. Except for the odd woman glimpsed in crowd scenes, it contains only five females, two of them girls. The first is the young girl who is blown up by a mobster's bomb. She represents frailty and vulnerability brutally destroyed by Capone's angel-of-evil lieutenant, Nitti (Billy Drago). Once Ness has begun his crusade, the girl's mother comes to his office to thank him. In an overwrought, overwritten monologue, she pathetically tells him how important it is to have a family man—one who understands about wives and children—doing the job he is doing. Ness's wife and his own young daughter are two of the remaining three females in the film, and they have scarcely more than an iconic function as females in peril. Interestingly enough, all these females are pointedly deprived of a husband or father to protect them in their hour of need.

The film's third protracted sequence, set in Chicago's Union Station, ties up many of these thematic threads. As Ness and Stone stalk Capone's accountant, a young mother, alone with her baby in this threatening place, slowly begins to drag the buggy up the wide marble stairway. Ness, on the alert for Capone's men, nevertheless takes pity on the struggling young woman, and goes to her aid. Just as he does so, the mobsters appear, and soon the carriage and its contents are bouncing their way down the staircase. Although the sequence is both well-directed and thematically justified, any viewer who has ever seen *Bronenosets Potyomkin* (1925; *The Battleship Potemkin*) will absolutely be wrenched away from Chicago and transported to Odessa. The self-indulgence of this sequence, in other words, is even greater than that of the crimebusters-on-the-range sequence.

The film's denouement consists of two major parts. In the first, Capone is finally brought to trial and convicted. De Palma resolves his opening mise-en-scène by showing the formerly expansive King of Crime now trapped like a hated rat by the press and the furious public in the courtroom. Meanwhile, Ness discovers that Capone's lieutenant, Nitti, was the man who slew his mentor, Malone, and he chases Nitti onto the rooftop, where they do battle. When Ness finally captures Nitti, the vicious murderer sneeringly taunts him with the difference between the monstrousness of his evil acts and the puny punishment he is likely to receive at the hands of the corrupt justice system in Chicago. It is Ness's final test, and he fails it. Succumbing to the way of lawlessness and violence—to Capone's way—he sends Nitti flying off the roof to meet his death on the pavement below.

R C Dale

Reviews
America. CLVII, August 1, 1987, p. 66.
Commonweal. CXIV, June 5, 1987, p. 354.
Films in Review. XXXVIII, August, 1987, p. 427.
The Humanist. XLVII, September, 1987, p. 43.
Los Angeles Times. June 3, 1987, VI, p. 1.
The Nation. CCXLIV, June 27, 1987, p. 900.
The New York Times. June 3, 1987, p. C17.
The New Yorker. LXIII, June 29, 1987, p. 70.
Time. CXXIX, June 22, 1987, p. 78.
Variety. CCCXXVII, June 3, 1987, p. 14.

WALL STREET

Production: Edward R. Pressman; released by Twentieth Century-Fox
Direction: Oliver Stone
Screenplay: Stanley Weiser and Oliver Stone
Cinematography: Robert Richardson
Editing: Claire Simpson
Production design: Stephen Hendrickson
Art direction: John Jay Moore and Hilda Stark; set decoration, Leslie
    Bloom and Susan Bode
Costume design: Ellen Mirojnick
Sound: Chris Newman
Music: Stewart Copeland
MPAA rating: R
Running time: 124 minutes

> *Principal characters:*
> Bud Fox .... Charlie Sheen
> Chuckie .... Chuck Pfeiffer
> Lou Mannheim .... Hal Holbrook
> Gordon Gekko .... Michael Douglas (AA)
> Carl Fox .... Martin Sheen
> Sir Larry Wildman................ Terence Stamp
> Darien Taylor .... Daryl Hannah
> Roger Barnes .... James Spader

History occasionally shines on Hollywood directors. With the Ivan Boesky insider-trading scandal still in the news, promotion for *Wall Street* began in earnest several months before the film's release. It is difficult to know how much Oliver Stone altered the script to capitalize on this *cause célèbre* in the world of high finance. Even if the initial conception remained unaltered in production—the plot and characters need not have been modeled on any particular event or corporate raider, as the stock of originals was plentiful— the immediate resonance for many audiences must be the revelations about insider trading that rocked both "the Street" and the world these past months. Then came Black Monday in October and the commercial success of *Wall Street* was relatively certain.

Stone's career as screenwriter and director has been on a steady upward trajectory ever since he won an Oscar for the screenplay for *Midnight Express* (1978). The box-office and critical success of *Platoon* (1986) propelled him into the superstar category of writers and directors, from which he can choose his associates, his projects, and his compensation. What is most eerie about his meteoric rise to fame and fortune is the way in which it recapitulates, at slightly reduced speed, the overnight success story of Bud Fox (Charlie Sheen) in *Wall Street*.

Wall Street does have its virtues, particularly when measured against previous *exposés* of financial speculation such as *Rollover* (1981; although it should be said that the latter's apocalyptic ending, with suicides by investment bankers and a replay of the 1929 forecast in fake news footage, no longer appears quite so outlandish). Among Stone's signal strengths as a filmmaker are his attention to detail and his commitment to filmic, if not dramatic, realism. The authenticity of the sets and locations, right down to the clothing, the fancy apartments and furnishings, and the frequently deployed background of the lower Manhattan skyline, gives the film the feel of its world. Particular attention has been paid to decoration and artworks, with originals by Jim Dine, Julian Schnabel, Joan Miró, and others prominently figuring in the establishment of what it means to live in the fast lane. Gordon Gekko (Michael Douglas) lectures to Bud on surplus value creation in late capitalism—"Things are worth whatever we say they're worth"—and suggests as one prominent example the inflation in price of the large painting that adorns his office wall. Nothing, the film ostensibly argues, is proof against the inexorable logic of free-market speculation, which makes exchange value the only measure of worth.

Yet *Wall Street* is first and foremost a morality play, and what escape the coercive power of money and greed are individual conscience and the ever-vigilant watchdogs of justice. The itinerary of Bud Fox from anonymous employee of a large brokerage and investment house to high-flying entrepreneur to indicted criminal is the chronicle of a young lad from the wrong side of the tracks who succumbs to temptation but ultimately sees the error of his ways and is willing to stand the punishment a just society metes out to those who transgress its rules. As Bud's father, Carl Fox (Martin Sheen), opines just before his son ascends the steps of the Fulton Street courthouse in the film's closing tracking shot, "Maybe it's the best thing after all." He is referring to Bud's impending jail term. Having paid his debt to society, Bud will likely go back to work at Blue Star Airlines, his father's employer and the means he first uses to attract Gekko's attention with some inside information. As Bud confesses to Gekko in the film's climactic scene in Central Park, "I tried to be Gordon Gekko, but I found out I was really just plain Bud Fox." Vindication not just for personal scruples, but for the superior morality of the working class.

Herein lies the most acute flaw in Stone's conception. The film is overlaid with a heavy dose of cocktail-party psychology, with Gekko assuming the role of Bud's father and mentor, displacing the working-class hero whose only concern is to defend his men from the predations of corporate vultures. Adding the mythic symbolism—Gekko's demoniac smile whenever he discloses for Bud a new scam or trick of the trade suggests his Mephistophelian origins and the nature of the pact Bud has made for his soul—the plot finally pivots around a small allegory of class: honesty, fairness, and loyalty are working-class values; ruthlessness, cunningness, and selfishness are the preserve of financiers. Bud's boss (James Karen), who has promoted and fawned over him in the brief moment of the young man's success, quickly dismisses him when the police arrive to handcuff Bud, intoning piously, "From the minute I laid eyes on you, I knew you were no good." Gekko's by-now-infamous "Greed is good" speech to the shareholders of soon-to-be-his Telstar Paper remains unrefuted at the film's end, at least from the perspective of the business world. Only the ridiculous homily by Lou Mannheim (Hal Holbrook) about man's ability to stare into the abyss—opposes the dominant amorality of corporate raiders among the characters whose preserve is the financial district. Bud's lawyer friend Roger Barnes (James Spader) demurs out of fear of getting caught, not from conscience. The streak of largesse demonstrated by Sir Larry Wildman (Terence Stamp) at the end of the film when he saves Blue Star from being carved up by Gekko carries the significant fillip of his revenge on his archenemy. In this film, the good guys do not merely wear three-piece suits or lunch at Le Cirque; nor, in Carl Fox's admonishing words to his son, is their worth "measured by the size of their wallet."

What, then, are we to make of the Bud Fox-Gordon Gekko relation? Or for that matter, of Sir Larry Wildman's reversion to his working-class origins when he addresses Gekko as "mate" during their contretemps in Gekko's home? Gekko says repeatedly that he sees in Bud—"buddy boy," he calls him—a younger version of himself. He alludes more than once to his own humble origins and takes considerable pleasure in putting in their place the more privileged of his competitors and associates. Gekko is the consummate arriviste, a buccaneer who scorns the more settled and established members of the corporate hierarchy (represented primarily by Holbrook's avuncular character, but also by Richard Dysart, who plays the hapless chief executive officer of Telstar), only to be undone by his own protégé, who first deceives him on the Blue Star deal and then helps federal agents entrap him. Why does Gekko fail? That is perhaps the most improbable aspect of an altogether implausible plot. Nothing in Gekko's character as it is presented in the film would suggest that he could be cheated by an inexperienced young man; his incautious trust of Bud in the Blue Star negotiations clashes with everything the audience has learned about him up to that point. The fact that he would confess to Bud, while they are walking in the park, the various high crimes and misdemeanors he committed does not seem logical. Does Stone really think Ivan Boesky and his ilk are rank fools? Surely not.

At work here is Stone's conviction that the world of contemporary high finance and securities trading has been contaminated by the likes of Gekko, whose real sin is to have gotten beyond himself. One ought to stay in the class one is born to, the film asserts, and the world will be just fine. *Wall Street* is dedicated to Stone's late father, who was himself a broker and economics writer, and his incarnation in the film would seem to be the redoubtable Lou Mannheim. A survivor from an older, more genteel era on the Street, Mannheim is the other surrogate father whose advice Bud derides on his way up, only to accept the consoling bromides once he falls. The film suggests, if only fleetingly, that things were once different among the financiers and corporate executives of America. Before Gordon Gekko there was Lou Mannheim; before reckless greed there was the slow, patient investment of capital that built the country. Mannheim says so (even Bud's father accepts the premise), defending the current management of Blue Star against Gekko's assertion that they are running the company into the ground. That makes for a nice fable about the history of corporate America, one that paints Charles Wilson, Gerard Swope, and David Rockefeller in rosy hues, while T. Boone Pickens and Carl Icahn get the tar brush. Only Felix Rohatyn could actually believe this story of an era of capitalist decency and good conduct prior to the current aberrant period of lawlessness. For those who go to see *Wall Street* seeking some insider information of their own on the psychology and the mores of the big players, a better suggestion is to read Matthew Josephson's unparalleled classic about nineteenth century American capitalism, *The Robber Barons* (1934). One will quickly see that nothing much has changed on the Street from that day to this.

Michael Sprinker

Reviews
America. CLVIII, January 30, 1988, p. 100.
Barrons. LXVII, December 14, 1987, p. 46.
Commonweal. CXV, February 12, 1988, p. 88.
The Economist. CCCV, December 19, 1987, p. 81.
The Nation. CCXLVI, January 23, 1988, p. 97.
The New Republic. CXCVIII, January 4, 1988, p. 24.
The New York Times. December 11, 1987, p. C3.
Time. CXXX, December 14, 1987, p. 82.
Variety. CCCXXIX, December 9, 1987, p. 13.
The Wall Street Journal. December 10, 1987, p. 27.

WEEDS

Production: Bill Badalato; released by De Laurentiis Entertainment Group
Direction: John Hancock
Screenplay: John Hancock and Dorothy Tristan
Cinematography: Jan Weincke
Editing: Dennis O'Connor, David Handman, Chris Lebenzon, and Jon Poll
Production design: Joseph T. Garrity
Art direction: Pat Tagliaferro; set decoration, Jerie Keiter
Costume design: Mary Kay Stolz
Sound: James Thorton
Music: Angelo Badalamenti
MPAA rating: R
Running time: 115 minutes

Principal characters:
Lee Umstetter .... Nick Nolte
Claude .... Lane Smith
Burt .... William Forsythe
Navarro .... John Toles-Bey
Bagdad .... Ernie Hudson
Dave .... Mark Rolston
Lazarus .... J. J. Johnson
Lillian .... Rita Taggart

The effectiveness of prison reform has long been one of the more challenging social debates. Although lawbreakers must be punished, former convicts often return to society as maladjusted individuals who pose a greater threat than when first incarcerated. Critics of the American penal system have claimed since its inception that it does little in the way of real reform, serving instead as a brutal holding pen for society's dropouts.

Weeds, directed by John Hancock (*Bang the Drum Slowly*, 1973) and written by him and his wife, Dorothy Tristan, examines the reformation of San Quentin inmate Lee Umstetter (Nick Nolte). Inspired by Tristan's story concerning the real-life experiences of former prisoner Rick Cluchey, Hancock spent a decade trying to adapt Cluchey's story to the screen. He met with Cluchey in prison and together they brought his play, *The Cage*, to the stage. It was produced by the San Francisco Actor's Workshop, of which Hancock was artistic director, and first performed outside prison walls in 1965. Drama critic Barbara Blayden succeeded in her campaign for Cluchey's release from San Quentin, where he was serving a stiff sentence for armed robbery. *The Cage* then toured the United States and Europe.

The film's opening sequence, reminiscent of a Marcel Marceau skit about a bumbling, suicidal man, shows Umstetter leaping from the second story of

San Quentin's atrium. The attempted suicide causes only some internal injuries. Released from isolation, he tries to hang himself in a cell shared by kindly embezzler Claude (Lane Smith). Failing a second time, Umstetter slouches into the prison library, asks for a book, "any book, as long as it is thick," and is handed Leo Tolstoy's *War and Peace* (1886). He goes on to read Jean-Paul Sartre, Albert Camus, and Jean Genet. One can see by now that this is no ordinary prison film. Something wonderful and unexpected happens: A hardened, repeat offender (who in the film is serving a life sentence without possibility of parole) is undergoing a transformation.

The ensuing years in prison pass quickly and Umstetter gradually changes from a person with no interest in living to a person committed to becoming a playwright and director. With Claude as his stage manager, Umstetter auditions other inmates, bringing together a motley cast made up of clownish shoplifter Burt (William Forsythe), murderer Bagdad (Ernie Hudson), pimp and extortionist Navarro (John Toles-Bey), exhibitionist Dave (Mark Rolston), and others. When drama critic Lillian (Rita Taggart) attends a prison performance of the play and gives it a rave review, Umstetter's life turns around. They begin a correspondence and eventually Lillian succeeds in getting him pardoned after he has served fourteen years of his sentence.

Once free, Umstetter contacts the old prison cast of *The Cage* and they begin rehearsing for a national tour. What develops is the gradual emergence of men who, for much of their lives, had no direction and little concern for others. Through the device of the theater, they mature in their self-awareness and sensitivity toward one another. At one point when the production is financially threatened, Navarro, the pimp, offers to sell his fancy car in order to pay production costs. He says to Umstetter, "I love you man, you're like a brother to me." Umstetter tells his cast that there will be no drugs, weapons, or alcohol on tour, but old habits are difficult to break. At one pitstop along the road, Burt weakens and steals several useless trinkets. Once back in the trailer they hear police sirens and must scramble to empty cupboards and pockets of guns and drugs. Reformation is far from complete.

Umstetter's cheating ways persist. Although *The Cage* finally reaches Off-Broadway, Umstetter is soundly chastised by a critic for emulating Jean Genet's *Haute Surveillance* (1949; *Deathwatch*, 1954). He rereads this play and decides that the guard should drop his French accent. In time and with Navarro's encouragement to rewrite the play so that it comes from him and not Genet, Umstetter sets it in an American prison. As Nolte's character develops, so does the play's authenticity, which was not as evident in earlier versions of the play. In the process of self-discovery, he also learns creative honesty. It is no great surprise that Umstetter identifies with Genet. He too was a repeat offender and became self-educated while serving time in France.

A salient point in the Cluchey story was the question-and-answer period after performances when the cast would talk candidly about prison life. In *Weeds*, one man says it was the dreaming that got him through, except when he awoke nothing had changed. Burt speaks of how he liked prison because it gave his days structure.

In John Frankenheimer's *Birdman of Alcatraz* (1962), there is a scene in which Robert Stroud (Burt Lancaster) and the warden (Karl Malden) argue about prison reform. The warden defends himself, stating that he strived throughout his career to better the lives of his inmates through structure. Birdman Stroud replies, "How, by having them make license plates?" This method of reform Stroud adds, only served to keep men at their most base level. While Burt in *Weeds* had his time structured, it did nothing to teach him self-determination.

The film completes a circle when the cast returns to San Quentin for a performance. While the character portraying the guard taunts the actors onstage, real guards with real guns patrol along catwalks above the audience. There are disquieting shots of tattooed men who become increasingly agitated with Umstetter's incitement. A mock fire is set inside the cage by the clever use of lights and fans as the actors and then the rowdy audience chant, "Burn it down! Burn it down!" Inmates pile wooden benches together and set them on fire. Tear gas is fired to disperse the mob. A full-scale riot then erupts, bursting forth into the yard. There is a horrifying moment when the actors are confused with the prisoners. Burt is clubbed, as is Umstetter's dear friend Claude. The guards keep swinging at him until Umstetter can no longer contain himself. He rushes to protect Claude and is hit with the full force of a club. Ironically, the play's notoriety for causing a prison riot helps to launch it on Broadway.

Nolte is not a virtuoso performer. He lacks the kind of subtle shadings to his acting which Lancaster captured so masterfully in *Birdman of Alcatraz*. What Nolte has to his credit is a heartfelt desire to realize the difficult progression of Umstetter's reformation. It is with Nolte's Umstetter that one comes to see the power of human will over extreme adversity. Despite its weaknesses, *Weeds* remains a vital film about people who will behave as decently or as barbarically as the prison system treats them.

Nika Cavat

Reviews
Chicago Tribune. October 16, 1987, VII, p. 52.
Los Angeles Times. October 16, 1987, VI, p. 1.
Macleans. C, November 2, 1987, p. 52.
The New York Times. October 16, 1987, p. C10.

The New Yorker. LXIII, November 2, 1987, p. 136.
Newsweek. CX, November 16, 1987, p. 109.
People Weekly. XXVIII, October 26, 1987, p. 14.
The Village Voice. November 3, 1987, p. 76.
The Wall Street Journal. October 22, 1987, p. 36.
The Washington Post. October 30, 1987, p. D7.

THE WHALES OF AUGUST

Production: Carolyn Pfeiffer and Mike Kaplan for Alive Films and Circle
  Associates
Direction: Lindsay Anderson
Screenplay: David Berry; based on his play of the same name
Cinematography: Mike Fash
Editing: Nicolas Gaster
Production design: Jocelyn Herbert
Art direction: K. C. Fox and Bob Fox; set decoration, Sosie Hublitz
Makeup: Julie Hewett
Costume design: Rudy Dillon
Sound: Donald Summer
Music direction: Derek Wadsworth
Music: Alan Price
MPAA rating: no listing
Running time: 90 minutes

> *Principal characters:*
> Libby Strong .... Bette Davis
> Sarah Webber .... Lillian Gish
> Mr. Maranov....................... Vincent Price
> Tisha Doughty...................... Ann Sothern
> Joshua Brackett................... Harry Carey, Jr.
> Mr. Beckwith .... Frank Grimes
> Old Randall .... Frank Pitkin
> Young Randall .... Mike Bush
> Young Libby...................... Margaret Ladd
> Young Tisha .... Tisha Sterling
> Young Sarah.................... Mary Steenburgen

Fans of Bette Davis and Lillian Gish were alternately charmed and sad-
dened by *The Whales of August* in that it showed both legendary actresses
still capable of compelling work but just as often too frail to rise to the
demands of certain scenes. No one expected these two empresses of the
cinema to be at the height of their powers nowadays, and what they have
accomplished under Lindsay Anderson's surprisingly delicate direction is
quite extraordinary. For two such different actresses—and personalities—as
Davis and Gish to convince the viewer that they are sisters and close
companions seems, on paper, an impossible task. Davis' biting sarcasm and
Gish's eternal sweetness complement each other surprisingly well, however,
and the century-and-a-half of experience they share between them invests
David Berry's rather schematic characters with an extra dimension of emotional urgency.

Director Anderson's unemphatic approach to the material also helps this octogenarian teapot tempest play better than it should. Eschewing the bombastic staging and black satire of his English Everyman trilogy—*If . . .* (1969), *O Lucky Man!* (1973) and *Britannia Hospital* (1982)—Anderson's one concession to cinematic stylishness in *Whales of August* is the use of repeated returns to the rugged Maine shoreline outside the sisters' summer cottage. The environment practically becomes the film's third major character, as waves lapping against the rocky coast evoke both the changelessness and the inexorable movement of time that so strongly informs the principals' twilight years. While some may accuse Anderson of just adding pretty postcard shots to an already sentimental enterprise, Anderson's deployment of these exterior transitions has a subtle intelligence that truly enhances the rhythm of the narrative, which would otherwise be confined to the house and its immediate surroundings and focused exclusively on the aged women's unremarkable conflicts. Berry's built-in invisible correlatives—whales that never come, an unseen picture window—do not do much to relieve the play's inherent claustrophobia. Anderson's camera performs the necessary task of opening up Berry's play in the most appropriate and unobtrusive manner imaginable; it is the kind of play that requires the occasional injection of fresh air.

Two long-widowed sisters from Philadelphia, Libby Strong (Davis) and Sarah Webber (Gish), have been summering at the family cottage on a holiday isle off the coast of Maine since they were young girls. Libby, blind and autocratic, now depends on Sarah for basic care—meals, clean clothes, and the like. Sarah, whose husband was killed in World War II, needs the financial support Libby's longer-lived spouse left her. As summer wanes, Sarah hopes to catch a glimpse of the migrating whales that passed by the island this time every year during their youth. The cynical Libby knows, correctly, that the whales disappeared decades ago.

One morning, the ingratiating Mr. Maranov (Vincent Price) comes by with fishing pole to ask if he can troll in the waters near the sisters' property. Sarah says of course and is flattered when he offers to share his catch with her. Inside the house, Sarah greets her dead husband's picture (it is their wedding anniversary day). Libby accuses her of talking to herself and continues in the same generally cranky tone throughout the morning.

Despite her astringence, Libby expresses a genuine need for Sarah that goes beyond the mere daily necessities. She fears Sarah's leaving her and for the first time expresses a recognition of her own mortality. Sarah, whose love for Libby is beautifully expressed by the gentle care with which she brushes her sister's long, white hair, is unnerved by Libby's talk of death.

Tisha Doughty (Ann Sothern), a chubby, impulsive neighbor and family friend of half a century, comes berry picking through the bushes, where she encounters Maranov. She expresses her condolences over the death of

Maranov's mistress, whose home he has been sharing. With resigned optimism, Maranov expresses certainty that he will soon find a new home.

At the house, Sarah, on the advice of handyman Joshua Brackett (Harry Carey, Jr.), suggests that they install a picture window. Libby immediately nixes the idea, claiming that it would cost too much and that they are too old for any changes.

Tisha arrives, and in private Sarah shares her concern over Libby's talk of dying. Tisha suggests that Libby should be turned over to her daughter's care and that Sarah sell the summer cottage to one of the new, younger tourist families who are taking over the island. In the parlor with Libby, they trade gossip (Maranov's circumstances) and jokes, Libby with the most caustic glee. As noisy handyman Joshua smashes about outside and under the house, Mr. Maranov drops by with the promised fish. Everyone, except Libby, loves the picture window idea. Sarah invites Maranov for dinner and moonlight, to Libby's loud protests that she will not eat his fish (earlier, she had characterized Maranov as a fraud).

Libby and Sarah argue over Maranov's intentions shortly before he returns to clean the fish. After his arrival, Libby sulks, but Sarah graciously invites him to watch the sunset with her and to look for whales in the morning. At dinner, Libby eats pork chops. Conversation eventually moves into the parlor. Maranov recounts his tragic adventures as a child of exiled Russian nobility. Sarah is enchanted, Libby unimpressed. She ends the evening by advising Maranov to start his search for a new refuge but warns him that he will not find it here. Out on the moonlit porch, Maranov tells Sarah—who is furious about her sister's ill manners—that he has spent his life visiting friends and is confident that he will find a new home. He will not be coming back in the morning.

Late that night, with candlelight, roses, and a glass of wine, Sarah celebrates her forty-sixth anniversary with Philip's photograph. She confesses to it that she cannot manage Libby much longer. Libby emerges from her room, frightened by a dream of seeing them both within death's reach. Upset, Sarah storms upstairs, proclaiming that life is not over for her. Alone, Libby feels the flowers on the table and wishes her absent sister a happy anniversary.

The following morning, Libby confronts Sarah about her intentions to leave. Sarah suggests that it might be best, and Libby reluctantly agrees to go to her daughter. She returns to her room.

Unexpectedly, Tisha drives over with a real estate agent, Mr. Beckwith (Frank Grimes). He recites the house's selling points to Sarah's growing ire. Sarah orders him and the presumptuous Tisha to leave, since she never agreed to sell the place. She tells her husband's photograph that they are not leaving home. Libby emerges from her room and accuses Sarah of talking to herself again. They reaffirm their love for each other but are interrupted by the resumed clanging of Joshua. Libby asks him to start working on the picture window as soon as possible.

Standing on the cliff by the shore, Libby asks Sarah if she can see whales. Sarah informs her that the whales have all gone. Shrugging, Libby says that one can never tell.

On every level, Anderson has made a more believable, less-cloying study of old age and family relations than the most recent film on the subject, *On Golden Pond* (1981). Any limitations Gish or Davis display are not the result of bad direction—as was the case with Henry Fonda and Katharine Hepburn in the earlier film—but of their physical frailty. Yes, Davis is unremittingly shrill throughout, and she puts the same arch, clipped spin on all of her lines, yet such an approach is perfect for her character. Although it may seem less artful than Gish's intuitive personification of Sarah, Davis' performance might actually be the more impressive. She evokes empathy for a highly unlikable person with a minimum of nuance and variety.

Gish is a delight, although she appears tired in a number of shots where she seems to be concentrating on remembering her lines more than on inhabiting Sarah. Nevertheless, there are a satisfying number of moments when her luminous soulfulness—most movingly at her solitary anniversary celebration—shines through as beautifully as it did in 1917.

Of the main supporting actors, John Ford repertory company alumnus Carey is the most natural as the crusty old handyman. Price is sly in the complex role of a highly civilized gentleman with a decidedly ungentlemanly way of life. Sothern's approach is a bit too theatrical in a loud way (as opposed to stylized, in the manner of Davis). Hers is the least adept of the formidable talents on display, and she obviously tries too hard in their company. It follows that she was the only member of the ensemble to receive an Academy Award nomination. Nevertheless, Gish and Davis' still-formidable acting gifts present a generally inspiring portrait of the human spirit's tenacity. Again, unlike *On Golden Pond*, *The Whales of August* is more about the bittersweet joy of life than it is about the problems of aging or the fear of death.

Robert Strauss

Reviews
America. CLVII, November 21, 1987, p. 384.
Daily Variety. May 13, 1987, p. 8.
Films in Review. XXXVIII, November, 1987, p. 551.
The Hollywood Reporter. October 26, 1987, p. 3.
Los Angeles. XXXII, November, 1987, p. 310.
Los Angeles Times. October 23, 1987, VI, p. 1.

The New Republic. CXCVII, November 2, 1987, p. 28.
The New York Times. October 16, 1987, p. C3.
Newsweek. CX, October 26, 1987, p. 88.
People Weekly. XXVIII, October 26, 1987, p. 14.
Variety. CCCXXVII, May 13, 1987, p. 23.
The Village Voice. October 27, 1987.
The Wall Street Journal. October 21, 1987, p. 34.

WISH YOU WERE HERE

Origin: Great Britain
Production: Sarah Radclyffe; released by Atlantic Releasing Corporation
Direction: David Leland
Screenplay: David Leland
Cinematography: Ian Wilson
Editing: George Akers
Art direction: Caroline Amies
Costume design: Shuna Harwood
Sound: Billy McCarthy
Music: Stanley Myers
MPAA rating: R
Running time: 90 minutes

> Principal characters:
> Lynda............................Emily Lloyd
> Hubert ....Geoffrey Hutchings
> Eric.................................Tom Bell
> Dave.............................Jesse Birdsall
> Dr. Holroyd ....Heathcote Williams
> Lynda's aunt ....Pat Heywood

If David Leland continues to be involved with films such as *Mona Lisa* (1986), *Personal Services* (1987), and *Wish You Were Here*, his services as writer and director will be much sought after by actresses in search of wonderful parts. Yet, even if he never acts in, writes for, or directs another motion picture, and even if Emily Lloyd does not triumphantly move on from her performance as the unhappy but irrepressible Lynda in *Wish You Were Here*, Leland will be remembered as the director who brought to the screen one of the most astounding first performances ever seen. *Wish You Were Here*, though, has more in its favor than Lloyd's performance, more than her fresh, young beauty and the glorious sunny days at the seashore; it also has a classic story of adolescent rebellion and self-discovery by a young girl who manages to do something to shock and amuse almost everyone.

In contrast, Lynda's father, Hubert (Geoffrey Hutchings), is a rather staid fellow, a pillar of the community who owns a local barber shop and who would like nothing better than to see his eldest child complete her apprenticeship as a hairdresser, so that he can get her off his hands. She, however, is bored with hairdressing school and quickly sees to it that her days there are numbered by deliberately damaging her volunteer customer's hair. On a daily basis, Lynda offends her father with language more appropriate to the sailor he once was. By riding her bicycle around town with her skirt tucked up to expose her Betty Grable legs, disrupting the adults' quiet entertainments, and teasing the men both young and old, Lynda soon finds herself unpopular with everyone around her, for they do not know what to make of her.

The one exception is a disreputable-looking fellow, a friend of her father's who appreciates the opportunity that Lynda offers to someone who is able to exploit it. A bookie and a loner, Eric (Tom Bell) initially finds Lynda unwilling; she even insults him and taunts him with the name of Long John Silver, making fun of his lanky figure and lame leg. He patiently waits for her, however, and boredom leads her to him, but not before she looks for love in the arms of a conceited young bus driver named Dave (Jesse Birdsall), whose lovemaking leaves her feeling that she is still practically a virgin. A date at the movies with one of the nice young boys around town leaves her angrily frustrated. Lynda's search for love through sex, in other words, leads to failure.

Various scenes in the film suggest that all was not so bad when Lynda was a child. During the war, when her mother was still alive, she was happier. Hubert constantly tries to shame Lynda by telling her that her mother would not have approved of her current behavior. Lynda might agree, but even as a child she rejected her father as a dull interloper in the happy relationship she shared with her mother. Lynda's first appearance in the film shows her as a child wearing a gas mask, refusing to remove it so as not to have to give her returning father a welcoming kiss. Although only a child, Lynda defiantly interrupts her parents' conversations with family and friends to characterize their interests as humbug, especially when her father tells yet again of having set the hair of some second-rate illustrious client. Although these scenes suggest that Lynda was happier with her mother in the halcyon days of yore, the film as a whole does not argue convincingly that Lynda would have been any happier had her mother lived.

Ignoring the underlying cause of Lynda's disruptions—her dissatisfaction with the narrow interests of the people around her and her own loneliness—and focusing on the superficial (her foul language), her father hopes that a psychiatrist can help Lynda adjust. In a hilarious sendup of psychiatric practices, the doctor asks Lynda to work her way through the alphabet naming all the foul words she can associate with each letter. Things go well until she gets to *f*, at which point she foils his expectations by insisting that she cannot think of any words. The psychiatrist abandons the exercise and discusses Lynda's behavior with Hubert, while she stands aside mugging and miming her sarcastic opinion of their inability to comprehend her behavior.

Disingenuously putting on a show of her legs and knickers for the men who work at the bus station (where her father next finds her a job), Lynda again gets herself fired, but not before beginning a flirtation with Dave, the young bus driver. Delighted to be going dancing with a handsome, cheeky young man, Lynda practically throws herself into Dave's bed, even if it is really his grandmother's bed in his grandmother's house, available to him for amorous purposes only through her absence. She is not so overwhelmed, however, as to have lost her sharp eye for humbug. Dave takes so long to prepare himself for bed that when he finally appears before her, foppishly dressed in yellow pajamas and carrying a long cigarette holder, she tells him that she is not half as impressed with him as he is with himself. When morning arrives, one of the film's most amusing scenes occurs. Dave's suspicious uncle comes to the house, and his dog finds a used condom under the bed. Although Lynda has also hid under the bed, she miraculously escapes detection, and she and Dave burst into laughter as, unnoticed, the dog carries the condom out into the street amid the Sunday pedestrian traffic.

Yet, all is not laughter and sunshine in *Wish You Were Here*. Having succumbed to Eric's advances, Lynda soon becomes pregnant and goes away to another seaside community, where she works in a painfully respectable tea room frequented by the reserved and middle-aged well-to-do. Again and again, she tries to reconcile herself to an abortion. Her aunt (Pat Heywood) comes to see her, offering advice and money for the abortion. In one of the film's most moving scenes, her aunt speaks the frank words of an older woman who, although understanding Lynda's needs and desires, also sees the potential for disaster in Lynda's current behavior. Sitting across from each other at a long, empty table, framed by a window separating them from the bleak and empty boardwalk, the two women seem imprisoned by the grim realities of their lives.

Lynda has two other visitors to her self-imposed exile. When Eric humbles himself to pursue her and to ask her to return to him, she tries first to avoid him by having another waitress serve him. When she is forced to confront him, however, the setting—lone figures viewed from a distance stalking along an empty pier and gesticulating angrily—again emphasizes the isolation and unhappiness of Lynda's situation. When her father pursues her to the tea room, though, the results are quite different. He provokes an argument and the two of them quarrel loudly, upsetting the guests and management, thrilling the other servers, and garnering applause from the elderly woman who has continued discreetly to play the piano.

After this uproarious scene, Lynda is fired once again, and the viewer is left wondering what decisions she will make. When she returns home and steps down from the bus wearing white gloves and a splendidly full-skirted yellow dress, that wonder grows. When it becomes clear that she is carrying a baby, which she transports home to her father's house in a magnificent new baby carriage, parading through the streets and defiantly saying to one and all, "Yes, it's mine," wonder may have turned to bewilderment. Lynda is once again radiantly beautiful and finally happy, but one questions if this well-being can be maintained.

It may be, as some reviewers have suggested, that Lynda's happiness derives from the fact that she has finally found something of her own to love that will love her in return. Having lost her own mother, she has found happiness in becoming a mother herself. Yet, from a realist's point of view, or from a feminist's point of view, this ending poses problems. It is true that in a small British town of the early 1950's a young woman such as Lynda would have had few outlets for her exuberance and that it would likely have manifested itself through her sexuality. What makes the ending of *Wish You Were Here* seem so implausible, though, is the uncertain question of her future and that of her child. After all, who will support Lynda and the baby? Is it believable that motherhood alone will miraculously make Lynda happy?

Wish You Were Here, despite the realism of its settings and supporting roles, seems in the final analysis to partake more of fantasy than of reality. In this it differs from films such as *Empire of the Sun* (1987; reviewed in this volume) and *Hope and Glory* (1987; reviewed in this volume). Although these two films deal with the specific effects of World War II on the average Briton's life both at home and in the colonies, they and *Wish You Were Here* seem part of a trend (along with such novels as Ronald Frame's *Sandmouth*, 1987) to reexamine middle-class British life under the pressures of the war and its aftermath. Of all these works, *Wish You Were Here* seems most like an abstraction and least grounded in specific reality. There is an element of Lynda's interaction with people that is reminiscent of the antic quality of the wantonly destructive females in Véra Chytilová's *Daisies* (1966). Granted, Leland's thematic scope and structure are smaller than Chytilová's, and Lloyd's performance must warm our hearts to Lynda. Yet, Lynda is a character not quite of this earth. Our sympathies must also go out to her father, an ordinary man who really has done nothing to deserve the fate of being responsible for such an impossibly bright and sharptongued young woman. For viewers who must deal with her for a few bright, shining moments, however, Lynda is a refreshingly honest joy and a delight.

Harriet Margolis

Reviews

Films in Review. XXXVIII, November, 1987, p. 547.
Los Angeles Times. July 30, 1987, VI, p. 1.
The Nation. CCXLV, September 12, 1987, p. 246.
The New Republic. CXCVII, August 3, 1987, p. 27.
New Statesman. CXIV, December 18, 1987, p. 34.
The New York Times. July 24, 1987, p. C7.
The New Yorker. LXIII, July 27, 1987, p. 63.
Newsweek. CX, August 3, 1987, p. 67.
Time. CXXX, September 7, 1987, p. 68.

THE WITCHES OF EASTWICK

Production: Neil Canton, Peter Guber, and Jon Peters; released by Warner Bros.
Direction: George Miller
Screenplay: Michael Cristofer, based on the novel of the same name by John Updike
Cinematography: Vilmos Zsigmond
Editing: Richard Francis-Bruce and Hubert C. De La Bouollerie
Art direction: Polly Platt
Special effects: Industrial Light and Magic
Makeup: Rob Bottin
Music: John Williams
MPAA rating: R
Running time: 122 minutes

Principal characters:
Daryl Van Horne .... Jack Nicholson
Alexandra Medford .... Cher
Jane Spofford.................... Susan Sarandon
Sukie Ridgemont .... Michelle Pfeiffer
Felicia Alden................ Veronica Cartwright
Clyde Alden .... Richard Jenkins
Walter Neff .... Keith Joakum
Fidel .... Carel Struycker

John Updike is a prestigious writer, and Hollywood is always ready to exploit prestige, even if not commonly prone to respect it. As often happens, the design of Updike's novel, *The Witches of Eastwick* (1984), was drastically modified to turn the story into a star vehicle for Jack Nicholson, who plays the Devil incarnate, Daryl Van Horne; Van Horne is not, however, the central character of Updike's novel. In Updike's original work, the Devil is a dupe and no match for the three clever women who dominate the narrative. As Pauline Kael remarked in *The New Yorker*, about Michael Cristofer's "rickety script," the film is little more than "a farce that resembles its source."

Understandably, then, Updike's readers were bound to be bothered and bewildered (though perhaps bewitched) by the film version directed by Australian George Miller in 1986, released in June of 1987, and only loosely based upon the novel. The film is little more than a cartoon reduction of the original story about three divorcées who discover that they have supernatural powers, which they use, sometimes spitefully, to terrorize people they dislike in the Rhode Island community where they live. Conventional notions of witchcraft are amusingly updated to the twentieth century.

The witches are led by the artist-earthmother Alexandra, who at thirty-eight, is the eldest of the three. She makes curious female figurines called "bubbies," sculpted with distinctive anatomical enlargements. Jane, who plays the cello, is the most malicious of the three. Sukie, the youngest, is a writer, hacking away as a journalist for a local paper, the Eastwick *Word*. All three have artistic temperaments, and in the novel, they know from the beginning that they have supernatural powers. The film reduces their bitchiness as well as their witchiness. It also diminishes their spirit.

Updike wickedly suggests that the power of witchcraft exists in all intelligent, independent, artistic women and that such power can be liberated by female frustration and contempt for men. The local men, whom they use for their carnal pleasures, are relatively stupid and defenseless against their charms. After the witches have worked terrible hexes on their local adversaries, other women in town start to hex them. The film ignores their nastier tendencies, making the women rather ordinary; it opts instead for a bland kind of bewitching comedy where they are concerned. Updike's comedy, often bordering on satire, is far more sophisticated than that of the film.

Updike's plot turns on the appearance of a wealthy, mysterious inventor who comes to town to purchase a local mansion, presumably summoned by the witches, testing their powers. His name is Daryl Van Horne and he seems to be the Devil. The film makes no mistake about his demoniac identity, taking the story one step beyond the reality that Updike meticulously creates, flattening it out and making it obvious. In both versions, the witches seem to have conjured him, and in both he takes possession of the three sexually. In the novel, however, he finally marries a young woman named Jenny, who is then hexed to death by the three very jealous witches.

The cinematic version omits the character of Jenny, consciously undercutting the malevolence of the three female leads, Cher as Alexandra, Susan Sarandon as Jane, and Michelle Pfeiffer as Sukie. Miller, best known for his Mad Max series, told an interviewer that he took on the project without having read the novel. If it is true that he had only read the screenplay and then went on to make modifications on its design, it is hardly surprising that the film wanders so far from its source.

The most major transformation, no doubt, concerns the Van Horne character, which is redesigned as yet another Nicholson loony, making the film look like an unnatural mating of *The Witches of Eastwick* and *The Shining* (1980). Updike's often-elegant and wickedly amusing novel is not exactly improved by a transformation that turns it into a Stephen King-styled Gothic tale about the Devil.

Nevertheless, it is often amusing to watch Nicholson overact and draw new business out of his evil bag of tricks. That wicked flamboyance surely justified whatever extravagance might have been budgeted for his salary. Nicholson's seduction scenes, first with Cher and later with Sarandon, are so outrageous that they are fascinating to watch.

The film builds to a spectacular conclusion, moreover, as the novel does not, as the three witches focus their powers to hex Van Horne out of their lives after he has attempted to punish them for turning their backs on him. The film's finale looks like something out of *Ghostbusters* (1984), only slightly more serious. Superior special effects create a ghastly spectacle that is all flash and trash.

In the novel, Van Horne forms an apparently homosexual attachment with Jenny's brother after she dies, and the two of them simply go away together. There is no big finale and no excuse for special effects. In the film, all three witches become pregnant and give birth to sons after they have sent Van Horne back to where he belongs. They continue to live in harmony together at his Eastwick estate and thwart his attempts to communicate with his offspring from the "other side." This conclusion, though flashy and good for a final laugh, has nothing to do with Updike, who almost keeps his narrative within the bounds of ordinary reality.

Clearly, the film was not made for the readers of John Updike but as an excuse for Nicholson to flaunt his extravagant tricks, including a replaying of his mad scene in *The Shining*, played here in a village street in the light of day. The film explodes with his energy, enhanced by special effects, while the witches merely provide entertaining support. Van Horne, a character of some mystery and magnitude in Updike's original, is simplified as a cartoon misogynist and a "horny little devil," made idiotic by his own words.

One discerns a potential problem of focus in Updike's novel. This problem is solved in the film rather crudely by compressing and reinventing the action and by decimating the characters. Cristofer's screenplay distances the witches that Updike so carefully individualized. It deprives the viewer of an adequate context, as when the witches victimize an obnoxious, self-righteous neighbor by having her spit up the sweepings from their kitchen floors. In the novel, their motive is sexual and spiteful. The film version attempts to simplify and improve this sequence by having Felicia (Veronica Cartwright) vomiting cherry pits (in church, no less), intercut with Nicholson feeding the witches cherries as they skinny-dip in his pool. The mischief here is inspired by Nicholson, not by the witches, and the film fails to make clear exactly what may be happening.

Moreover, in the novel Van Horne is not the only man in the witches' lives, just as they are not the only women in his, though he is, to be sure, the most exciting. Updike's witches are not merely sexually repressed singles, just waiting for a sexy devil to detonate them. Regardless of Nicholson's flamboyant lechery (which is clearly played for laughs), the film is relatively chaste when compared to the rampant adultery that dominates the novel. Cher's Alexandra, the dominant character in the novel, is easily eclipsed in the film by Sarandon's Jane, who turns into a ravishing sexpot after Nicholson has fiddled with her.

Updike did not bother to see this motion picture, but after friends had told him that the filmed treatment only slightly resembled his text, he wrote a piece for *The New York Times* entitled "Seen the Movie? Read the Book!" Updike took the commonsensical position that novelists who sell the rights to their work to Hollywood thereafter lose control over the alterations that usually follow.

He took solace in the fact, however, that "the text is always there, for the ideal reader to stumble upon, to enter, to reanimate, . . . readily recoverable and potentially as alive as on the day it was first scribbled." Books will be sold, and filmmakers "owe nothing to the authors of books they adapt except the money they have agreed to pay them." Regardless, books are eternal, and the text will survive for those curious enough to seek out the author's original intention, and his irony, elegance, and wit. The worst Hollywood can do is to create mistaken impressions about a book's merits. The best Hollywood can do is to send intelligent viewers scurrying to their local booksellers.

Evaluated purely as a film, however, *The Witches of Eastwick* is far better than the usual Hollywood demoniac horror vehicle: it is made visually interesting by Vilmos Zsigmond's cinematography and is sometimes distractingly amusing because of director Miller's sinister comic approach. The major drawing card is Nicholson, at his flamboyant best, who seems to be overcompensating for his lackluster performance in his last motion picture, *Heartburn* (1986). This film, in short, has plenty to offer a popular audience, though it has little to do with Updike, whose text survives, beyond commercialization, for serious readers.

James M. Welsh

Reviews

Commonweal. CXIV, July 17, 1987, p. 421.
Fantasy and Science Fiction. LXXIII, October, 1987, p. 74.
Films in Review. XXXVIII, October, 1987, p. 490.
Literature/Film Quarterly. XV, number 3, p. 151.
Los Angeles Times. June 12, 1987, VI, p. 1.
The New York Times. June 12, 1987, p. C3.
The New Yorker. LXIII, June 29, 1987, p. 72.
Newsweek. CIX, June 15, 1987, p. 71.
Time. CXXIX, June 22, 1987, p. 76.
The Washington Post. June 12, 1987, p. D1.

WITHNAIL AND I

Origin: Great Britain
Released: 1986
Released in U.S.: 1987
Production: Paul M. Heller for HandMade Films; released by Cineplex Odeon Films
Direction: Bruce Robinson
Screenplay: Bruce Robinson
Cinematography: Peter Hannan
Editing: Alan Strachan
Production design: Michael Pickwoad
Art direction: Henry Harris
Special effects: Paul Corbould
Costume design: Andrea Galer
Music: David Dundas and Rick Wentworth
MPAA rating: R
Running time: 108 minutes

Principal characters:
Withnail . . . . Richard E. Grant
Marwood . . . . Paul McGann
Uncle Monty . . . . Richard Griffiths
Danny . . . . Ralph Brown
Jake . . . . Michael Elphick
Irishman . . . . Daragh O'Mallery
Isaac Parkin . . . . Michael Wardle
Mrs. Parkin . . . . Una Brandon-Jones
General . . . . Noel Johnson
Waitress . . . . Irene Sutcliffe

Withnail and I marks the directorial debut of Bruce Robinson (scriptwriter of *The Killing Fields*, 1984), who is also the author of its screenplay. The film is set in 1969 and concerns the adventures of two starving actors, Withnail (Richard E. Grant) and Marwood (Paul McGann), the "I" of the title, who inhabit a decrepit apartment in Camden Town, London. As the film opens, the two men have reached a totally abject state caused by their experience of cold and hunger and by the effects of the drugs and alcohol which they consume in order to endure the squalor of their environment. In desperation, Marwood proposes that they take a rejuvenating trip to the country. In order to effect their plan, they visit Withnail's highly eccentric, flamboyantly homosexual Uncle Monty (Richard Griffiths) and procure the key to Uncle Monty's place in the country.

Upon arriving in the country, Withnail and Marwood discover that Uncle Monty's country seat is not much more than a glorified hovel, and they are left to endure the same kind of struggle against cold and hunger which had characterized their life in London. While in the country, Withnail and Marwood encounter various eccentric characters, including Jake (Michael Elphick), the village poacher, who refuses to sell them any food and who ominously threatens to pay the two a visit some night. Later, when Withnail and Marwood spot Jake prowling around their cottage, they determine to return to London. During the night before their intended departure, the two friends hear someone breaking into the cottage. That someone proves to be Uncle Monty, who finds the men crouched in the same bed, paralyzed with fear.

Withnail and Marwood realize that Uncle Monty's motivation for visiting them is sexual rather than paternal, and Marwood now lives in dread of Uncle Monty's advances. The following night, after the intoxicated Withnail has been put to bed, Marwood's worst fears are confirmed as Uncle Monty corners him and virtually forces himself on Marwood. Although both Marwood and Withnail are heterosexual, Marwood fends off Uncle Monty with the fiction that he and Withnail are lovers and that any infidelity on Marwood's part would kill Withnail. The sensitive Uncle Monty is shattered at having, as he thinks, almost come between the lovers, and he desists in his advances on Marwood. The next morning, Withnail and Marwood discover that the only trace of the vanished Uncle Monty is a letter in which he attributes his departure to his desire not to come between the friends. Withnail and Marwood are interrupted in their discussion of Uncle Monty by the arrival of a telegram for Marwood requesting his presence at a theatrical audition. The telegram precipitates their immediate return to London. Back in town, Marwood unexpectedly lands the lead in a play that will open in Manchester, forcing the friends to separate.

Withnail and I constitutes yet one more testimony to the vitality of recent British cinema. Like Hanif Kureishi (screenwriter of *My Beautiful Laundrette*, 1985, and *Sammy and Rosie Get Laid*, 1987) and David Leland (screenwriter of *Mona Lisa*, 1986, and *Personal Services*, 1987), Robinson is a highly skilled screenwriter who combines verbal wit with a keen pictorial sense. As *Withnail and I* begins, the way in which the camera pans the debris-glutted flat of Withnail and Marwood immediately suggests the depths to which the pair have sunk. Soon after, in keeping with his predilection for making extreme, histrionic gestures, Withnail drinks lighter fluid. He then accuses Marwood of being in possession of some antifreeze, to which Marwood retorts, "You should never mix your drinks."

The antisentimental, darkly comic tone of the opening scenes dominates the film as a whole and suggests affinities between *Withnail and I* and numerous recent British films, including *Letter to Brezhnev* (1985) and *Sid and Nancy* (1986). In *Withnail and I*, the black comedy arises from an absurdist, tongue-in-cheek treatment of the battle that Withnail and Marwood wage against poverty, cold, and hunger, and such comedy functions to demystify a popular, nostalgic vision of the 1960's. Like *Prick Up Your Ears* (1987; reviewed in this volume) and *Wish You Were Here* (1987; reviewed in this volume), *Withnail and I*'s vision of a past era is colored by the filmmaker's sensitivity to the hard realities of the contemporary British scene. This implicit link between the 1960's and the 1980's is most strongly suggested at the end of the film when Danny (Ralph Brown), the strangely visionary drug dealer, remarks upon the fact that the decade of the 1960's is nearing an end and prophesies, "London is a country coming down from her trip."

Another indication of Robinson's craftsmanship is that, despite its apparent looseness, *Withnail and I* is constructed in a highly organized manner. The film's tripartite and circular structure comprises an introductory segment set in London, a central section focusing on the adventures of Withnail and Marwood in the country, and a conclusion set back in London. This basic structure is punctuated by the way in which the film's middle is framed by sequences of Withnail and Marwood traveling on the road in their dilapidated Jaguar. Such structural symmetry is further accentuated by the fact that the two friends head out of London to the strains of one Jimi Hendrix standard, "All Along the Watchtower," and return to the strains of another, "Voodoo Chile."

The central section of the film, involving the rural hiatus, is in turn divided roughly in half. In the first part, before Uncle Monty's arrival, the humor is mainly a darkly comic slapstick which arises from the total inability of Withnail and Marwood to cope with country life. In one hilarious sequence, the two men use a double-barreled shotgun in an unsuccessful attempt to shoot fish in a stream. Here the incongruity between the pastoral environment and the urban intruders with their gun is truly absurd.

Uncle Monty's arrival in the country signals a shift in the film's comic strategy from slapstick to a kind of homosexual sex farce. These episodes, however, which exploit for comic purpose both the image of Marwood's homophobia and a caricature of homosexuality in the person of Uncle Monty, exemplify a fundamental problem with the film's tone. On the one hand, the film's manipulative purpose seems to be merely to evoke the audience's laughter, and to this end Robinson has masterfully exploited a number of time-honored comic devices. For example, Withnail and Uncle Monty can be seen as contemporary versions of traditional comic eccentrics, characters whose behavior functions on the basis of hyperbole. Not even the brilliant performances of Grant and Griffiths can disguise the fact that Withnail and Uncle Monty are essentially characters in the Jonsonian tradition of humors. The basic plot reworks an archetypal comic situation involving urbanites in the country, a situation that merely reverses the old pattern, which focuses on country bumpkins who find themselves in the sophisticated city.

Yet, working against a characterization of the film as mere entertainment are numerous traces of a more serious purpose. There are, for example, allusions to entrapment and the need for escape running throughout the film. Withnail and Marwood must first escape the confines of their apartment and therefore plan an escape to the country. In the country, however, Withnail and Marwood encounter only a different version of the same struggle with hunger and poverty, and, as Marwood discovers, "country folk are no more receptive to strangers than city people."

Withnail and I's puzzling ambiguity of tone is most forcefully apparent in the film's final moments. After encouraging Withnail not to accompany him to the station, Marwood exits, leaving a drunken Withnail to stand alone in the rain. As if to punctuate his awareness of his own continued imprisonment, Withnail walks over to a high wire fence which encages some wild wolves and utters the famous speech from William Shakespeare's *Hamlet* which begins, "I have of late . . . lost all my mirth." It is a moment in which Withnail's delightfully outrageous histrionics turn sour, a moment in which the blackness and bleakness inherent in the comedy of the film rises disturbingly to the surface. Like Withnail, the film has lost all of its mirth, and also like Withnail, the filmmaker seems to have something profound to say, but his message remains elusive.

Paul W. Salmon

Reviews
Films in Review. XXXVIII, October, 1987, p. 495.
Los Angeles Times. June 30, 1987, VI, p. 1.
Macleans. C, July 6, 1987, p. 55.
The New Republic. CXCVII, July 13, 1987, p. 26.
The New York Times. June 19, 1987, p. C10.
Time. CXXX, September 7, 1987, p. 68.
Variety. CCCXXVI, February 11, 1987, p. 17.
Vogue. CLXXVII, July, 1987, p. 40.
The Wall Street Journal. July 16, 1987, p. 26.

MORE FILMS OF 1987

Abbreviations: *Pro.* = Production *Dir.* = Direction *Scr.* = Screenplay *Cine.* = Cinematography *Ed.* = Editing *Mu.* = Music *P.d.* = Production design *A.d.* = Art direction *S.d.* = Set decoration *R.t.* = Running time *MPAA* = MPAA rating

ADVENTURES IN BABYSITTING
Pro. Debra Hill and Lynda Obst; Buena Vista *Dir.* Chris Columbus *Scr.* David Simkins *Cine.* Ric Waite *Ed.* Fredric Steinkamp and William Steinkamp *Mu.* Michael Kamen *P.d.* Todd Hallowell *A.d.* Barbara Dunphy *S.d.* Dan May *R.t.* 99 min. *MPAA* PG-13. *Cast:* Elisabeth Shue, Maia Brewton, Keith Coogan, Anthony Rapp, Calvin Levels, Vincent D'Onofrio, Penelope Ann Miller, George Newbern, John Ford Noonan, Bradley Whitford.

A babysitter (Elisabeth Shue) takes her charges with her when she goes to pick up a friend at the downtown Chicago bus station.

ALADDIN (*Superfantagenio.* Italy, 1987)
Pro. Ugo Tucci; Italian International Film *Dir.* Bruno Corbucci *Scr.* Mario Amendola, Marcello Fondato, and Bruno Corbucci *Cine.* Silvano Ippoliti *Ed.* Daniele Alabiso *Mu.* Fabio Frizzi *R.t.* 100 min. *Cast:* Bud Spencer, Luca Venantini, Janet Agren, Umberto Raho, Julian Voloshin, Daimy Spencer.

A teenage boy working in a junk shop calls up a genie when he polishes a rusty oil lamp.

ALIEN PREDATOR (also known as *The Falling*)
Pro. Deran Sarafian and Carlos Aured; Trans World Entertainment *Dir.* Deran Sarafian *Scr.* Deran Sarafian; based on the screenplay *Massacre at R. V. Park*, by Noah Blogh *Cine.* Tote Trenas *Ed.* Dennis Hill *Mu.* Chase/Rucker Productions *R.t.* 90 min. *MPAA* R. *Cast:* Dennis Christopher, Martin Hewitt, Lynn-Holly Johnson, Luis Prendes, J. O. Bosso.

Three youths are threatened by an alien that came to Earth as the result of the Skylab crash and that drives its human hosts mad.

ALL-AMERICAN HIGH
Pro. Keva Rosenfeld and Linda Maron; Direct Cinema *Dir.* Keva Rosenfeld *Cine.* Kevin O'Brien and Robert Wise *Ed.* Keva Rosenfeld *Mu.* Ethan James *R.t.* 59 min.

This documentary focuses on the social activities and nonscholarly electives offered at upper-middle-class Torrance High School in California, as seen through the eyes of a Finnish exchange student.

ALLAN QUATERMAIN AND THE LOST CITY OF GOLD
Pro. Menahem Golan and Yoram Globus; Cannon Group *Dir.* Gary Nelson *Scr.* Gene Quintano; based on the novel by H. Rider Haggard *Cine.* Alex Phillips and Frederick Elmes *Ed.* Gary Griffen and Dan Loewenthal *Mu.* Michael Linn and Jerry Goldsmith *P.d.* Trevor Williams and Leslie Dilley *S.d.* Patrick Willis and Portia Iversen *R.t.* 99 min. *MPAA* PG. *Cast:* Richard Chamberlain, Sharon Stone, James Earl Jones, Henry Silva, Robert Donner, Doghmi Larbi, Aileen Marson, Cassandra Peterson, Martin Rabbett, Rory Kilalea.

Allan Quatermain (Richard Chamberlain) and his fiancée (Sharon Stone) search for his brother (Martin Rabbett), who has found descendants of Phoenicians living in a City of Gold in Africa's jungles.

THE ALLNIGHTER

Pro. Tamar Simon Hoffs; Universal *Dir.* Tamar Simon Hoffs *Scr.* Tamar Simon Hoffs and M. L. Kessler *Cine.* Joseph Urbanczyk *Ed.* Dan M. Rich *Mu.* Charles Bernstein *P.d.* Cynthia Sowder *S.d.* Debra Combs *R.t.* 92 min. *MPAA* PG-13. *Cast:* Susanna Hoffs, Dedee Pfeiffer, Joan Cusack, John Terlesky, James Anthony Shanta, Michael Ontkean, Pam Grier, Kaaren Lee, Janelle Brady.

The Allnighter follows the antics of three beach-house roommates on the eve of their college graduation.

ALPINE FIRE (Switzerland, 1987)

Pro. Bernard Lang; Vestron Entertainment *Dir.* Fredi M. Murer *Scr.* Fredi M. Murer *Cine.* Pio Corradi *Ed.* Helena Gerber *Mu.* Mario Beretta *R.t.* 125 min. *MPAA* R. *Cast:* Thomas Nock, Johanna Lier, Dorothea Moritz, Rolf Illig, Tilli Breidenbach, Joerg Odermatt.

The isolation of farm life high in the Swiss Alps propels Belli (Johanna Lier) and her deaf brother (Thomas Nock) into a precarious sexual relationship.

AMAZING GRACE AND CHUCK

Pro. David Field; Tri-Star Pictures *Dir.* Mike Newell *Scr.* David Field *Cine.* Robert Elswit *Ed.* Peter Hollywood *Mu.* Elmer Bernstein *P.d.* Dena Roth *A.d.* John Myhre *S.d.* Michael J. Taylor *R.t.* 115 min. *MPAA* PG. *Cast:* Jamie Lee Curtis, Alex English, Gregory Peck, William L. Petersen, Joshua Zuehlke, Dennis Lipscomb, Lee Richardson, Frances Conroy.

After seeing a missile silo, Chuck (Joshua Zuehlke) refuses to take the mound in his Little League game as a form of protest over nuclear weapons. Soon others throughout the world join Chuck's stand, and the United States and Soviet governments are forced to agree to nuclear disarmament.

AMAZON WOMEN ON THE MOON

Pro. Robert K. Weiss; Universal *Dir.* Joe Dante, Carl Gottlieb, Peter Horton, John Landis, and Robert K. Weiss *Scr.* Michael Barrie and Jim Mulholland *Cine.* Daniel Pearl *Ed.* Bert Lovitt, Marshall Harvey, and Malcolm Campbell *A.d.* Alex Hajdu *S.d.* Julie Kaye Towery *R.t.* 85 min. *MPAA* R. *Cast:* Henny Youngman, Charlie Callas, Steve Allen, Lou Jacobi, Arsenio, Donald Muhich, Monique Gabrielle, Erica Yohn, Michelle Pfeiffer, Peter Horton, Griffin Dunne, Joe Pantoliano, Stanley Brock, Steve Forrest, Robert Colbert, Rip Taylor, Joey Travolta, Slappy White, David Alan Grier, B. B. King, Jackie Vernon, Rosanna Arquette, Steve Guttenberg, Henry Silva, Archie Hahn, Al Lohman, Roger Barkley, Ed Begley, Jr., John Ingle, Angel Tompkins, Terence McGovern, Carrie Fisher, Marc McClure, Matt Adler, Kelly Preston, Ralph Bellamy, Ira Newborn, Karen Montgomery, Sybil Danning, Justin Benham, Erica Gayle, Russ Meyer, Belinda Balaski, T. K. Carter, Philip Proctor.

The short skits in this anthology are strung together with segments of a science-fiction parody.

AMERICAN NINJA 2: THE CONFRONTATION

Pro. Menahem Golan and Yoram Globus; Cannon Group *Dir.* Sam Firstenberg *Scr.* Gary Conway and James Booth; from a story by Gary Conway; based on characters created by Avi Kleinberger and Gideon Amir *Cine.* Gideon Porath *Ed.* Michael J. Duthie *Mu.* George S. Clinton *P.d.* Holger Gross *A.d.* Robert Jenkinson *R.t.* 89 min. *MPAA* R. *Cast:* Michael Dudikoff, Steve James, Larry Poindexter, Gary Conway, Jeff Weston, Michelle Botes, Michael Stone, Len Sparrowhawk, Jonathan Pienaar.

Two ninja-trained army rangers (Michael Dudikoff and Steve James) are sent to a Caribbean island to investigate the disappearance of several United States marines.

ANGEL DUST (*Poussière d'ange.* France, 1987)
Pro. Jacques-Eric Strauss; UGC *Dir.* Edouard Niermans *Scr.* Edouard Niermans, Jacques Audiard, and Alain Le Henry *Cine.* Bernard Lutic *Ed.* Yves Deschamps and Jacques Witta *Mu.* Leon Senza and Vincent-Marie Bouvot *A.d.* Dominique Maleret *R.t.* 94 min. *Cast:* Bernard Giraudeau, Fanny Bastien, Fanny Cottencon, Jean-Pierre Sentier, Michel Aumont, Gerard Blain, Luc Lavandier, Veronique Silver, Daniel Laloux, Yveline Ailhaud, Patrick Bonnel, Bertie Cortez, Henri Marteau, Daniel Russo.

An alcoholic detective (Bernard Giraudeau) becomes involved with a young woman (Fanny Bastien) who is determined to kill everyone connected with the murder of her mother, a prostitute.

ANGUISH (*Angustia.* Spain, 1987)
Pro. Pepón Coromina; Samba P. C. and Luna Films *Dir.* Bigas Luna *Scr.* Bigas Luna *Cine.* José María Civit *Ed.* Tom Sabin *Mu.* J. M. Pagan *P.d.* Andreu Coromina *S.d.* Felipe de Paco *R.t.* 89 min. *Cast:* Zelda Rubinstein, Michael Lerner, Talia Paul, Angel José, Clara Paster, Isabel García Lorca.

In this horror film, two mad killers stalk members of a theater audience who are watching a horror film.

L'ANNÉE DES MEDUSES (France, 1987)
Pro. Alain Terzian; European Classics *Dir.* Christopher Frank *Scr.* Christopher Frank; based on his novel of the same name *Cine.* Renato Berta *Ed.* Nathalie Lafaurie *Mu.* Alain Wisniak *A.d.* Jean-Jacques Caziot *R.t.* 110 min. *Cast:* Valerie Kaprisky, Bernard Giraudeau, Caroline Gellier, Jacques Perrin, Beatrice Agenin, Betty Assenza, Charlotte Kadi, Pierre Vaneck, Philippe Lemaire, Antoine Nikola.

A teenager and her mother compete sexually.

APRIL IS A DEADLY MONTH (*Les Mois d'avril sont meurtriers.* France, 1987)
Pro. Louis Grau; Sara/CDF *Dir.* Laurent Heynemann *Scr.* Laurent Heynemann, Bertrand Tavernier, and Philippe Boucher; based on *The Devil's Home on Leave*, a novel by Robin Cook *Cine.* Jean-Francis Gondre *Ed.* Armand Psenny *Mu.* Philippe Sarde *A.d.* Valerie Grall *R.t.* 88 min. *Cast:* Jean-Pierre Marielle, Jean-Pierre Bisson, François Berleand, Brigitte Rouan, Guylaine Pean.

A policeman (Jean-Pierre Marielle) stalks a professional killer (Jean-Pierre Bisson) against whom there is no evidence.

ASSASSINATION
Pro. Pancho Kohner; Cannon Group *Dir.* Peter Hunt *Scr.* Richard Sale *Cine.* Hanania Baer *Ed.* James Heckert *Mu.* Robert O. Ragland and Valentine Mc-Callum *P.d.* William Cruise *A.d.* Joshua S. Culp *R.t.* 88 min. *MPAA* PG-13. *Cast:* Charles Bronson, Jill Ireland, Stephen Elliott, Jan Gan Boyd, Randy Brooks, Erik Stern, Michael Ansara, James Staley, Kathryn Leigh Scott, James Acheson.

Jay Killian (Charles Bronson) tries to protect the First Lady (Jill Ireland), a spoiled woman who has become the target of assassins.

BABETTE'S FEAST (Denmark, 1987)
Pro. Gabriel Axel; Orion Classics *Dir.* Gabriel Axel *Scr.* Gabriel Axel; based on a story from *Anecdotes of Destiny*, by Isak Dinesen *Cine.* Henning Kristiansen *Ed.* Finn Henriksen *Mu.* Per Norgard *P.d.* Eugenio Zanetti *R.t.* 105 min. *Cast:* Stephane Audran, Birgitte Federspiel, Bodil Kjer, Vibeke Hastrup, Hanne Stensgard, Jarl Kulle, Gudmar Wivesson, Jean-Philippe Lafont, Bibi Andersson.

Two spinster sisters take in a widowed refugee, Babette (Stephane Audran), who rewards their charity with a breathtaking surprise.

BACK TO THE BEACH
Pro. Frank Mancuso, Jr.; Paramount Pictures *Dir.* Lyndall Hobbs *Scr.* Peter Krikes, Steve Meerson, and Christopher Thompson; based on a story by James Komack and characters created by Lou Rusoff *Cine.* Bruce Surtees *Ed.* David Finfer *Mu.* Steve Dorff *P.d.* Michael Helmy *R.t.* 92 min. *MPAA* PG. *Cast:* Annette Funicello, Frankie Avalon, Connie Stevens, Lori Loughlin, Tommy Hinkley, Demian Slade, John Calvin, Joe Holland, David Bowe, Bob Denver, Don Adams, Tony Dow, Jerry Mathers, Pee-wee Herman, Steve Ray Vaughan, Dick Dale, O. J. Simpson.

Annette (Annette Funicello) and Frankie (Frankie Avalon) return to the beaches of Los Angeles to find their daughter living with her surfer boyfriend.

BACKFIRE
Pro. Danton Rissner *Dir.* Gilbert Cates *Scr.* Larry Brand and Rebecca Reynolds *Cine.* Tak Fujimoto *Ed.* Melvin Shapiro *Mu.* David Shire *P.d.* Dan Lomino *R.t.* 91 min. *Cast:* Karen Allen, Keith Carradine, Jeff Fahey, Bernie Casey, Dean Paul Martin, Dinah Manoff.

A rich Vietnam veteran (Jeff Fahey) has recurring nightmares about combat in the war, and although he believes that his wife is his one support, she seems to be involved in intrigue against him.

THE BARBARIANS
Pro. John Thompson; Cannon International *Dir.* Ruggero Deodato *Scr.* James R. Silke *Cine.* Lorenzo Battaglia *Ed.* Eugene Alabiso *Mu.* Pino Donaggio *P.d.* Giuseppe Mangano *R.t.* 87 min. *MPAA* R. *Cast:* David Paul, Peter Paul, Richard Lynch, Eva La Rue, Virginia Bryant, Sheeba Alahani, Michael Berryman.

Twin brothers (David Paul and Peter Paul) escape the slavery under which they have grown up and regroup with their former friends to rescue their queen (Virginia Bryant).

BATTERIES NOT INCLUDED
Pro. Ronald L. Schwary; Universal *Dir.* Matthew Robbins *Scr.* Matthew Robbins, Brad Bird, Brent Maddock, and S. S. Wilson; based on a story by Mick Garris *Cine.* John McPherson *Ed.* Cynthia Scheider *Mu.* James Horner *P.d.* Ted Haworth *A.d.* Angelo Graham *S.d.* George R. Nelson *R.t.* 116 min. *MPAA* PG. *Cast:* Hume Cronyn, Jessica Tandy, Frank McRae, Elizabeth Pena, Michael Carmine, Dennis Boutsikaris.

Steven Spielberg's space-alien fantasy features two aliens that come to the rescue of tenants in a rundown Manhattan brownstone.

THE BEAT
Pro. Julia Phillips, Jon Klik, and Nick Wechsler; Vestron Entertainment *Dir.* Paul

Mones *Scr.* Paul Mones *Cine.* Tom Di Cillo *Ed.* Elizabeth Kling *Mu.* Carter Burwell *P.d.* George Stoll *R.t.* 98 min. *MPAA* R. *Cast:* John Savage, David Jacobson, William McNamara, Kara Glover, Jeffrey Horowitz.

A class of rebellious kids at first ridicule and then follow the strange philosophy of a student who seems to believe that all the adults of the world are dead and that he is a mystical hero.

THE BEAT GENERATION—AN AMERICAN DREAM

Pro. Janet Forman; Renaissance Motion Pictures *Dir.* Janet Forman *Cine.* Tom Houghton *Ed.* Peter Odabashian *Mu.* David Amram *R.t.* 90 min. *Cast:* David Amram, Amiri Baraka, Ray Bremser, William S. Burroughs, Carolyn Cassidy, Clark Coolidge, Gregory Corso, Robert Creeley, Diane di Prima, Allen Ginsberg, Larry Fagin, Abbie Hoffman, Lawrence Ferlinghetti, Herbert Huncke, Hettie Jones, Jan Kerouac, Timothy Leary, Neal Cassidy, Peter Orlovsky, Thelonious Monk, Carl Solomon, Anne Waldman, Jack Kerouac.

Steve Allen narrates this documentary on the beatniks of the 1950's which includes interviews with participants in the movement as well as old film footage.

THE BELIEVERS

Pro. John Schlesinger, Michael Childers, and Beverly Camhe; Orion Pictures *Dir.* John Schlesinger *Scr.* Mark Frost; based on the book *The Religion*, by Nicholas Conde *Cine.* Bobby Muller *Ed.* Peter Honess *Mu.* J. Peter Robinson *P.d.* Simon Holland *A.d.* John Kasarda and Carol Spier *S.d.* Susan Bode and Elinor Rose Galbraith *R.t.* 110 min. *MPAA* R. *Cast:* Martin Sheen, Helen Shaver, Harley Cross, Robert Loggia, Elizabeth Wilson, Harris Yulin, Lee Richardson, Richard Masur, Carla Pinza, Jimmy Smits.

A police psychologist discovers the perpetrators of a series of ritualistic murders: members of an African voodoo cult who practice child sacrifice and devil worship in midtown Manhattan.

BELLY OF AN ARCHITECT

Pro. Colin Callender and Walter Donohue; Hemdale Film Corp. *Dir.* Peter Greenaway *Scr.* Peter Greenaway *Cine.* Sacha Vierny *Ed.* John Wilson *Mu.* Wim Mertens *A.d.* Luciana Vedovelli *R.t.* 108 min. *Cast:* Brian Dennehy, Chloe Webb, Lambert Wilson, Sergio Fantoni, Stephania Cassini, Vanni Corbellini, Alfredo Varelli, Geoffrey Coppleston, Francesco Carnelutti.

Stourley Kracklite (Brian Dennehy), an architect, gradually slips into insanity, becoming obsessed with abdomens.

BENJI THE HUNTED

Pro. Ben Vaughn; Buena Vista *Dir.* Joe Camp *Scr.* Joe Camp *Cine.* Don Reddy *Ed.* Karen Thorndike *Mu.* Euel Box and Betty Box *A.d.* Bob Riigs and Ray Brown *R.t.* 88 min. *MPAA* G. *Cast:* Benji, Red Steagall, Nancy Francis, Mike Francis, Frank Inn.

Lost after a fishing accident, Benji finds his way through the Northwest woods, cares for four orphaned cougar cubs, and outsmarts a wolf and Kodiak bear.

BIG SHOTS

Pro. Joe Medjuck and Michael C. Gross; Twentieth Century-Fox *Dir.* Robert Mandel *Scr.* Joe Eszterhas *Cine.* Miroslav Ondricek *Ed.* Bill Anderson, Sheldon Kahn, and Dennis Virkler *Mu.* Bruce Broughton *P.d.* Bill Malley *R.t.* 90 min. *MPAA* PG-13. *Cast:* Ricky Busker, Darius McCrary, Robert Joy, Jerzy

Skolimowski, Brynn Thayer, Robert Prosky, Paul Winfield.

A white suburban boy (Ricky Busker), lost and threatened in Chicago's inner city, is rescued and befriended by a black youth (Darius McCrary). Together they embark on a dangerous adventure.

THE BIG TOWN

Pro. Martin Ransohoff; Columbia Pictures *Dir.* Ben Bolt *Scr.* Robert Roy Pool; based on the novel *The Arm*, by Clark Howard *Cine.* Ralf D. Bode *Ed.* Stuart Pappe *Mu.* Michael Melvoin *P.d.* Bill Kenney *A.d.* Dan Yarhi *R.t.* 109 min. *MPAA* R. *Cast:* Matt Dillon, Diane Lane, Tommy Lee Jones, Bruce Dern, Lee Grant, Tom Skerritt, Suzy Amis, David Marshall Grant.

Crapshooter J. C. Cullen (Matt Dillon) tries his luck in the gambling halls of Chicago and falls in with a dangerous crowd.

BLOOD DINER

Pro. Jimmy Maslion; Vestron Entertainment *Dir.* Jackie Kong *Scr.* Michael Sonye *Cine.* Jurg Walther *Ed.* Thomas Meshelski *Mu.* Don Preston *P.d.* Ron Petersen *A.d.* Keith Barrett *R.t.* 90 min. *MPAA* R. *Cast:* Rick Burks, Carl Crew, Roger Dauer, Sheba Jackson, Lisa Guggenheim.

A pair of brothers carve up women's bodies in order to assemble a body for the ancient goddess Sheetar to inhabit.

BLUE MONKEY

Pro. Martin Walters; Spectrafilm *Dir.* William Fruet *Scr.* George Goldsmith *Cine.* Brenton Spencer *Ed.* Michael Fruet *Mu.* Patrick Coleman and Paul Novotny *A.d.* Reuben Freed *S.d.* Brendan Smith *R.t.* 98 min. *MPAA* R. *Cast:* Steve Railsback, Gwynyth Walsh, Susan Anspach, John Vernon, Joe Flaherty, Robin Duke, Don Lake, Sandy Webster, Helen Hughes, Joy Coghill.

A caterpillar regurgitated by a man in a hospital examining room grows into a hideous, slimy monster.

BODY SLAM

Pro. Shel Lytton and Mike Curb; De Laurentiis Entertainment Group *Dir.* Hal Needham *Scr.* Shel Lytton and Steve Burkow; based on a story by Shel Lytton *Cine.* Mike Shea *Ed.* Randy Thornton *Mu.* Michael Lloyd and John D'Andrea *A.d.* Pamela Warner *R.t.* 89 min. *Cast:* Dirk Benedict, Tanya Roberts, Roddy Piper, Captain Lou Albano, Barry Gordon, Charles Nelson Reilly, Billy Barty, John Astin, Deni Janssen, Sam (Tama) Fatu, Dennis Fimple.

A sly promoter (Dirk Benedict) almost accidentally links rock and roll and wrestling in his promotions and is quickly successful.

BORN IN EAST L. A.

Pro. Peter Macgregor-Scott; Universal *Dir.* Cheech Marin *Scr.* Cheech Marin *Cine.* Alex Phillips *Ed.* Don Brochu *Mu.* Lee Holdridge *A.d.* J. Rae Fox, Lynda Burbank, and Hector Rodriguez *S.d.* Steven Karatzas and Enrique Estevez *R.t.* 84 min. *MPAA* R. *Cast:* Cheech Marin, Paul Rodriguez, Daniel Stern, Kamala Lopez, Jan-Michael Vincent, Neith Hunter, Alma Martinez, Tony Plana.

Rudy (Cheech Marin), a Los Angeles native, becomes the victim of an immigration service mistake and is deported to Mexico.

THE BRAVE LITTLE TOASTER

Pro. Donald Kushner and Thomas L. Wilhite *Dir.* Jerry Rees *Scr.* Jerry Rees and Joe Ranft; based on a screen story by Jerry Rees, Joe Ranft, and Brian McEntee and the novella of the same name by Thomas M. Disch *Mu.* David Newman and Van Dyke Parks *A.d.* Brian McEntee *R.t.* 80 min. *Voices:* Jon Lovitz, Tim Stack, Timothy E. Day, Thurl Ravencroft, Deanna Oliver, Phil Hartman, Jonathon Berair, Joe Ranft.

In this animated children's story, five appliances from Rob's summer cabin—a lamp, a toaster, a vacuum cleaner, an electric blanket, and a radio—set out for the city to find their long-absent master.

BURGLAR

Pro. Kevin McCormick and Michael Hirsh; Warner Bros. *Dir.* Hugh Wilson *Scr.* Joseph Loeb III, Matthew Weisman, and Hugh Wilson; based on novels by Lawrence Block *Cine.* William A. Fraker *Ed.* Fredric Steinkamp and William Steinkamp *Mu.* Sylvester Levay *P.d.* Todd Hallowell *A.d.* Michael Corenblith *S.d.* Daniel Loren May *R.t.* 102 min. *MPAA* R. *Cast:* Whoopi Goldberg, Bobcat Goldthwait, G. W. Bailey, Lesley Ann Warren, James Handy, Anne DeSalvo, John Goodman, Elizabeth Ruscio, Vyto Ruginis, Larry Mintz.

A former cat burglar (Whoopi Goldberg) is blackmailed by a crooked policeman into doing some work for him. When a far more serious crime is committed while she is doing the job, she must find the real culprit before she is blamed.

BURKE AND WILLS (Australia, 1987)

Pro. Graeme Clifford and John Sexton; Hemdale Film Corp. *Dir.* Graeme Clifford *Scr.* Michael Thomas *Cine.* Russell Boyd *Ed.* Tim Wellburn *Mu.* Peter Sculthorpe *P.d.* Ross Major *R.t.* 140 min. *MPAA* PG-13. *Cast:* Jack Thompson, Nigel Havers, Greta Scacchi, Matthew Farger, Ralph Cotterill, Drew Forsythe, Chris Haywood, Monroe Reimers.

In this chronicle of the first trek by white men across Australia, Jack Thompson and Nigel Havers star as the forceful adventurer and the introspective scientist who led the arduous expedition.

BURNIN' LOVE

Pro. Michael Gruskoff; De Laurentiis Entertainment Group *Dir.* John Moffitt *Scr.* Terrence Sweeney and Lanier Laney *Cine.* Mark Irwin *Ed.* Danford B. Greene *Mu.* Charles Fox *P.d.* Roy Forge Smith *A.d.* Gordon White *S.d.* Brendan Smith *R.t.* 83 min. *Cast:* Patrick Cassidy, Kelly Preston, Bud Cort, David Graf, Stuart Pankin, Dave Thomas, Barbara Carrera, Georgia Brown, Annie Golden, Audrie Neenan, Jayne Eastwood, Dr. Joyce Brothers.

Two young lovers almost become victims in a witch-hunt hysteria orchestrated by the local judge and mayor in an effort to confiscate land to be used in a real-estate scheme.

BUSTED UP

Pro. Damian Lee and David Mitchell; Shapiro Entertainment *Dir.* Conrad E. Palmisano *Scr.* Gary Zubeck *Cine.* Ludvik Bogner *Ed.* Gary Zubeck *Mu.* Charles Barnett *A.d.* Stephen Surjik *R.t.* 90 min. *MPAA* R. *Cast:* Paul Coufos, Irene Cara, Stan Shaw, Tony Rosato.

A young man attempts to win a series of boxing matches in order to save the rundown gym he owns.

THE CALLER

Pro. Frank Yablans; Empire Pictures *Dir.* Arthur Seidelman *Scr.* Michael Sloan *Cine.* Armando Nannuzzi *Ed.* Bert Glatstein *Mu.* Richard Band *P.d.* Giovanni

Natalucci *R.t.* 98 min. *Cast:* Malcolm McDowell, Madolyn Smith.

A young woman living in an isolated cabin is reluctant at first to let a man enter her home. Soon, however, they begin an affair, but his actual function is as a lifelike police robot gathering information about her husband's death.

CAMPUS MAN

Pro. Peggy Fowler and Jon Landau; Paramount Pictures *Dir.* Ron Casden *Scr.* Matt Dorff, Alex Horvat, and Geoffrey Baere; based on a story by Matt Dorff and Alex Horvat *Cine.* Francis Kenny *Ed.* Steven Polivka *Mu.* James Newton Howard *P.d.* David Gropman *A.d.* Karen Schulz *S.d.* J. Allen Highfill *R.t.* 94 min. *MPAA* PG. *Cast:* John Dye, Steve Lyon, Kim Delaney, Kathleen Wilhoite, Miles O'Keeffe, Morgan Fairchild, John Welsh, Josef Rainer, Dick Alexander, Steve Archer, Eden Brandy.

A college business student (John Dye) who needs to raise ten thousand dollars for tuition persuades his roommate (Steve Lyon), who is on the diving team, to pose for a calendar. When the roommate is kicked off the team by the NCAA for posing, the trouble begins.

CAN'T BUY ME LOVE

Pro. Thom Mount; Buena Vista *Dir.* Steve Rash *Scr.* Michael Swerdlick *Cine.* Peter Lyons Collister *Ed.* Jeff Gourson *Mu.* Robert Folk *P.d.* Donald L. Harris *S.d.* Christian W. Russhon and Andrew Bernard *R.t.* 94 min. *MPAA* PG-13. *Cast:* Patrick Dempsey, Amanda Peterson, Courtney Gains, Seth Green, Tina Caspary, Devin Devasquez, Darcy DeMoss, Eric Bruskotter.

Desperate for an entry to the "in" crowd at school, Ronald (Patrick Dempsey) strikes an agreement with popular Cindi (Amanda Peterson): He will pay her one thousand dollars to act as his girlfriend for a month.

CAPTIVE HEARTS

Pro. John A. Kuri; Metro-Goldwyn-Mayer/United Artists *Dir.* Paul Almond *Scr.* Patrick N. Morita and John A. Kuri; based on an original screenplay by Sargon Tamimi *Cine.* Thomas Vamos *Ed.* Yurij Luhovy *Mu.* Osamu Kitajima *P.d.* Steve Sardanis and François DeLucy *S.d.* Claudine Charbonneau and Anne Galea *R.t.* 97 min. *MPAA* PG. *Cast:* Noriyuki (Pat) Morita, Chris Makepeace, Mari Sato, Michael Sarrazin, Seth Sakai, Denis Akiyama.

Shot down near a remote Japanese village during World War II, two United States airmen cope in different ways: One antagonizes his captors and tries to escape, while the other befriends the village elder and falls in love with a local woman.

THE CARE BEARS ADVENTURE IN WONDERLAND (Canada, 1987)

Pro. Michael Hirsh, Patrick Loubert, and Clive A. Smith; Cineplex Odeon Films *Dir.* Raymond Jafelice *Scr.* Susi Snooks and John Deklein; based on a story by Patrick Loubert and Peter Sauder *Mu.* Trish Cullen *R.t.* 75 min. *Voices:* Colin Fox, Bob Dermer, Eva Almos, Dan Hennessey, Jim Henshaw, Maria Lukofsky, Luba Goy, Keith Knight, Tracey Moore.

The Care Bears join Alice in Wonderland in this animated film.

CHINA GIRL

Pro. Michael Nozik; Vestron Entertainment *Dir.* Abel Ferrara *Scr.* Nicholas St. John *Cine.* Bojan Bazelli *Ed.* Anthony Redman *Mu.* Joe Delis *P.d.* Dan Leigh *S.d.* Leslie Rollins *R.t.* 88 min. *Cast:* James Russo, Sari Chang, Richard Panebianco, David Caruso, Russell Wong, Joey Chin, James Hong, Judith Malina.

Set in New York City, this film takes the *Romeo and Juliet* theme and sets it in the midst of a gang war between Chinese and Italian gangs.

THE CHIPMUNK ADVENTURE

Pro. Ross Bagdasarian; Samuel Goldwyn Company *Dir.* Janice Karman *Scr.* Janice Karman and Ross Bagdasarian *Mu.* Randy Edelman *P.d.* Carol Holman Grosvenor *R.t.* 90 min. *MPAA* G. *Voices:* Ross Bagdasarian, Janice Karman, Dody Goodman, Susan Tyrell, Anthony DeLongis, Frank Welker.

In this animated film, the Chipmunks challenge the Chipettes, a female trio, to a race around the world based on their favorite video game.

CHUCK BERRY: HAIL! HAIL! ROCK 'N' ROLL

Pro. Stephanie Bennett and Chuck Berry; Universal *Dir.* Taylor Hackford *Cine.* Oliver Stapleton *Ed.* Lisa Day *Mu.* Keith Richards *P.d.* Kim Colefax *S.d.* Rosemary Brandenburg *R.t.* 120 min. *MPAA* PG. *Cast:* Chuck Berry, Keith Richards, Linda Ronstadt, Julian Lennon, Robert Cray, Eric Clapton, Etta James, Little Richard, Bruce Springsteen, Jerry Lee Lewis, John Lennon, Roy Orbison, Don Everly, Phil Everly, Bo Diddley.

Rock star Chuck Berry talks about his years in music; superb concert footage and interviews with other musicians are included.

COLD STEEL

Pro. Lisa M. Hansen; CineTel Films *Dir.* Dorothy Ann Puzo *Scr.* Michael D. Sonye and Moe Quigley; based on a story by Michael D. Sonye, Dorothy Ann Puzo, and Lisa M. Hansen *Cine.* Tom Denove *Ed.* David Bartlett *Mu.* David A. Jackson *A.d.* Maxine Shepard *S.d.* Scott Ambrose *R.t.* 90 min. *MPAA* R. *Cast:* Brad Davis, Sharon Stone, Jonathan Banks, Jay Acovone, Adam Ant, Eddie Egan, Sy Richardson, Anne Haney, Ron Karabatsos.

Johnny Modine (Brad Davis), a Los Angeles policeman, pursues the murderer of his father.

COMMANDO SQUAD

Pro. Alan Amiel; Trans World Entertainment *Dir.* Fred Olen Ray *Scr.* Michael D. Sonye *Cine.* Gary Graver *Ed.* Kathie Weaver *A.d.* Corey Kaplan *R.t.* 89 min. *MPAA* R. *Cast:* Brian Thompson, Kathy Shower, William Smith, Sid Haig, Robert Quarry, Ross Hagen, Marie Windsor, Mel Welles, Benita Martinez, Dawn Wildsmith, Russ Tamblyn, Tane McClure, Michael D. Sonye.

On a mission to destroy a cocaine factory in Mexico, a pair of government drug enforcement agents (Kathy Shower and Brian Thompson) confront dealers and gunrunners.

COP

Pro. James B. Harris and James Woods; Atlantic Entertainment Group *Dir.* James B. Harris *Scr.* James B. Harris; based on the novel *Blood on the Moon*, by James Ellroy *Cine.* Steve Dubin *Ed.* Anthony Spano *Mu.* Michel Colombier *P.d.* Gene Rudolf *R.t.* 110 min. *MPAA* R. *Cast:* James Woods, Lesley Ann Warren, Charles Durning, Charles Haid, Raymond J. Barry, Randi Brooks, Steve Lambert, Annie McEnroe, Vicki Wauchope, Jan McGill.

Policeman Lloyd Hopkins (James Woods) is already suffering estrangement from his wife (Jan McGill) and young daughter (Vicki Wauchope) when a tough serial murder case threatens to send him over the edge.

CREEPOZOIDS

Pro. David DeCoteau and John Schouweiler; Urban Classics *Dir.* David DeCoteau *Scr.* Burford Hauser and David DeCoteau *Cine.* Thomas Callaway *Ed.* Miriam L. Preissel *Mu.* Guy Moon and Jonathan Scott Bogner *P.d.* Royce Mathew *R.t.* 71 min. *MPAA* R. *Cast:* Linnea Quigley, Ken Abraham, Michael Aranda, Richard Hawkins, Kim McKamy, Joi Wilson.

Several years after a nuclear war, five army deserters who seek refuge in an abandoned building are assaulted by a deadly monster.

CREEPSHOW 2

Pro. David Ball; New World Pictures *Dir.* Michael Gornick *Scr.* George A. Romero; based on stories by Stephen King *Cine.* Dick Hart and Tom Hurwitz *Ed.* Peter Weatherly *Mu.* Les Reed *P.d.* Bruce Miller *R.t.* 89 min. *MPAA* R. *Cast:* Lois Chiles, George Kennedy, Dorothy Lamour, Tom Savini, Domenick John, Frank S. Salsedo, Holt McCallany, David Holbrook, Don Harvey, Paul Satterfield, Jeremy Green, Daniel Beer, Page Hannah, David Beecroft, Tom Wright, Richard Parks, Stephen King, Joe Silver.

Three episodes based on Stephen King tales tell the stories of a wooden Indian out to avenge the deaths of two shopowners; a blob in a mountain lake that eats four teenagers; and a woman who is haunted by the hitchhiker she ran over.

CRITICAL CONDITION

Pro. Ted Field and Robert Cort; Paramount Pictures *Dir.* Michael Apted *Scr.* Denis Hamill and John Hamill; based on a story by Denis Hamill, John Hamill, and Alan Swyer *Cine.* Ralf D. Bode *Ed.* Robert K. Lambert *Mu.* Alan Silvestri *P.d.* John Lloyd *S.d.* George Robert Nelson *R.t.* 90 min. *MPAA* R. *Cast:* Richard Pryor, Rachel Ticotin, Ruben Blades, Joe Mantegna, Bob Dishy, Sylvia Miles, Joe Dallesandro, Randall "Tex" Cobb, Bob Saget, Garrett Morris.

A man (Richard Pryor) who has attempted an insanity plea is about to be sent back to jail when the lights go out in the hospital where he is being held. To escape, he pretends to be the doctor in charge of the hospital.

CROSS MY HEART

Pro. Lawrence Kasdan; Universal *Dir.* Armyan Bernstein *Scr.* Armyan Bernstein and Gail Parent *Cine.* Thomas Del Ruth *Ed.* Mia Goldman *Mu.* Bruce Broughton *P.d.* Lawrence G. Paull *A.d.* Bill Eliot *S.d.* Joanne MacDougall *R.t.* 90 min. *MPAA* R. *Cast:* Martin Short, Annette O'Toole, Paul Reiser, Joanna Kerns, Jessica Puscas, Lee Arenberg.

David (Martin Short) and Kathy (Annette O'Toole), on their third date, come into conflict as they begin to uncover painful facts about each other.

CRYSTAL HEART

Pro. Carlos Vasallo; New World Pictures *Dir.* Gil Bettman *Scr.* Linda Shayne; based on a story by Alberto Vázquez-Figueroa *Cine.* Alexander Ulloa *Ed.* Nicholas Wentworth *Mu.* Joel Goldsmith *P.d.* José María Alarcón *R.t.* 103 min. *MPAA* R. *Cast:* Lee Curreri, Tawny Kitaen, Lloyd Bochner, May Heatherly, Simon Andreu, Marina Saura, Lagena Lookabill.

A young man (Lee Curreri), who has spent his life in a sealed environment because of his lack of an immune system, and a prospective rock singer fall in love.

THE CURE IN ORANGE

Pro. Gordon Lewis; Movie Visions *Dir.* Tim Pope *Cine.* Chris Ashbrook *Ed.*

Peter Goddard *R.t.* 96 min. *Cast:* Robert Smith, Simon Gallup, Porl Thompson, Boris Williams, Laurence Tolhurst.

Members of The Cure perform twenty-three songs at a concert staged in the Roman ruins near Provence, France.

CYCLONE

Pro. Paul Hertzberg; CineTel Films *Dir.* Fred Olen Ray *Scr.* Paul Garson; based on a story by Fred Olen Ray *Cine.* Paul Elliott *Ed.* Robert A. Ferretti *Mu.* David A. Jackson *A.d.* Maxine Shepard *R.t.* 83 min. *MPAA* R. *Cast:* Heather Thomas, Jeffrey Combs, Ashley Ferrare, Dar Robinson, Martine Beswicke, Robert Quarry, Martin Landau.

A new top-secret weapon, a high-tech motorcycle with a transformer that converts hydrogen to energy, is coveted by villainous arms merchants who have no qualms about murdering its inventor.

DANCERS

Pro. Menahem Golan and Yoram Globus; Cannon Group *Dir.* Herbert Ross *Scr.* Sarah Kernochan *Cine.* Ennio Guarnieri *Ed.* William Reynolds *Mu.* Adolphe Adam and Pino Donaggio *P.d.* Gianni Quaranta *A.d.* Luigi Marchione *S.d.* Elio Altamura *R.t.* 99 min. *MPAA* PG. *Cast:* Mikhail Baryshnikov, Alessandra Ferri, Leslie Browne, Thomas Rall, Lynn Seymour, Victor Barbee, Julie Kent, Mariangela Melato, Leandro Amato, Gianmarco Tognazzi, Desmond Kelly, Chrisa Keramidas, Amy Werba, Jack Brodsky, Robert Argand, Amanda McKerrow, Bonnie Moore, Artists of the American Ballet Theatre.

A jaded womanizer and ballet dancer (Mikhail Baryshnikov) is refreshed by his relationship with a young ballerina (Julie Kent) as the ballet *Giselle* is being staged by their dance company.

DATE WITH AN ANGEL

Pro. Martha Schumacher; De Laurentiis Entertainment Group *Dir.* Tom McGloughlin *Scr.* Tom McGloughlin *Cine.* Alex Thomson *Ed.* Marshall Harvey *Mu.* Randy Kerber *P.d.* Craig Stearns *A.d.* Jeffrey S. Ginn *R.t.* 105 min. *MPAA* PG. *Cast:* Michael E. Knight, Phoebe Cates, Émmanuelle Béart, David Dukes, Phil Brock, Albert Macklin, Pete Kowanko, Vinny Argiro, Bibi Besch.

Date with an Angel is a romantic comedy about a young man (Michael E. Knight), newly engaged, who wakes the morning after an impromptu bachelor party to find an angel (Émmanuelle Béart) among the debris.

DEAD OF WINTER

Pro. John Bloomgarden and Marc Shmuger; Metro-Goldwyn-Mayer *Dir.* Arthur Penn *Scr.* Marc Shmuger and Mark Malone *Cine.* Jan Weincke *Ed.* Rick Shaine *Mu.* Richard Einhorn *P.d.* Bill Brodie *S.d.* Mark S. Freeborn *R.t.* 100 min. *MPAA* R. *Cast:* Mary Steenburgen, Roddy McDowall, Jan Rubes, William Russ, Mark Malone, Ken Pogue, Wayne Robson.

A young woman who believes that she is to be the replacement for an ailing actress becomes a pawn in a blackmailing scheme.

DEADLINE

Pro. Elisabeth Wolters-Alfs; Skouras Pictures *Dir.* Nathaniel Gutman *Scr.* Hanan Peled *Cine.* Amnon Salomon and Thomas Mauch *Ed.* Peter Przygodda *Mu.* Jacques Zwart and Hans Jansen *A.d.* Yoram Barzily *R.t.* 100 min. *MPAA* R. *Cast:* Christopher Walken, Hywel Bennett, Marita Marschall, Arnon Zadok, Amos

Lavie, Ette Ankri, Martin Umback, Moshe Ivgi, Sason Gabay, Shahar Cohen, Shlomo Bar-Aba, Gaby Shoshan, Igal Naor, Jerry Weinstock, Reuven Dayan, Nader Masraawi, David Menachem, Shlomo Tarshish, Moni Mushonov.

Reporter Don Stevens (Christopher Walken) tries to warn the Israelis about the Lebanese Christian Phalangists in time to prevent the refugee-camp massacre of Palestinians.

DEADLY ILLUSION

Pro. Irwin Meyer; CineTel Films *Dir.* William Tannen and Larry Cohen *Scr.* Larry Cohen *Cine.* Daniel Pearl *Ed.* Steve Mirkovich and Ronald Spang *Mu.* Patrick Gleeson *A.d.* Marina Zurkow and Ruth Lounsbury *R.t.* 87 min. *MPAA* R. *Cast:* Billy Dee Williams, Vanity, Morgan Fairchild, John Beck, Joe Cortese, Dennis Hallahan, Jenny Cornuelle, Michael Wilding, Jr., Allison Woodward, Joe Spinell, Michael Emil.

This homage to film noir has Billy Dee Williams playing an unlicensed detective who is taken for a ride by a crook posing as a businessman (Dennis Hallahan) who wants his wife murdered.

DEAR AMERICA

Pro. Bill Couturie and Thomas Bird *Dir.* Bill Couturie *Scr.* Richard Dewhurst and Bill Couturie *Cine.* No listing; stock footage from NBC Video Archives *Ed.* Stephen Stept *Mu.* Todd Boekelheide *R.t.* 87 min. *Voices:* Tom Berenger, Ellen Burstyn, J. Kenneth Campbell, Richard Chaves, Josh Cruze, Willem Dafoe, Robert De Niro, Brian Dennehy, Kevin Dillon, Matt Dillon, Robert Downey, Jr., Michael J. Fox, Mark Harmon, John Heard, Fred Hirz, Harvey Keitel, Elizabeth McGovern, Judd Nelson, Sean Penn, Randy Quaid, Tom Quill, Eric Roberts, Ray Robertson, Howard Rollins, Jr., John Savage, Martin Sheen, Tucker Smallwood, Roger Steffens, Jim Tracy, Kathleen Turner, Tico Wells, Robin Williams, Raphael Sbarge.

This documentary weaves together 1960's newsreels and popular music with readings of letters sent home by American soldiers fighting in Vietnam.

DEATH BEFORE DISHONOR

Pro. Lawrence Kubik; New World Pictures *Dir.* Terry J. Leonard *Scr.* Frank Capra, Jr., Lawrence Kubik, and John Gatliff *Cine.* Don Burgess *Ed.* Steve Mirkovich *Mu.* Brian May *P.d.* Kuli Sandor *S.d.* Doron Efrat *R.t.* 95 min. *MPAA* R. *Cast:* Fred Dryer, Brian Keith, Paul Winfield, Joanna Pacula, Kasey Walker, Rockne Tarkington, Joey Gian, Peter Parros, Sasha Mitchell, Dan Chodos, Muhamad Bakri.

American marines in the fictional Middle Eastern country of Jemal search for their colonel, who has been kidnapped by terrorists.

DEATH WISH 4: THE CRACKDOWN

Pro. Pancho Kohner; Cannon Group *Dir.* J. Lee Thompson *Scr.* Gail Morgan Hickman; based on characters created by Brian Garfield *Cine.* Gideon Porath *Ed.* Peter Lee Thompson *Mu.* Paul McCallum, Valentine McCallum, and John Bisharat *A.d.* Whitney Brooke Wheeler *S.d.* Mark Andrew *R.t.* 92 min. *MPAA* R. *Cast:* Charles Bronson, Kay Lenz, John P. Ryan, Perry Lopez, George Dickerson, Soon-Teck Oh, Dana Barron, Jesse Dabson.

After his girlfriend's daughter overdoses on crack, an architect (Charles Bronson) seeks revenge, attempting to eliminate the Los Angeles underground drug trade.

DIARY OF A MAD OLD MAN (The Netherlands, Belgium, and France, 1987) *Pro*. Henry Lange, Pierre Drouot, and Fons Rademakers; Cannon Group *Dir*. Lili Rademakers *Scr*. Hugo Claus and Claudine Bouvier; based on the novel by Jun'ichiro Tanizaki *Cine*. Paul van den Bos *Ed*. Ton de Graaff *Mu*. Egisto Macchi *P.d*. Philippe Graff *R.t*. 91 min. *Cast:* Ralph Michael, Beatie Edney, Suzanne Flon, Derek de Lint, Dora van der Groen, Ina van der Molen.

This moody film depicts the erotic obsession of an old man for his beautiful daughter-in-law.

DISORDERLIES
Pro. Michael Schultz, George Jackson, and Michael Jaffe; Warner Bros. *Dir*. Michael Schultz *Scr*. Mark Feldberg and Mitchell Klebanoff *Cine*. Rolf Kesterman *Ed*. Ned Humphreys *Mu*. Art of Noise *A.d*. George Costello *R.t*. 96 min. *MPAA* PG. *Cast:* Damon Wimbley, Darren Robinson, Mark Morales, Ralph Bellamy, Tony Plana, Anthony Geary, Marco Rodriguez, Troy Beyer.

A ruthless conniver (Anthony Geary) hires three incompetent orderlies (The Fat Boys: Damon Wimbley, Darren Robinson, and Mark Morales) to care for his rich uncle (Ralph Bellamy), in the hope that the old man will die under their care.

DOLLS
Pro. Brian Yuzna; Empire Pictures *Dir*. Stuart Gordon *Scr*. Ed Naha *Cine*. Mac Ahlberg *Ed*. Lee Percy *Mu*. Fuzzbee Morse *P.d*. Giovanni Natalucci *S.d*. Becky Block-Cummins and Martangella Capunao *R.t*. 77 min. *MPAA* R. *Cast:* Ian Patrick Williams, Carolyn Purdy-Gordon, Carrie Lorraine, Guy Rolfe, Hilary Mason, Bunty Bailey, Cassie Stuart, Stephen Lee.

When a family, a businessman, and two hitchhikers take refuge from a storm at a dollmaker's house, the dolls come to life and exact a bloody punishment on the evildoers in the group.

DOWN TWISTED
Pro. Menahem Golan and Yoram Globus; Cannon Films *Dir*. Albert Pyun *Scr*. Gene O'Neill and Noreen Tobin; based on a story by Albert Pyun *Cine*. Walt Lloyd *Ed*. Dennis O'Connor *Mu*. Berlin Game *P.d*. Chester Kaczenski *A.d*. Richard Hummel and Douglas H. Leonard *R.t*. 97 min. *MPAA* R. *Cast:* Carey Lowell, Charles Rocket, Trudi Dochtermann, Thom Mathews, Norbert Weisser, Linda Kerridge, Nicholas Guest, Gaylyn Gorg.

When her roommate's boyfriend doublecrosses a group of thieves who have stolen a religious relic, Maxine (Carey Lowell) is dragged into a web of violence and deceit that she does not really understand.

DUDES
Pro. Herb Jaffe; New Century/Vista Film Company *Dir*. Penelope Spheeris *Scr*. J. Randal Johnson *Cine*. Robert Richardson *Ed*. Andy Horvitch *P.d*. Robert Ziembicki *R.t*. 90 min. *MPAA* R. *Cast:* Jon Cryer, Daniel Roebuck, Flea, Lee Ving, Catherine Mary Stewart, Billy Ray Sharkey, Glenn Withrow, Michael Melvin, Axxel G. Reese, Marc Rude, Calvin Bartlett, Pete Willcox, Vance Colvig, Pamela Gidley.

When their pal is murdered by a Western outlaw, New York punkers Grant (Jon Cryer) and Biscuit (Daniel Roebuck) seek revenge.

D. U. I.
Pro. Cathleen Doyle and Spike Stewart *Dir*. Spike Stewart *Cine*. Cathleen Doyle,

Spike Stewart, Patrick Stewart, David Vaught, and Karl Marderian *Ed*. Linda Henry *R.t.* 80 min. *Cast:* Severed Head in a Bag, Tequila Mockingbird, Jon Wayne, Three Day Stubble, Ugly Janitors of America, Debt of Nature, John Trubee, Thra's Dumbos, Krew Kuts Klan, Lopez Beatles, Whitehouse, The Free Bass Ensemble, Wurm.

This documentary includes performances by punk/performance art bands on the outer fringes of Los Angeles' music scene.

EDDIE MURPHY RAW

Pro. Robert D. Wachs and Keenen Ivory Wayans; Paramount Pictures *Dir*. Robert Townsend *Scr*. Eddie Murphy *Cine*. Ernest Dickerson *Ed*. Lisa Day *P.d*. Wynn P. Thomas *S.d*. James T. Fredericks *R.t.* 91 min. *MPAA* R. *Cast:* Eddie Murphy.

In *Raw*, a concert film directed by Robert Townsend, Eddie Murphy offers his own brand of humor for ninety minutes. The performance is replete with the standard anatomical jokes and parodies of famous personalities, such as fellow comic Bill Cosby.

EMMANUELLE 5 (France, 1987)

Pro. Alain Siritzky; AAA *Dir*. Walerian Borowezyk *Scr*. Walerian Borowezyk and Alex Cunningham; based on an original idea by Émanuelle Arsan *Cine*. Max Montheillet *Ed*. Franck Mathieu *Mu*. Pierre Bachelet *A.d*. Alain Faure *R.t.* 78 min. *Cast:* Monique Gabrielle, Dana Burns Westberg, Crofton Hardester, Yaseen Khan.

This fifth installment in the mildly erotic Emmanuelle series has the main character (Monique Gabrielle) scandalize the Cannes Film Festival attendees with her new film before being pursued by both a billionnaire and a sheikh.

THE EMPEROR'S NEW CLOTHES (USA and Israel, 1987)

Pro. Menahem Golan and Yoram Globus; Cannon Films *Dir*. David Irving *Scr*. Anna Mathias, Len Talan, and David Irving; based on a story by Hans Christian Andersen *Cine*. David Gurfinkel *Ed*. Tova Neeman *Mu*. David Kriveshei *P.d*. Marek Dobrowolski *A.d*. Avi Avivi *R.t.* 80 min. *Cast:* Sid Caesar, Robert Morse, Jason Carter, Lysette Anthony, Clive Revill, Julian Joy Chagrin, Eli Gorenstein, Israel Gurion, Susan Berlin-Irving.

Based on Hans Christian Andersen's fairy tale, this film tells the story of an emperor who is deceived into believing that his nonexistent clothes actually are beautiful finery.

END OF THE LINE (*Terminus*. France and West Germany, 1987)

Pro. Anne François; AAA and Hemdale Film Corp. *Dir*. Pierre-William Glenn *Scr*. Pierre-William Glenn and Patrice Duvic; based on an orginal story by Alain Gillot *Cine*. Jean-Claude Vicquery *Ed*. Thierry Derocles *Mu*. David Cunningham *A.d*. Alain Challier *R.t.* 115 min. *Cast:* Karen Allen, Johnny Hallyday, Jürgen Prochnow, Gabriel Damon, Julie Glenn, Louise Vincent, Dieter Schidor, Janos Kulka, Dominique Valera, Jean-Luc Montama, Ray Montama, Bruno Ciarrochi, David Jalil, Andre Nocquet.

Stump (Johnny Hallyday) substitutes in a driving race for a woman who was killed when she strayed off course, and he is soon involved in a game of more complexity than he had thought.

ENEMY TERRITORY

Pro. Cynthia de Paula and Tim Kincaid; Empire Pictures *Dir*. Peter Manoogian

Scr. Stuart M. Kaminsky and Bobby Liddell; based on a story by Stuart M. Kaminsky *Cine.* Ernest Dickerson *Ed.* Peter Teschner *Mu.* Sam Winans and Richard Koz Kosinski *P.d.* Medusa Studios and Marina Zurkow *A.d.* Joanna Basinger *R.t.* 90 min. *MPAA* R. *Cast:* Gary Frank, Ray Parker, Jr., Jan-Michael Vincent, Frances Foster, Tony Todd, Stacey Dash, Deon Richmond, Tiger Haynes, Charles Randall, Peter Wise, Robert Lee Rush.

An insurance salesman calls on a woman who lives in a dangerous part of town and is threatened by a gang of hoodlums called the Vampires.

ERNEST GOES TO CAMP
Pro. Stacy Williams; Buena Vista *Dir.* John R. Cherry III *Scr.* John R. Cherry III and Coke Sams *Cine.* Harry Mathias and Jim May *Ed.* Marshall Harvey *Mu.* Shane Keister *A.d.* Kathy Emily Cherry *R.t.* 93 min. *MPAA* PG. *Cast:* Jim Varney, Victoria Racimo, John Vernon, Iron Eyes Cody, Lyle Alzado, Gailard Sartain, Daniel Butler, Hakeem Abdul-Samad, Patrick Day, Scott Menville, Jacob Vargas.

Ernest (Jim Varney), familiar from television commercials, becomes a counselor for a group of delinquents at a summer camp and leads them in a fight to save the camp from some land developers.

EVIL DEAD II: DEAD BY DAWN
Pro. Robert G. Tapert; Rosebud Releasing Corp. *Dir.* Sam Raimi *Scr.* Sam Raimi and Scott Spiegel *Cine.* Peter Deming *Ed.* Kaye Davis *Mu.* Joseph Lo Duca *A.d.* Philip Duffin and Randy Bennett *S.d.* Elizabeth Moore *R.t.* 85 min. *Cast:* Bruce Campbell, Sarah Berry, Dan Hicks, Kassie Wesley, Theodore Raimi, Denise Bixler, Richard Domeier, John Peaks, Lou Hancock.

A young man (Bruce Campbell) takes his girlfriend (Sarah Berry) to a cabin in the woods, and they are beset by the dead, who want to escape limbo by inhabiting living bodies.

EXTREME PREJUDICE
Pro. Buzz Feitshans; Tri-Star Pictures *Dir.* Walter Hill *Scr.* Deric Washburn and Harry Kleiner; based on a story by John Milius and Fred Rexer *Cine.* Matthew F. Leonetti *Ed.* Freeman Davies *Mu.* Jerry Goldsmith *P.d.* Albert Heschong *A.d.* Joseph C. Nemec III *R.t.* 104 min. *MPAA* R. *Cast:* Nick Nolte, Powers Boothe, Michael Ironside, Maria Conchita Alonso, Rip Torn, Clancy Brown, William Forsythe, Matt Mulhern, Larry B. Scott, Dan Tullis, Jr.

Two former friends end up on opposite sides of the law: Jack (Nick Nolte) is a Texas Ranger, and Cash (Powers Boothe) is a drug runner. Their confrontation is complicated by a commando group performing a covert operation on the Texas-Mexico border.

FACES OF WOMEN (Ivory Coast, 1987)
Pro. Désiré Écare; New Yorker *Dir.* Désiré Écare *Scr.* Désiré Écare *Cine.* François Migeat and Dominique Gentil *Ed.* Giselle Miski, Madame Dje-dje, and Nicholas Barrachin *R.t.* 105 min. *Cast:* Eugénie Cisse Roland, Sidiki Bakaba, Albertine N'Guessan, Kouadio Brou, Mahile Veronique, Carmen Levry, Anny Brigitte, Alexis Leatche, Désiré Bamba, Fatou Sall.

Scenes of a street festival frame two stories, one of a woman whose husband is unjustifiably jealous, the other of hardworking Bernadette, who supports her husband and relatives despite all manner of setbacks.

FAT GUY GOES NUTZOID

Pro. Emily Dillon; Troma *Dir.* John Golden *Scr.* John Golden and Roger Golden *Cine.* John Drake *Ed.* Jeff Wolf *Mu.* Leo Kottke *P.d.* Martin de Maat *R.t.* 78 min. *Cast:* Tibor Feldman, Peter Linari, John Mackay, Douglas Stone, Max Alexander.

When Roger (Tibor Feldman) causes trouble at the camp for the retarded where his brother (Douglas Stone) works, they are kicked out, and more trouble results when Dave (Peter Linari), nicknamed "The Mouka," a camper, stows away in their truck.

FATAL BEAUTY

Pro. Leonard Kroll; Metro-Goldwyn-Mayer *Dir.* Tom Holland *Scr.* Hilary Henkin and Dean Riesner; based on a story by Bill Svanoe *Cine.* David M. Walsh *Ed.* Don Zimmerman *Mu.* Harold Faltermeyer *P.d.* James William Newport *S.d.* Rick Simpson *R.t.* 104 min. *MPAA* R. *Cast:* Whoopi Goldberg, Sam Elliott, Ruben Blades, Harris Yulin, John P. Ryan, Jennifer Warren, Brad Dourif, Mike Jolly, Charles Hallahan.

Narcotics detective Rita Rizzoli (Whoopi Goldberg) takes to the streets to fight a pair of drug dealers (Brad Dourif and Mike Jolly).

FEEL THE HEAT

Pro. Don Van Atta; Trans World Entertainment *Dir.* Joel Silberg *Scr.* Stirling Silliphant *Cine.* Nissim Nitcho and Frank Harris *Ed.* Christopher Holmes and Darren Holmes *Mu.* Thomas Chase and Steven Rucker *P.d.* Jorge Marchegiani *R.t.* 87 min. *Cast:* David Dukes, Tiana Alexandra, Rod Steiger, Brian Thompson, Jorge Martinez, John Hancock, Brian Libby, Jessica Schultz, Toru Tanaka.

A female government narcotics agent (Tiana Alexandra) trained in the martial arts goes undercover in Buenos Aires at a dance club suspected of being a drug-smuggling headquarters.

FIRE AND ICE

Pro. Willy Bogner; Concorde Pictures *Dir.* Willy Bogner *Scr.* Willy Bogner *Cine.* Willy Bogner *Ed.* Petra Von Oelffen and Claudia Travnecek *Mu.* Harold Faltermeyer, Gary Wright, Panarama, Alan Parsons, and John Denver *R.t.* 80 min. *MPAA* PG. *Cast:* John Evans, Suzy Chaffee.

John (John Evans) pursues Suzy (Suzy Chaffee) to various international skiing locations, and his fantasies and pursuit involve many fancy ski stunts.

FIRE FROM THE MOUNTAIN

Pro. Adam Friedson and Deborah Shaffer *Dir.* Deborah Shaffer *Scr.* Based on the book *Fire from the Mountain*, by Omar Cabezas *Cine.* Frank Pineda *Ed.* Gina Reticker *Mu.* Charlie Hoden *R.t.* 60 min. *Cast:* Tony Plana.

The life and political journey of Nicaraguan activist Omar Cabezas is the subject of this documentary.

FIVE CORNERS

Pro. Forrest Murray and Tony Bill *Dir.* Tony Bill *Scr.* John Patrick Shanley *Cine.* Fred Murphy *Ed.* Andy Blumenthal *Mu.* James Newton Howard *P.d.* Adrianne Lobel *R.t.* 92 min. *MPAA* R. *Cast:* Jodie Foster, Tim Robbins, Todd Graff, John Turturro, Elizabeth Berridge, Rose Gregorio, Gregory Rozakis, John Seitz, Kathleen Chalfant.

Set in 1964 in the Bronx, *Five Corners* depicts the intertwined lives of several youths whose happiness is threatened by the release from prison of a man seeking revenge.

A FLAME IN MY HEART (*Une Flamme dans mon coeur.* France and Switzerland, 1987)
Pro. Paolo Branco; Bac Films *Dir.* Alain Tanner *Scr.* Myriam Almeida and Alain Tanner *Cine.* Acacio de Almeida *Ed.* Laurent Uhler *Mu.* Johann Sebastian Bach and Neil Gotkovsky *R.t.* 112 min. *Cast:* Myriam Mezieres, Aziz Kabouche, Benoit Regent, Biana, Jean-Yves Berthelot, Andre Marcon, Anne Ruckl, Jean-Gabriel Nordmann.

A love-hungry actress, rid of an abusive lover, takes up with a journalist, who takes her to Egypt.

FLOWERS IN THE ATTIC
Pro. Sy Levin and Thomas Fries *Dir.* Jeffrey Bloom *Scr.* Jeffrey Bloom; based on the novel of the same name by V. C. Andrews *Cine.* Frank Byers and Gil Hubbs *Ed.* Gregory F. Plotts *Mu.* Christopher Young *P.d.* John Muto *S.d.* Michele Starbuck *R.t.* 95 min. *MPAA* PG-13. *Cast:* Louise Fletcher, Victoria Tennant, Kristy Swanson, Jeb Stuart Adams, Ben Granger, Lindsay Parker, Marshall Colt, Nathan Davis, Alex Koba.

As their mother schemes to wangle an inheritance from their crusty grandfather, four children are forced to remain for weeks in a guest room and its adjoining attic.

FOREVER, LULU
Pro. Amos Kollek; Tri-Star Pictures *Dir.* Amos Kollek *Scr.* Amos Kollek *Cine.* Lisa Rinzler *Ed.* Jay Freund *P.d.* Stephen McCabe *S.d.* Victor Zolfo *R.t.* 85 min. *MPAA* R. *Cast:* Hanna Schygulla, Deborah Harry, Alec Baldwin, Annie Golden, Paul Gleason, Ruth Westheimer, Raymond Serra, George Kyle, Harold Guskin, Bill Corsair, Jonathan Freeman, Amos Kollek, Charles Ludlam, Cathy Gati, Beatrice Pons, Sally June Heit.

A German immigrant woman works as a secretary by day and writes novels by night. Her success is complicated by an encounter with murder, money, and a mysterious woman.

FROM THE HIP
Pro. Rene Dupont and Bob Clark; De Laurentiis Entertainment Group *Dir.* Bob Clark *Scr.* David E. Kelley and Bob Clark; based on a story by David E. Kelley *Cine.* Dante Spinotti *Ed.* Stan Cole *Mu.* Paul Zaza *P.d.* Michael Stringer *A.d.* Dennis Bradford *S.d.* Edward (Tantar) LeViseur *R.t.* 111 min. *MPAA* PG. *Cast:* Judd Nelson, Elizabeth Perkins, John Hurt, Darren McGavin, Dan Monahan, David Alan Grier, Nancy Marchand, Allan Arbus, Edward Winter, Richard Zobel, Ray Walston, Robert Irvin Elliott, Beatrice Winde, Art Hindle, Priscilla Pointer.

Robin Weathers (Judd Nelson), a young, brash lawyer, is assigned to defend a college professor who is charged with murdering a woman, and Robin's ethics are challenged by the case.

THE GARBAGE PAIL KIDS MOVIE
Pro. Rod Amateau; Atlantic Entertainment Group *Dir.* Rod Amateau *Scr.* Melinda Palmer and Rod Amateau *Cine.* Harvey Genkins *Ed.* Leon Carrere *Mu.* Michael Lloyd *P.d.* Robert I. Jillson *S.d.* Hub Braden *R.t.* 100 min. *MPAA* PG. *Cast:* Anthony Newley, Mackenzie Astin, Katie Barberi, Ron MacLachlan, Kevin Thompson, Phil Fondacaro, Robert Bell, Larry Green, Arturo Gil, Sue Rossitto,

Debbie Lee Carrington.

Those creatures of slime, the Garbage Pail Kids, are set loose to create anarchy and messes wherever they go.

GOOD MORNING, BABYLON (Italy, France, and USA, 1987)
Pro. Giuliani G. De Negri; Vestron Entertainment *Dir.* Paolo Taviani and Vittorio Taviani *Scr.* Paolo Taviani and Vittorio Taviani; based on an idea by Lloyd Fonvielle *Cine.* Giuseppe Lanci *Ed.* Roberto Perpignani *Mu.* Nicola Piovani *A.d.* Gianni Sharra *R.t.* 115 min. *Cast:* Vincent Spano, Joaquim de Almeida, Greta Scacchi, Desiree Becker, Omero Antonutti, Charles Dance, Berangere Bonvoisin, Margarita Lozano, David Brandon, Brian Freilino.

Two Italian immigrants are hired to help D. W. Griffith (Charles Dance) design the sets for the film *The Fall of Babylon.*

GOOD WEATHER, BUT STORMY LATE THIS AFTERNOON (France, 1987)
Pro. Coralie Films International *Dir.* Gerard Frot-Coutaz *Scr.* Gerard Frot-Coutaz and Jacques Davila *Cine.* Jean-Jacques Bouhoun *Ed.* Paul Vecchiali and Franck Mathieu *Mu.* Roland Vincent *R.t.* 85 min. *Cast:* Micheline Presle, Claude Pieplu, Xavier Deluc, Tonie Marshall.

A middle-class suburban French couple, nearly forty years into a stormy but loving marriage, air their foibles on the occasion of their son's visit with his new lady friend.

LA GRAN FIESTA (Puerto Rico, 1987)
Pro. Robert Gándara and Marcos Zurinaga; Zaga Films *Dir.* Marcos Zurinaga *Scr.* Ana Lydia Vega and Marcos Zurinaga *Cine.* Marcos Zurinaga *Ed.* Roberto Gándara *Mu.* Angel "Cucco" Peña *R.t.* 100 min. *Cast:* Daniel Lugo, Miguelángel Suárez, Luis Prendes, Cordelia González, Laura Delano, Raul Carbonell, Jr., Carlos Augusto Cestero, Raul Dávila, Raul Julia, E. G. Marshall, Julian Pastor.

Passion and political intrigue ferment in the casino of San Juan, Puerto Rico, as the United States Navy prepares to take it over in 1942.

GRAND CANYON: THE HIDDEN SECRETS
Pro. Kieth Merrill and O. Douglas Memmott *Dir.* Kieth Merrill *Scr.* Kieth Merrill *Cine.* Reed Smoot *Ed.* Stephen L. Johnson *Mu.* Bill Conti *P.d.* Roger Crandall *R.t.* 36 min. *Cast:* Bruce Simballa, Daniel T. Majetich, Coby Jordan, Martin Litton.

This IMAX film provides majestic panoramas of the Grand Canyon with reenactments of several historic expeditions.

GROUND ZERO (Australia, 1987)
Pro. Michael Pattinson; Hoyts *Dir.* Michael Pattinson and Bruce Myles *Scr.* Jan Sardi and Mac Gudgeon *Cine.* Steve Dobson *Ed.* David Pulbrook *Mu.* Chris Neal *P.d.* Brian Thomson *R.t.* 109 min. *Cast:* Colin Friels, Jack Thompson, Donald Pleasence, Natalie Bate, Simon Chilvers, Neil Fitzpatrick, Bob Maza, Peter Cummins.

Searching for the truth about his father's death thirty years before, Harvey Denton (Colin Friels) stumbles across information that British agents are desperate to keep secret.

HAMBURGER HILL
Pro. Marcia Nasatir and Jim Carabatsos; Paramount Pictures *Dir.* John Irvin *Scr.* Jim Carabatsos *Cine.* Peter MacDonald *Ed.* Peter Tanner *Mu.* Philip Glass *P.d.* Austen Spriggs *A.d.* Toto Castillo *R.t.* 110 min. *MPAA* R. *Cast:* Anthony

Barrile, Michael Patrick Boatman, Don Cheadle, Michael Dolan, Don James, Dylan McDermott, M. A. Nickles, Harry O'Reilly, Daniel O'Shea, Tim Quill, Tommy Swerdlow, Courtney Vance, Steven Weber, Tegan West, Kieu Chinh, Doug Goodman, J. C. Palmore, J. D. Van Sickle.

Ordered to take Hamburger Hill in Vietnam, a squadron of American soldiers persists for an agonizing eleven days, suffering many casualties.

THE HANOI HILTON
Pro. Menahem Golan and Yoram Globus; Cannon Films *Dir.* Lionel Chetwynd *Scr.* Lionel Chetwynd *Cine.* Mark Irwin *Ed.* Penelope Shaw *Mu.* Jimmy Webb *P.d.* R. Clifford Searcy *A.d.* Carol Bosselman *S.d.* Ian Cramer *R.t.* 130 min. *MPAA* R. *Cast:* Michael Moriarty, Jeffrey Jones, Paul Le Mat, Stephen Davies, Lawrence Pressman, Aki Aleong, Gloria Carlin, John Diehl, Rick Fitts, David Soul, David Anthony Smith, Ken Wright, Doug Savant, John Vargas, Michael Russo.

This film attempts to portray the plight of American servicemen being held in a prisoner-of-war camp in North Vietnam.

HANSEL AND GRETEL
Pro. Menahem Golan and Yoram Globus; Cannon Group *Dir.* Len Talan *Scr.* Nancy Weems and Len Talan *Cine.* Ilan Rosenberg *Ed.* Irit Raz *Mu.* Michael Cohen; based on an opera by Engelbert Humperdinck *P.d.* Marek Dobrowolski *R.t.* 86 min. *Cast:* Hugh Pollard, Nicola Stapleton, Emily Richard, David Warner, Cloris Leachman, Eugene Kline, Warren M. Feigin, Josh Buland, Lutuf Nouasser, Beatrice Shimshoni.

This is a retelling of the classic fairy tale.

HAPPY '49 (Yugoslavia, 1987)
Pro. Union Film, Makedonija Film, and Gradski Kina *Dir.* Stole Popov *Scr.* Gordan Mihic *Cine.* Misco Samoilovski *Ed.* Laki Cermcev *Mu.* Ljupco Konstantinov *S.d.* Nikola Lazarevski *R.t.* 128 min. *Cast:* Sveto Cvetkovich, Meto Jovanovski, Vladica Milosavljic, Aco Gjorcev, Petar Arsovski, Goce Todorovski, Dushan Kostovski.

The love/hate relationship of two brothers that is played out in their attraction to the same woman and their conflicting and confused ideologies echoes the conflicts taking place in 1949 Yugoslavia.

HAPPY HOUR
Pro. J. Stephen Peace and John De Bello; The Movie Store Pictures *Dir.* John De Bello *Scr.* John De Bello, Constantine Dillon, and J. Stephen Peace *Cine.* Kevin Morrisey *Ed.* John De Bello *Mu.* Rick Patterson and Neal Fox *P.d.* Constantine Dillon *R.t.* 86 min. *MPAA* R. *Cast:* Richard Gilliland, Jamie Farr, Tawny Kitaen, Ty Henderson, Rich Little, Eddie Deezen, Kathi Diamant, Debbie Gates, James Newell, Beverly Todd, Debi Fares, Eric Christmas.

Blake Teegarden (Richard Gilliland) invents an irreproducible formula for beer that is addictive. A rival beer company steals half the existing liquid.

HAPPY NEW YEAR
Pro. Jerry Weintraub; Columbia Pictures *Dir.* John G. Avildsen *Scr.* Warren Lane; based on the film *La Bonne Année*, directed by Claude Lelouch *Cine.* James Crabe *Ed.* Jane Kurson *Mu.* Bill Conti *P.d.* William J. Cassidy *A.d.* William F. Matthews *S.d.* Don Ivey *R.t.* 85 min. *MPAA* PG. *Cast:* Peter Falk, Charles Durning, Wendy Hughes, Tom Courtenay, Joan Copeland, Tracy Brooks Swope,

Daniel Gerroll, Bruce Malmuth, The Temptations, Peter Sellars, Anthony Heald, Claude Lelouch.

Nick (Peter Falk) and Charlie (Charles Durning), career criminals, set up an elaborate plan to rob a West Palm Beach jewelry store.

HARD TICKET TO HAWAII

Pro. Arlene Sidaris; Malibu Bay Films *Dir.* Andy Sidaris *Scr.* Andy Sidaris *Cine.* Howard Wexler *Ed.* Michael Haight *Mu.* Gary Stockdale *P.d.* Sal Grasso and Peter Munneke *R.t.* 96 min. *MPAA* R. *Cast:* Ronn Moss, Dona Speir, Hope Marie Carlton, Harold Diamond, Rodrigo Obregon, Cynthia Brimhall, Patty Duffek, Wolf Larson, Lory Green, Rustam Branaman, David DeShay, Michael Andrews, Andy Sidaris, Kwan Hi Lim, Joseph Hieu, Peter Bromilow, Glen Chin, Russell Howell, Richard Lepore, Joey Meran, Shawne Zarubica.

Two women who run an air-freight service in Hawaii unwittingly become involved with diamond smugglers, drug traffickers, and a poisonous snake; Rowdy Abilene (Ron Moss) and Jake (Harold Diamond) effect a hilarious rescue.

HARRY AND THE HENDERSONS

Pro. Richard Vane and William Dear; Universal *Dir.* William Dear *Scr.* William Dear, William E. Martin, and Ezra D. Rappaport *Cine.* Allen Daviau *Ed.* Donn Cambern *Mu.* Bruce Broughton *P.d.* James Bissell *A.d.* Don Woodruff *S.d.* Linda DeScenna *R.t.* 105 min. *MPAA* PG. *Cast:* John Lithgow, Melinda Dillon, Margaret Langrick, Joshua Rudoy, Kevin Peter Hall, David Suchet, Lainie Kazan, Don Ameche, M. Emmet Walsh, Bill Ontiverous, David Richardt.

A vacationing family accidentally injures Bigfoot (Kevin Peter Hall) with their car; they take him home, dub him Harry, and nurse him back to health.

HEART

Pro. Randy Jurgensen; New World Pictures *Dir.* James Lemmo *Scr.* James Lemmo and Randy Jurgensen *Cine.* Jacek Laskus *Ed.* Lorenzo Marinelli *Mu.* Geoff Levin and Chris Many *P.d.* Vicki Paul *A.d.* Susan Raney *R.t.* 90 min. *MPAA* R. *Cast:* Brad Davis, Frances Fisher, Steve Buscemi, Robinson Frank Adu, Jesse Doran, Sam Gray, Bill Costello.

An aging boxer (Brad Davis) agrees to fight a much younger man (Bill Costello).

HEARTS OF FIRE

Pro. Richard Marquand, Jennifer Miller, and Jennifer Alward; Lorimar *Dir.* Richard Marquand *Scr.* Scott Richardson and Joe Eszterhas *Cine.* Alan Hume *Ed.* Sean Barton *Mu.* John Barry and Beau Hill *A.d.* Kit Surrey and Barbara Dunphy *R.t.* 95 min. *MPAA* R. *Cast:* Bob Dylan, Rupert Everett, Fiona, Julian Glover, Suzanne Bertish, Ian Dury, Richie Havens, Larry Lamb, Tim Cappello.

Bob Dylan stars as a reclusive rock star in this last film by the late Richard Marquand.

HEAT

Pro. Keith Rotman and George Pappas; New Century/Vista Film Company *Dir.* R. M. Richards *Scr.* William Goldman; based on his novel of the same name *Cine.* James Contner *Ed.* Jeffrey Wolf *Mu.* Michael Gibbs *A.d.* Jerry Wunderlich *S.d.* Bobby Bernhardt *R.t.* 101 min. *MPAA* R. *Cast:* Burt Reynolds, Karen Young, Peter MacNicol, Howard Hesseman, Neill Barry, Diana Scarwid, Joe Mascolo, Alfie Wise.

Nick Escalante (Burt Reynolds) attempts to overcome his addiction to gambling while protecting a young millionaire and while trying to find the man who attacked a friend.

HEAVEN
Pro. Joe Kelly; Island Pictures *Dir.* Diane Keaton *Cine.* Frederick Elmes and Joe Kelly *Ed.* Paul Barnes *Mu.* Howard Shore *A.d.* Barbara Ling *R.t.* 80 min. *MPAA* PG-13.

Director Diane Keaton interviewed approximately one hundred people, including fundamentalists, old people, and children, on their concepts of heaven to produce this documentarylike film.

HELLO AGAIN
Pro. Frank Perry; Buena Vista *Dir.* Frank Perry *Scr.* Susan Isaacs *Cine.* Jan Weincke *Ed.* Peter C. Frank and Trudy Ship *Mu.* William Goldstein *P.d.* Edward Pisoni *A.d.* William Barclay *S.d.* Robert J. Franco *R.t.* 96 min. *MPAA* PG. *Cast:* Shelley Long, Judith Ivey, Gabriel Byrne, Corbin Bernsen, Sela Ward, Austin Pendleton, Carrie Nye, Robert Lewis, Madeleine Potter, Thor Fields.

Lucy Chadman (Shelley Long) is brought back to life by her occultist sister a year after her death.

HELLO MARY LOU: PROM NIGHT II
Pro. Peter Simpson and Bruce Pittman; Samuel Goldwyn Company *Dir.* Bruce Pittman *Scr.* Ron Oliver *Cine.* John Herzog *Ed.* Nick Rotundo *Mu.* Paul Zaza *R.t.* 96 min. *MPAA* R. *Cast:* Lisa Schrage, Wendy Lyon, Michael Ironside, Richard Monette, Justin Louis.

The 1957 prom queen of Hamilton High (Lisa Schrage), burned to death in a jealous rage by her boyfriend, returns to her old school to possess the body of a 1980's student and take revenge on her enemies.

HELLRAISER (Great Britain, 1987)
Pro. Christopher Figg; New World Pictures *Dir.* Clive Barker *Scr.* Clive Barker; based on his novel, *The Hellbound Heart Cine.* David Worley *Ed.* Christopher Young *A.d.* Jocelyn James *R.t.* 90 min. *Cast:* Andrew Robinson, Clare Higgins, Ashley Laurence, Sean Chapman, Oliver Smith, Robert Hines, Antony Allan, Leon Davis, Michael Cassidy, Frank Baker, Kenneth Nelson, Gay Baynes, Niall Buggy.

An adventurer, who unleashes evil when he finds a magic box, becomes one of the undead and seeks to devour human flesh in order to regain his own human form. His sister-in-law, who was his former lover, helps him.

HER NAME IS LISA
Pro. Rachid Kerdouche *Dir.* Rachid Kerdouche *Scr.* Ron Gott; based on a story by Frank Boccio and Rachid Kerdouche *Cine.* Klaus Quinn-Hoch and Wayne McDaniel *Mu.* Richard Sohl *S.d.* Charles Mission *R.t.* 79 min. *Cast:* Bill Rice, Rockets Redglare, Lisa Wujnovich.

A middle-aged, naïve farmer from Vermont goes to New York to search for the young woman with whom he is in love.

HE'S MY GIRL
Pro. Lawrence Taylor Mortorff and Angela Schapiro; Scotti Bros. Entertainment *Dir.* Gabrielle Beaumont *Scr.* Taylor Ames and Charles F. Bohl *Cine.* Peter Lyons Collister *Ed.* Roy Watts *A.d.* Cynthia Kay Charette *S.d.* Gary D. Randall *R.t.* 104 min. *MPAA* PG-13. *Cast:* T. K. Carter, David Hallyday, Misha McK, Jennifer Tilly, Warwick Sims, David Clennon, Monica Parker.

Singer Bryan Peters (David Hallyday) allows his manager, Reggie (T. K. Carter), to dress in drag to accompany him on a week-long Hollywood promotional tour.

THE HIDDEN
Pro. Robert Shaye, Gerald T. Olson, and Michael Meltzer; New Line Cinema and Heron Communications *Dir.* Jack Sholder *Scr.* Bob Hunt *Cine.* Jacques Haitkin *Ed.* Michael Knue *Mu.* Michael Convertino *P.d.* C. J. Strawn and Mick Strawn *S.d.* James Barrows *R.t.* 96 min. *MPAA* R. *Cast:* Michael Nouri, Kyle MacLachlan, Ed O'Ross, Clu Gulagar, Claudia Christian, Clarence Felder, William Boyett, Richard Brooks, Catherine Cannon, Larry Cedar, John McCann, Chris Mulkey.

Los Angeles detective Tom Beck (Michael Nouri) chases down a malevolent reptilian alien that forces itself down the throats of its victims, then forces them to commit crimes.

HIDING OUT
Pro. Jeff Rothberg; De Laurentiis Entertainment Group *Dir.* Bob Giraldi *Scr.* Joe Menosky and Jeff Rothberg *Cine.* Daniel Pearl *Ed.* Edward Warschilka *Mu.* Anne Dudley *P.d.* Dan Leigh *A.d.* Carol Wood *S.d.* Leslie Rollins *R.t.* 98 min. *MPAA* PG-13. *Cast:* Jon Cryer, Keith Coogan, Annabeth Gish, Gretchen Cryer, Oliver Cotton, Lou Walker, Tim Quill.

A Wall Street yuppie (Jon Cryer) disguises himself as a high school student in order to evade the mobsters who have him on their hit list.

HOME IS WHERE THE HART IS
Pro. John M. Eckert, Atlantic Entertainment Group *Dir.* Rex Bromfield *Scr.* Rex Bromfield *Cine.* Robert Ennis *Ed.* Michael Todd *Mu.* Eric N. Robertson *A.d.* Jill Scott *S.d.* Lesley Beale *R.t.* 94 min. *MPAA* PG. *Cast:* Valri Bromfield, Stephen E. Miller, Deanne Henry, Martin Mull, Eric Christmas, Ted Stidder, Leslie Nielsen, Joe Austin.

Belle Haimes (Valri Bromfield) schemes to reverse her ailing fortunes by marrying a senile billionaire (Joe Austin).

HOME REMEDY (also known as *Xero*)
Pro. Kathie Hersch *Dir.* Maggie Greenwald *Scr.* Maggie Greenwald *Cine.* Thomas H. Jewett *Ed.* Pamela Scott Arnold *Mu.* Steve Katz *R.t.* 100 min. *Cast:* Seth Barrish, Maxine Albert, Richard Kidney, David Feinman, John Tjakonas, Alexa, Cynde Kahn.

Nancy (Maxine Albert), a suburban housewife, intrudes upon Richie (Seth Barrish) as he pursues a self-imposed program of boredom.

HOT PURSUIT
Pro. Pierre David and Theodore R. Parvin; Paramount Pictures *Dir.* Steven Lisberger *Scr.* Steven Lisberger and Steven Carabatsos; based on a story by Steven Lisberger *Cine.* Frank Tidy *Ed.* Mitchell Sinoway *Mu.* Rareview *P.d.* William J. Creber *A.d.* Fernando Ramirez and Chris Dorrington *R.t.* 93 min. *MPAA* PG-13. *Cast:* John Cusack, Robert Loggia, Jerry Stiller, Wendy Gazelle, Monte Markham, Shelly Fabares, Ben Stiller, Dah-ve Chodan, Keith David, Paul Bates.

A teenage boy (John Cusack) misses his plane and tries to catch up with his girlfriend and her family, who are sailing amid the Caribbean Islands.

HOTEL COLONIAL (USA and Italy, 1987)
Pro. Mauro Berardi and William M. Siegel; Columbia Pictures *Dir.* Cinzia Torrini

Scr. Enzo Monteleone *Cine.* Giuseppe Rotunno *Ed.* Nino Baragli *Mu.* Pino Donaggio *A.d.* Giantito Burchilliaro *R.t.* 104 min. *Cast:* John Savage, Robert Duvall, Rachel Ward, Massimo Trolsi, Anna Galiena.

Marco (John Savage) journeys to Colombia to find that his brother is not dead, as he had been told, but has disappeared. In Marco's search for him, he encounters drug smugglers and scalp hunters.

HOTSHOT
Pro. Steve Pappas; International Film Marketing *Dir.* Rick King *Scr.* Joe Sauter and Rick King, with additional material by Ray Errol Fox and Bill Guttentag *Cine.* Greg Andracke and Edgar Moura *Ed.* Stan Salfas *Mu.* William Orbit *P.d.* Ruth Ammon and Berta Segall *S.d.* Betsy Klompus *R.t.* 91 min. *MPAA* PG. *Cast:* Jim Youngs, Pele, Billy Walock, Leon Russom, David Groh, Rutanya Alda, Peter Henry Schroeder.

A rich young man who wants to be a soccer player rather than follow his parents' plans for him travels to Brazil to take lessons from soccer star Pele.

HOUSE II: THE SECOND STORY
Pro. Sean S. Cunningham; New World Pictures *Dir.* Ethan Wiley *Scr.* Ethan Wiley *Cine.* Mac Ahlberg *Ed.* Marty Nicholson *Mu.* Henry Manfredini *P.d.* Gregg Fonseca *R.t.* 85 min. *MPAA* R. *Cast:* Arye Gross, Jonathan Stark, Royal Dano, Bill Maher, John Ratzenberger, Lar Park Lincoln, Amy Yasbeck, Gregory Walcott, Dwier Brown, Lenora May, Devin Devasquez.

In the house in which his parents were murdered twenty-five years earlier, Jesse McLaughlin (Arye Gross) exhumes the body of one of his ancestors, who returns to life and battles an evil spirit.

THE HOUSEKEEPER (Canada, 1987)
Pro. Harve Sherman; Castle Hill Productions *Dir.* Ousami Rawi *Scr.* Elaine Waisglass; based on the novel *A Judgment in Stone*, by Ruth Rendell *Cine.* David Herrington *Ed.* Stan Cole *Mu.* Paul Zaza *R.t.* 96 min. *MPAA* R. *Cast:* Rita Tushingham, Ross Petty, Shelley Peterson, Jonathan Crombie, Jessica Steen, Jackie Burroughs, Tom Kneebone, Peter MacNeill, Donald Ewer, Joyce Gordon, Aisha Tushingham.

A woman who has grown up scarred by her inability to read takes a job as a housekeeper and, slipping over the edge into madness, murders her employers because of their sinful life-style.

HUNK
Pro. Marilyn J. Tenser; Crown International Pictures *Dir.* Lawrence Bassoff *Scr.* Lawrence Bassoff *Cine.* Bryan England *Ed.* Richard E. Westover *Mu.* David Kurtz *A.d.* Catherine Hardwicke *R.t.* 102 min. *MPAA* PG. *Cast:* John Allen Nelson, Steve Levitt, Deborah Shelton, Rebeccah Bush, James Coco, Robert Morse, Avery Schreiber.

A computer programmer (Steve Levitt) is granted his wish of becoming strong and handsome, but he learns that there is a steep price if he wants to stay that way.

I WAS A TEENAGE ZOMBIE
Pro. Richard Hirsh and John Elias Michalakias; Horizon Releasing *Dir.* John Elias Michalakias *Scr.* James Martin *Cine.* Peter Lownes *Ed.* John Elias Michalakias *Mu.* Jonathan Roberts and Craig Seaman *R.t.* 92 min. *Cast:* Michael Ruben, George Seminara, Steve McCoy, Peter Bush, Cassie Madden, Cindy Keiter, Gwyn

Drischell, Allen L. Rickman, Lynnea Benson, Ray Stough.

A teenager, victimized by toxic marijuana, dies; his body, dumped in the river, is reanimated by nuclear waste, and he reappears as a green-faced zombie.

IT'S ALIVE III: ISLAND OF THE ALIVE

Pro. Paul Stader; Warner Bros. *Dir.* Larry Cohen *Scr.* Larry Cohen *Cine.* Daniel Pearl *Ed.* David Kern *Mu.* Laurie Johnson and Bernard Herrmann *R.t.* 91 min. *Cast:* Michael Moriarty, Karen Black, Laurene Landon, Gerrit Graham, James Dixon, Neal Israel, Art Lund, Ann Dane, Macdonald Carey.

A father (Michael Moriarty) prevents his child, a monster deemed a threat to the community, from being executed. Instead, the child is sent to a remote island with several other monster children.

I'VE HEARD THE MERMAIDS SINGING

Pro. Patricia Rozema and Alexandra Raffe; Miramax Films *Dir.* Patricia Rozema *Scr.* Patricia Rozema *Cine.* Douglas Koch *Ed.* Patricia Rozema *Mu.* Mark Korven *A.d.* Valanne Ridgeway *R.t.* 81 min. *Cast:* Sheila McCarthy, Paule Baillargeon, Ann-Marie McDonald, John Evans, Brenda Kamino, Richard Monette.

A naïve, elfin young woman (Sheila McCarthy) falls in love with her boss (Paule Baillargeon), owner of an art gallery.

JAWS—THE REVENGE

Pro. Joseph Sargent; Universal *Dir.* Joseph Sargent *Scr.* Michael de Guzman; based on a character created by Peter Benchley *Cine.* John McPherson *Ed.* Michael Brown *Mu.* Michael Small and John Williams *P.d.* John J. Lloyd *A.d.* Don Woodruff *S.d.* Hal Gausman and John Dwyer *R.t.* 98 min. *MPAA* PG-13. *Cast:* Lorraine Gary, Lance Guest, Mario Van Peebles, Karen Young, Michael Caine, Judith Barsi, Lynn Whitfield, Mitchell Anderson.

When one son is killed by a great white shark, Ellen Brody (Lorraine Gray), griefstricken, travels to join her other son in the Bahamas, but it seems the shark will go to any lengths to pursue his vendetta against the family.

JIM AND THE PIRATES (*Jim and Piraterna Blom.* Sweden, 1987)

Pro. Waldemar Bergendal; Svensk Filmindustri *Dir.* Hans Alfredson *Scr.* Hans Alfredson and Stellan Skarsgard *Cine.* Ralph Evers and Bertil Rosengren *Ed.* Jan Persson *Mu.* Stefan Nilsson *P.d.* Stig Boquist *R.t.* 91 min. *Cast:* Johan Akerblom, Ewa Froling, Stellan Skarsgard, Hans Alfredson, Jan Malmsjo, Stig Olin, Carl Billquist, Lena T. Hansson, Kenneth Milldorf, Jesper Danielsson, Sten Hellstrom, Christina Schultzberg, Rolf Adolfsson, My Skarsgard, Sam Skarsgard, Licka Sjoman, Dora Soderberg, Borje Norrman, Mats Bergman, Vanja Rodefeldt, Jim Hughes.

A young boy copes with the death of his father by imagining that his father is still there to give him advice—advice that usually involves the boy's powers of fantasy.

JOCKS

Pro. Ahmet Yasa; Crown International Pictures *Dir.* Steve Carver *Scr.* Michael Lanahan and David Oas *Cine.* Adam Greenberg *Ed.* Tom Siiter *Mu.* David McHugh *A.d.* Randy Ser *S.d.* Greg Melton *R.t.* 91 min. *MPAA* R. *Cast:* Scott Strader, Perry Lang, Mariska Hargitay, Richard Roundtree, R. G. Armstrong, Christopher Lee, Stoney Jackson, Adam Mills, Trinidad Silva, Don Gibb, Katherine Kelly Lang, Tom Shadyac, Christopher Murphy.

A high school tennis team attends a tournament held in Las Vegas and becomes involved in all sorts of escapades.

JOHN AND THE MISSUS (Canada, 1987)
Pro. Peter O'Brian and John Hunter *Dir.* Gordon Pinsent *Scr.* Gordon Pinsent; based on his novel *Cine.* Frank Tidy *Ed.* Bruce Nyznik *Mu.* Michael Conway Baker *A.d.* Earl Preston *S.d.* Jeanie M. Staple *R.t.* 100 min. *Cast:* Gordon Pinsent, Jackie Burroughs, Randy Follett, Jessica Steen, Roland Hewgill, Timothy Webber, Neil Munro, Michael Wade, Jerry Doyle.

A man refuses to move from the town in which he was born when the government asks the inhabitants to resettle in another town.

JOHN HUSTON AND THE DUBLINERS
Pro. Lilyan Sievernich *Dir.* Lilyan Sievernich *Cine.* Lisa Rinzler *Ed.* Miroslav Janek *Mu.* Alex North *R.t.* 60 min. *Cast:* John Huston, Anjelica Huston, Tony Huston, Roberto Silvi, Tom Shaw, Donal McCann, Rachael Dowling, Helena Carroll, Cathleen Delany, Ingrid Craigie, Dan O'Herlihy, Marie Kean, Donal Donnelly, Katherine O'Toole, Sean McClory, Frank Patterson.

Filmed on the set of *The Dead*, this documentary pays homage to the late director John Huston.

KANGAROO (Australia, 1987)
Pro. Ross Dimsey; Cineplex Odeon Films *Dir.* Tim Burstall *Scr.* Evan Jones; based on the novel of the same name by D. H. Lawrence *Cine.* Dan Burstall *Ed.* Eward McQueen-Mason *Mu.* Nathan Waks *P.d.* Tracy Watt *R.t.* 105 min. *MPAA* R. *Cast:* Colin Friels, Judy Davis, John Walton, Julie Nihill, Hugh Keays-Byrne, Peter Hehir, Peter Cummins, Tim Robertson.

Based on D. H. Lawrence's novel, *Kangaroo* depicts the different reactions of a writer and his wife to Australia. The writer becomes involved with a fascist who wants to stamp out the country's growing labor movement.

THE KID BROTHER (Canada and Japan, 1987)
Pro. Kiyoshi Fujimoto *Dir.* Claude Gagnon *Scr.* Claude Gagnon *Cine.* Yudai Kato *Ed.* André Corriveau *Mu.* François Dompierre *P.d.* Bill Bilowit *R.t.* 95 min. *Cast:* Kenny Easterday, Caitlin Clarke, Liane Curtis, Zack Grenier, Jesse Easterday, Jr., Tom Reddy, Alain St-Alix, John Carpenter.

A boy born without legs or lower torso (Kenny Easterday) stars in this unusual film about the struggles of a family to deal with their handicapped son.

KIDNAPPED
Pro. Marlene Schmidt *Dir.* Howard Avedis *Scr.* Howard Avedis *Cine.* Tom Denove *Ed.* Michael Luciano and Lloyd Nelson *Mu.* Ron Jones *R.t.* 98 min. *Cast:* David Naughton, Barbara Crampton, Lance LeGault, Chick Vennera, Kim Evenson, Jimmie Walker, Kin Shriner, Michelle Rossi, Robert Dryer, Gary Wood, Charles Napier.

When her sister is kidnapped by a photographer who works for a gangster who makes pornographic films, Bonnie (Barbara Crampton) enlists the aid of a maverick policeman (David Naughton).

THE KILLING TIME
Pro. Peter Abrams and Robert L. Levy; New World Pictures *Dir.* Rick King *Scr.* Don Bohlinger, James Nathan, and Bruce Franklin Singer *Cine.* Paul H. Goldsmith *Ed.* Lorenzo de Stefano *Mu.* Paul Chihara *P.d.* Bernt Amadeus Capra *S.d.* Byrnadette Di Santo *R.t.* 95 min. *MPAA* R. *Cast:* Beau Bridges, Kiefer Suther-

land, Wayne Rogers, Joe Don Baker, Camelia Kath, Janet Carroll, Michael Madsen.

A small-town sheriff (Beau Bridges) and his lover (Camelia Kath) scheme to murder her domineering husband (Wayne Rogers).

THE KINDRED

Pro. Jeffrey Obrow; F/M Entertainment *Dir.* Stephen Carpenter and Jeffrey Obrow *Scr.* Stephen Carpenter, Jeffrey Obrow, John Penney, Earl Ghaffari, and Joseph Stefano *Cine.* Stephen Carpenter *Ed.* John Penney and Earl Ghaffari *Mu.* David Newman *P.d.* Chris Hopkins *A.d.* Becky Block *S.d.* Susan Emshwiller *R.t.* 91 min. *MPAA* R. *Cast:* David Allen Brooks, Rod Steiger, Amanda Pays, Talia Balsam, Kim Hunter, Timothy Gibbs, Peter Frechette, Julia Montgomery, Bunki Z, Charles Grueber.

When his dying mother asks him to destroy her research project, John (David Allen Brooks) finds that she has created a terrifying monster by splicing his genes with a marine animal.

KING LEAR (USA and Switzerland, 1987)

Pro. Menahem Golan and Yoram Globus; Cannon Films *Dir.* Jean-Luc Godard *Scr.* Jean-Luc Godard *Cine.* Sophie Maintigneux *R.t.* 90 min. *Cast:* Burgess Meredith, Peter Sellars, Molly Ringwald, Jean-Luc Godard, Woody Allen, Norman Mailer, Kate Miller.

Jean-Luc Godard's first feature in English is a surrealistic exploration of the boundaries of reality and perception.

KISS DADDY GOOD NIGHT

Pro. Maureen O'Brien and William Ripka *Dir.* Peter Ily Huemer *Scr.* Peter Ily Huemer and Michael Gabrieli; based on a story by Peter Ily Huemer *Cine.* Bobby Bukowski *Ed.* Ila von Hasperg *Mu.* Don King and Duncan Lindsay *R.t.* 80 min. *Cast:* Uma Thurman, Paul Dillon, Paul Richards, Steve Buscemi, Annabelle Gurwitch, David Brisbin.

Uma Thurman plays Lisa, a beautiful blonde who gains entry to men's apartments, then drugs and robs them; Paul Richards plays William, her neighbor, who is obsessed with her resemblance to his daughter.

THE KITCHEN TOTO (Great Britain, 1987)

Pro. Ann Skinner; Cannon Group *Dir.* Harry Hook *Scr.* Harry Hook *Cine.* Roger Deakins *Ed.* Tom Priestley *Mu.* John Keane *P.d.* Jamie Leonard *R.t.* 95 min. *Cast:* Bob Peck, Phyllis Logan, Edwin Mahinda, Kirsten Hughes, Robert Urquhart, Nicholas Chase, Job Seda, Leo Wringer.

In this film set in Kenya in 1950, a young black boy (Edwin Mahinda), whose father has been murdered by a black radical group, is taken in by a white policeman. The boy is torn between his tribal loyalties and his debt to the whites who have been kind to him.

LADY BEWARE

Pro. Tony Scotti and Lawrence Taylor-Mortorff; Scotti Bros. Entertainment *Dir.* Karen Arthur *Scr.* Susan Miller and Charles Zev Cohen *Cine.* Tom Neuwirth *Ed.* Roy Watts *Mu.* Craig Safan *S.d.* Tom Wells *R.t.* 108 min. *MPAA* R. *Cast:* Diane Lane, Michael Woods, Cotter Smith, Peter Nevargic, Edward Penn, Tyra Ferrell.

Designer Katya Yarno (Diane Lane), who has just moved to Pittsburgh, is dogged by a man who becomes obsessed with her.

THE LAST DAY OF WINTER (People's Republic of China, 1987)
Pro. China Film Export and Import Corporation *Dir.* Wu Ziniu *Scr.* Qiao Xuezhu *Cine.* Yang Wei *Mu.* Wang Xilin *R.t.* 94 min. *Cast:* Li Ling, Tao Zeru, Yu Meng, Hong Yuzhou, Zhang Xiaomin.

Three young people travel to a prison camp in northern China to visit siblings interned there.

THE LAST STRAW (Canada, 1987)
Pro. David Wilson and Giles Walker; Cinema International Canada *Dir.* Giles Walker *Scr.* Giles Walker and David Wilson *Cine.* Andrew Kitzanuk *Ed.* David Wilson *Mu.* Robert Lauzon and Fernand Martel *R.t.* 98 min. *Cast:* Salverio (Sam) Grana, Fernanda Tavares, Maurice Podbrey, Beverley Murray, Stefan Wodoslawsky, Christine Pak, Wally Martin.

Alex (Salverio Grana) is in great demand as a sperm donor when it is discovered that he is the world's most potent man.

LATE SUMMER BLUES (*Blues Lahofesh Hagadol.* Israel, 1987)
Pro. Ilan de Fries, Renen Schorr, and Doron Nesher *Dir.* Renen Schorr *Scr.* Doron Nesher *Cine.* Ethan Harris *Ed.* Shlomo Hazan *Mu.* Rafi Kadishsohn *R.t.* 101 min. *Cast:* Dor Zweigenbaum, Yoav Tzafir, Noa Goldenberg, Vered Cohen, Shahar Segal, Sharon Bar-Ziv, Ada Ben Nahum, Edna Fliedel, Miki Kam, Moshe Havatzeleth, Amith Gazith.

In the summer of 1970, a group of Israeli teenagers plan high school graduation celebrations as they struggle with their feelings about being drafted into the army.

THE LAW OF DESIRE (*La ley del deseo.* Spain, 1987)
Pro. El Deseo S. A. and Laurenfilm S. A. *Dir.* Pedro Almodovar *Scr.* Pedro Almodovar *Cine.* Angel Luis Fernández *Ed.* José Salcedo *S.d.* Javier Fernández *R.t.* 101 min. *Cast:* Eusebio Poncela, Carmen Maura, Antonio Banderas, Miguel Molina, Manuel Velasco, Bibi Andersson, Fernando Guillén, Nacho Martínez, Helga Line, Fernando G. Cuervo, Germán Cobos, Maruchi Leon, Marta Fernández Muro.

Antonio (Antonio Banderas) falls in love with a famous film director (Eusebio Poncela) and pushes his rival (Miguel Molina) off a cliff.

LEMON SKY
Pro. Marcus Viscidi *Dir.* Jan Egleson *Scr.* Lanford Wilson *Cine.* James Glennon *Ed.* Jeanne Jordan and William A. Anderson *Mu.* Pat Metheny *A.d.* Dianna Freas *R.t.* 106 min. *Cast:* Kevin Bacon, Tom Atkins, Lindsay Crouse, Kyra Sedgwick, Laura White, Casey Affleck, Peter Macowan.

When Alan (Kevin Bacon) comes to live with his father and stepmother, tensions arise that prove destructive to the family.

LEONARD PART 6
Pro. Bill Cosby; Columbia Pictures *Dir.* Paul Weiland *Scr.* Jonathan Reynolds; based on a story by Bill Cosby *Cine.* Jan DeBont *Ed.* Gerry Hambling *Mu.* Elmer Bernstein *P.d.* Geoffrey Kirkland *A.d.* Blake Russell *S.d.* Jim Poynter *R.t.* 85 min. *MPAA* PG. *Cast:* Bill Cosby, Tom Courtenay, Joe Don Baker, Moses Gunn, Pat Colbert, Gloria Foster, Victoria Rowell, Anna Levine, David Maier, Grace Zabriskie, Hal Bokar, George Maguire, John Hostetter, William Hall, George Kirby, Jane Fonda.

A wealthy retired spy (Bill Cosby) is called on to save the world from a maniacal villainess (Gloria Foster) and her hordes of avenging frogs, fish, cats, and lobsters.

Meanwhile, the spy's own family is falling apart.

LES PATTERSON SAVES THE WORLD (Australia, 1987)

Pro. Sue Milliken; Hoyts *Dir.* George Miller *Scr.* Barry Humphries and Diane Millstead *Cine.* David Connell *Ed.* Tim Wellburn *Mu.* Tim Finn *P.d.* Graham Walker *R.t.* 95 min. *Cast:* Barry Humphries, Pamela Stephenson, Thaao Penghlis, Andrew Clarke, Henri Szeps, Hugh Keays-Byrne, Elizbeth Melvor, Garth Meade, Arthur Sherman, Josef Drewnaak, Joan Rivers, Esben Storm, Joy Westmore, Connie Hobbs, Paul Jennings, Graham Kennedy, John Clarke, David Whitney, Sally Tayler, Peter Collingwood.

Corpulent Australian diplomat Sir Les Patterson (Barry Humphries) is sent in disgrace to a small Arab country just before a military coup takes place. After the coup, Patterson must confront a plot to infect the world with disease by exporting contaminated toilet seats.

LESS THAN ZERO

Pro. Jon Avnet and Jordan Kerner; Twentieth Century-Fox *Dir.* Marek Kanievska *Scr.* Harley Peyton; based on the novel by Bret Easton Ellis *Cine.* Edward Lachman *Ed.* Peter E. Berger and Michael Tronick *Mu.* Thomas Newman *P.d.* Barbara Ling *A.d.* Stephen Rice *S.d.* Nancy Nye *R.t.* 98 min. *MPAA* R. *Cast:* Andrew McCarthy, Jami Gertz, Robert Downey, Jr., James Spader, Michael Bowen, Nicholas Pryor, Tony Bill.

A trio of wealthy Los Angeles young people (Andrew McCarthy, Jami Gertz, and Robert Downey, Jr.) struggle to make sense of the round of drugs, parties, and sex that makes up their lives.

LIFE CLASSES (Canada, 1987)

Pro. Stephen Reynolds; Cinephile *Dir.* William D. MacGillivray *Scr.* William D. MacGillivray *Cine.* Lionel Simmons *Ed.* William D. MacGillivray *Mu.* Alexandra Tilley *A.d.* Mary Steckle *R.t.* 117 min. *Cast:* Jacinta Cormier, Leon Dubinsky, Evelyn Garbary, Mary Izzard, Francis Knickle, Jill Chatt, Leo Jessome, Caitlyn Colquhoun.

A young Cape Breton woman becomes a mother and discovers herself as an artist.

LIGHT OF DAY

Pro. Rob Cohen and Keith Barish; Tri-Star Pictures *Dir.* Paul Schrader *Scr.* Paul Schrader *Cine.* John Bailey *Ed.* Jacqueline Cambas *Mu.* Thomas Newman *P.d.* Jeannine Claudia Oppewall *S.d.* Lisa Fischer *R.t.* 107 min. *MPAA* PG-13. *Cast:* Michael J. Fox, Gena Rowlands, Joan Jett, Michael McKean, Thomas G. Waites, Cherry Jones, Michael Dolan, Paul J. Harkins, Billy Sullivan, Jason Miller.

A brother and sister (Michael J. Fox and Joan Jett) try to succeed in rock and roll despite their depressing daily lives.

THE LIGHTHORSEMEN (Australia, 1987)

Pro. Ian Jones and Simon Wincer; Cinecom International *Dir.* Simon Wincer *Scr.* Ian Jones *Cine.* Dean Semler *Ed.* Adrian Carr *Mu.* Mario Millo *P.d.* Bernard Hides *R.t.* 128 min. *Cast:* Jon Blake, Peter Phelps, Tony Bonner, Bill Kerr, John Walton, Gary Sweet, Tim McKenzie, Sigrid Thornton, Anthony Andrews, Anthony Hawkins, Gerard Kennedy, Shane Briant, Ralph Cotterill, John Heywood, Di O'Connor, Grant Piro, Patrick Frost, Adrian Wright, Anne Scott-Pendlebury, Brenton Whittle, Jon Sidney, Graham Dow, James Wright, Gary Stalker, Scott Bradley, Peter Merrill, Peter Browne.

This story of four young Australian cavalrymen climaxes with the charge of the Light Horse on the Turks and Germans at Beersheba.

LIKE FATHER LIKE SON

Pro. Brian Grazer and David Valdes; Tri-Star Pictures *Dir.* Rod Daniel *Scr.* Lorne Cameron and Steven L. Bloom *Cine.* Jack N. Green *Ed.* Lois Freeman-Fox *Mu.* Miles Goodman *P.d.* Dennis Gassner *S.d.* John T. Walker *R.t.* 98 min. *MPAA* PG-13. *Cast:* Dudley Moore, Kirk Cameron, Sean Astin, Patrick O'Neal, Margaret Colin, Catherine Hicks.

A stuffy surgeon (Dudley Moore) and his carefree teenage son (Kirk Cameron) exchange personalities when the father unknowingly imbibes brain transference serum.

LIONHEART

Pro. Stanley O'Toole and Talia Shire; Orion Pictures *Dir.* Franklin J. Shaffner *Scr.* Menno Meyjes and Richard Outten; based on a story by Menno Meyjes *Cine.* Alec Mills *Ed.* David Bretherton and Richard Haines *Mu.* Jerry Goldsmith *P.d.* Gil Parrondo *R.t.* 104 min. *MPAA* PG. *Cast:* Eric Stoltz, Gabriel Byrne, Nicola Cowper, Dexter Fletcher, Deborah Barrymore, Nicholas Clay, Bruce Purchase, Neil Dickson.

A band of medieval teenagers meet with danger and adventure in their quest to join King Richard II and help to recapture the Holy Land.

LIVING ON TOKYO TIME

Pro. Lynn O'Donnell and Dennis Hayashi *Dir.* Steven Okazaki *Scr.* John McCormick and Steven Okazaki *Cine.* Steven Okazaki and Zand Gee *Ed.* Steven Okazaki *R.t.* 83 min. *Cast:* Minako Ohashi, Ken Nakagawa, Mitzie Abe, Bill Bonham, Brenda Aoki, Kate Connell, John McCormick, Sue Matthews, Jim Cranna, Alex Herschlag, Keith Choy, Judi Nihei, Lane Nishikawa.

A young Japanese woman (Minako Ohashi) visits the United States after her arranged marriage plans fall through and becomes involved with a second generation Japanese man who dreams of becoming a rock star.

THE LOST BOYS

Pro. Harvey Bernhard; Warner Bros. *Dir.* Joel Schumacher *Scr.* Janice Fischer, James Jeremias, and Jeffrey Boam; based on a story by Janice Fischer and James Jeremias *Cine.* Michael Chapman *Ed.* Robert Brown *Mu.* Thomas Newman *P.d.* Bo Welch *A.d.* Tom Duffield *S.d.* Chris Westlund *R.t.* 92 min. *MPAA* R. *Cast:* Jason Patric, Corey Haim, Dianne Wiest, Barnard Hughes, Edward Herrmann, Kiefer Sutherland, Jami Gertz, Corey Feldman, Jamison Newlander, Brooke McCarter, Billy Wirth, Alexander Winter, Chance Michael Corbitt.

Sam (Corey Haim) enlists the aid of two young friends to combat a gang of vampire bikers who have ensnared his older brother.

MAID TO ORDER

Pro. Herb Jaffe and Mort Engelberg; New Century/Vista Film Company *Dir.* Amy Jones *Scr.* Amy Jones, Perry Howze, and Randy Howze *Cine.* Shelly Johnson *Ed.* Sidney Wolinsky *Mu.* Georges Delerue *P.d.* Jeffrey Townsend *R.t.* 93 min. *MPAA* PG. *Cast:* Ally Sheedy, Beverly D'Angelo, Michael Ontkean, Valerie Perrine, Dick Shawn, Tom Skerritt, Merry Clayton, Begona Plaza.

Suddenly thrown on her own resources, spoiled party girl Jessie Montgomery (Ally Sheedy) finds a job as a maid in the home of a Malibu couple.

THE MALADY OF LOVE (*Le Mal d'aimer*. France and Italy, 1987)
Pro. Lisa Fayolle and Paolo Zaccaria; AAA *Dir.* Giorgio Treves *Scr.* Vincenzo Cerami and Pierre Dumayet *Cine.* Giuseppe Ruzzolini *Ed.* Carla Simoncelli *Mu.* Egisto Macchi *A.d.* Lorenzo Baraldi *R.t.* 88 min. *Cast:* Robin Renucci, Isabelle Pasco, Carole Bouquet, Piera Degli Esposti, Erland Josephson, Andrzej Seweryn.

Set in a fifteenth century leper colony, this film involves a physician who defies authority by running away with a seemingly pure girl who has been suspected of contracting syphilis.

THE MALIBU BIKINI SHOP
Pro. Gary Mehlman and J. Kenneth Rotcop; International Film Marketing *Dir.* David Wechter *Scr.* David Wechter *Cine.* Tom Richmond *Ed.* Jean-Marc Vasseur *Mu.* Don Perry *A.d.* Dian Perryman *S.d.* Kayla Koeber *R.t.* 99 min. *MPAA* R. *Cast:* Michael David Wright, Bruce Greenwood, Barbra Horan, Debra Blee, Jay Robinson, Gaylyn Gorg, Ami Julius, Frank Nelson.

Two brothers, one a businessman and the other a beach bum, inherit a shop.

MALONE
Pro. Leo L. Fuchs; Orion Pictures *Dir.* Harley Cokliss *Scr.* Christopher Frank; based on the novel *Shotgun*, by William Wingate *Cine.* Gerald Hirschfeld *Ed.* Todd Ramsay *Mu.* David Newman *P.d.* Graeme Murray *S.d.* Barry Brolly *R.t.* 92 min. *MPAA* R. *Cast:* Burt Reynolds, Cliff Robertson, Kenneth McMillan, Cynthia Gibb, Scott Wilson, Lauren Hutton, Philip Anglim, Tracey Walter, Dennis Burkley.

Disillusioned CIA agent Malone (Burt Reynolds) finds himself in a small Oregon town that is threatened by a rich rancher (Cliff Robertson) who is attempting to buy everyone's land in order to establish a paramilitary base there.

A MAN IN LOVE
Pro. Michel Seydoux; Cinecom International *Dir.* Diane Kurys *Scr.* Diane Kurys *Cine.* Bernard Zitzermann *Ed.* Joele Van Effenterre *Mu.* Georges Delerue *A.d.* Dean Tavoularis *R.t.* 108 min. *MPAA* R. *Cast:* Peter Coyote, Greta Scacchi, Peter Riegert, John Berry, Vincent Lindon, Jean Pigozzi, Elia Katz, Constantin Alexandrov, Michele Melega, Jean-Claude de Goros, Claudia Cardinale, Jamie Lee Curtis.

An American actor (Peter Coyote) and a Parisian actress (Greta Scacchi) meet on a film set and begin a clandestine affair.

MANNEQUIN
Pro. Art Levinson; Twentieth Century-Fox *Dir.* Michael Gottlieb *Scr.* Michael Gottlieb and Edward Rugoff *Cine.* Tim Suhrstedt *Ed.* Richard Halsey *Mu.* Sylvester Levay *P.d.* Josan Russo *A.d.* Richard Amend *S.d.* Elise Rowland *R.t.* 89 min. *MPAA* PG. *Cast:* Andrew McCarthy, Kim Cattrall, Estelle Getty, G. W. Bailey, James Spader, Meshach Taylor, Carole Davis, Stephen Vinovich, Christopher Maher, Phyllis Newman.

A young man (Andrew McCarthy) achieves success when the mannequin (Kim Cattrall) he sculpted comes to life and helps him make a store profitable; his career is threatened by his supervisor, who is also in the pay of a rival shop.

MARILYN MONROE: BEYOND THE LEGEND
Pro. Gene Feldman and Suzette Winter *Dir.* Gene Feldman *Scr.* Gene Feldman and Suzette Winter *Cine.* Rick Robertson and Richard Francis *Ed.* Les Mulkey *R.t.* 60 min. *Cast:* Richard Widmark, Robert Mitchum, Shelley Winters, Joshua Lo-

gan, Susan Strasberg, Don Murray, Celeste Holm, Sheree North, Clark Gordon, John Springer, Laszlo Willinger.

Gene Feldman's documentary uses film clips and interviews to examine Marilyn Monroe's acting career.

THE MARSUPIALS: THE HOWLING III (Australia, 1987)

Pro. Charles Waterstreet and Philippe Mora; Bacannia Entertainment *Dir.* Philippe Mora *Scr.* Philippe Mora; based on the book *The Howling III*, by Gary Brander *Cine.* Louis Irving *Ed.* Lee Smith *Mu.* Allan Zavod *P.d.* Ross Major *R.t.* 94 min. *Cast:* Barry Otto, Imogen Annesley, Dasha Blahova, Max Fairchild, Ralph Cotterill, Leigh Biolos, Frank Thring, Michael Pate, Barry Humphries, Carole Skinner, Brian Adams, Bill Collins, Christopher Pate.

In this parody of the werewolf genre, Professor Beckmeyer (Barry Otto) studies a tribe of marsupial werewolves, some of whom make their way from the Australian bush into Sydney, where they cause all manner of mayhem.

MASTERS OF THE UNIVERSE

Pro. Menahem Golan and Yoram Globus; Cannon Group *Dir.* Gary Goddard *Scr.* David Odell *Cine.* Hanania Baer *Ed.* Anne V. Coates *Mu.* Bill Conti *P.d.* William Stout *A.d.* Robert Howland *R.t.* 106 min. *MPAA* PG. *Cast:* Dolph Lundgren, Frank Langella, Meg Foster, Billy Barty, Courteney Cox, James Tolkan, Christina Pickles, Robert Duncan McNeil, Jon Cypher, Chelsea Field.

A young Earth couple help He-Man (Dolph Lundgren) to retrieve the cosmic key that will help him to defeat the evil Skeletor (Frank Langella).

MEATBALLS III

Pro. Don Carmody and John Dunning; The Movie Store Pictures *Dir.* George Mendeluk *Scr.* Michael Paseornek and Bradley Kesden *Cine.* Peter Benison *Ed.* Debra Karen *Mu.* Paul Zaza *R.t.* 94 min. *MPAA* R. *Cast:* Sally Kellerman, Patrick Dempsey, Al Waxman, Isabelle Mejias, Shannon Tweed, Jan Taylor, George Buza.

A teenage boy (Patrick Dempsey) has the help of a guardian angel (Sally Kellerman) in finding an appropriate girlfriend.

THE MESSENGER (USA and Italy, 1987)

Pro. Fred Williamson and Pier Luigi Circiaci; Snizzlefritz *Dir.* Fred Williamson *Scr.* Brian Johnson, Conchita Lee, and Anthony Wisdom; based on a story by Fred Williamson *Cine.* Giancarlo Ferrando and Craig Greene *Ed.* No listing *Mu.* William Stuckey *R.t.* 92 min. *MPAA* R. *Cast:* Fred Williamson, Sandy Cummings, Val Avery, Michael Dante, Chris Connelly, Cameron Mitchell, Peter Turner, Joe Spinell.

A former Green Beret, musical prodigy, and burglar (Fred Williamson) avenges the murder of his wife.

MILLION DOLLAR MYSTERY

Pro. Stephen F. Kesten; De Laurentiis Entertainment Group *Dir.* Richard Fleischer *Scr.* Tim Metcalfe, Miguel Tejada-Flores, and Rudy DeLuca *Cine.* Jack Cardiff *Ed.* John W. Wheeler *Mu.* Al Gorgoni *P.d.* Jack G. Taylor, Jr. *R.t.* 95 min. *MPAA* PG. *Cast:* Eddie Deezen, Wendy Sherman, Rick Overton, Mona Lyden, Douglas Emerson, Royce D. Applegate, Pam Matteson, Daniel McDonald, Penny Baker, Tawny Fere, LaGena Hart, Tom Bosley, Mack Dryden, Jamie Alcroft, Rich Hall, Gail Neely, Kevin Pollak, H. B. Hagerty, Bob Schott.

Clues to the whereabouts of a million dollars are hidden in this comedy about people who make fools of themselves trying to track down a dead con man's fortune.
MISS MONA (France, 1987)
Pro. Michele Ray-Gravras; K. G. Distribution and AAA *Dir.* Mehdi Charef *Scr.*
Mehdi Charef *Cine.* Patrick Blossier *Ed.* Kenout Peltier *Mu.* Bernard Lubat *R.t.*
98 min. *Cast:* Jean Carmet, Ben Smail, Albert Delpy, Daniel Schad, Francis Frappat, André Chaumeau, Albert Klein, Philippe de Brugada, Yvette Petit, Michel Peyleron, Maximilien Decroux, Kader Boukhanef, Remi Martin.

This film describes the relationship between an aging, gay, transvestite prostitute and a young Arab—when the Arab kills a man they had robbed, the transvestite uses the money to buy him an identity card, but the police capture him first.
MISS . . . OR MYTH?
Pro. Geoffrey Dunn, Mark Schwartz, and Claire Rubach *Dir.* Geoffrey Dunn and Mark Schwartz *Scr.* Geoffrey Dunn *Cine.* Mark Schwartz *Ed.* Mark Schwartz
Mu. Liz Story *R.t.* 60 min. *Cast:* Lee Ann Meriwether, Ann Simonton.

Feminists, pageant directors, and beauty queens offer their opinions on the merits of beauty pageants during the 1985 Miss California contest in Santa Cruz.
MONSTER IN THE CLOSET
Pro. David Levy and Peter L. Bergquist; Troma *Dir.* Bob Dahlin *Scr.* Bob Dahlin; based on a story by Bob Dahlin and Peter L. Bergquist *Cine.* Ronald W. McLeish
Ed. Raja Gosnell and Stephanie Palewski *Mu.* Barrie Guard *P.d.* Lynda Cohen
R.t. 92 min. *MPAA* PG. *Cast:* Donald Grant, Denise DuBarry, Henry Gibson, Howard Duff, Donald Moffat, Claude Akins, Paul Walker, Frank Ashmore, John Carradine, Stella Stevens, Kevin Peter Hall.

Horror film clichés are gently satirized in this story of a reporter, a biology teacher, and an Einsteinian scientist tracking down a ravenous monster that devours its human prey in closets.
THE MONSTER SQUAD
Pro. Jonathan A. Zimbert; Tri-Star Pictures *Dir.* Fred Dekker *Scr.* Shane Black and Fred Dekker *Cine.* Bradford May *Ed.* James Mitchell *Mu.* Bruce Broughton
P.d. Albert Brenner *A.d.* David M. Haber *R.t.* 81 min. *MPAA* PG-13. *Cast:* Andre Gower, Robby Kiger, Stephen Macht, Duncan Regehr, Tom Noonan, Brent Chalem, Ryan Lambert, Ashley Bank, Michael Faustino, Mary Ellen Trainor.

Young members of a club devoted to monsters do battle against Count Dracula, the Wolfman, the Mummy, and other ghouls who have joined in a quest for an ancient amulet.
A MONTH IN THE COUNTRY (Great Britain, 1987)
Pro. Kenith Trodd; Orion Classics *Dir.* Pat O'Connor *Scr.* Simon Gray; based on the novel by J. L. Carr *Cine.* Kenneth Macmillan *Mu.* Howard Blake *P.d.* Leo Austin *R.t.* 96 min. *MPAA* PG-13. *Cast:* Colin Firth, Kenneth Branagh, Natasha Richardson, Patrick Malahide, Tony Haygarth, Jim Carter, Richard Vernon.

Two soldiers still troubled by their experiences in World War I find that the time they spend in a small Yorkshire town is helping to heal their emotional wounds.
MORGAN STEWART'S COMING HOME
Pro. Stephen Friedman; New Century/Vista Film Company *Dir.* Alan Smithee
Scr. Ken Hixon and David Titcher *Cine.* Richard Brooks *Ed.* Bob Letterman *Mu.*
Peter Bernstein *P.d.* Charles Bennett *S.d.* Victor Kempster *R.t.* 96 min. *MPAA*

PG-13. *Cast:* Jon Cryer, Lynn Redgrave, Nicholas Pryor, Viveka Davis, Paul Gleason, Andrew Duncan, Savely Kramorov, John David Cullum.

A teenage boy (Jon Cryer) is brought home from school in order to give his father's Congressional campaign a family image, and he does manage to pull together his unsympathetic family.

MOSCOW FAREWELL (*Mosca addio.* Italy, 1987)

Pro. Roseo Film; Istituto Luce and Italnoleggio *Dir.* Mauro Bolognini *Scr.* Enrico Roseo and Marcello Andrei *Cine.* Ennio Guarnieri *Ed.* Nino Baragli *Mu.* Ennio Morricone *R.t.* 102 min. *Cast:* Liv Ullmann, Daniel Olbrychski, Aurore Clement, Francesca Ciardi, Carmen Scarpitta, Nino Fuscagni, Saverio Vallone.

A woman denied emigration with her family protests and is sent to a camp in Siberia. When she returns to Moscow, she has nowhere to live and no job, and she finally takes refuge in a small town.

MUNCHIES

Pro. Roger Corman; Concorde Pictures *Dir.* Bettina Hirsch *Scr.* Lance Smith *R.t.* 85 min. *MPAA* PG. *Cast:* Harvey Korman, Charles Stratton, Nadine Van Der Velde, Alix Elias, Charlie Phillips, Jon Stafford, Hardy Rawis.

A scientist (Harvey Korman) finds an unusual creature in a cave in Peru and brings it home. His brother (Harvey Korman) discovers the malevolent side of the cute beast when he pushes it too far.

MY AFRICAN ADVENTURE

Pro. Menahem Golan and Yoram Globus; Cannon Group *Dir.* Boaz Davidson *Scr.* Menahem Golan *Cine.* Joseph Wain *Ed.* Natan Zahavi and Bruria Davidson *R.t.* 93 min. *Cast:* Dom De Luise, Jimmie C. Walker, David Mendenhall, Deep Roy, Warren Berlinger, Herbert Lom, Len Sparrowhawk, Peter Elliott, Fats Dibeco, Graham Armitage, Mike Westcott, Phillip Van Der Byl, Bobby Porter, Irene Frangs.

An American boy, his guardian, and an African tour guide cooperate to save a talking chimp from a local police chief and a circus owner in this family-oriented comedy.

MY DARK LADY

Pro. Carole Terranova and Stratton Rawson; Film Gallery *Dir.* Frederick King Keller *Scr.* Fred A. Keller, Gene Brook, and Frederick King Keller; based on an original story by Fred A. Keller *Cine.* Thom Marini *Ed.* Darren Kloomok *Mu.* Ken Kaufman *P.d.* Stratton Rawson *S.d.* Gary Matwijkow *R.t.* 104 min. *Cast:* Fred A. Keller, Lorna Hill, Raymond Holder, John Buscaglia, Evan Perry, Barbara Cady, Stuart Roth, Tess Spangler, Steven Cooper.

A Shakespearean actor down on his luck moves into the home of a prostitute and gives her son acting lessons. When the boy enters a preparatory school on scholarship, the headmaster makes trouble because of his background.

MY DEMON LOVER

Pro. Robert Shaye; New Line Cinema *Dir.* Charles Loventhal *Scr.* Leslie Ray *Cine.* Jacques Haitkin *Ed.* Ronald Roose *Mu.* David Newman *P.d.* Brent Swift *A.d.* Douglas Dick *R.t.* 86 min. *MPAA* PG-13. *Cast:* Scott Valentine, Michelle Little, Arnold Johnson, Robert Trebor, Alan Fudge, Gina Gallego, Calvert DeForest, Eva Charney, Dan Patrick Brady.

A young man (Scott Valentine) is afflicted with a mysterious curse that literally turns him into various demons when he is sexually aroused.

MY TRUE LOVE, MY WOUND (*Mon bel Amour, ma dechirure.* France, 1987)
Pro. Yannick Bernard; Bac Films *Dir.* Jose Pinheiro *Scr.* Louis Calaferto, Sotha, and Jose Pinheiro *Cine.* Richard Andry *Ed.* Claire Pinheiro-L'Heveder *Mu.* Romano Musumarra *A.d.* Theo Meurisse *R.t.* 107 min. *Cast:* Stephane Ferrara, Catherine Wilkening, Vera Gregh, Veronique Barrault, Jacques Castaldo, Philippe Manesse, Jacky Sigaux, Mouss.

An actress enters into a passionate clandestine affair with a street ruffian.

NEAR DARK
Pro. Steven-Charles Jaffe; De Laurentiis Entertainment Group *Dir.* Kathryn Bigelow *Scr.* Eric Red and Kathryn Bigelow *Cine.* Adam Greenberg *Ed.* Howard Smith *Mu.* Tangerine Dream *P.d.* Stephen Altman *A.d.* Dian Perryman *R.t.* 95 min. *MPAA* R. *Cast:* Adrian Pasdar, Jenny Wright, Lance Henriksen, Bill Paxton, Jenette Goldstein, Tim Thomerson, Joshua Miller, Marcie Leeds.

A young cowboy (Adrian Pasdar) falls in with a gang of vampires, who eventually threaten members of his family.

NIAGARA FALLS: MIRACLES, MYTHS AND MAGIC
Pro. Nicholas Gray *Dir.* Kieth Merrill *Scr.* Kieth Merrill *Cine.* David Douglas *Ed.* Ben Burtt *R.t.* 40 min. *Cast:* Vanessa Boyack, Philippe Petit, Robert Sims.

This IMAX film re-creates several key events in the history of Niagara Falls.

NICE GIRLS DON'T EXPLODE
Pro. Doug Curtis and John Wells; New World Pictures *Dir.* Chuck Martinez *Scr.* Paul Harris *Cine.* Steven Katz *Ed.* Wende Phifer Mate *Mu.* Brian Banks and Anthony Marinelli *P.d.* Sarina Rotstein *R.t.* 92 min. *MPAA* PG. *Cast:* Barbara Harris, Michelle Meyrink, William O'Leary, Wallace Shawn, James Nardini, Margot Gray, Jonas Baugham, William Kuhlke.

A possessive mother arranges for fires and explosions whenever her daughter falls in love, and she manages to persuade her daughter that the fires are caused by a genetic mutation caused by the mother drinking a toxic substance while pregnant.

THE NIGHT OF THE PENCILS (*La noche de los lapices.* Argentina, 1987)
Pro. Fernando Ayala *Dir.* Hector Olivera *Scr.* Hector Olivera and Daniel Kon; based on the historical essay by Maria Seoane and Hector Ruiz Nuñez *Cine.* Leonardo Rodríguez Solis *Ed.* Miguel Mario López *Mu.* José Luis Castineira de Dios *R.t.* 101 min. *Cast:* Alejo García Pintos, Vita Escardo, Pablo Novarro, Leonardo Sbaraglia, José María Monje Berbel, Pablo Machado, Adriana Salonia, Hector Bidonde, Tina Serrano, Lorenzo Quinteros, Alfonso de Grazia, Manuel Callau, Francisco Cocuzza, Juan Manuel Tenuta, Andrea Bonelli, Rubens Correa, Angela Ragno.

This Argentinian film, based on true events, depicts the incarceration and torture of seven high school students who protested for student bus passes after the fall of Isabel Perón.

NIGHTFLYERS
Pro. Robert Jaffe; New Century/Vista Film Company; *Dir.* T. C. Blake (Robert Collector) *Scr.* Robert Jaffe; based on the novella by George R. R. Martin *Cine.* Shelly Johnson *Ed.* Tom Siiter *Mu.* Doug Timm *P.d.* John Muto *A.d.* Mike Bingham *S.d.* Anne Huntley-Ahrens *R.t.* 89 min. *MPAA* R. *Cast:* Catherine Mary Stewart, Michael Praed, John Standing, Lisa Blount, Glenn Withrow, James Avery, Helene Udy, Annabel Brooks, Michael Des Barres.

A team of scientists lease an old spaceship that turns out to be inhabited by a malevolent being (Michael Des Barres).

NIGHTMARE AT SHADOW WOODS

Pro. Marianne Kanter; Film Concept Group *Dir.* John W. Grissmer *Scr.* Richard Lamden *Cine.* Richard E. Brooks *Ed.* Michael R. Miller *Mu.* Richard Einhorn *P.d.* Jim Rule *R.t.* 84 min. *MPAA* R. *Cast:* Louise Lasser, Mark Soper, Marianne Kanter, Julie Gordon, Jayne Bentzen, William Fuller.

Terry (Mark Soper), a psychopath, wields hatchet and machete to murder any number of victims, pinning all the crimes on his shy twin brother Todd (Mark Soper).

A NIGHTMARE ON ELM STREET 3: DREAM WARRIORS

Pro. Robert Shaye; New Line Cinema *Dir.* Chuck Russell *Scr.* Wes Craven, Bruce Wagner, Chuck Russell, and Frank Darabont; based on a story by Wes Craven and Bruce Wagner; from characters created by Wes Craven *Cine.* Roy H. Wagner *Ed.* Terry Stokes and Chuck Weiss *Mu.* Angelo Badalamenti *A.d.* Mick Strawn and C. J. Strawn *S.d.* James Barrows *R.t.* 96 min. *MPAA* R. *Cast:* Heather Langenkamp, Patricia Arquette, Larry Fishburne, Priscilla Pointer, Craig Wasson, Robert Englund, Brooke Bundy, Rodney Eastman, Bradley Gregg, Ira Heiden, Ken Sagoes, Penelope Sudrow, Jennifer Rubin, John Saxon, Clayton Landey, Nan Martin, Stacey Alden, Kristin Clayton, Sally Piper, Rozlyn Sorrell, Dick Cavett, Zsa Zsa Gabor.

Freddy (Robert Englund) comes back to haunt seven teenagers who are, therefore, afraid to go to sleep; an intern tries to help by prescribing a dream-inhibiting drug.

NIGHTSTICK (also known as *Calhoun*)

Pro. Martin Walters; Production Distribution Company *Dir.* Joseph L. Scanlan *Scr.* James J. Docherty *Cine.* Robert Fresco *Ed.* Richard Wells and Daniel Radford *Mu.* Robert O. Hagland *A.d.* Reuben Freed *S.d.* Tony Duggan-Smith *R.t.* 92 min. *MPAA* R. *Cast:* Bruce Fairbairn, Kerrie Keane, Robert Vaughn, John Vernon, Leslie Nielsen, Walker Boone, Tony De Santis, David Mucci.

Police officer Jack Calhoun (Bruce Fairbairn) pursues three crooks who are threatening to blow up a bank. The case becomes more personal when the thugs kidnap Calhoun's girlfriend (Kerrie Keane) and hold her hostage.

NO MAN'S LAND

Pro. Joseph Stern and Dick Wolf; Orion Pictures *Dir.* Peter Werner *Scr.* Dick Wolf *Cine.* Hiro Narita *Ed.* Steve Cohen and Daniel Hanley *Mu.* Basil Poledouris *P.d.* Paul Peters *S.d.* Ethel Robins Richards *R.t.* 106 min. *MPAA* R. *Cast:* Charlie Sheen, D. B. Sweeney, Randy Quaid, Lara Harris, Bill Duke, R. D. Call, Arlen Dean Snyder, M. Emmet Walsh.

Assigned to work undercover to expose the illegal dealings of the owner of a Porsche garage (Charlie Sheen), a young policeman (D. B. Sweeney) is drawn into a compromising friendship with the targeted criminal.

NO PICNIC

Pro. Doris Kornish *Dir.* Philip Hartman *Scr.* Philip Hartman *Cine.* Peter Hutton *Ed.* Grace Tankersley *Mu.* Ned Sublette and The Raunch Hands *A.d.* Tina Chaden *R.t.* 84 min. *Cast:* David Brisbin, Myoshin, Anne D'Agnillo.

A man on the edge of the music industry encounters many odd characters while trying to fulfill his dream.

NORTH SHORE

Pro. William Finnegan; Universal *Dir*. William Phelps *Scr*. Tim McCanlies and William Phelps; based on a story by William Phelps and Randal Kleiser *Cine*. Peter Smokler *Ed*. Robert Gordon *Mu*. Richard Stone *P.d*. Marc Balet *S.d*. Wally White *R.t*. 96 min. *MPAA* PG. *Cast:* Matt Adler, Gregory Harrison, Nia Peeples, John Philbin, Gerry Lopez, Laird Hamilton, Robbie Page, Mark Occhilupo, John Parragon.

Rick (Matt Adler) gets more than he bargains for when he travels to Oahu to surf the waves of the North Shore.

NOWHERE TO HIDE

Pro. Andras Hamori; New Century/Vista Film Company *Dir*. Mario Azzopardi *Scr*. Alex Rebar and George Goldsmith; based on a story by Alex Rebar *Cine*. Vic Sarin *Ed*. Rit Wallis *Mu*. Brad Fiedel *R.t*. 90 min. *MPAA* R. *Cast:* Amy Madigan, Daniel Hugh-Kelly, Robin MacEachern, Michael Ironside, John Colicos, Chuck Shamata, Clark Johnson.

When her marine-officer husband (Daniel Hugh Kelly) is murdered, Barbara Cutter (Amy Madigan) takes up his investigation of military corruption.

NUMBER ONE WITH A BULLET

Pro. Menahem Golan and Yoram Globus; Cannon Films *Dir*. Jack Smight *Scr*. Gail Morgan Hickman, Andrew Kurtzman, Rob Riley, and James Belushi; based on a story by Gail Morgan Hickman *Cine*. Alex Phillips *Ed*. Michael J. Duthie *Mu*. Alf Clausen *P.d*. Norman Baron *R.t*. 101 min. *MPAA* R. *Cast:* Robert Carradine, Billy Dee Williams, Valerie Bertinelli, Peter Graves, Doris Roberts, Bobby DiCicco, Ray Girardin, Barry Sattels, Mykel T. Williamson.

A pair of policemen, one unorthodox (Robert Carradine), the other suave (Billy Dee Williams), go after a drug dealer who is an important figure in the community.

O. C. AND STIGGS

Pro. Robert Altman and Peter Newman; Metro-Goldwyn-Mayer/United Artists *Dir*. Robert Altman *Scr*. Donald Cantrell and Ted Mann; based on a story by Tod Carroll and Ted Mann *Cine*. Pierre Mignot *Ed*. Elizabeth Kling *Mu*. King Sunny Ade and His African Beats *P.d*. Scott Bushnell *A.d*. David Gropman *S.d*. John Hay *R.t*. 109 min. *MPAA* R. *Cast:* Daniel H. Jenkins, Neill Barry, Paul Dooley, Jane Curtin, Jon Cryer, Ray Walston, Louis Nye, Tina Louise, Martin Mull, Dennis Hopper, Melvin Van Peebles, Donald May, Carla Borelli, Cynthia Nixon.

Two teenagers will stop at nothing to make life miserable for a heartless insurance executive.

ONCE WE WERE DREAMERS (Israel, 1987)

Pro. Ben Elkerbout, Ludi Boeken, and Katriel Schory; Hemdale Film Corp. *Dir*. Uri Barbash *Scr*. Benny Barbash *Cine*. Amnon Salomon *Ed*. Tova Asher *Mu*. Misha Segal *P.d*. Eilon Levy *R.t*. 110 min. *Cast:* Kelly McGillis, John Shea, Christine Boisson.

Idealistic founders of a Jewish commune in Palestine after World War I find their aspirations challenged by infighting and romantic rivalries.

OPERA (Italy, 1987)

Pro. Marlo Cecchi Gori and Vittorio Cecchi Gori; CDI *Dir*. Dario Argento *Scr*. Dario Argento and Franco Ferrini *Cine*. Ronnie Taylor *Ed*. Franco Fraticelli *Mu*.

Davide Bassan *R.t.* 90 min. *Cast:* Christine Marsillach, Urbano Barberini, Daria Nicolodi, Ian Charleson, Antonella Vitale, William McNamara.

Betty (Christine Marsillach), a young opera singer making her debut, is forced to watch the murders of her lover and her costume designer.

ORPHANS

Pro. Alan J. Pakula; Lorimar *Dir.* Alan J. Pakula *Scr.* Lyle Kessler; based on a play by Lyle Kessler *Cine.* Donald McAlpine *Ed.* Evan Lottman *Mu.* Michael Small *P.d.* George Jenkins *R.t.* 120 min. *MPAA* R. *Cast:* Albert Finney, Matthew Modine, Kevin Anderson, John Kellogg, Anthony Heald, Novella Nelson, Elizabeth Parrish, B. Constance Barry, Frank Ferrara, Clifford Feari.

A stranger brings hope into the dark world of a sociopath (Matthew Modine) and the younger brother whom he terrorizes (Kevin Anderson).

THE OUTING

Pro. Warren Chaney; TMS Pictures *Dir.* Tom Daley *Scr.* Warren Chaney *Cine.* Herbert Raditschnig *Ed.* Claudio Cutry *Mu.* Joel Rosenbaum and Bruce Miller *P.d.* Robert Burns *R.t.* 85 min. *MPAA* R. *Cast:* Deborah Winters, James Huston, Andra St. Ivanyi, Scott Bankston, Mark Mitchell, Andre Chimene, Damon Merrill, Barry Coffing, Tracye Walker, Raan Lewis, Hank Amigo, Brian Floores, Michelle Watkins.

Released from five thousand years' imprisonment in a lamp, a genie embarks on a campaign of revenge.

OVER THE TOP

Pro. Menahem Golan and Yoram Globus; Warner Bros. *Dir.* Menahem Golan *Scr.* Stirling Silliphant and Sylvester Stallone; based on a story by Gary Conway and David C. Engelbach *Cine.* David Gurfinkel *Ed.* Don Zimmerman and James Symons *Mu.* Giorgio Moroder *P.d.* James Schoppe *A.d.* William Skinner *S.d.* Cloudia *R.t.* 93 min. *MPAA* PG. *Cast:* Sylvester Stallone, Robert Loggia, Susan Blakely, Rick Zumwalt, David Mendenhall, Chris McCarty, Terry Funk.

Trucker Lincoln Hawk (Sylvester Stallone) reunites with his estranged young son (David Mendenhall) and enters an arm-wrestling tournament in Las Vegas.

OVERBOARD

Pro. Anthea Sylbert and Alexandra Rose; Metro-Goldwyn-Mayer *Dir.* Garry Marshall *Scr.* Leslie Dixon *Cine.* John A. Alonzo *Ed.* Dov Hoenig and Sonny Baskin *Mu.* Alan Silvestri *A.d.* James Shanahan and Jim Dultz *R.t.* 112 min. *MPAA* PG. *Cast:* Goldie Hawn, Kurt Russell, Edward Herrmann, Katherine Helmond, Michael Hagerty, Roddy McDowall, Jared Rushton, Jeffrey Wiseman, Brian Price, Jamie Wild, Frank Campanella, Harvey Alan Miller.

A self-centered millionaire (Goldie Hawn) suffers amnesia after a boating accident; her life is changed completely when a carpenter (Kurt Russell) decides to claim her as his wife in order to exact revenge for her previous ill-treatment of him.

PATTI ROCKS

Pro. Gwen Field and Gregory M. Cummins; FilmDallas *Dir.* David Burton Morris *Scr.* David Burton Morris, Chris Mulkey, John Jenkins, and Karen Landry; based on characters created by Victoria Wozniak in the film *Loose Ends* *Cine.* Gregory M. Cummins *Ed.* Gregory M. Cummins *Mu.* Doug Maynard *A.d.* Charlotte Whitaker *R.t.* 87 min. *MPAA* R. *Cast:* Chris Mulkey, John Jenkins, Karen Landry.

Billy (Chris Mulkey) enlists his friend Eddie (John Jenkins) to help him tell his pregnant girlfriend (Karen Landry) that he has a wife and family. Director David Burton Morris has constructed a biting examination of male egos and sexual attitudes.

PELLE THE CONQUEROR (*Pelle Erobreren*. Denmark and Sweden, 1987) *Pro.* Per Holst; Karne Film *Dir.* Bille August *Scr.* Bille August; based on a novel by Martin Andersen Nexo *Cine.* Jorgen Persson *Ed.* Janus Billeskov Jansen *Mu.* Stefan Nilsson *P.d.* Anna Asp *R.t.* 160 min. *Cast:* Max Von Sydow, Pelle Hvenegaard, Erik Paaske, Bjorn Granath, Axel Strobye, Astrid Villaume, Troels Asmussen, John Wittig, Anne Lise Hirsch Bjerrum, Sofie Grabol, Lena Pia Bernhardsson, Kristina Tornquist, Buster Larsen, Henrik Bodker, Lars Simonsen, Thure Lindhardt, Benjamin Holck Henricksen, Nis Bank-Mikkelsen.

Pelle Erobreren follows the fates of an elderly Swedish farmer (Max Von Sydow) and his son Pelle (Pelle Hvenegaard) as they leave their impoverished life for an even harder one of near-slavery in the land of plenty, Denmark.

PENITENTIARY III
Pro. Jamaa Fanaka and Leon Isaac Kennedy; Cannon International *Dir.* Jamaa Fanaka *Scr.* Jamaa Fanaka *Cine.* Marty Ollstein *Ed.* Ed Harker *A.d.* Craig Freitag *P.d.* Marshall Toomey *R.t.* 91 min. *MPAA* R. *Cast:* Leon Isaac Kennedy, Anthony Geary, Steve Antin, Ric Mancini, Kessler Raymond, Jim Bailey, Magic Schwarz, Windsor Taylor Randolph, Rick Zumwalt, Janct Rotblatt, Madison Campudoni, Bert Williams, Mark Kemble, Jack Rader.

Thrown into jail for killing an opponent while in a drug-induced mania, boxer Too Sweet (Leon Isaac Kennedy) finds that the rules of prison boxing are brutal.

THE PERFECT MATCH
Pro. Mark Deimel; Airtight *Dir.* Mark Deimel *Scr.* Nick Duretta, David Burr, and Mark Deimel *Cine.* Bob Torrance *Ed.* Craig Colton *Mu.* Tim Torrance *P.d.* Maxine Shepard *R.t.* 92 min. *MPAA* PG. *Cast:* Marc McClure, Jennifer Edwards, Diane Stilwell, Rob Paulsen.

Tim (Marc McClure) and Nancy (Jennifer Edwards) are two lonely urban singles who meet through a personal ad. They lie about their interests and abilities in an attempt to appear more attractive, but eventually they find their way to romance.

PERSONAL SERVICES (Great Britain, 1987)
Pro. Tim Bevan; Universal International Pictures *Dir.* Terry Jones *Scr.* David Leland *Cine.* Roger Deakins *Ed.* George Akers *P.d.* Hugo Luczyc-Wyhowski *A.d.* Jane Coleman *R.t.* 105 min. *MPAA* R. *Cast:* Julie Walters, Alec McCowen, Shirley Stelfox, Danny Schiller, Victoria Hardcastle, Tim Woodward, Dave Atkins, Leon Lissek.

In this satire on two-faced attitudes toward prostitution, the director of a genteel brothel (Julie Walters) is dragged into court and recognizes the judge as one of her regular clients.

PETER VON SCHOLTEN (Denmark, 1987)
Pro. Nina Crone; Metronome *Dir.* Palle Kjarulff-Schmidt *Scr.* Sven Holm *Cine.* Mikael Salomon *Ed.* Kasper Schyberg *Mu.* Bent Fabricius-Bjerre *P.d.* Soren Krag Sorensen *R.t.* 112 min. *Cast:* Ole Ernst, Etta Cameron, Jesper Langberg, Preben Kristensen, Olaf Ussing, Bodil Udsen, Torben Jensen, Dale Smith, Soren Pilmark, Preben Neergaard, Leonard Malone, Henning Moritzen, Karen-Lise Mynster, Arne Hansen, Lars Lunoe, Raymond Adjavon, Bodil Lassen, Guido Paevatalu, Dick

Kaysoe, John Larsen, Henning Jensen, Torbon Jetsmark, Anna Adair, Hans Henrik Krause, Edwin Donoghue, Birgit Conradi, Hans Christian Agidius, Fritze Hedemann.

This historical drama describes the fight of Peter Von Scholten (Ole Ernst) to grant emancipation to the slaves of the Danish Virgin Islands in the 1800's.

THE PICK-UP ARTIST

Pro. David L. MacLeod; Twentieth Century-Fox *Dir.* James Toback *Scr.* James Toback *Cine.* Gordon Willis *Ed.* David Bretherton and Angelo Corrao *Mu.* Georges Delerue *P.d.* Paul Sylbert *A.d.* Bill Groom *S.d.* John Alan Hicks *R.t.* 81 min. *MPAA* PG-13. *Cast:* Molly Ringwald, Robert Downey, Jr., Dennis Hopper, Danny Aiello, Mildred Dunnock, Harvey Keitel, Brian Hamill, Tamara Bruno, Vanessa Williams, Angie Kempf, Polly Draper, Frederick Koehler, Robert Towne, Victoria Jackson, Lorraine Bracco, Bob Gunton, Clemenze Caserta, Christine Baranski, Joe Spinell, Tony Conforti, Jilly Rizzo, Tom Signorelli.

A womanizer (Robert Downey) becomes obsessed with an unresponsive young woman (Molly Ringwald), whose gambler father has piled up enormous debts in Atlantic City.

THE PIMP (*Zegen*. Japan, 1987)

Pro. Yoshiniko Sugiyama, Kunio Takeshige, and Jire Ooba; Tosi Co. *Dir.* Shohei Imamura *Scr.* Shohei Imamura and Kota Okaba *Cine.* Masao Tochizawa *Mu.* Shinichiro Ikebe *A.d.* Yoshinaha Yokoo *R.t.* 124 min. *Cast:* Ken Ogata, Mitsuko Baisho, Nerihei Miki, Taiji Toneyama, Mami Kumagaya, Ko Chun-Hsiung.

Based on the adventures of a historical figure, this film depicts the life of a patriotic scoundrel who opens a series of brothels to help enrich the emperor of Japan.

PINOCCHIO AND THE EMPEROR OF THE NIGHT

Pro. Lou Scheimer; New World Pictures *Dir.* Hal Sutherland *Scr.* Robby London, Barry O'Brien, and Dennis O'Flaherty *Cine.* Ervin L. Kaplan *Ed.* Jeffrey Patrick Gehr *Mu.* Anthony Marinelli and Brian Banks *A.d.* John Gruso *R.t.* 87 min. *MPAA* G. *Voices:* Edward Asner, Tom Bosley, Lana Beeson, Linda Gary, Jonathan Harris, James Earl Jones, Ricky Lee Jones, Don Knotts, William Windom.

Pinocchio, now a flesh-and-blood boy, is still susceptible to smooth-talking swindlers and his own impulsive urges.

POLICE ACADEMY 4: CITIZENS ON PATROL

Pro. Paul Maslansky; Warner Bros. *Dir.* Jim Drake *Scr.* Gene Quintano; based on characters created by Neal Israel and Pat Proft *Cine.* Robert Saad *Ed.* David Rawlins *Mu.* Robert Folk *P.d.* Trevor Williams *A.d.* Rhiley Fuller *S.d.* Steve Shewchuk *R.t.* 87 min. *MPAA* PG. *Cast:* Steve Guttenberg, Bubba Smith, Michael Winslow, David Graf, Tim Kazurinsky, Sharon Stone, Leslie Easterbrook, Marion Ramsey, Lance Kinsey, G. W. Bailey, Bobcat Goldthwait, George Gaynes, Billie Bird.

The regulars from the previous three *Police Academy* films direct the training for a citizen's crime-control group.

POSITIVE I. D.

Pro. Andy Anderson; Universal *Dir.* Andy Anderson *Scr.* Andy Anderson *Cine.* Jack Parsons *Ed.* Andy Anderson and Robert J. Castaldo *Mu.* Steven Jay Hoey *A.d.* Terri Cummings and Patty Newton *R.t.* 95 min. *MPAA* R. *Cast:* Stephanie Rascoe, John Davies, Steve Fromholz, Laura Lanc, Gail Cronauer, Audeen Casey,

Matthew Sacks, Steven Jay Hoey, John Williamson, Erin White, April White, Terry Leeser.

Traumatized by rape, Julie (Stephanie Rascoe) decides to adopt a new identity and seek revenge.

A PRAYER FOR THE DYING (Great Britain, 1987)
Pro. Peter Snell; Samuel Goldwyn Company *Dir.* Mike Hodges *Scr.* Edmund Ward and Martin Lynch; based on a novel by Jack Higgins *Cine.* Mike Garfath *Ed.* Peter Boyle *Mu.* Bill Conti *P.d.* Evan Hercules *R.t.* 107 min. *MPAA* R. *Cast:* Mickey Rourke, Bob Hoskins, Alan Bates, Sammi Davis, Christopher Fulford, Liam Neeson, Alison Doody, Camille Coduri, Ian Bartholomew, Mark Lambert, Cliff Burnett, Anthony Head, David Lumsden, Lenny Tero.

An Irish Republican Army (IRA) hit man finds himself trapped between his IRA bosses, a gangster, the police, and a priest who witnesses a murder he carries out.

PRETTYKILL (also known as *Tomorrow's a Killer*)
Pro. John R. Bowey and Martin Walters; Spectrafilm *Dir.* George Kaczender *Scr.* Sandra K. Bailey *Cine.* Joao Fernandes *Ed.* Tom Merchant *Mu.* Robert O. Ragland *A.d.* Andris Hausmanis *S.d.* Jeff Cutler *R.t.* 95 min. *MPAA* R. *Cast:* David Birney, Season Hubley, Susannah York, Yaphet Kotto, Suzanne Snyder, Germaine Houde, Lenore Zann, Vito Rezza, Marsha Moreau, Sarah Polley, O. L. Duke, Heather Smith, Erik King, Richard Fitzpatrick, Ron White, Gary Majchrizak, Louis Turenne, Philip Akin.

A policeman (David Birney) whose girlfriend (Season Hubley) is a prostitute finds himself jeopardizing his career and her life when his drug case links with the investigation of a serial murder of prostitutes.

PRINCE OF DARKNESS
Pro. Larry Franco; Universal *Dir.* John Carpenter *Scr.* Martin Quatermass *Cine.* Gary G. Kibbe *Ed.* Steve Mirkovich *Mu.* John Carpenter and Alan Howarth *P.d.* Daniel Lomino *R.t.* 110 min. *MPAA* R. *Cast:* Donald Pleasence, Jameson Parker, Victor Wong, Lisa Blount, Dennis Dun, Susan Blanchard, Anne Howard, Ann Yen, Ken Wright, Dirk Blocker, Jessie Lawrence Ferguson, Peter Jason, Alice Cooper.

A secret canister, hidden in a church for hundreds of years, is found to contain a devil, who shocks innocent passersby by raining caterpillars and spiders on them.

THE PRINCESS ACADEMY
Pro. Sandra Weintraub; Empire Pictures *Dir.* Bruce Block *Scr.* Sandra Weintraub; based on an idea by Fred Weintraub *Cine.* Kent Wakeford *Ed.* Martin Cohen *Mu.* Roger Bellon *R.t.* 90 min. *MPAA* R. *Cast:* Eva Gabor, Lar Park Lincoln, Lu Leonard, Richard Paul, Carole Davis, Badar Howar, Barbara Rovsek, Yolande Palfrey, Britt Helfer.

A female juvenile delinquent is given a scholarship to a finishing school in Switzerland where the main subject seems to be sex.

THE PRINCIPAL
Pro. Thomas H. Brodek; Tri-Star Pictures *Dir.* Christopher Cain *Scr.* Frank Deese *Cine.* Arthur Albert *Ed.* Jack Hofstra *Mu.* Jay Gruska *P.d.* James T. Davis *A.d.* Mark Billerman *S.d.* Rick Brown *R.t.* 109 min. *MPAA* R. *Cast:* James Belushi, Louis Gossett, Jr., Rae Dawn Chong, Michael Wright, J. J. Cohen, Esai Morales, Troy Winbush, Jacob Vargas, Thomas Ryan, Reggie Johnson, Kelly Minter.

James Belushi stars as the new principal of a tough inner-city school that is run by gangs.

PRIVATE INVESTIGATIONS

Pro. Steven Golin and Sigurjon Sighvatsson; Metro-Goldwyn-Mayer/United Artists *Dir.* Nigel Dick *Scr.* John Dahl and David Warfield *Cine.* David Bridges *Ed.* Scott Chestnut *Mu.* Murray Munro *P.d.* Piers Plowden *A.d.* Nick Rafter *R.t.* 90 min. *MPAA* R. *Cast:* Clayton Rohner, Ray Sharkey, Paul Le Mat, Talia Balsam, Phil Morris, Martin Balsam, Anthony Zerbe, Robert Ito, Vernon Wells, Anthony Geary.

A young architect is drawn into a dangerous showdown with drug-dealing policemen in Los Angeles.

PROGRAMMED TO KILL

Pro. Don Stern and Allan Holzman; Trans World Entertainment *Dir.* Allan Holzman, with additional scenes directed by Robert Short *Scr.* Robert Short *Cine.* Nitcho Lion Nissim and Ernest Holzman *Ed.* Michael Kelly *Mu.* Jerry Immel and Craig Huxley *S.d.* Michael Parker and Pola Schreiber *R.t.* 92 min. *MPAA* R. *Cast:* Robert Ginty, Sandahl Bergman, James Booth, Alex Courtney, Paul W. Walker, Louise Caire Clark, Peter Bromilow, George Fisher, Jim Turner.

A female terrorist captured by the CIA and given an operation that programs her to kill other terrorists suddenly realizes that she has killed all her friends and travels back to the United States to seek revenge.

PROJECT X

Pro. Walter F. Parkes and Lawrence Lasker; Twentieth Century-Fox *Dir.* Jonathan Kaplan *Scr.* Stanley Weiser; based on a story by Stanley Weiser and Lawrence Lasker *Cine.* Dean Cundey *Ed.* O. Nicholas Brown *Mu.* James Horner *P.d.* Lawrence G. Paull *S.d.* Rick Simpson *R.t.* 108 min. *MPAA* PG. *Cast:* Matthew Broderick, Helen Hunt, Bill Sadler, Johnny Ray McGhee, Jonathan Stark, Robin Gammell, Stephen Lang, Jean Smart, Chuck Bennett, Daniel Roebuck, Mark Harden, Duncan Wilmore.

A young air force pilot assigned to train chimpanzees to fly simulated airplanes discovers that the chimps are later used in radiation experiments, and he tries to save them.

PUPPETOON MOVIE

Pro. Arnold Leibovit; Expanded Entertainment *Dir.* George Pal *Scr.* Arnold Leibovit *Cine.* Gene Warren, Jr. *Ed.* Arnold Leibovit *Mu.* Buddy Baker *R.t.* 80 min.

The much-beloved Gumby introduces this sequence of nine George Pal shorts, small individual vignettes featuring three-dimensional animation.

QUEEN CITY ROCKER (New Zealand, 1987)

Pro. Larry Parr; Spectrafilm *Dir.* Bruce Morrison *Scr.* Bill Baer *Cine.* Kevin Hayward *Ed.* Michael Hacking *Mu.* David McCartney *P.d.* Mike Becroft *R.t.* 92 min. *Cast:* Matthew Hunter, Mark Pilisi, Ricky Bribiesca, Kim Willoughby, Rebecca Saunders, Peter Bland.

A young gang leader (Matthew Hunter) becomes disillusioned with the violence and aimlessness of his life when his best friend is killed in retribution for destroying a nightclub.

RACHEL RIVER
Pro. Timothy Marx *Dir*. Sandy Smolan *Scr*. Judith Guest; based on the stories of Carol Bly *Cine*. Paul Elliott *Ed*. Susan Crutcher *Mu*. Arvo Part *P.d*. David Wasco *R.t*. 90 min. *Cast:* Zeljko Ivanek, Pamela Reed, Craig T. Nelson, James Olson, Alan North, Viveca Lindfors, Jo Henderson, Jon DeVries, Ailene Cole, Courtney Kjos, Ollie Osterberg, Wellington Nelson, Richard Jenkins, Michael Gallagher, Richard Reihle, Ron Duffy, Don Cosgrove, Stephen Yoakum, Cliff Rakerd, Patricia Mary Van Oss.

A single mother and radio journalist (Pamela Reed), researching the life of a widow who has just died, makes discoveries about herself and about the quiet depth of relationships among people in her small Minnesota town.

RADIUM CITY
Pro. Carole Langer *Dir*. Carole Langer *Cine*. Luke Sacher *Ed*. Carole Langer *Mu*. Tim Cappello *R.t*. 120 min.

This documentary investigates the high rates of cancer and death among women who painted numbers in radium onto clock faces in the town of Ottawa, Illinois.

RAGE OF HONOR
Pro. Don Van Atta; Trans World Entertainment *Dir*. Gordon Hessler *Scr*. Robert Short and Wallace Bennett; based on a story by Robert Short *Cine*. Julio Bragado *Ed*. Robert Gordon *Mu*. Stelvio Cipriani *P.d*. Adrian Gorton *A.d*. Kirk Demusiak and Abel Fogellio *R.t*. 91 min. *MPAA* R. *Cast:* Sho Kosugi, Lewis Van Bergen, Robin Evans, Gerry Gibson, Chip Lucia, Richard Wiley, Carlos Estrada, Alan Amiel.

A narcotics investigator (Sho Kosugi) travels to Buenos Aires in search of the people who murdered his assistant.

RAMPAGE
Pro. David Salven; De Laurentiis Entertainment Group *Dir*. William Friedkin *Scr*. William Friedkin; based on the novel by William P. Wood *Cine*. Robert D. Yeoman *Ed*. Jere Huggins *Mu*. Ennio Morricone *P.d*. Buddy Cone *A.d*. Carol Clements *S.d*. Nancy Nye *R.t*. 97 min. *MPAA* R. *Cast:* Michael Biehn, Alex McArthur, Nicholas Campbell, Deborah Van Valkenburgh, John Harkins, Art Lafleur, Billy Greenbush, Royce D. Applegate, Grace Zabriskie, Roy London, Donald Hotton, Andy Romano.

An assistant district attorney who opposes the death penalty (Michael Biehn) is assigned to prosecute a psychopath (Alex McArthur) who has committed five grisly murders.

RAWHEADREX
Pro. Kevin Attew and Don Hawkins; Empire Pictures *Dir*. George Pavlou *Scr*. Clive Barker *Cine*. John Metcalfe *Ed*. Andy Horvitch *Mu*. Colin Towns *A.d*. Len Huntingford *R.t*. 89 min. *MPAA* R. *Cast:* David Dukes, Kelly Piper, Ronan Wilmot, Niall Toibin, Heinrich Von Schellendorf, Niall O'Brien, Hugh O'Connor, Cora Lunny.

An American historian (David Dukes) in Ireland must use his knowledge to destroy RawHeadRex (Heinrich Von Schellendorf), a monster from the pre-Christian era who is destroying everything in his path.

REAL MEN
Pro. Martin Bregman; United Artists *Dir*. Dennis Feldman *Scr*. Dennis Feldman

Cine. John A. Alonzo *Ed.* Malcolm Campbell and Glenn Farr *A.d.* William J. Cassidy and James Allen *S.d.* Tom Pedigo *R.t.* 86 min. *MPAA* PG-13. *Cast:* James Belushi, John Ritter, Barbara Barrie, Bill Morey, Isa Andersen, Gail Barle, Mark Herrier, Matthew Brooks.

In this take-off on spy films, CIA agents match wits with Russians and extraterrestrials.

REPENTANCE (*Pokayaniye.* USSR, 1987)

Pro. Studio Gruzia Film *Dir.* Tengiz Abuladze *Scr.* Tengiz Abuladze, Rezo Kveselava and Nana Dzhanelidze *Cine.* Mikhail Agranovitj *Ed.* Nana Dzhanelidze *P.d.* Georgi Mikeladze *R.t.* 145 min. *Cast:* Avtandil Makharadze, Ija Ninidze, Merab Ninidze, Zejnab Botsvadze, Ketevan Abuladze, Edisher Giorgobiani, Kahki Kavsadze, Nino Zakoriadze, Nato Otjigava, Dato Kemkhadze.

This symbolic film depicts the actions of a son who is conscience-stricken over his late father's deeds as dictator.

RETURN TO HORROR HIGH

Pro. Mark Lisson; New World Pictures *Dir.* Bill Froehlich *Scr.* Bill Froehlich, Mark Lisson, Dana Escalate, and Greg H. Sims *Cine.* Roy Wagner *Ed.* Nancy Forner *Mu.* Stacy Widelitz *P.d.* Greta Grigorian *R.t.* 95 min. *MPAA* R. *Cast:* Lori Lethin, Brendan Hughes, Alex Rocco, Scott Jacoby, Andy Romano, Richard Brestoff, Al Fann, Pepper Martin, Maureen McCormick, Vince Edwards.

A film crew goes to a high school to shoot the story of the murders that took place there five years before and ends up stalked by the same killer.

REVENGE OF THE NERDS II: NERDS IN PARADISE

Pro. Ted Field, Robert Cort, and Peter Bart; Twentieth Century-Fox *Dir.* Joe Roth *Scr.* Dan Guntzelman and Steve Marshall; based on characters created by Tim Metcalfe, Miguel Tejada-Flores, Steve Zacharias, and Jeff Buhai *Cine.* Charles Correll *Ed.* Richard Chew *Mu.* Mark Mothersbaugh, Gerald V. Casale, and Devo *P.d.* Trevor Williams *R.t.* 92 min. *MPAA* PG-13. *Cast:* Robert Carradine, Curtis Armstrong, Larry B. Scott, Timothy Busfield, Courtney Thorne-Smith, Andrew Cassese, Donald Gibb, Bradley Whitford, Ed Lauter, Barry Sobel.

The nerds are back, encountering frat-rat resistance at a fraternity convention in Fort Lauderdale.

THE RIGHT HAND MAN (Australia, 1987)

Pro. Steven Grives, Tom Oliver, and Basil Appleby; New World Pictures *Dir.* Di Drew *Scr.* Helen Hodgeman; based on the novel of the same name by Kathleen Peyton *Cine.* Peter James *Ed.* Don Saunders *Mu.* Allan Zavod *P.d.* Neil Angwin *R.t.* 100 min. *Cast:* Rupert Everett, Hugo Weaving, Catherine McClements, Arthur Dignam, Jennifer Claire.

In this film set in Australia in the 1860's, a young man (Rupert Everett) stricken with diabetes hires a stagecoach driver (Hugo Weaving) to raise his horses.

RIMINI RIMINI (Italy, 1987)

Pro. Augusto Caminito; Medusa *Dir.* Sergio Corbucci *Scr.* Bernardino Zapponi, Sergio Corbucci, Bruno Corbucci, Mario Amendola, Marco Risi, Gianni Romoli, and Massimo Franciosa *Cine.* Danilo Desideri *Ed.* Tatiana Casini Morigi *A.d.* Marco Dentici *R.t.* 116 min. *Cast:* Paolo Villaggio, Serena Grandi, Eleonora Brigliadori, Laura Antonelli, Jerry Cala, Gigi and Andrea, Paolo Bonacelli, Maurizio Micheli, Sylva Koscina, Elvire Audray.

Several comedy stories involving sexual escapades take place in the Italian beach town of Rimini.

RITA, SUE AND BOB TOO (Great Britain, 1987)
Pro. Sandy Leiberson; Orion Classics *Dir.* Alan Clarke *Scr.* Andrea Dunbar; based on her plays *The Arbor* and *Rita, Sue and Bob Too Cine.* Ivan Strasburg *Ed.* Stephen Singleton *Mu.* Michael Kamen *R.t.* 95 min. *Cast:* Michelle Holmes, Siobhan Finneran, George Costigan, Lesley Sharp, Willie Ross, Patti Nicholls, Ghir Kulvindar.

Bob persuades the two girls who babysit for him and his wife to enter into a triangular adulterous affair, but they all profess innocence when Bob's wife finds out.

ROBERT WILSON AND THE CIVIL WARS (USA and West Germany, 1987)
Pro. Markas Trebitsch, Orin Wechsberg, and Howard Brookner; Unisphere *Dir.* Howard Brookner *Scr.* Howard Brookner *Cine.* Ira Brenner, Bob Chappell, and Tom Di Cillo *Ed.* Michelle Bahlke *R.t.* 90 min.

This documentary examines the life and work of controversial playwright/director Robert Wilson, focusing on his attempt to coordinate the production of his play *the CIVIL warS*.

THE ROMANCE OF BOOK AND SWORD (Hong Kong, 1987)
Pro. Lee Ping Wang *Dir.* Ann Hui *Scr.* Ann Hui; based on a novel by Jin Yung *Cine.* Chow Muk leung *Ed.* Chow Muk-leung *R.t.* 180 min. *Cast:* Zhang Duo Fu, Da Shi Chang, Ai Nuo, Liu Jia.

Two brothers, separated in infancy, are brought together as warriors of opposing factions at the time of the overthrow of the Ming dynasty in China.

THE ROSARY MURDERS
Pro. Robert G. Laurel and Michael Mihalich *Dir.* Fred Walton *Scr.* Elmore Leonard and Fred Walton *Cine.* David Golia *Ed.* Sam Vitale *Mu.* Bobby Laurel and Don Sebesky *R.t.* 105 min. *MPAA* R. *Cast:* Donald Sutherland, Charles Durning, Josef Sommer, Belinda Bauer, James Murtaugh, John Danelle, Addison Powell, Kathleen Tolan, Tom Mardirosian, Anita Barone.

A priest silenced by information learned in the confessional begins an investigation himself into the murders of several priests and nuns.

THE RUMBA (*La Rumba*. France, 1987)
Pro. Christine Gouze-Renal; Hachette Première and Universal International Pictures *Dir.* Roger Hanin *Scr.* Roger Hanin and Jean Curtelin *Cine.* Jean Penzer *Ed.* Youchef Tobni *Mu.* Claude Bolling *P.d.* Bernard Evein *R.t.* 92 min. *Cast:* Roger Hanin, Michel Piccoli, Niels Arestrup, Guy Marchand, Patachou, Corinne Touzet, Sophie Michaud, Stéphane Jobert, Karim Allaoui, Vivian Reed, Lino Ventura.

Beppo Manzoni (Roger Hanin), who owns several nightclubs in Paris and has ties to the Mafia, fights against fascism in 1938.

RUMPELSTILTSKIN
Pro. Menahem Golan and Yoram Globus; Cannon Group *Dir.* David Irving *Scr.* David Irving *Cine.* David Gurfinkel *Ed.* Tova Neeman *Mu.* Max Robert *P.d.* Marek Dobrowolski *S.d.* Albert Segal *R.t.* 84 min. *MPAA* G. *Cast:* Amy Irving, Billy Barty, Clive Revill, Priscilla Pointer, John Moulder-Brown, Yael Uziely, Robert Symonds.

This retelling of the Rumpelstiltskin fairy tale adds several songs to the story.

THE RUNNING MAN
Pro. Tim Zinnemann and George Linder; Tri-Star Pictures *Dir.* Paul Michael Glaser *Scr.* Steven E. de Souza; based on the novel by Richard Bachman (Stephen King) *Cine.* Thomas Del Ruth *Ed.* Mark Roy Warner, Edward A. Warschilka, and John Wright *Mu.* Harold Faltermeyer *P.d.* Jack T. Collis *S.d.* Jim Duffy *R.t.* 101 min. *MPAA* R. *Cast:* Arnold Schwarzenegger, Maria Conchita Alonso, Richard Dawson, Yaphet Kotto, Jim Brown, Jesse Ventura, Erland Van Lidth, Marvin J. McIntyre, Gus Rethwisch, Toru Tanaka, Mick Fleetwood, Dweezil Zappa, Karen Leigh Hopkins, Sven Thorsen.

Ben Richards (Arnold Schwarzenegger) escapes from prison only to become the quarry of a manhunt sponsored by a popular television show.

RUSSKIES
Pro. Mark Levinson and Scott Rosenfelt; New Century/Vista Film Company *Dir.* Rick Rosenthal *Scr.* Alan Jay Glueckman, Sheldon Lettich, and Michael Nankin; based on a story by Sheldon Lettich and Michael Nankin *Cine.* Reed Smoot *Ed.* Antony Gibbs *Mu.* James Newton Howard *P.d.* Linda Pearl *A.d.* John Myhre *R.t.* 99 min. *MPAA* PG. *Cast:* Whip Hubley, Leaf Phoenix, Peter Billingsley, Stefan DeSalle, Susan Walters, Patrick Kilpatrick, Vic Polizos, Charles Frank, Susan Blanchard, Benjamin Hendrickson, Carole King, Vojo Goric, Al White, Patrick Mickler, Summer Phoenix, Leo Rossi, Gene Scherer.

A Soviet sailor (Whip Hubley), separated from his comrades by a storm, is found and befriended by three young Americans (Leaf Phoenix, Peter Billingsley, and Stefan DeSalle).

SAMMY AND ROSIE GET LAID (Great Britain, 1987)
Pro. Tim Bevan and Sarah Radclyffe; Cinecom International *Dir.* Stephen Frears *Scr.* Hanif Kureishi *Cine.* Oliver Stapleton *Ed.* Mick Audsley *Mu.* Stanley Myers *P.d.* Hugo Luczyc-Wyhowski *R.t.* 100 min. *Cast:* Shashi Kapoor, Claire Bloom, Ayub Khan Din, Frances Barber, Roland Gift, Wendy Gazelle, Suzette Llewellyn, Meera Syal, Badi Uzzaman.

Sammy (Ayub Khan Din) and Rosie (Frances Barber), Londoners who have an open marriage, are visited by Sammy's Pakistani father (Shashi Kapoor), who attempts to make amends for his abandonment of the family.

SATURDAY NIGHT AT THE PALACE (South Africa, 1987)
Pro. Robert Davies *Dir.* Robert Davies *Scr.* Paul Slabolepszy and Bill Flynn; based on a play by Paul Slabolepszy *Cine.* Robert Davies *Ed.* Lena Farugia and Carla Sandrock *Mu.* Johnny Cleff *A.d.* Wayne Attrill and Sandy Attrill *R.t.* 88 min. *Cast:* Bill Flynn, John Kani, Paul Slabolepszy.

A bigoted racist terrorizes a dignified black man at a restaurant as the black man is about to close the place.

SEASON OF DREAMS (also known as *Stacking*)
Pro. Martin Rosen; Spectrafilm *Dir.* Martin Rosen *Scr.* Victoria Jenkins *Cine.* Richard Bowen *Ed.* Patrick Dodd *Mu.* Patrick Gleeson *P.d.* David Wasco *A.d.* Sharon Seymour *S.d.* Sandy Reynolds Wasco *R.t.* 109 min. *MPAA* PG. *Cast:* Christine Lahti, Frederic Forrest, Megan Follows, Jason Cedrick, Ray Baker, Peter Coyote, James Gammon, Kaiulani Lee, Jacqueline Brookes, Irene Dailey, Pat Coggins.

A teenage girl (Megan Follows) tries to save the family farm with the help of the town drunk (Frederic Forrest), who had once been in love with her mother, while her parents try to resolve their own problems.

THE SECRET POLICEMAN'S THIRD BALL (Great Britain, 1987)
Pro. Neville Bolt and Tony Hollingsworth; Virgin Films *Dir.* Jen O'Neill *Cine.* Stephen Foster *Ed.* John Hackney *Mu.* Paul Gambaccini, Bill Wyman, and Terry Taylor *A.d.* Dennis de Groot *R.t.* 92 min. *Cast:* Bob Hoskins, Joan Armatrading, Jackson Browne, Paul Brady, Kate Bush, David Gilmour, Nick Mason, John Cleese, Robbie Coltrane, Phil Cool, Bob Geldof, Lenny Henry, Nik Kershaw, Mark Knopfler, Chet Atkins, Emo Philips, Lou Reed, Spitting Image, Ruby Wax, Duran Duran, Stephen Fry, Hugh Laurie, Ben Elton, Peter Gabriel, Youssou N'Dour.

This comedic and musical revue was put together as an Amnesty International benefit.

SEVEN WOMEN, SEVEN SINS (West Germany, France, USA, Austria, and Belgium, 1987)
Pro. Brigitte Kramer, Maya Constantine, and Maxi Cohen *Dir.* Helke Sander, Bette Gordon, Maxi Cohen, Chantal Akerman, Valie Export, Laurence Gavronn, and Ulrike Ottinger *Scr.* Helke Sander, Bette Gordon, Maxi Cohen, Chantal Akerman, Valie Export, Laurence Gavronn, Ulrike Ottinger, and Doerte Haak *Cine.* Nurif Aviv, Frank Prinzi, Luc Benhamou, Joel Gold, Edgar Osterberger, Ulrike Ottinger, and Martin Schaetter *Ed.* Elizabeth Kling, Bettina Baehler, Ewa Fichtel, and Monique Prim *R.t.* 120 min. *Cast:* Evelyne Did, Gabriela Herz, Delphine Seyrig, Kate Valk, Roberta Wallach, Susanne Widl, Irm Hermann, Chantal Akerman.

Seven female directors depict examples of the seven deadly sins.

SHADEY (Great Britain, 1987)
Pro. Otto Plaschkes; Skouras Pictures *Dir.* Philip Saville *Scr.* Snoo Wilson *Cine.* Roger Deakins *Ed.* Chris Kelly *Mu.* Colin Towns *P.d.* Norman Garwood *R.t.* 90 min. *MPAA* PG-13. *Cast:* Antony Sher, Billie Whitelaw, Patrick Macnee, Leslie Ash, Bernard Hepton, Larry Lamb, Katherine Helmond, Jon Cartwright, Jesse Birdsall.

Oliver Shadey (Antony Sher), an auto mechanic whose psychic visions are revealed on 8mm film, is exploited by an evil millionaire who puts his extrasensory gifts to work for military intelligence.

SHE MUST BE SEEING THINGS
Pro. Sheila McLaughlin *Dir.* Sheila McLaughlin *Scr.* Sheila McLaughlin *Cine.* Mark Daniels *Ed.* Ila Von Hasperg *Mu.* John Zorn *A.d.* Leigh Kyle *R.t.* 90 min. *Cast:* Lois Weaver, Sheila Dabney, Kyle DeCamp, John Erdman.

The eleventh International Lesbian and Gay Film Festival screened this film about the relationship of a lesbian lawyer who jealously fantasizes about her lover's affairs.

SHY PEOPLE
Pro. Menahem Golan and Yoram Globus; Cannon Films *Dir.* Andrei Konchalovsky *Scr.* Gérard Brach, Andrei Konchalovsky, and Marjorie David; based on a story by Andrei Konchalovsky *Cine.* Chris Menges *Ed.* Alain Jakubowicz *Mu.* Tangerine Dream *P.d.* Steve Marsh *A.d.* Leslie McDonald *S.d.* Leslie Morales *R.t.* 118 min. *MPAA* R. *Cast:* Jill Clayburgh, Barbara Hershey, Martha Plimpton, Merritt Butrick, Don Swayze, Pruitt Taylor Vince, Mare Winningham, Michael Audley, Brad Leland, Paul Landry.

A mother and daughter at odds with each other travel to Louisiana to meet some distant relatives for a story the mother (Jill Clayburgh) is writing. They find an unusual family grouping and serve as catalysts for chaotic events.

THE SICILIAN

Pro. Michael Cimino and Joann Carelli; Twentieth Century-Fox *Dir.* Michael Cimino *Scr.* Steve Shagan; based on the novel of the same name by Mario Puzo *Cine.* Alex Thomson *Ed.* Françoise Bonnot *Mu.* David Mansfield *P.d.* Wolf Kroeger *A.d.* Stefano Ortolani *S.d.* Joseph Mifsud Chevalier *R.t.* 115 min. *MPAA* R. *Cast:* Christopher Lambert, Terence Stamp, Joss Ackland, John Turturro, Richard Bauer, Barbara Sukowa, Giulia Boschi, Ray McAnally, Barry Miller, Andreas Katsulas, Michael Wincott, Derrick Branche, Richard Venture, Ramon Bieri, Stanko Molnar, Oliver Cotton, Joe Regalbuto, Tom Signorelli, Aldo Ray, Nicholas Kepros, Justin Clark, Trevor Ray.

This film is based on the life of Salvatore Giuliano (Christopher Lambert), an Italian Robin Hood who threatened and kidnapped wealthy landowners in order to obtain land for Sicilian peasants.

SIESTA

Pro. Gary Kurfirst; Lorimar *Dir.* Mary Lambert *Scr.* Patricia Louisianna Knop; based on the novel by Patrice Chaplin *Cine.* Bryan Loftus and Michael Lund *Ed.* Glenn A. Morgan *Mu.* Marcus Miller and Miles Davis *P.d.* John Beard *A.d.* Jose Maria Tapiador and Jon Hutman *S.d.* Kara Lindstrom *R.t.* 97 min. *MPAA* R. *Cast:* Ellen Barkin, Gabriel Byrne, Julian Sands, Isabella Rossellini, Martin Sheen, Alexi Sayle, Grace Jones, Jodie Foster.

Claire (Ellen Barkin), a skydiver, travels to Spain in a desperate quest to reunite with her former lover, Augustine (Gabriel Byrne).

SIGN O' THE TIMES

Pro. Robert Cavallo, Joseph Ruffalo, and Steven Fragnoli; Cineplex Odeon Films *Dir.* Prince *Cine.* Peter Sinclair and Jerry Watson *Ed.* Steve Purcell *Mu.* Billy Youdelman and Susan Rogers *P.d.* Leroy Bennett *R.t.* 85 min. *MPAA* PG-13. *Cast:* Prince, Sheila E., Sheena Easton, Dr. Fink, Miko Weaver, Levi Seacer, Jr., Wally Safford, Gregory Allen Brooks, Boni Boyer, Eric Leeds, Atlanta Bliss, Cat.

Prince and several of his musical protegés frolic through hard-driving, sexy performances of fourteen songs.

SILENT NIGHT, DEADLY NIGHT PART II

Pro. Lawrence Appelbaum; Silent Night Releasing Corp. and Ascot Entertainment Group *Dir.* Lee Harry *Scr.* Lee Harry and Joseph H. Earle; from a story by Lee Harry, Joseph H. Earle, Dennis Paterson, and Larry Appelbaum; based on a character created by Michael Hickey and Paul Caimi *Cine.* Harvey Genkins *Ed.* Lee Harry *Mu.* Michael Armstrong *R.t.* 88 min. *MPAA* R. *Cast:* Eric Freeman, James L. Newman, Elizabeth Clayton, Jean Miller.

Ricky (Eric Freeman) goes on an insane killing spree when he discovers that his parents were murdered by a psychotic dressed as Santa Claus.

SISTER, SISTER

Pro. Walter Coblenz; New World Pictures *Dir.* Bill Condon *Scr.* Bill Condon, Joel Cohen, and Ginny Corrella *Cine.* Stephen M. Katz *Ed.* Marion Rothman *Mu.* Richard Einhorn *P.d.* Richard Sherman *R.t.* 91 min. *MPAA* R. *Cast:* Eric Stoltz, Jennifer Jason Leigh, Judith Ivey, Dennis Lipscomb, Anne Pitoniak, Benjamin

Mouton, Natalia Nogulich, Richard Minchenberg, Bobby Pickett, Jason Saucier, Jerry Leggio, Fay Cohn, Ashley McMurray, Ben Cook, Casey Levron, Aggie.

Lucy (Jennifer Jason Leigh), who runs a Louisiana guesthouse with her sister Charlotte (Judith Ivey), becomes involved in an affair with Matt Rutledge (Eric Stoltz), a neighbor.

'68

Pro. Dale Djerassi, Isabel Maxwell, and Steven Kovacs *Dir.* Steven Kovacs *Scr.* Steven Kovacs *Cine.* Daniel Lacambre *Ed.* Cari Coughlin *Mu.* John Cipollina and Shony Alex Braun *A.d.* Joshua Koral *S.d.* Kris Boxell *R.t.* 97 min. *MPAA* R. *Cast:* Eric Larson, Robert Locke, Sandor Tecsi, Anna Dukasz, Miran Kwun, Terra Vandergaw, Shony Alex Braun, Donna Pecora, Elizabeth De Charay, Jan Nemec, Rusdi Lane, Nike Doukas, Neil Young.

This film attempts to connect a Hungarian family's trials and experiences as immigrants in San Francisco with the turbulent events of the late 1960's.

SLAM DANCE

Pro. Rupert Harvey and Barry Opper; Island Pictures *Dir.* Wayne Wang *Scr.* Don Opper *Cine.* Amir Mokri *Ed.* Lee Percy *Mu.* Mitchell Froom *P.d.* Eugenio Zanetti *A.d.* Philip Dean Foreman *R.t.* 99 min. *MPAA* R. *Cast:* Tom Hulce, Mary Elizabeth Mastrantonio, Virginia Madsen, Millie Perkins, Adam Ant, Don Opper, Harry Dean Stanton, Herta Ware, John Doe, Robert Beltran, Judith Barsi.

When his girlfriend turns up dead, C. C. Drood (Tom Hulce) is the prime suspect. The investigative trail leads to a political sex scandal involving a retiring detective and a high-ranking police officer.

SLATE, WYN, AND ME (Australia, 1987)

Pro. Tom Burstall; Hemdale Film Corp. *Dir.* Don McLennan *Scr.* Don McLennan; based on the novel *Slate and Wyn and Blanche McBride*, by Georgia Savage *Cine.* David Connell *Ed.* Peter Friedrich *Mu.* Peter Sullivan *P.d.* Paddy Reardon *R.t.* 90 min. *Cast:* Sigrid Thornton, Simon Burke, Martin Sacks, Tommy Lewis, Lesley Baker, Harold Baigent, Michelle Torres, Murray Fahey, Taya Straton, Julia MacDougall, Peter Cummins, Reg Corman.

Two outlaw brothers kidnap a schoolteacher who has witnessed their shooting of a policeman.

SLAVE GIRLS FROM BEYOND INFINITY

Pro. Ken Dixon; Urban Classics *Dir.* Ken Dixon *Scr.* Ken Dixon *Cine.* Ken Wiatrak and Thomas Callaway *Ed.* Bruce Stubblefield and James A. Stewart *Mu.* Carl Dante and Jonathan Scott Bogner *A.d.* Escott Norton *R.t.* 72 min. *MPAA* R. *Cast:* Elizabeth Cayton, Cindy Beal, Brinke Stevens, Don Scribner, Carl Horner, Kirk Graves, Randolph Roehbling.

Three beautiful women (Elizabeth Cayton, Cindy Beal, and Brinke Stevens) escape their captors by commandeering a spaceship. They land on another planet, where they must battle the malevolent Zed (Don Scribner).

SOMEONE TO LOVE

Pro. M. H. Simonsons *Dir.* Henry Jaglom *Scr.* Henry Jaglom *Cine.* Hanania Baer *R.t.* 109 min. *Cast:* Orson Welles, Henry Jaglom, Andrea Marcovicci, Michael Emil, Sally Kellerman, Oja Kodar, Stephen Bishop, Dave Frishberg, Geraldine Baron, Michael Kaye, Ronee Blakely, Miles Kreuger, Barbara Flood, Amnon Meskin, Pamela Goldblum, Robert Hallak, Sunny Meyer, Kathryn Harrold, Monte

Hellman, Jeremy Kagan, Peter Rafelson, Ora Rubens, Katherine Wallach.

A director (Henry Jaglom), frustrated at his girlfriend's unwillingness to settle down, throws a party at which he asks guests why they are still alone.

SOMEONE TO WATCH OVER ME

Pro. Thierry De Ganay and Harold Schneider; Columbia Pictures *Dir.* Ridley Scott *Scr.* Howard Franklin *Cine.* Steven Poster *Ed.* Claire Simpson *Mu.* Michael Kamen *P.d.* Jim Bissell *S.d.* Linda Descenna *R.t.* 106 min. *MPAA* R. *Cast:* Tom Berenger, Mimi Rogers, Lorraine Bracco, Jerry Orbach, John Rubinstein, Andreas Katsulas, Tony DiBenedetto, James Moriaraty, Mark Moses, Daniel Hugh-Kelly, Harley Cross.

Assigned to protect aristocratic Claire Gregory (Mimi Rogers), who has witnessed a murder, police officer Mike Keegan (Tom Berenger) becomes involved romantically with her and finds his own life—and those of his wife and child—in danger.

SORORITY HOUSE MASSACRE

Pro. Ron Diamond; Concorde Pictures *Dir.* Carol Frank *Scr.* Carol Frank *Cine.* Marc Reshovsky *Ed.* Jeff Wishengrad *Mu.* Michael Wetherwax *A.d.* Susan Emshwiller *S.d.* Gene Serdena *R.t.* 73 min. *MPAA* R. *Cast:* Angela O'Neill, Wendy Martel, Pamela Ross, Nicole Rio, John C. Russell, Marcus Vaughter, Vincent Bilancio, Joe Nassi, Gillian Frank.

Beth (Angela O'Neill) tries to recover from a massacre at a sorority house where, unremembered by her, her family was slaughtered thirteen years earlier by her deranged brother.

SOUTH OF RENO (also known as *Darkness, Darkness*)

Pro. Robert Tinnell *Dir.* Mark Rezyka *Scr.* Mark Rezyka and T. L. Lankford *Cine.* Bernard Auroux *Ed.* Marc Grossman *Mu.* Nigel Holton and Clive Wright *P.d.* Philip Duffin *A.d.* Elizabeth Moore *R.t.* 94 min. *Cast:* Jeffrey Osterhage, Lisa Blount, Joe Phelan, Lewis Van Bergen, Julia Montgomery, Brandis Kemp, Danitza Kingsley, Mary Grace Canfield, Bert Remsen.

A lonely, daydreaming desert dweller (Jeffrey Osterhage) decides to take revenge for his wife's infidelity.

SPACEBALLS

Pro. Mel Brooks; Metro-Goldwyn-Mayer/United Artists *Dir.* Mel Brooks *Scr.* Mel Brooks, Thomas Meehan, and Ronny Graham *Cine.* Nick McLean *Ed.* Conrad Buff IV *Mu.* John Morris *P.d.* Terence Marsh *A.d.* Harold Michelson and Diane Wager *S.d.* John Franco, Jr. *R.t.* 96 min. *MPAA* PG. *Cast:* Mel Brooks, John Candy, Rick Moranis, Bill Pullman, Daphne Zuniga, Dick Van Patten, George Wyner, Michael Winslow, Joan Rivers, Lorene Yarnell, John Hurt.

Spaceballs, about the war between the planets Spaceball and Druidia, is a parody of the space western.

SQUARE DANCE

Pro. Daniel Petrie; Island Pictures *Dir.* Daniel Petrie *Scr.* Alan Hines; based on his novel *Cine.* Jacek Laskus *Ed.* Bruce Green *Mu.* Bruce Broughton *P.d.* Jan Scott *S.d.* Erica Rogalla *R.t.* 112 min. *MPAA* PG-13. *Cast:* Jason Robards, Jane Alexander, Winona Ryder, Rob Lowe, Deborah Richter, Guich Koock, Elbert Lewis.

A young girl (Winona Ryder) who finds solace only in church activities, as she feels unwanted by her dour grandfather, runs away to Fort Worth to live with her mother, who does not know what to do with her.

THE SQUEEZE

Pro. Rupert Hitzig and Michael Tannen; Tri-Star Pictures *Dir.* Roger Young *Scr.* Daniel Taplitz *Cine.* Arthur Albert *Ed.* Harry Keramidas *Mu.* Miles Goodman *P.d.* Simon Waters *A.d.* Christopher Nowak *S.d.* Ted Glass *R.t.* 101 min. *MPAA* PG-13. *Cast:* Michael Keaton, Rae Dawn Chong, Liane Langland, Leslie Bevis, John Davidson, Meat Loaf, Ronald Guttman.

Harry Berg (Michael Keaton) is thrown into a dangerous role when he discovers a dead man in his former wife's closet but neglects to call the police.

STEELE JUSTICE

Pro. John Strong; Atlantic Releasing Corp. *Dir.* Robert Boris *Scr.* Robert Boris *Cine.* John M. Stephens *Ed.* John O'Connor and Steve Rosenblum *Mu.* Misha Segal *P.d.* Richard N. McGuire *R.t.* 95 min. *MPAA* R. *Cast:* Martin Kove, Sela Ward, Ronny Cox, Bernie Casey, Joseph Campanella, Soon-Teck Oh, Jan Gan Boyd David Froman, Sarah Douglas.

A Vietnam veteran (Martin Kove) encounters the same evil Vietnamese official he clashed with during the war on the streets of Los Angeles. The officer is now a top drug dealer.

THE STEPFATHER

Pro. Jay Benson; New Century/Vista Film Company *Dir.* Joseph Ruben *Scr.* Donald E. Westlake *Cine.* John W. Lindley *Ed.* George Bowers *Mu.* Patrick Moraz *P.d.* James William Newport *A.d.* Davie Willson *S.d.* Kimberly Richardson *R.t.* 88 min. *MPAA* R. *Cast:* Terry O'Quinn, Jill Schoelen, Shelley Hack, Charles Lanyer, Stephen Shellen.

A psychopathic man kills his family when they do not live up to his ideal. He marries again, and his stepdaughter begins to suspect that all is not well.

STRAIGHT TO HELL (Great Britain, 1987)

Pro. Eric Fellner; Island Pictures *Dir.* Alex Cox *Scr.* Alex Cox and Dick Rude *Cine.* Tom Richmond *Ed.* Dave Martin *Mu.* The Pogues *P.d.* Andrew McAlpine *R.t.* 86 min. *Cast:* Sy Richardson, Joe Strummer, Dick Rude, Courtney Love, Dennis Hopper, Elvis Costello, Grace Jones, Jim Jarmusch, Biff Yeager, Zander Schloss, Sara Sugarman, The Pogues, Juan Torres.

Having broken their assassination contract because of oversleeping, three scruffy outlaws and their female companion rob a bank instead. Their car breaks down, so they must take refuge in a sleepy little town in this parody of a typical Western.

THE STRANGER (USA and Argentina, 1987)

Pro. Hugo Lamonica; Columbia Pictures *Dir.* Adolfo Aristarain *Scr.* Dan Gurskis *Cine.* Horacio Maira *Ed.* Eduardo Lopez *Mu.* Craig Safan *S.d.* Abel Fagellio *R.t.* 88 min. *MPAA* R. *Cast:* Bonnie Bedelia, Peter Riegert, Barry Primus, David Spielberg, Marcos Woinski, Julio de Grazia, Cecilia Roth, Arturo Maly, Ricardo Darin, Adrian Chio, Tito Mendoza, Federico Luppi, Jacques Arndt, Milton James, Marina Magali, Ernesto Larrese, Sacha Favelevic.

In this psychological thriller, a woman (Bonnie Bedelia) witnesses three brutal murders and then suffers from amnesia after a car accident, so that she is unable to identify the killers.

STREET TRASH

Pro. Roy Frumkes *Dir.* Jim Muro *Scr.* Roy Frumkes *Cine.* David Sperling *Ed.*

Dennis Werner *Mu.* Rick Ulfik *P.d.* Rob Marcucci *A.d.* Denise Labelle and Tom Molinelli *R.t.* 91 min. *Cast:* Bill Chepil, Mike Lackey, Vic Noto, Mark Sferrazza, Jane Arakawa, Nicole Potter, R. L. Ryan, Clarenze Jarmon, Bernard Perlman, Miriam Zucker, M D'Jango Krunch, James Lorinz, Morty Storm, Tony Darrow.

When some skid row inhabitants drink some very bad liquor, they self-destruct.

STRIPPED TO KILL

Pro. Andy Ruben, Mark Byers, and Matt Leipzig; Concorde Pictures *Dir.* Katt Shea Ruben *Scr.* Katt Shea Ruben *Cine.* John Leblanc *Ed.* Zach Staenberg *Mu.* John O'Kennedy *A.d.* Paul Raubertas *R.t.* 84 min. *MPAA* R. *Cast:* Kay Lenz, Greg Evigan, Norman Fell, Tracy Crowder, Athena Worthey, Carlyle Byron, Debbie Nassar, Lucia Nagy Lexington, Michelle Foreman, Pia Kamakahi, Tom Ruben, Daina Bellamy, Peter Scranton, Brad David, J. Bartell, Andy Ruben, Debra Lamb.

A Los Angeles policewoman (Kay Lenz) is assigned to go undercover as a stripper in order to help catch a serial murderer.

STUDENT CONFIDENTIAL

Pro. Richard Horian; Troma *Dir.* Richard Horian *Scr.* Richard Horian *Cine.* James Dickson *Ed.* Richard Horian *Mu.* Richard Horian *P.d.* David Wasco *A.d.* Robert Joyce *R.t.* 94 min. *MPAA* R. *Cast:* Eric Douglas, Marlon Jackson, Susan Scott, Elizabeth Singer, Ronee Blakley, Richard Horian, Paula Sorenson, John Milford, Kip King, Sarina Grant, Billie Jean Thomas, Joel Mills, Corwyn Anthony.

Student Confidential is the story of three high school students whose lives are changed by a wealthy man (Richard Horian) introduced to them by their principal.

SULLIVAN'S PAVILION

Pro. Fred G. Sullivan *Dir.* Fred G. Sullivan *Scr.* Fred G. Sullivan *Cine.* Hal Landen *Ed.* Fred G. Sullivan *Mu.* Kenneth Higgins and James Calabrese *A.d.* Susan Neal *R.t.* 83 min. *Cast:* Polly Sullivan, Tate Sullivan, Katie Sullivan, Kirk Sullivan, Ricky Sullivan, Fred G. Sullivan, Jon Granik, James R. Hogue, Jan Jalcnak, Judith Mayes, Don Samuels, Roberta Schwebel.

This comic memoir portrays a filmmaker's family life as he struggles to continue releasing films without ever being very successful.

SUMMER CAMP NIGHTMARE

Pro. Robert T. Crow and Emilia Lesniak-Crow; Concorde Pictures *Dir.* Bert L. Dragin *Scr.* Bert L. Dragin and Penelope Spheeris; based on the novel *The Butterfly Revolution*, by William Butler *Cine.* Don Burgess *Ed.* Michael Spence *Mu.* Ted Neeley and Gary Chase *P.d.* Richard McGuire *A.d.* Barry Franenberg *S.d.* Jennifer Pray *R.t.* 87 min. *MPAA* PG-13. *Cast:* Chuck Connors, Charles Stratton, Adam Carl, Harold P. Pruett, Melissa Brennan, Tom Fridley, Stuart Rogers, Shawn McLemore, Samantha Newark, Nancy Calabrese, Michael Cramer, Rick Fitts.

A camp counselor (Charles Stratton), rebellious at the strict discipline of the camp's director (Chuck Connors), takes over and begins to run the place like a neo-fascist.

SUMMER HEAT

Pro. William Tennant; Atlantic Releasing Corp. *Dir.* Michie Gleason *Scr.* Michie Gleason; based on the novel *Here to Get My Baby Out of Jail*, by Louise Shivers *Cine.* Elliot Davis *Ed.* Mary Bauer *Mu.* Richard Stone *P.d.* Marsha Hinds *A.d.* Bo Johnson *S.d.* Jan K. Bergstrom *R.t.* 80 min. *MPAA* R. *Cast:* Lori Singer, Anthony Edwards, Bruce Abbott, Kathy Bates, Clu Gulager, Jessie Kent, Noble

Willingham, Nesbitt Blaisdell, Jane Cecil, Matt Almond, Miriam Byrd-Nethery, Jessica Leigh Mann, Michael Mattick, Conrad McLaren.

Roxy (Lori Singer), a young farm woman, is drawn into an affair with a handsome farmhand, who murders her husband. The trial brings Roxy into the public eye, and she must cope with community censure.

SUMMER NIGHT WITH GREEK PROFILE, ALMOND EYES, AND SCENT OF BASIL (Italy, 1987)
Pro. Gianni Minervini; New Line Cinema *Dir.* Lina Wertmuller *Scr.* Lina Wertmuller *Cine.* Camillo Bazzoni *Mu.* Bixio CEMSA *A.d.* Enrico Job *R.t.* 94 min. *Cast:* Mariangela Melato, Michele Placido, Roberto Herlitzka, Massimo Wertmuller.

Wealthy, voluptuous Fulvia (Mariangela Melato) kidnaps a radical terrorist (Michele Placido); sexual fireworks ensue.

SUMMER SCHOOL
Pro. George Shapiro and Howard West; Paramount Pictures *Dir.* Carl Reiner *Scr.* Jeff Franklin; based on a story by Stuart Birnbaum, David Dashev, and Jeff Franklin *Cine.* David M. Walsh *Ed.* Bud Molin *Mu.* Danny Elfman *P.d.* David L. Snyder *A.d.* Joe Wood *R.t.* 98 min. *MPAA* PG-13. *Cast:* Mark Harmon, Kirstie Alley, Robin Thomas, Patrick Labyorteaux, Courtney Thorne-Smith, Dean Cameron, Gary Riley, Kelly Minter, Ken Olandt, Shawnee Smith.

Gym teacher Freddy Shoop (Mark Harmon), roped into teaching remedial English in summer school, gains self-esteem as he helps his students.

SUPERMAN IV: THE QUEST FOR PEACE
Pro. Menahem Golan and Yoram Globus; Warner Bros. *Dir.* Sidney J. Furie *Scr.* Lawrence Konner and Mark Rosenthal; based on a story by Christopher Reeve, Lawrence Konner, and Mark Rosenthal *Cine.* Ernest Day *Ed.* John Shirley *Mu.* John Williams and Alexander Courage *P.d.* John Graysmark *A.d.* Leslie Tomkins *S.d.* Peter Young *R.t.* 89 min. *MPAA* PG. *Cast:* Christopher Reeve, Gene Hackman, Jackie Cooper, Marc McClure, Jon Cryer, Sam Wanamaker, Mark Pillow, Mariel Hemingway, Margot Kidder.

Superman targets his greatest enemy yet: nuclear weapons.

SURF NAZIS MUST DIE
Pro. Robert Tinnell; Troma *Dir.* Peter George *Scr.* Jon Ayre *Cine.* Rolf Kesterman *Ed.* Craig Colton *Mu.* Jon McCallum *A.d.* Byrnadette Di Santo *R.t.* 95 min. *MPAA* R. *Cast:* Gail Neely, Robert Harden, Barry Brenner, Dawn Wildsmith, Michael Sonye, Joel Hile, Tom Shell, Bobbie Briese, Gene Mitchell.

When a young black man (Robert Harden) is killed by a gang of surfer fascists, the boy's mother goes after the gang.

SURRENDER
Pro. Aaron Spelling and Alan Greisman; Warner Bros. *Dir.* Jerry Belson *Scr.* Jerry Belson *Cine.* Juan Ruiz-Anchia *Ed.* Wendy Greene Bricmont *Mu.* Michel Colombier *P.d.* Lilly Kilvert *A.d.* Jon Hutman *R.t.* 95 min. *MPAA* PG. *Cast:* Sally Field, Michael Caine, Steve Guttenberg, Peter Boyle, Jackie Cooper, Julie Kavner, Louise Lasser, Iman.

An impoverished artist (Sally Field) and a jaded novelist (Michael Caine) fall in love, endure separation, and are reunited.

SWEET COUNTRY
Pro. Michael Cacoyannis; Cinema Group Pictures *Dir.* Michael Cacoyannis *Scr.* Michael Cacoyannis; based on the novel by Caroline Richards *Cine.* Andreas Bellis *Ed.* Dinos Katsourides and Michael Cacoyannis *Mu.* Stavros Xarhakos *S.d.* Antonis Kyriakoulis *R.t.* 150 min. *MPAA* R. *Cast:* Jane Alexander, John Cullum, Carole Laure, Franco Nero, Joanna Pettet, Randy Quaid, Irene Papas, Jean-Pierre Aumont, Pierre Vaneck.

An American woman (Jane Alexander) in Chile with her husband (John Cullum), a doctor, becomes involved with a leftist underground group after the overthrow of President Allende.

SWEET LORRAINE
Pro. Steve Gomer; Angelika Films *Dir.* Steve Gomer *Scr.* Michael Zettler and Shelly Altman; based on a story by Michael Zettler, Shelly Altman, and George Malko *Cine.* Rene Ohashi *Ed.* Laurence Solomon *Mu.* Richard Robbins *P.d.* David Gropman *A.d.* Karen Schulz *S.d.* Richard Hoover *R.t.* 91 min. *MPAA* PG-13. *Cast:* Maureen Stapleton, Trini Alvarado, Lee Richardson, John Bedford Lloyd, Freddie Roman, Giancarlo Esposito, Edith Falco, Todd Graff, Evan Handler, Tamara Tunie.

The owner of an old resort hotel in the Catskills realizes that she must sell the place because it is no longer profitable, but she keeps it open for one more season.

SWEET REVENGE
Pro. Steve Stabler; Concorde Pictures *Dir.* Mark Sobel *Scr.* Steven Krauzer and Tim McCoy *Cine.* Shane Kelly *Ed.* Michael S. Murphy *Mu.* Ernest Troost *P.d.* Vic Dabao *R.t.* 78 min. *MPAA* R. *Cast:* Nancy Allen, Ted Shackelford, Martin Landau, Sal Landi, Michelle Little, Gina Gershon, Lotis Key, Stacey Adams, Leo Martinez.

Reporter Jillian Grey (Nancy Allen), investigating a white-slavery ring, is kidnapped by its propagators.

THE TALE OF RUBY ROSE (Australia, 1987)
Pro. Bryce Menzies and Andrew Wiseman; Hemdale Film Corp. *Dir.* Roger Scholes *Scr.* Roger Scholes *Cine.* Steve Mason *Mu.* Paul Schutze *A.d.* Bryce Perrin *R.t.* 101 min. *Cast:* Melita Jurisic, Chris Haywood, Rod Zuanic, Martyn Sanderson, Sheila Florance.

A woman living in a remote mountain cabin with her husband and son retreats from her fears into a fantasy world. She finds help from the grandmother she had never met when she visits the valley.

TESTIMONY (Great Britain, 1987)
Pro. Tony Palmer *Dir.* Tony Palmer *Scr.* David Rudkin and Tony Palmer; based on the *Memoirs of Dmitri Shostakovich*, edited by Soloman Bolkov *Cine.* Nic Knowland *Ed.* Tony Palmer *Mu.* Dmitri Shostakovich *P.d.* Tony Palmer *A.d.* Paul Tompleman, Chris Bradley, and Chris Browning *R.t.* 157 min. *Cast:* Ben Kingsley, Sherry Baines, Magdalen Asquith, Mark Asquith, Terence Rigby, Ronald Pickup, John Shrepnel, Robert Reynolds.

Testimony is director Tony Palmer's lengthy account of the life of Russian composer Dmitri Shostakovich (Ben Kingsley) and of his stormy relationship with Joseph Stalin (Terence Rigby). Shostakovich was successful until his opera *Lady Macbeth* offended the Soviet leader, who then persecuted the unfortunate composer.

THEY STILL CALL ME BRUCE

Pro. Johnny Yune and James Orr *Dir.* Johnny Yune and James Orr *Scr.* Johnny Yune and James Orr *Cine.* R. Michael Delahoussaye *Ed.* Roy Watts *Mu.* Morton Stevens *A.d.* Jeff McManus *R.t.* 91 min. *MPAA* PG. *Cast:* Johnny Yune, David Mendenhall, Pat Paulsen, Joey Travolta, Robert Guillaume, Bethany Wright, Carl Bensen.

Korean Bruce Won (Johnny Yune) arrives in Houston looking for the G.I. who saved his life during the Korean War. Mayhem ensues as he becomes entangled in romance with a call girl, cases of mistaken identity, and martial arts competitions.

THREE FOR THE ROAD

Pro. Herb Jaffe and Mort Engelberg; New Century/Vista Film Company *Dir.* B. W. L. Norton *Scr.* Richard Martini, Tim Metcalfe, and Miguel Tejada-Flores; based on a story by Richard Martini *Cine.* Steve Posey *Ed.* Christopher Greenbury *Mu.* Barry Goldberg *P.d.* Linda Allen *A.d.* William Buck *S.d.* Linda Allen *R.t.* 90 min. *MPAA* PG. *Cast:* Charlie Sheen, Kerri Green, Alan Ruck, Sally Kellerman, Blair Tefkin, Raymond J. Barry, Alexa Hamilton, Bert Remsen, James Avery, Eric Bruskotter.

A political aide (Charlie Sheen) is asked to escort a senator's daughter to a psychiatric school and soon learns that the senator is not as admirable as he seems.

THREE KINDS OF HEAT

Pro. Michael J. Kagan; Cannon International *Dir.* Leslie Stevens *Scr.* Leslie Stevens *Cine.* Terry Cole *Ed.* Bob Dearberg *Mu.* Michael Bishop, with Scott Page *P.d.* Duncan Cameron *A.d.* Alan Hunter Craig *S.d.* Robyn Hamilton-Doney *R.t.* 87 min. *MPAA* R. *Cast:* Robert Ginty, Victoria Barrett, Shakti, Sylvester McCoy, Barry Foster, Jeannie Brown, Paul Gee, Malcolm Connell, Trevor Martin, Mary Tamm, Keith Edwards, Jack Hedley, Bridget Khan.

A state department agent (Robert Ginty) and policewomen from New York and Hong Kong (Victoria Barrett and Shakti) collaborate on an Interpol mission to track down Harry Pimm (Sylvester McCoy).

THREE O'CLOCK HIGH

Pro. David E. Vogel; Universal *Dir.* Phil Joanou *Scr.* Richard Christian Matheson and Thomas Szollosi *Cine.* Barry Sonnenfeld *Ed.* Joe Anne Fogle *Mu.* Tangerine Dream *P.d.* Bill Matthews and Tom Bugenhaven *R.t.* 97 min. *MPAA* PG-13. *Cast:* Casey Siemaszko, Anne Ryan, Stacey Glick, Jonathan Wise, Richard Tyson, Jeffrey Tambor, Liza Morrow, Phillip Baker Hall, John P. Ryan.

Jerry Mitchell (Casey Siemaszko), assigned to do an interview with the school bully (Richard Tyson) for his high school newspaper, is challenged to a fight by the boy and spends the rest of the day in terror.

A TIGER'S TALE

Pro. Peter Douglas; Atlantic Entertainment Group *Dir.* Peter Douglas *Scr.* Peter Douglas; based on a novel by Allen Hanney III *Cine.* Tony Pierce-Roberts *Ed.* David Campling *Mu.* Lee Holdridge *P.d.* Shay Austin *R.t.* 97 min. *MPAA* R. *Cast:* Ann-Margret, C. Thomas Howell, Charles Durning, Kelly Preston, Ann Wedgeworth, William Zabka, James Noble, Tim Thomerson, Steven Kampmann, Traci Lin, Angel Tompkins.

A nineteen-year-old boy (C. Thomas Howell) falls in love with his girlfriend's mother (Ann-Margret).

TOO MUCH

Pro. Menahem Golan and Yoram Globus; Cannon Group   *Dir.* Eric Rochat   *Scr.* Eric Rochat   *Cine.* Daisaku Kimura   *Ed.* Alain Jakubowicz   *Mu.* George S. Clinton   *A.d.* Tsunco Kantake   *R.t.* 89 min.   *MPAA* PG.   *Cast:* Bridgette Andersen, Masato Fukazama, Hiroyuki Watanabe, Char Fontanta, Uganda, Joan Laine.

Accompanying her parents on their Tokyo business trip, Suzy (Bridgette Andersen) is given a robot (Masato Fukazama), which she names "Too Much."

TOO OUTRAGEOUS! (Canada, 1987)

Pro. Roy Krost; Spectrafilm   *Dir.* Richard Benner   *Scr.* Richard Benner   *Cine.* Fred Guthe   *Ed.* George Appleby   *Mu.* Russ Little   *A.d.* Andris Hausmanis   *R.t.* 100 min.   *MPAA* R.   *Cast:* Craig Russell, Hollis McLaren, David McIlwraith, Ron White, Lynne Cormack, Michael J. Reynolds, Timothy Jenkins, Paul Eves, Frank Pellegrino, Barry Flatman.

In a sequel to the 1977 hit *Outrageous*, female impersonator Robin Turner (Craig Russell) is gaining success on the gay club circuit, but his schizophrenic girlfriend Liza (Hollis McLaren) becomes involved in a relationship with an unscrupulous bartender (Frank Pellegrino).

TOUGH GUYS DON'T DANCE

Pro. Menahem Golan and Yoram Globus; Cannon Films   *Dir.* Norman Mailer   *Scr.* Norman Mailer; based on his novel   *Cine.* John Bailey   *Ed.* Debra McDermott   *Mu.* Angelo Badalamenti   *P.d.* Armin Ganz   *S.d.* Gretchen Rau   *R.t.* 108 min.   *MPAA* R.   *Cast:* Ryan O'Neal, Isabella Rossellini, Debra Sandlund, Wings Hauser, John Bedford Lloyd, Clarence Williams III, Lawrence Tierney, Penn Jillette, Frances Fisher, R. Patrick Sullivan, Stephen Morrow, John Snyder.

This film noir picture involves a man (Ryan O'Neal) with the events surrounding a drug deal, corrupt policemen, and a former pornographic film star.

TRAVELLING AVANT (also known as *Dolly In*; France, 1987)

Pro. Claude Abeille; UGC   *Dir.* Jean-Charles Tacchella   *Scr.* Jean-Charles Tacchella   *Cine.* Jacques Assuerus   *Ed.* Marie-Aimée Debril   *Mu.* Raymond Allesandrini   *A.d.* Georges Levy   *R.t.* 144 min.   *Cast:* Thierry Fremont, Simon de La Brosse, Ann-Gisel Glass, Sophie Minet, Laurence Cote, Luc Lavandier, Nathalie Mann, Jacques Serre, Alix de Konopka.

The friendship of two film buffs disintegrates when their attempt to form a film club fails.

TRAVELLING NORTH (Australia, 1987)

Pro. Ben Cannon; CEL   *Dir.* Carl Schultz   *Scr.* David Williamson; based on his play of the same name   *Cine.* Julian Penny   *Ed.* Henry Dangar   *Mu.* Alan John   *P.d.* Owen Paterson   *R.t.* 96 min.   *MPAA* PG-13.   *Cast:* Leo McKern, Julia Blake, Graham Kennedy, Henri Szeps, Michele Fawdon, Diane Craig, Andrea Moor, Drew Forsythe, John Gregg.

A retired man (Leo McKern) grasps at love and happiness in a new marriage and a move north to Queensland, but his health begins to deteriorate.

THE TROUBLE WITH DICK

Pro. Gary Walkow   *Dir.* Gary Walkow   *Scr.* Gary Walkow   *Cine.* Daryl Studebaker   *Ed.* G. A. Walkowishky   *Mu.* Roger Bourland   *P.d.* Eric Jones and Pui Pui Li   *R.t.* 86 min.   *Cast:* Tom Villard, Susan Dey, Elaine Giftos, Elizabeth Gorcey, David Clennon, Jack Carter, Marianne Muellerleile.

A young science-fiction writer has an emotional breakdown over his writing, which he cannot get published, and his sex life, which has become increasingly confusing as both a mother and her daughter enter his romantic life.

THE TROUBLE WITH SPIES (also known as *Trouble at the Royal Rose*)
Pro. Burt Kennedy; De Laurentiis Entertainment Group *Dir.* Burt Kennedy *Scr.* Burt Kennedy; based on the book *Apple Spy in the Sky*, by Marc Lovell *Cine.* Alex Phillips *Ed.* Warner E. Leighton *Mu.* Ken Thorne *P.d.* Jose Maria Tapiador *R.t.* 91 min. *MPAA* PG. *Cast:* Donald Sutherland, Ned Beatty, Ruth Gordon, Lucy Gutteridge, Michael Hordern, Robert Morley, Gregory Sierra, Suzanne Danielle, Fima Noveck.

In *The Trouble with Spies*, Appleton Porter (Donald Sutherland), an inept British intelligence agent, is sent on a mission to entrap Soviet spies.

UNDER COVER
Pro. Menahem Golan and Yoram Globus; Cannon Group *Dir.* John Stockwell *Scr.* John Stockwell and Scott Fields *Cine.* Alexander Gruszynski *Ed.* Sharyn L. Ross *Mu.* Todd Rundgren *P.d.* Becky Block *R.t.* 94 min. *MPAA* R. *Cast:* David Neidorf, Jennifer Jason Leigh, Barry Corbin, David Harris, Kathleen Wilhoite, David Denney, Brent Hadaway, John Philbin, Brad Leland, Mark Holton, Carmen Argenziano.

Narcotics agents (David Neidorf and Jennifer Jason Leigh) work under cover in a high school to bring to justice the drug dealer who murdered their colleague.

UNDER THE SUN OF SATAN (*Sous le soleil de Satan*. France, 1987)
Pro. Claude Abeille; Gaumont *Dir.* Maurice Pialat *Scr.* Sylvie Danton and Maurice Pialat; based on the novel by Georges Bernanos *Cine.* Willy Kurant *Ed.* Yann Dedet *Mu.* Henri Dutilleux *P.d.* Katia Vischkof *R.t.* 98 min. *Cast:* Gérard Depardieu, Sandrine Bonnaire, Maurice Pialat, Alain Artur, Yann Dedet, Brigitte Legendre, Jean-Claude Bourlat.

A Roman Catholic priest (Gérard Depardieu), obsessed with purity and moral strength, goes on a journey and encounters a young woman with a sordid past.

UNSANE (*Tenebrae*. Italy, 1987)
Pro. Claudio Argento; Bedford Entertainment and Film Gallery *Dir.* Dario Argento *Scr.* Dario Argento and George Kemp; based on a story by Dario Argento *Cine.* Luciano Tovoli *Ed.* Franco Fraticelli *Mu.* Claudio Simonetti, Fabio Pignatelli, and Massimo Morante *A.d.* Giuseppe Bassan *S.d.* Maurizio Garrone *R.t.* 100 min. *MPAA* R. *Cast:* Anthony Franciosa, John Saxon, Daria Nicolodi, Giuliano Gemma, Mirella D'Angelo, Veronica Lario, John Steiner, Lara Wendel, Christian Borromeo, Ania Pieroni, Eva Robins, Mirella Banti, Isabella Amadeo, Carola Stagnaro.

A novelist (Anthony Franciosa), whose books have been accused of being too violent, is threatened by a killer who is committing murders in the style of the author's latest book.

URSULA
Pro. Heikki Takkinen *Dir.* Jakko Pyhala *Scr.* Jakko Pyhala; based on the novel *Puuluola*, by Kim Weckstrom *Cine.* Pertti Mutanen *Mu.* Antti Hytti and Raine Salo *R.t.* 100 min. *Cast:* Ville Virtanen, Heidi Kilpelainen, Petri Aalto, Tomi Salmela, Ahmed Riza, Chris af Enehielm, Pekka Uotila, Eija Vilpas, Johan Donner, Sauli Poljakoff, Resika Nordin, Raine Salo.

Two young people attempt to escape their lives as drug addicts or dealers.

VERNE MILLER

Pro. Ann Broke Ashley; Alive Films *Dir.* Rod Hewitt *Scr.* Rod Hewitt *Cine.* Misha Suslov *Ed.* John O'Connor *Mu.* Tom Chase and Steve Rucker *P.d.* Victoria Paul *R.t.* 95 min. *Cast:* Scott Glenn, Barbara Stock, Thomas G. Waites, Ed O'Ross, Andrew Robinson.

Verne Miller recounts the story of a sheriff (Scott Glenn) who turned to crime and became Al Capone's hired killer.

THE VIOLINS CAME WITH THE AMERICANS

Pro. David Greene *Dir.* Kevin Conway *Scr.* M. Quiros (Mila Burnette) *Cine.* Benjamin Davis *Ed.* John Tintori *Mu.* Fred Weinberg *S.d.* Sue Raney *R.t.* 94 min. *Cast:* Mila Burnette, Joaquim de Almeida, Jose Ferrer, Maria Norman, Kevin Conway, Norma Candal, Iris Martinez, Paula Trueman, Alba Oms.

A woman who recently separated from her husband returns to her family in the South Bronx and explores her Puerto Rican roots.

THE VIRGIN QUEEN OF ST. FRANCIS HIGH (Canada, 1987)

Pro. Crown International Pictures *Dir.* Francesco Lucente *Scr.* Francesco Lucente *Cine.* Joseph Bitonti and Kevin Alexander *Ed.* Francesco Lucente *Mu.* Danny Lowe, Brad Steckel, and Brian Island *R.t.* 94 min. *MPAA* PG. *Cast:* Joseph R. Straface, Stacy Christensen, J. T. Wotton, Anna-Lisa Iapaolo, Lee Barringer, Bev Wotton.

The Virgin Queen of St. Francis High concerns a high school boy who makes a bet with his buddy that he can deflower the title character, a popular blonde, before the end of the summer.

WAITING FOR THE MOON (also known as *The Trail of the Lonesome Pine*)

Pro. Sandra Schulberg; Skouras Pictures *Dir.* Jill Godmilow *Scr.* Mark Magill; based on a story by Jill Godmilow and Mark Magill *Cine.* Andre Neau *Ed.* Georges Klotz *Mu.* Michael Sahl *P.d.* Patrice Mercier *R.t.* 87 min. *MPAA* PG. *Cast:* Linda Hunt, Linda Bassett, Andrew McCarthy, Bernadette Lafont, Bruce McGill, Jacques Boudet.

This portrait of Alice B. Toklas (Linda Hunt) and Gertrude Stein (Linda Bassett) does not claim to be biographical, but it depicts the relationship of the two and their interactions with friends.

WALK LIKE A MAN

Pro. Leonard Kroll; Metro-Goldwyn-Mayer/United Artists *Dir.* Melvin Frank *Scr.* Robert Klane *Cine.* Victor J. Kemper *Ed.* Bill Butler and Steve Butler *Mu.* Lee Holdridge *P.d.* Bill Malley *A.d.* Mary Ann Biddle *R.t.* 86 min. *MPAA* G. *Cast:* Howie Mandel, Christopher Lloyd, Cloris Leachman, Colleen Camp, Amy Steel.

A man (Howie Mandel) reared by wolves in the wilderness is discovered to be the heir of a large fortune. An animal behaviorist tries to teach him to be human before his brother (Christopher Lloyd) swindles him out of the inheritance.

A WALK ON THE MOON

Pro. Dina Silver *Dir.* Raphael Silver *Scr.* William B. Mai *Cine.* Adam Greenberg *Ed.* Peter Frank *Mu.* Paul Chihara *P.d.* Holger Gross *R.t.* 95 min. *Cast:* Kevin Anderson, Terry Kinney, Laila Robins, Patrice Martinez, Pedro Armendariz, Roberto Sosa.

A young Peace Corps volunteer (Kevin Anderson) goes to a small Colombian village, where he is astounded by the cynicism of his predecessor and the indifference of the natives.

WALKER

Pro. Lorenzo O'Brien and Angel Flores Marini; Universal and Northern Distribution Partners *Dir.* Alex Cox *Scr.* Rudy Wurlitzer *Cine.* David Bridges *Ed.* Carlos Puente Ortega and Alex Cox *Mu.* Joe Strummer *P.d.* Bruno Rubeo *A.d.* Cecilia Montiel and Jorge Sainz *S.d.* Bryce Perrin and Suzie Frishette *R.t.* 95 min. *MPAA* R. *Cast:* Ed Harris, Richard Masur, René Auberjonois, Keith Szarabajka, Sy Richarson, Xander Berkeley, John Diehl, Peter Boyle, Marlee Matlin, Alfonso Arau, Pedro Armendariz, Roberto Lopez Espinoza, Gerrit Graham, William O'Leary, Blanca Guerra, Alan Bolt, Miguel Sandoval.

This version of the life and strange career of William Walker, the American who invaded Nicaragua in 1855 and ruled there for two years, makes a political point about policies of Ronald Reagan's adminstration.

THE WANNSEE CONFERENCE (*Die Wannseekonferenz*. West Germany, 1987)

Pro. Manfred Korytowski; Rearguard *Dir.* Heinz Schirk *Scr.* Paul Mommertz *Cine.* Horst Schier *Ed.* Ursula Mollinger *A.d.* Robert Höfer-Ach and Barbara Siebner *R.t.* 87 min. *Cast:* Robert Artzorn, Friedrich Beckhaus, Gerd Bockmann, Jochen Busse, Hans W. Bussinger, Harald Dieti, Peter Fitz, Reinhard Glemnitz, Dieter Groest, Martin Lüttge, Anita Mally, Dietrich Mattausch, Gerd Rigauer, Franz Rudnick, Günter Sporrle, Rainer Steffen.

This historical drama recounts the discussions at the Wannsee Conference, at which the participants codified the Nazi approach to the destruction of the Jews.

WANTED: DEAD OR ALIVE

Pro. Robert C. Peters; New World Pictures *Dir.* Gary Sherman *Scr.* Michael Patrick Goodman, Brian Taggert, and Gary Sherman *Cine.* Alex Nepomniaschy *Ed.* Ross Albert *Mu.* Joseph Renzetti *P.d.* Paul Eads *A.d.* Jon Hutman *R.t.* 104 min. *MPAA* R. *Cast:* Rutger Hauer, Gene Simmons, Robert Guillaume, Mel Harris, William Russ, Susan McDonald, Jerry Hardin, Hugh Gillin, Robert Harper.

A former CIA agent (Rutger Hauer) searches for an Arab terrorist (Gene Simmons) who is blowing up various locations in Los Angeles.

WARM NIGHTS ON A SLOW MOVING TRAIN (Australia, 1987)

Pro. Ross Dimsey and Patric Juillet; Filmpac Holdings *Dir.* Bob Ellis *Scr.* Bob Ellis and Denny Lawrence *Cine.* Yuri Sokol *Ed.* Tim Lewis *Mu.* Peter Sullivan *P.d.* Tracy Watt *R.t.* 91 min. *Cast:* Wendy Hughes, Colin Friels, Norman Kaye, John Clayton, Rod Zuanic, Lewis Fitz-gerald, Steve J. Spears, Grant Tilly, Peter Whitford, Chris Haywood, John Flaus, Peter Carmody.

A prostitute who works a suite on a train every weekend falls in love with one man, and he persuades her to help him assassinate a politician.

WARNING BANDITS (*Attention Bandits*. France, 1987)

Pro. Claude Lelouch; AAA *Dir.* Claude Lelouch *Scr.* Claude Lelouch and Pierre Uytterhoeven *Cine.* Jean-Yves Le Mener *Ed.* Hughes Darmois *Mu.* Francis Lai *A.d.* Jacques Bufnoir *R.t.* 108 min. *Cast:* Jean Yanne, Marie-Sophie Pochat, Patrick Bruel, Charles Gérard, Corinne Marchand, Christine Barbelivien, Hélène Surgere, Hervé Favre.

When Marie-Sophie (Marie-Sophie Pochat) discovers that her long-absent father is an outlaw, it completely changes her life.

WARRIOR QUEEN
Pro. Harry Alan Towers; Seymour Borde and Associates *Dir*. Chuck Vincent *Scr*. Rich Marx; based on a story by Peter Welbeck *Cine*. Lorenzo Battaglia *Ed*. Chuck Vincent, Joel Bender, Jim Sanders, and Tony Delcampo *Mu*. Ian Shaw and Kai Joffe *P.d*. Lucio Parise *R.t*. 69 min. *MPAA* R. *Cast:* Sybil Danning, Donald Pleasence, Richard Hill, J. J. Jones, Tally Chanel, Stasia Micula, Suzanne Smith, David Haughton, Mario Cruciani, Marco Tulio Cau.

Berenice (Sybil Danning), the mistress of the Roman emperor, spends her days in Pompeii trying to save two young slave girls.

A WEDDING IN GALILEE (*Noce en Galilee*. Belgium, France, and Palestine, 1987)
Pro. Michel Khleifi and Bernard Lorain; Lasa Films *Dir*. Michel Khleifi *Scr*. Michel Khleifi *Cine*. Walther van den Ende *Ed*. Marie Castro Vasquez *Mu*. Jean-Marie Senia *A.d*. Yves Brover *R.t*. 113 min. *Cast:* Ali Mohammed Akiki, Nazih Akly, Mabram Khouri, Anna Achdian, Sonia Amar, Emtiaz Diab, Georges Khleifi, Hassan Diab, Abkas Himas.

An Arab wedding set to take place in a village on Israel's West Bank must allow for the presence of the Israeli governor and his staff in order to have the celebration go on past curfew.

WHEN THE WIND BLOWS (Great Britain, 1986)
Pro. John Coates; Recorded Releasing *Dir*. Jimmy Murakami *Scr*. Raymond Briggs; based on his book *Mu*. David Bowie, Roger Waters, Genesis, Paul HardCastle, Squeeze, and Hugh Cornwall *A.d*. Richard Fawdry *R.t*. 85 min. *Voices:* Peggy Ashcroft, John Mills.

This animated film portrays an elderly British couple who follow the government's instructions on protecting the household in case of nuclear war but do not really understand the ramifications of a nuclear blast.

WHERE THE HEART ROAMS
Pro. George Csicsery; Film Arts Foundation *Dir*. George Csicsery *Scr*. George Csicsery *Cine*. John Knoop *R.t*. 83 min. *Cast:* Barbara Cartland, Janet Dailey, Bill Dailey, Chelley Kitzmiller, Ted Kitzmiller, Gina Kitzmiller, Kathryn Falk, Jude Deveraux, Rebecca Brandewyne, John Gfeller, Hilari Cohen, Vivian Stephens, Diane Dunaway, Lori Herter, Jerry Herter, Brenda Trent, Kathryn Davis, Lida Lunt, Chamisa James, Maralys Wills, E. Jean Carroll, Linda Wisdom, Robert Pearson.

Documentary filmmaker George Csicsery rides the "love train" from Los Angeles to New York, interviewing writers and fans of historical romance novels and attending the 1983 Romantic Booklover's Conference.

THE WHISTLE BLOWER (Great Britain, 1987)
Pro. Geoffrey Reeve; Hemdale Film Corp. *Dir*. Simon Langton *Scr*. Julian Bond; based on a novel by John Hale *Cine*. Fred Tammes *Ed*. Bob Morgan *P.d*. Morley Smith *A.d*. Chris Burke *R.t*. 100 min. *MPAA* PG. *Cast:* Michael Caine, James Fox, Nigel Havers, Felicity Dean, John Gielgud, Kenneth Colley, Gordon Jackson, Barry Foster, David Langton.

With the murder of his idealistic son (Nigel Havers), who had been reluctantly working in British intelligence, Frank Jones (Michael Caine) finds his pragmatic patriotism shaken to the core.

WHITE OF THE EYE (Great Britain, 1987)
Pro. Cassian Elwis and Brad Wyman; Cannon Group *Dir.* Donald Cammell *Scr.* Donald Cammell and China Cammell; based on the novel *Mrs. White*, by Margaret Tracy *Cine.* Alan Jones and Larry McConkey *Ed.* Terry Rawlings *Mu.* Nick Mason and Rich Fenn *R.t.* 110 min. *MPAA* R. *Cast:* David Keith, Cathy Moriarty, Art Evans, Alan Rosenberg, Alberta Watson, Michael Greene, Mark Hayashi, William Schilling, David Chow, Danielle Smith, China Cammell.

A man who is having marital problems is suspected of committing a series of murders of wealthy housewives.

WHITE WINTER HEAT
Pro. Warren Miller; Eric/Chandler *Dir.* Warren Miller *Scr.* Warren Miller *Cine.* Brian Sisselman, Gary Nate, Larry Gebhardt, Stephen Jackson, and Fletcher Manley *Ed.* Michael Usher and Ray Laurent *Mu.* Brooks Arthur and Daniel Segal *R.t.* 91 min. *Cast:* Warren Miller.

A documentary celebrating skiing and skiers, *White Winter Heat* features amazing stunts filmed in beautiful locations.

WHO'S THAT GIRL
Pro. Rosilyn Heller and Bernard Williams; Warner Bros. *Dir.* James Foley *Scr.* Andrew Smith and Ken Finkleman; based on a story by Andrew Smith *Cine.* Jan De Bont *Ed.* Pembroke Herring *Mu.* Stephen Bray *P.d* Ida Random *A.d.* Don Woodruff *S.d.* Cloudia *R.t.* 94 min. *MPAA* PG. *Cast:* Madonna, Griffin Dunne, Haviland Morris, John McMartin, Robert Swan, Drew Pillsbury, Coato Mundi, Dennis Burkley, John Mills.

Loudon Trutt (Griffin Dunne), assigned to assist a former convict (Madonna), finds himself falling in love with her as she completely disrupts his life.

THE WILD PAIR
Pro. Paul Mason and Randall Torno; Trans World Entertainment *Dir.* Beau Bridges *Scr.* Joseph Gunn; based on a story by Joseph Gunn and John Crowther *Cine.* Peter Stein *Ed.* Chris Holmes *Mu.* John Debney *P.d.* Stephen Berger *R.t.* 88 min. *MPAA* R. *Cast:* Beau Bridges, Bubba Smith, Lloyd Bridges, Gary Lockwood, Raymond St. Jacques, Danny De La Paz, Lela Rochon, Ellen Geer, Angelique De Windt, Creed Bratton, Randy Boone, Greg Finley, Andrew Parks.

Undercover agent Joe Jennings (Beau Bridges) and Los Angeles detective Benny Avalon (Bubba Smith) work together as they pursue a drug dealer and a mass murderer.

WILD THING
Pro. David Calloway and Nicolas Clermont; Atlantic Releasing Corp. *Dir.* Max Reid *Scr.* John Sayles; based on a story by John Sayles and Larry Stamper *Cine.* Rene Verzier *Ed.* Battle Davis and Steven Rosenblum *Mu.* George S. Clinton *P.d.* John Meighen and Jocelyn Joli *A.d.* Ross Schorer *R.t.* 92 min. *MPAA* PG-13. *Cast:* Rob Knepper, Kathleen Quinlan, Robert Davi, Maury Chaykin, Betty Buckley, Guillaume Lemay-Thivierge, Robert Bednarski, Clark Johnson, Sean Hewitt, Teddy Abner, Cree Summer Francks, Shawn Levy.

A boy escapes the scene of the murder of his parents by a drug dealer and a corrupt policeman and grows up in "the zone," a dangerous section of town in which the uncommunicative youth finally joins a group organized against the evil man who runs the zone.

WINNERS TAKE ALL
Pro. Christopher W. Knight and Tom Tatum; Apollo Pictures *Dir.* Fritz Kiersch
Scr. Ed Turner; based on a story by Tom Tatum and Christopher W. Knight *Cine.*
Fred V. Murphy II *Ed.* Lorenzo De Stefano *Mu.* Doug Timm *P.d.* Steven P.
Sardanis *S.d.* Tom Talbert *R.t.* 102 min. *MPAA* PG-13. *Cast:* Don Michael Paul,
Kathleen York, Robert Krantz, Deborah Richter, Peter DeLuise, Courtney Gains,
Paul Hampton, Gerardo Mejia, Tony Longo, Isabel Grandin.

Rick Melon (Don Michael Paul) is pitted against "Bad" Billy Robinson (Robert
Krantz), his boyhood buddy, in a Supercross motorcycle race, with more than biking
at stake.

WITCHBOARD
Pro. Gerald Geoffray; Cinema Group Pictures *Dir.* Kevin S. Tenney *Scr.* Kevin S.
Tenney *Cine.* Roy H. Wagner *Ed.* Steve Waller and Dan Duncan *Mu.* Dennis
Michael Tenney *R.t.* 98 min. *MPAA* R. *Cast:* Todd Allen, Tawny Kitaen, Stephen
Nichols, Kathleen Wilhoite, Burke Byrnes, Rose Marie.

A Ouija board unleashes an evil spirit that attempts to use Linda (Tawny Kitaen)
as a vehicle for rebirth. Jim (Todd Allen) and Brandon (Stephen Nichols) patch up
their friendship to save her.

WITH LOVE TO THE PERSON NEXT TO ME (Australia, 1987)
Pro. John Cruthers *Dir.* Brian McKenzie *Scr.* Brian McKenzie *Cine.* Ray Argall
Ed. Ray Argall and David Greig *P.d.* Kerith Holmes *R.t.* 98 min. *Cast:* Kim
Gyngell, Paul Chubb, Barry Dickins, Sally McKenzie, Beverley Gardiner, Phil
Motherwell.

Wallace (Kim Gyngell), a lonely cab driver, tapes the monologues of his customers, who are also bereft of love.

WITNESS TO A KILLING (Sri Lanka, 1987)
Pro. Jayantha Jayatilaka *Dir.* Chandran Rutnam *Scr.* Chandran Rutnam *Cine.*
Daryn Okada *Ed.* Gladwin Fernando *Mu.* Sarath Fernando *A.d.* Errol Kelly *R.t.*
72 min. *Cast:* Razi Anwer, Tony Ranasinghe, Swineetha Weerasinghe, Ravindra
Randeniya, Anojo Weerasinghe.

A small boy, unable to convince his parents that he saw a neighbor committing
murder, is pursued by the killer.

WORKING GIRLS
Pro. Lizzie Borden and Andi Gladstone; Miramax Films *Dir.* Lizzie Borden *Scr.*
Lizzie Borden, with Sandra Kay; based on a story by Lizzie Borden *Cine.* Judy
Irola *Mu.* David van Tieghem *R.t.* 90 min. *Cast:* Louise Smith, Ellen McElduff,
Amanda Goodwin, Marusia Zach, Janne Peters, Helen Nicholas.

Almost documentarylike in content, this film examines the lives and work of a
group of prostitutes at an upscale bordello.

THE WRONG COUPLES (Hong Kong, 1987)
Pro. John Sham; D and B Films *Dir.* John Chiang *Scr.* John Chan *Cine.* Tee Tung
Lung *A.d.* Fong Ying *R.t.* 98 min. *Cast:* Josephine Siu Fong Fong, Richard Ng,
Paul Chiang, Pauline Kwan, Maggie Li, Dennis Li.

Richard Ng plays a sailor who is shocked when he returns home to find that his
wife has left him and rented the apartment to a spinster (Josephine Siu Fong Fong).

THE YEAR MY VOICE BROKE (Australia, 1987)
Pro. George Miller, Doug Mitchell, and Terry Hayes *Dir.* John Duigan *Scr.* John

Duigan *Cine.* Geoff Burton *Ed.* Neil Thompston *Mu.* Christine Woodruff *P.d.* Roger Ford *R.t.* 103 min. *Cast:* Noah Taylor, Leone Carmen, Ben Mendelsohn, Graeme Blundell, Lynette Curran, Malcolm Robertson, Judi Farr, Tim Robertson, Bruce Spence, Harold Hopkins, Nick Tate, Vincent Ball, Anja Coleby, Kylic Ostara, Kelly Dingwall, Dorothy St. Heaps, Coleen Clifford, Kevin Manser, Mary Regan, Queenie Ashton, Helen Lomas, Emma Lyle, Louise Birgan, Matthew Ross, Allan Penney, Robert Carlton.

An adolescent boy (Noah Taylor) is confused and distraught by the actions of his lifelong friend, Freya (Leone Carmen), who shuns him to go out with an older boy, becomes pregnant, and moves to the city.

YOU TALKIN' TO ME?
Pro. Michael Polaire; Metro-Goldwyn-Mayer/United Artists *Dir.* Charles Winkler *Scr.* Charles Winkler *Cine.* Paul Ryan *Ed.* David Handman *Mu.* Joel McNeely *R.t.* 97 min. *MPAA* R. *Cast:* Jim Youngs, James Noble, Mykel T. Williamson, Faith Ford, Bess Motta, Rex Ryon, Brian Thompson, Alan King.

An out-of-work actor (Jim Youngs) is corrupted by the money and success he achieves as the host of a racist, right-wing television show.

ZJOEK (The Netherlands, 1987)
Pro. Kees Kasander and Denis Wigman *Dir.* Eric van Zuylen *Scr.* Marietta de Vries; based on *The Mind of a Mnemonist* and *The Man with the Shattered World*, by Alexander R. Luria *Cine.* Witold Sobocinski and Piotr Sobocinski *Ed.* Jan Dop *Mu.* Henk Hofstede *A.d.* Jan Roelfs and Ben van Os *R.t.* 90 min. *Cast:* Hans Dagelet, Felix-Jan Kuypers, Guusje van Tilborgh, Rudolf Lucieer.

This film contrasts the cases of a showman who has devised methods of remembering everything and of an injured soldier who can no longer remember the meanings of words.

ZOMBIE HIGH
Pro. Marc Toberoff and Aziz Chazal; Cinema Group Pictures *Dir.* Ron Link *Scr.* Tim Doyle, Elizabeth Passerelli, and Aziz Ghazal *Cine.* David Lux and Brian Coyne *Ed.* Shawn Hardin and James Whitney *Mu.* Daniel May *P.d.* Matthew Kozinets *A.d.* Hisham Abed *S.d.* Martin Jones and Todd Stevens *R.t.* 91 min. *MPAA* R. *Cast:* Virginia Madsen, Richard Cox, Kay Kuter, James Wilder, Sherilynn Fenn, Paul Feig, T. Scott Coffey, Paul Williams, Henry Sutton.

A boarding school's professors lobotomize their students, creating serum from the brain tissue that gives them eternal life.

RETROSPECTIVE
FILMS

ALL I DESIRE

Released: 1953
Production: Ross Hunter for Universal International
Direction: Douglas Sirk
Screenplay: James Gunn and Robert Blees; from an adaptation by Gina Kaus of the novel *Stopover*, by Carol Brink
Cinematography: Carl Guthrie
Editing: Milton Carruth
Art direction: Bernard Herzbrun and Alexander Golitzen; set decoration, Russell A. Gausman and Julia Heron
Costume design: Rosemary Odel
Choreography: Kenny Williams
Music: Joseph Gershenson
Song: David Lieber, "All I Desire"
Running time: 79 minutes

Principal characters:
Naomi Murdoch .... Barbara Stanwyck
Henry Murdoch .... Richard Carlson
Dutch Heineman .... Lyle Bettger
Joyce Murdoch .... Marcia Henderson
Lily Murdoch .... Lori Nelson
Sara Harper .... Maureen O'Sullivan
Russ Underwood .... Richard Long
Ted Murdoch .... Billy Gray
Lena Engstrom .... Lotte Stein

A provocative melodrama, *All I Desire* benefits from the fruitful teaming of Douglas Sirk, a great director, and Barbara Stanwyck, a great actress. The film is a key work for both, leading Sirk into the genre in which he would be most creative and showing off Stanwyck in one of her most affecting performances. Between them, director and star bring inflections to the material at hand which give it maximum expressiveness and continuing resonance.

In the 1950's, such an accomplishment could be easily underrated, for *All I Desire* is, to put it simply, a domestic soap opera or woman's picture, and a long-standing critical prejudice against that particular subgenre of melodrama was at its most pronounced during this period. Retrospectively, however, this type of film has been accorded the respect it deserves in most currents of critical thought, for it requires considerable stylistic grace and a keen understanding of the complexities of inner emotional life in order to be artistically successful. It is widely acknowledged that by purveying what were perceived to be women's fantasies, the Hollywood cinema of the classical era was also—given the insight and intelligence of individual filmmakers—bringing to light, in an aesthetically pleasing way, the complexities and contradictions within women that such fantasies intimate.

All I Desire is an excellent, if imperfect, example of this, for it dramatizes a conflict between various possible ways of living for an individual woman without persuasively resolving the conflict. In the protagonist's belated integration into a serene family life, one fantasy is fulfilled—possibly the one that most needs to be fulfilled—but there is the sense that this integration carries a condition that no further individual evolution will ever be allowed to her. The positive tone of this resolution may seem too complacent to underscore powerfully the eloquent ambiguity of the whole, but it does not completely undermine that ambiguity. Exposition of plot and character is essentially credible throughout, supporting a central portrait that piercingly reveals the emotions of a woman dimensional enough to be real.

The woman is Naomi Murdoch (Stanwyck), who lives in a turn-of-the-century world in which moral values are supposed to be absolute and one must passively harmonize with the prevailing way of life or actively rebel against it. Possessed of a strong-willed and unsettled spirit, Naomi could not adjust to her role as a conventional wife and mother of three in a small Wisconsin town. An extramarital affair had been one symptom of her discontent, and finally, she had broken with her family and left town to pursue a career as an actress.

Ten years later, as the film begins, she is again discontent, performing in a seedy theater on the vaudeville circuit and ruefully musing over her choices. Impulsively, she returns home to see her younger daughter Lily (Lori Nelson) perform in a school play. Her husband, Henry (Richard Carlson), and oldest daughter Joyce (Marcia Henderson) have not forgiven her for her desertion, but Lily, who has romanticized her, welcomes her, and her son Ted (Billy Gray), only a baby when she abandoned the family, quickly warms up to her despite his incomprehension of her past behavior. The visit stirs Naomi's deep yearning to reclaim what she has scorned, and Henry, though he is wary of her and more or less engaged to a single teacher, Sara Harper (Maureen O'Sullivan), still loves her. Slowly, the romance is rekindled and reconciliation begins to appear possible, while Naomi gradually wins over the reserved Joyce by helping her to become more alluring to her ambivalent boyfriend Russ (Richard Long), gives Lily a sobering perspective on her dreams of emulating her mother's theatrical glory, and makes a sincere effort to explain herself to Ted. Unfortunately, her former lover, Dutch (Lyle Bettger), is around, too, tempting her to resume their old relationship. Naomi finally realizes that she no longer wants him, though her impulse to confront him with her intentions at the scene of their past meetings results in an accidental shooting in which Dutch is wounded. Showing that he will no longer threaten her present life with exposure of the past, Dutch paves the way for Naomi to return home for good, and she is at last happily reunited with her husband and children.

The novel on which the film was based is Carol Brink's *Stopover* (1951), and adapter Gina Kaus retained both the title and a conclusion in which Naomi's return home does not work out and she leaves once again. Sirk would have preferred that ending and would have liked to keep the original title even without it, in order to undercut ironically a resolution he personally did not see as a happy one. That helps to explain why the final scene, which convention dictates should be romantic and reassuring, is somewhat pallid. Already a master of the form of melodrama in most respects, Sirk had not quite learned how to elicit intense audience empathy in the face of arbitrary narrative decisions (something he does do in later films, when the melodramatic curve of a subject is often much less sober than it is here) while projecting the kind of ambivalence that makes the material interesting and meaningful. On the whole, though, he is quite sympathetic to this story and impressively discerning in balancing the viewer's responses to it.

Sirk sees the home, family, and town to which Naomi returns as implicitly repressive; at the same time, perhaps because he is so pessimistic about her fulfillment, he invests her yearning for this domestic ideal with a considerable amount of intense and positive emotion. In his beautifully textured black-and-white images, in the lovingly decorated interiors of the Murdoch home, and in the fluidly staged orchestration of the interaction between family members within the dominant domestic space, he sees wish fulfillment—not quite within Naomi's grasp for most of the film but close enough to be felt—as possible.

It is this desperate hope of reality bending to inner desire which fascinates Sirk, and he does not need to simplify Naomi or any other character in order to vivify it. Henry does seem to be quite a conservative and narrow man, yet his love for his wife, when it surfaces, seems deep and genuine; conceivably, he could evolve in his understanding and become the man she wants him to be. By contrast, Dutch is not a simple antagonist, but a man of real feeling who at one time did appreciate Naomi in a way others did not. Naomi's two daughters—Lily, vibrant yet naïve, and Joyce, uncomfortably pushing herself to be responsible and mature at some cost to her self-expressiveness—are reflective in different ways of their mother's conflicted inner nature. Naomi herself is especially complex, and the counterpoint between melodramatic illumination of a possible course for her and an opposing sense of how difficult it must be to still some aspects of a free-spirited inner self so that others might thrive artfully addresses concerns that women surely felt in the era the film describes, in the era in which it was made, and, in a still different way, in a continuing present. The most cynical interpretation of the film might hold that Naomi, an actress, finally finds in life the perfect role and plays it with conviction. Even in that interpretation, however, it would have to be acknowledged that her motives are understood and appreciated, and her actions sympathetically observed.

Few people in Hollywood (and fewer critics) were aware when Sirk became a contract director at Universal-International in 1950 that he was an uncommonly cultured man who had been a major force in the German theater—and, to some extent, cinema—of the 1920's and 1930's. In retrospect, it may seem bizarre to some that his career took the direction it did at this time. Yet this studio, once thought of as so artistically humble, was the perfect place for a mature Sirk's distinctive gifts to flower and achieve their fullest expression. For one thing, the look of its art direction, sets, and lighting—so openly and brilliantly stylized—lent itself to his ideas about a sophisticated, multileveled approach to melodrama. *All I Desire* was Sirk's ninth film there and the first to be comfortably situated in the genre that would draw forth his best efforts. With its producer, Ross Hunter, Sirk moved on the following year to a remake of the improbable and outrageous *Magnificent Obsession* (1954), the film in which he decisively turned Hollywood's conception of melodrama to his own advantage. That film's great commercial success encouraged him to approach his subsequent work with a higher level of boldness, conviction, and purpose which resulted in six masterpieces, climaxed by *Imitation of Life* in 1959, after which he left Hollywood, never to return.

All I Desire, while tentative in some ways, displays the essentials of his perfected style—dramatic high-contrast lighting (which he retained, unlike most directors, in his color films, as well as in later black-and-white ones), deep-focus compositions which permit remarkably intricate staging in long takes, a sharp foregrounding of objects or effective placing of actors in diagonal patterns, supple camera work combined with a considerable amount of movement within the frame, and unashamedly emotional playing so marked by sincerity that it never feels unnatural. Although not all the distancing devices Sirk would refine through experience—mirrors, metaphorical figures, emotionally charged inanimate objects—are conspicuously present, the impulse to bring a more dispassionate perspective to the material is evoked in the character of the Scandinavian maid, Lena (Lotte Stein), who is sympathetic to Naomi and serves as a kind of Greek chorus. While it cannot compare to such awesome cinematic experiences as *Written on the Wind* (1956) and *The Tarnished Angels* (1957), this is no less clearly a work deeply instilled with Sirk's sensibility and distinguished by its own solid virtues.

The most outstanding of these virtues, undoubtedly, is Stanwyck's radiant performance as Naomi. Sirk was a superb director of most actors, as attested here by his guidance of contract ingenues Henderson and Nelson, who thrive under his guidance as they did not elsewhere. He did not simply instruct Stanwyck, however, now a veteran with years of consummate professionalism behind her who had never failed to attract good projects and remained a strong romantic lead while her contemporaries were turning to character roles. Like most of her other directors, and almost all of her colleagues on both sides of the camera, Sirk especially admired and appreciated her. Skillfully projecting attributes which seem to originate in her own evolved spirit—an aching vulnerability betraying itself within an aura of independence, self-possession, and grave beauty—she imparts to the role of Naomi a special quality which evokes something profoundly essential about the nature of all women. Between them, Sirk and Stanwyck bring cinematic magic to the film's finest moment: Naomi's nocturnal walk to the house she left years before, where inside the members of her family, unaware of her, mingle at the dinner table while she looks at them through a window. Stanwyck's face, in the film's only full-frame close-up, briefly and silently expresses a sudden, sublime response in which eager yearning and deep pain struggle in uncertainty, before Sirk quickly and discreetly cuts away.

Blake Lucas

Reviews
Commonweal. LVIII, August 14, 1953, p. 466.
The Hollywood Reporter. June 19, 1953, p. 3.
McCalls. LXXX, June, 1953, p. 12.
National Parent-Teacher. XLVIII, September, 1953, p. 38.
The New York Times. August 29, 1953, II, p. 10.
Theatre Arts. XXXVII, July, 1953, p. 87.
Variety. June 24, 1953, p. 6.

GLORIA

Released: 1980
Production: Sam Shaw; released by Columbia Pictures
Direction: John Cassavetes
Screenplay: John Cassavetes
Cinematography: Fred Schuler
Editing: George C. Villaseñor
Production design: John Godfrey
Art direction: Rene D'Auriac
Special effects: Connie Brink, Al Griswald, and Ron Ottensen
Makeup: Vince Callahan
Costume design: Peggy Farrell
Sound: Dennis Maitland, Sr., and Jack Jocobsen
Music direction: Bill Conti
Music: Tony Ortega and Tommy Tedesco
Title design: Sam Shaw
MPAA rating: PG
Running time: 121 minutes

Principal characters:
Gloria Swenson	Gena Rowlands
Phil Dawn	John Adames
Jack Dawn	Buck Henry
Jeri Dawn	Julie Carmen
Tony Tanzini	Basilio Franchina
Sill	Val Avery

Although *Gloria* is clearly John Cassavetes' easiest and most accessible film, it is still a hard film for most audiences to appreciate. One of the things that makes Cassavetes' work so difficult for many viewers is that it combines two apparently contradictory qualities: simple, almost primitive plots used to launch stunningly subtle explorations of emotional relationships between characters. Since the emotional events take place, as it were, underneath the actions, between the lines of the dialogue, in the pauses and beats of the acting, it is easy to miss them. One's attention to the fairly routine events of the film can actually get in the way of understanding of what is really going on in it.

The plot of *Gloria* is as simple and schematic as the plot of a dream or a fairytale: A six-year-old Puerto Rican boy named Phil (John Adames) is marked for assassination by the mob after the rest of his family is wiped out in a gangland massacre which they believe he witnessed. In hiding, he is put into the hands of a street-smart gangster's paramour and former gun moll, Gloria (Gena Rowlands). Thus thrown together and far from fond of each other, Cassavetes' odd couple hides from the mobsters pursuing them—by day searching for a way out of New York City, by night sleeping and passing the time in cheap hotels. With hit men hot on their heels, they flee across Manhattan and northern New Jersey. The plot can be encapsulated that simply. It certainly cannot be called new.

On this old and rickety scaffolding, Cassavetes builds an almost unfathomably complex structure of emotional interactions between his mismatched central pair. What distinguishes *Gloria* from a sentimental piece such as *Little Miss Marker* (1934; remade 1980) is this complexity and subtlety.

Cassavetes teaches his viewer to see and hear a film in unaccustomed ways. One learns to see and hear the secret impulses that lie beneath characters' brave public expressions. One hears the special tone that comes into Gloria's voice when she mentions the name of her former lover, Tony Tanzini (Basilio Franchina). Underneath Phil's tough-guy posturing, one hears and sees his deep need for Gloria, which he denies even to himself. One sees the profound emotional dependence of these two figures on each other in the moments when they most passionately protest their autonomy.

It seems positively necessary for Cassavetes to reduce to a minimum the practical, worldly events in his work in order to make room for the spiritual and emotional events which most interest him. Freed from close attention to plot, his viewers are invited to enter into an imaginative, speculative relationship with the material of his films. In minimizing or downplaying the plot, Cassavetes' goal is to open up his scenes to the registration of imaginative impulses and swerves of feeling that would be lost or suppressed in a flurry of physical events and interactions. As pint-sized Phil and hardened Gloria flee through the boroughs of New York, the events that interest Cassavetes are the inward, almost invisible, emotional transactions between them involving their oscillations of love and hate, attraction and repulsion, need and pride. *Gloria* is less interested in the codes of gangland warfare than in the endless warfare that takes place between characters' desires for independence and self-sufficiency and their emotional susceptibilities and needs for one another.

If one had to summarize all Cassavetes' work in one sentence, one might say that his films are studies of characters' fundamental confusions about themselves and their needs for others. The problem with that description, however, is that it makes his work sound too much like that of Neil Simon or Woody Allen. Bickering, frightened, half-in-love Phil and Gloria might seem to be a star-crossed, screwball pair in the tradition of Oscar and Felix, Annie and Alvy. Cassavetes' characters, however, represent confusions of feeling much deeper than those in Allen's or Simon's work. While these filmmakers' characters are always relatively sane, rational, and verbally coherent, Cassavetes' characters embody muddles of contradictory impulses far beyond their capacities to articulate. Simon's or Allen's characters are never allowed to become as confused or confusing—to themselves, to others in their films, or to their audiences—as Cassavetes' characters. Characters in a Simon or Allen film can nearly always explain themselves and their actions. Cassavetes' characters, however—such figures as Cosmo Vitelli or Gloria Swenson or Robert Harmon—do not even know when they are confused or mistaken or unhappy, and they certainly cannot theorize about their emotional states or verbalize their problems.

More fundamentally, Cassavetes' work suggests that the clarity of purpose and expression that one encounters in an Allen or Simon film represents a lie about the basic truths of people's emotional lives. One cannot step outside oneself to see one's own most important problems. One cannot remove oneself far enough from one's own feelings to verbalize one's confusions. Cassavetes' films open to view a realm of emotional bewilderments and cross-purposes whose essence is that they will not be brought to full consciousness, will not be expressed verbally, will not be known abstractly. Cassavetes' films utterly deny the faith in reason and language as a means of understanding upon which Simon's and Allen's films are predicated.

To cultivate the complexity of feelings and beliefs which he is interested in dramatizing, Cassavetes presents what might be called "unanalyzed" behavior. That is to say, his characters display behaviors too multivalent or muddled or changeable to be reduced to a leading trait or theme. In contrast, at a given moment in a Simon or Allen picture, one can almost always locate a particular problem by which the star performer is victimized. Like all Cassavetes' principal characters, Gloria and Phil, and their relationship with each other, defy abstract analysis.

Their relationship resists analysis in the same way that events and persons in life outside of films do. It resists being organized into a predictable pattern or an abstract trajectory of development. The result, as all Cassavetes' films demonstrate, is relationships and scenes continuously on the move. Like parts of a Calder mobile, Gloria and Phil rotate around each other at constantly changing distances, endlessly—and often unconsciously—readjusting their positions.

At the beginning of the film, Gloria is snugly ensconced in her womblike apartment high above her decaying Bronx neighborhood. Surrounded by her memorabilia, she has built herself a cozy world of emotional comfort and stability. Her taffy-colored cat is the only love in her life—a love that makes no demands that cannot be instantly and easily met. Phil not only forces her down out of her sanctuary to negotiate the littered pavements of New York, but, more important, he also forces her to renegotiate emotional territory that she had long since left behind. In Cassavetes' work, the repressed always returns. Phil salutarily messes up Gloria's life by bringing out in her maternal and sexual feelings that she thought she had forever forgotten.

In a nicely understated symbolic touch, as Gloria passes through the glass doors of her apartment building out onto the mess and confusion of the street, she accidentally drops her cat as she reaches out to help Phil. The fact that a viewer sees it happen while Gloria remains ignorant of the exchange only adds to the emotional importance of the moment. Without realizing it, Gloria has irrevocably given up one sort of relationship for another.

The subtlest adjustments of relationship in *Gloria*, however, are not presented abstractly or symbolically, but locally, in the second-by-second development of each scene. Notwithstanding the action-heavy genre requirements of his film, Cassavetes makes time and space for the registration of the tiniest fluxes of feeling. Thus, the scenes upon which he lavishes the most care are those in which almost nothing external is happening: scenes in which Phil and Gloria bide their time in a hotel room, one in which they visit a cemetery together, several in which they argue with each other on the street.

All Cassavetes' work addresses the need to exhume and exorcise the emotional ghosts that individuals have buried or suppressed. For Cassavetes, it is in owning such feelings, in not screening them out or aspiring to a merely mechanical consistency of behavior, that people are true to themselves. It is a moral imperative in his work that one must remain continuously open to influences and susceptibilities, that one must face the truth of one's own muddlements of feelings. Moreover, to do that one must throw away all of the predetermined "scripts" and prescriptive "stage directions" that would limit one's responsiveness.

Though *Gloria* is concerned superficially with the way two people avoid physical entrapment or capture through an inventive course of eccentrically improvised actions, the true subject of the film is the way the human heart avoids entrapment, or capture, or prediction. It is about the way two people can open up to each other emotionally, even as the world closes down around them physically. Gloria and Phil reveal grand, operatic possibilities of emotional movement even in situations of the most daunting physical confinement. Cassavetes gives his characters possibilities of life and growth in the most oppressive circumstances. As not only the ending, but the whole of *Gloria* suggests, one can find emotional and imaginative openings out of even the most frightening or worldly dead ends.

In the largest sense, what *Gloria* teaches is that if one would attempt to "beat the system" that threatens to regiment the soul or imprison the heart, one must become a postmodern personality. One must become as mercurial and slippery as the improvised meanings that people continuously make and remake, as open to one's spontaneous impulses and feelings as Gloria shows herself to be by the end of the film.

Even the unitary "self"—as it exists in works of "well-made" drama and in the theoretical postulates of psychology—becomes something that must be discarded, left behind. It is a dead end for development. As Gloria reveals in this film—and as all Cassavetes' other works also show—to survive one must become an improviser of one's own endlessly shifting identity.

As Gloria gloriously, ebulliently demonstrates, American heroism ultimately requires that one leave all homes behind. One must hit the road and be willing to make all meaning and significant relationships on the run. One must learn to live on what William James called "the perilous edge" of experience—continuously breasting nonentity, continuously threatened with slipping back into nonentity. One must, in Cassavetes' dramatic universe, embrace an ethic of endless, unstable, uncomfortable improvisation—in the emotional, the physical, and the theatrical senses of the word. One must find one's comfort in that anxious, endless state of struggle and redefinition, if comfort is to be found at all.

Raymond Carney

Reviews
American Film. VI, January/February, 1981, p. 18.
Chicago Tribune. October 14, 1980, III, p. 2.
The Christian Century. XCVII, December 24, 1980, p. 1277.
Films in Review. XXXI, October, 1980, p. 475.
Los Angeles. XXV, October, 1980, p. 250.
Los Angeles Times. October 19, 1980, p. C37.
The New York Times. October 1, 1980, III, p. 19.
Newsweek. XCVI, October 6, 1980, p. 72.
Saturday Review. VII, October, 1980, p. 93.
Sight and Sound. L, Winter/Spring, 1981, p. 42.
Time. CXVI, October 6, 1980, p. 92.
Variety. September 10, 1980, p. 30.

THE HASTY HEART

Released: 1949
Production: Howard Lindsay and Russel Crouse for Warner Bros.
Direction: Vincent Sherman
Screenplay: Ranald MacDougall; based on the play "The Hasty Heart," by
　John Patrick
Cinematography: Wilkie Cooper
Editing: E. B. Jarvis
Art direction: Terence Verity
Costume design: Peggy Henderson
Sound: Harold V. King
Music direction: Louis Levy
Music: John Beaver
Running time: 102 minutes

> *Principal characters:*
> Yank .... Ronald Reagan
> Sister Margaret Parker .... Patricia Neal
> Lachlen "Lachie" McLachlen .... Richard Todd
> Colonel Dunn .... Anthony Nicholls
> Tommy .... Howard Crawford
> Kiwi .... Ralph Michael
> Digger .... John Sherman
> The Orderly .... Alfred Bass
> Blossom .... Orlando Martins

"Sorrow is born in the hasty heart." As true as that may be, a man can use this kind of sentiment to isolate himself from the world around him. It can be used to protect him against his fellowman, leaving him unable to give of himself because he is afraid of what he might receive from others. When he is finally confronted with the selfless generosity of true friendship, he changes.

To remain closed and thereby impervious to the goodness of men or to open one's heart and risk the pain of rejection—this is the basic conflict of *The Hasty Heart*. The decision rests with Lachlen McLachlen (Richard Todd), a young Scot who is fatally wounded in the Burmese jungle during the last days of World War II. When he learns that he is facing certain death, he no longer has the luxury of time to weigh and measure his decisions. He must open his heart or meet death alone.

McLachlen is hospitalized and assigned to the care of Sister Parker (Patricia Neal), a Canadian nurse who oversees a ward of five men: Yank (Ronald Reagan), a brash American whose self-righteous Scottish grandfather has left him with a sour taste in his mouth for all Scots; Tommy (Howard Crawford), a fat and jolly Englishman; Kiwi (Ralph Michael), a scruffy, bearded New Zealander; Digger (John Sherman), the Australian in the group; and an African from Basutoland whom the men have nicknamed Blossom (Orlando Martins) because it is the only word of English he knows.

McLachlen has not been told that he has only a few weeks to live. Sister Parker and the men know that he has lost a kidney and that the remaining one is defective. The men are asked to befriend him for the time he has left. They nickname the Scot "Lachie," offering him chocolate, cigarettes, and books to read. The irascible loner is suspicious of all men, chooses to bunk alone, and isolates himself from the group. He proudly declares that he "dunna" make friends freely and that he places little value in conversation.

When Sister Parker discovers that Lachie is a member of the Cameron Highlanders but owns no kilt, she and the men purchase one for him for his twenty-fourth birthday. He accepts the gift with great reluctance, admitting that no one ever gave him "tuppence for nothing" and that he is a poor man and cannot hope to repay their kindness.

That night, Lachie privately tells Sister Parker of his lonely youth. A foundling with no education, the world seemed to be against him. Until now he suffered alone but for the first time in his life he feels alive. He confesses he has "shared a moment with kings" and he realizes he has fallen in love with her. Unskilled at friendship, Lachie's newfound feelings cause him to overreact. He becomes unbearably gregarious with the men and mistakes Sister Parker's kindness for love, asking her to marry him. She is overcome with emotion and cannot say no.

The camp commander, Colonel Dunn (Anthony Nicholls), receives a communication that Lachie should be told of his illness and can be flown to Scotland if he wishes, so the doctor finally tells the Scot that he has only a week or two to live. Furious because he believes that the men and Sister Parker have only pitied him and that he has sacrificed his pride for false friendship, Lachie decides to leave the camp even though it means dying alone in Scotland.

Lachie will not listen to Sister Parker when she explains her feelings and the genuine affection the men have for him. Reverting to his closed and angry self, Lachie refuses Yank's farewell handshake. When Blossom offers Lachie a necklace and he flings it back at the African, Yank loses control of his temper. He upbraids the Scot for his ingratitude and meanness, reminding him that Blossom never understood that he was dying and that the gift came from the African's heart, not from pity.

At first, the stubborn Scot stands by his decision to leave, but finally he breaks into tears, admitting that he does not want to die alone. The other men grant his humble request to stay. He dons his kilt and as the group poses for Sister Parker's camera, Lachie slips Blossom's necklace over his head and Yank rests his arm on Lachie's shoulder.

The picture was filmed entirely in England at Elstreet Studios to utilize Warner's "frozen funds," profits held in that country after World War II. It was financed partially by Warner Bros. and partially by Associated British Pictures Corporation. Director Vincent Sherman (who is listed as a producer in the British credits for the film) and Warner contract players Reagan and Neal were sent from Hollywood. The remainder of the cast and crew were British.

A Scot named Gordon Jackson was strongly recommended to play Lachie, but when Sherman met Richard Todd at a cocktail party he was convinced that Todd would be perfect as the taciturn Scot. Although the actor was Irish and had dark hair (studio head Jack Warner thought all Scots were sandy-haired), his outstanding portrayal made Todd an international film star overnight.

Neal was also a relative newcomer to the screen. According to Sherman, she lacked confidence about her ability to play the Canadian nurse, but she succeeded in overcoming her insecurities to create a subtly blended character. At one moment she is a no-nonsense professional woman. In the next she is a nurturing mother. By moonlight, she is the angel of mercy and understanding that inspires Lachie's love.

Along with *King's Row* (1941), *The Hasty Heart* stands out as one of Reagan's best performances. Yank's freshness and quick temper gave Reagan the opportunity for a broad range of scenes. Particularly memorable is his recitation of the books of the Old Testament, in which he demonstrates to the other men the lasting effects of his Scottish grandfather's discipline.

Filmed on a modest budget of $800,000, the picture was faithful to the play and only a few establishing scenes of documentary war footage were added to "open up" the confined drama. Sherman's direction gives the drama the pace it needs to overcome the limitations of a theatrical script. His camera angles and compositions successfully develop the tenuous relationship between the group and Lachie, visually complementing Ranald MacDougall's beautifully constructed adaptation of John Patrick's play. Always working against the physical and psychic confinement of the hospital ward, the drama moves effortlessly through character revelation and reversals. Much of the story's tension comes from the relationship between Yank and Lachie. In his own way, Yank reflects the stubbornness of the Scot. He is as hard-bent on being friendly as Lachie is determined to be lonely.

The original characters in Patrick's play were based on the writer's experiences in combat in Burma. There he met a crusty Scottish sergeant who was the basis for Lachie's character. Like Yank, Patrick contracted malaria and recovered in a military hospital in India. He wrote the play in only twelve days on his way home from North Africa.

As in other war films, such as *Destination Tokyo* (1943) and *A Walk in the Sun* (1945), *The Hasty Heart* surrounds the three central characters with "types" rather than individuals. The men are identified by their nationalities and nicknames, retaining the anonymity of war even in the intimacy of the hospital ward. Poignantly, the soldiers, who have been living with death for years at the front and have seen hundreds of men brutally killed in action, are deeply moved when they learn that such a young man will die from uremic poisoning. Whatever horrors they have witnessed during war, the process of one individual facing death still has profound meaning to them. Yet, while the picture is full of sentiment and tearful moments, it is the comic touch which audiences have fondly remembered. What does a Scot wear under his kilt? In the film's closing scene, the men learn the answer when Tommy lifts Lachie's kilt, but Lachie's secret is slyly kept from the audience.

The Hasty Heart received excellent reviews, and was especially popular in England. The readers of the London *Daily Mail* awarded the picture its National Film Award for 1950.

Joanne L. Yeck

Reviews
The Christian Century. LXVII, February 8, 1950, p. 191.
Commonweal. LI, February 3, 1950, p. 464.
Film Daily. December 2, 1949, p. 7.
Films in Review. I, March, 1950, p. 32.
The New Republic. CXXII, February 6, 1950, p. 22.
The New York Times. January 22, 1950, II, p. 1.
The New Yorker. XXV, January 28, 1950, p. 74.
Newsweek. XXXV, January 30, 1950, p. 72.
Time. LV, February 13, 1950, p. 88.
Variety. September 2, 1949, p. 8.

SEVEN MEN FROM NOW

Released: 1956
Production: Andrew V. McLaglen and Robert E. Morrison for Batjac Productions; released by Warner Bros.
Direction: Budd Boetticher
Screenplay: Burt Kennedy
Cinematography: William H. Clothier
Editing: Everett Sutherland
Art direction: Leslie Thomas
Sound: Earl Crain, Jr.
Music: Henri Vars
Running time: 77 minutes

Principal characters:
Ben Stride .... Randolph Scott
Annie Greer .... Gail Russell
Masters .... Lee Marvin
John Greer .... Walter Reed
Pate Bodeen .... John Larch
Clete .... Donald Barry

Perhaps the Western has yet to yield all of its secrets. Once the most popular genre in American cinema, it was finally debased in the 1970's, then in the 1980's virtually disappeared save for a few works (*Silverado* and *Pale Rider*, both 1985, are conspicuous examples) which attempted its resurrection but were so simplistic in their comprehension of classical models that the results were coarse to the point of seeming almost parodistic. Few tasks could prove more rewarding to the film critic, film scholar, film buff, or general filmgoer than to rediscover the innate sensitivity which guides the Western at its most formally refined; for in the simple stories, which follow deeply traditional patterns and demand an iconography as worn by use as the leather on an old saddle, there may exist a tonic, even visionary perception of human experience as a rite of passage in which the potential rewards are a higher understanding and a renewal of harmony with the earth and with the male-female duality that seeks vital expression on earth.

When conscientiously executed, Westerns are not ceaseless displays of action—for a few well-played violent confrontations are all the action needed to create a catharsis—nor do they illustrate a pure hero who unwaveringly rights all wrongs and rides on, immune to feelings which might compromise his sense of mission. The greater task of the Western hero is to perceive the limits of his virtue and to acknowledge his fallibility, so that he may finally transcend his physical actions and manifest a rare spiritual enlightenment. No one is more important in aiding him in this task than the heroine, whose superficially peripheral role in the broad outline of the narrative allows her to be treated with a stimulating flexibility. Chastely or not, she is waiting for the fullest expression of her femininity until some subtle shift of consciousness, shared by hero and heroine even if unarticulated, allows him to become the man he was always capable of being. In the beauty of that exchange also lies the truth that the genre is not predominantly an expression of masculine fantasy, formerly thought, but a form more capable than any of evoking a pristine romanticism. Further, a third essential figure, the villain—who may even be the most compelling of the three—exists not only to be the manifestation of a morally corrupt male alternative but also, more crucially, to be a catalytic force in drawing hero and heroine to each other. Without the tension his presence creates, they would drift on separately, too reticent to acknowledge the ideal of their fulfilled love.

Seven Men from Now is a great Western partly because its perfect understanding of these inherent truths of the genre is exhibited without a trace of pretension. Story and cinematic realization are imaginative and stylish, yet simple and direct. In common with other journey Westerns which focus primarily or exclusively on a small group of characters—the narrative is very concentrated and characterization is central, so that the allusion to an existential quest arises naturally out of a straightforward presentation of the literal journey and its tangible objectives.

Former sheriff Ben Stride (Randolph Scott) is seeking revenge against the seven men who killed his wife while holding up a Wells Fargo office in Silver Springs; he also seeks to recover the strongbox full of gold which they stole. After killing two of the outlaws in a shoot-out, he comes to the aid of an Eastern couple, John (Walter Reed) and Annie Greer (Gail Russell), who are traveling by wagon to the town of Flora Vista, en route to California. At a stagecoach station, the group is joined by Masters (Lee Marvin) and his henchman Clete (Donald Barry); not among the men for whom Stride is looking, they intend to take possession of the gold by force when he finds it. The loquacious Masters is an old adversary of the taciturn Stride and enjoys taunting him in various ways as the journey continues, but he also saves Stride's life by killing the third of the outlaws in a mysterious encounter. When Masters savors telling a story to Stride and the Greers as the four drink coffee inside the wagon one rainy night—the story involves a wife who leaves her gentle husband for a stronger man, and Masters pointedly underscores the resemblances between the alleged real people he is describing and the people he is telling the story to—Stride forcefully suggests that he and Clete ride on alone. Stride then discovers that John Greer has been transporting the gold for the outlaws, and he unloads the strongbox in a patch of desert between some high rocks and waits for them. Arriving in

Flora Vista, a guilt-ridden Greer—aware of Annie's disappointment in him and her unspoken affection for Stride—refuses to cooperate any further with the outlaw leader, Pate Bodeen (John Larch), and Bodeen kills him when he attempts to go to the sheriff's office. A three-way showdown over the gold ensues among Bodeen and his remaining partners, Stride, and Masters and Clete; and after all the others are dead, Masters—who has even ruthlessly shot his own ally—emerges from the rocks and challenges a wounded Stride, who kills him in open confrontation. Departing from Flora Vista to return the gold, Stride says goodbye to Annie, but their mutual hope to meet again becomes an expressed intention.

Especially impressive in director Budd Boetticher's knowing treatment of Burt Kennedy's skillfully conceived original screenplay are the flamboyance of Masters and the delicately understated eroticism of the relationship between Stride and Annie, elements of the film which are effectively contrasted with each other while also being interdependent. Masters may not be in all respects Stride's satanic double—as bereft of both inhibitions and morals as Stride is ruled by them—but to a great extent, he knows the other (much of what the viewer learns about Stride one learns from him), speaks for him (telling his story, he stares at Annie with undisguised pleasure, seductively emphasizing ways in which the other woman was "a lot like you—but not near as pretty"), and derives a perverse pleasure from the ambivalence of their relationship (he confronts Stride fairly in the climax partly out of a need for the other's respect, and Stride kills him with visible regret). Visually defined by his ostentatious bright green scarf, Masters so consistently manifests a ready affability and reckless unpredictability that he is, up to a point, a more attractive character than the hero and one whose villainy generates a complex response. While he knows all the details of Stride's immediate past, he is too insensitive to appreciate Stride's inner feelings, revealed in an intimate confession to Annie—Stride's wife took the job at the Wells Fargo office, which resulted in her death, because after losing the election for sheriff, he was too proud to take a lesser job that might diminish his masculine self-image. In Annie, Stride finds again a womanly softness and understanding which might free him from the guilt he suffers for having tragically disdained those same qualities in his wife (and in himself). Annie's loyalty to her husband, despite Greer's evident unmanly cowardice (which Stride, though more quietly than Masters, also despises), contains a lesson he must absorb.

Ironically, Stride's emotional progress parallels Greer's moral progress, for Greer gains belated courage when he renounces the moral weakness that is probably the greater cause of his wife's diminished love, while in an ironic echo of this, total moral weakness is what makes Masters the villain and, for all of his bravado and charisma, a man who is never alluring to Annie. Though always honorable, Stride is not the representative of masculine wholeness that he might be until he has found revenge to be an empty experience and is ready to re-create his life out of a newly enlightened spirit. Therefore, the awakening love he shares with Annie must, until then, remain mute and restrained, but it is for that reason so charged with emotion that the most innocent touch—Stride lifting Annie off her horse—can evoke more passion than a torrid love scene.

In a drama as much moral and sexual as physical, the sophistication with which themes and attitudes are explored is admirably casual, contained within a frame in which the emphasis is on humor, picturesque images, and narrative clarity. Boetticher makes the landscape through which the characters journey—rocks and desert, prairie and rivers—seem primal and captivatingly innocent, allows a relaxed atmosphere to prevail as the characters drift into the incidental sharing of thoughts that their enforced intimacy encourages, and waits with steady composure for the sequence of decisive action, staged with exhilarating flair when it finally arrives, which resolves Stride's melancholy quest.

Seven Men from Now benefits throughout from a happy confluence of talent. Boetticher, who earlier had only imprinted an appreciable measure of his personality on two films about bullfighting (*The Bullfighter and the Lady,* 1951, based on his own experiences, and *The Magnificent Matador,* 1955), finally found the perfect vehicle to reveal him as a major cinematic artist of impressive individuality. Special, too, are the performances of the three leads. Russell, one of the most beautiful and appealingly sweet actresses of the 1940's, had been long absent from the screen because of personal problems, but registers here as the same tender, haunting presence. Marvin was in the best phase of his career, as a supporting actor specializing in colorful villains, and has never been more memorable. Exemplary of the silver-haired, lean-faced actor's uncommon skill in this kind of role is the way in which he turns Masters' death into what is almost a ballet of dazed disbelief. Innately dignified and gentlemanly, Scott, entering his twilight years on the screen, possesses an understated authority and an aura of mature goodness that make his introspective protagonist a figure of mythical beauty; irreplaceable, Scott ranks with John Wayne, James Stewart, and Joel McCrea among the classical Western's strongest heroes.

A series of seven Boetticher-directed Scott Westerns—now commonly known as the Ranown cycle (though only five of the films were made by the Randolph Scott-Harry Joe Brown production company from which the name was derived)—began with this Batjac production. *The Tall T* (1957), *Ride Lonesome* (1959), and *Comanche Station* (1960) were once again written by Kennedy; *Decision at Sundown* (1957), *Buchanan Rides Alone* (1958), and *Westbound* (1959; a Warner Bros. studio project) are the other three works. The series is now considered one of the major achievements of the genre, to the extent that Boetticher is commonly accorded the kind of critical acknowledgment in studies of the Western that such imposing figures as John Ford, Howard Hawks, and Anthony Mann enjoy. In truth, the Ranown cycle is less even than, for example, Mann's James Stewart series, though, along with *Seven Men from Now*, *Ride Lonesome*, and *Comanche Station* are also masterpieces which magnificently refine and explore in new ways the motifs of this seminal work—the journey, the lost or dead wife, definitions of masculinity and femininity, ambivalent villainy, revenge, solitude, and existential morality. The later works are emotionally bleaker, with the Scott hero characteristically alone once more at the fadeout. No less aware of this potential for a tragic isolation, *Seven Men from Now* is more poised at the edge of hopefulness, offering—in a final parting which evokes those of such other great Westerns as Ford's *My Darling Clementine* (1946) and Mann's *The Man from Laramie* (1955)—an intimation that the painful past may be laid to rest and the future is glowing with bright promise.

Blake Lucas

Reviews
Cahiers du cinéma. LXXIV, August/September, 1957.
The Hollywood Reporter. July 11, 1956, p. 3.
National Parent-Teacher. LI, October, 1956, p. 39.
Variety. July 11, 1956, p. 6.

THEY WON'T BELIEVE ME

Released: 1947
Production: Joan Harrison for RKO Radio Pictures
Direction: Irving Pichel
Screenplay: Jonathan Latimer; based on an unpublished story by Gordon McDonell
Cinematography: Harry J. Wild
Editing: Elmo Williams
Art direction: Albert S. D'Agostino and Robert Boyle; set decoration, Darrell Silvera and William Magginetti
Music: Roy Webb
MPAA rating: no listing
Running time: 95 minutes

> *Principal characters:*
> Larry Ballentine . . . . Robert Young
> Verna Carlson . . . . Susan Hayward
> Janice Bell . . . . Jane Greer
> Gretta . . . . Rita Johnson
> Trenton . . . . Tom Powers
> Lieutenant Carr . . . . George Tyne
> Thomason . . . . Don Beddoe
> Cahill . . . . Frank Ferguson
> Judge Fletcher . . . . Harry Harvey

In a hot Los Angeles courtroom, defense attorney Cahill (Frank Ferguson) is presenting his case. He summons his client, Larry Ballentine (Robert Young), to the stand to tell his story; Ballentine is accused of murdering Verna Carlson (Susan Hayward). In a flashback, occasionally narrated in voice-over, Larry recounts the events.

In New York City, during a previous summer, Ballentine is talking to Janice Bell (Jane Greer) in a secluded café. It is a regular afternoon liaison, and they discuss a yacht Ballentine is buying with the intention of using it to further their illicit relationship. On his way home to his wife, Ballentine buys a cigarette case for Janice, to replace a broken one. On arriving at his apartment, however, Ballentine discovers that he has forgotten to buy his wife, Gretta (Rita Johnson), an anniversary present and gives her the cigarette case. Soon after, he and Janice meet again in the café. The magazine for which she writes is transferring her to Montreal and she asks Larry to go with her and resolve the current difficult triangle situation. He agrees.

That night, Ballentine is surprised by Gretta while packing. She is amazingly good-humored, saying that she knows about his leaving but does not blame him. Ironically, she says, she has just purchased a half interest for Ballentine in a West Coast stock brokerage. Ballentine reconsiders, and the viewer next encounters him and his wife on a train bound for California. In a conversation in their Pullman car, Gretta reveals that she has known of Larry's infidelity for a long time.

Larry is next seen in his role as a partner at Trenton and Ballentine in Los Angeles. His partner, Trenton (Tom Powers), considers him lazy and shiftless. A secretary, Verna Carlson (Susan Hayward), gets him out of a jam with Trenton by drafting and sending a prospectus to a client whom Larry had forgotten. (It is intimated that Verna had been Trenton's lover in the past.) While having drinks later at Verna's house, they coyly discuss her golddigging, and it is clear that she is pursuing him.

During the course of his affair with Verna, Gretta announces that she is moving to a remote mountain ranch, as someone has advised her of Larry's relationship with the secretary. He is invited to accompany her or give up any claim to her money.

Surrendering his position at the brokerage, Larry accompanies Gretta to the ranch, which is completely isolated, without even a phone. There Gretta makes friends with a horse which has a habit of waiting for her as she visits a steep, rocky canyon. After some time, Gretta relents and decides to have visitors at the ranch, sending Larry to Los Angeles to arrange for an extra room to be built. From the general store near the ranch, he telephones Verna and arranges to meet her in Los Angeles. There, he tells her of his scheme to embezzle his wife's money and arranges to meet her later at the general store. The store owner, Thomason (Don Beddoe), notices them together.

As they elope to Reno, they are involved in an accident in which Verna is killed. Unconscious, Larry is dragged from the wreck. Awakening in the hospital days later, he discovers that it is believed that Gretta perished in the wreck, the wedding ring being the crucial evidence for this assumption.

Larry decides to go ahead with the deception and kill Gretta, who he presumes is still at the remote ranch. On arriving at Thomason's, he discovers that the people of the mountain community also believe Gretta is dead; she has not been seen. Borrowing Thomason's truck, he drives to the house. Larry looks for Gretta and finds her dead at the bottom of the canyon on the property, watched over by her horse. He drops her body into the pool at the base of the canyon.

After a connecting reference to the framing story in the courtroom, Larry is next seen in Jamaica, where he is extremely depressed and appears to be contemplating suicide. He meets Janice by an apparent coincidence (she has since relocated to Los Angeles), and they begin dating again. They fly back to Los Angeles together. That evening, Larry arrives to pick up Janice and discovers her meeting Trenton, discussing an ongoing investigation of Larry and his actions. It is clear, however, that Janice is sympathetic to Larry.

Soon after, a woman named Susan Haines, who claims to be Verna's roommate, visits Larry, ostensibly to track down Verna for back rent. When Larry tells her that he has no knowledge of Verna's whereabouts, she tells him that she will take the matter to the police. Larry, shaken, pays the small bill himself. Later, he confronts Trenton, who now holds the check he had given Haines. Trenton accuses Larry of killing Verna in order to avoid her blackmailing him, then driving off to have the accident that killed his wife. Thomason is brought in, seemingly corroborating this version of events. Los Angeles police are summoned.

Larry is then taken to the ranch, which is being searched. A policeman spots Gretta's horse, lying at the bottom of the canyon. At the moment the suffering horse is to be shot Gretta's body is discovered; it is battered beyond recognition.

Resuming the framing story, Larry is completing his testimony. The body in the canyon is assumed to be Verna's. During a recess, Janice tells Larry, who is in a holding cell, that she will stand by him after the trail. He refuses her help, saying he has already decided his guilt for himself. The next day, the jury returns its verdict. Before it can be read, Larry tries to jump out of the courtroom window, and a policeman shoots him to death. The verdict is read not guilty.

They Won't Believe Me was shot during the period of Dore Schary's reign as head of production at RKO, the golden age of *film noir* at the studio, a time which also saw the release of films such as *Out of the Past* (1947) and *They Live by Night* (1949). Perhaps as a result of its exclusive company at the studio, *They Won't Believe Me* has gone unrecognized. The film was designed to complete Young's conversion from smooth-faced juvenile (a role of which he had tired at Metro-Goldwyn-Mayer) to a tougher, more adult *persona*, a process begun in RKO's *The Enchanted Cottage* (1945) and *Crossfire* (1947).

The film is also a study of RKO's production team in high gear. Four men—Nicholas Musuraca, George Diskant, Robert DeGrasse, and Harry Wild—shot nearly all the studio's major *films noirs* and borrowed freely from one another to create a remarkably unified visual style. In *They Won't Believe Me*, Wild's shooting of mountain lakes, canyons, and other exteriors is clearly modeled on Musuraca's similar work in *Out of the Past*—crystal clear landscapes and medium shots. The bizarre, selective focus wide-angle close-ups are Wild's own contributions, however.

The entire film is remarkable in that it shows the rich resources and technical capabilities of the studio at work on an average, rather than an extraordinary project.

For director Irving Pichel, this combination of talents was particularly fortuitous. Pichel (1891-1954) was one of the earliest theorists among Hollywood directors of a complex theory of point-of-view, one that did not depend on specious definitions of realism. Instead, his writings draw a distinction between character-centered viewpoints and narrational devices linked to story structure and presentation of plot material. For *They Won't Believe Me*, he was fortunate to be teamed with producer Joan Harrison, a former Hitchcock protegé whose previous work had displayed a clear proclivity toward experimentation in this area. In such films as *Phantom Lady* (1944), *Uncle Harry* (1945), and *Nocturne* (1946), she had dealt with the shifting attributes of truth-telling, through rigidly objective storytelling methods in which versions of criminal events are provided by a revolving group of suspects. In *They Won't Believe Me*, the strategy is taken to an extreme; Ballentine is an utter heel, a Don Juan who steals from and murders his lovers. Yet other characters in *They Won't Believe Me* are presented as equally morally culpable at times. Janice conspires with Trenton to deceive Larry; Verna is a self-admitted golddigger; Gretta cold-bloodedly, obsessively buys Larry's affections; even Thomason, the grocery store owner, is presented as a meddlesome busybody. These judgments, however, are rendered clinically, without harsh cuts to close-ups or musical cues, or even a break from the highly restrained, almost expressionless acting style Pichel enforces on his cast.

It is Larry's attorney, at the beginning of the film, who first sets up this ambivalence. As he introduces the witnesses against Larry, each is given a full-face close-up. Each consciously averts his or her eyes from the camera; one, a detective, manages to sit with his back completely turned to the camera. When the jury is seated, at the very end of the film, rigidly formalized, identical shots of each member give utterly no hint of their opinion; in fact, they have decided that Ballentine is not guilty. Only in Janice's final reaction shot is a hint of the film's ultimate sympathy given.

Visually and narratively, the story is told in a laconic, low-key manner. As with all films of crime and detection, the plot turns on several coincidences and passing ironies. It is from the moral weight of events, however, and a final rendering of judgment on them, that the film draws its power as well as the sense of genuine climax that underlies the theatrical last-second shooting.

Wild's cinematography depends on day shooting and minimal camera movement to develop a deceptively placid surface. Wild also frames Ballentine in shots which somehow seem always to isolate him in his surroundings, whether it is a medium shot of a crowded office, an extreme long shot of a Sierra canyon, or the occasional too-tight close-up.

Screenwriter Jonathan Latimer, a well-known mystery writer, contributes to this sense of near existential alienation; Ballentine often speaks in voice-over during scenes crowded with people whose conversation is pushed off the sound track by Ballentine's meditations. Latimer relies primarily on extended description delivered in Young's flat monotone to establish an unemotional accompaniment to the decisions Ballentine makes. Yet these descriptions always have a sense of the grotesque and a foreboding tone.

In the sequence in which the ranch is searched for Verna's body, the extraordinarily coincidental nature of the discovery of Gretta's body is perfectly in keeping with the various ironies that have already accreted around Ballentine. Unlike other Harrison films, particularly *Uncle Harry*, the film's photo-finish, while technically unmotivated by the plot, serves not to resolve the dilemmas the film poses, but to suspend them permanently over an abyss of the questionable morality of everyone Ballentine has killed, and those he has left behind.

Kevin Jack Hagopian

Reviews

Commonweal. XLVI, August 1, 1947, p. 386.
Life. XXII, March 10, 1947, p. 59.
The New York Times. July 17, 1947, II, p. 16.
The New Yorker. XXIII, July 26, 1947, p. 57.
Newsweek. XXX, August 11, 1947, p. 89.
Theatre Arts. XXXI, September, 1947, p. 14.
Time. XLIX, June 23, 1947, p. 93.
Variety. July 23, 1947, p. 10.

OBITUARIES

Yves Allégret (October 13, 1907-January 31, 1987). Allégret was an important French director in the years immediately following World War II. He was married to actress Simone Signoret from 1944 to 1949, and his films helped make her a star. Working in the *film noir* genre, he made *Les Démons de l'aube* (1946), *Dédée d'Anvers* (1948), and *Manèges* (1950), each featuring Signoret as a woman of questionable virtue. He often worked with screenwriter Jacques Sigurd; they collaborated on *Une Si Jolie Petite Plage* (1949; also known as *Riptide*), which is often cited as Allégret's best work. His last important film was *Les Orgueilleux* (1953), based on a story by Jean-Paul Sartre. Attacked by François Truffaut in a 1954 essay that launched the auteur movement, Allégret's reputation declined quickly, although he continued to make films for another twenty years. His additional films include *Mam'zelle Nitouche* (1954), *Oasis* (1955), *Johnny Banco* (1967), and *Mords pas—on t'aime* (1976).

Irving Allen (November 24, 1905-December 17, 1987). Born in Poland, producer-director Allen moved to the United States as a youth. He began his film career as an editor for Paramount, Republic, and Universal studios. Next he directed short subjects for RKO and Warner Bros., winning an Academy Award nomination for the single reel *Forty Boys and a Song* (1941), and winning the award itself for the two-reeler *Climbing the Matterhorn* (1947). His first feature film was *Strange Voyage* (1945), which he followed with a series of low-budget dramas such as *Avalanche* (1946) and *Slaughter Trail* (1951), his last film as a director. He formed Warwick Films with British producer Albert R. Broccoli in 1953, and produced such Alan Ladd vehicles as *Black Night* (1954) and *Hell Below Zero* (1954). Allen's partnership with Broccoli was dissolved in the early 1960's, shortly before the British producer embarked upon the incredibly successful James Bond series of films. Allen countered with an action-adventure series of his own, starring Dean Martin as Matt Helm in *The Silencers* (1966), *The Ambushers*, (1967), and *The Wrecking Crew* (1969). He also directed *High Conquest* (1947) and *16 Fathoms Deep* (1948). His credits as a producer include *The Red Beret* (1953), *Safari* (1956), *Killers of Kilimanjaro* (1959), *Genghis Khan* (1965), *Cromwell* (1970), and *Eyewitness* (1971).

Leslie Arliss (1901-December 30, 1987). Born Leslie Andrews, Arliss was a British director who achieved his greatest success in the 1940's. The son of actor George Arliss, Arliss broke into films as a screenwriter in the early 1930's, working on *Tonight's the Night* (1932), *Jack Ahoy* (1936), and *The Foreman Went to France* (1942). He codirected *The Farmer's Wife* (1941) with Norman Lee, and his *The Man in Grey* (1943), *Love Story* (1944), and *The Wicked Lady* (1945) helped launch the careers of James Mason, Stewart Granger, and Margaret Lockwood, respectively. He also directed *The Night Has Eyes* (1942), *Idol of Paris* (1948), *See How They Run* (1955), and *Miss Tulip Stays the Night* (1955).

Fred Astaire (May 10, 1899-June 22, 1987). Born Frederick Austerlitz, Astaire was an actor, singer, dancer, and choreographer. He is almost universally conceded to have been the greatest dancer in the history of cinema.

Astaire was the son of Austrian immigrants; he was born in Omaha, Nebraska, but moved to New York before his fifth birthday with his mother and older sister Adele. The two children were given dancing lessons, beginning a partnership that lasted for a quarter of a century. Fred and Adele polished their act on the vaudeville circuit, and in 1916 made their Broadway debut in *Over the Top*, which earned for them rave reviews. Their first starring stage vehicle was *Lady Be Good* in 1924; other noteworthy Broadway successes were *Funny Face* and *The Band Wagon*, which was to be the act's last show. Adele married a British nobleman and retired from show business in 1932, while Astaire danced alone in *The Gay Divorcée* (1934) to mixed reviews.

Astaire's stage success attracted the attention of Hollywood talent scouts. Although they were unimpressed with his screen test ("Can't act. Slightly bald. Can dance a little."), he won a small part opposite Joan Crawford in *Dancing Lady* (1933), in which he wore the top hat and tails that were to become his trademark. That same year, he appeared in *Flying Down to Rio* (1933). Although he received only sixth billing, he was paired with Ginger Rogers, who was a last-minute replacement for a dancer named Dorothy Jordan. Their lengthy duet in "The Carioca" was a sensation; the film's success saved its studio, RKO, from bankruptcy; and Astaire and Rogers began a partnership that was to last for ten more films and leave an indelible mark on film history. Astaire formed another important association during the filming of *Flying Down to Rio*: He met Hermes Pan, a choreographer with whom he would work extensively for the rest of his career.

RKO quickly cast Astaire and Rogers in the film version of *The Gay Divorcée*, in which Astaire played an impetuous but affable dancer who falls in love with an initially reluctant Rogers; she spars with him throughout the film but is eventually won over. This basic formula was to serve Astaire and Rogers well throughout their partnership. *The Gay Divorcée* featured Cole Porter's score (including "Night and Day" and "The Continental"), and Astaire's pleasant, if untrained, voice added to the film's success.

Roberta (1935), with its Jerome Kern score, solidified the pair's success. *Top Hat* (1935), *Follow the Fleet* (1936), *Swing Time* (1936, featuring the pair's finest dancing), *Shall We Dance* (1937), *Carefree* (1938), and *The Story of Vernon and Irene Castle* (1939) are all landmarks in the genre of the film musical. At that point, the partnership dissolved, with Rogers concentrating on dramatic parts and Astaire, who was concerned about being identified too closely with Rogers, acting and dancing with other partners.

His new costars included Eleanor Powell in *Broadway Melody of 1940* (1940), and Rita Hayworth twice, in *You'll Never Get Rich* (1941) and *The Sky's the Limit* (1943). He spent the next few years entertaining American troops in USO shows, made three uninspired and financially unsuccessful films, and announced his retirement in 1946.

Astaire came out of retirement in 1948 at the behest of Metro-Goldwyn-Mayer whose new dancing star Gene Kelly had broken his ankle shortly after the start of production of *Easter Parade* (1948). Astaire replaced Kelly opposite costar Judy Garland, the film was an artistic and financial success, and Astaire's film career resumed. When Garland's health proved to be too fragile to permit her to work with Astaire in *The Barkleys of Broadway* (1949), he was paired with Ginger Rogers one last time after a ten-year hiatus.

Astaire continued to make films regularly for the next twenty years. He performed creditably in his first dramatic role in *On the Beach* (1959), and this led to other nonmusical roles, including *The Towering Inferno* (1974), for which he received an Academy Award nomination as Best Supporting Actor. His last dancing film was Francis Coppola's ill-conceived *Finian's Rainbow* (1968), in which the director placed Astaire's disembodied dancing feet on the screen for the first time. Astaire had always insisted on longer shots that did not fragment his dancing. He cohosted MGM's two successful retrospectives of the golden age of Hollywood musicals, *That's Entertainment* (1974) and *That's Entertainment II* (1976). His last film was *Ghost Story* (1981).

Fred Astaire has been the subject of several biographies; in 1960, he published an autobiography, *Steps in Time*. He appeared on television occasionally, winning two Emmy Awards for his work in that medium. Over the years, Astaire's name has become synonymous with grace. Certainly no other dancer has had such an impact on film audiences. In 1949, Hollywood honored Astaire with a special Academy Award "for his unique artistry and his contributions to the technique of musical pictures." His additional film appearances include *A Damsel in Distress* (1937), *Second Chorus* (1940), *Holiday Inn* (1942), *Blue Skies* (1946), *Daddy Long Legs* (1955), *Funny Face* (1957), *Silk Stockings* (1957), and *Midas Run* (1969).

Mary Astor (May 3, 1905-September 25, 1987). Born Lucille Vasconcellos Langhanke, Astor was a talented actress who survived a series of scandals to star in numerous films in a forty-five-year acting career that bridged the silent and sound eras. Her father encouraged her to study acting, moving his family to Hollywood to further his daughter's career. She landed a film contract in 1920 and soon won several bit parts in minor films.

John Barrymore chose her to play opposite him in *Beau Brummel* (1924), and the role made her a star; though the actor was twenty-four years her senior, she also became his mistress. Astor made more than twenty films through the end of the silent era. With the advent of sound, she went back to the stage to improve her vocal delivery, and by 1930, her talents were again in demand.

In 1935, she entered into an unpleasant divorce and child-custody battle with her second husband, who introduced what was purported to be Astor's diary as evidence of her unsuitability as a mother. The diary, which Astor claimed was forged, revealed intimate details of her affair with writer George S. Kaufman, but her studio head, Sam Goldwyn, gave her public support, and her career survived the scandal.

The late 1930's and early 1940's were the most productive years of her career. She appeared in *Dodsworth* (1936), *The Prisoner of Zenda* (1937), and *The Great Lie* (1941), for which she won an Academy Award as Best Supporting Actress opposite Bette Davis. That same year, she appeared as Brigid O'Shaughnessy opposite Humphrey Bogart's Sam Spade in *The Maltese Falcon* (1941), the role for which she is best remembered.

By 1949, her problems with alcohol were serious enough to prevent her from working, and in 1951, she nearly died from an overdose of sleeping pills. She entered psychotherapy and conquered her illness; as part of her therapy, she wrote a frank autobiography, *My Story*, which was published in 1959. She also began acting again, appearing in a series of popular melodramas such as *Return to Peyton Place* (1961) and *Youngblood Hawke* (1964). Her last film was *Hush Hush . . . Sweet Charlotte* (1965), in which she once again appeared with Bette Davis. Astor published four novels in the 1960's, and a second volume of memoirs, *A Life on Film*, in 1967. Her additional acting credits include *Puritan Passions* (1923), *Don Juan* (1926), *Red Dust* (1932), *The Hurricane* (1937), *The Palm Beach Story* (1942), *Little Women* (1949), *A Kiss Before Dying* (1956), and *Stranger in My Arms* (1959).

Sherwood Bailey (August 6, 1923-August 6, 1987). Bailey was a freckled child actor who played the role of Spud in the Our Gang comedies of the 1930's. As a teenager, he acted in such films as *Too Many Parents* (1936) and *Young Thomas Edison* (1940).

Alfred Bass (April 8, 1921-July 15, 1987). Bass was a British character actor who specialized in comedy, often playing Cockney roles. His first film was *Johnny Frenchman* (1945), and he appeared in dozens of films in a career that spanned thirty-five years. His additional acting credits include *The Hasty Heart* (1949), *The Lavender Hill Mob* (1951), *Help!* (1965), *Alfie* (1966), *A Funny Thing Happened on the Way to the Forum* (1966), and *Revenge of the Pink Panther* (1978).

Spencer Gordon Bennet (January 5, 1893-October 8, 1987). Bennet was a director who specialized in Saturday matinee serials. He broke into film in 1912 as a stuntman and worked with George B. Seitz, who directed many popular serials between 1916 and 1925. Bennet directed *The Green Archer* (1925), *The Masked Marvel* (1943), *Superman* (1948, codirected with Thomas Carr), and *Captain Video* (1951, codirected with Wallace Grissell). He directed more than one hundred films in a career that spanned forty-five years. His serials include *The Tiger Woman* (1944) and *Blackhawk* (1952). Other films include *Calling All Cars* (1935), *Arizona Bound* (1941), and *Lone Texas Ranger* (1945).

Alessandro Blasetti (July 3, 1900-February 2, 1987). Blasetti was an important Italian director whose career spanned forty years. Dissatisfied as a lawyer, Blasetti became first a film critic and then a filmmaker. His first film, *Sole* (1929), was produced by a film collective which he helped found. His masterpiece was *1860* (1934), an account of Giuseppe Garibaldi's conquest of Sicily from the point of view of two peasants. His *Quattro passi fra le nuvole* (1942) is often cited as the precursor of the neorealist film, which blossomed in Italy after World War II, and his *Altri Tempi* (1952), which consisted of a series of episodes, created a genre that was to remain prominent in Italian cinema for two decades. Blasetti wrote or cowrote many of his films and acted in several as well. He also played himself in Luchino Visconti's *Bellissima* (1951), which satirized the Italian film industry. Blasetti's additional films include *Vecchia Guardia* (1935), *La corona di ferro* (1941), *Fabiola* (1948), *Prima Communione* (1950), and *Tempi nostri* (1954).

Ray Bolger (January 10, 1904-January 15, 1987). Bolger was a dancer and actor who gave a memorable performance as the Scarecrow in Victor Fleming's classic *The Wizard of Oz* (1939). As a vaudeville dancer, Bolger learned to use his loose-limbed gait to comic effect, and he was a successful Broadway performer in the early 1930's. Although the bulk of his career was spent on the stage, he made more than a dozen films, most of which were musicals. In 1952, he reprised his starring Broadway role in the film version of *Where's Charley?* (1952), which contained his signature tune, "Once in Love with Amy." The sad-eyed comic also appeared in *The Great Ziegfeld* (1936), *Four Jacks and a Jill* (1942), *Stage Door Canteen* (1943), *The Harvey Girls* (1946), *April in Paris* (1953), and *Babes in Toyland* (1961). He played a priest in a straight dramatic role in *The Runner Stumbles* (1979), and his last film appearance was as narrator of *That's Dancing* (1985), an anthology which featured one of

Bolger's dance scenes that had been cut from *The Wizard of Oz*.

William Bowers (January 17, 1916-March 27, 1987). Bowers was a screenwriter whose career spanned a quarter of a century and more than forty films. He was nominated twice for Academy Awards: with André De Toth for *The Gunfighter* (1950) and with James Edward Grant for *The Sheepman* (1958). In addition to his writing, he also produced *Support Your Local Sheriff* (1969) and acted in *The Godfather, Part II* (1974). His additional writing credits include *My Favorite Spy* (1942), *Night and Day* (1946), *My Man Godfrey* (1957), and *Way. . . Way Out* (1966).

Lou Breslow (1900-November 10, 1987). Breslow was a screenwriter who specialized in comedy writing for such stars as Laurel and Hardy, Bob Hope, the Three Stooges, and Abbott and Costello. His screenwriting credits include *Five of a Kind* (1938), *A-Haunting We Will Go* (1942), *Blondie Goes to College* (1942), *Whispering Ghosts* (1942), and *Abbott and Costello in Hollywood* (1945).

Clarence Brown (May 10, 1890-August 17, 1987). Brown was a director and producer who was best known for his work with Greta Garbo. Educated as an engineer, Brown became interested in film and studied under director Maurice Tourneur from 1915 to 1920. His first film as a director was *The Great Redeemer* (1920), which featured John Gilbert. He also directed Rudolph Valentino in *The Eagle* (1925).

Brown signed with Metro-Goldwyn-Mayer, and his first film for the studio, with which he would be associated for the remainder of his career, was *Flesh and the Devil* (1927), starring Gilbert and MGM's hottest female star, Greta Garbo. The studio regarded Garbo as temperamental, but Brown worked well with her, and they were teamed in one more silent film, *A Woman of Affairs* (1928), and in five of Garbo's best sound films. *Anna Christie* (1930) was the star's first talkie; she and Brown were both nominated for Academy Awards for that picture and for *Romance*, which was released the same year. Perhaps because they were competing against themselves, neither artist won the award. Brown's three additional films with Garbo were *Inspiration* (1931), *Anna Karenina* (1935), and *Conquest* (1937).

Brown spent a quarter of a century making films for MGM, and he was known for the high quality of his productions. He was nominated for Academy Awards as Best Director four more times, for *A Free Soul* (1931), *The Human Comedy* (1943), *National Velvet* (1945), and *The Yearling* (1946). After 1947, Brown produced most of the films he directed. He retired from filmmaking in 1953, a wealthy man as a result of judicious real estate investments. Brown's additional film credits include *Ah, Wilderness!* (1935), *The Rains Came* (1939), *Edison the Man* (1940), *The White Cliffs of Dover* (1944), *Song of Love* (1947), *Intruder in the Dust* (1950), and *Angels in the Outfield* (1951).

Madeleine Carroll (February 26, 1906-October 2, 1987). Born Marie-Madeleine Bernadette O'Carroll, Carroll was a British actress best known for roles in two early Alfred Hitchcock films. After a year on the London stage, she made her film debut in *The Guns of Loos* (1928). She made more than a dozen films in the next six years, usually in roles calling for sophisticated blondes. Roles in Hitchcock's *The Thirty-nine Steps* (1935) and *Secret Agent* (1936) brought offers from Hollywood, and she moved to the United States, where she made *Café Society* (1939) and *My Favorite Blonde* (1942, opposite Bob Hope), among other films. She was married to actor Sterling Hayden from 1942 to 1946. Carroll retired from film after making *The Fan* (1949); her additional acting credits include *School for Scandal* (1930), *Lloyds of*

London (1936), and *The Prisoner of Zenda* (1937).

William Buster Collier, Jr. (February 12, 1902-February 6, 1987). Collier, son of actor William Collier, Sr., was a child actor who became a popular leading man of the silent era. He made his film debut in 1914 in *The Bugle Call*. As a juvenile lead, he starred in such films as *Wine of Youth* (1924) and *Devil's Cargo* (1925). As he matured, he developed into a romantic lead in *Beware of Bachelors* (1928) and *Bachelor Girl* (1929). He made a successful transition to sound, notably in character roles in films such as *Cimarron* (1931) and *Little Caesar* (1931). After making *The People's Enemy* (1935), he retired from acting and became a successful agent. Collier's additional acting credits include *The Wanderer* (1925), *The Donovan Affair* (1929), *The College Coquette* (1929), and *All of Me* (1934).

Olive Cooper (1893-June 12, 1987). Born Olive Cooper Curtis, Cooper was a screenwriter who wrote Westerns for Roy Rogers and Gene Autry. She wrote more than thirty scripts for Republic Studios between 1937 and 1950, including *Down Mexico Way* (1941) and *Cowboy Serenade* (1942) for Autry and *The Border Legion* (1940) and *King of the Cowboys* (1943) for Rogers. Her additional writing credits include *Cocoanut Grove* (1938), *The Bamboo Blonde* (1946), *Sioux City Sue* (1947), and *Hills of Oklahoma* (1950).

F. R. Budge Crawley (1912-May 13, 1987). Crawley was a Canadian film producer who made twenty-five hundred documentary films in a career that spanned nearly fifty years. He is best known for *The Man Who Skied Down Everest* (1975), which won an Academy Award as Best Documentary Feature.

Viola Dana (June 28, 1897-July 3, 1987). Born Virginia Flugrath, Dana was a popular actress of the silent era. A child star, she won fame in Broadway's *Poor Little Rich Girl* at the age of sixteen. She appeared in more than sixty films, mostly for Metro-Goldwyn-Mayer. Her career effectively ended with the advent of sound, and her last film was *The Show of Shows* (1929). Her additional film credits include *Molly the Drummer Boy* (1914), *Rosie O'Grady* (1917), *A Chorus Girl's Romance* (1920), *Merton of the Movies* (1924), and *Naughty Nanette* (1927).

Ruby Dandridge (1900-October 17, 1987). Dandridge was a black actress who began her entertainment career as a singer and dancer in vaudeville. Her daughter was the actress Dorothy Dandridge, who died in 1965. Ruby Dandridge appeared in *Carmen Jones* (1954), in which her daughter starred. Her additional film credits include *Cabin in the Sky* (1943), *Junior Miss* (1945), *My Wild Irish Rose* (1947), and *A Hole in the Head* (1959).

Henri Decaë (July 31, 1915-March 7, 1987). Decaë was a French cinematographer who worked with such important directors as François Truffaut, Claude Chabrol, and Louis Malle in the heyday of the French New Wave. After directing and photographing short subjects during World War II, he teamed with director Jean-Pierre Melville on *Le Silence de la mer* (1947). He worked with a variety of French, American, and British filmmakers during the next three and a half decades. Decaë was equally at home in color or black-and-white film, and he worked successfully with big-budget studio films as well as with avant-garde directors. His film credits include *Le Beau Serge* (1958), *The 400 Blows* (1959), *Sundays and Cybèle* (1962), *Viva Maria* (1965), *Bobby Deerfield* (1977), and *The Boys from Brazil* (1978).

King Donovan (1918-June 30, 1987). Donovan was a character actor who appeared in numerous films between the late 1940's and the early 1980's. He was most active in the 1950's. He also directed *Promises, Promises* (1963), a sex comedy which garnered some notoriety at the time of its release because of a brief nude scene involving the film's star, Jayne Mansfield. Donovan was the husband of actress Imogen Coca. His acting credits include *All the King's Men* (1949), *Singin' in the Rain* (1952), *Invasion of the Body Snatchers* (1956), *The Defiant Ones* (1958), *The Perfect Furlough* (1958), and *Nothing Lasts Forever* (1982).

Richard Egan (July 29, 1921-July 20, 1987). Egan was an actor who specialized in leading roles in action films in the 1950's and early 1960's. He had a master's degree in theater and was discovered by a Warner Bros. talent scout while acting in a dramatic production at Stanford University. His first film was *The Damned Don't Cry* (1950), and the tall, handsome actor starred in numerous films for Twentieth Century-Fox during the next decade. He is perhaps best remembered for costarring in *Love Me Tender* (1956), opposite Elvis Presley in the singer's screen debut. His additional acting credits include *Up Front* (1951), *Demetreus and the Gladiators* (1954), *The Revolt of Mamie Stover* (1956), *A Summer Place* (1959), *Pollyanna* (1960), and *The Sweet Creek County War* (1979).

Benson Fong (October 10, 1916-August 1, 1987). Fong was a Chinese-American character actor who specialized in playing Asian villains in American films. He was especially in demand during World War II, when he played Japanese characters in such films as *Behind the Rising Sun* (1943), *Thirty Seconds over Tokyo* (1944), and *First Yank into Tokyo* (1945). After the war, Fong continued to be in demand, appearing a wide variety of films, including *Flower Drum Song* (1961), *Girls! Girls! Girls!* (1962), and *The Love Bug* (1969). He was a regular in the television series *Kung Fu* and ran a chain of Chinese restaurants in the Los Angeles area. His additional acting credits include *Charlie Chan in the Secret Service* (1944), *Peking Express* (1951), *Our Man Flint* (1966), and *Oliver's Story* (1978).

Bob Fosse (June 23, 1927-September 23, 1987). Fosse was a director, dancer, and choreographer. Although he spent the bulk of his career working on Broadway, he had a major impact on film in his relatively short career as a director. A hard drinker, a heavy smoker, and a confessed womanizer, Fosse brought a ferocious energy to the dances he choreographed and to the films he directed. He was the son of a vaudeville performer, and he grew up dancing on the burlesque circuit. His first Broadway appearance came in 1949, and after moving to Hollywood he appeared in three films for Metro-Goldwyn-Mayer in a single year: *Give a Girl a Break* (1953), *The Affairs of Dobie Gillis* (1953), and *Kiss Me Kate* (1953).

Fosse returned to Broadway to choreograph *The Pajama Game* and *Damn Yankees* in the mid-1950's, winning Tony Awards for his work on both plays. When the two plays were filmed, in 1957 and 1958, respectively, he choreographed the screen versions as well. Fosse also won Tony Awards for *Redhead*, which he also directed, in 1959; *Little Me*, in 1962; *Sweet Charity*, in 1966; and *Pippin*, in 1973.

Fosse was well-known for his sensual, rhythmic dance sequences, and in 1969 he brought *Sweet Charity* to the screen in his first effort at directing as well as choreographing a film. His second picture, *Cabaret* (1972), was a tour de force. Both a commercial and critical success, the film starred Liza Minnelli and was nominated for nine Academy Awards. It won eight, including Best Director for Fosse. That award, plus two Tonys for *Pippin* and an Emmy for his television special *Liza with a Z* (also featuring Minnelli), gave him an unprecedented single-year sweep of the major American entertainment awards.

Fosse's next film, *Lenny* (1974), starred Dustin Hoffman as controversial comedian and social commentator Lenny Bruce. The stark black-and-white film was a distinct change of pace for the flashy Fosse; both he and Hoffman were nominated for Academy Awards for their work on the picture.

Five years later, Fosse delivered another tour de force—the autobiographical *All That Jazz* (1979). Starring Roy Scheider as a self-destructive choreographer, *All That Jazz* was a dazzling, if occasionally self-indulgent, public airing of Fosse's personality, including the less impressive aspects. The film was nominated for nine Academy Awards and won four. As it turned out, *All That Jazz* represented the peak of Fosse's career. His final film, *Star 80* (1983), received mixed reviews, and his last original Broadway play, *Big Deal*, closed after sixty-two shows in 1986. Fosse was producing a revival of *Sweet Charity*, featuring his former wife Gwen Verdon, at the time of his death. His additional film credits include *My Sister Eileen* (1955), *The Little Prince* (1974, both as actor and choreographer), and *Thieves* (1977).

Hugo Fregonese (April 18, 1908-January 18, 1987). Born in Argentina, Fregonese was a director best known for his visually striking B-Westerns. After making *Pampa Barbara* (1943) and two other films in Argentina, he moved to Hollywood, where he made several Westerns and other action films for Universal. These included *Saddle Tramp* (1950) and *Apache Drums* (1951). He made a prison comedy, *My Six Convicts* (1952), for Stanley Kramer at Columbia Pictures; a year later, he moved to Twentieth Century-Fox, where he made *Man in the Attic* (1953), *The Raid* (1954), and *Black Tuesday* (1955), a gangster film. His films were admired by critics, but Fregonese was forced to go to Europe to find work as a director. His European films are regarded as minor. His directorial credits include *One Way Street* (1950), *Blowing Wild* (1953), *Decameron Nights* (1953), *Marco Polo* (1962), and *Shatterhand* (1964).

Gustav Fröhlich (March 21, 1902-December 26, 1987). Fröhlich was a German actor best known for his first film role—that of the idealistic Freder Fredersen in Fritz Lang's *Metropolis* (1927). A romantic dispute between Fröhlich and Nazi propaganda minister Joseph Goebbels about an actress led to an interruption in Fröhlich's career in the mid-1940's, but he returned to acting after the war. He appeared in more than one hundred films and also directed eight films between 1933 and 1955. His acting credits include *Barcarole* (1935) and *Die Suenderin* (1951). He directed *Leb'wohl Christina* (1945), *Die Luge* (1950), and *Seine Tochter ist der Peter* (1955), among other films.

Pál Gábor (1932-October 21, 1987). Gábor was a Hungarian director best known for *Angi Vera* (1979), a sensitive look at trust and betrayal set in a political "re-education" camp in 1948. After serving a brief apprenticeship as assistant director in the early 1960's, Gábor began making short subjects and then feature-length films. *Visit* (1968) was a documentary; *Horizon* (1971) was his first film to be shown widely in the United States. His additional films include *Forbidden Ground* (1968), *Journey with Jacob* (1973), *Epidemic* (1975), and *Wasted Lives* (1981).

Wynne Gibson (July 3, 1905-May 15, 1987). Winifred "Wynne" Gibson was an actress who parlayed her stage experience into a film career in the early days of sound. Her first film was *Nothing but the Truth* (1929), and she made more than forty films for Paramount Pictures, Universal, and RKO. She specialized in playing hard-boiled characters, and her acting credits included *The Gang Buster* (1931), *If I Had a Million* (1932), *Gangs of New York* (1938), and *The Falcon Strikes Back* (1943).

Hermione Gingold (December 9, 1897-April 30, 1987). Gingold was a British actress and comedienne who appeared on Broadway and in films and television. She made her London stage debut before the age of ten and made three films in England between 1936 and 1952, before coming to the United States. She attracted attention in supporting roles in three major musicals: *Around the World in 80 Days* (1956); *Gigi* (1958), in which she and Maurice Chevalier sang "I Remember It Well"; and *The Music Man* (1962). She had a distinctive voice and appeared on the soundtrack of the animated feature *Gay Purr-ee* (1963). Her last film was *Garbo Talks* (1984). Gingold's additional acting credits include *Someone at the Door* (1936), *The Butler's Dilemma* (1943), *The Pickwick Papers* (1952), *Bell, Book and Candle* (1958), and *A Little Night Music* (1977).

Jackie Gleason (February 26, 1916-June 24, 1987). Gleason was an actor and comedian who was one of the most popular television stars of the 1950's. He had begun performing in vaudeville by the time he was fifteen; by his mid-twenties he had moved to Hollywood, where he appeared in minor roles for Warner Bros. and Twentieth Century-Fox in films such as *Navy Blues* (1941) and *Orchestra Wives* (1942).

Stardom came to Gleason in 1952, when *The Jackie Gleason Show* was introduced on CBS television. The hourlong series came to dominate the Saturday evening ratings, and "The Honeymooners" segment, featuring Gleason as the irascible Brooklyn bus driver Ralph Kramden, was to provide him with his most enduring role.

Gleason returned to films in the early 1960's. His portrayal of the pool shark Minnesota Fats in *The Hustler* (1961) earned for him an Academy Award nomination as Best Supporting Actor. He also appeared in straight dramatic roles in *Requiem for a Heavyweight* (1962), *Soldier in the Rain* (1963), and *Nothing in Common* (1986).

In 1962, he wrote and starred in *Gigot* (1962), a sensitive film in which he played a deaf-mute. He also appeared in such comedies as *Papa's Delicate Condition* (1963), *Skidoo* (1969), and *The Sting II* (1982). Gleason's most popular recent role, however, was that of the redneck Southern Sheriff Buford T. Justice opposite Burt Reynolds in *Smokey and the Bandit* (1977) and its sequels *Smokey and the Bandit II* (1980) and *Smokey and the Bandit Part 3* (1983, in which Reynolds did not appear).

The rotund comic was also a musician; he led his own orchestra and recorded thirty-five albums of his own lush, romantic compositions. He won a Tony Award in 1959 for his work in the Broadway musical *Take Me Along*, and his old television shows are still popular in syndication and on videotape. Nicknamed "The Great One" by Orson Welles, Gleason's additional film credits include *Larceny, Inc.* (1942), *All Through the Night* (1942), *The Desert Hawk* (1950), *Don't Drink the Water* (1969), and *The Toy* (1983).

Lorne Greene (February 12, 1915-September 11, 1987). Greene was a Canadian actor best known for his starring role in the popular television series *Bonanza*. He had a rich, resonant voice and was a top Canadian radio newscaster in the early 1950's, when he moved to the United States. He quickly found work as an actor onstage and in television and film. He appeared in *The Silver Chalice* (1954) and *Peyton Place* (1957), among other films. The success of *Bonanza*, which ran from 1959 to 1972, kept him out of film until 1974; he appeared in a handful of films until

1979, when a new television series, *Battlestar Galactica*, again claimed most of his time. His additional film credits include *Autumn Leaves* (1956), *The Buccaneer* (1958), *Earthquake* (1974), *Tidal Wave* (1975), and *Klondike Fever* (1979).

Joan Greenwood (March 4, 1921-February 2, 1987). Greenwood was a British actress who worked extensively onstage as well as in film. She is best known for her roles opposite Alec Guinness in the classic British comedies *Kind Hearts and Coronets* (1949) and *The Man in the White Suit* (1951). She also appeared in *Whiskey Galore* (1949), *The Importance of Being Ernest* (1952), *The Detective* (1954, again opposite Guinness), and *Tom Jones* (1963).

Paul Groesse (1907-May 4, 1987). Born in Hungary, Groesse was an award-winning art director. He came to the United States at the age of six. Trained as an architect, he began working for Metro-Goldwyn-Mayer in the mid-1930's. He and colleague Cedric Gibbons won three Academy Awards: for *Pride and Prejudice* (1940), *The Yearling* (1946), and *Little Women* (1949). He was nominated for eight other Academy Awards, often in collaboration with Gibbons (in the 1950's) or George W. Davis (in 1963 and 1966): *Madame Curie* (1943), *Annie Get Your Gun* (1950), *Too Young to Kiss* (1951), *The Merry Widow* (1952), *Lili* (1953), *The Music Man* (1962), *Twilight of Honor* (1963), and *Mister Buddwing* (1966).

Bernhard Grzimek (1911-March 13, 1987). Grzimek was a German documentary filmmaker who won an Academy Award for *Serengeti Shall Not Die* (1959). Grzimek was responsible for numerous books, films, and television productions, all of which concern the protection of wildlife. His additional films include *No Place for Wild Animals* (1956).

Morton Haack (1930-March 22, 1987). Haack was a costume designer whose work was nominated for three Academy Awards: *The Unsinkable Molly Brown* (1964), *Planet of the Apes* (1968), and *What's the Matter with Helen?* (1971). His additional film credits include *Please Don't Eat the Daisies* (1960), *Walk, Don't Run* (1966), and *Buona Sera, Mrs. Campbell* (1968).

Irene Handl (December 27, 1901-November 29, 1987). Handl was a British actress who specialized in comedy and often played eccentric Cockney roles. She began acting in her late thirties, and her first film was *The Girl in the News* (1940). She continued to act on the British stage throughout her career; in addition, she was a popular television star in Great Britain and published two novels. Her film credits include *The Belles of St. Trinian's* (1954), *I'm All Right Jack* (1959), *Morgan* (1966), *On a Clear Day You Can See Forever* (1970), and *The Last Remake of Beau Geste* (1977).

Elizabeth Hartman (December 23, 1941-June 10, 1987). Hartman was an actress best known for her role in *A Patch of Blue* (1965), in which she played a blind girl who fell in love with a black man, played by Sidney Poitier. This was her first film role, and it earned for her an Academy Award nomination as Best Actress. She appeared in five other films, notably Francis Coppola's *You're a Big Boy Now* (1967), but her career foundered after *Walking Tall* (1973), and her only other screen credit was a voice part in the animated feature *The Secret of NIMH* (1982). She had been receiving psychiatric treatment prior to her death by suicide. Her additional films were *The Group* (1966), *The Fixer* (1968), and *The Beguiled* (1971).

Rita Hayworth (October 17, 1918-May 14, 1987). Born Margarita Carmen Cansino, Hayworth was an actress and one of Hollywood's reigning sex symbols of the 1940's. She was the daughter of a Spanish dancer; her mother, whose maiden name was Haworth, had been a Ziegfeld showgirl. Hayworth was born and reared in Brooklyn, New York, where she began dancing at an early age. When she was ten, her family moved to Southern California. As a teenager, she danced professionally in a number of Mexican nightclubs, where she was discovered by a talent scout for Twentieth Century-Fox. Beginning at the age of sixteen, Hayworth appeared in small roles in ten films, including *Under the Pampas Moon* (1935) and *Trouble in Texas* (1937).

Her career was foundering when she met Edward C. Judson, whom she married in 1937. Judson, a promoter, dyed the actress' hair red, altered her hairline, and changed her name to Rita Hayworth. Harry Cohn at Columbia Pictures was impressed enough to offer her a contract, and her first important role came in Howard Hawks's *Only Angels Have Wings* (1939) opposite Cary Grant. On loan to Warner Bros., she starred opposite James Cagney in *The Strawberry Blonde* (1941). Yet her biggest break came later that year when she was cast with Fred Astaire in the musical *You'll Never Get Rich* (1941); the pair were teamed again in *You Were Never Lovelier* (1942), and Astaire once called Hayworth his favorite dancing partner.

Hayworth was known throughout her career for her tangled romantic life; by 1943 she had left Judson and was planning to marry Victor Mature, her costar in *My Gal Sal* (1942). Instead, she married Orson Welles that same year. In the meantime, Hayworth had emerged as one of the screen's most popular sex symbols. A *Life* magazine cover of her posed kneeling on a bed in a negligee made her one of the two most popular pinup girls of World War II; Betty Grable was her only serious rival.

Hayworth's best-remembered film was probably *Gilda* (1946), in which a sizzling strip tease to "Put the Blame on Mame" solidified her status as a screen siren. She once ruefully noted the extent of her identification with the film by remarking that the men in her life "fell in love with Gilda and woke up with me." She gave another strong performance in *The Lady from Shanghai* (1948), directed by Orson Welles as the couple's marriage was disintegrating. Although the film earned a disappointing reception on its release, it is regarded today as a classic.

After her divorce from Welles, Hayworth married the wealthy Muslim playboy Aly Khan in 1949; the marriage lasted two years. By this time, Hayworth's romantic affairs were causing disruptions in her career. She continued to command starring roles, but the years were taking their toll. Beginning with *Pal Joey* (1957), she was cast as more mature women. Some of her best acting during this period came in *Separate Tables* (1958) and *They Came to Cordura* (1959).

Hayworth continued to act throughout the 1960's and early 1970's, but neither the films nor her roles in them were memorable. Her last picture was *The Wrath of God* (1972). The last years of her life were spent in the fog of a disease which was initially assumed to be alcoholism, but which was finally diagnosed as Alzheimer's disease. Hayworth will be remembered as the woman who symbolized Hollywood glamour in the 1940's, just as Marilyn Monroe did in the 1950's. Her additional acting credits include *Tales of Manhattan* (1942), *Cover Girl* (1944), *The Loves of Carmen* (1948), *Affair in Trinidad* (1952), *Salome* (1953), *Miss Sadie Thompson* (1953), and *Fire Down Below* (1957).

Leon Hirszman (1937-September 15, 1987). Hirszman was a Brazilian director who was active in the *Cinema Novo* movement, which sparked the rebirth of the Brazilian film industry in the 1960's. His best-known film is *They Don't Wear Black Tie* (1981), which won the special jury prize at the Venice Film Festival. He died of AIDS, which he reportedly contracted from a blood transfusion. His additional films include *The São Diogo Quarry* (1962), *Absolute Majority* (1964), *The Girl from Ipanema* (1967), and *São Bernardo* (1972).

John Huston (August 5, 1906-August 28, 1987). Huston, an actor, screenwriter, and director, was a towering figure in American cinema. His career spanned more than half a century, and his work was both critically and commercially successful for virtually the entire period. He was the son of actor Walter Huston. Sickly as a child, Huston took up boxing as a teenager and grew to a robust manhood.

Through his father's influence, he was able to land small roles in several films in the early sound era, and in 1931 he tried his hand at screenwriting with increasingly impressive results: *Jezebel* (1938), *The Amazing Dr. Clitterhouse* (1938), *Juarez* (1939), and *High Sierra* (1941). His work on *Dr. Ehrlich's Magic Bullet* (1940) and *Sergeant York* (1941) earned for him his first two Academy Award nominations.

In 1941, Huston convinced Warner Bros. to let him direct his own adaptation of Dashiell Hammett's mystery *The Maltese Falcon* (1941). With Humphrey Bogart starring as Sam Spade and a memorable supporting cast which included Mary Astor, Peter Lorre, and Sydney Greenstreet, the film became an instant classic. It was nominated for an Academy Award as Best Picture, and Huston was nominated for his screenplay. He directed Bogart, Astor, and Greenstreet in *Across the Pacific* (1942) and then joined the army signal corps, where he made three distinguished documentaries about the war effort: *Report from the Aleutians* (1943), *The Battle of San Pietro* (1945), and *Let There Be Light* (1946). The latter film was so stark in its portrayal of the effects of shell shock that it was suppressed until 1980.

After the war, Huston entered a very productive decade. Working once again with Bogart, he wrote, directed, and acted in *The Treasure of the Sierra Madre* (1948). Huston won his two Academy Awards as director and writer of this film; his father, who also appeared in the picture, won the award for Best Supporting Actor. That same year, Huston made his last film for Warner Bros. *Key Largo* also starred Bogart; Claire Trevor won an Academy Award as Best Supporting Actress for her work in the film.

Huston then went to work for Metro-Goldwyn-Mayer. His first film for the studio was *The Asphalt Jungle* (1950), which he also produced and cowrote. This crime film, which features exceptional ensemble acting by Sterling Hayden, Sam Jaffe, Jean Haden, James Whitmore, and Marilyn Monroe, is often cited as the best distillation of Huston's recurring theme of the failure of dreams.

A year later, Huston produced another classic, *The African Queen* (1951), starring Bogart and Katharine Hepburn. Bogart won his own Academy Award for his performance, and both Huston and Hepburn were nominated for their work. Huston's next film, *Moulin Rouge* (1952), was based on the life of French painter Henri Toulouse-Lautrec. It was also a success, earning seven Academy Award nominations and winning two awards. *Beat the Devil* (1954, and Huston's last collaboration with Bogart), *Moby Dick* (1956, for which he was named best director by the New York Film Critics and the National Board of Review), and *Heaven Knows Mr. Allison* (1957) completed an extremely successful decade for the filmmaker.

Huston slumped a bit during the next five years; only *The Misfits* (1961), in which Marilyn Monroe and Clark Gable made their final screen appearances, stands out. In 1963, however, Huston took an acting job in *The Cardinal* (1963). His performance won for him an Academy Award nomination as Best Supporting Actor and resurrected his acting career. Some of his roles appeared to have been chosen whimsically—*Battle for the Planet of the Apes* (1973), for example—but his role as the villain in Roman Polanski's *Chinatown* (1974) was a tour de force.

Huston continued to direct noteworthy films at a relatively advanced age. *A Walk with Love and Death* (1969, which included his daughter Anjelica's first film appearance) marked the beginning of a comeback after fifteen years of uncertain inspiration. *Fat City* (1972), *The Man Who Would Be King* (1975), *Wise Blood* (1979), and *Under the Volcano* (1984) were all significant films. His primary late-career success, however, was *Prizzi's Honor* (1986). The film was nominated for eight Academy Awards, and Anjelica Huston won the award for Best Supporting Actress, making her the third generation of Huston Oscar winners. Huston's last film, an adaptation of James Joyce's "The Dead," was released posthumously in 1987.

Huston was a larger-than-life figure. Known as a hard-living man, he lived into his eighties, working productively until the end. He had a reputation as a maverick, but he was honored repeatedly by the establishment at which he occasionally scoffed. He published his autobiography, *An Open Book*, in 1980, and he was active during the final year of his life in fighting the colorization of black-and-white films. His additional films include *The Red Badge of Courage* (1951), *The Unforgiven* (1960), *The Night of the Iguana* (1964), *Reflections in a Golden Eye* (1967), and *The Life and Times of Judge Roy Bean* (1972).

Claude Jutra (March 11, 1930-April 23, 1987). Jutra was a French Canadian director who began making films as a teenager. He first attracted wide attention via a collaboration with animator Norman McLaren on *A Chairy Tale* (1957). He subsequently made documentaries and feature films and appeared in several productions—both his own and those of other filmmakers—as an actor. His best-known film is *Mon Oncle Antoine* (1971), which was named Best Picture at the Canadian Film Awards. Jutra was known to have Alzheimer's disease and is believed to have committed suicide. His additional films include *Le Niger—Jeune Republique* (1960), *A tout prendre* (1963), *Wow!* (1969), and *Kamouraska* (1974).

Milt Kahl (1910-April 19, 1987). Kahl was an animator who worked for the Disney Studios for more than four decades. One of the studio's top draftsmen, Kahl was usually assigned the most challenging characters, and his work appeared in such Disney classics as *Snow White and the Seven Dwarfs* (1938), *Pinocchio* (1940), *Song of the South* (1946), *Alice in Wonderland* (1951), *Peter Pan* (1953), *Lady and the Tramp* (1955), *Sleeping Beauty* (1959), and *101 Dalmations* (1961).

Danny Kaye (January 18, 1913-March 3, 1987). Born David Daniel Kaminski, Kaye was a comedian who found success on Broadway, in television, and in film. He grew up in Brooklyn, New York, and entered show business as a singer and dancer in the nightclub and vaudeville circuit. The red-haired actor developed a keen sense of comic timing and was known for his ability to speak very rapidly, often in doubletalk. Kaye's first brush with fame came in the 1941 Broadway play *Lady in the Dark*, in which he performed a song called "Tchaikovsky," which consisted of the rapid-fire recitation of fifty-four Russian names.

Signed by Sam Goldwyn to a film contract in 1943, Kaye appeared in several musical comedies in the 1940's and 1950's which displayed his talents to a growing legion of fans. One of the best was *The Secret Life of Walter Mitty* (1947), in which Kaye was able to portray the film's hero as six different characters. Other hits from this period include *The Kid from Brooklyn* (1946), *Hans Christian Andersen* (1952), *White Christmas* (1954), and *The Five Pennies* (1959).

After 1960, Kaye took his talents to television, where he starred in his own Emmy-winning variety program from 1963 to 1967. He also began to devote more time to philanthropy; he had been the ambassador-at-large for UNICEF since the 1950's. Kaye was much honored in his lifetime for his good works as well as for his accomplishments in various fields of entertainment. He was given an honorary Academy Award in 1954 "for his unique talents, his service to the Academy, the motion picture industry, and the American people." In 1982, the Academy gave him its Jean Hersholt Humanitarian Award as a performer "whose humanitarian efforts have brought credit to the industry." His additional acting credits include *Up in Arms* (1944), *A Song Is Born* (1948), *The Inspector General* (1949), *Merry Andrew* (1958), *On the Double* (1961), and *The Madwoman of Chaillot* (1969).

Harry Keller (February 22, 1913-February 22, 1987). Keller was a producer and director who worked in television as well as film. He specialized in low-budget films, many of which were Westerns. He broke into film as an editor, and his first directorial effort was *The Blonde Bandit* (1949). Between 1951 and 1954, he made twelve Westerns; he also directed *Tammy Tell Me True* (1961) and *Tammy and the Doctor* (1963). He began producing films in 1964; these include *Kitten with a Whip* (1964), *The Skin Game* (1971), and *Class of '44* (1973). His additional directing credits include *Fort Dodge Stampede* (1951), *El Paso Stampede* (1953), *The Female Animal* (1958), and *In Enemy Country* (1968).

Madge Kennedy (April 19, 1891-June 9, 1987). Kennedy was an actress who starred in the silent era and made a comeback in character roles in the 1950's. She made a name for herself as a teenager on Broadway and was signed to a film contract by Sam Goldwyn in 1917. She appeared in twenty-one films, including *Baby Mine* (1917), *The Girl with the Jazz Heart* (1921), and *Oh Baby!* (1926). After a few theatrical appearances between 1929 and 1932, she abandoned acting. A quarter of a century later, she returned to film in George Cukor's *The Marrying Kind* (1952) and appeared in nearly a dozen films before retiring again after *The Marathon Man* (1976). Her additional acting credits include *Nearly Married* (1917), *Scandal Street* (1925), *The Rains of Ranchipur* (1955), *Lust for Life* (1956), *Let's Make Love* (1960), and *They Shoot Horses Don't They?* (1969).

Esmond Knight (May 4, 1906-February 23, 1987). Knight was a British actor who appeared in both leading and supporting roles onstage and in film during a span of forty-five years. His first film was *The Ringer* (1931); he appeared in supporting roles in Laurence Olivier's three major Shakespearean films: *Henry V* (1944), *Hamlet* (1948), and *Richard III* (1956). Knight was temporarily blinded while serving in the British Navy during World War II, and he published an autobiography, *Seeking the Bubble*, in 1943. His additional acting credits include *Pagliacci* (1937), *A Canterbury Tale* (1944), *The Red Shoes* (1948), *The Spy Who Came in from the Cold* (1965), and *Robin and Marian* (1976).

Arthur Lake (April 17, 1905-January 9, 1987). Born Arthur Silverlake, Lake was an actor who grew up in a show business family and made his first film at the age of twelve. After *Jack and the Beanstalk* (1917), he played juvenile roles into his early adulthood and appeared in one of director Mervyn LeRoy's earlier films, *Harold Teen* (1928). He is best remembered for his portrayal of Dagwood Bumstead in Columbia Picture's long-running series based on the comic strip "Blondie." From the original *Blondie* (1938) through *Beware of Blondie* (1950), he starred opposite Penny Singleton in twenty-seven of these films, which are credited with saving the studio from financial collapse. His acting credits include *The Irresistible Lover* (1927), *Topper* (1937), *Blondie Plays Cupid* (1940), *Blondie's Blessed Event* (1942), and *Blondie Knows Best* (1946).

Mervyn LeRoy (October 15, 1900-September 13, 1987). LeRoy was an actor, director, and producer who directed some of the most memorable films of the 1930's and 1940's for Warner Bros. and Metro-Goldwyn-Mayer. Born and reared in San Francisco, he was a twelve-year-old newsboy when one of his customers gave him a bit part in a play. This led to a vaudeville act and a move to Los Angeles at the age of nineteen. He soon earned supporting and lead roles in films such as *Double Speed* (1920) and *The Ghost Breaker* (1922). In 1924, he began to write screenplays, and by 1927 he was directing for First National, a Warner Bros. subsidiary. His early films included *Harold Teen* (1928) and *Showgirl in Hollywood* (1930).

In 1931, he was given his first major assignment: *Little Caesar* (1931), starring Edward G. Robinson. The tremendous success of LeRoy's film provided the driving force behind the gangster genre, at which Warner Bros. excelled in the 1930's. LeRoy made several other important social dramas for the studio in the early 1930's, including *Five Star Final* (1931), again starring Robinson, this time in an exposé of corrupt newspaper practices; and *I Am a Fugitive from a Chain Gang* (1932), which featured Paul Muni in an indictment of prison conditions in the South. He also gave Warner Bros. its biggest musical success of the early 1930's, the influential *Gold Diggers of 1933* (1933), and showed his flair for comedy by directing Marie Dressler and Wallace Beery in *Tugboat Annie* (1933) for MGM in the same year.

In 1938, LeRoy established a more lasting relationship with MGM. As a producer, he developed the Marx Brothers comedy *At the Circus* (1939) and initiated one of the studio's most enduringly popular films, *The Wizard of Oz* (1939). He directed *Waterloo Bridge* (1940), one of Vivien Leigh's best films, as well as *Random Harvest* (1942), *Madame Curie* (1943), and *Thirty Seconds over Tokyo* (1944). He won an Academy Award for his documentary short, *The House That I Live In* (1945), which utilized the talents of Frank Sinatra to promote its theme of tolerance and social responsibility.

LeRoy continued to make films for another twenty years, although his material was only occasionally inspiring. Highlights of this period include *Quo Vadis* (1951), *Mister Roberts* (1955, which he took over when the film's original director, John Ford, became ill), *The Bad Seed* (1956), *No Time for Sergeants* (1958), *The FBI Story* (1959), and the musical *Gypsy* (1962).

LeRoy was active in film for nearly fifty years, and his work included several films which are among Hollywood's finest. At the 1975 Academy Award ceremonies, LeRoy was honored with the Irving Thalberg Memorial Award, given "to creative producers whose body of work reflects a consistently high quality of motion picture production." His additional films include *Anthony Adverse* (1936), *They Won't Forget*

(1937), *Escape* (1940), *Blossoms in the Dust* (1941), *Little Women* (1949), *The Devil at 4 O'Clock* (1961), and *Moment to Moment* (1965).

Joseph E. Levine (September 9, 1905-July 31, 1987). Levine was a producer who was a major force in international cinema in the 1960's and 1970's. Born in Boston, Levine got into the motion-picture business as a theater owner and film distributor in New England. His first venture in filmmaking was *Gaslight Follies* (1955), an unsophisticated anthology of scenes from film classics of the silent era, which he released through his own company, Embassy Pictures. The next year, he purchased the American rights to the Japanese horror film *Godzilla, King of the Monsters* (1956) for twelve thousand dollars and turned it into a huge hit.

Next, Levine looked to Italy for films he could sell to American audiences. He purchased *Hercules* (1959), which starred bodybuilder Steve Reeves; this film was another substantial money-maker and served as the model for a succession of similar action films based very loosely on Greek legends. Although he spent very little for the rights to these films, Levine spared no expense in promoting them and usually wound up with considerable profits.

Levine pioneered the technique of opening a film simultaneously in thousands of theaters across the country, a practice that is now commonplace. Though he produced more than his share of forgettable films, he was also responsible for introducing American audiences to Vittorio De Sica's *Two Women* (1961), which featured an Academy Award-winning performance by Sophia Loren; *Divorce—Italian Style* (1963); and Federico Fellini's classic *8½* (1963). Other films released by Levine and Embassy Pictures in the 1960's include the Academy Award-winning documentary *The Sky Above, The Mud Below* (1961), and *Darling* (1965), which included Julie Christie's Academy Award-winning performance.

By the mid-1960's, Levine had begun to produce his own films. His early efforts were mostly steamy potboilers such as *The Carpetbaggers* (1964) and *Harlow* (1965), but as executive producer he developed several distinguished films, including *The Graduate* (1967), *The Producers* (1968), *The Lion in Winter* (1968), and *Carnal Knowledge* (1971).

Levine spent two and a half years and 25 million dollars on the World War II epic *A Bridge Too Far* (1977), which featured brief (and expensive) cameo roles by dozens of top stars. The film failed to earn back its expenses, and that marked the beginning of the end of Levine's career. He produced a few more films and announced plans for many others, but his years as a pacesetter in the film industry were over. His additional credits as a producer or executive producer include *Sands of the Kalahari* (1965), *The Tenth Victim* (1965), *The Oscar* (1966), *Soldier Blue* (1970), *A Touch of Class* (1973), *And Justice for All* (1979), and *Tattoo* (1981).

John Paul Livadary (1898-April 7, 1987). Livadary was a pioneer in the field of sound films. He was hired by Columbia Pictures in 1928 to head its sound department, a position which he held until his retirement in 1959. He was nominated for sixteen Academy Awards and won two, for *The Jolson Story* (1946) and *From Here to Eternity* (1953). In addition, he received special Academy Awards in 1937, 1944, 1950, and 1954 for technical contributions to cinema. His additional film credits include *Mr. Deeds Goes to Town* (1936), *Lost Horizon* (1937), *Mr. Smith Goes to Washington* (1939), *The Caine Mutiny* (1954), and *Pal Joey* (1957).

Norman McLaren (April 11, 1914-January 27, 1987). Born in Scotland, McLaren was an animator who joined the Canadian National Film Board in 1941; by 1943, he headed the board's animation unit. He worked in a variety of styles and is remembered for having perfected the animation technique of drawing directly onto film. He won an Academy Award for his short subject *Neighbors* (1952). His additional films include *Seven till Five* (1933), *Dots* (1940), *Blinkity Blank* (1954), *Rhythmetic* (1956), *A Chairy Tale* (1957), and *Striations* (1970).

Rouben Mamoulian (October 8, 1898-December 4, 1987). Born in Russia, Mamoulian was a director known for his inventive camera work in some of the most distinguished films of the early sound era. He studied drama at the University of London and came to the United States in 1923. In 1927, he directed the play *Porgy* on Broadway.

Mamoulian was asked by Paramount Pictures to direct *Applause* (1929), one of its earliest talkies. The conventional wisdom of the time held that film cameras needed to be housed in soundproof booths to prevent extraneous noise from entering the soundtrack. Mamoulian rejected this notion, and his camera work was a striking contrast to the static films of the early sound era. *City Streets* (1931), a gangster film, continued to break ground with its innovative camera movement, as did *Dr. Jekyll and Mr. Hyde* (1932), and *Love Me Tonight* (1932).

In 1933, Mamoulian made films with cinema's two most prominent foreign actresses. Marlene Dietrich starred in *Song of Songs*, and Greta Garbo gave what is generally regarded as her finest performance in *Queen Christina*. In 1935, Metro-Goldwyn-Mayer asked Mamoulian to direct its first three-color Technicolor film, *Becky Sharp* (1935), which remains a remarkably striking film.

Also in 1935, Mamoulian returned to Broadway to direct the musical version of his earlier success. *Porgy and Bess*, featuring George Gershwin's songs, became a landmark of American theater. He returned to Broadway a number of times during the next decade, directing such classics as *Oklahoma!* in 1943 and *Carousel* in 1945, both Rodgers and Hammerstein musicals.

Mamoulian was a director who insisted on making films his way or not at all, and by the mid-1940's, he was beginning to clash with equally headstrong studio executives. He was replaced as the director of *Laura* (1944), the film version of *Porgy and Bess* (1959), and *Cleopatra* (1963) as a result of these disagreements. Mamoulian made only two films after World War II. *Summer Holiday* (1948) was a disappointing musical remake of *Ah, Wilderness!* (1935). *Silk Stockings* (1957), itself a remake of *Ninotchka* (1939), however, was a light and airy musical that paired Cyd Charisse with Fred Astaire in the dancer's last great musical.

In 1935, Mamoulian helped found the Screen Directors Guild of America, later known simply as Directors Guild of America. In 1982, the organization gave Mamoulian its coveted D. W. Griffith Award in recognition of his achievements. His additional films include *We Live Again* (1934), *The Gay Desperado* (1936), *Golden Boy* (1939), *The Mark of Zorro* (1940), and *Blood and Sand* (1941).

Lee Marvin (February 19, 1924-August 29, 1987). Marvin was an actor who specialized in tough-guy roles in a career that lasted three and a half decades. After a stint in the Marine Corps during World War II, Marvin took up acting and appeared in minor roles onstage and in television. His first film was *You're in the Navy Now* (1951). He began attracting notice for supporting roles in films such as *The Wild One* (1954), in which he played a menacing hoodlum on a motorcycle, and *Bad Day* *at Black Rock* (1955) and *The Man Who Shot Liberty Valance* (1962), both Westerns in which he played sadistic cowboys.

Another Western, *Cat Ballou* (1965), made Marvin famous. This film, which starred Jane Fonda, was played strictly for laughs, and Marvin had two parts: a drunken gunfighter and his evil twin, a man who dressed in black and wore a silver nose to replace one that had been bitten off in a fight. Marvin won an Academy Award as Best Actor for his performance, and thereafter he was a star.

He continued to specialize in tough-guy roles. *The Dirty Dozen* (1967) was a very popular World War II action film, and *Point Blank* (1967), a tale of revenge and organized crime, has come to be regarded as one of the finest dramas of its time. Marvin occasionally strayed from his métier; he performed creditably in the musical *Paint Your Wagon* (1969) and in the drama *The Iceman Cometh* (1973). Nevertheless, he was at his best in action films; he gave his last great performance in Samuel Fuller's *The Big Red One* (1980), in which he brought great depth to the role of a grizzled infantry sergeant during World War II.

In addition to his film career, Marvin also appeared frequently on television, most notably as one of the stars of "M Squad," a police drama that ran from 1957 to 1960. He also made legal history of sorts in 1979, when actress Michelle Triola, a former girlfriend who had lived with him for six years, sued him for alimony after their relationship ended. A judge awarded Triola $104,000 in what came to be known as a "palimony" decision. Marvin's additional acting credits include *The Caine Mutiny* (1954), *Pete Kelly's Blues* (1955), *The Comancheros* (1961), *Donovan's Reef* (1963), *The Killers* (1964), *Ship of Fools* (1965), *Hell in the Pacific* (1968), *Monte Walsh* (1970), and *Pocket Money* (1972).

David Maysles (January 10, 1932-January 3, 1987). Maysles was a documentary filmmaker who, along with his older brother Albert, was one of the pioneers of *cinéma vérité*. The Maysles brothers called their style "direct cinema" and used small, hand-held cameras to film their subjects going about their daily routines, rather than in staged scenes. Often they filmed celebrities—*What's Happening: The Beatles in the USA* (1964), *Meet Marlon Brando* (1965), and *Gimme Shelter* (1970), which featured the Rolling Stones and their disastrous concert at Altamont, California. Other films, however, focused on less glamorous topics: *Salesman* (1969) and *Grey Gardens* (1975). The Maysles brothers received an Academy Award nomination for *Christo's Valley Curtain* (1972). Their other films include *With Love from Truman* (1966) and *Running Fence* (1977).

Pola Negri (December 31, 1894-August 1, 1987). Born Barbara Apollonia Chalupiec, in Poland, Negri was one of the most popular actresses of the silent film era. She studied ballet and drama in Russia and began acting on the Polish stage in 1913. A year later she was appearing in films, and in 1917 she moved to Berlin to pursue her acting career there. She met director Ernst Lubitsch, who cast her in *The Eyes of the Mummy* (1918) and *Carmen* (1918). In both films she portrayed a femme fatale who destroyed her helpless lovers. This sort of woman became known as a vamp, and Negri epitomized the style.

As soon as Hollywood filmmakers became aware of Negri's European success, they brought her to America, where she appeared in such hits as *Bella Donna* (1923), *The Spanish Dancer* (1923), and *Lily of the Dust* (1924). She also made news offscreen. Paramount trumped up a feud between its two biggest stars, Negri and

Gloria Swanson, and Negri willingly played along. She had a brief and well-publicized affair with Charlie Chaplin and was engaged to marry Rudolph Valentino at the time of his death in 1926.

Negri's exotic style was widely imitated, and she is credited with introducing such fashion developments as turbans, boots, and painted toenails to American audiences. She made twenty films of varying quality in the United States between 1923 and 1928. Among the better ones were Lubitsch's *Forbidden Paradise* (1924) and Raoul Walsh's *East of Suez* (1925). By the end of the decade, American audiences began to lose their fondness for her stylized characterizations, and the advent of sound revealed a thick accent that effectively ended her popularity in this country.

Negri returned to Europe where she made one film in France, *Fanatisme* (1932), and several in Germany. *Mazurka* (1935) was reportedly one of Adolf Hitler's favorite films. She returned to the United States at the outbreak of World War II but made only two more films, appearing in the comedy *Hi Diddle Diddle* (1943) and as the villain in *The Moonspinners* (1964).

Negri became an American citizen in 1951 and published her autobiography, *Memoirs of a Star*, in 1970. Her additional acting credits include *Love and Passion* (1914), *Madame Dubarry* (1919), *Sumurun* (1920), *A Woman of the World* (1925), *Good and Naughty* (1926), *Loves of an Actress* (1928), *A Woman Commands* (1932), and *Madame Bovary* (1937).

Ralph Nelson (August 12, 1916-December 21, 1987). Nelson was a director who made his name in television and subsequently made feature films. He directed more than a thousand dramatic shows on such "golden age" television shows as "Playhouse 90" and "General Electric Theater"; he won an Emmy in 1958 for his production of *Requiem for a Heavyweight*. His first feature film was also *Requiem for a Heavyweight* (1962). He produced, directed, and acted in *Lilies of the Field* (1963), for which Sidney Poitier won an Academy Award; and *Charly* (1968), for which Cliff Robertson won an Academy Award. Nelson was married for a time to actress Celeste Holm. His additional film credits include *Soldier in the Rain* (1963), *Father Goose* (1964), *Soldier Blue* (1970), and *A Hero Ain't Nothin' but a Sandwich* (1977).

Geraldine Page (November 22, 1924-June 13, 1987). Page was an actress whose film and stage appearances were noteworthy for their consistently high quality. She had a small role in the film *Out of the Night* (1947) but first attracted national attention in an Off-Broadway production of Tennessee Williams' *Summer and Smoke* in 1952. Her performance earned for her a New York Drama Critics award; she won the same award in 1959 for her role opposite Paul Newman in Williams' *Sweet Bird of Youth*.

Page's first significant film role came in *Hondo* (1953), a Western originally released in 3-D and starring John Wayne. She played a young widow saved by Wayne from an Indian uprising, and her performance earned for her an Academy Award nomination as Best Supporting Actress. Oddly enough, it was eight years before she appeared in another film. Page blamed the hiatus on Hollywood conservatism during the McCarthy years.

She remained active onstage, and when *Summer and Smoke* (1961) was brought to the screen, Page starred as the lovelorn spinster, earning another Academy Award nomination, this time as Best Actress. She and Newman reprised their stage roles in the film version of *Sweet Bird of Youth* (1962), which resulted in another Best Actress nomination. She was also nominated for supporting roles in Francis Coppola's *You're a Big Boy Now* (1967), *Pete and Tillie* (1972), and *The Pope of Greenwich Village* (1984), and as Best Actress for her work in Woody Allen's *Interiors* (1978). She finally won the Best Actress award for *The Trip to Bountiful* (1985).

Page was one of the leading advocates of the Method school of acting, and her performances were always memorable. She was also known to be choosy about her roles, which is one reason that her filmography is relatively brief. In addition to her stage and film honors, Page also won two Emmy Awards for her work on television. She was married to actor Rip Torn. Her additional film credits include *Taxi* (1953), *Toys in the Attic* (1963), *What Ever Happened to Aunt Alice?* (1969), *The Beguiled* (1971), *The Day of the Locust* (1975), *White Nights* (1985), and *Native Son* (1986).

Robert Paige (December 2, 1910-December 21, 1987). Born John Arthur Paige Paige was an actor who began his film career using the name David Carlyle. He worked as a leading man in a number of B-films and musicals, most of which were made for Universal. As David Carlyle, he appeared in *Annapolis Farewell* (1935), *Cain and Mabel* (1936), and *Smart Blonde* (1937). As Robert Paige, his acting credits include *Highway Patrol* (1938), *Golden Gloves* (1940), *Hellzapoppin* (1941), *Pardon My Sarong* (1942), *Son of Dracula* (1943), *Marriage-Go-Round* (1960), and *Bye Bye Birdie* (1963).

Robert Preston (June 8, 1918-March 21, 1987). Born Robert Preston Meservey, Preston was a Broadway and film actor best known for his starring role in the stage and screen versions of *The Music Man* (1962). Preston grew up in Hollywood, and his early acting career was in film, playing supporting roles in Paramount Pictures films of the late 1930's and early 1940's. His first film was *King of Alcatraz* (1938), and he worked his way up to second-lead roles before entering the military in 1942. After the war, he appeared in films—often Westerns—for a variety of studios, still in second-lead roles.

Bored with the direction his career was taking, Preston left Hollywood for New York and continued acting in television and onstage. His work earned for him increasing respect, and when he was cast as Professor Harold Hill (a role turned down by Gene Kelly, Danny Kaye, and Ray Bolger, among others) in Meredith Wilson's play *The Music Man*, his career was made. He won a Tony Award for his work as the musical con man. Hollywood was still a bit skeptical about Preston's ability to carry a major film, and when Warner Bros. was casting the film version of the play, Preston's name was not high on its list. He fought for and won the part, however, and the film was a resounding success, both critically and financially.

Preston continued to act in films, although sporadically, for the rest of his life. In the immediate aftermath of *The Music Man*'s success, he appeared in *How the West Was Won* (1962), *Island of Love* (1963), and *All the Way Home* (1963). It was nine years before his next film, *Junior Bonner* (1972). In the 1980's, his notable appearances included two Blake Edwards comedies, *S.O.B.* (1981) and *Victor/Victoria* (1982). Interspersed with his films were numerous appearances on Broadway, most notably in *I Do, I Do* with Mary Martin in 1966 and 1967, and *Mack and Mabel* in 1974. His additional film credits include *Union Pacific* (1939), *Beau Geste* (1939), *This Gun for Hire* (1942), *Blood on the Moon* (1948), *My Outlaw Brother* (1951), *The Dark at the Top of the Stairs* (1960), and *Semi-Tough* (1977).

John Qualen (December 8, 1899-September 12, 1987). Born John Oleson, Qualen was a thin character actor who specialized in playing farmers and weak-willed victims. Best known for the role of Muley Graves in *The Grapes of Wrath* (1940), Qualen appeared in more than one hundred films in a career that spanned four decades. His acting credits include *Arrowsmith* (1931), *His Girl Friday* (1940), *Casablanca* (1943), *The High and the Mighty* (1954), *The Searchers* (1956), *Anatomy of a Murder* (1959), and *The Man Who Shot Liberty Valance* (1962).

William Rose (1918-February 10, 1987). Rose was a screenwriter who was born in the United States and settled in Scotland after World War II. He wrote for British films between 1948 and 1957; his most noteworthy films of this era were *Genevieve* (1953) and the black comedy *The Lady Killers* (1955), which featured Peter Sellers and Alec Guinness. Rose earned Academy Award nominations for both of these films. He began writing for Hollywood with *It's a Mad Mad Mad Mad World* (1965); earned a third Academy Award nomination for *The Russians Are Coming the Russians Are Coming* (1966); and won the award for the screenplay of *Guess Who's Coming to Dinner* (1967). His additional credits include *Once a Jolly Swagman* (1948), *The Maggie* (1954), *The Flim-Flam Man* (1967), and *The Secret of Santa Vittoria* (1969).

Russell Rouse (1916-October 2, 1987). Rouse was a screenwriter and director whose career included highly experimental films as well as conventional Hollywood features. His first film, which he codirected with Leo Popkin, was *The Well* (1951), a study in mob psychology which earned for Rouse and his longtime collaborator Clarence Greene an Academy Award nomination for their script. *The Thief* (1952), which starred Ray Milland, was filmed entirely without dialogue. Rouse and Greene won an Academy Award for their work on *Pillow Talk* (1959). As a writer only, Rouse worked on *Nothing but Trouble* (1945), *D.O.A.* (1950), and *Color Me Dead* (1969). As a director and writer, his credits include *New York Confidential* (1955), *A House Is Not a Home* (1964), and *The Oscar* (1966).

Waldo Salt (October 18, 1914-March 7, 1987). Salt was an Academy Award-winning screenwriter whose career was disrupted by the anticommunist blacklist in the early 1950's. Working for Metro-Goldwyn-Mayer, his collaboration on the script of *Shopworn Angel* (1938) marked his first screen credit. He was scheduled to testify before the House Committee on Un-American Activities in 1951 on his alleged Communist affiliations, but the committee was disbanded before he was called as a witness. Nevertheless, Salt became *persona non grata* in Hollywood; during the next decade he wrote for British and American television under various pseudonyms. As the blacklist lifted, he wrote for Hollywood once again. He won Academy Awards for his screenplays of *Midnight Cowboy* (1969) and *Coming Home* (1978); he shared the latter award with Robert C. Jones. Salt was given the Laurel Award for lifetime achievement by the Writers Guild of America. His additional screen credits include *The Wild Man of Borneo* (1941), *M* (1951), *Taras Bulba* (1962), *Serpico* (1973), and *The Day of the Locust* (1975).

Will Sampson (1934-June 3, 1987). Sampson was a Native American actor who was best known for the role of Chief Broom in *One Flew Over the Cuckoo's Nest* (1975). A massive man—six feet, seven inches tall and 260 pounds—Sampson played American Indians in numerous films, including *The Outlaw—Josey Wales* (1976), *Buffalo Bill and the Indians* (1976), *Orca* (1977), *Poltergeist II* (1986), and *Firewalker* (1986).

Denis Sanders (January 21, 1929-December 10, 1987). Sanders was a screenwriter and documentary producer-director whose work won two Academy Awards. Along with his brother Terry, Sanders produced the Academy Award-winning short subject *A Time Out of War* (1954). The Sanders brothers adapted Norman Mailer's *The Naked and the Dead* (1958) for film. His feature film work, however, was less successful than his documentaries, which included *Elvis—That's the Way It Is* (1970) and *Czechoslovakia 1968* (1969), for which Sanders and Robert M. Fresco shared the Academy Award for Best Documentary Short Subject. Sanders' additional film credits include *Crime and Punishment USA* (1959), *War Hunt* (1961), *Soul to Soul* (1971), and *Invasion of the Bee Girls* (1973).

Randolph Scott (January 23, 1898-March 3, 1987). Born Randolph Crane, Scott was an actor who appeared in nearly one hundred films in a thirty-three-year screen career; he was closely identified with the Western genre. There is some dispute as to the year of his birth; most biographers cite 1903, but family sources suggest that 1898 is accurate. Scott was born to financially secure parents in Virginia and was known throughout his career as a classic Southern gentleman. He served in World War I and settled in Southern California, where he took up acting. His occasional golfing partner, Howard Hughes, got him small parts in such films as *The Far Call* (1929) and *The Virginian* (1929).

In 1932, the lanky actor signed a seven-year contract with Paramount, which promptly put him to work. He made eleven films in 1933, often with director Henry Hathaway in remakes of Westerns of the silent era. His early Westerns included *The Thundering Herd* (1933), *The Last Roundup* (1934), and *Wagon Wheels* (1934). Scott also appeared in other types of films, including *Roberta* (1935), and *Follow the Fleet* (1936), two Fred Astaire-Ginger Rogers musicals. He also starred opposite Shirley Temple in *Rebecca of Sunnybrook Farm* (1937).

Nevertheless, Westerns continued to be his bread and butter. Passed over for the role of Ashley Wilkes in *Gone with the Wind* (1939), he starred in *Jesse James* (1939) and *Frontier Marshal* (1939) instead. By the late 1940's, he had settled into a comfortable career starring in B-Westerns for such directors as Andre de Toth and Budd Boetticher, for whom he made seven films which are generally regarded as his finest. In these films, which include *Decision at Sundown* (1957), *Buchanan Rides Alone* (1958), and *Comanche Station* (1960), Scott brought a gritty integrity to his roles which came to epitomize the "good guy" in the Western genre. He made one last film, Sam Peckinpah's *Ride the High Country* (1962), in which he costarred with Joel McCrea. Scott had originally been cast as the hero, but he and McCrea discussed the script and persuaded Peckinpah to let them switch roles; thus his final screen role was that of a villain.

One reason Scott was able to retire so early was that he had invested his earnings wisely in oil and Southern California real estate. His net worth at the time of his death has been estimated at well above $100 million. Scott's additional acting credits include *Go West Young Man* (1936), *Virginia City* (1940), *Western Union* (1941), *Colt .45* (1950), *Sugarfoot* (1951), *The Tall T* (1957), *Shootout at Medicine Bend* (1957), and *Ride Lonesome* (1959).

Joan Shawlee (March 5, 1929-March 22, 1987). Shawlee was an actress who specialized in comic supporting roles. In her first films, including *Lover Come Back* (1946) and *Buck Privates Come Home* (1947), she used the name Joan Fulton. A large woman, she was often described as Amazonian. Shawlee was best known for her role as the leader of the all-girl band in *Some Like It Hot* (1959). She also appeared in *Prehistoric Women* (1950), *A Star Is Born* (1954), *A Farewell to Arms* (1957), *The Apartment* (1960), *Irma La Douce* (1963), and *The Wild Angels* (1966).

Dick Shawn (December 1, 1923-April 17, 1987). Born Richard Schulefand, Shawn was an actor and comedian who appeared in film, television, nightclubs, and Broadway plays in the course of his career. His first film was *The Opposite Sex* (1956), and his most notable recent appearance was in Francis Coppola's 3-D short, *Captain Eo* (1986), which featured singer Michael Jackson. His additional film credits include *It's a Mad Mad Mad Mad World* (1963), *What Did You Do in the War Daddy?* (1966), *The Producers* (1968), and *Love at First Bite* (1979).

Jacques Sigurd (June 15, 1920-December 20, 1987). Sigurd was a French screenwriter who worked on many of the best French films of the late 1940's and early 1950's, often with director Yves Allégret. Two Sigurd and Allégret collaborations, *Dédée d'Anvers* (1948) and *Manèges* (1950), were the vehicles that launched actress Simone Signoret's acting career. His additional film credits include *Une Si Jolie Petite Plage* (1949), *Lucrèce Borgia* (1953), *La Belle Otéro* (1954), and *Les Tricheurs* (1958).

Douglas Sirk (April 26, 1900-January 14, 1987). Born Claus Detlef Sierck in Hamburg, Germany, Sirk was a director who was known for his ability to inject life into seemingly unpromising material. He was active in the German theater in the 1920's, and by the mid-1930's he was directing films. A political leftist with a Jewish wife, Sirk grew increasingly uncomfortable in Germany as Nazi repression intensified. He left the country in 1937 and eventually settled in the United States.

Initially, the only film work he could find in Hollywood was screenwriting (none of his efforts was filmed). In an effort to Americanize himself, he changed his name to Douglas Sirk, and by the mid-1940's he was directing in Hollywood. His first effort was the anti-Nazi *Hitler's Madman* (1943), but the films that followed were romances of various types: *Summer Storm* (1944), *A Scandal in Paris* (1946), and *Slightly French* (1949).

In 1949, Sirk signed with Universal-International. His first films for the studio were largely unmemorable, but when he was permitted to work with such talent as Rock Hudson, Barbara Stanwyck, and Robert Stack, he demonstrated an ability to transcend the limitations of his scripts and turn mediocre soap operas into stylish films. Highlights of this final period of his film career include *Magnificent Obsession* (1954) and *All That Heaven Allows* (1956), both of which featured Hudson and Jane Wyman; *All I Desire* (1953) and *There's Always Tomorrow* (1956), starring Barbara Stanwyck; and *Written on the Wind* (1957) and *The Tarnished Angels* (1958), both featuring Hudson and Stack. The latter film was an adaptation of William Faulkner's *Pylon* (1935), and Sirk considered it his finest film.

His last film was his most commercially successful. *Imitation of Life* (1959) starred Lana Turner and concerned a light-skinned, young black woman who passed as a Caucasian. As with his earlier films, Sirk's skill lifted this picture above its melodramatic plot.

By this time, Sirk was tiring of the Hollywood system. He left the United States and returned to Germany, where he changed his name back to Detlef Sierck and worked in the theater and as an instructor in the Munich Film School. He was much admired by the generation of German filmmakers that rose to prominence in the 1970's; Rainer Werner Fassbinder was particularly enthusiastic about the elder statesman of German cinema. Indeed, in the late 1980's, Sirk's work has undergone a worldwide critical reappraisal, and he is now regarded as one of the most important filmmakers of the 1950's. His additional films include *April April* (1935), *Das Mädchen von Moorhof* (1935), *Sleep My Love* (1948), *Meet Me at the Fair* (1952), *Captain Lightfoot* (1955), *Interlude* (1957), and *A Time to Love and a Time to Die* (1958).

David Susskind (December 19, 1920-February 22, 1987). Susskind was a producer best known for his work in television and Broadway. He specialized in high-quality dramatic productions and won twenty Emmy Awards during his career. He also hosted a syndicated talk show for twenty years. His film productions include *A Raisin in the Sun* (1961), *Requiem for a Heavyweight* (1962), *All Creatures Great and Small* (1974), *Alice Doesn't Live Here Anymore* (1975), *Buffalo Bill and the Indians* (1976), and *Fort Apache, the Bronx* (1981).

Kent Taylor (May 11, 1907-April 11, 1987). Born Louis Weiss, Taylor was an actor who was a leading man in numerous B-pictures. His first film was *Road to Reno* (1931), and he made thirty films in the next five years, usually playing a suave ladies' man. In the early 1950's, he starred in television's *Boston Blackie* series and often appeared as the second-lead in major film productions. By the 1960's, he had returned to B-pictures, often in supporting roles. His acting credits include *I'm No Angel* (1933), *Ramona* (1936), *The Gracie Allen Murder Case* (1939), *Tangier* (1946), *Ghost Town* (1956), *The Day Mars Invaded Earth* (1963), and *Satan's Sadists* (1969).

Verree Teasdale (March 15, 1906-February 17, 1987). Teasdale was an actress who specialized in playing glamorous blondes. Her first film was *Syncopation* (1929), and she married actor Adolphe Menjou in 1934. Teasdale continued to appear in films through 1941; her additional acting credits include *The Sap from Syracuse* (1930), *Madame DuBarry* (1934), *A Midsummer Night's Dream* (1939), and *Come Live with Me* (1941).

Alice Terry (July 24, 1899-December 22, 1987). Born Alice Frances Taafe, Terry was a talented actress of the silent era. She made her film debut as a teenager in *Not My Sister* (1916) and also appeared in Cecil B. De Mille's *Old Wives for New* (1921). She married director Rex Ingram in 1921; that same year, he cast her opposite Rudolph Valentino in *The Four Horsemen of the Apocalypse* (1921), where her cool style contrasted nicely with Valentino's flamboyance. Terry and Ingram repeated this formula in *The Arab* (1924), in which she starred with Ramon Novarro. She began appearing almost exclusively in films directed by her husband, and both their careers effectively ended with the advent of sound, although the couple codirected *Love in Morocco* (1933), in which Ingram, but not Terry, acted. Her last film was the Spanish production *Asilo Naval* (1935). Terry's additional acting credits include *Hearts Are Trumps* (1920), *The Prisoner of Zenda* (1922), *Scaramouche* (1923), *The Magician* (1926), and *The Garden of Allah* (1927).

Raquel Torres (November 11, 1908-August 10, 1987). Born Paula Osterman in Mexico, Torres was an actress who played exotic beauties. She grew up in Los Angeles, and her first film appearance was a costarring role in W. S. Van Dyke's *White Shadows in the South Seas* (1928), Metro-Goldwyn-Mayer's first full-sound film. She appeared in several pictures during the next five years, but she retired soon after her marriage to a businessman. Her additional film credits include *The Bridge of San Luis Rey* (1929), *Aloha* (1931), *Duck Soup* (1933), and *Red Wagon* (1934).

Charles van der Linden (1911-July 20, 1987). Van der Linden was a Dutch director who specialized in short subjects. He moved to the United States in the 1920's and made dozens of films, including *Dutch in Seven Lessons* (1948), which was Audrey Hepburn's first film. His *Building Game* (1963) won the Berlin Film Festival prize as best documentary, and *This Tiny World* (1972) won the Academy Award for Best Documentary Short Subject. His additional films include *Young Hearts* (1936), *Dutch at the Double* (1948), *Flower of the Nation* (1956), *Big City Blues* (1963), and *Search for Peace* (1968).

Lino Ventura (July 14, 1919-October 23, 1987). Born Lino Borrini, Ventura was a French actor who specialized in tough-guy roles. A former professional boxer, he began acting in the early 1950's. He moved quickly from minor parts to leading roles and worked for filmmakers in France, Italy, Germany, England, and the United States. He appeared in Louis Malle's first feature film, *Frantic* (1958); in Vittorio De Sica's *Il Giudizio Universale* (1961); in Claude Lelouch's *Money Money Money* (1972); and in Dino De Laurentiis' *The Valachi Papers* (1972). His additional acting credits include *Touchez pas au Grisbi* (1954), *The Threepenny Opera* (1963), *Le Deuxième Souffle* (1966), *A Pain in the A . . .* (1973), and *The Medusa Touch* (1978).

Andy Warhol (August 8, 1927-February 21, 1987). Born Andrew Warhola, Warhol was an artist and filmmaker who transferred his pop art sensibilities to cinema. He had been a successful commercial artist for a decade when his 1962 exhibits of silkscreened prints of such cultural artifacts as Campbell's soup cans and photographs of Marilyn Monroe made him famous. A year later, he began to make films. *Kiss* (1963), *Eat* (1963), *Sleep* (1963), and *Haircut* (1963) were all fixed-camera shots of Warhol associates kissing, eating, sleeping (for eight hours), and getting a haircut, respectively. Critics called the films exercises in terminal boredom, but the New York avant-garde loved them.

Warhol began to attract bohemians of all stripes to his New York headquarters, which he called the Factory in partial ironic acknowledgment of the assembly-line nature of his art. Many of his friends adopted stage names such as Viva, Ultra Violet, Ingrid Superstar, and Candy Darling, and were featured in his films.

Warhol's films often featured nudity and a wide variety of explicit sexual behavior; gradually they also developed some semblance of a plot. *The Chelsea Girls* (1966) was the first Warhol film to be distributed commercially; it consisted of two separate films shown side by side and was a hit at art houses and colleges. His ****, (1967; also known as *Four Stars* after the *New York Daily News*' best-film rating) used the same technique. Its running time was more than twenty-four hours, although it was later released in a 102-minute version.

Warhol began to lose his avant-garde status with a trio of comedies in 1967, as some of his earlier supporters believed that he was abandoning experimentalism for commercial success. On June 5, 1968, Valerie Solanis, who had appeared in *I, a Man* (1967), shot Warhol and nearly killed him. While she initially claimed to represent a militant feminist group, the motives behind her act remain murky.

While Warhol spent months convalescing, his associate Paul Morrissey took over Warhol's filmmaking chores. Abandoning all vestiges of experimentalism in favor of campy comedy, Morrissey directed the six most commercially successful films to be released under Warhol's name: *Flesh* (1968), *Trash* (1970), *Heat* (1972), *Andy Warhol's Frankenstein* (1974), *Andy Warhol's Dracula* (1974), and *Andy Warhol's Bad* (1977). The exact extent of Warhol's participation in these films is a matter of conjecture.

Warhol's films reawakened interest in avant-garde cinema in the 1960's; their explicit sexuality paved the way for similar scenes in more conventional films. His Morrissey-era comedies foreshadowed such late-night cult classics as *The Rocky Horror Picture Show* (1975). Warhol once said that "in the future, everyone will be famous for fifteen minutes." Indeed, Warhol spent the last years of his life functioning mainly as a celebrity, remaining active in New York art circles until his death. His additional films include *Empire* (1965), *Poor Little Rich Girl* (1965), *Nude Restaurant* (1967), and *Lonesome Cowboys* (1968).

Emlyn Williams (November 26, 1905-September 25, 1987). Williams was a Welshman who was best known for his autobiographical play *The Corn Is Green*, first staged in 1938. He also worked in films as an actor and screenwriter, with more than forty films to his credit. He acted in *The Frightened Lady* (1932), *The Iron Duke* (1935), *They Drive by Night* (1939), *Major Barbara* (1941), *Ivanhoe* (1952), and *I Accuse!* (1958). His screenwriting credits include *The Man Who Knew Too Much* (1934), *This England* (1941), and *The Last Days of Dolwyn* (1949), which he also directed.

LIST OF AWARDS

Academy Awards
Best Picture: The Last Emperor (Columbia Pictures)
Direction: Bernardo Bertolucci (*The Last Emperor*)
Actor: Michael Douglas (*Wall Street*)
Actress: Cher (*Moonstruck*)
Supporting Actor: Sean Connery (*The Untouchables*)
Supporting Actress: Olympia Dukakis (*Moonstruck*)
Original Screenplay: John Patrick Shanley (*Moonstruck*)
Adapted Screenplay: Mark Peploe and Bernardo Bertolucci (*The Last Emperor*)
Cinematography: Vittorio Storaro (*The Last Emperor*)
Editing: Gabriella Cristiani (*The Last Emperor*)
Production Design: Ferdinando Scarfiotti (*The Last Emperor*)
Art Direction: Bruno Cesari and Oswaldo Desideri (*The Last Emperor*)
Special Visual Effects: Dennis Muren, William George, Harley Jessup, and Kenneth Smith (*Innerspace*)
Sound: Bill Rowe and Ivan Sharrock (*The Last Emperor*)
Makeup: Rick Baker (*Harry and the Hendersons*)
Costume Design: James Acheson (*The Last Emperor*)
Original Score: Ryuichi Sakamoto, David Byrne, and Cong Su (*The Last Emperor*)
Original Song: "(I've Had) the Time of My Life" (*Dirty Dancing:* music and lyrics, Franke Previte, John DeNicola, and Donald Markowitz)
Foreign-Language Film: Babette's Feast (Denmark)
Short Film, Animated: The Man Who Planted Trees (Société Radio-Canada)
Short Film, Live Action: Ray's Male Heterosexual Dance Hall (Chanticleer Films)
Documentary, Feature: The Ten-Year Lunch: The Wit and the Legend of the Algonquin Round Table (Direct Cinema)
Documentary, Short Subject: Young at Heart (Sue Marx Films)

Directors Guild of America Award
Director: Bernardo Bertolucci (*The Last Emperor*)

Writers Guild Awards
Original Screenplay: John Patrick Shanley (*Moonstruck*)
Adapted Screenplay: Steve Martin (*Roxanne*)

New York Film Critics Awards
Best Picture: Broadcast News (Twentieth Century-Fox)
Direction: James L. Brooks (*Broadcast News*)

Actor: Jack Nicholson (*Broadcast News*, *Ironweed*, and *The Witches of East-wick*)
Actress: Holly Hunter (*Broadcast News*)
Supporting Actor: Morgan Freeman (*Street Smart*)
Supporting Actress: Vanessa Redgrave (*Prick Up Your Ears*)
Screenplay: James L. Brooks (*Broadcast News*)
Cinematography: Vittorio Storaro (*The Last Emperor*)
Foreign-Language Film: My Life as a Dog (Sweden)

Los Angeles Film Critics Awards
Best Picture: Hope and Glory (Columbia Pictures)
Direction: John Boorman (*Hope and Glory*)
Actor: Steve Martin (*Roxanne*) and Jack Nicholson (*Ironweed*), tie
Actress: Holly Hunter (*Broadcast News*) and Sally Kirkland (*Anna*), tie
Supporting Actor: Morgan Freeman (*Street Smart*)
Supporting Actress: Olympia Dukakis (*Moonstruck*)
Screenplay: John Boorman (*Hope and Glory*)
Cinematography: Vittorio Storaro (*The Last Emperor*)
Music: Ryuichi Sakamoto, David Byrne, and Cong Su (*The Last Emperor*)
Foreign-Language Film: Au Revoir les Enfants (France)

National Society of Film Critics Awards
Best Picture: The Dead (Vestron Entertainment)
Direction: John Boorman (*Hope and Glory*)
Actor: Steve Martin (*Roxanne*)
Actress: Emily Lloyd (*Wish You Were Here*)
Supporting Actor: Morgan Freeman (*Street Smart*)
Supporting Actress: Kathy Baker (*Street Smart*)
Screenplay: John Boorman (*Hope and Glory*)
Cinematography: Philippe Rousselot (*Hope and Glory*)

National Board of Review Awards
Best English-Language Film: Empire of the Sun (Warner Bros.)
Direction: Steven Spielberg (*Empire of the Sun*)
Actor: Michael Douglas (*Wall Street*)
Actress: Lillian Gish (*The Whales of August*) and Holly Hunter (*Broadcast News*), tie
Outstanding Juvenile Performance: Christian Bale (*Empire of the Sun*)
Supporting Actor: Sean Connery (*The Untouchables*)
Supporting Actress: Olympia Dukakis (*Moonstruck*)
Foreign-Language Film: Jean de Florette and *Manon of the Spring* (France)

Golden Globe Awards

Best Picture, Drama: The Last Emperor (Columbia Pictures)
Best Picture, Comedy or Musical: Hope and Glory (Columbia Pictures)
Direction: Bernardo Bertolucci (*The Last Emperor*)
Actor, Drama: Michael Douglas (*Wall Street*)
Actress, Drama: Sally Kirkland (*Anna*)
Actor, Comedy or Musical: Robin Williams (*Good Morning, Vietnam*)
Actress, Comedy or Musical: Cher (*Moonstruck*)
Supporting Actor: Sean Connery (*The Untouchables*)
Supporting Actress: Olympia Dukakis (*Moonstruck*)
Screenplay: Mark Peploe and Bernardo Bertolucci (*The Last Emperor*)
Original Score: Ryuichi Sakamoto, David Byrne, and Cong Su (*The Last Emperor*)
Foreign-Language Film: My Life as a Dog (Sweden)

Golden Palm Awards (Cannes International Film Festival)

Gold Palm: Pelle the Conqueror (Bille August)
Grand Special Jury Award: A World Apart (Chris Menges)
Actor: Forest Whitaker (*Bird*)
Actress: Barbara Hershey, Jodhi May, and Linda Mvusi (*A World Apart*)
Direction: Fernando Solanas (*The South*)

British Academy Awards

Best Picture: Jean de Florette (Cannon)
Direction: Oliver Stone (*Platoon*)
Actor: Sean Connery (*The Name of the Rose*)
Actress: Anne Bancroft (*Eighty-four Charing Cross Road*)
Supporting Actor: Daniel Auteuil (*Jean de Florette*)
Supporting Actress: Susan Wooldridge (*Hope and Glory*)
Original Screenplay: David Leland (*Wish You Were Here*)
Adapted Screenplay: Claude Berri and Gerard Brach (*Jean de Florette*)
Cinematography: Bruno Nuytten (*Jean de Florette*)
Editing: Ian Crawford (*Platoon*)
Production Design: Santo Loquasto (*Radio Days*)
Special Visual Effects: Michael Owens (*The Witches of Eastwick*)
Costume Design: Jeffray Kurland (*Radio Days*)
Sound: Jonathon Bates, Simon Kaye, and Gery Humphreys (*Cry Freedom*)
Original Score: Ennio Morricone (*The Untouchables*)
Best Foreign-Language Film: The Sacrifice (France and Sweden)

MAGILL'S CINEMA ANNUAL

TITLE INDEX

509

TITLE INDEX

TITLE INDEX

DIRECTOR INDEX

DIRECTOR INDEX

DIRECTOR INDEX

519

DIRECTOR INDEX

SCREENWRITER INDEX

SCREENWRITER INDEX

CRAVEN, WES
Nightmare on Elm Street 3   423
CRISTOFER, MICHAEL
Witches of Eastwick, The   381
CRUICKSHANK, JIM
Three Men and a Baby   347
CSICSERY, GEORGE
Where the Heart Roams   447
CUNNINGHAM, ALEX
Emmanuelle 5   402
CURTELIN, JEAN
Rumba, The   432

DAHL, JOHN
Private Investigations   429
DAHLIN, BOB
Monster in the Closet   420
D'AMICO, SUSO CECCHI
Dark Eyes   91
DANTON, SYLVIE
Under the Sun of Satan   444
DARABONT, FRANK
Nightmare on Elm Street 3   423
DAVID, MARJORIE
Shy People   434
DAVILA, JACQUES
Good Weather, But Stormy Late This
Afternoon   406
DEAR, WILLIAM
Harry and the Hendersons   408
DEARDEN, JAMES
Fatal Attraction   118
DE BELLO, JOHN
Happy Hour   407
DECOTEAU, DAVID
Creepozoids   398
DEESE, FRANK
Principal, The   428
DE GUZMAN, MICHAEL
Jaws—The Revenge   412
DEIMEL, MARK
Perfect Match, The   426
DEKKER, FRED
Monster Squad, The   420
DEKLEIN, JOHN
Care Bears Adventure in Wonderland, The   396
DELUCA, RUDY
Million Dollar Mystery   419
DE SOUZA, STEVEN E. See SOUZA, STEVEN
E. DE.
DE VRIES, MARIETTA
Zjoek   450
DEWHURST, RICHARD
Dear America   400
DILLON, CONSTANTINE
Happy Hour   407
DIXON, KEN
Slave Girls from Beyond Infinity   436
DIXON, LESLIE
Outrageous Fortune   267
Overboard   425
DOCHERTY, JAMES J.
Nightstick   423

DORFF, MATT
Campus Man   396
DOUGLAS, PETER
Tiger's Tale, A   442
DOYLE, TIM
Zombie High   450
DRAGIN, BERT L.
Summer Camp Nightmare   439
DUIGAN, JOHN
Year My Voice Broke, The   449
DUMAYET, PIERRE
Malady of Love, The   418
DUNBAR, ANDREA
Rita, Sue and Bob Too   432
DUNN, GEOFFREY
Miss . . . or Myth?   420
DURANG, CHRISTOPHER
Beyond Therapy   67
DURETTA, NICK
Perfect Match, The   426
DUVIC, PATRICE
End of the Line   402
DZHANELIDZE, NANA
Repentance   431

EARLE, JOSEPH H.
Silent Night, Deadly Night Part II   435
ÉCARE, DÉSIRÉ
Faces of Women   403
ELLIS, BOB
Warm Nights on a Slow Moving Train   446
EPPS, JACK, JR.
Secret of My Success, The   315
ESCALATE, DANA
Return to Horror High   431
ESZTERHAS, JOE
Big Shots   393
Hearts of Fire   408
EVANS, BRUCE A.
Made in Heaven   223
EXPORT, VALIE
Seven Women, Seven Sins   434

FANAKA, JAMAA
Penitentiary III   426
FELDBERG, MARK
Disorderlies   401
FELDMAN, DENNIS
Real Men   430
FELDMAN, GENE
Marilyn Monroe   418
FERGUSON, LARRY
Beverly Hills Cop II   63
FERRINI, FRANCO
Opera   424
FIELD, DAVID
Amazing Grace and Chuck   390
FIELDS, SCOTT
Under Cover   444
FINKLEMAN, KEN
Who's That Girl   448
FISCHER, JANICE
Lost Boys, The   417

SCREENWRITER INDEX

SCREENWRITER INDEX

OPPER, DON
Slam Dance 436
ORR, JAMES
They Still Call Me Bruce 442
Three Men and a Baby 347
OTTINGER, ULRIKE
Seven Women, Seven Sins 434
OUTTEN, RICHARD
Lionheart 417

PALMER, MELINDA
Garbage Pail Kids Movie, The 405
PALMER, TONY
Testimony 441
PARENT, GAIL
Cross My Heart 398
PARKER, ALAN
Angel Heart 29
PASEORNEK, MICHAEL
Meatballs III 419
PASSERELLI, ELIZABETH
Zombie High 450
PEACE, J. STEPHEN
Happy Hour 407
PELED, HANAN
Deadline 399
PENNEY, JOHN
Kindred, The 414
PEPLOE, MARK
Last Emperor, The 205
PETRIE, DANIEL, JR.
Big Easy, The 71
PEYTON, HARLEY
Less Than Zero 416
PHELPS, WILLIAM
North Shore 424
PIALAT, MAURICE
Under the Sun of Satan 444
PINHEIRO, JOSE
My True Love, My Wound 422
PINSENT, GORDON
John and the Missus 413
PONICSAN, DARRYL
Nuts 262
POOL, ROBERT ROY
Big Town, The 394
PROSER, CHIP
Innerspace 188
PYHALA, JAKKO
Ursula 444

QIAO XUEZHU
Last Day of Winter, The 415
QUATERMASS, MARTIN
Prince of Darkness 428
QUIGLEY, MOE
Cold Steel 397
QUINTANO, GENE
Allan Quatermain and the Lost City of
Gold 389
Police Academy 4 427
QUIROS, M.
Violins Came with the Americans, The 445

RAIMI, SAM
Evil Dead II 403
RANFT, JOE
Brave Little Toaster, The 394
RAPPAPORT, EZRA D.
Harry and the Hendersons 408
RAY, LESLIE
My Demon Lover 421
REBAR, ALEX
Nowhere to Hide 424
RED, ERIC
Near Dark 422
REES, JERRY
Brave Little Toaster, The 394
REYNOLDS, JONATHAN
Leonard Part 6 415
REYNOLDS, REBECCA
Backfire 392
REZYKA, MARK
South of Reno 437
RICHARDSON, SCOTT
Hearts of Fire 408
RIESNER, DEAN
Fatal Beauty 404
RILEY, ROB
Number One with a Bullet 424
RISI, MARCO
Rimini Rimini 431
ROBBINS, MATTHEW
Batteries Not Included 392
ROBINSON, BRUCE
Withnail and I [1986] 385
ROBINSON, PHIL ALDEN
In the Mood 183
ROCHAT, ERIC
Too Much 443
ROMERO, GEORGE A.
Creepshow 2 398
ROMOLI, GIANNI
Rimini Rimini 431
ROSE, WILLIAM
Obituaries 497
ROSENTHAL, MARK
Superman IV 440
ROSEO, ENRICO
Moscow Farewell 421
ROTH, ERIC
Suspect 335
ROTHBERG, JEFF
Hiding Out 410
ROUSE, RUSSELL
Obituaries 497
ROZEMA, PATRICIA
I've Heard the Mermaids Singing 412
RUBEN, KATT SHEA
Stripped to Kill 439
RUDE, DICK
Straight to Hell 438
RUDKIN, DAVID
Testimony 441
RUGOFF, EDWARD
Mannequin 418
RUSSELL, CHUCK
Nightmare on Elm Street 3 423

SCREENWRITER INDEX

CINEMATOGRAPHER INDEX

CINEMATOGRAPHER INDEX

KELLY, JOE
Heaven 409
KELLY, SHANE
Sweet Revenge 441
KEMPER, VICTOR J.
Walk Like a Man 445
KENNY, FRANCIS
Campus Man 396
KESTERMAN, ROLF
Disorderlies 401
Surf Nazis Must Die 440
KIBBE, GARY G.
Prince of Darkness 428
KIESSER, JAN
Made in Heaven 223
Some Kind of Wonderful 323
KIMBALL, JEFFREY L.
Beverly Hills Cop II 63
KIMURA, DAISAKU
Too Much 443
KITZANUK, ANDREW
Last Straw, The 415
KNOOP, JOHN
Where the Heart Roams 447
KNOWLAND, NIC
Testimony 441
KOCH, DOUGLAS
I've Heard the Mermaids Singing 412
KOLTAI, LAJOS
Gaby—A True Story 139
KRISTIANSEN, HENNING
Babette's Feast 392
KURANT, WILLY
Under the Sun of Satan 444

LACAMBRE, DANIEL
'68 436
LACHMAN, EDWARD
Less Than Zero 416
Making Mr. Right 227
LANCI, GIUSEPPE
Good Morning, Babylon 406
LANDEN, HAL
Sullivan's Pavilion 439
LASKUS, JACEK
Heart 408
Square Dance 437
LASZLO, ANDREW
Innerspace 188
LEBLANC, JOHN
Stripped to Kill 439
LE MENER, JEAN-YVES
Warning Bandits 446
LEONETTI, MATTHEW F.
Dragnet 104
Extreme Prejudice 403
LHOMME, PIERRE
Maurice 241
LINDLEY, JOHN
In the Mood 183
Stepfather, The 438
LLOYD, WALT
Down Twisted 401
LOFTUS, BRYAN
Siesta 435

LOWNES, PETER
I Was a Teenage Zombie 411
LUND, MICHAEL
Siesta 435
LUTIC, BERNARD
Angel Dust 391
LUX, DAVID
Zombie High 450

MCALPINE, DONALD
Fringe Dwellers, The [1986] 127
Orphans 425
Predator 275
MCCONKEY, LARRY
White of the Eye 448
MCDANIEL, WAYNE
Her Name Is Lisa 409
MACDONALD, PETER
Hamburger Hill 406
MCLEAN, NICK
Spaceballs 437
MCLEISH, RONALD W.
Monster in the Closet 420
MACMILLAN, KENNETH
Month in the Country, A 420
MCPHERSON, JOHN
Batteries Not Included 392
Jaws—The Revenge 412
MAEDA, YONEZA
Funeral, The [1984] 135
MAINTIGNEUX, SOPHIE
King Lear 414
MAIRA, HORACIO
Stranger, The 438
MANLEY, FLETCHER
White Winter Heat 448
MARDERIAN, KARL
D. U. I. 401
MARINI, THOM
My Dark Lady 421
MASON, STEVE
Tale of Ruby Rose, The 441
MATHIAS, HARRY
Ernest Goes to Camp 403
MAUCH, THOMAS
Deadline 399
MAY, BRADFORD
Monster Squad, The 420
MAY, JIM
Ernest Goes to Camp 403
MEHEUX, PHIL
Fourth Protocol, The 122
MENGES, CHRIS
Shy People 434
METCALFE, JOHN
Rawheadrex 430
MIGEAT, FRANÇOIS
Faces of Women 403
MIGNOT, PIERRE
Beyond Therapy 67
O. C. and Stiggs 424
MILLS, ALEC
Lionheart 417
Living Daylights, The 214

CINEMATOGRAPHER INDEX

537

SAAD, ROBERT
Police Academy 4   427
SACHER, LUKE
Radium City   430
SALOMON, AMNON
Deadline   399
Once We Were Dreamers   424
SALOMON, MIKAEL
Peter Von Scholten   426
SAMOILOVSKI, MISCO
Happy '49   407
SANCHEZ, LEON
Predator   275
SARIN, VIC
Nowhere to Hide   424
SCHAEFFER, MARTIN
Seven Women, Seven Sins   434
SCHIER, HORST
Wannsee Conference, The   446
SCHULER, FRED
Gloria [1980]   458
SCHWARTZ, MARK
Miss . . . or Myth?   420
SEALE, JOHN
Stakeout   327
SEMLER, DEAN
Lighthorsemen, The   416
SERESIN, MICHAEL
Angel Heart   29
SHEA, MIKE
Body Slam   394
SIMMONS, LIONEL
Life Classes   416
SINCLAIR, PETER
Sign o' the Times   435
SISSELMAN, BRIAN
White Winter Heat   448
SMOKLER, PETER
North Shore   424
SMOOT, REED
Grand Canyon   406
Russkies   433
SOBOCINSKI, PIOTR
Zjoek   450
SOBOCINSKI, WITOLD
Zjoek   450
SOKOL, YURI
Warm Nights on a Slow Moving Train   446
SOLIS, LEONARDO RODRÍGUEZ
Night of the Pencils, The   422
SONNENFELD, BARRY
Raising Arizona   294
Three O'Clock High   442
Throw Momma from the Train   351
SOUTHON, MIKE
Gothic   159
SOVA, PETER
Good Morning, Vietnam   154
Tin Men   355
SPANG, RONALD
Deadly Illusion   400
SPENCER, BRENTON
Blue Monkey   394
SPERLING, DAVID
Street Trash   438

SPINOTTI, DANTE
From the Hip   405
STAPLETON, OLIVER
Chuck Berry: Hail! Hail! Rock 'n' Roll   397
Prick Up Your Ears   280
Sammy and Rosie Get Laid   433
STEIN, PETER
Wild Pair, The   448
STEPHENS, JOHN M.
Steele Justice   438
STEWART, PATRICK
D. U. I.   401
STEWART, SPIKE
D. U. I.   401
STORARO, VITTORIO
Ishtar   196
Last Emperor, The   205
STRADLING, HARRY
Blind Date   79
STRASBURG, IVAN
Rita, Sue and Bob Too   432
STUDEBAKER, DARYL
Trouble with Dick, The   443
SUHRSTEDT, TIM
Mannequin   418
SURTEES, BRUCE
Back to the Beach   392
SUSLOV, MISHA
Verne Miller   445

TAMMES, FRED
Whistle Blower, The   447
TAMURA, MASAKI
Tampopo [1986]   343
TAYLOR, GIL
Bedroom Window, The   53
TAYLOR, RONNIE
Cry Freedom   87
Opera   424
TEE TUNG LUNG
Wrong Couples, The   449
THOMSON, ALEX
Date with an Angel   399
Sicilian, The   435
TIDY, FRANK
Hot Pursuit   410
John and the Missus   413
TOCHIZAWA, MASAO
Pimp, The   427
TORRANCE, BOB
Perfect Match, The   426
TOVOLI, LUCIANO
Unsane   444
TRENAS, TOTE
Alien Predator   389

ULLOA, ALEXANDER
Crystal Heart   398
URBANCZYK, JOSEPH
Allnighter, The   390

VACANO, JOST
Robocop   303
VAMOS, THOMAS
Captive Hearts   396
Gate, The   147

CINEMATOGRAPHER INDEX

EDITOR INDEX

541

EDITOR INDEX

543

EDITOR INDEX

EDITOR INDEX

ART DIRECTOR INDEX

ART DIRECTOR INDEX

ESTEVEZ, ENRIQUE
  Born in East L. A.   394
  Predator   275
EVEIN, BERNARD
  Rumba, The   432

FAGELLIO, ABEL
  Rage of Honor   430
  Stranger, The   438
FARQUHAR, MELBA KATZMAN
  Hollywood Shuffle   166
FAURE, ALAIN
  Emmanuelle 5   402
FAWDRY, RICHARD
  When the Wind Blows [1986]   447
FERNÁNDEZ, JAVIER
  Law of Desire, The   415
FETTIS, GARY
  Gardens of Stone   143
FISCHER, DAVID
  Roxanne   311
FISCHER, LISA
  Big Easy, The   71
  Light of Day   416
FONG YING
  Wrong Couples, The   449
FONSECA, GREGG
  House II   411
FORD, MICHAEL
  Empire of the Sun   113
  Living Daylights, The   214
FORD, ROGER
  Year My Voice Broke, The   449
FOREMAN, PHILIP DEAN
  Slam Dance   436
FOX, BOB
  Whales of August, The   372
FOX, J. RAE
  Born in East L. A.   394
FOX, K. C.
  Whales of August, The   372
FRANCO, JOHN, JR.
  Spaceballs   437
FRANCO, ROBERT J.
  Angel Heart   29
  Hello Again   409
FRANENBERG, BARRY
  Summer Camp Nightmare   439
FREAS, DIANNA
  Lemon Sky   415
FREDERICKS, JAMES T.
  Eddie Murphy Raw   402
FREEBORN, MARK S.
  Dead of Winter   399
FREED, REUBEN
  Blue Monkey   394
  Nightstick   423
FREITAG, CRAIG
  Penitentiary III   426
FRISHETTE, SUZIE
  Walker   446
FULLER, RHILEY
  Police Academy 4   427
FURST, ANTON
  Full Metal Jacket   131

GALBRAITH, ELINOR ROSE
  Believers, The   393
GALEA, ANNE
  Captive Hearts   396
GANZ, ARMIN
  Angel Heart   29
  Tough Guys Don't Dance   443
GARBUGLIA, MARIO
  Dark Eyes   91
GARRITY, JOSEPH T.
  Weeds   368
GARRONE, MAURIZIO
  Unsane   444
GARWOOD, NORMAN
  Princess Bride, The   285
  Shadey   434
GASSNER, DENNIS
  In the Mood   183
  Like Father Like Son   417
GAUSMAN, HAL
  Jaws—The Revenge   412
  Untouchables, The   359
GAUSMAN, RUSSELL A.
  All I Desire [1953]   453
GENTZ, RICK T.
  Outrageous Fortune   267
GERVASI, CARLO
  Dark Eyes   91
GIBESON, BRUCE
  No Way Out   258
GINN, JEFFREY S.
  Date with an Angel   399
GIOVAGNONI, GIANNI
  Last Emperor, The   205
GLASS, TED
  Squeeze, The   438
GODDARD, RICHARD C.
  Innerspace   188
GODFREY, JOHN
  Gloria [1980]   458
GOLITZEN, ALEXANDER
  All I Desire [1953]   453
GORTON, ADRIAN
  Rage of Honor   430
GOULD, ROBERT
  Robocop   303
GRAFF, PHILIPPE
  Diary of a Mad Old Man   401
GRAHAM, ANGELO
  Batteries Not Included   392
GRAHAM, MARLENE
  Gate, The   147
GRALL, VALERIE
  April Is a Deadly Month   391
GRASSO, SAL
  Hard Ticket to Hawaii   408
GRAY, MAGGIE
  Princess Bride, The   285
GRAYSMARK, JOHN
  Superman IV   440
GRIFFITH, CLAY
  Dirty Dancing   100
GRIGORIAN, GRETA
  Return to Horror High   431

ART DIRECTOR INDEX

ART DIRECTOR INDEX

ART DIRECTOR INDEX

559

MUSIC INDEX

MUSIC INDEX

MUSIC INDEX

MUSIC INDEX

PERFORMER INDEX

AALTO, PETRI
Ursula   444
ABBOTT, BRUCE
Summer Heat   439
ABDUL-SAMAD, HAKEEM
Ernest Goes to Camp   403
ABE, MITZIE
Living on Tokyo Time   417
ABNER, TEDDY
Wild Thing   448
ABRAHAM, KEN
Creepozoids   398
ABULADZE, KETEVAN
Repentance   431
ACHDIAN, ANNA
Wedding in Galilee, A   447
ACHESON, JAMES
Assassination   391
ACKLAND, JOSS
Sicilian, The   435
ACOVONE, JAY
Cold Steel   397
ADAIR, ANNA
Peter Von Scholten   426
ADAMES, JOHN
Gloria [1980]   458
ADAMS, BRIAN
Marsupials, The   419
ADAMS, DON
Back to the Beach   392
ADAMS, JEB STUART
Flowers in the Attic   405
ADAMS, STACEY
Sweet Revenge   441
ADELE, JAN
High Tide   163
ADJANI, ISABELLE
Ishtar   196
ADJAVON, RAYMOND
Peter Von Scholten   426
ADLER, MATT
Amazon Women on the Moon   390
North Shore   424
ADOLFSSON, ROLF
Jim and the Pirates   412
ADU, ROBINSON FRANK
Heart   408
AF ENEHIELM, CHRIS. *See* ENEHIELM,
CHRIS AF.
AFFLECK, CASEY
Lemon Sky   415
AGENIN, BEATRICE
Année des meduses, L'   391
AGGIE
Sister, Sister   435
AGIDIUS, HANS CHRISTIAN
Peter Von Scholten   426
AGREN, JANET
Aladdin   389

AI NUO
Romance of Book and Sword, The   432
AIELLO, DANNY
Moonstruck   245
Pick-Up Artist, The   427
AILHAUD, YVELINE
Angel Dust   391
AKERBLOM, JOHAN
Jim and the Pirates   412
AKERMAN, CHANTAL
Seven Women, Seven Sins   434
AKIKI, ALI MOHAMMED
Wedding in Galilee, A   447
AKIN, PHILIP
Prettykill   428
AKINS, CLAUDE
Monster in the Closet   420
AKIYAMA, DENIS
Captive Hearts   396
AKLY, NAZIH
Wedding in Galilee, A   447
ALAHANI, SHEEBA
Barbarians, The   392
ALBANO, CAPTAIN LOU
Body Slam   394
ALBERT, MAXINE
Home Remedy   410
ALCROFT, JAMIE
Million Dollar Mystery   419
ALDA, RUTANYA
Hotshot   411
ALDEN, STACEY
Nightmare on Elm Street 3   423
ALEANDRO, NORMA
Gaby—A True Story   139
ALEONG, AKI
Hanoi Hilton, The   407
ALEXA
Home Remedy   410
ALEXANDER, DICK
Campus Man   396
ALEXANDER, JANE
Square Dance   437
Sweet Country   441
ALEXANDER, MAX
Fat Guy Goes Nutzoid   404
ALEXANDRA, TIANA
Feel the Heat   404
ALEXANDROV, CONSTANTIN
Man in Love, A   418
ALFREDSON, HANS
Jim and the Pirates   412
ALLAN, ANTONY
Hellraiser   409
ALLAOUI, KARIM
Rumba, The   432
ALLEN, KAREN
Backfire   392
End of the Line   402
Glass Menagerie, The   150

PERFORMER INDEX

PERFORMER INDEX

BONNEL, PATRICK
  Angel Dust   391
BONNER, TONY
  Lighthorsemen, The   416
BONVOISIN, BERANGERE
  Good Morning, Babylon   406
BOONE, RANDY
  Wild Pair, The   448
BOONE, WALKER
  Nightstick   423
BOOTH, CONNIE
  Eighty-four Charing Cross Road   108
BOOTH, JAMES
  Programmed to Kill   429
BOOTHE, POWERS
  Extreme Prejudice   403
BORELLI, CARLA
  O. C. and Stiggs   424
BORROMEO, CHRISTIAN
  Unsane   444
BOSCHI, GIULIA
  Sicilian, The   435
BOSCO, PHILIP
  Suspect   335
  Three Men and a Baby   347
BOSLEY, TOM
  Million Dollar Mystery   419
  Pinocchio and the Emperor of the Night   427
BOSSO, J. O.
  Alien Predator   389
BOTES, MICHELLE
  American Ninja 2   390
BOTSVADZE, ZEJNAB
  Repentance   431
BOTTOMS, SAM
  Gardens of Stone   143
BOUCHAUD, JEAN
  Manon of the Spring [1986]   232
BOUDET, JACQUES
  Waiting for the Moon   445
BOUKHANEF, KADER
  Miss Mona   420
BOUQUET, CAROLE
  Malady of Love, The   418
BOURLAT, JEAN-CLAUDE
  Under the Sun of Satan   444
BOUTSIKARIS, DENNIS
  Batteries Not Included   392
BOVASO, JULIE
  Moonstruck   245
BOWE, DAVID
  Back to the Beach   392
BOWEN, MICHAEL
  Less Than Zero   416
BOYACK, VANESSA
  Niagara Falls   422
BOYAR, SULLY
  Best Seller   58
BOYD, JAN GAN
  Assassination   391
  Steele Justice   438
BOYER, BONI
  Sign o' the Times   435
BOYETT, WILLIAM
  Hidden, The   410

BOYLE, PETER
  Surrender   440
  Walker   446
BRACCO, LORRAINE
  Pick-Up Artist, The   427
  Someone to Watch over Me   437
BRADFORD, RICHARD
  Untouchables, The   359
BRADLEY, SCOTT
  Lighthorsemen, The   416
BRADY, DAN PATRICK
  My Demon Lover   421
BRADY, JANELLE
  Allnighter, The   390
BRADY, PAUL
  Secret Policeman's Third Ball, The   434
BRANAGH, KENNETH
  Month in the Country, A   420
BRANAMAN, RUSTAM
  Hard Ticket to Hawaii   408
BRANCHE, DERRICK
  Sicilian, The   435
BRANDEWYNE, REBECCA
  Where the Heart Roams   447
BRANDON, DAVID
  Good Morning, Babylon   406
BRANDON-JONES, UNA
  Withnail and I [1986]   385
BRANDY, EDEN
  Campus Man   396
BRANTLEY, BETSY
  Fourth Protocol, The   122
BRATTON, CREED
  Wild Pair, The   448
BRAUN, SHONY ALEX
  '68   436
BREIDENBACH, TILLI
  Alpine Fire   390
BREMSER, RAY
  Beat Generation—An American Dream,
    The   393
BRENNAN, MELISSA
  Summer Camp Nightmare   439
BRENNAN, TOM
  Fatal Attraction   118
BRENNER, BARRY
  Surf Nazis Must Die   440
BRESTOFF, RICHARD
  Return to Horror High   431
BREWTON, MAIA
  Adventures in Babysitting   389
BRIANT, SHANE
  Lighthorsemen, The   416
BRIBIESCA, RICKY
  Queen City Rocker   429
BRIDGES, BEAU
  Killing Time, The   413
  Wild Pair, The   448
BRIDGES, JEFF
  Nadine   254
BRIDGES, LLOYD
  Wild Pair, The   448
BRIESE, BOBBIE
  Surf Nazis Must Die   440

575

PERFORMER INDEX

BUSH, PETER
I Was a Teenage Zombie 411
BUSH, REBECCAH
Hunk 411
BUSKER, RICKY
Big Shots 393
BUSSE, JOCHEN
Wannsee Conference, The 446
BUSSINGER, HANS W.
Wannsee Conference, The 446
BUTLER, DANIEL
Ernest Goes to Camp 403
BUTRICK, MERRITT
Shy People 434
BUZA, GEORGE
Meatballs III 419
BYRD-NETHERY, MIRIAM
Summer Heat 439
BYRNE, GABRIEL
Gothic 159
Hello Again 409
Lionheart 417
Siesta 435
BYRNES, BURKE
Witchboard 449
BYRON, CARLYLE
Stripped to Kill 439

CAAN, JAMES
Gardens of Stone 143
CADY, BARBARA
My Dark Lady 421
CAESAR, SID
Emperor's New Clothes, The 402
CAGE, NICOLAS
Moonstruck 245
Raising Arizona 294
CAINE, MICHAEL
Fourth Protocol, The 122
Jaws — The Revenge 412
Surrender 440
Whistle Blower, The 447
CALA, JERRY
Rimini Rimini 431
CALABRESE, NANCY
Summer Camp Nightmare 439
CALL, R. D.
No Man's Land 423
CALLAS, CHARLIE
Amazon Women on the Moon 390
CALLAU, MANUEL
Night of the Pencils, The 422
CALLOW, SIMON
Maurice 241
CALVIN, JOHN
Back to the Beach 392
CAMERON, CANDACE
Some Kind of Wonderful 323
CAMERON, DEAN
Summer School 440
CAMERON, ETTA
Peter Von Scholten 426
CAMERON, KIRK
Like Father Like Son 417

CAMMELL, CHINA
White of the Eye 448
CAMP, COLLEEN
Walk Like a Man 445
CAMPANELLA, FRANK
Overboard 425
CAMPANELLA, JOSEPH
Steele Justice 438
CAMPBELL, BRUCE
Evil Dead II 403
CAMPBELL, J. KENNETH
Dear America 400
CAMPBELL, NICHOLAS
Rampage 430
CAMPION, CRIS
Beyond Therapy 67
CAMPUDONI, MADISON
Penitentiary III 426
CANDAL, NORMA
Violins Came with the Americans, The 445
CANDY, JOHN
Planes, Trains, and Automobiles 271
Spaceballs 437
CANFIELD, MARY GRACE
South of Reno 437
CANNON, CATHERINE
Hidden, The 410
CANTOR, MAX
Dirty Dancing 100
CAPPELLO, TIM
Hearts of Fire 408
CARA, IRENE
Busted Up 395
CARBONELL, RAUL, JR.
Gran Fiesta, La 406
CARDINALE, CLAUDIA
Man in Love, A 418
CAREY, HARRY, JR.
Whales of August, The 372
CAREY, MACDONALD
It's Alive III 412
CARL, ADAM
Summer Camp Nightmare 439
CARLIN, GEORGE
Outrageous Fortune 267
CARLIN, GLORIA
Hanoi Hilton, The 407
CARLSON, RICHARD
All I Desire [1953] 453
CARLSON, SARA
Bedroom Window, The 53
CARLSSON, ING-MARI
My Life as a Dog [1985] 250
CARLTON, HOPE MARIE
Hard Ticket to Hawaii 408
CARLTON, ROBERT
Year My Voice Broke, The 449
CARMEN, JULIE
Gloria [1980] 458
CARMEN, LEONE
Year My Voice Broke, The 449
CARMET, JEAN
Miss Mona 420

577

PERFORMER INDEX

PERFORMER INDEX

PERFORMER INDEX

587

PERFORMER INDEX

PERFORMER INDEX

PERFORMER INDEX

PERFORMER INDEX

PERFORMER INDEX

KABOUCHE, AZIZ
Flame in My Heart, A 405
KADI, CHARLOTTE
Année des meduses, L' 391
KAGAN, JEREMY
Someone to Love 436
KAHN, CYNDE
Home Remedy 410
KAM, MIKI
Late Summer Blues 415
KAMAKAHI, PIA
Stripped to Kill 439
KAMINO, BRENDA
I've Heard the Mermaids Singing 412
KAMPMANN, STEVEN
Tiger's Tale, A 442
KANE, CAROL
Ishtar 196
Princess Bride, The 285
KANI, JOHN
Saturday Night at the Palace 433
KANTER, MARIANNE
Nightmare at Shadow Woods 423
KAPELOS, JOHN
Roxanne 311
KAPOOR, SHASHI
Sammy and Rosie Get Laid 433
KAPRISKY, VALERIE
Année des meduses, L' 391
KARABATSOS, RON
Cold Steel 397
KARMAN, JANICE
Chipmunk Adventure, The 397
KARVAN, CLAUDIA
High Tide 163
KATH, CAMELIA
Killing Time, The 413
KATO, YOSHI
Tampopo [1986] 343
KATSULAS, ANDREAS
Sicilian, The 435
Someone to Watch over Me 437
KATZ, ELIA
Man in Love, A 418
KAVNER, JULIE
Radio Days 290
Surrender 440
KAVSADZE, KAHKI
Repentance 431
KAYE, DANNY
Obituaries 489
KAYE, MICHAEL
Someone to Love 436
KAYE, NORMAN
Warm Nights on a Slow Moving Train 446
KAYSOE, DICK
Peter Von Scholten 426
KAZAN, LAINIE
Harry and the Hendersons 408
KAZURINSKY, TIM
Police Academy 4 427
KEAN, MARIE
Dead, The 95
John Huston and the Dubliners 413
Lonely Passion of Judith Hearne, The 219

KEANE, KERRIE
Nightstick 423
KEATON, DIANE
Baby Boom 41
KEATON, MICHAEL
Squeeze, The 438
KEAYS-BYRNE, HUGH
Kangaroo 413
Les Patterson Saves the World 416
KEENER, ELIOT
Angel Heart 29
KEHOE, JACK
Untouchables, The 359
KEITEL, HARVEY
Dear America 400
Pick-Up Artist, The 427
KEITER, CINDY
I Was a Teenage Zombie 411
KEITH, BRIAN
Death Before Dishonor 400
KEITH, DAVID
White of the Eye 448
KELLER, FRED A.
My Dark Lady 421
KELLER, MARTHE
Dark Eyes 91
KELLERMAN, SALLY
Meatballs III 419
Someone to Love 436
Three for the Road 442
KELLOGG, JOHN
Orphans 425
KELLY, DESMOND
Dancers 399
KEMBLE, MARK
Penitentiary III 426
KEMKHADZE, DATO
Repentance 431
KEMP, BRANDIS
South of Reno 437
KEMPF, ANGIE
Pick-Up Artist, The 427
KENNEDY, GEORGE
Creepshow 2 398
KENNEDY, GERARD
Lighthorsemen, The 416
KENNEDY, GRAHAM
Les Patterson Saves the World 416
Travelling North 443
KENNEDY, KRISTINA
Baby Boom 41
KENNEDY, LEON ISAAC
Penitentiary III 426
KENNEDY, MADGE
Obituaries 490
KENNEDY, MICHELLE
Baby Boom 41
KENT, JESSIE
Summer Heat 439
KENT, JULIE
Dancers 399
KEPROS, NICHOLAS
Sicilian, The 435
KERAMIDAS, CHRISA
Dancers 399

597

PERFORMER INDEX

PERFORMER INDEX

PERFORMER INDEX

MOREY, BILL
  Real Men 430
MORGAN, HARRY
  Dragnet 104
MORGAN, WENDY
  Eighty-four Charing Cross Road 108
MORIARATY, JAMES
  Someone to Watch over Me 437
MORIARTY, CATHY
  White of the Eye 448
MORIARTY, MICHAEL
  Hanoi Hilton, The 407
  It's Alive III 412
MORIER-GENOUD, PHILIPPE
  Au Revoir les Enfants 37
MORITA, NORIYUKI (PAT)
  Captive Hearts 396
MORITZ, DOROTHEA
  Alpine Fire 390
MORITZEN, HENNING
  Peter Von Scholten 426
MORLEY, ROBERT
  Trouble with Spies, The 444
MORRIS, GARRETT
  Critical Condition 398
MORRIS, HAVILAND
  Who's That Girl 448
MORRIS, PHIL
  Private Investigations 429
MORROW, LIZA
  Three O'Clock High 442
MORROW, STEPHEN
  Tough Guys Don't Dance 443
MORSE, ROBERT
  Emperor's New Clothes, The 402
  Hunk 411
MOSES, MARK
  Someone to Watch over Me 437
MOSS, RONN
  Hard Ticket to Hawaii 408
MOSTEL, JOSH
  Matewan 236
  Radio Days 290
MOTHERWELL, PHIL
  With Love to the Person Next to Me 449
MOTTA, BESS
  You Talkin' to Me? 450
MOULDER-BROWN, JOHN
  Rumpelstiltskin 432
MOUSS
  My True Love, My Wound 422
MOUTON, BENJAMIN
  Sister, Sister 435
MUCCI, DAVID
  Nightstick 423
MUELLERLEILE, MARIANNE
  Trouble with Dick, The 443
MUHICH, DONALD
  Amazon Women on the Moon 390
MULGREW, KATE
  Throw Momma from the Train 351
MULHERN, MATT
  Extreme Prejudice 403
MULKEY, CHRIS
  Hidden, The 410
  Patti Rocks 425

MULL, MARTIN
  Home Is Where the Hart Is 410
  O. C. and Stiggs 424
MUNDI, COATO
  Who's That Girl 448
MUNDY, MEG
  Fatal Attraction 118
MUNRO, NEIL
  John and the Missus 413
MURNEY, CHRISTOPHER
  Secret of My Success, The 315
MURO, MARTA FERNÁNDEZ
  Law of Desire, The 415
MURPHY, CHRISTOPHER
  Jocks 412
MURPHY, EDDIE
  Beverly Hills Cop II 63
  Eddie Murphy Raw 402
MURRAY, BEVERLEY
  Last Straw, The 415
MURRAY, DON
  Made in Heaven 223
  Marilyn Monroe 418
MURTAUGH, JAMES
  Rosary Murders, The 432
MUSHONOV, MONI
  Deadline 399
MYEROVICH, ALVIN
  Dirty Dancing 100
MYERS, KIM
  In the Mood 183
MYNSTER, KAREN-LISE
  Peter Von Scholten 426
MYOSHIN
  No Picnic 423

NAKAGAWA, KEN
  Living on Tokyo Time 417
NANCE, JACK
  Barfly 49
NAOR, IGAL
  Deadline 399
NAPIER, CHARLES
  Kidnapped 413
NARDINI, JAMES
  Nice Girls Don't Explode 422
NASSER, DEBBIE
  Stripped to Kill 439
NASSI, JOE
  Sorority House Massacre 437
NAUGHTON, DAVID
  Kidnapped 413
NAUGHTON, JAMES
  Glass Menagerie, The 150
NAYYAR, HARSH
  Making Mr. Right 227
N'DOUR, YOUSSOU
  Secret Policeman's Third Ball, The 434
NEAL, PATRICIA
  Hasty Heart, The [1949] 463
NEELY, GAIL
  Million Dollar Mystery 419
  Surf Nazis Must Die 440

607

PERFORMER INDEX

PENN, SEAN
Dear America 400
PENNEY, ALLAN
Year My Voice Broke, The 449
PENNY, LEAH
Housekeeping 179
PERKINS, ELIZABETH
From the Hip 405
PERKINS, MILLIE
Slam Dance 436
PERLMAN, BERNARD
Street Trash 438
PERRIN, JACQUES
Année des meduses, L' 391
PERRINE, VALERIE
Maid to Order 417
PERRY, EVAN
My Dark Lady 421
PERSKY, LISA JANE
Big Easy, The 71
PETERS, JANNE
Working Girls 449
PETERSEN, WILLIAM L.
Amazing Grace and Chuck 390
PETERSON, AMANDA
Can't Buy Me Love 396
PETERSON, CASSANDRA
Allan Quatermain and the Lost City of
Gold 389
PETERSON, LENKA
Dragnet 104
PETERSON, SHELLEY
Housekeeper, The 411
PETIT, PHILIPPE
Niagara Falls 422
PETIT, YVETTE
Miss Mona 420
PETTET, JOANNA
Sweet Country 441
PETTY, ROSS
Housekeeper, The 411
PETTY, TOM
Made in Heaven 223
PEYLERON, MICHEL
Miss Mona 420
PFEIFFER, CHUCK
Wall Street 364
PFEIFFER, DEDEE
Allnighter, The 390
PFEIFFER, MICHELLE
Amazon Women on the Moon 390
Witches of Eastwick, The 381
PHELAN, JOE
South of Reno 437
PHELPS, PETER
Lighthorsemen, The 416
PHILBIN, JOHN
North Shore 424
Under Cover 444
PHILIPS, EMO
Secret Policeman's Third Ball, The 434
PHILLIPS, CHARLIE
Munchies 421
PHILLIPS, LESLIE
Empire of the Sun 113

PHILLIPS, LOU DIAMOND
Bamba, La 45
PHOENIX, LEAF
Russkies 433
PHOENIX, SUMMER
Russkies 433
PIALAT, MAURICE
Under the Sun of Satan 444
PICARDO, ROBERT
Innerspace 188
PICCOLI, MICHEL
Rumba, The 432
PICKETT, BOBBY
Sister, Sister 435
PICKLES, CHRISTINA
Masters of the Universe 419
PICKUP, RONALD
Testimony 441
PIENAAR, JONATHAN
American Ninja 2 390
PIEPLU, CLAUDE
Good Weather, But Stormy Late This
Afternoon 406
PIERONI, ANIA
Unsane 444
PIGOZZI, JEAN
Man in Love, A 418
PILISI, MARK
Queen City Rocker 429
PILLOW, MARK
Superman IV 440
PILLSBURY, DREW
Who's That Girl 448
PILMARK, SOREN
Peter Von Scholten 426
PINES, LARRY
Anna 33
PINSENT, GORDON
John and the Missus 413
PINTOS, ALEJO GARCÍA
Night of the Pencils, The 422
PINVIDIC, MARGOT
Housekeeping 179
PINZA, CARLA
Believers, The 393
PIPER, KELLY
Rawheadrex 430
PIPER, RODDY
Body Slam 394
PIPER, SALLY
Nightmare on Elm Street 3 423
PIRO, GRANT
Lighthorsemen, The 416
PITKIN, FRANK
Whales of August, The 372
PITONIAK, ANNE
Best Seller 58
Housekeeping 179
Sister, Sister 435
PLACIDO, MICHELE
Summer Night with Greek Profile, Almond
Eyes, and Scent of Basil 440
PLANA, TONY
Born in East L. A. 394

611

PERFORMER INDEX

615

PERFORMER INDEX

617

PERFORMER INDEX

PERFORMER INDEX

PERFORMER INDEX

627

SUBJECT INDEX

The selection of subject headings combines standard Library of Congress Subject Headings and common usage in order to aid the film researcher. Cross references, listed as *See* and *See also*, are provided when appropriate. While all major themes, locales, and time periods have been indexed, some minor subjects covered in a particular film have not been included.

SUBJECT INDEX

SUBJECT INDEX